NUMBER 653

THE ENGLISH
EXPERIENCE

ITS RECORD IN EARLY PRINTED BOOKS
PUBLISHED IN FACSIMILE

JOHN DOWNAME

THE CHRISTIAN WARFARE

LONDON, 1604

WALTER J. JOHNSON, INC.
THEATRUM ORBIS TERRARUM, LTD.
AMSTERDAM 1974 NORWOOD, N.J.

The publishers acknowledge their gratitude to
the Curators of the Bodleian Library, Oxford,
for their permission to reproduce the Library's
copy, Shelfmark: Vet.A. 2, e.381

BV
4500
·D66
1974

S.T.C. No. 7133

Collation: π^4, A-Z^8, Aa-Vv^8, Xx^2

Published in 1974 by

Theatrum Orbis Terrarum, Ltd.
O.Z. Voorburgwal 85, Amsterdam

&

Walter J. Johnson, Inc.
355 Chestnut Street
Norwood, New Jersey
07648

Printed in the Netherlands

ISBN 90 221 0653 5

Library of Congress Catalog Card Number:
74-80174

THE CHRISTIAN WARFARE.

WHEREIN IS FIRST GENERALLY SHEWED THE MALICE, POWER AND

politike ſtratagems of the ſpirituall enemies of our ſaluation, Sathan and his aſſiſtants the world and the fleſh ; with the meanes alſo whereby the Chriſtian *may vvithſtand and defeate them.*

AND AFTERWARDS MORE SPE CIALLIE THEIR PARTICVLAR TEMPTATI-

ons, againſt the ſeuerall cauſes and meanes of our ſaluation, whereby on the one ſide they allure vs to ſecurity and preſumption, and on the other ſide, draw vs to doubting and deſperation, are expreſ- ſed and anſwered.

WRITTEN ESPECIALLY FOR THEIR SAKES

who are exerciſed in the ſpirituall conflict of temptations, and are afflicted in conſcience in the ſight *and ſenſe of their ſinnes.*

By I. Dovvname Preacher of Gods word.

Put on the whole armour of God, that ye may be able to ſtand againſt the aſſaults of the Diuell. Epheſ.6.11.

AT LONDON
Imprinted by Felix Kyngston, for Cuthbert Burby, and are to be ſold at his ſhop in Paules Church-yard at the ſigne of the Swan. 1 6 0 4.

TO THE GODLY,

ZEALOVS, AND SIN-
CERE PROFESSORS OF GODS
TRVE RELIGION, SIR I oun Scot,
Sir Thomas Smith,and their Ladies;Maiſter Ro-
bert Chamberlaine Eſquire, and Miſtris
Anne Chamberlaine his wife,his welbeloued and
moſt reſpected friends: I. D. wiſheth the fruition of all the true comforts of this life,
and eternall happineſſe in
the life to come.

Anifold (right Worſhipfull)
and moſt daungerous are the
temptations and aſſaults of
our ſpirituall enemies, whereby they labour to hinder the
ſaluation of Gods elect, and to
increaſe the greatneſſe of their
helliſh dominions, by with-
drawing(if it were poſſible)Gods ſeruants from their
ſubiection and alleageance, and making them their
ſlaues and perpetuall vaſſals.To this end they take indefatigable paines, going continually about ſeeking
whom they may deuour; ſometimes like roaring
Lions, compelling by violent force, and ſometimes

¶ 2   like

like old Serpents, alluring and deceiuing with treacherous policies. Neither doe they reſt in the time
of our reſt, but waking and ſleeping they ſet vpon vs,
one while inticing vs to ſwallow the poyſon of
ſinne, with the ſugred baites of worldly vanities,
and another while driuing vs into their ſnares of perdition, with the ſharpe pricking goades of miſerie and affliction. Before vs they ſet carnall pleaſures,
deceiuing riches, and vaine honours, to allure vs to
come into the broad way that leadeth to deſtruction: and behind vs they hold the three-ſtringed whip
of loſſe, ſhame, and puniſhment, to keepe vs from going backe, and to haſten vs with winged ſpeede to
run forward in this helliſh iourney. Neither do they
greatly care what path we chuſe in this common way
of perdition ; whether the ſpatious way of ſecuritie and preſumption, or the ſtrait path of horror
and deſperation, whether the toyling way of vnſati-
able couetouſneſſe, or the ſoft faire way of bewitch-
ing pleaſures, whether the open way of worldlineſſe
and atheiſme, or through the hidden thickets of hypocriſie and diſſimulation: in a word they regard
not in what way we walke, ſo we goe forward in the
waies of ſinne, for though they ſeeme diuers and
contrarie one to another, yet they haue all the ſame
end, meeting together in hell and deſtruction. And
howſoeuer they cannot with all their malice, power
and policies attaine vnto their deſires, by bringing
Gods elect and faithfull ones to perdition and endleſſe miſerie; becauſe God their heauenly father
who hath taken vpon him their protection, fruſtra-
teth all their ſubtill policies with his all-ſeeing wiſedome, and withſtandeth all their might with his almightie

mightie power, yet doe they exceedingly with their assaults and temptations, foyle, vexe and trouble them; by working in some, forgetfulnesse of God and of themselues, securitie, and carelesse retchlesnesse; and turmoyling others with horrible feares, desperat doubting, and bitter agonies. Whereby it commeth to passe, that the one sort securely goe on in sinne, forgetting the end of their creation, redemption, and holy vocation, vnto which God hath called them, vntill with *Salomon* they haue found in the end of their worldly delights, nothing but vanitie and vexation of spirit: and the other are so affrighted, astonished, and continually tormented with doubtings, feares, and the continuall assaults of their spirituall enemies, that they goe mourning all the day long, pining away in griefe and anguish of mind, till at last they grow wearie of their liues, thinking their soules an intollerable burthen to their bodies, and their bodies to the earth. The consideration of which lamentable and too too miserable effects, as it shall moue all christians to stand vpon their guard, and to arme themselues with the spirituall armour, that they may not be ouercome of their temptations, and fall into these great mischiefes: so should it moue Gods faithfull ministers (whose dutie it is, not onely themselues to walke in the waies of righteousnesse, but also as spirituall guides to leade others with them) in discharge of their conscience before God, and in christian commiseration and compassion towards their brethren, to vse all good meanes both by speaking and writing, whereby they may bee preserued and freed from these snares which their spirituall enemies doe lay to intrap them; by beating

downe

downe with the cannon-fhot of Gods threatnings, the high forts of their proud prefumption, and rouzing them out of the deepe flumber of retchleffe fecuritie; as alfo by raifing vp and comforting thofe that mourne in Syon, ftooping, yea lying groueling vnder the heauie burthen of their finnes. The which howfoeuer it is performed by many, in refpect of their feuerall charges committed to them; and fome alfo haue briefely touched fome poynts in writing, which concerned the comforting and raifing vp of their priuate friends: yet not any (that I know of) haue in our language largely and generally handled thefe controuerfies, and fpirituall conflicts betweene the chriftian and the enemies of his faluation, for the common good of the whole Church. And therefore hauing with *Elihu* long waited to fee if thofe who were more auncient, better experienced, and more richly furnifhed with Gods gifts and graces than my felfe, would vndertake this worke, which is to God moft acceptable, and to his faints and children fo profitable and neceffarie: at length after others long filence, I refolued to fpeake, and no longer to conceale fuch true comforts as God hath reuealed vnto me; to the end that hereby I might releeue and comfort thofe who are poore in fpirit, and humbled in the fight of finne; or at leaft by offering willingly to this vfe my fmall mite, I might giue an occafion vnto others better able, to vnlocke and open their rich treafuries, that they may beftow vpon their poore brethren their great talents and gifts of better valew. The which my labors as I did not rafhly vndertake them, fo I haue not fuddenly finifhed them; for almoft three yeeres fince I purpofed to take this

worke

worke in hand, which I haue now by Gods affiftance
finifhed; but at the firft (I confeffe) I intended not
that it fhould come in to publike view; but onely
(as others before me)propounded as the end of my
labours, the comforting and raifing vp of a moft
faithfull feruant of God, and my moft deare friend,
who hath bound me with many benefits to the performance of all chriftian duties. But afterwards finding it to grow to fuch a volume that it was too
great to paffe in a written coppie, and hoping that
that which was profitable for one might bee beneficiall vnto many, at length I refolued to make
my labours publike by committing them to the
preffe. The principall things that I propounded
to my felfe in this treatife are thefe; firft and efpecially I indeauour to comfort thofe who are afflicted
in confcience, in the fight and fence of their finnes,
by offering vnto them certaine affurance, that their
finnes are remitted, and that themfelues are elected
to eternall life, in the ftate of grace, reconciled vnto
God in Chrift and receiued in his loue and fauour.
Secondly, I labour to leade the chriftian in an euen
courfe, vnto the hauen of eternall happineffe; that
he may not runne afide, neither on the right hand,
and fo falling vpon the rockes of prefumption make
fhipwracke of his foule, nor yet on the left hand, and
fo plunge himfelfe into the gulfe of defperation.
Wherein I haue purpofely and aduifedly auoyded
their practife, who fcatter their confolations they
know not where, to bee applyed they care not by
whom; whereof it commeth to paffe that thofe that
are moft fecure and prefumptuous arrogate them,
to whom they doe not appertaine; and thofe that
are

are afflicted and humbled dare not appropriate them
to themselues, becaufe they are deliuered indefinitly
to all, without all caution or any condition, whereby they might bee reftrained rather to them than
any other in whom finne yet liueth and raigneth.
Wherein they refemble negligent phyfitions, who
hauing made a good medicine for a ficke man,
doe not giue it vnto him, but caft it careleſly into
fome corner, whether the ficke patient in refpect of
his faintneffe and weakeneffe is likely neuer to come:
which being found and greedily drunken vp by
thofe who haue no neede of it, in ftead of doing
them good doth turne to their baine and vtter deftruction. Laftly, I haue defired to giue folid and
fubftantiall confolations, which are firmely grounded vpon Gods vndoubted truth, and fuch infallible
reafons as cannot bee gainfaid; and haue withall
deliuered the conditions, vpon which they are to be
receiued, and the vndoubted fignes and markes of
thofe, to whom of right they appertaine; to the end
that thofe who finde thefe things in themfelues, may
not doubt to apply them to their wounded confciences, whereby they may bee foundly cured and
throughly comforted; and that thofe who finde no
fuch condition obferued by them, nor any fuch figne
or marke in them, may be debarred from participa-
ting of thefe confolations, which would nourifh in
them fecuritie and prefumption : and contrariwife
examining themfelues according to thefe rules, and
finding no correfpondencie betweene themfelues
and them, may hereby be awakened out of their lethargie of fecuritie, and attaining vnto a fight and
fenfe of their miferable eftate may neuer be at reft,

till

till by vsing all good meanes for this purpose, they
may finde these markes and signes of their election,
vocation, iustification, and sanctification in them, that
so they may boldly and fitly apply vnto themselues
these comforts and consolations as rightly and truly
appertaining vnto them. All which my labours I
thought good to dedicate vnto your worships, partly because I desired to giue this testimonie of my
true thankefulnesse, for those manifold benefits
which from some of you I haue receiued, and of
mine vnfained loue which I beare to you all, for your
vertues and approued godlinesse ; and partly because I thought none fitter to whom I might commend this discourse of the *Christian Warfare*, than
your selues who are olde experienced souldiars in
fighting these spirituall battailes, and therefore haue
iudiciall feeling and sensible apprehension, of those
things which I haue written and commended to
your patronage. Now the Lord our God who is the
fountaine of all goodnesse, and the sole giuer of all
true consolation, increase in you more and more the
gifts and graces of his sanctifying spirit, and so fill
your hearts with all sound spirituall comfort, and the
ioy in the holy Ghost, that you may through the
course of your whole liues, chearefully goe forward
in the profession and sincere practise of his religion
and true godlinesse, and after this life may receiue
that crowne of righteousnesse, which is prepared and
laid vp for you in his kingdome of eternall glorie.
Amen.

Your Worships in the Lord most assured.

IOHN DOVVNAME.

THE CONTENTS OF
THIS BOOKE.

THE CHIEFE POINTS HANDLED
in the firſt Booke.

                         A 2   may

THE CONTENTS.

How

THE CONTENTS.

A 3   2.*Assured*

THE CONTENTS.

CHAP. XXIII.

THE CHIEFE POINTS HANDLED
in the second Booke.

CHAP. I.

Temporall

THE CONTENTS.

in

THE CONTENTS.

Thirdly,

THE CONTENTS.

ueth

THE CONTENTS.

Of

THE CONTENTS.

How

THE CONTENTS.

THE CONTENTS.

That

THE CONTENTS.

That

THE CONTENTS.

THE CONTENTS OF THE
third Booke.

The

THE CONTENTS.

FINIS.

THE FIRST BOOKE
INTREATING OF THE POWER
and policies of our ſpirituall enemies,and of the
meanes how we may withſtand the one
and defeate the other.

CHAP. I.

*That all the godly are aſſaulted with the ſpirituall enemies of
their ſaluation.*

THE Apoſtle hauing ſhewed the myſterie §. *Sect.*1.
of our ſaluation and the cauſes thereof
for the confirmation of our faith in the
three firſt chapters of his Epiſtle to the
Epheſians, and afterwards in the other
chapters hauing ſet downe diuers duties
both generally belonging to all Chri-
ſtians, and alſo particularly appertaining to men of ſundrie
conditions, that he might moue them to repentance and a-
mendment of life ; in the next place like the Lords Centinell
doth diſcouer and giue vs warning of the approch of mighty
enemies, willing vs to arme our ſelues at all points in our
owne defence, and couragiouſly to ſtand vnder the ſtanderd
of Chriſt Ieſus,that we may be continually in readines to endure the encounter,chap.6.10,11,&c. Whereby he giueth vs *All that will*
to vnderſtand, that as ſoone as we ſeeke for aſſurance of ſal- *liue like Gods*
uation in Chriſt, and endeuour to ſerue the Lord in a holie *ſeruants muſt*
and a Chriſtian life, wee are to prepare our ſelues for a com- *prepare them-*
bat,vnleſſe we would ſuddenly be ſurpriſed ; for the ſpiritual *ſelues for the*
ſpirituall com-
enemies of our ſaluation bandie themſelues againſt vs as *bat.*

B   ſoone

2   *That all the godly are affaulted with tentations.*

foone as we haue giuen our names vnto God, and taken vpon vs the profeffion and practife of Chriftianitie, which are the liuerie and cognifance of our heauenly Lord and Mafter. And this is manifeft by the example of Gods children from time to time,who although they liued in peace and fecuritie before they were intertained into Gods familie, yet no fooner were they admitted to be of Gods houfehold feruants, but Sathan and the world haue raged againft them,laboring both by inward temptations and outward furie, either to withdraw them from Gods feruice by flattring inticements, or vtterly to deftroy and ouerthrow them by open violence.

Gen.4.

No fooner had *Abel* offered a facrifice of fweete fmelling fauour vnto God, but Sathan ftirreth vp *Cain* to become his butcher: whileft *Mofes* was contented to be reputed the fonne of *Pharaohs* daughter he enioyed all profperitie,but as foone as hee ioyned himfelfe to Gods people and Church, *Pharaoh* feeketh his life : as long as the Ifraelites worfhipped the Egyptian Idols,they fate by their flefh-pots in peace,and quietly enioyed the fruites of the land; but as foone as they made but a motion of feruing the Lord, the King ftirred vp by the diuell,doth rage againft them with more then barbarous crueltie: whileft *Paul* perfecuted the Church of God, Sathan did not fo much trouble him either outwardly in bodie or inwardly in minde; but no fooner was he truly conuerted to the faith and preached the Gofpell, but prefently he fetteth his wicked impes on worke to take away his life, which the Lord not permitting, he mooueth them to perfecute him by imprifoning, whipping, and ftoning him; and not content with thefe outward afflictions, he fendeth his

2.Cor.12.

meffenger to buffet him, that he might be no leffe vexed inwardly in minde then outwardly in bodie. Yea he fpared not our Sauiour Chrift himfelfe, but as foone as he began to fhew himfelfe to be the fonne of God and redeemer of mankinde, in perfourming the duties of his calling, then efpecially hee bendeth all his force againft him, he tempteth and affaulteth

Matth.4.

him fortie daies together, and taking the foyle himfelfe, hee ftirreth vp his wicked inftruments to perfecute him, and at length to take away his life.

Whofoeuer

Whofoeuer therefore refolue to be Gods feruants, muft make account to be his fouldiers alfo; and whileft with *Ne-hemias* followers, with one hand they perfourme the workes of their callings and Chriftianitie, they muft with the other hand hold their weapons to repell their fpirituall enemies, who continually labour to hinder the Lords buildings : for no fooner doe we become friends to God, but prefently Sathan affaulteth vs as his enemies ; no fooner doe we receiue the Lords preffe money and fet foote into his campe, but Sathan aduanceth againft vs his flagges of defiance, labouring both by fecret treacherie, and outward force, to fupplant and ouercome vs.

Here therefore is inftruction for fecure worldlings, and §. *Sect.*2. confolation and incouragement for Gods children. Worldly *The two-fold* men in fteed of fighting the Lords battailes, fpend their time *vfe of this doc-* in chambering and wantonnes, in lufts and vncleannes, in *trine.* Muficke and daliance, in furfetting and all voluptuoufnes, in couetoufnes and idlenes, as though there were no enemie to affault them, and as if Sathan were fome meeke lambe and not a roring lion readie to deuoure them ; fo that good *Mo-fes* comming neere them cannot heare the noife of them that haue the victorie, nor the noife of them that are ouercome, but the noife of finging and meriment, for they are not figh- Exod. 32. ting the battailes of the Lord of hoafts, but folemnifing a Sabbath to the golden Calfe, fitting downe to eate and drink and rifing vp to play. The fpirituall Cananites are quite forgotten, and they remember not the bleffed land of promife, whereunto like pilgrimes they fhould bee trauailing, but make this world, this wildernes of fin, the place of their ioy and delight. In a word, they flourifh in their outward ftates, and neuer in their mindes feele any vexation of Sathans temtations. And what is the caufe of all this ? If you aske them they will fay, that they haue fuch a ftrong faith and peace of confcience, that Sathans temptations haue no power ouer *That the world-* them; neither were they euer troubled with any of his en- *lings peace pro-* counters. And not content with thefe bragges of their owne *ceedeth not* happie eftate, they cenfure and condemne Gods children, *from ftrength,* accounting their ftate moft defperate who are molefted with *curitie.*

Sathans

Sathans temptations, and goe mourning vnder the burthen of sinne all the day long; supposing either that they are in Sathans power, and haue more grieuously sinned then other men, or that they are mad and frantick so to vexe themselues with such needlesse sorrow. But let such men know that of all others their state is most daungerous, for they are grieuously sicke, and haue no sense of their disease, their wounds are so mortall that they depriue them of all feeling; they are assaulted, yea taken prisoners whilest they sleepe soundly in securitie, and discerne not the approch of the enemie. *Non ergo repugnant quia se impugnari ignorant:* They make no resistance because they are ignorant of the assault. And what can be more daungerous then to haue the enemie approch and lay hands on vs before we be aware? But this is the state

Hierom.

of those men: for as one saith, *Tum maximè impugnantur cum se impugnari nesciant:* They are most assaulted when they feele no assault. Let them know, that they are not the Lords souldiers but the diuels reuellers, and therefore he fighteth not against them because they are his friends. For there was neuer any of Christs souldiers in the Militant Church which haue not been exercised in this warfare; there was neuer any so strong in faith but Sathan durst encounter him, euen the Apostles, yea *Adam* in the state of innocencie, yea our Sauiour Christ himselfe; there were neuer any so constant in the course of Christianitie, but the world hath sought to draw them out of the right way by her baites of prosperitie, or to force them to sinne by threatning aduersitie; there were neuer any that haue had in them one sparke of Gods spirit (Christ excepted) who haue not felt it assaulted and often foiled by the flesh. For *the flesh lusteth against the spirit, and the spirit against the flesh, and they are contrarie the one to the other,*

Galat.5.17.
Rom.7.23.

as it is Galath.5.17. Yea the Apostle *Paul* himselfe when he was most sanctified, *saw another law in his members rebelling against the law of his minde, leading him captiue to the law of sin,* as appeareth Rom.7.23.

§. Sect.3.

It is not therefore their strength of faith, but their carnall securitie which so lulleth them asleepe in the cradle of worldly vanities that they cannot discerne this fight; it is not their

peace

peace with God nor the peace of confcience which makes
them thus quiet, for *there is no* (fuch) *peace, faith my God, to
the wicked,*Efa.57.21. but it is a peace which they haue made   Efa.57.21.
with Sathan,*a couenant with death and an agreement with hell,*
as the Prophet fpeaketh, Efa.28.15. *When the ftrong armed* Efa.28.15.
man Sathan (quietly) *keepes the houfe, the things that he poffeffeth are in peace ; but when a ftronger then he commeth* to dif-
poffeffe him,he will neuer lofe his poffeffion without a fight,
and we cannot chufe but feele the blowes in fo fharpe an incounter. Luk.11.21. If a man neuer enter the field to fight a- Luk.11.21.
gainft Sathan, or if at the firft encounter he yeeld himfelfe
prifoner, and be content to be tied in the pleafing fetters of
finne, it is no marueile that hee doth not rage in his confcience, when as alreadie hee is in his captiuitie readie to perfourme all thofe workes of darknes wherein he employeth
him ; but if when Chrift the redeemer is preached vnto them
by his Ambaffadours , they would fhew any defire of comming out of his thraldome , furely this fpirituall *Pharaoh*
would neuer lofe their feruice but by force and compulfion,
neither can fo ftrong a man be forced but wee muft needes
feele the conflict. While the prifoner lieth in the dungeon,
loaded with bolts and tied in chaines,the keeper fleepeth fecurely, becaufe he knoweth he is fafe; but if his bolts being
filed off and his chaines loofed,he haue efcaped out of prifon, then the Iaylor beginneth to buftle and purfueth him
fpeedely with Huean crye : fo whileft Sathan holdeth vs im-
prifoned in the darke dungeon of ignorance,loaded and tied
with the heauie bolts and chaines of finne, hee is retchleffe
and fecure ; but if our Sauiour by his Ambaffadours in the
preaching of the word, loofe and vnburthen vs of thefe
chaines and bolts, and by the light of his fpirit fo illuminate
the eyes of our vnderftanding, that we fee the way out of Sathans dungeon of ignorance, and fo efcape out of his captiuitie, then he rageth againft and purfueth vs as *Pharaoh* did
the Ifraelites, that either he may bring vs backe againe into
his bondage, or els deftroy vs, if we make refiftance. Laftly
they feele not any fight betweene the flefh and the fpirit, becaufe the flefh wholie ruleth them, and like a flood which

           hath

hath a cleere current carrieth them wholie into a sea of sinne without any stop or resistance, and therfore no marueile they feele not this fight, when the spirit which is one of the combatants hath no force nor residence in them.

Secondly, Gods children who continually feele the assaults of their spirituall enemies, and see the breaches which are made in their soules with the continuall batterie of their temptations, may receiue no small consolation hereby, when as they consider that all who professe themselues Gods seruants, and resolue to serue the Lord in holines and righteousnes are thus tempted and tried. *For the Dragon is wroth with the woman* (that is Gods Church) *and her seede which keepe the commandements of God, and haue the testimonie of Iesus Christ,* as is Reuel. 12. 17. and like a roring lion seeketh their destruction, because they haue renounced him, and fight vnder the standard of the Lord of hoasts whom hee maligneth : and hence it is that whilest we liue without sense of sinne, we eate and drinke and take our ease without disturbance, but after we make any conscience of our waies and endeuour to serue the Lord, then Sathan casteth against vs the firie darts of his temptations, and we feele many conflicts betweene the flesh and the spirit, with which the worldly man is neuer troubled. So that when we are thus tempted and assaulted by Sathan, the world, and our corrupt flesh, it is a strong argument to perswade vs that wee are intertained for Gods souldiers, and haue receiued the presse money of his spirit; for Sathans kingdome is not diuided, neither doth he fight against those who are his friends and seruants, but against those who wage warre against him and fight vnder the Lords standerd. True it is, that when his seruants haue committed such abominable and grieuous sinnes, as haue made deepe wounds in their seared consciences, whereby they are awakened out of their sleepie lethargie of securitie, then Sathan filleth them with horrour and despaire, that hee may keepe them from true repentance, when he can hide from them their sinnes no longer; and the Lord in his iust iudgement, and for the example of others, doth suffer Sathan to begin in them the torments of hell in this life ; but if hee can by any meanes hide

their

their sinnes and keepe them quietly in his kingdome, he will neuer vexe them. And hence it is that whereas one perisheth through despaire, many thousands perish through presumption and securitie. Let all those therefore who feele the burthen of their sinnes, and are vexed with the continuall assaults of their spirituall enemies comfort themselues; for hereby they haue assurance that they are members of the Church militant, into which none but souldiers are intertained, and that now they begin to be Gods friends and seruants when as Sathan opposeth himselfe against them.

Chap. II.

Why God suffereth his seruants to be exercised in the spirituall conflict of tentations.

Vt here it may be demaunded, why the Lord will suffer his seruants to be thus tempted and assaulted, whereas the wicked are free from such conflicts. I answere, first for his owne glorie, for whereas our enemies are strong and mighty and we weake and feeble, hereby is the Lords omnipotent power manifested to all the world, by whose assistance such impotent wretches conquer and subdue such furious and puissant enemies.

Secondly, God suffereth his children to be tempted, that so those spirituall graces which he hath bestowed vpon them may the more cleerely shine to his glorie. For who can know whether they be Gods golden vessels before they be brought to the touchstone of temptation? Who could know the faith, patience and valour of Gods souldiers, if they alwaies lay quietly in garrison and neuer came to the skirmish? Who could feele the odoriferous smell of these aromaticall spices, if they were not punned and brused in the morter of afflictions? For example, who would haue discerned *Abrahams* faith, *Dauids* pietie, *Iobs* patience, *Pauls* courage and constancie, if they had been neuer tempted, which now to the glorie of God shine to all the world?

And

And as the Lord suffereth Sathan and his impes to trie his children for his owne glorie, so also for their spirituall and euerlasting good: for first hereby he chastizeth them for their sinnes past, and recalleth them to their remembrance, that so they may truly repent of them. And this cause *Iob* speaketh of: Iob.13.26. *Thou writest* (saith he) *bitter things against me, and makest me to possesse the iniquities of my youth.*

Iob.13.26.

Secondly, hereby hee manifesteth vnto vs our secret and hidden sinnes, which the blind eyes of our iudgement would not discerne, if their sight were not quickned with this sharp water of temptation. For so long as wee liue in peace, our secure consciences neuer summon vs to the barre of Gods iudgement; but when wee are roused vp by temptation, wee enter into a more straight examination of our selues, and search what secret sinnes lie lurking in the hidden corners of our hearts, that so wee may repent of them and make our peace with God, without whose assistance wee can haue no hope to stand in any temptation.

Thirdly, the Lord hereby preuenteth our sinnes to come : for when we haue experience, that the most sharp weapons, which Sathan vseth to inflict deepe wounds in our consciences, are our sinnes; this will make vs most carefull to abstaine from them, least thereby we strengthen him for our owne ouerthrow. And as these temptations of Sathan are in this regard so many bridles to restraine vs from sinne ; so also they are so many prickes to let out the winde of vaine glorie, wherewith like bladders we be puffed vp, as wee may see in the example of *Paul, who lest he should be exalted out of measure through the abundance of reuelations, receiued a pricke in the flesh, the messenger of Sathan to buffet him.* 2.Cor.12.7.

2.Cor.12.7.

Fourthly, the Lord suffereth Sathan to assault vs, that wee may hereby come to the sight of our owne weaknesse and infirmities, when wee haue receiued many foiles; and learne to relie vpon his helpe and assistance in all our dangers; for so proud we are by nature, that before we come to the fight we think that we can repell the strongest assaults, and ouercome all enemies which oppose themselues against vs by our owne power ; but when wee see our selues vanquished and foiled

with

with euery small temptation, wee learne to haue a more humble conceit of our owne abilitie, and to depend wholy vpon the Lord. And this end is set downe, Deut.8.2.and 13.3. Deut.8.2. and 13.3.

Fiftly, the Lord permitteth Sathan continually to assaile vs with his temptations, to the end we may continually buckle vnto vs the whole armour of God, that we may be readie for the battaile. For as those who haue no enemies to encounter them, cast their armour aside and let it rust, because they are secure from daunger; but when the enemies are at hand and sound the alarum, they both wake and sleepe in their armour readie for the assault : so, if we should not continually skirmish with our spirituall enemies, we would lay aside the spirituall armour; but when wee haue continuall vse of it, both day and night we keepe it fast buckled vnto vs, that being armed at all points, we may be able to make resistance that we be not surprised at vnawares.

Lastly, by this conflict the Lord strengthneth and increaseth all his graces in vs : for as by exercise the strength of the body is preserued and augmented, and in short time decaieth through idlenesse and sloth; so the gifts of Gods spirit, faith, affiance, hope, patience and the rest languish in vs, if they bee not exercised with temptations. *For tribulation bringeth forth* Rom.5.3.4. *patience, and patience experience, and experience hope, and hope maketh not ashamed,* as it is Rom.5.3,4,5. For when once wee haue been tempted and tried, and the Lord hath mercifullie deliuered vs from the temptation, afterwards being so assaulted wee patiently endure it, hoping for the Lords assistance, 1.Sam.17.37. beleeuing and assuring our selues that the Lord who hath deliuered vs will againe deliuer vs, as it is Psal.27.9. Moreouer, when wee see the great neede of the graces of Gods spirit, this will be a strong motiue to intice vs to a carefull vse of all good meanes whereby we may attaine vnto them, whereas if we were free from this spirituall conflict, we should not so cleerely see nor apprehend the vse and necessitie of them.

Psal.27.9.

CHAP.

CHAP. III.

Arguments whereby we may be encouraged to enter into this ſpirituall conflict.

§. *Sect*.1.

Nd thus haue I ſhewed that al that will be Gods ſeruants muſt fight his battailes againſt his and our ſpirituall enemies, and the cauſes why the Lord preſſeth vs to this ſeruice ; now that wee may goe couragiouſly into the field, let vs conſider of ſome reaſons and motiues which may make vs reſolute and valiant. The firſt is the iuſtneſſe of our cauſe. For though ſouldiers be neuer ſo ſtrong and well furniſhed, yet if their conſciences tell them that they fight in a bad quarrell, it will much abate their courage, and make them cowardly and timorous. But our cauſe is moſt iuſt, and our warre moſt lawfull, for God who is iuſtice it ſelfe hath proclaimed it by his Heraulds the Apoſtles. So Ephe.6.10. *Finally my brethren be ſtrong in the Lord, and in the power of his might.* 11. *Put on the whole armour of God, that ye may be able to ſtand againſt the aſſaults of the diuell, &c.* And Iam.4.7. *Reſiſt the diuell and he will flie from you.* And 1.Pet.5.8. *Be ſober and watch for your aduerſarie the diuell as a roring lion walketh about ſeeking whom he may deuoure : 9.Whom reſiſt ſtedfaſt in the faith.*

Eph.6.10.

Iam.4.7.
1.Pet.5.8.

The cauſe of our ſpirituall warre of great importance.

Secondly, the cauſe of our warre is of great waight, as namely for the glory of God and our owne ſaluation ; for in all ſathans skirmiſhes, he ſeeketh to impeach Gods glory with falſe imputations, and to bring vs to vtter deſtruction. And this may appeare by his firſt conflict with our mother *Eue*, Gen.3.4.5. where he accuſeth God of a lye, who is truth it ſelfe; and of impotencie and enuious diſdaine, ſaying, that the cauſe why he did forbid them to eate of the fruite of the tree of the knowledge of good and euill, was not (as he had ſaid) becauſe they ſhould die, but becauſe he knew that when they ſhould eate thereof, their eyes ſhould be opened, and they ſhould be as Gods knowing good and euill. Where firſt he ſeeketh to dimme the beames of Gods glorie by accuſing him

Gen.3.4.5.

him of a lie, and to perswade them that he was not omnipotent, seeing that he was not able to hinder them from being
Gods, if they tasted of this fruite : lastly, that he therefore for-
bad them to eate thereof, because he enuied them so glorious
an estate. And secondly he laboureth to destroy our first parents both bodie and soule, by tempting them to disobedience and the transgression of Gods commandement : and
therefore our Sauiour Christ Ioh.8.44. doth very fitly ioyne   Ioh.8.44.
these two together, saying, that he was a liar and a manslaier
from the beginning. A liar, in that he falsely accused God of
lying; a manslaier, because he did it to this end, that he might
murther our first parents and all their posteritie both bodie
and soule. So that you see that the end of Sathans fight is to
dishonour God and destroy vs, and therefore if wee haue any
regard of Gods glorie (which should be more deare vnto vs
then our owne soules) or any respect of our owne saluation, if
we would not treacherously betray them both by our sloth-
fulnes or cowardize into the hands of Gods and our enemie;
let vs valiantly enter the field, and neuer cease our couragious
fight till we haue obtained a full victorie.

The second reason to moue vs to vndertake this fight is   §. Sect.2.
the profit which will accrew vnto vs thereby : for if the get-   *The profit of*
ting of some bootie and prize, or the receiuing of some trife-   *this spirituall*
ling pay will moue the souldiers of earthly Princes to vnder-   *fight.*
goe all daungers, and with wonderfull perill of life to fight
euen at the Cannons mouth ; how much more should the
stipend of our heauenly king moue vs to fight this combat
how terrible soeuer it seemeth to flesh and bloud ? For first
that is truly here verified, *Pax belli filia*, Peace is the daughter
of warre, neither can we sooner enter the field to fight against
these enemies, but presently we shall haue peace with God,
and soone after the fruite thereof the peace of conscience.
Whereas if we betray Gods cause to Sathan and our soules to
sinne, well may wee be lulled asleepe in carnall securitie, but
we shall neuer enioy this peace with God and peace of con-
science : for *there is no peace, saith my God, to the wicked.*Esa.57.   Esa.57.21.
And whosoeuer haue taken this treacherous truce with Sa-
than, shall finde that he will breake it for his best aduantage,
                                                              if

if not in the whole courfe of their liues, yet at the houre of death when as they fhall be able to make no refiftance.

Promifes made to thofe that fight.
A poc.2.& 3.
Secondly, if wee fight againft thefe enemies and valiantly ouercome, the Lord hath promifed to giue vs to eate of the tree of life which is in Paradice, and the Manna that is hid, and that he will write our names in the booke of life, Apoc.2 and 3 .that is, he will in this life beftow on vs all his fpirituall graces, and in the life to come replenifh vs with fuch *ioyes as*
1.Cor.2.9.
neither eye hath feene, nor eare heard, nor heart of man conceiued, 1.Cor.2.9. Let vs therefore ftriue that wee may ouercome, *Nam breuis eft labor, premium verò æternum:* Our labour is but fhort, but our reward fhall be eternall. On the other fide, if wee confider Sathans pay which he giueth vnto his fouldiers, we fhall finde that it is nothing but the pleafures of fin for a feafon, and in the end euerlafting death and deftruction of bodie and foule : *For the wages of finne is death,* as it is
Rom.6.23.
Rom.6.23. Who therefore is fo flothfull and cowardly that would not be encouraged, to fight the Lords battailes againft our fpirituall enemies, with fuch promifes made by him who is truth it felfe and cannot deceiue vs ? Who is fo defperate and foole-hardie as to fight vnder Sathans banner, feeing the pay which he giueth is euerlafting death, and vtter confufion ?

§. Sect.3.
The honor that will accompany our victorie.
The third reafon to moue vs to this fight, is the honour which will accompanie this victorie : for if earthly fouldiers will purchafe honour with the loffe of life, which is nothing els but the commendation of the Prince, or applaufe of the vaine people; what hazard fhould we not vndergo in fighting the fpirituall combat, feeing our grand Captaine the Lord of hoafts, & infinite multitudes of bleffed Angels look vpon vs and behold our combat, whofe praife and approbation is our chiefe felicitie ? What peril fhould we feare, to obtaine a crowne of glorie which is promifed to all that ouercome, and to become heires apparant of Gods kingdome ? On the other fide, the fhame and confufion of face which fhall ouertake them who cowardly forfake the Lords ftanderd and yeeld vnto Sathan, when as they fhall not dare to looke the Lord in the face whofe caufe they haue betrayed, fhould

serue

serue as a ftrong motiue to encourage vs to the fight.

The fourth reafon to perfwade vs, is the neceffitie of vndertaking this combat. There is no man fo cowardly that wil
not fight when there is no hope in flight, no mercie to be expected in the enemie, no outrage and crueltie which will not
be committed. But fuch is our enemie that we cannot poffi-
blie flee from him, his malice is vnreconcilable, his crueltie
outragious, for hee fighteth not againft vs to the end that hee
may obtaine foueraigntie alone, abridge vs of our libertie,
fpoyle vs of our goods; but he aimeth at our death and deftruction of bodie and foule : if therefore wee fo carefully
arme our felues againft earthly enemies, who when they haue
done their vttermoft rage can but fhorten a miferable life,
how much more carefully fhould we refift this enemie, who
feeketh to depriue vs of euerlafting life, and to plunge vs into an euerdying death?

Secondly, this fight is neceffarie, becaufe in our Baptifme
we haue taken a militarie facrament, and promifed faithfullie
vnto the Lord, that wee will continue his faithfull fouldiers
vnto the end, fighting his battailes againft the flefh, the
world and the diuell. There wee haue giuen our names vnto
Chrift, to whom wee owe our felues and liues by a double
right, both becaufe he hath giuen them vnto vs, and alfo reftored them the fecond time when wee had loft them. There
wee are put in minde of his bloudfhed for our redemption,
which fhould encourage vs to fight couragioufly, that wee
may be preferued from falling againe into the cruell flauerie
of finne and Sathan.

Thirdly, vnleffe wee fight this fpirituall combat, and in
fighting ouercome, wee fhall neuer be crowned with the
crown of glory: for it is not giuen vnto any to triumph, who
haue not fought valiantly and fubdued their enemies. The
euerlafting peace of Gods kingdome is not promifed to
fuch cowards as neuer entred the field, or being entred haue
prefently yeelded themfelues to be the captiues of Sathan:
but vnto thofe that fight couragioufly and glorioufly ouercome. *If any man* (faith the Apoftle) *ftriue for a maisterie, he is
not crowned except he ftriue as he ought to doe,* 2. Tim. 2. 5. So
the

the Apostle *Iames* chap.1.verf.12. pronounceth the man *blef-*
fed that endureth tentation; for when he is tried(or rather as the
words are,when by triall he shall be found approued) *he shall*
receiue a crowne of life, which the Lord hath promised to them
that loue him. Whereby it appeareth, that none are crowned
vnlesse they striue as they ought , and therefore much lesse
they which striue not at all ; that none are blessed but those
who are tempted, and being tempted endure the temptation ; that first we must be tried,and by triall approoued,be-
fore we can receiue the crowne of life.

§. *Sect.5.*   Lastly, wee may be encouraged to this fight by certaine
Those that will hope of victorie,for we fight vnder the standerd of Christ Ie-
fight against sus,who alone is mightier then all our enemies that assault
our spirituall vs. If wee did indeede regard our enemies strength and our
enemies are
sure of victorie. owne weaknes onely, wee might well be discouraged from
vndertaking this combat, but if wee looke vpon our grand
Captaine Christ, whose loue towards vs is no lesse then his
power,and both infinite,there is no cause of doubting,for he
that exhorteth vs to the fight, will so helpe vs that we may
August.   ouercome; *Deficientes sublenat & vincentes coronat :* When
wee faint he sustaineth vs, and crowneth vs when wee ouercome. He hath alreadie ouercome our enemies to our hand,
and hath cooled their courage and abated their force. He
hath brused the serpents head,so that he shall not be able to
ouercome the least of his followers,well may he hisse against
them, but he cannot hurt them, for his sting is taken away.
Sathan was the strong man who possessed all in peace, but
our Sauiour Christ who was a stronger then he,comming vpon him hath ouercome him, and taken from him all his armour wherein he trusted and diuided his spoiles, Luk.11.21,
22. We fought against mightie enemies and great poten-
tates,Eph.6.12. but our Sauiour hath *spoiled principalities and*
powers,and hath made a shew of them openly,and hath triumphed
ouer them vpon the crosse, Col.2.15. *and so through death hath*
destroyed him that had the power of death, that is the diuell, that
he might deliuer all them which for feare of death were all their
life subiect to bondage, as it is Heb.2.14,15. He was indeede a
Iosh.10.24.25.mightie prince of this worldly Canaan, but our good *Ioshua*
hath

hath subdued him, and hath left nothing for vs to doe who are his souldiers and followers, but to tread in his necke in token of victorie. But we alas are faint-harted, like vnto *Iether* the first borne of *Gedeon*, Iudg.8.20,21. for though our Sauiour Christ hath conquered these our spirituall enemies, and hath put the sword of his spirit into our hands, wherewith we might also vanquish them, yet we are afraid to draw the sword, because we are but fresh water souldiers and white liuered; and therefore we had need to encourage our selues, not onely by looking on the victorie of our chiefe Captaine, but also on the conquest of our fellow souldiers, who were weake and fraile like our selues. So likewise Christ hath ouercome the world, and willeth vs to be of good comfort, seeing we shall be partakers with him in his triumph, if we wil ioyne with him in his fight, Ioh.16.33. And though our flesh be a treacherous enemie and stronger to vs then the spirit, yet so we will fight against the lusts thereof we shall be sure of victorie, for he will assist vs with his holie spirit, and therewith enable vs more and more to mortifie this old man and bodie of sinne. Well may we take a foyle in this spirituall combat, but the Lord wil raise vs vp againe; *For though we fall, yet shall we not be cast off, because the Lord putteth vnder his hand,* as it is Psal.37.24. And the Lord hath promised, that he will not suffer *vs to be tempted aboue our power, but will giue the issue with the tentation that we may be able to beare it,* as it is 1.Cor.10.13. and he that hath promised is faithfull and true, yea truth it selfe, and therefore he will be as good as his word. Though therefore Sathan incounter vs with all furie, let vs not be faint-harted, but couragiously endure his assaults, and so in the end the victorie will be ours: for if wee *resist the diuell he will flie from vs,* Iam.4.7. if we fight the Lords battailes valiantly, *the God of peace shall tread Sathan vnder our feete shortly,* as it is Rom.16.20. For the promise of brusing the serpents head made by the Lord, Gen.3.15. doth belong not onely to Iesus Christ our head, but also to all those who are members of his bodie.

Let vs not therefore feare to fight against beaten and conquered enemies, slothfully pretending our weaknes to withstand

§. Sect.6.

a Ioh.16.33.

Erasm. in En-chir. milit. Christ.

stand these sonnes of *Anakim*, for as one saith: *Nemo hic non vincet nisi qui vincere noluit:* Euery one shall be a conqueror who desireth the conquest. For if we will be the Lords soul-diers, he will not suffer himselfe to be so much disgraced, as to let vs be ouercome by his mortall enemies. He hath ar-med vs himselfe with his owne armour, and sent vs out to fight his battailes, and therefore he will not haue vs vanqui-shed, being fortified with his strength, for so should himselfe be ouercome in vs, and his weapons would be esteemed weake and insufficient. Yea he hath ingrafted vs into his own bodie, and we are liuely members thereof, and therefore let vs neuer think that all the power of hell shall be able to ouer-come vs : for what head can with patience suffer his found members to be pulled from his bodie, if he be able to defend them?

Chap. IIII.

Of the malice of our spirituall enemie Sathan.

§. Sect. 1.

And so much concerning the reasons which may encourage vs to vndertake this combat; now we are to speake of the spirituall warfare it self, wherein (as in all other warres) we are to consi-der of our preparation to the conflict, and the conflict it selfe. In our preparation we are first to consider of the state, qualitie, and condition of our enemies, and of our meanes how we may withstand and ouercome them.

Concerning the first, in an enemie who proclaimeth warre against vs we are to consider two things : first of his will, and secondly of his power. For if he haue will to hurt vs and no power, he is not to be greatly regarded; if power and no ma-litious and vnreconcilable will, he is not so much to be fea-red, but if his power be great and puissant, and his will mali-tious, then is it time to looke about vs, and to muster all our forces, that we may be readie to endure the incounter.

First therefore concerning the will of our grand and arch enemie Sathan, if wee consider thereof aright, wee shall finde

that

that it is moſt malitiouſly bent againſt vs, ſo that there is no
hope of truce or reconciliation with him, though wee could
finde in our cowardly hearts to labour and ſue for a diſhono-
rable peace with Gods and our enemie. For his malice is not
newly conceiued but inueterate, euen as ancient within a few
daies as the world it ſelfe, and much more durable ; for the
world ſhall haue an end, but Sathans malice to mankinde is
endleſſe, becauſe the cauſe thereof, namely the loue and fauour of God toward the faithfull (whoſe eſtate he doth enuie
and maligne, himſelfe being eternally reprobated) ſhall be
endleſſe and eternall. And this appeareth in the example of
our firſt parents, who were no ſooner placed in the garden of
pleaſure, and poſſeſſed of Paradiſe, but Sathan being almoſt
burſt with enuie to ſee their happie eſtate, neuer reſted till he
had diſgorged his malice, and diſpoſſeſſed them of that happineſſe which they enioyed. Neither doth he leſſe maligne
and hate thoſe who being fallen in *Adam* are raiſed vp in
Chriſt, and haue the fee ſimple of euerlaſting glorie, purchaſed by Chriſts merit, aſſured vnto them by the ſpirit of God
and a liuely faith. And hence it is that the Lord knowing Sathans malice towards his children, and that whether he fawneth or frowneth, he alwaies ſeeketh their deſtruction, hath
proclaimed open warres betweene vs, Gen.3.15.that we may
alwaies ſtand vpon our guard, and not be ſurpriſed at vnawares; that alſo wee may not entertaine a thought of peace,
though Sathan offer it on whatſoeuer conditions : for what
peace can there be betweene the children of God and the
children of Belial, betweene the ſeede of the woman and the
ſeede of the ſerpent, ſeeing God himſelfe from the beginning hath put enmitie betweene them ?

But as the malice of Sathan is inueterate, ſo alſo it is mortall and deadly, not to be ſatisfied by offering a ſmall iniurie,
by taking away our goods and good name, or afflicting vs
with ſickneſſe, no not by taking away our liues ; for nothing
will ſatisfie him but our finall deſtruction of body and ſoule.
And this his malice is liuely deciphered vnto vs by diuers
names which are giuen him in the Scriptures. For he is called
Sathan, that is an aduerſarie, ſtill readie to croſſe vs in all our
ſuites

Zach.3.1.
Matth.13.39.

suites which we make vnto God, as he did *Iehoshua* the high
Prieſt,Zach.3.1. He is called an enemie,Matth.13.39.and that
a malitious one; for where Chriſt the good husbandman
ſoweth wheate, there hee ſoweth tares, that is,hypocrites a-
mongſt true profeſſors, to the diſhonour of God, the diſcredit of the Goſpell, and the reproch of the true profeſſours
thereof.

And leaſt we ſhould thinke that he is ſome milde natured
enemie who will be ſatisfied with ſome ſmall reuenge, he is
called a murtherer and a manſlayer, as though this were his
profeſſion and occupation. And leaſt we ſhould imagine him
to be one lately fallen to this trade, our Sauiour telleth vs that

Ioh.8.44.

he hath been ſo from the beginning, ſo that like an old hangman he is fleſht in bloud and crueltie; and therefore ſeeing
wee can hope for no mercie at his hands, let vs ſo much the
more couragiouſly oppoſe our ſelues againſt him.

But for as much as the moſt ſauage man hath ſome reliques of humanitie left in him, therefore the holie Ghoſt
compareth him to beaſts,that wee may expect nothing from
him but brutiſh crueltie; as firſt to a lion, yea a lion roring
after his pray, who is ſo hungrie and rauenous, that he deſireth nothing more then to ſeaze vpon that which he purſu-

1.Pet.5.8.

eth,1.Pet.5.8. Now who would not be moſt carefull to keepe
himſelfe out of the pawes of ſuch a rauenous beaſt? or if hee
were incountred by him,who would not reſiſt him if hee had
any hope of victorie?

But in truth Sathan is farre more cruell then the roring
lion, who (if wee may giue credit to hiſtories) ſpareth thoſe
that fall downe flat before him; whereas if he ſhould get vs
at ſuch aduantage, he would proudly trample vs vnder foot,
and make vs ſure for euer riſing;and therefore leaſt we ſhould
looke for any mercie at his hands by ſubmiſſion,the holie

Apoc.12.3.

Ghoſt calleth him the *great red dragon,* Apoc.12.3. which
beaſt beareth ſuch naturall malice to mankinde, that he deuoureth them not onely for hunger, but alſo for ſport or hatred, in ſatisfying whereof hee taketh great delight ; ſuch a
beaſt is our enemie, who is ſo fleſht in bloud and crueltie,
and ſo ouercaried with malice and hatred, that he eſteemeth

it

it his chiefe fport and paftime to deftroy vs. Yea he is far more daungerous, for the other rageth but againft the bodie, this againft both body and foule; that beaft we may eafily auoid, but it is impoffible to flee from this winged Dragon, and therefore there is no other meanes to efcape his furie, but by arming our felues ftrongly, and fighting valiantly til we haue put him to flight.

And thus you fee Sathans malice ioyned with crueltie and raging violence, which he vfeth when hee hath any hope of furprifing vs by affault; but if hee finde vs ftrongly fortified with Gods graces, and at all points armed with the com-pleate armour of a Chriftian, if he perceiue that we are hed-ged in and fenced on all fides (as he fpeaketh of *Iob* chap.1. 10) that is, guarded and protected by Gods almightie and al-ruling prouidence, fo that he hath no hope of ouercomming vs by affault and force, then he fheweth no leffe malice and more fubtiltie in feeking our deftruction, by fauning vpon vs, and alluring vs to finne, by offering the baites of honour, pleafure and commoditie, that fo he may make entrance as it were by a pofterne gate, and fubdue vs while we are aban-doned of the Lords affiftance, and difarmed of our fpirituall weapons, whereby we fhould make refiftance. And thus hee dealt with our firft parents, who being inticed to finne, and alfo yeelding to the inticement, and fo being depriued of Gods protection and the breaft-plate of rightcoufnes, were laid open to thofe deadly wounds which he inflicted on them. For affoone as they had tafted of the forbidden fruite, they perceiued their nakednes, and therefore couered them-felues with figge leaues, too weake an armour to repell the firie darts of Sathan. Thus he difarmed the Ifraelites, by temp-ting them to worfhip the golden Calfe, fo that *Mofes* faw that they were naked, that is, difarmed of Gods fauour and protection, Exod.32.25. And this his policie hee taught his feruant *Balaam*, who when he could not curfe them whom God had bleffed, gaue this curfed counfaile to *Balaak*, that the Moabitifh women fhould intice the Ifraelites to commit with them firft carnall and then fpirituall whoredome, know-ing that to be the onely meanes to bring Gods curfe vpon

§. Sect.3. Sathans malice ioyned with treacherous falfehood.

Iob.1.10.

Exod. 32.25.

them.

Numb.25.1.2. and 31.16. Apoc.2.14. them. As wee may fee if we compare Numb.25.1,2. with the 31.chapter and 16.verfe, and Apoc.2.14. And thus alfo this wilde boare would haue broken downe the hedge which defended *Iob*, by tempting him to blafpheme God. And thus our fubtill enemie *Sinon*-like inticeth vs with deceiuing allurements, euen with our owne hands to breake downe the wall of our defence, and to make an open paffage for whole troupes of finnes to enter and furprize vs, whileft we (ouercome with a falfe ioy) glut and make our felues drunke with the cup of voluptuous pleafures, and lie fnorting in the dead fleepe of carnall fecuritie, not fo much as once dreaming of our approching ruine and deftruction.

§. Sect.4.

Matth.4.2. 1.Theff.3.5. And hereof he hath the name of tempter giuen him, yea he is not onely called a tempter, but, κατ᾽ ἐξοχὴν, ὁ πειράζων *the tempter*, becaufe he is a tempter of tempters, and as it were a tempter by profeffion, Matth.4.2. 1.Theff.3.5.

The confideration whereof fhould make vs moft carefull to withftand all his temptations, whereby he allureth vs vnto finne. For if we yeeld vnto them, he will furely difarme vs of Gods fauour and protection, and fo deadly wound our foules when he hath made them naked. There is no wife man will put off his armour and caft away his weapons in the prefence of his cruell enemie, though hee perfwade him thereto with many flattring fpeeches and faire promifes; and fhall we let Sathan difarme vs, becaufe he allureth vs thereto, by promifing fome vnlawfull profit or vaine pleafure, efpecially feeing we know him to be an enemie no leffe treacherous then malitious?

But as he is a tempter to intice vs vnto finne, fo alfo he is our accufer after that we haue finned, requiring of God that he will execute his iuftice vpon the offenders who haue deferued punifhment. Of this there neede no further proofe Iob.1.7. then his owne teftimonie, Iob.1.7. where hee profeffeth that he had been compaffing the earth about; like a promoter to fpie out faults, that he might informe againft the offenders. But becaufe wee will not reft in his teftimonie, who is the father of lies, wee will adde thereunto another of vndoubted Apoc.12.10. authoritie: for Apoc.12.10. it is faid, that the Saints *reioyce, becaufe tauſe Sathan, who was the accuſer of their brethren, was caſt downe, which accuſed them before God day and night.* So that Sathan can ſpare no time, from accuſing vs for ſinne, but that which hee imployeth in tempting vs thereunto, or in inflicting thoſe puniſhments which God permitteth him to lay vpon vs. Whereby we may perceiue the malice and treachery of our enemie, who though he be the chiefe cauſe which moueth vs to ſinne, yet himſelfe is the firſt that accuſeth vs for it, and that vnceſſantly. Which may ſerue as a ſtrong argument to make vs warie of our waies, leaſt falling into ſinne, we giue Sathan occaſion to inſult ouer vs, and to preferre bils of inditement before our heauenly Iudge, whoſe exact iuſtice will not let ſinne goe vnpuniſhed. If there were a promoter continually prying into all our actions, who were moſt maliciouſly diſpoſed againſt vs, and readie to infourme of all our miſdemeanour vnto the Magiſtrate, how fearefull would wee be to doe any thing which would bring vs within the compaſſe of the law? But ſuch an informer continually obſerueth all our behauiour, euen in our ſecret chambers; who will not faile to accuſe vs euen of thoſe ſinnes which he himſelfe hath tempted vs vnto: and therefore ſeeing this malitious blab ſtill prieth into our actions, this ſhould be of more force to withhold vs from all ſinne, then if all the world did look vpon vs.

But he is not onely an accuſer, but a ſlaunderer alſo, and thereof he hath his name διάϐολ﹩. If therefore he can ſpie but an apparance of euill in vs, he will not ſticke to ſay, that wee haue or will commit that euill which he ſuſpecteth vs of, for he will wreſt and miſconſter all we do to the worſt ſenſe, and make of euery molehill an huge mountaine. Thus wrongfully did he ſlaunder *Iob*, that hee ſerued God for that end for which *Demetrius* ſeru'd his Goddeſſe, namely for aduantage, becauſe he preſerued him and bleſſed all he had; affirming that if he would take away his goods, and a little afflict his bodie, he would blaſpheme him to his face, Iob.1.10. And this alſo teacheth vs to look warily to our actions, abſtaining not onely from euill, but alſo from all apparance thereof, as the Apoſtle exhorteth, that ſo wee giue not to our malitious enemie the leaſt aduantage. Iob.1.10. 1.Theſſ.5.22.

C 3 Neither

Neither is Sathan onely an accufer and flaunderer, but alfo
an executioner or hangman, readie with all alacritie and fa-
uage crueltie to inflict that punifhment the which the Lord
adiudgeth vs vnto, as wee may fee in the hiftorie of *Iob* ; and
this alfo fheweth vnto vs the extreame malice of our enemy,
which maketh him to forget that glorious ftate wherein hee
was created, & with al willingnes to execute fo bafe an office.

§. *Sect.5.*
Eph.6.12.

By all which appeareth that our enemie Sathan is moft
malitious, yea *malitioufneffe* it felfe, as he is called Eph.6. 12.
that is, the father and author of all malice and enuie, who laboureth might and maine to difhonour God and worke our
deftruction. The confideration whereof fhould rouze vs out
of our carnall fecuritie (whereby men behaue themfelues, as
though either they had no enemie at all, or els fuch a gentle
natured one, that they may haue peace with him at their own
pleafure) feeing there is no hope of peace and truce, vnleffe
we can be content to liue in his thraldome to our vtter deftruction: for whomfoeuer he keepeth as his prifoners in this
life, he will at the houre of death and iudgement bring out to
execution.

Let vs therefore oppofe againft Sathans malice, Chriftian
refolution; ftedfaftly purpofing and endeuouring to continue
our fight in refifting Sathan to our liues end, how troublefome foeuer it feemeth to flefh and bloud. For feeing there is
no truce to be hoped for, nor to be defired if it were offered,
by reafon of the enmitie which is betweene vs and our enemie; feeing his malice is fo inueterate and mortall, that there
is no mercie to be expected, but all barbarous and raging
crueltie; feeing alfo wee fight the Lords battailes, who hath
affured vs of victorie in the end: This fhould make vs fo refolute, that though we be foyled, wounded, and as it were beaten downe on our knees, yet wee fhould neuer yeeld, but
make refiftance euen to the laft gafpe. For what more honorable death then to dye in fighting the Lords battailes?
What death more profitable, feeing by dying we fhall ouercome and obtaine a finall victorie ouer all our enemies, and
receiue the crowne of glory, euerlafting happineffe, promifed
to all thofe who fight valiantly in this combat vnto the end ?

CHAP.

CHAP. V.

Of the strength of our spirituall enemie Sathan.

Nd thus haue I shewed the malitious will of our enemie ; let vs now confider of his power. For though he be most malitious,yet if hee wanted power to execute his malice, wee might well contemne him,and rest secure,making no great preparation to resist his weake assault.

But with our enemie it is farre otherwise : for as his will is most malitioufly bent to hurt, so is he strong and mightie to effect his will. And this his power and abilitie to execute his will,confisteth partly in his strength, and partly in his skill and warlike policie,whereby he imployeth all his strength to his best aduantage. His strength may be confidered both in himfelfe and in his aides.

In respect of his owne strength he is very mightie, so that *Of Sathans* if the Lord permitteth him he is able to raife the winds, ftirre *strength confi-* vp tempests, bring downe fire from heauen, and vtterly de-*dered in him-* ftroy vs in a moment. And this his strength the holie Ghost *selfe.* expresseth, by comparing him to things most strong, either in the fea or on the land, that fo we may be more carefull to arme our felues against him.He is compared to the great *Le-* *Esa 27.1.* *uiathan* or Whale, Esa.27.1. whose inuincible force is defcri-*Iob.41.* bed by the Lord himfelfe,Iob.41.

He is compared to a lion, yea to a *roring lion,* 1.Pet.5.8. *1.Pet.5.8.* which rauenoufly hunting after his pray hath his force re-doubled with his hunger. And also to a *great red Dragon,*ha-uing feuen heads and tenne hornes, whofe strength is fo great, that with his very taile hee drew the third part of the ftarres of heauen,and caft them to the earth, Apoc.12.4. that *Apoc.12.4.* is, he vanquifheth and fubdueth many in the vifible Church which make fome profeffion of religion, but in their liues denie the power thereof. And this his ftrength is fo much the more dangerous,by reafon of his mortall malice and deadly poyfon which he cafteth out of his mouth in great abundáce.

§. *Sect.2.*

And leaſt we ſhould contemne this brutiſh might,which a weake man may with policie defeate, therefore he is compared to *a ſtrong armed man*, Luk.11.21. who keepeth in peace all that he poſſeſſeth. And leaſt wee ſhould deſpiſe him becauſe hee is but one, the holie Ghoſt telleth vs that hee is a mightie prince,not of one land or countrie, but of the whole world,Ioh.12.31. who therefore hath infinite multitudes at his commaundement, neither is there one of theſe princes alone, but huge multitudes of them ; and therefore the holie Ghoſt ſpeaking of them vſeth the plurall number, ſaying, that we *fight againſt principalities, againſt powers, and againſt the worldly gouernours,&c.*Whereas therefore the holie Ghoſt doth call him the ſtrong man,Sathan,and the diuel in the ſingular number;he would not haue vs to conceiue that there is onely one,but it is partly to note the chiefe of the kingdome of darknes,according to that Matth.25.41. *Depart from me ye accurſed into euerlaſting fire, which is prepared for the diuell and his angels.* And in this ſenſe he is called Beelzebub the prince of diuels,Matth.12.24. And partly to intimate vnto vs their great conſent and agreement in ſeeking the deſtruction of mankinde ; for though they be an huge multitude, yet they combine themſelues together,as if they were but one,in ſeeking our deſtruction.

Otherwiſe the Scriptures euidently ſhew vs, that there is not one alone,but many to aſſault vs. Matth.12.45.One ſpirit taketh vnto him ſeuen more,and they al enter into one man. Mark.16.9.It is ſaid that Chriſt had caſt out of *Mary Magdalen* ſeuen, that is, many diuels. So Luk.8.30. there is mention made of a man poſſeſſed with an whole legion, that is, with an huge multitude. So that as our enemies are powerful in ſtrength,ſo are they in numbers numberleſſe, enow to beſet vs all,on all ſides and in all places,and therefore our fight muſt needes be daungerous : which daunger the Apoſtle aggrauateth, by telling vs that they are the princes of darknes, and therefore as well able to aſſault vs in the night as in the day, which fight of all other is moſt terrible,when we cannot ſee our enemies, and therefore cannot tell on which ſide to defend our ſelues.

Secondly,

Luk.11.21.

Ioh.12.31.

Eph.6.12.

Matth.25.41.

Matth.12.24.

Matth.12.45.

Mark.16.9.
Luk.8.30.

Eph.6.12.

Secondly, he telleth vs that wee wraſtle not with enemies of fleſh and bloud like vnto our ſelues, but with ſpirituall wickedneſſes, which are moſt daungerous; becauſe being ſpirits they can with incredible ſwiftnes paſſe from place to place which are farre diſtant, and therfore the more fitly take all aduantages, either in aſſaulting vs at their pleaſure, or withdrawing themſelues when they finde reſiſtance; being ſpirits they can lie ſecretly in ambuſhment, euen in our bedchambers, and ſo ſurprize vs when they finde vs moſt retchleſſe and ſecure, for we cannot diſcouer them before we feele their aſſaults.

Thirdly, he telleth vs that they are in high places, to note vnto vs that they haue gotten the aduantage of the vpper ground; and therefore the fight muſt be daungerous, when our enemie fighteth againſt vs from an high place or fort, we ſtanding ſo low that we are ſcarce able to reach him. But becauſe earthly things cannot ſufficiently ſhew the power of our enemie Sathan, therefore he is called *the god of this world,* 2.Cor.4.4 2.Cor. 4.4 to note vnto vs, that in reſpect of worldly ſtrength and humane reſiſtance, hee is after a ſort omnipotent, that is, able to doe what he liſt, if he were not reſtrained by Gods diuine power, who alone is omnipotent, and ouerruled by no ſuperiour.

And thus you ſee the puiſſant power of this our ſpirituall enemie; but though he were ſtrong, yet if withall he were a daſtard and voide of courage, he were the leſſe to be feared; but as he is very ſtrong, ſo alſo he is exceeding deſperate and audacious, for there was neuer man that liued, who he durſt not encounter, yea and that after (by Gods aſſiſtance) he had taken many ouerthrowes. Though *Dauid* were a moſt holie man and according to Gods owne hart, yet he aſſaulted him, and gaue him diuers foyles, by tempting him to adulterie, murther, and in pride of heart to number the people. Though *Iob* was by Gods owne teſtimonie the iuſteſt man on earth, and therefore the beſt armed with the breaſt-plate of righteouſnes, yet Sathan durſt encounter him as long as God would ſuffer him. He reſiſted *Iehoſhua* the good high Prieſt, Zach.3.1. He buffeted *Paul* the choſen veſſell of the Lord,

§. *Sect.3.*
Of the courage and audaciouſnes of Sathan.

Zach.3.1.
2.Cor.

2.Cor.12.7. Yea ſo ventrous hee is, that he aſſaulted our firſt parents in the ſtate of innocencie, when they were armed with free will, and might if they would haue reſiſted his temptations. Nay, ſo deſperately audacious is this our ene-mie, that he durſt encounter our grand Captaine Chriſt Ieſus, who was God and man able to deſtroy him with a word of his mouth; and that not once but many times, after he was ſhamefully foyled and ouerthrowne : yea ſo inſolent and foole-hardie he is, that he did not onely aſſault him here on earth when he was in the ſhape of a ſeruant, and whereas in reſpect of his outward ſtate he might haue ſome hope of pre-uailing; but alſo he wageth warre againſt him in heauen, ſit-ting at the right hand of his father in all glorie, power and maieſtie, when as he hath no appearance of hope to preuaile, but is moſt ſure that he ſhall haue the ouerthrow. And this

appeareth Apoc.12.7. *And there was a battaile in heauen: Mi-chael and his angels fought againſt the dragon; and the dragon fought and his angels,but they preuailed not,&c.* Where by *Mi-chael* we are to vnderſtand Chriſt himſelfe, for he onely is the prince of Angels ; and this name ſignifying ſuch an one as is equall with God almightie, can agree to no other but vnto Chriſt alone. And by the Dragon wee are to vnderſtand Sa-than, as appeareth verſ.9. who fought againſt our Sauiour, though he preuailed not.

If therefore hee durſt encounter the moſt valiant ſouldiers that euer fought the Lords battailes, yea if hee durſt ſet vpon our Sauiour Chriſt himſelfe; then ſurely there is no doubt but that he hath courage enough to ſet vpon vs who are weake and feeble, altogether vnable in our ſelues to make reſiſtance.

Seeing therefore our enemies are ſo puiſſant in ſtrength, ſo innumerable in multitude,ſo dangerous and ſo audacious, let vs ſhake off all ſecuritie, and continually ſtand in readines to endure the encounter : for what follie is it for vs with ſe-cure worldlings to contemne, and make no reckoning of ſuch enemies ? Seeing euery one of vs muſt reſiſt a huge mul-titude; ſeeing wee which are weake and feeble are to with-ſtand thoſe which are ſtrong and mightie; ſeeing wee which are fleſh and bloud muſt enter combat with thoſe which are

ſpirituall

fpirituall wickedneffes, principalities, powers,and princes of
darknes; feeing wee who are cowardly and fearefull muft fuftaine the encounter of thofe who are defperate and audacious; laftly,feeing wee haue in our felues no aduantages a-
gainft them, and they want no aduantages againft vs : let vs
not therefore foolifhly contemne fuch puiffant enemies, but
with all care and diligence let vs arme our felues againft
them,and *worke out our faluation with feare and trembling,* as
the Apoftle exhorteth, Phil.2.12. Phil.2.12.

§. Sect.4.

But as we are not fecurely to contemne thefe enemies : fo
we are not faintly to yeeld vnto them, nor cowardly to defpaire of victorie. For as all thofe which fecurely contemning
them neuer ftand vpon their guard, are moft fure to be furprifed and ouerthrowne; fo whofoeuer arme themfelues a-
gainft them, and enter into the fpirituall combat with a defire to ouercome , fhall moft certainly obtaine victorie : for
though their power be great , yet it is not infinite, and that
which they haue, it is not from themfelues but from the
Lord, who fo curbeth them with his all-ruling prouidence,
that they are not able to goe one iot further then he loofeth
out the raines ; as it plainly appeareth both by examples and
teftimonies of Scripture. Though Sathan were moft malitioufly difpofed againft *Iob*, fo that he did with all extremi-
tie execute that which God fuffered him to doe,yet he could
not goe one iot further then his commiffion, he could not
touch his fubftance till the Lord had faid, *All that he hath is
in thy hand,*Iob.1.12. And therefore not preuailing againft
him by depriuing him of his goods and fubftance, he commeth againe to the Lord to haue his commiffion inlarged,
Iob.2.1. and then hauing gotten authoritie to afflict his bodie,yet could he not touch his life, becaufe the Lord had not
giuen him fo much liberty.Though *Saul* were a wicked man,
yet Sathan could not hurt or vexe him,till the Lord fent him,
1.Sam.16.14.And hence it is that he is called the *fpirit of God,*
verf.15.and chap.18.10. becaufe he is Gods flaue and wholie
at his appointment. So hee could not deceiue the falfe prophets of *Ahab*,till he had gotten licence of the Lord,1.King.
22.22. Nay, fo farre is Sathan from hauing abfolute authoritie

tie and power ouer the faithfull, that it is limited and restrained in respect of the meanest creatures; for a whole legion
of diuels could not so much as enter into one heard of swine,
till by earnest intreatie they had obtained leaue of our Sauiour Christ, Luk. 8.31,32. And therefore much lesse can they
preuaile against any of Gods children, seeing the very haires
of their head are numbred, Matth. 10.29. Well may Sathan
maligne vs and earnestly desire our destruction; well may he
secke to sift vs like wheate, as hee did *Peter*; but our Sauiour
Christ maketh intercession for vs, so that our faith shall neuer
faile, Luk. 22.31.

This also is manifest by plaine testimonies. *Iude 6.* it is
said, that the Lord hath *reserued the wicked angels in euerlasting chaines vnder darknes, vnto the iudgement of the great day.*
2. Pet. 2.4. *God spared not the Angels that had sinned, but cast
them downe into hell, and deliuered them into chaines of darknes
to be kept vnto damnation.* So Apoc. 20. 2. Sathan is said to haue
been bound by the Angell of the Lord for a thousand yeres,
so that hee could not stirre till the Lord suffered him to be
loosed. By all which the holie Ghost noteth vnto vs, that Sathan is no more able to doe vs hurt, then a malefactor who
being bound hand and foote is cast into a deepe dungeon, or
then a band-dog which is fast tied vp in strong chaines, till
the Lord looseth him and giueth him leaue.

But here some man may obiect, that Sathan is said in the
Scriptures, to resist God and to oppose himselfe against him,
and euen to fight a battaile against our Sauiour Christ himselfe and his blessed Angels, Apoc. 12.7. I answere, that this
resistance and fight dependeth on Gods permissiue prouidence, neither could hee so much as stirre against God, if hee
did not suffer him. He is indeede most malitiously disposed
against the Lord, and by this his malice is stirred vp to doe
those things which hee thinketh most displeasant in Gods
eyes: but because the Lord chaineth and curbeth him in with
his omnipotent power, he is onely able to doe those things
that God permitteth him, and, will he nill he, he is constrai-
ned to obey his Creator and to be at his commandement.

Seeing therefore Sathans power is restrained by the omnipotent

nipotent power of God, this may ſerue as a ſtrong reaſon to ſtrengthen our faith in the aſſurance of victorie; eſpecially conſidering that the Lord is not only omnipotent in power, but alſo in reſpect of his will moſt readie to aide and ſupport vs in all our conflicts. For he hath promiſed vs, that wee ſhall not *be tempted aboue our power, for he will giue a good iſſue to the* 1.Cor.10.13. *temptation,* though the beginning and middle are dangerous and troubleſome, 1.Cor.10.13. He hath promiſed, that if wee will but reſiſt the diuell, wee ſhall put him to flight, Iam.4.7. Iam.4.7. Though therefore in our ſelues wee are very weake, yet God will aſſiſt vs in this combat, which as well concerneth his owne glorie as our good, and being armed with his power, the gates of hell cannot preuaile againſt vs. Well may the Lord ſuffer vs to take a foyle, that thereby learning to know our owne weakenes, wee may the more carefully reſt on his power, and more earneſtly craue his aſſiſtance, but then hee will raiſe vs vp though wee be neuer ſo feeble; for the more apparant our infirmities are, the more cleerely will the omnipotent power of the Lord ſhine vnto all the world, when by his helpe we haue obtained victorie.

Would we therefore reſiſt Sathans force and ſtrength? then §. *Sect.*5. let vs not goe armed in our owne power, for we are ſo weak- *If we will o-* ned with ſinne and corruption, that wee are not able to with- *uercome we* ſtand his leaſt aſſault; but deſpairing in our owne abilitie, let *muſt wholy re-* vs relie our ſelues wholie on the Lord : *for we are ſtrengthened* *lie on the Lord.* *with all might through his glorious power,* as it is Col.1.11. and Col.1.11. though in our ſelues wee are able to doe nothing, *yet wee are* *able to doe all things, through the helpe of Chriſt which ſtrengthe-* *neth vs,* as it is Phil.4.13. Of our ſelues we are not able to en- Phil.4.13. dure the leaſt incounter of our ſpirituall enemies; but yet if wee truſt in the Lord, he *will giue vs victorie through Ieſus* 1.Cor.15.57. *Chriſt,* 1.Cor.15.57. And hence it is that the Apoſtle prepa- ring vs for this ſpirituall combat, doth exhort vs to *be ſtrong* Rom.8.37. *in the Lord, and in the power of his might; and to put on the whole* *armour of God, that we may be able to ſtand againſt the aſſaults* Eph.6.10.11. *of the diuell,* Epheſ.6.10,11. If therefore wee would be ſafely protected from the furie of Sathans power, let vs not oppoſe againſt it our owne ſtrength, for then ſurely we ſhall be ouer- come,

but let vs relie our selues on the almightie power of God,
professing with the Prophet *Dauid*,Pfal.18.2.that the *Lord is*

Pfal.18.2.
*our rocke and fortreſſe,and he that deliuereth vs.our God and our
ſtrength,in him will we truſt, our ſhield, the horne of our ſaluation
and our refuge.* Let vs with him call vpon *God which is worthie
to be praiſed,*and ſo ſhal we be ſafe from al our enemies,ver.3.

In like manner, when wee conſider of the infinite number
of our enemies, which daily aſſault euery one of vs, let vs
thereby be awakened out of the ſlumber of careleſſe retch-
leſnes, and be ſtirred vp to ſtand vpon our guard more carefully : but yet let not this diſcourage vs from the fight, becauſe there are many to one, *for the Lord is with vs* whileſt we
fight his battailes, and therefore *what mattreth it who oppoſe
themſelues againſt vs ?* Rom.8.31. *The Lord will fight for vs,*

Rom.8 31.
Exod.14.14.
*therefore let vs hold our peace,*Exod.14.14.*The battell is not
ours but Gods, and therefore let vs not be afraid of this great*

2.Chro.20.15.
*multitude,*as it is 2.Chro.20.15. for the greater the number is
which fighteth againſt vs, the more will the Lord glorifie
himſelfe in our victorie, the greatnes of his power ſhining ſo
much the more cleerely in the weakenes of the meanes, and
our infirmities ſeruing as a foile, to make the riches of his
omnipotencie and glorie appeare more glorious. So that the
Lord ſtanding on our ſide, it is not materiall how many wicked ſpirits aſſaults vs ; if he take vpon him our preſeruation,
we neede not care though the whole power of hell ſeeke our
deſtruction. But if ſuch be the frailtie of our faith, that wee
would oppoſe number againſt number,let vs conſider that if
we will fight the Lords battailes,he wil ſend as many bleſſed
Angels to our aid & reſcue, as there are wicked ſpirits which
aſſault vs ; *for the Angels of the Lord pitch their tents round*

Pfal.34.7.
*about them that feare him,and deliuer them,*as it is Pfal.34.7.So
that if the Lord open our eyes, as hee did the eyes of *Eliſhaes*
ſeruant,we ſhall plainly perceiue that there are more with vs

2 King.6.16.
§. Sect.6.
then againſt vs,2.King.6.16,17.

So when we conſider that we wreſtle not againſt fleſh and
bloud, but againſt ſpirituall wickedneſſes, this ſhould make
vs labour that our care and diligence may counteruaile the
diſaduantage which we haue in the fight. But wee are not to
be

be difcouraged hereby from entring the combat: for though
we be but flefh and bloud, yet the fpirit of God dwelling in
vs,can eafily difcerne and defeate all Sathans ambufhments;
for light and darknes are to him alike. And whereas Sathan
can with great agilitie giue the affault and retire back for his
beft aduantage,Gods fpirit farre excelleth him, for he is prefent in all places at all times; fo that Sathan can no fooner offer to ftrike, but Gods fpirit is readie to defend; no fooner
can the diuell tempt,then the Lord enableth vs to endure the
temptation. And though Sathan fighteth from high places,
and fo taketh the aduantage of the vpper ground, yet let not
this difmay vs in our fight,for there is one higher then hee
who laugheth him to fcorne, and maketh fruftrate all his en-
terprifes.

Laftly,when we confider that our enemie is defperate and
audacious, wee are not to caft away our fpirituall weapons
and forfake the field, but let it rather serue as a ftrong motiue to make vs arme our felues with Chriftian refolution :
for feeing fathan is fo audacious and venterous in the affault,
furely we fhould be as valiant and bold in giuing him the repulfe; if he be defperate in feeking our deftruction,it behooueth vs to be refolute in feeking our preferuation,feeing this
much more concerneth vs then the other him; efpeciallie
confidering that though wee take many foyles, and be often
beaten downe with the violent blowes of his temptations,
yet in the end we fhall haue affured victorie. And why therefore fhould Sathan fhew more refolution when he is fure to
be vanquifhed,then we who are fure of the victorie,if we doe
not cowardly yeeld ?

Chap. VI.
Of Sathans aides : and firft of the world.

A Nd fo much concerning Sathans ftrength, being con- §. Sect. r.
fidered in himfelf.But befides himfelf he hath the aide
of other enemies to fupplant vs,who though they doe
not make fo terrible a fhew, yet they are no leffe dangerous,

and

and all thefe are led vnder the conduct of two Captaine Ge-
nerals,the World and the Flefh.

By the world I vnderftand impious carnall and vnbeleeuing men,with all their baites and inticements vnto vanitie,
and all their difcouragements,afflictions and miferies wherewith they hinder Gods children in trauailing the path of
righteoufnes which leadeth to Gods kingdome.This wicked
world, the diuels darling and chief champion,doth affault vs
How the world on both fides ; on the right hand it encountreth vs with pro-
tempteth by- fperitie, offering vs the baite of pleafure, that thereby it may
profperitie. allure vs to fwallow the hooke of finne; it cafteth before vs
the golden apples of riches,that by ftooping down to gather
them,we may be hindred in running the Chriftian race, and
fo lofe the goale and garland of euerlafting glorie ; it tempteth vs with the honours and glorie thereof to difhonour
God,and to fall before Sathan,worfhipping him by our fins;
in a word, it promifeth whatfoeuer our corrupt mindes defire,if we will liue in finne, and turne afide out of the narrow
path into the broad way, which leadeth to deftruction. And
how prone wee are to liften to thefe Syrens fongs, it is but
too manifeft by lamentable experience : for doth not our
firft loue waxe cold, and our former zeale of Gods glorie
freeze as foone as the world fauneth vpon vs, and quencheth
in vs the heate of Gods fpirit, by cafting on vs the watrifh
vanities of pleafures,honours and riches ? Doe not hereby religious feruants become irreligious mafters? and yong faints
in fhew,old diuels in truth ? Doe we not fee that as foone as
Demas hath imbraced the world, he forfaketh Chrift ? yea
that *Peter* himfelfe denieth his Mafter, when he hath bafted
himfelfe by the fire of this wicked *Caiphas*.? Are there not
many who haue been forward profeffors in the time of their
aduerfitie and want, which caft off the cloake of their profeffion as foone as the warme funne of profperitie hath fhined
vpon them ? Is there not many amongft vs who in the time
of affliction could not be inforced by torments to prophane
Gods name, by fwearing an idle oath; or his Sabbaoths by
following their pleafures, or by doing the workes of their
callings; and yet the fame men after they haue fallen into
                                                        wicked

wicked companie, who haue inticed them by their words
and euil examples to tafte of the world and the vanities therof, will not fticke to fweare with the fwearer, and follow their
pleafures on the Lords Sabbaoth with the moft prophane?
fo hard a thing it is to refift the world when it fauneth on vs.

But how hard foeuer it feemeth to flefh and bloud, yet
muft wee oppofe our felues againft this enemie alfo : for
without a fight wee can neuer obtaine victorie, and without
victorie we fhall neuer receiue the crowne of glorie. And to
the end that we may be prouoked to fight againft the world
and the vanities thereof, we are to know, that though it faune
vpon vs, yet it is our mortall enemie ; though it flatteringly
profeffe it felfe our friend, yet in truth it fighteth againft our
foules vnder Sathans banner, for hee is the prince thereof,
Ioh.12.31. though it haue hony in the mouth, yet there is
deadly poyfon in the taile, for the end thereof bringeth deftruction ; though it offer vs many pleafing things to allure
vs, yet they are but baites which intice vs to come within the
compaffe of Sathans nets of perdition. Let vs confider, that
though it maketh a fhew, and feemeth a pleafant place like
the paradife of God, yet it is a Sodome of finne, which one
day the Lord will deftroy with fire and brimftone : and therfore let vs with righteous *Lot* hafte out of it, neuer turning
back with a defire to enioy the vanities thereof ; for *the world
wholy lieth in wickedneffe*, as it is 1.Ioh.5.19. Let vs remember
that it is impoffible *to ferue God and this Mammon*, Mat.6.24.
to loue the world and God alfo: *For if any man loue the world,
the loue of the father is not in him*, 1.Ioh.2.15. and as the A-
poftle *Iames* telleth vs, *The amitie of the world is enmitie with
God : and whofoeuer will be a friend of the world, maketh himfelfe
the enemie of God*, Iam.4.4. Neither let vs defire the loue of the
world, for it *loueth thofe onely which are her owne, as for thofe
whom Chrift hath chofen out of it, thofe the world hateth* : nay
therefore hateth them becaufe Chrift hath chofen them, as it
is Ioh.15.19.

Let vs remember ỹ it wil be to fmal purpofe to enioy thefe
worldly pleafures of finne for a feafon, and in the end plunge
our felues into euerlafting death ; that the worlds muficke is

§. *Sect.*2.
*How we muft
refift the temp-
tations of pro-
fperitie.*

Ioh.12,31.

Gen.13.10.

1.Ioh.5.19.

Matth.6.24
1.Ioh.2.15.

Iam.4.4.

Ioh.15.19.

D   but

but the Syrens fong, which allureth vs to make fhipwrack of
our foules on the rockes of finne, and while it tickleth the
eare it woundeth vs to the very heart; that though the cup
which it offereth be of gold, and the drinke fweete in tafte,
yet it is deadly poyfon in operation; for they that drinke
thereof are fo lulled afleepe in pleafures and fecuritie; that
they neuer awake out of their fpirituall lethargie; or if they
doe, yet like *Sampfon,* without ftrength to refift the fpirituall
Philiftines, after the world (like *Dalila*) hath lulled them a
while in her lap of carnall pleafures. Let vs remember, that
they who drinke of this cup of voluptuous vanities, muft afterwards drinke of that cup fpoken of Pfal.75.8. that is, the
cup of Gods wrath; and fhall be tormented in fire and brimftone for euermore, as it is expounded Apoc.14.10. Let vs remember that the worlds chiefe good is vncertaine in getting,
and momentanie and mutable in the poffeffion, it being euery day readie to leaue vs, or wee to leaue it. Laftly, let vs remember that for this fhort, inconftant, and vaine ioy, we lofe
an eternall waight of vnfpeakable glorie, and plunge our
felues into grieuous and endleffe miferie. What therefore *will
it profit vs to gaine the whole world, and lofe our owne foules,* as
our Sauiour fpeaketh, Mark.8.36.

     And if wee haue thefe meditations continually running in
our mindes, then fhall we eafily ftop our eares at the firft hearing of this Syrens fong; then fhall we conftantly go forward
in our pilgrimage towards our heauenly home: and though
honours ftand before vs, riches on the one hand, pleafures on
the other, alluring vs to enter into the broad way which leadeth to deftruction; yet fhall we not forfake the ftraight path
which leadeth vnto life euerlafting, how vnpleafant foeuer it
feemeth to flefh and bloud.

     But if the world cannot thus preuaile, then doth fhe turne
her fmiles into frowns, her allurements into threats, her beds
of pleafures, into miferies and afflictions, her glorious offers
of honours and riches, to proude menacings of pouertie and
ignominie; all which being terrible in the eyes of flefh and
bloud fo farre preuaile with fome, that they moue them to
make fhipwracke of faith and a good confcience; and being

                                         wearie

Marginal notes:

Pfal.75.8.

Apoc.14.10.

Mark.8.36.

§. Sect.3.
*How the world
tempteth by ad-
uerfitie.*

wearie in trauailing through this defart and vnpleafant wildernefle vnto the land of promife, they defire to returne back
into the bondage of the fpirituall *Pharaoh*, that they may
quietly fit by the flefh-pots of Egypt, and glut themfelues
with the cucumbers and pepons of carnall pleafures: that is,
they chufe rather to walke in the broad way which leadeth
to deftruction, becaufe it is delightfull, than in the narrow
way which leadeth to euerlafting life, becaufe they muft
paffe through the briars of affliction and thornes of tribulation, before they can receiue the crowne of glorie; they preferre the pleafures of fin for a feafon, before the recompence
of reward, which God hath promifed, euen the eternall ioyes
of the kingdome of glorie. So vnpleafant a thing it is for flefh
and bloud to denie it felfe, and to take vp the croffe and follow Chrift.

But though the world be farre more terrible to looke vpon
when it frowneth, then when it fawneth, yet is it farre leffe
dangerous. For oftentimes this poyfon of aduerfitie is fo
tempered and corrected with thofe holefome preferuatiues
of faith, hope, patience and humilitie, that in fteed of killing
vs, it doth but purge away our corrupt humours of finne;
though the world whip vs, yet thereby it correcteth vs, and
makes vs better; though it burne vs in the fire of afflictions,
yet it doth not confume, but rather refine vs from our
droffe; though like a ftormie winde it fhaketh vs, yet in fteed
of blowing vs downe, it caufeth vs to take more deepe roote
in all vertue and goodnes: in a word, as it plaieth the fchool-
mafter in fcourging vs, fo alfo in inftructing & teaching vs to
know God, and to know our felues; to know the vanitie of
the world, and to labour after a more permanent felicitie.

Notwithstanding, howfoeuer by the grace and bleffing of
God, aduerfitie (the worlds churlifh fonne) oftentimes worketh thefe good effects; yet in it felfe it is a temptation, and
that a ftrong one, to draw vs from God, by caufing vs to
murmure and repine: yea as Sathan faid of *Iob*, to curfe God
to his face, to enuie all who feeme vnto vs more happie then
our felues, to defpaire of Gods mercie, and to vfe vnlawfull
meanes, that thereby we may better our eftate. And therefore

Numb.11.5.

§. *Sect.*4.
How we are to
arme our felues
againſt aduer-
ſitie.

it behoueth vs to arme our selues against the violence of this enemie also, least building our houses vpon the sands of securitie they be ouerturned, when the winds of afflictions and floods of aduersitie and persecution blow and beate against vs. And to this end we are to remember, first, that these fatherly corrections are euident testimonies to assure vs that we are not bastards, but Gods deare children, whom he gently cha-

Hcb.12.6,7,8. stiseth, that wee may not be destroyed with the world; that now Christ hath chosen vs out of the world, seeing the world

Ioh.15.19. hateth vs; that now wee are the friends of God, when the world (Sathans eldest sonne) becommeth our enemie: for so long as we are of the world the world loueth vs, for it loueth her owne. Secondly, let vs continually remember the recompence of reward, & then shal we with *Moses* volūtarily chuse

Heb.11.25.26. *rather to suffer aduersitie with the people of God, than to enioy the pleasures of sin for a season; esteeming the rebuke of Christ greater riches, than the treasures of Egypt,* as it is Heb.11.25,26. Thē shall we endure to be tried and purified in the fornace of afflictions, if we know that after we are found to be pure gold, the Lord will lay vs vp in his treasurie of euerlasting happines. Lastly, let vs remember, that eternall blessednesse is promised to those that mourne with a godly sorrow, and eternal woe denounced against those who pamper themselues with

Matth.5.4.10. worldly delights. Matth.5.4. *Blessed are they that mourne, for they shall be comforted.* So vers.10. *Blessed are they which suffer persecution for righteousnes sake, for theirs is the kingdome of*

Luk.6.21,25. *heauen.* Luk.6.21. *Blessed are ye which hunger now, for ye shall be satisfied: blessed are ye that weepe now, for ye shall laugh.* And vers.25. *Woe be vnto you that are full, for ye shall hunger: woe vnto you that now laugh, for ye shall waile and weepe.* And least the tediousnesse of our troubles should discourage vs, or the waight of them presse vs downe, the Apostle telleth vs, that

2.Cor.4.17. they are but light and momentanie, causing notwithstanding vnto vs a farre most excellent and eternall waight of glorie, 2.Cor.4.17. Why therefore should this little spot of foule way, cause vs to stand still, or goe out of our course, which leadeth to euerlasting happines?

CHAP.

CHAP. VII.

Of the flesh, and the strength thereof.

Nd so much concerning the world. The second enemie which assisteth Sathan against vs is the flesh, which is that inborne traytor which wee nourishing in our selues, doth ope a gate in our soules, into which Sathan and the world may easily send whole troupes of temptations to enter and surprize vs. By the flesh we are not to vnderstand the bodie alone and the flesh thereof, but that corruption of nature which hath defiled both bodie and soule, being spread and mixed with euery part of both, euen as the light is mingled with darknes in the twilight or dawning of the day; whereby wee are made prone to all sinne, and readie to entertaine all temptations, which promise the satisfying of any of the lusts thereof. This secret traytor conspiring with Sathan and the world to worke our destruction, doth entertaine and further all their temptations; it fighteth and lusteth against the spirit, it rebelleth against the law of our mindes, and leadeth vs captiue to the law of sinne, it hindreth vs from doing the good we would, and maketh vs commit the euill which wee hate, as it is notably set downe Rom.7. So Gal.5.17. *The flesh lusteth against the spirit, and the spirit against the flesh, and these are contrarie the one to the other, so that ye cannot doe the same things that ye would.*

§. *Sect.*1.

VVhat the flesh is.

Rom.7.
Galat.5.17.

This enemie the holy Ghost in the Scriptures deciphereth by diuers names; for it is called the old man, the old *Adam,* the earthly, carnall, and naturall man, the sinne which is inherent and dwelleth in vs, the adioyning euill, the law of the members, the lusts of the flesh which fight against the soule; by all which is signified our corruption of nature, which is deriued from our first parents, whereby wee are made backward vnto all good, and prone vnto all euill, vnapt to entertaine any good motions of Gods spirit, but most readie to receiue and imbrace all the suggestions and temptations of

the

the world and the diuell, as the waxe the print of the seale, or the tindar fire. And this the Apostle *Iames* sheweth chap. 1.14

Iam.1.14.15. *Euery man is tempted when he is drawne away by his owne concupiscence and is enticed: 1 5. Then when lust hath conceiued, it bringeth foorth sinne, and sinne when it is finished bringeth foorth death.* So that as Sathan is the father, so the flesh is the mother of sinne, which receiuing Sathans temptations as it were into a fruitfull wombe, doth conceiue, nourish, and bring forth sinne, which no sooner is borne, but like a deadly stinging serpent, it bringeth death to bodie and soule, vnlesse the poyson thereof be ouercome and taken away by the precious bloud of Christ.

§. Sect.2. The treacherie of the flesh. And thus you see what the flesh is, and how it conspireth with Sathan in seeking our destruction, whereby appeareth the treacherie and dangerousnes of this our enemie. The treacherie thereof is hereby manifest, in that being in outward shew a deare friend, and more neere than an *alter idem*, another selfe, it notwithstanding aideth Sathan to our owne ouerthrow. So as wee may complaine with *Dauid*, Psal.41.9.

Psal.41.9. *My familiar friend whom I trusted, which did eate my bread, hath lift vp the heele against me.* For this *Iudas* which daily followeth vs, and eateth, drinketh and sleepeth with vs, doth betray vs into the hands of those enemies who seeke our life; and that, when it seemeth louingly and kindly to kisse vs.

And as it is most treacherous, so also most dangerous, and hard to be ouercome, for as much as it is in our self, and the greatest part of our selfe, and therefore we cannot forsake it,

Mark.8.34. That the flesh is a most dangerous enemie. vnlesse we forsake our selues; we cannot fight against it, vnlesse we raise intestine and ciuill warres in our owne bowels; we cannot vanquish it, vnlesse wee subdue our selues; and if we seeke to runne away from it, wee might as easily flee from our owne shadowes, yea from our selues, for wee carrie it in our owne bosomes. How hard therefore is this enemie to be ouercome? how dangerous and irksome must this fight needs be, wherein our selues must be enemie to our selues? So that we cannot obtaine the victorie, vnlesse we be ouercome; we cannot be sure of life, vnlesse we mortifie and kill our greatest part; we cannot sustaine our selues, but we nourish our ene-

mie;

mie; we cannot famish our enemie, but we our selues shall pine with hunger. Who would not thinke the estate of those citizens to be most dangerous, who being besieged by forraine forces, harbour amongst them more traytors which are hourely in readines to open the gates and betray the citie into their enemies hands, than true subiects and loyall citizens to stand in their defence? But this is our case, we are besieged with forraine forces, the world and the diuell; and we nourish in vs secret traytors, euen the flesh, with whole legions of the lusts thereof, which are continually readie to open the gates of our soules, euen our senses of seeing, hearing, touching, tasting, smelling, whereby whole troupes of temptations enter and surprize vs.

The consideration whereof should make vs most watchfully to stand vpon our guard, and to vse such Christian policie to withstand our enemies, and preuent their treacherous attempts, as true-hearted citizens would vse in the like case; who if they were besieged with forraine forces, and knew that they harboured traytors, who sought all opportunities of betraying their citie into their enemies hand, they would if they were strong enough lay hand on them, draw them to the place of iudgement, condemne and put them to death; but if they found them too great and strong a partie, then they would vse all good policie to make them weaker, by depriuing them of their foode and prouision, weapons, armour and munition, and all other meanes wherein consisted their chiefe strength; and then they would set vpon them being thus disabled, and proceede in the course of iustice before mentioned: so we being in continuall danger to haue the citie of our soules sacked through the treacherousnes of our flesh, must, if wee be strong enough and powerfull through Gods spirit, mortifie, kill, and abolish the flesh, and the lusts thereof; but if we finde the spirit weake and the flesh strong, we are to disable it by fasting and watchfulnes in prayer, by withdrawing from it the foode with which it is nourished, that is, voluptuous pleasures and worldly delights, but especially being weake in our selues, wee are to implore the aide and assistance of Gods spirit, whereby we may be strengthe-

§. Sect.3.
How the flesh is to be weakned.

ned

1.Pet.2.11.

ned and enabled to subdue and mortifie the lusts of the flesh, which rebell and fight againſt our ſoules, being aſſured by Gods mercifull promiſe, that if we aske and deſire his ſpirit, Luk.11.13. he will giue it vs, Luk.11.13. and hauing the ſpirit of God to aſſiſt vs, we ſhall be ſure of victorie.

But if in ſteede of mortifying and taming the fleſh and the luſts thereof, wee pamper them like Epicures with all volup-Pro.24.21. tuous delights; wee ſhall but ſtrengthen our enemies to cut our owne throtes : if wee delicately bring vp this ſeruant, which we ſhould vſe as a ſlaue, at length it will be not onely as our ſonne, but a tyrannous Lord and maſter, which will binde vs hand and foote in the fetters of ſinne, and caſt vs into the priſon of hell. What follie therefore is it to nouriſh and arme our enemie to our owne deſtruction?

CHAP. VIII.

Of Sathans policie.

§. Sect.1.

Nd thus much of the fleſh, which is the ſecond enemie that ioyneth with Sathan in working our deſtruction; and thus much alſo concerning the firſt part of our enemies power, which con-ſiſteth in the ſtrength either of himſelf or of his aides: now we are to conſider of the ſecond part, which con-ſiſteth in his warlike policie and skill, in imploying this his ſtrength to his beſt aduantage.

If our enemie had great ſtrength, and yet wanted policie, he might the more eaſily be reſiſted, and the ſooner vanqui-ſhed; for ſtrength without wit is like a giant without eyes. But as our enemie is exceeding ſtrong, ſo is hee alſo no leſſe ſubtill and politike, in imploying all his ſtrength to his beſt aduantage; and therefore as in regard of his ſtrength he is called in the Scriptures a lion, and a mightie dragon; ſo in reſpect of his ſubtiltie and wilines he is called a ſerpent, yea an old ſerpent, which being the ſubtilleſt of beaſts, hath his Apoc.12.9. craft redoubled by his age and experience, Apoc.12.9. and hereof he is called in the Scriptures, δαίμων & δαιμόνων *quaſi* δαή-μων, to ſignifie vnto vs his great knowledge.

No

No marueile therefore though Sathan fhould be an expert fouldier, feeing he is not onely of wonderfull ftrength, but alfo of great knowledge by creation; which though in refpect of good things it was much decreafed by his fall, yet in fleights and ftratagems it is much increafed by his long experience from the beginning of the world, euen almoft fixe thoufand yeeres; which is fufficient to make one wife that is by nature foolifh and fimple, and therefore much more Sathan, who is by nature very politike ; being alfo a fpirit, and hereby fit to diue as it were into the fecrets of nature, and with incredible fwiftnes to paffe from place to place, readie to intrude himfelfe into all companies fecretly, and to learne the nature, qualities and difpofitions of al men, againft whom he fighteth. And though he cannot know our thoughts directly and certainly, for this is proper to God alone to bee the fearcher of hearts, yet he hath fuch intelligence from our affections, lufts, inclinations and outward actions, that hee can fhrewdly geffe at them, if he doe but a while keepe vs companie, and fee our difpofition and conuerfation. So that wee cannot giue Sathan the leaft aduantage, but he is readie to take it and make vfe thereof to our ouerthrow ; we can lay no plot againft him but he difcerneth it, and is readie to preuent it. And therefore in this refpect our ftate is like the king of Arams, 2.King.6.12. for Sathan our enemie knoweth all our counfailes and confultations which wee take and hold in our moft fecret chambers. *2.King.6.12.*

And thus you fee what Sathans policie is : againft which we muft oppofe no leffe wifedome and skill, if wee will haue the victorie. Whereas therefore wee are foolifh by nature, or wilie to beguile our felues; that wifedome which we haue naturally being worldly and carnall, which is enmitie againft God, Rom.8.7. and therefore more fit to betray vs into the hands of our enemie, than to defend vs from him ; it behooueth vs to goe out of our felues into the Lords treafurie of wifedome, and there to furnifh vs with fuch fpirituall fauing wifedome, as fhall be fit to oppofe againft the fubtill policie of our fpirituall enemie. That is, wee muft continually heare and meditate in Gods word, which will make vs wife and skilfull. *§. Sect.2.* *How we may defeate Sathans policie.* *Rom.8.7.*

skilfull in defcrying all Sathans ftratagems, and alfo in preuenting them being difcouered. For howfoeuer in the darke
night of ignorance and error we may eafily fall into his ambufhments, yet the light of Gods word fhining vnto vs, will
plainly difclofe them to the eyes of the moft fimple.

But befides this theoreticall wifedome feated in the vnderftanding, there is alfo a practicall or operatiue wifedome required in Gods word, which fheweth it felfe in our affections
and actions. And it confifteth in the feare of the Lord, that is,
true godlineffe and finceritie of heart. Of this *Iob* fpeaketh,

Iob.28.28.
Pfal.111.10.
chap.28.verf.28. *The feare of the Lord is wifedome, and to depart
from euill is vnderftanding.* So Pfalm.111.10. *The feare of the
Lord is the head or beginning of wifedome.* And Pro.28.7. he is

Pro.28.7.
called *a wife fonne which keepeth the law.* So that our chiefe
wifedome confifteth in the feare of the Lord, and in a godlie
endeuour of performing obedience to the Lords commandements.

If therefore we would attaine vnto fuch fpirituall wifedom
that we may refift our fpirituall enemie, wee muft be conuerfant in hearing and reading the word of God, meditating

Pfal.1.2.
therein with the Prophet *Dauid both day and night* ; and
withall we muft by all meanes feeke the feare of the Lord, labouring to leade our liues in a conftant courfe of true godlines. And though wee are full of infirmities, yet at leaft let vs
haue an holie endeuour to performe feruice vnto God, in
truth, vprightnes, and integritie of heart. And fo wee may affure our felues that though we be neuer fo fimple and foolifh
by nature, yet fhall wee be wife enough to withftand and o-
uercome our fpirituall enemies: for the Lord who is wifedome it felfe will direct vs in our waies, and he alfo will fo in-
fatuate this curfed *Achitophel,* and turne his wifedome into
foolifhnes, that wee fhall neuer thereby be hurt or circumuented.

But on the other fide, though wee be neuer fo wife in carnall wifedome, and though our heads be a ftorehoufe of politike ftratagems, yet if wee neglect Gods word, and voluntarily giue our felues ouer vnto finne and difobedience, we fhal
be fo befotted with follie, that Sathan will eafily deceiue and
                                            circumuent

circumuent vs. An example whereof wee haue in our firſt parents, who though they were more wiſe by creation than euer were any liuing (Chriſt excepted) yet when they caſt the word of God behinde their backe, giuing more credit to Sathans ſuggeſtions, and withall tranſgreſſed Gods commandement; their wiſedome was turned into ignorance and follie, and they became an eaſie pray to their malitious enemie. And whereas they thought by that meanes to haue gone beyond the Lord in policie, and to haue obtained a farre greater meaſure of knowledge and glorie,they were in ſteed therof beſotted with follie, and ouerwhelmed with ignominie and ſhame, by being made the bondſlaues of ſinne and Sathan.And thus alſo the heathen neglecting the true worſhip of God, and giuing themſelues to idolatrie, became fooles, whileſt they profeſſed themſelues very wiſe, as the Apoſtle witneſſeth,Rom.1.22. for the *Lord deſtroyeth the wiſedome of the wiſe,and caſteth away the vnderſtanding of the prudent,* as it is 1.Cor.1.19.

Rom. 1.22.

1.Cor.1.19.

Seeing then our chiefe wiſedome conſiſteth in the ſtudie of Gods word,and in vprightnes of hart,integritie,Chriſtian ſinceritie and ſimplicitie,and in a holie care of perfourming obedience to Gods will, let vs therefore continually meditate in Gods word, and with the Prophet *Dauid* make it our counſellor, Pſal.119. And whenſoeuer Sathan doth aſſault and tempt vs to ſinne, let vs haue recourſe to this our counſellor the word of God, there inquiring whether that whereunto we are tempted be lawfull or no ; and if it tell vs that it is a ſinne, let vs with all care and conſcience auoide it : for though Sathan lay ouer it neuer ſo faire a gloſſe, and intice vs to the committing thereof, by offering vnto vs the greateſt pleaſures,riches and honours of the world, yet let vs aſſure our ſelues that he thereby ſeeketh to circumuent vs;and to purchaſe worldly vanities,he inticeth vs to ſell our ſoules; and therefore in Chriſtian wiſedome let vs auoide his ſtratagems.

Pſal.119.

CHAP.

Chap. IX.

*Of the spirituall armour described,*Eph.6.

§. *Sect*.1.

And thus haue I shewed the nature and qualitie of our enemie against whom wee must fight; both in respect of his wil, and also his power, consisting in his strength and policie; and also I haue shewed some meanes which in our preparation against him we must vse carefully, that wee may withstand him; namely, by opposing against his malitious will, christian resolution; against his strength, the omnipotent power of Gods might; against his subtil policie, christian wisedom, consisting in the knowledge of Gods word, and true integritie and simplicitie of heart.

That the weapons of our Christian warfare must be spirituall.

Now wee are to speake of the last meanes which we are to vse in our preparation immediatly before our combat; that is, we are to arme our selues against the encounter.: and to this end (because we are but fresh-water-souldiers & of small experience) let vs take the counsaile and aduice of the Apostle *Paul,* one of Gods chiefe champions and expert souldiers, as he setteth it downe, Eph.6.11,12,13,14,&c.where first he describeth the quality, and as it were the mettall of our armour; in which respect hee telleth vs, that wee must put on the armour of God which is spirituall, and that our weapons and armour must not be carnall. For being of this nature, though they were neuer so strög, they were to no purpose, seeing our enemie is spiritual; neither do we *wrestle against flesh & blood, but against principalities, powers and spirituall wickednesses,* as it is Eph.6.12. In vaine therfore it were with the Papists to seeke to defend our selues with holy water, or Crucifixes, or ragges and reliques of Saints, from the violent assaults of this our enemie; or els with desperate hacksters to trust in our sword, buckler and speare: for well is that verified of this spirituall Leuiathan, which the Lord speaketh of the earthly Leuiathan, Iob.41.17.20. *When the sword doth touch him, he will not rise vp, and he laugheth at the shaking of the speare.* And therefore when we are to encounter this great Goliah, we are to

Eph.6.11.&c.

2.Cor.10.4.

Eph.6.12.

Iob.41.17.20.

lay

lay aside the carnall weapons of *Saul*, which are altogether 1.Sam. 17.39.
vnfit for a Christian, seruing rather to burthen and so hinder 44.
him, than to defend and further him in this spiritual combat;
and we are to go against him in the name of the Lord, strengthened in the power of his might, putting on vs the armour
of God, that is, such diuine and spirituall armour as the Lord
hath giuen and appointed vs to vse. For it is not sufficient
that we prepare vs this armour, if we let it lie by vs, or suffer it
(as it were) to hang vpon the walles, there to rust without
vse; but we are to put it on, and keepe it fast buckled vnto vs
both night and day, that wee may be alwaies in readines to
endure the assault of our enemies.

Neither is it enough that wee put on one peece of the ar- §. Sect. 2.
mour, and like young souldiers leaue off the rest for lightnes *That we must*
sake, or els through foole-hardines to shew needlesse valour; *put on the*
we must not put on the helmet of saluation, and leaue off the *whole armour*
breast-plate of righteousnes; nor take vnto vs the girdle of *of God.*
veritie and the shield of faith, and cast away from vs the
sword of the spirit, but we are to put on the whole armour of
God, and like valiant souldiers, who meane indeede to stand
to it, wee are to arme our selues at all points in compleat armour of proofe, which will keepe vs from fleeing, and our e-
nemie from ouercomming. For if we take none of the Christian armour, or but some of the lightest parts, if wee take the
shield of faith, and leaue behinde vs the breast-plate of righteousnes, we shal either desperatly fight and be ouerthrowne
in the battaile, or els cowardly runne away and forsake the
field. But on the other side, if we buckle vnto vs the whole armour of God, we shall not neede to flee away for feare, being
so well defended; nor to doubt of victorie, for we shall surely
ouercome; the Lord hauing hauing giuen, and we hauing receiued this armour to this end, as the Apostle noteth vnto vs
in these words; *that you may be able to stand against the assaults*
of the diuell, or his treacherous ambushments, as the word
here vsed, signifieth. So that the Lord hath giuen vs this armour, and we put it on, to the end that we may be enabled to
resist Sathan; and therefore seeing it is armour of Gods own
making and bestowing, we may assure our selues that he will
not

not suffer his workmanship and gift to be so much disgraced, as that sathan should pearce thorow it and wound vs. For the Lord knoweth the force of Sathans darts, & bullets of temptation; and he hath made his armour high proofe; and therefore strong enough to repell all the batterie of Sathans suggestions.

§. Sect.3.
The necessitie of the spirituall armour.

And that we may be the rather stirred vp with all care and diligence to prouide and buckle fast to vs the armour which he after describeth, he sheweth the necessitie thereof, by describing the daungerousnes of our enemies, who being not flesh and blood, but principalities, powers, worldly gouernours, princes of the darknes of this world, and spirituall wickednesses, which are in high places, cannot possibly be resisted by our owne strength and meanes. And (therefore) for this cause he willeth vs to take vnto vs the whole armour of God, that we may be able to resist in the euill day, that is, the time of temptation, which is therefore called the euill day, partly because therein Sathan tempteth vs vnto euill, and partly because it is a time of trouble, aduersitie and affliction, when Sathan sifteth vs with his temptations. And thus the euill day is taken Psal.41.1. *The Lord will deliuer him in the euill day,* that is, (as our translation also reades it) in the time of trouble. And thus also it is vsed Eph.5.16. *Redeeming the time, because the daies are euill,* that is, full of troubles and afflictions. And therefore *Beza* doth translate in this place ἐν τῇ ἡμέρᾳ τῇ πονηρᾷ, *tempore aduerso,* the time of aduersitie.

VVhat is meant by the euill day.

Psal.41.1.

Eph.5.16.

By which we learne not to esteeme our spirituall fight as a May-game, but as a time of trouble and aduersitie, wherein wee are assaulted by mightie enemies, and oftentimes foyled and wounded; and therefore we must not voluntarily runne into temptations, seeing the time of them is euill and full of trouble; but rather feruently pray vnto the Lord that hee will not leade vs into temptation, considering our owne weaknes and our enemies power; or if it please him to make triall of vs, that he will not suffer vs to fall therein, but that he will deliuer vs from euill, for as much as the kingdome and power and glorie is his alone, and therefore he is of power sufficient to saue and deliuer vs.

But

But as we are not securely to rush into the field of tempta- *That we must*
tion against our spirituall enemies, so wee are not when our *not cowardly*
enemies sound the alarum to battaile and assault vs, coward- *flee in the spi-*
ly to cast downe our weapons and to runne away : for the A- *rituall conflict.*
postle would not take away from vs true valour and Chri-
stian fortitude,but carnall securitie and retchlesnes;and therfore though our enemies be mightie, and the time of temptation full of trouble,yet he biddeth vs not to cast off our armour and to runne away, wholie despairing of victorie, but
he exhorteth vs for this cause , to take vnto vs the whole armour of God, that wee may be able to resist in the euill day,
and hauing finished all things may stand fast; that is, hauing
put our enemies to flight and obtained the victorie, we may
like conquerors stand last in the field, as it were triumphant-
ly insulting ouer them ; whereby hee intimateth thus much,
that if wee will take vnto vs the whole armour of God,how
weake soeuer wee be in our selues,yet shall wee be enabled
to resist our spirituall enemies in the euill day; and not onely
so,but also obtaine victorie and triumph ouer them.

And therefore hee willeth vs not to be dismaied, neither §. *Sect.4.*
with our enemies power,nor our owne trouble, but to stand *That euery one*
to it,saying,vers.14.*Stand therefore :*by which word hee inti- *must abide in*
mateth vnto vs diuers duties: first,as in the campe euery man *his vocation.*
hath his place appointed him, and his proper colours vnder
which he is to keep him ; so all Christian souldiers haue their
stations,that is, their vocations whereunto they are called of
God, within the limits whereof they are to containe themselues : and these are first their generall calling whereby they
are intertained into the Church militant , which is Gods
campe or armie,where they are to fight vnder the standerd of
their captaine Christ : and secondly their speciall callings,
whereby there is appointed to euery member of the militant
Church,a certaine standing,and particular and proper duties
and functions which he is to execute, as it is in the armies of
earthly princes. First therefore wee must containe our selues
within our generall vocation and station, that is, wee must
keepe vs in Gods armie and campe,the Church militant : for
as those stragling souldiers who depart from the armie and

raunge

raunge abroad to forrage, or get some bootie, are easily vanquished by their enemies ; so those who depart and make an
apostasie from Gods Church, to gaine or retaine their pleasures and worldly preferments , are easily ouerthrowne, falling into Sathans ambushments. And secondly, euery one is
to containe himselfe within the limits of his speciall vocation, and to keepe his peculiar standing appointed him by
God ; for as there is nothing more pernitious to an armie
than disorder, when as some intrude themselues into others
place, as when the common souldier will be an officer, the
Lieutenant Captaine, and the Captaine, Generall of the armie ; so nothing is more hurtfull to the Church militant,
than when disorderly one vsurpes another place and office,as
when the Ministers will be Magistrates, and the Magistrates
Ministers,and when the common people vsurpe the office of
them both.

Secondly,when as he biddeth vs stand in our places,he re-
straineth vs from two extreames : the one, that wee doe not
wilfully thrust our selues into the combat of temptations before we be assaulted, and so as it were runne out of our standings to seeke an enemie : and secondly, that when wee are
assaulted we doe not flee away, but stand to it valiantly and
endure the violence of the assailants. Lastly, he exhorteth vs
to watchfulnes and painfull diligence,for we must not drowsily and securely lay vs downe and giue our selues to sleepe,
nor yet sit idlely as though wee had nothing to doe; but wee
are to stand vpon our guard, and to watch continually, that
wee may alwaies be in readines to withstand the assaults of
our enemies ; otherwise if wee sleepe in securitie,they will
suddenly set vpon vs and surprize vs at vnawares.

<hr/>

CHAP. X.

*Of the particular parts of the Christian armour : and first of
the girdle of veritie.*

§.Sect.1.   ANd thus the Apostle hauing taken away all retchlesse
securitie and foole-hardines, and also strengthened vs
with

with true valour and Chriſtian fortitude, in the next place he *Of the girdle of*
deſcribeth the armour of God which wee are to buckle vnto *veritie.*
vs. Where firſt wee are generally to obſerue, that wee are not
curiouſly and ſcrupulouſly to ſearch out the reaſon why ſuch
and ſuch vertues are likened to theſe or thoſe peeces of armour : as for example, why he calleth truth a girdle, righteouſnes a breaſt-plate, faith a ſhield,&c. for it was not the A-
poſtles purpoſe ſo exactly to fit the ſimilitudes, as may appeare 1.Theſſ.5.8. where he indifferently aſcribeth the name
of breaſt-plate both to faith and charitie, by which here hee
vnderſtandeth righteouſneſſe; but onely briefly and generally to ſhew what vertues and graces of Gods ſpirit are moſt
neceſſarie for a Chriſtian, wherewith hee. may be enabled to
reſiſt his ſpirituall enemies, continuing his former allegorie
taken from warres.

But let vs come to the armour it ſelfe, which is both de-
fenſiue and offenſiue : the firſt part is the girdle of veritie.The
word here vſed ſignifieth a broad ſtudded belt vſed in warres
in ancient times, wherewith the ioynts of the breaſt-plate,
and that armour which defended the bellie, loynes and
thighes were couered.And by this,truth is reſembled:where-
by ſome vnderſtand the truth of religion and of the doctrine
which we profeſſe, others vnderſtand hereby truth and vprightnes of heart, or the integritie of a good conſcience,
whereby wee perfourme all duties of religion belonging to
God and our neighbour in ſimplicitie, without all hypocriſie
and diſſimulation. But becauſe both are notable and neceſſarie parts of our Chriſtian armour , I ſee no reaſon why wee *VVhat we are*
may not take it in both ſenſes, ſeeing the Apoſtle doth of *to vnderſtand*
purpoſe ſet downe vnder theſe metaphoricall words, the *by the girdle of*
chiefe vertues and graces wherewith wee are to arme our *veritie.*
ſelues againſt our ſpirituall enemies.Firſt therfore here is required truth of our religion which we profeſſe : and ſecondly,
that we profeſſe it truly,that is,with vpright & ſimple hearts.

For the firſt : it is the foundation vpon which all other du- §. *Sect.2.*
ties to God or man are to be built; for if they be not groun- *That our reli-*
ded on Gods truth,but deuiſed by mans braine, they are but *gion muſt be*
humane dotages which the Lord will not accept ; neither is *grounded on*
Gods truth.

E   it it to any purpose that wee shew our selues earnest and forward in religion, vnlesse it be true and consonant to Gods word. For as the faster that those trauaile which are out of the way, the further they are from their iourneys end; so the more earnest and forward that wee are in trauailing the by-paths of error, the further we are from Gods kingdome : and therefore Sathan careth not greatly whether we be of no religion or of a false religion, whether wee worship no God at all, or a false God, or at least the true God after a false manner, whether wee perfourme no dueties vnto God, or such as being not agreeable to Gods truth are abominable vnto him. First then wee must containe all our actions within the compasse of Gods word, and whatsoeuer wee professe and practise, it must haue his ground and warrant from this truth, if wee will be accounted true members of Gods militant

1.Tim 3.15. Church, which is therefore called *the pillar of truth*, 1.Tim.3. 15. because contemning all errours and doctrines of men, it faithfully keepeth the truth of Gods word. And as souldiers were girt about with that strong and broad studded belt, wherewith their loynes were strengthened, and so enabled to sustaine the fight without werines; so wee are to compasse our selues about with truth, whereby wee may be strengthened when as we know that we fight in a iust quarrell; neither shall wee easily be deceiued with Sathans temptations and false suggestions, if we be girt about with the girdle of verity. And hereby appeareth the necessitie of this peece of armour: for seeing Sathan is a liar from the beginning, it behooueth vs to be compassed about with truth, that the bright beames thereof may discouer and disperse all the foggie mists of Sathans errors and lies.

§. *Sect.3.*
That we must professe the truth, in truth and simplicitie of heart.

But it is not sufficient that wee professe the truth, vnlesse it be in truth, that is, in integritie and simplicitie of heart, without all hypocrisie and dissimulation. For how glorious soeuer our profession euen of the true religion be before men, yet it is abominable in the eyes of God, if it be not in truth and from an vpright heart, but counterfeite and hypocriticall. Whatsoeuer duties and good workes we perfourme, though neuer so excellent in theselues, yet are they not acceptable in

Gods

Gods fight,if they be not ioyned with integritie and fimplicitie. For example,prayer is a notable part of Gods worfhip;
but if we doe not call vpon God in truth,but with fained and
deceitfull lips,that we may haue the praife of men,our praiers Matth.6.
are odious and Pharifaicall,Matth.6. Thankfgiuing is an excellent dutie, but if with the Pharifie wee giue thankes rather
to boaft of our gifts,then to fhew true thankfulnes to the gi- Luk.18.
uer,we fhall not be approoued of God. Giuing of almes is a
worke acceptable vnto God,for it is a facrifice wherewith he
is well pleafed,Heb.13.16. but if they be not giuen in fimpli- Heb.13.16.
citie of heart,but in hypocrifie,that we may be feene of men,
it fhall haue the hypocrites reward, Matth.6. In a word, this Matth.6.
truth and fimplicitie of heart is fo neceffarie, that without it,
whatfoeuer we doe it is not regarded; for *God is a spirit, and* Ioh.4.24.
*he will be worshipped in spirit and in truth,*Ioh.4.24. According
to that,Iofh.24.14. *Feare the Lord, and serue him in vprightnes* Iofh.24.14.
*and in truth.*Which if wee perfourme,our feruice of God will
be acceptable in his fight,though perfourmed in great weaknes, and mingled with many imperfections : otherwife,
though wee offer thoufands of rammes,and whole riuers of
oyle,that is,omit no outward coft and labour in Gods wor- Mich.6.7.8.
fhip, yet will it be abominable in his eyes,Mich.6.7.8. Let vs
therefore with our Sauiour pray vnto God,that wee may bee Ioh.17.17.
fanctified with his truth, that not onely whatfoeuer wee doe
may be grounded on Gods truth, but that wee may doe it in
truth and vprightnes of heart.

Chap. XI.

Of the breast-plate of righteousnes,and Gospell of peace.

He fecond part of our armour is the breaft-plate §. *Sect.*1.
of righteoufnes; whereby we are to vnderftand
a good confcience,true fanctification and a godly life,which alfo we are to put on according to
the example of our grand Captaine Chrift. Efa.59.17. *He put*
on righteoufnes as an habergeon, and an helmet of faluation vpon Efa.59.17.
his

his head. And then ſhall not Sathans darts pearce vs, ſo long as we are armed with a good conſcience, and a godly and innocent life. Yea as long as our breaſts and hearts are armed with righteouſnes, though our other members fall into ſinne, our wounds ſhall not be mortall : for as the breaſt-plate doth defend the breaſt and vitall parts of a ſouldier, ſo the ſtudie and holie endeuour of a Chriſtian to liue in righteouſneſſe and true ſanctification, doth ſo arme his minde, that Sathan cannot deadly wound the heart with any of his temptations. True it is that the Saints doe recciue wounds and foyles, when as Sathan hath drawne them to commit ſinne, but they are not wounded at the heart, becauſe they doe not ſinne with full conſent of will ; for they allow not that which they doe, neither doe they what they would, but what they hate, and they delight in the law of God concerning the inner man, when the fleſh leadeth them captiue to the law of ſin.

Rom. 7. 15. 22.

And hence it is that *Paul* ſaith he did not tranſgreſſe Gods law, but ſinne that dwelled in him, Rom. 7. 17. And the A-

Rom. 7. 17.

poſtle *Iohn* affirmeth, that *they who are borne of God ſinne not,*

1. Ioh. 3. 9. and verſ. 6. 8.

1. Ioh. 3. 9. and that *they who are in Chriſt ſinne not :* and that *whoſoeuer ſinneth is of the diuell,* verſ. 6. 8. Not that Gods children are exempted from all ſinne, but becauſe they ſinne not with the full conſent and ſwinge of their will ; and when they doe fall, their hearts are defended with the breaſt-plate of righteouſnes, that is, with an holie endeuour and deſire of ſeruing God. *Dauid,* a man according to Gods owne heart, may be a notable example hereof : for euen after he was indued with the knowledge of the truth, and had this godlie endeuour of ſeruing God, he notwithſtanding fell grieuouſly many times, and was wounded often with Sathans darts ; but his wounds were not mortall, neither did they pearce the heart, becauſe he was armed with the breaſt-plate of righteouſnes ; for he kept Gods law in his heart, and it was ſweeter

Pſal. 119.

than honey vnto his mouth, he meditated therein, and ſought after it continually, as appeareth Pſal. 119. Would we therefore be preſerued from the deadly wounds of Sathans darts of temptation ? then let vs ſtudie and labour after true holines, let vs keepe a good conſcience ; and howſoeuer wee fall

often

often through infirmitie, yet let the heart alwaies be armed with the breaſt-plate of righteouſnes, that is, with an earneſt deſire and holie endeuour of ſeruing God; and ſo ſhall Sathan neuer mortally wound vs.

But on the other ſide, if we once lay aſide the breaſt-plate of righteouſnes, not ſo much as endeuouring to ſerue the Lord in holines of life, but imbrace ſinne with full conſent of will, we ſhall lay our breaſts open and naked to all Sathans thruſts, yea and as it were put ſwords in his hands wherewith hee may wound and murther vs: for vntill wee diſarme our ſelues, and put weapons into the hands of Sathan by our ſinnes, he cannot hurt vs; as wee may ſee in the example of our firſt parents, who whileſt they continued in their righteouſnes and integritie, Sathan could not offer them any violence by aſſault and force, and therefore he allured them to entertaine a treacherous parley, wherein hauing inticed them to diſarme themſelues of this breaſt-plate of righteouſnes, by wilfull tranſgreſſing Gods commandement, hee inflicted on them deadly wounds, pearcing them through to the verie heart, and ſo like *Ioab* whileſt he ſeemed louingly to imbrace them, he did moſt treacherouſly ſtab them.

That the lacke of this armour is moſt pernicious.

The conſideration whereof ſhould make vs repell moſt carefully all Sathans temptations, whereby he inticeth vs to ſinne; but eſpecially let vs neuer bee allured to put off the breaſt-plate of righteouſnes, and then though Sathan wound our ſoules with ſinne, yet his wounds will not be mortall ſo long as wee doe not fall into ſinne with full conſent of will, but through infirmitie; in the meane time loathing the ſinne which wee commit, and delighting our ſelues in the law of God, in reſpect of the inner man: for though we fall, yet the Lord will raiſe vs vp by vnfained repentance, ſo that though ſinne dwell in vs, yet ſhall it neuer raigne in vs.

E 3   CHAP.

CHAP. XII.

Of the preparation of the Goſpell of peace.

THe third part of our Chriſtian armour is, that wee haue our feete ſhod with the preparation of the Goſpel of peace ; where he alludeth to the cuſtome of ſouldiers in former times,who going into the field,ſtrongly armed their legges and feete with legge-harneſſe, wargreaues or buskins, to preſerue them from the iniurie of the weather,the pearcing of briars,thornes,and ſuch other things as might hurt them in their way as they marched, and from the violence alſo of their enemies blowes when they were incountred ; for all which vſes the Goſpell ſerueth in our ſpirituall warfare : for they who are armed with the true knowledge thereof,and are aſſured of the merciful promiſes therein contained , they will walke and march valiantly in the waies of godlineſſe and Chriſtianitie, though they are full of the briars and thornes of afflictions and perſecution ; preferring the rebuke of Chriſt before the riches of Egypt,becauſe they haue an eye to the recompence of reward, which they ſhall receiue at the end of their iourney. And this maketh them little to regard the foulenes and vnpleaſantnes of the way ; and though Sathan trouble them in their march, ſetting vpon and aſſaulting them, yet they eaſily reſiſt the furie of his temptations,and goe on forward in the profeſſion and practiſe of Chriſtianitie, if they be armed with the knowledge of the Goſpell of peace ; for it is therefore called the

Luk.10.5.

Goſpell of peace, becauſe it bringeth peace to our ſoules, not onely as it is the ambaſſage of God, whereby wee being

Rom.10.15.
Luk.1.7.9.

reconciled vnto God, haue peace with him, from the aſſurance whereof we haue the peace of conſcience, but alſo becauſe if we be armed therewith, we ſhall obtaine a finall victorie ouer our ſpirituall enemies , after which ſhall follow euerlaſting peace, which ſhall not ſo much as be diſturbed with the attempts of any enemies.

But it is not ſufficient that we know and beleeue this Goſpell

pell of peace, vnleſſe we be alwaies prepared to make confeſ
ſion and profeſſion therof, though thereby we incurre worldly ſhame, loſſes, afflictions and perſecution. And this the Apoſtle ſignifieth, by telling vs that our feete muſt be ſhod *VVhat it is to*
with the preparation of the Goſpell of peace; that is, as thoſe *be prepared*
who are well ſhod are in readines to goe through rough and *pell.*
vnpleaſant waies : ſo thoſe that are indued with the knowledge of the Goſpell, muſt alwaies be in readines to make
profeſſion thereof in the middeſt of affliction and perſecution. *For as with the heart man beleeueth vnto righteouſnes, ſo* Rom.10.10.
with the mouth he muſt confeſſe vnto ſaluation, Rom.10.10.
And this is that which the Apoſtle *Peter* requireth of vs, 1.Pet.3.15.
1.Epiſt.3.15. That we doe not onely ſanctifie the Lord in our
hearts, but alſo that *we be readie alwaies to giue an anſwere to*
euery man that asketh vs a reaſon of the hope that is in vs.

But if we lay aſide this armour, we ſhal be as vnfit to trauell
in the afflicted way which leadeth to Gods kingdome, as
thoſe ſouldiers who are barefoote be vnfit to march through
waies which are full of briars and thornes ; neither ſhall wee
be readie to make confeſſion and profeſſion of our faith in
the time of perſecution and trouble, but rather to ſlide backe
into a generall apoſtaſie from all religion, vnleſſe we be confirmed and comforted with the ſweete promiſes of the Goſpell, made to thoſe who ſuffer affliction for Chriſts ſake,
namely, that *if we confeſſe him before men, he will confeſſe vs be-* Matth.10.32.
fore his father in heauen, Matth.10.32. That *whoſoeuer ſhall loſe* Mark.8.35.
his life for Chriſts ſake and the Goſpels, ſhall ſaue it, Mark.8.35.
That *whoſoeuer ſhall forſake houſes, or brethren, or ſiſters, or fa-* Matth.19.29.
ther or mother, or wife and children, or lands for his names ſake,
ſhall receiue an hundred fold more, and ſhall inherit euerlaſting
life, Matth.19.29.

Chap. XIII.

Of the ſhield of faith.

THe fourth peece of the Chriſtian armour which the A- §. Sect.1.
poſtle exhorteth vs aboue all to put on, is the ſhield of
faith, which of all other parts is moſt neceſſarie, becauſe how

weake

weake soeuer it be in it selfe, yet it doth defend and protect vs against all the temptations of Sathan; for he that putteth on faith, doth put on Iesus Christ also, it being a propertie inseparable of faith, to applie vnto vs Christ Iesus and all his benefits, that is, his merits and righteousnes, and euerlasting life it selfe. And this will be not onely a glorious garment to couer our deformitie out of Gods sight, to preserue vs from the heate of Gods wrath, and to obtaine the euerlasting blessing of our heauenly father, but also it is armour of proofe to defend vs from the violent assaults of our spirituall enemies. Let vs therefore take vnto vs the shield of faith, that wee may also *put on the Lord Iesus Christ*, as the Apostle exhorteth vs, Rom.13.14. for hauing him wee shall want nothing, which may either defend our selues or offend our enemies; the Lord himselfe will be our shield and buckler, and therefore it will be impossible for our foes to preuaile against vs.

Rom.13.14.

What is meant by quenching Sathans firie darts.

But let vs consider further of the excellencie and necessitie of this shield of faith, which appeareth by the vertue thereof, in repelling all the firie darts of Sathan. The Apostle saith, *that thereby wee may quench his firie darts*, alluding to the custome of souldiers in ancient time, who malitiously poysoned their darts, whereby the bodies of those who were wounded were so inflamed, that they could hardly be cured, or eased of their raging and burning paine. And such darts are all Sathans temptations, whereby wee are wounded with sinne; for if they bee not repelled and quenched with the shield of faith, they will inflame our lusts to sinne, and one sinne will inflame our hearts to another, till there be kindled in vs a world of wickednesse. And this wee may see in the example of *Dauid*, who after that he gaue himselfe to idlenesse and sloth, and so was pearced with one of Sathans firie darts, it presently inflamed his heart to commit adulterie, and hauing giuen place to that, hee was prouoked to murther; so that if wee admit one of these firie darts, they will inflame vs to receiue another, and so our burning wounds will torment our consciences, and most hardly admit of any cure.

And therefore it behooueth vs to take vnto vs the shield of faith, whereby we may quench these firie darts. But why doth

doth the Apostle vse this improper speech, seeing the shield doth not quench, but repell the darts that beate vpon it? I answere, partly to shew the nature of our enemies temptations, namely, that they are firie, mortall, raging, and pernitious (as before I said) and partly to set foorth a double vertue of faith; for first thereby wee repell and beate backe his temptations, and so *resist him stedfastly in the faith,* as the Apostle speaketh, 1. Pet. 5. 9. And secondly, if Sathans darts haue pearced and wounded vs, faith also doth coole the scorching heate of sinne, by applying vnto vs the precious baulme of Christs blood, so that our wounds are not mortall vnto vs, though mortall in themselues, if they were not cured by this soueraigne salue of sinne, which being applied by faith, doth ease the burning torments of our euill consciences, and preserueth vs from all danger of death. The first of these vertues is signified hereby, in that he calleth faith a shield, which repelleth Sathans temptations, as the shield doth the darts that are cast against it: the second by the word (quenching) namely, that as water quencheth the fire, so faith quencheth the firie darts of Sathans temptations, as is aforesaid. — 1. Pet. 5. 9.

Lastly, wee are to note that he calleth Sathan the wicked one, to shew vnto vs that hee is the father and author of all wickednesse and sinne, both by sinning himselfe, and prouoking others to sinne by his temptations. And therefore he is called the wicked or euill one both here and Matth. 6. 13. *But deliuer vs from the euill one.* So Matth. 13. 38. *The tares are the children of the wicked one,* as also Ioh. 8. 44. — *VVhy Sathan is called the wicked one.* Matth. 6. 13. and 13. 38. Ioh. 8. 44.

Chap. XIIII.

Of the helmet of saluation.

He fist peece of our Christian armour is the helmet of saluation, which is so called by a metonymie of the effect, because it bringeth saluation to them that weare it, for we are saued by hope, as it is Rom. 8. 24. which we are to vnderstand by the helmet of saluation, as appeareth 1. Thess. 5. 8. — Esa. 59. 17. Rom. 8. 24. 1. Thess. 5. 8.

where

Hope,the hel-
met of falua-
tion.

where he exhorteth vs to put on the hope of faluation for an
helmet. As therefore fouldiers when they goe into the field
put on their helmet, that thereby they may defend their
head,which is their chiefe part,from the cruell blowes of the
enemie; fo we being to fight the fpirituall battaile, muft put
on hope both of victorie, and the glorious crowne belonging thereunto, and fo fhall wee neuer turne our backes when
wee are affaulted, feeing by the Lords affiftance we doe affuredly hope for victorie, and through his mercie and the merits of Chrift do expect after our combat is finifhed,the garland of euerlafting happines,promifed to all that ouercome.
For though Sathan affault vs on the one fide, by offering vnto vs the riches, honours and pleafures of the world, that
thereby he may intice vs to finne, and fo yeeld our felues his
captiues,he fhall not preuaile againft vs, if we be armed with
this helmet of faluation: for as no man in his right wits
would fell his certaine intereft vnto a goodly inheritance for
a bright fhining counter; fo much leffe will any man, who is
not ftarke mad, fell his affured hope of the eternall kingdom
of glorie,by yeelding himfelfe the flaue of finne and Sathan,
to purchafe for the prefent the worlds counterfaite fhining
excellencies, which are in truth but mutable, or at leaft momentanie vanities. And though he affault vs on the other fide
with afflictions, croffes and perfecutions as he did *Paul,* yet
wee will with him,for the hope of Ifrael, be content to bee
bound in the chaines of miferie and affliction. For the hea-
uieft croffe will feeme tolerable,yea an eafie yoke and a light
burthen, to thofe who doe expect and hope for a farre moft
excellent and an eternall waight of glorie; neither can the
ftraight way and the narrow gate difcourage thofe, that in
the end of their iourney affuredly expect a palace of pleafure
and neuer fading felicitie. But on the other fide,if we doe not
put on this helmet, wee fhall not dare to lift vp our heads in
the day of battaile : for as thofe who are encouraged with
hope of victorie and the fpoyle enfuing, doe fight valiantly;
fo thofe who are quite forfaken of hope, doe forfake alfo the
field,and cafting downe their armour and weapons, doe either runne away,or cowardly yeeld vnto the enemie.

A&.28.20.

2 Cor.4.17.

                                          CHAP.

Chap. XV.

Of the sword of the spirit.

Nd so much for the defensiue armour which wee must put on; that which followeth is both defensiue and offensiue, fit to defend our selues, and repell and foyle the enemie. The first is *the sword of the spirit, the word of God.* This the Apostle calleth the sword of the spirit, because it is a spirituall and not a carnall weapon, which the spirit of God himself hath as it were tempered, made, sharpened, and put into our hands, to repell our spirituall enemies whensoeuer they assault vs. If therefore we would defend our selues and driue backe Sathan, wee must not onely buckle vnto vs the defensiue armour before spoken of (for he that standeth altogether vpon defence, standeth vpon no defence) but wee must take vnto vs the sword of the spirit, wherewith we may repell and deadly wound our spirituall enemies. Wherein we are to imitate the example of our chiefe Captaine Iesus Christ, who though he was able to haue confuted Sathan by other arguments, or to haue confounded him by the omnipotent power of his deitie, yet as he suffered himselfe to be tempted in all things like vnto vs, so he vsed also the same weapons, which he hath appointed vs to vse in this spirituall combat of temptations, to the end that we might be taught how to handle them, hauing his example for our imitation, and also may conceiue assured hope of victorie, considering that our Captaine subdued Sathan with the selfesame weapons. *Matth.* 4.

Whensoeuer therefore wee are assaulted by Sathan, let vs draw out the sword of the spirit, that wee may defend our selues, and giue him the foyle, as being the most fit weapon for this purpose: for if Sathan seeke to blind the eyes of our vnderstanding with ignorance, that thereby hee may leade vs as it were hoodwinkt into sinne, the word of God is a lanthorne to our feete, and a light vnto our pathes to discouer Sathans darke illusions and secret ambushments, and to

§. *Sect.*2.
*That the sword
of the spirit is
a most fit wea-
pon to repell
Sathans temp-
tations.*

guide

guide our feete in the way of peace. If he seeke to deceiue vs
with his lies, and to seduce vs into errors; the word of God
is the touchstone of truth, by which wee discerne the pure
golden veritie from the drossie conceits of humane inuentions; and the subtill delusions of Sathans probable false-
hoods, from the vndoubted certaintie of Gods infallible
truth. If he transforme himselfe into an angell of light, Gods
word doth pull off his vizard, and maketh him appeare in his
owne likenes: if he come vpon vs like a roring lion to deuoure vs, it protecteth vs from danger, and maketh vs strong
enough to withstand his violence. Seeing therefore this weapon is so excellent, let vs most highly esteeme it, and manful-
How we are to ly vse it whensoeuer Sathan doth assault vs and tempt vs vnto
vse the sword sinne. For example, when he inticing vs to commit sinne, doth
of the spirit in extenuate and mince it as though it were but a May-game
the conflict of and a tricke of youth which God regardeth not; let vs draw
temptations. out the sword of the spirit, saying, it is written, that all they
are accursed who continue not in all that is written in the
booke of the law to doe it, Gal.3.10. that they who liue ac-
Galat.3 10. cording to the flesh, cannot please God, Rom.8.8. that the
Rom.8.8. burthen of sinne cannot be light, seeing it pressed out of
Christ himselfe a bloudie sweate, &c.

On the other side, if hee aggrauate the hainousnes of our
sins, to the end hee may draw vs into despaire of Gods mer-
Ezec.18.23.32 cie; let vs say, it is written, *I will not the death of a sinner* (saith
the Lord) *but that he repent and liue,* Ezech.18.23.32. And, *that*
1.Tim.1.15. *Iesus Christ came into the world to saue sinners,* 1.Tim.1.15. And
Matth.9.13. *that he came not to call the righteous, but sinners to repentance,*
Matth.9.13. Ioh.3.16. If he tempt vs to the loue of the world,
and to the seruice of this vnrighteous Mammon; let vs answer
Matth.6.24. him, that it is impossible to *serue two masters* of such contrarie
disposition, as it is written Matth.6.24. *That if wee loue the*
1.Ioh.2.15. *world, the loue of the father abideth not in vs* 1.Ioh.2.15. That
Iam.4.4. *the amitie of the world is enmitie against God,* Iam.4.4.

Contrariwise, if renouncing the world, and endeuouring
to serue the Lord in vprightnes and in truth, hee seeke to
draw vs from our integritie, by threatning afflictions and
persecution; wee are to strengthen our selues and resist him
with

with the sword of the spirit, remembring that they are *blessed* *which suffer persecution for righteousnes sake, for theirs is the* Matth.5.10. *kingdō of heauen*,Mat.5.10.That *all that will liue godly in Christ* 1.Tim.3.12. *Iesus shall suffer persecutiō*,1.Tim.3.12.That *whosoeuer loseth a-* *ny thing for Christs sake,shall receiue in recompence an hundreth* Matth.19.29. *fold more,and haue euerlasting life* to boote,Matth.19.29.

If he tempt vs to the neglect of Gods word,wee are to tell him, that all Christs *sheepe heare his voyce and follow him,* Ioh. Ioh.10.27. 10.27.That *whosoeuer is of God heareth Gods words*,Ioh.8.47. Ioh.8.47. that they who know God heare his ministers, whereas he that is not of God heareth them not,1.Ioh.4.6.And if he ob- 1.Ioh.4.6. iect that wee cannot heare it without great labour and cost, wee are to remember, that whosoeuer is a wise Merchant fit for the kingdome of God, will rather sell all he hath to buy this precious pearle,than be without it,Matth.13.44,45,46. Mat.13.44.45.

On the other side,if he tempt vs to content our selues with the bare hearing thereof, neglecting obedience thereunto, we are to tell him,that *not the hearers of the word, but the doers* Rom.2.13. *thereof shall be iustified*,Rom.2.13. that they who are hearers of the word and not doers also, doe deceiue themselues,if Iam.1.22. they thinke hereby to haue any assurance of eternall life,Iam. 1.22.That *not euery one who saith Lord,Lord*, (that is,maketh a Matth.7.21. goodly profession of religion) *shall enter into the kingdome of heauen, but he that doth the will of the father who is in heauen.* Matth.7.21.

So when he tempteth vs to pride, wee are to say vnto him, Sathan I may not yeeld vnto thy temptation, for it is writ- ten ; *God resisteth the proude, but giueth his grace to the humble,* 1.Pet.5.5. 1.Pet.5.5. If he tempt vs to couetousnes, we are to resist him, saying, it is written, that *the desire of money is the roote of all* 1.Tim.6.10. *euill*, 1.Tim.6.10. If to carking care, wee are to tell him; that the Apostle exhorteth vs to *cast all our care on the Lord,for he* 1.Pet.5.7. *careth for vs*, 1.Pet.5.7. If to vnthriftie mispending of Gods gifts, and carelesse consuming of our estates, wee are to tell him, that he *that prouideth not for his familie, is worse than an* 1.Tim.5.8. *Infidell*,1.Tim.5.8.

And thus may we repell the violence of all Sathans temp- §. Sect.3. tations and giue him the foyle, if wee will take vnto vs the sword

That it behooueth vs to be skilfull in handling the sword of the spirit.

sword of the spirit, and skilfully vse the same in the fight; for it is not sufficient that we haue this sword lying by vs, nor to be able to shew the goodnes thereof in discourse, if in the meane time we neuer draw it out to fight the spirituall combat, but let it rust in the scabberd; but we must alwaies haue it readie for the combat, and (as it were) naked in our hands, that wee may strike home, and cut off all the temptations of Sathan, and the lusts of our owne flesh when they doe assault vs. And to this end we must be skilfull in the vse thereof: for though a man haue an excellent weapon, yet if he know not how to vse it, it will little helpe him either to defend himselfe or offend his enemie: so if a man haue this two edged sword of Gods word, and haue no skill to rule it, he will strike flatlong and not cut, and sometime wound himselfe in stead of hurting his enemie; yea so politike a warriour is Sathan, against whom we fight, that if wee be not skilfull in the vse of this sword, he will turne the edge and point thereof against our selues, and so in stead of defending vs, it will, like the sword of *Goliah*, be readie for the enemie to cut off our owne head. And therefore it behooueth vs to come into Gods schoole continually, that there we may learne how to vse and handle this sword of Gods word so cunningly, that wee may resist Sathan in all his assaults, and giue him no aduantage in the fight. Otherwise he will vse it to our own ouerthrow; for if hee durst fight against our Sauiour Christ with his owne weapon the word of God, whose knowledge was exquisite and without measure, saying, It is written; how much more busie will he be in vsing it against vs, who haue not attained vnto the least part of his skill?

The folly of those who neglect this spirituall weapon.

Whereby appeareth first the carnall retchlesnesse of many men, who, as though there were no enemie to assault them, haue not this weapon in their houses at all, or if they haue, yet they bestow more time in prophane exercises, than in studie how to vse the sword of the spirit for their owne defence; or at least trusting to their owne skill as sufficient in it selfe, they seldome come to the Lords schoole, where they might learne to vse the weapon of Gods word for their best aduantage.

Secondly,

Secondly, hereby appeareth the wicked practiſe of the enemies of Gods truth, who take from Gods people this ſword of the ſpirit, which the Lord hath giuen vnto all for their defence. Neither doth the Apoſtle in this place exhort onely the Clergie to take this weapon, but all Chriſtians whatſoeuer, who are aſſaulted with their ſpirituall enemies : but they notwithſtanding conſpiring with Sathan to worke the ouerthrow of Gods Church, depriue them of the vſe of the ſword of the ſpirit, the word of God, and ſo betray them into the power of Sathan, being able to make no reſiſtance, when their chiefe weapon is taken from them.

CHAP. XVI.

Of Prayer.

He laſt and chiefe meanes wherby we may both defend our ſelues and offend our enemie, is feruent and effectual prayer, which the Apoſtle exhorteth vs to vſe, Eph.6.18. *And pray alwaies with &c.* The neceſſitie and profit of which exercise is exceeding great in this ſpirituall combat, becauſe thereby we doe obtaine all our ſtrength to fight, and victorie alſo ouer our enemies. For firſt wee cannot endure the leaſt aſſault of Sathan by our owne ſtrength, vnleſſe wee be armed with the power of Gods might, as before I haue ſhewed. And the Lords aſſiſtance, whereby onely we can ouercome, is obtained by earneſt and effectuall prayer, according to that Pſal.50.15. *Call vpon me in the day of trouble; ſo will I deliuer thee, and thou ſhalt glorifie me.* And our Sauiour preſcribeth vs this meanes to free our ſelues from temptation, or at leaſt from being ouercome by them, by crauing the Lords aſſiſtance, ſaying, *Leade vs not into temptation, but deliuer vs from euill,*Matth.6.13. So hee exhorteth his diſciples vnto *prayer, leaſt they ſhould enter into temptation.*Luk.22.40,46.

Secondly, we cannot obtaine the ſpirituall armour (before deſcribed) by any meanes of our owne, but thoſe graces of Gods ſpirit are his gifts, from whom euery good and perfect gift

§. Sect.1.
Eph. 6.18.
That prayer is the meanes of obtaining Gods aſſiſtance, and the reſt of the ſpirituall armour.

Pſal.50.15.

Matth.6.13

Luk.22.40.

Iam.1.17.

Matth.7.7.

Ioh.16.23.

Verf.24.
Luk.11.13.

gift defcendeth, Iam.1.17. and therefore are to be begged at his hands by earneft and effectuall prayer, we hauing his gracious promife, that if we aske we fhall receiue, Math.7.7. And our Sauiour hath affured vs, that whatfoeuer wee aske the father in his name, he will giue it vs, Ioh.16.23. And to this his promife he addeth his commandement in the verfe following, faying, *Aske and you fhall receiue.* Yea, if we doe but truly defire the holy Ghoft, the Father will giue him vnto vs, Luk.11.13. And hee commeth not alone, but bringeth with him our fpirituall armour, euen all his graces fit for to arme vs in the fpirituall combat, againft all the affaults of Sathan and his affiftants.

§. Sect.2.
The reft of the fpirituall armour is not fufficient without prayer.

But whereas thefe graces are in this life but weake and imperfect in vs; our truth being mixt with will-worfhip and hypocrifie; the puritie of our confcience being ftained with our corruption; our knowledge of the Gofpell but in part, and fhadowed with the vaile of ignorance; our faith mixt with doubting, and weakened with incredulitie; our hope fhaken from our anker-hold, when the promifes of God are delaied; and whereas we alfo are vnskilfull to vfe this fpiritual armour for our beft aduantage; therefore it behooueth vs after wee haue armed our felues at all points, not to truft altogether in our armour, but to haue our recourfe vnto our grand Captaine Chrift Iefus, acknowledging our owne weakeneffe, and defiring his aide and affiftance, that being armed with his power, we may obtaine a glorious victorie ouer our fpirituall enemies. And as *Mofes* ioyned with *Iofuahs* fword his owne effectual prayer, which was of farre greater efficacie; for when he held vp his hands in prayer, Ifrael preuailed; but when he fainted, *Amaleck* had the vpper hand: fo wee being to fight againft the fpirituall Amalekites, are not wholie to truft in our fpirituall weapons, but we are to implore continually the Lords affiftance by heartie prayer, affuring our felues that if we lift vp our hands and hearts vnto God, we fhal in the end obtaine a full victorie; but if we faint, the fpirituall *Amaleck* will preuaile againft vs. Whileft our mindes lie groueling on the earth, it is an eafie matter for thefe fpirituall wickedneffes to ouercome vs, feeing they fight againft vs from high places;

ces; but if wee lift vp our hearts in prayer vnto God, our mindes and foules fhall be as it were tranfported into heauen, which is a tower of ftrength, into which our fpirituall enemies cannot approch. Whenfoeuer therefore wee are affaulted by Sathan, let vs lift vp our foules into heauen by effectuall prayer, and fo we fhall be out of his reach.

Now that our prayers may bee effectuall, there are diuers §. *Sect.3.* conditions and properties required in them by the Apoftle in this place. Firft, that wee pray continually, which alfo our Luk.18.1. Sauiour Chrift enioyneth vs, Luk.18.1. And *Paul* alfo 1.Theff. 1.Theff.5.17. 5.17. not that wee muft neglect all other exercifes and doe *The properties* nothing but pray; for there is a time to heare the word, to do *required in* the workes of mercie and of our callings; but his meaning is *prayer.* that we be alwaies readie to pray vpon all good occafions: efpecially in the time of temptation this dutie is required, according to that Pfal.50.15. And therefore the Apoftle faith Pfal.50.15. not, that wee muft pray ἐν παντὶ χρόνῳ, in euery particular time and feafon, but ἐν παντὶ καιρῷ, in euery fit time when iuft occafion and opportunitie is offered. Seeing therefore in the time of temptation we doe efpecially need the Lords helpe; therefore, that aboue al other is the opportune and conuenient time wherein we are to implore the Lords affiftance. Where by the way the ftinted prayers of the popifh rabble, which they reftraine to fet houres is confuted, for the Apoftle willeth vs alwaies to be in readines when any fit occafion is offered.

The fecond thing required, is, that wee pray with all manner of prayers and fupplication. The former word here vfed is προσευχή, which fignifieth the earneft defiring of any good thing: the other is δέησις, which is the deprecation of fome euill; fo that whether wee want any thing that is good, or would be deliuered from any thing which is euill, wee muft haue recourfe vnto God by prayer, that we may obtaine the one and auoide the other; but more efpecially when we feele the want or weaknes of any part of the fpirituall armour, the graces of Gods fpirit, wee are to begge them at Gods hand, that fo wee may be enabled to ftand in the encounter; and when wee apprehend the extreame malice, ioyned with the

F   great

great power and cunning policie of our fpirituall enemies, wee are earneftly to pray that the Lord will not leade vs into temptation ; or if he doe, yet that he will not fuffer vs to fall therein and to be ouerthrowne. And thefe our prayers muft not onely be publike in the Church, but alfo priuate in our chambers ; neither muft wee be alwaies begging thefe benefits at Gods hand, but hauing obtained them, we muft be as readie to giue him thankes , and to afcribe the glorie of all vnto him, who is the author and beftower of all vertue and grace which is in vs ; and fo calling vpon God with all manner of prayer, he will be continually readie to affift vs in our fpirituall combat.

The third thing required, is, that we pray in or by the fpirit, for the word here vfed may fignifie both. Firft therefore we muft pray in the fpirit ; to which is required firft that we pray with vnderftanding ; in which refpect the ignorant Papifts offend, who pray in an vnknowne tongue ; and the ignorant Proteftants alfo, who though they pray in their owne language, yet know not the fenfe and meaning of that they fpeake.

Efa.29.13.

Secondly, that we pray with attentiue mindes, ioyning our hearts with our tongues, and thoughts with words ; to which is oppofed the prayer of the lippes alone, when as wee draw neere vnto God with our mouthes, our hearts in the meane time being farre from him, as it is Efa.29.13. Which kinde of prayer is odious and abominable vnto God : for what more groffe difcord than when the tongue and heart difagree from one another, which fhould be tuned in vnifone ? And as the carcaffe being feuered from the foule is prefently corrupt and ftinketh ; fo the prayer of the lips being feuered from the prayer of the heart, which is the life and foule of it, is but a dead carcaffe of prayer, and ftinketh in Gods noftrels.

2.Tim.2.8.

Thirdly, that we pray with a pure confcience and faith vnfained, *lifting vp pure hands to God, without wrath or doubting,* as it is 1.Tim. 2. 8. to which is oppofed prayer proceeding from a polluted confcience, when as men liue in their finnes without any true forrow for thofe which are paft, or any fincere purpofe to forfake them in the time to come ; which

prayers

prayers muſt needes proceede from an heart full of incredulitie, ſeeing they haue no promiſe in the word whereupon
they may ground their faith : nay, contrariwiſe it is ſaid, that
God heareth not ſinners, Ioh.9.31. that is, ſuch as go on in their
ſinnes without repentance, hauing no purpoſe of heart to
leaue and forſake them. *Ioh.9.31.*

And thus you ſee what it is to pray in the ſpirit, which wee
cannot perfourme, vnleſſe we pray through and by the ſpirit
of God, which helpeth our infirmities , and teacheth vs to
pray as wee ought , yea it ſelfe maketh requeſt for vs with
ſighes which cannot be expreſſed, as it is Rom.8.26. *Rom.8 26.*

The fourth thing required is watchfulnes; which dutie is
required ioyntly with prayer in many places. Our Sauiour
three times ioyneth them together, ſaying, *Watch and pray*
that ye enter not into temptation, Matth.26. And the Apoſtle
Peter 1.Epiſt 4.7. ſaith, *Now the end of all things is at hand : Be*
ye therefore ſober and watching vnto prayer. As though hee
ſhould ſay, your enemie the diuell as a roring lion walketh
about, ſeeking whom he may deuoure, and therefore it behooueth you at all times like valiant and carefull ſouldiers,
who are ſtill in daunger to be aſſaulted by their enemies, to
be ſober and watch, as it is 1.Pet.5.8. but now more eſpecially ſeeing the end of all things is at hand, for Sathan knowing
that his time is but ſhort, will redouble all his forces to work
our deſtruction, euen as ſouldiers will moſt fiercely aſſault a
town, when as they cannot long lie at the ſiege, either by reaſon of winter drawing on, or the approching of new forces to
relieue the towne or raiſe the ſiege. Seeing therefore Sathan
redoubleth his force and care in working our deſtruction, let
vs redouble our care and watchfulnes in ſeeking to preuent
his force and malice. For if Sathan watch continually that he
may murther vs, ſhall not wee be watchfull in withſtanding
his aſſaults ? He is continually in armes to ouerthrow vs, and
ſhall not wee watch night and day in our Chriſtian armour,
that we may defeate his forces and obtaine victorie ?

§. Sect.4.
Of watchfulnes
Matth.26.

1.Pet.4.7.

1.Pet 5.8.

Now this our watchfulnes is partly of the bodie, and partly of the ſoule. The bodily watching is the abſtaining from
naturall ſleepe, to the end that wee may giue our ſelues vnto

prayer;

Pfal.6.6.
Pfal.88.1.

Pfal.119.62.
prayer; when as with *Dauid* we water our couch with teares,
Pfal.6.6. and call vpon God not onely in the day, but in the
night alfo, as it is Pfal.88.1. And whē as euen at midnight we
rouze vp our felues to giue thankes vnto God for his mercie
and benefits, as it is Pfal.119.62. The watchfulnes of the foule
is when as wee doe not fleepe in our finnes, being rocked in
the cradle of carnall fecuritie, but fhake off our drowfines by
vnfained repentance, rifing vp to newnes of life. And to this

Eph.5.14.
watchfulnes the Apoftle exhorteth vs Eph.5.14. *Awake thou*
that fleepeft, and ftand vp from the dead, and Chrift fhall giue
thee light,&c. for wee are dead in our finnes, till Chrift by his

Eph.2.1.
fpirit mortifie them and reuiue vs, raifing vs vp to newnes of
life, as it is Eph.2.1. Though therefore wee take our reft and

1.Theff.5.6.
fleepe in that meafure which nature requireth, yet *let vs not*
fleepe as doe other, (to wit, in carnall fecuritie) *but let vs watch*
and be fober, as it is 1.Theff.5.6. becaufe in this refpect it is
time that we fhould arife from fleepe, for the darke night of
ignorance is paft; and the bright fun-fhine day of the Gofpel

Rom.13.12.
&c.
is come, *let vs therefore caft away the workes of darknes, and let*
vs put on the armour of light : So that we walke honeftly as in the
day : not in gluttony and drunkennes, neither in chambering and
wantonneffe, nor in ftrife and enuying: but putting on the Lord Ie-
fus Chrift, taking no thought for the flefh, to fulfill the lufts there-
of, as it is Rom.13.12,13,14.

And this is the Chriftian watch which we are to ioyne with
prayer : but as I would not haue vs put our whole confidence
in the fpirituall armour, fo much leffe in our owne care and
watchfulnes; for wee muft relie our felues vpon God onely,
defiring him to watch ouer vs while we fleepe; but yet with
the Lords affiftance wee muft ioyne our endeuour, and not
drowfily and fleepely receiue his aide : and as the godly huf-
bandman expecteth the fruites of the earth from the bleffing
of God, and yet notwithftanding vfeth all paines, care and
diligence in plowing, harrowing and fowing his ground; fo
we are to feeke deliuerance from the force and malice of our
fpirituall enemies of God alone, but yet wee are to ioyne our
good endeuour carefully and diligently, vfing all the good
meanes which are ordained of God for this purpofe.

                                                          The

The fift thing required is perseuerance in prayer: for it is not sufficient to pray earneftly and feruently for a spirt, but we muft continue therein, expecting the Lords leifure. And vnto this we are exhorted Rom.12.12. *continuing in prayer.* So the Prophet *Dauid* perfwadeth to expect and waite for the Lord, and to bee ftrong in continuing conftantlie in our courfe, and then in the end God will comfort our hearts, Pfal.27.14 And the Apoftle *Paul* willeth vs to pray inceffantly, like importunate fuiters who will haue no nay, though they receiue many denials. To this dutie our Sauiour encourageth vs by the parable of the vnrighteous Iudge, who though hee neither cared for man nor feared God, yet was moued through importunitie to do the poore widow iuftice; and therefore our heauenly father will much more graunt the importunate fuites of his elect, efpecially hauing bound himfelfe thereunto by his moft gracious promifes. True it is that the Lord doth many times deferre to graunt the prayers of his children, as though he heard or regarded them not; when as in truth he neuer delayeth any of their lawfull fuites, vnleffe it be to this end that hee may thereby either conuay vnto them greater benefits than they defire, as when hee giueth fpirituall graces in ftead of earthly benefits;or els that thereby he may moue them to pray more feruently, and fo exercife and increafe their faith, hope and patience; or that he may fhew thefe his graces to the praife of his glorie who hath beftowed them, both to others and the parties themfelues; or that hee may moue vs more thankfully to receiue and highly to efteeme his benefits,after by long fuite wee haue obtained them, which wee would not fo greatly regard if he beftowed them at the firft motion. A notable example hereof we haue in the Canaanitifh woman,both for our comfort and imitation, Matth.15.To whofe prayers our Sauiour Chrift gaue(as it feemed) no eare; and when he did take notice of her fuite he giueth her a double repulfe,firft by telling her that he was fent onely to the loft fheepe of the houfe of Ifrael; and when this would not moue her to furceafe her fuite,he vfeth a more bitter deniall,telling her that it was not fit to take the childrens bread and to caft it to whelpes: but

§. Sect.5.
Of perfeue-rance in praier.
Rom.12.12.
Pfal.27.14.
1.Theff.5.17.
Luk.18.1.
VVhy the Lord delaieth to graunt the pe-titions of his children.
Matth.15.

when

when fhe was not hereby difcouraged, nor her faith extin-
guifhed, but rather of a fparke increafed to a great flame, at
the laft fhe doth not onely receiue what fhe defired, but alfo
was fent away with great commendation. But wherefore did
not our Sauiour graunt her petition at the firft hearing? Surely not that he grudged her her fuite,or was loth to entertaine
it,but to the end that he might make her more earneftly implore his helpe, and manifeft to all the world her fingular
faith ; and laftly, that fhe might be an example to vs for our
imitation,both to encourage vs in asking of God the fupplie
of our wants, and alfo to perfeuere in prayer, though at the
firft God feemeth not to regard vs, yea though wee receiue
diuers repulfes and many difcouragements : which if we perfourme wee fhall haue a notable teftimonie of a true faith,
when as we can patiently abide the Lords leifure,though hee
doe deferre his helpe,for *he that beleeueth, will not make hafte,*
as it is Efa.28.16. and in the end wee fhall be fure to obtaine
our godly and honeft defires,if not as we would,yet as it fhal
be moft for our good,and withall eternall bleffednes. *For the
Lord is the God of iudgement ; and bleffed are all they that waite
for him,*as it is Efa.30.18.

Efa.28.16.

Efa.30.18.

    When therefore we are affaulted by our fpiritual enemies,
and readie to faint in the combat of temptations, let vs call
vpon the Lord for his affiftance, that wee may be freed from
danger and deliuered from them ; and if the Lord doe feeme
to deferre his helpe, and fuffer vs ftill to beare the brunt of
the battaile, after wee haue many times implored his affiftance,yet let vs not be difcouraged,but conftantly perfeuere
in prayer,affuring our felues that the Lord will either free vs
from the temptation, or els giue vs ftrength to endure and
ouercome it : for hee hath promifed that he will not fuffer vs
to be tempted aboue our power,but that he will giue a good
iffue to the temptation that wee may be able to beare it,and
he is faithfull and true of his word : as it is 1.Cor.10.13. It
may be that the Lord wil not quite free vs from the skirmifh
of temptation,though we haue often defired it of him, either
becaufe he would further trie our Chriftian valour,and exercife our faith, or reftraine vs from finne, efpecially fpirituall
                                                             pride,

1.Cor.10.13.

pride,to which wee are too too fubiect; as wee may fee in the
example of *Paul,* who being buffeted by the meffenger of
Sathan, befought the Lord thrice that he might depart from
him : bnt the Lord anfwered,that his grace which he beftowed on him was fufficient,and that his power was made manifeft in the Apoftles weaknes,as appeareth 2.Cor.12.8,9. Now 1.Cor.12.8,9.
the caufe why the Lord would not altogether releafe him,
was,that he might be humbled hereby,the pricke of the flefh
letting out the winde of vaine glorie,which would haue puffed him vp, by reafon of the multitude of reuelations
which hee had receiued. Let vs not therefore fend for the
Lords affiftance (as it were) by pofte;and prefcribe the Lord
a time with the Bethulians, wherein if we be not relieued we
will faint and cowardly yeeld : for that which the Prophet
fpeaketh from the Lord concerning the vifion,may fitly bee
fpoken of the Lords aide and helpe ; *Though it tarie, watch* ; Hab.2.3.
*for it fhall furely come and not ftay,*Habac.2.3.

The laft thing required in our prayers,is,that wee doe not §. Sect.6.
onely pray for our felues, but alfo for all the Saints. For wee *Prayer to be*
are fellow members of the fame bodie, wee are fellow foul- *made for all*
diers which fight vnder the fame Captaine Iefus Chrift, and *the Saints.*
confequently their victorie is our victorie, and their foyles
are our foyles. As therefore fouldiers do not only ftand vpon
their feuerall guards, but ioyne their forces together, whereby it commeth to paffe,that they who being fcattered might
eafily be ouercome, hauing vnited their forces are vnrefiftable ; fo wee are not onely to ftand vpon our owne defence,
but to ioyne in prayer with the whole Church militant, and
then fhall not our fpirituall enemies ftand againft vs : for if
the praier of one righteous man auaileth much,being feruent Iam.5.16.
and effectuall; of what efficacie and power are the prayers of
all the righteous ioyned together ?

And thus haue I defcribed the Chriftian armour, which e- *No armour ap-*
uery man is to put on before hee enter into the combat with *pointed for the*
our fpirituall enemies : amongft all which there is not any *backe.*
peece appointed for the backe, to note vnto vs that wee muft
neuer retire, but manfully ftand to it euen in the face of our
enemie. For if wee refift Sathan, he will flee from vs,Iam.4.7. Iam.4.7.

but

but if we giue ground and betake our selues to flight, he will
pursue vs swiftly and deadly wound vs; for wee haue no armour on the backe to defend vs from the violence of his
blowes, neither will the Lord protect such faint-hearted cowards as runne away from his standerd, not daring to trust
and relie vpon his almightie power and neuer failing assistance, which he hath promised to all that fight his battailes.
Seeing therefore there is no safetie in flight, and assured victorie to those that faint not but endure the brunt of the skirmish vnto the end, let vs manfully stand vpon our guard, neither fleeing nor yeelding to our spirituall enemies; for where
can wee be more safe, than vnder the Lords standerd? where
can we be more honourably imployed, than in fighting his
battailes? how can our state be more dangerous, than when
we flee and Sathan pursueth vs? how can it be more desperate, than when wee yeeld our selues captiue to Sathan to be
bound in the fetters of sinne, vntill the sentence of condemnation be pronounced on vs in the general sessions at the day
of Christs appearing?

<hr />

Chap. XVII.
Of Sathans stratagems.

§. Sect. I.

ANd so much concerning our spirituall armour, as
also our preparation to the spirituall warfare; now
we are to speake of the battaile it selfe: where first
we are to consider of Sathans stratagems, and the
manner of his fight; and secondly, of the speciall conflicts or
temptations wherewith he assaileth vs. Concerning Sathans
stratagems, wee are to know that they are many and dangerous; with which he will easily circumuent and ouerthrow vs,
if wee doe not carefully preuent or cunningly auoide them.

Sathan wor-
keth vpon our
owne corrupt
affections.

For first he dealeth not with all alike, neither vseth the same
weapons to foyle euery one, but he obserueth the qualitie
and disposition of his enemies, and accordingly he fitteth his
temptations, so as they may be most forcible to preuaile a-
gainst them. And to this end he obserueth to what sinnes wee
are

are moſt inclined, either by nature, or by preſent occaſion,
and to thoſe he inciteth vs, thruſting vs as it were downe the
hill,where we are apt to runne headlong of our owne accord;
and ſeconding his aſſault with the aide of our corrupt fleſh,
which intertaineth willingly his ſuggeſtions, and vrgeth vs
violently to yeeld to his temptations. So that Sathan neuer
ſtriueth againſt the ſtreame, but vſeth the tide of our affections to carrie vs ſwiftly into a ſea of ſinne.

For example, if he finde a man ambitiouſly affected, then
he couereth his hooke with the baite of honours : and thus
he tempted *Abimelech* to murther all his worthie brethren, Iudg.9.
that hee might obtaine the ſoueraigntie : thus hee tempted
Ioab to ſtab traiterouſly *Abner* and *Amaſa,* that hee might
ſtill be Captaine Generall : thus he tempted *Abſalon* to vſurp 1.Sam.14.
the kingdome, though it were by the vtter deſtruction of his
owne father.And thus he tempted our Sauiour Chriſt to worſhip him, by offering him all the kingdomes of the world,
thinking belike that he was inclined to ambition, ſeeing hee
profeſſed himſelfe a great King, and had no worldly kingdome in his poſſeſſion. So in our daies he tempteth the ambitious ſubiect to aſpire, without iuſt title, to the Crowne of
their lawfull Princes; and thoſe who are Kings alreadie to
affect a Monarchie, by vſurping wrongfully their neighbour
kingdomes : ſo hee tempteth the Spiritualtie to come by
Church-preferments, rather commended by the gifts of the
purſe than of the minde ; and the Laytie to buy great offices
at ſo high a rate that they cannot liue of them, vnleſſe they
ſell iuſtice by taking bribes to betray the innocent,and their
honeſtie alſo by vſing all extorſion.

If he find that men are addicted to voluptuouſnes,then he
tempteth them to ſinne by offering carnall pleaſures; and
thus hee tempted *Noah* to drunkennes, *Dauid* to adulterie,
Salomon to idolatrie and all wickedneſſe. And thus now hee
tempteth ſome to good fellowſhip, that is, to ſpend their
whole time in drunkennes, belly-cheare, and all riotous ex-
ceſſe and Epicuriſme ; ſome to luſt,incontinencie,and all voluptuous pleaſures of the fleſh.Or if he cannot bring them to
ſuch carnall groſſnes, hee will intice them to vſe lawfull re-
creations

creations vnlawfully, and immoderatly spending all their time in pleasure, which they should bestow in the seruice of God, by imploying themselues in the generall duties of Christianitie, and in the speciall duties of their callings.

§. Sect.2.

1.Tim 6.9.10.
How Sathan worketh vpon mens couetousnes.

But if he finde that men are giuen to couctousnesse, then hath hee matter enough to worke vpon: for as the Apostle saith, 1.Tim.6.9,10. *They that will be rich fall into temptations and snares, and into many foolish and noisome lusts, which drowne men in perdition and destruction: for the desire of money is the roote of all euill.* With this baite hee allured *Laban* to deale churlishly and vniustly with *Iacob*, and his owne children; and to inrich himselfe by impouerishing them, for whose sake he should haue gathered his riches. He inticed *Balaam* to curse the people whom God had blessed, by offring him money the wages of wickednesse. He tempted *Gehazi* to take the talent and chaunge of raiment of *Naaman*, selling for this small trifle Gods honour and his masters credit. He allured *Achab* to murther *Naboth*, that he might purloyne his vineyard, and so purchase the iuyce of the grape with the blood of his faithfull subiect. With this baite he inticed *Iudas* to betray his master, selling him for thirtie peeces of siluer, whose worth could not be valued with many worlds. And hereby

Act.19.25.

also hee prouoked *Demetrius* to oppose himselfe to the preaching of the Gospell, because hee would not lose his gaine in making siluer shrines to the Idoll, Act.19.25. Neither was this argument drawne from profit forcible onely in former times, but now also it doth no lesse perswade to sinne. For whom almost doth not Sathan catch, or at least intangle in this golden net? Doth he not insnare as well professors of religion, as professed worldlings, so that in greedie seeking of gaine it is not easie to discerne the one from the other? Doth hee not ouercome all sorts and conditions of men, as well those who abound in al things, as those that enioy little, by proportionating his offers of riches, according to their seuerall estates; much to those that haue much, and little to those that possesse little? For hee commeth to Princes, and promiseth them huge summes of money, if they will lay intollerable taxations on their subiects, or rob the Church of

her

her liuings, that is, God himselfe of his right. He commeth to
Magiftrates and Iudges, and offreth vnto them great bribes,
if they will peruert iuftice, and so putteth out their eyes that
they cannot fee right from wrong; for, *reward blindeth the*   Deut. 16.19.
eyes of the wife, and peruerteth the words of the iuft, as it is Deut.
16.19. If he fee one in office couetous, he promifeth great re-
uenewes and ftately houfes, if hee will deceiue the Prince of
their right, and oppreffe the fubiect with grieuous extortion:
and the like offers he maketh to couetous gentlemen, if they
will build their houfes with the blood of their tenants, and
by grinding the faces of the poore, and by inhaunfing their
rents, and increasing their fines to fuch vnreafonable rates,
that the poore tenant can fcarce with the fweate of his face
earne his bread.

Neither doth hee angle with this baite in the Court and
countrie onely, but he thinketh it fit for the citie alfo : for he
commeth to the couetous Merchant, and promifeth him that
in fuch a countrie he fhall haue good trafficke, if hee will dif-
femble his religion, that is, denie Chrift before men : he offereth to the fhop-keeper increafe of wealth, if hee will vfe falfe
waights & meafures, and falfe lights, or els fell fuch wares as
are neither profitable for the Church nor Common-wealth;
or adulterate and falfifie his ftuffe by mixing bad with good;
or aske double the price, fwearing that it coft him more than
afterwards himfelfe is contented to take: in a word, if in buy-
ing and felling he will vfe fraud, lying, fwearing and forfwea-
ring, hee promifeth to make him a rich man, though oftentimes hee deceiueth him, for in ftead of increafing in wealth
by thefe vngodly practifes, oftentimes he becomes banke-
rupt, the Lord laying his curfe on thofe wicked meanes, without whofe bleffing the builder buildeth and the labourer la-
boureth but in vaine, as it is Pfal. 127. 1. 2. So alfo he commeth   Pfal. 127. 1. 2.
to the Artificer, and telleth him that if he will be rich, he muft
make fale ware : and what is that ? fuch as is fleight and altogether vnfit for vfe; as though that were moft fit for fale
which is fleight and altogether vnprofitable. And fo common nowadaies is this fault, that no greater difpraife can be
giuen, than to fay it is fale ware, as though now nothing
which

which is good and substantiall were fit to be sold. And with these and such like snares doth Sathan intangle those that are couetous, and haue set their hearts vpon the earthly Mammon; which I haue the longer stood vpon, because it is a temptation most dangerous; neither doth Sathan by any meanes more easily sacke our soules, and spoile vs of Gods graces,than when hee ascendeth by these golden ladders, or maketh a breach in our hearts with these rich bullets.

§. Sect.3.
How Sathan tempteth the vaine-glorious to sinne.

If Sathan see men proud and vaine-glorious, then he inticeth them to sinne, by offring them gorgeous attire farre vnfitting their state and callings, and so causeth them to commit a great absurditie: for whereas our Sauiour Christ saith, that the bodie is of more worth than raiment, they make their raiment of more worth than their bodies,in other mens iudgement, and preferre gay apparell before the health of their soules, in their owne estimation; for that they may iet it out in rich attire, they vse vnlawful meanes,either by iniuring and oppressing their inferiours, or at least by keeping the poore from their right: (for their superfluitie of wealth was not giuen them to spend in such excesse, but that they should like the Lords Almners relieue the poore with their surplussage) and by both,they wound their soules with sinne, and without repentance plunge them into euerlasting death.

So also Sathan taketh aduantage of our complexion and temperature; by tempting the Sanguine to pleasure and lust; the Flegmaticke to idlenes and sloth; the Melancholicke to enuie and malice; the Cholericke man he prouoketh to quarrels and braules, and inticeth him to take reuenge by aggrauating the iniurie, and suggesting that it will be great disparagement to put vp such a wrong. In a word,Sathan carefully obserueth to what sinne we are most prone by nature,custom or occasion;and to that he eggeth vs forward vnto which our owne lusts leade vs,changing his temptations as we change our affection.And therefore the Apostle *Iames* telleth vs,that whosoeuer is tempted,is drawne away by his owne concupiscence, because Sathan neuer assaulteth vs, but he is sure that the flesh will further him in his temptations.

Iam. 1. 14.

§. Sect.4.

And thus haue I discouered Sathans first stratagem, which
he

he vseth in tempting vs to sinne; which if wee would withstand and defeate, we are as carefully to obserue our own nature and disposition, that wee may finde to what vices we are
most prone, and so with greater watchfulnes we may auoide
them. For as when a citie is besieged, the inhabitants will
most strongly man that place, which by nature is most weake
and assaultable, because they know that the enemie will giue
the onset there where he is like to finde the easiest entrance :
so wee being besieged with our spirituall enemies, are most
carefully to obserue where our soules are weakest to make
resistance, and ouer that part wee are to watch with greatest
diligence, assuring our selues that there Sathan will plant all
his engines of batterie, that hauing made a breach hee may
enter and surprize vs. And because the heart of man is deceit- Ierem.17.9.
full aboue all things, and none but God know it, let vs summon it often before the throne of Gods iudgement, and examine it by his law, that thereby wee may see our secret corruptions, and after labour to kill and mortifie them.

If we finde that wee be ambitiously affected, wee are to vse
all good meanes that true humilitie may bee wrought in our
hearts, and whensoeuer (honours being offred) we are tickled
with ambitious and aspiring thoughts, let vs suspect that vnder honour Sathan hath hid a hooke to catch vs. And therefore before wee accept it, wee are to examine our selues whether we be fit for so high a place, and whether we can attaine
thereto by honest and lawfull meanes, and whether the place
it selfe be such, that therein we may glorifie God, benefit his
Church, and keepe a good conscience.

So if we finde that we are addicted vnto pleasures, wee are
with all care to studie and practise true mortification; and
when any pleasures are offred vs, wee are to looke narrowly
into them, that we may discerne if Sathan hath not laid vnder
them a snare to intrap vs, either by tempting vs to pleasures
which are vnlawfull, or to the immoderate vse of those which
be lawfull; and as we loue the saluation of our soules, let vs
auoide the baite when we see the snare.

In like manner if wee finde that we are prone to couetousnes, let vs carefully labour to weane our selues from this vice,

by

1.Tim.6.9.10.
Eph. 5.5.
Col.3.5.
Matth.19.24.

Luk.12.20.

by conſidering that it is idolatrie, and the roote of all euill; that the rich(that is,ſuch as ſet their hearts vpon riches) ſhall as hardly enter into Gods kingdome as a Camell thorow an needels eye; that riches are momentanie and mutable, and wee mortall, and therefore haue no aſſurance of them for the ſpace of one day. And when any commoditie is offred vs,we are to looke twice on it before we accept thereof, examining whether wee may compaſſe it by honeſt and good meanes, and without the hurt of our brethren, and then wee may take it as ſent from God ; otherwiſe we may aſſure our ſelues,that how pleaſantly ſoeuer the baite looketh, yet Sathan hath hid vnder it a deadly hooke,and therfore if we ſwallow the baite the hooke will choake vs.

And thus alſo are we to behaue our ſelues in reſpect of all other ſinnes, to which we finde after due examination we are addicted, if wee will be ſafe from the diuels malice and cunning furie, knowing that where we are moſt weake, there he will giue the moſt violent aſſaults.

CHAP. XVIII.

How Sathan fitteth his temptations to our
ſtate and conditions.

§. Sect.1.

 Vt as Sathan fitteth his temptations to our nature and diſpoſition, ſo alſo to our ſtate and condition: for this alſo he obſerueth, and according to the qualitie thereof he tempteth vs to ſuch ſinnes,as by reaſon thereof wee are moſt inclinable : and this he doth both in reſpect of our worldly and alſo our ſpirituall eſtate. In regard of our worldly eſtate,he obſerueth whether we are in proſperitie or aduerſitie. If we be in proſperitie,then he tempteth vs

How Sathan fit-
teth his temp-
tations to our
worldly eſtate.

to thoſe ſinnes whereunto that eſtate is moſt ſubiect, namely to pride and forgetfulnes of God,to contempt of our poore brethren,to the loue of the world,to coldnes in religion, and carnall ſecuritie ; for he will perſwade vs, how wickedly ſoeuer we liue,that we are highly in Gods fauour, otherwiſe he
would

would not beſtow ſo great and manifold benefits vpon vs, as pawnes and pledges of his loue.

If we be in aduerſitie, then he will labour to perſwade vs to vſe vnlawfull meanes for the repairing of our eſtates, diſtruſting in Gods al-ruling prouidence and neuer decceiuing promiſes. If we be poore, he inticeth vs to ſteale, defraud and oppreſſe our brethren, that ſo wee may become rich by others ſpoyles. If wee haue loſt any thing by theeues or other caſualtie, he tempteth vs to goe to witches and wizards, that ſo we may hazard our ſoules, which are of more value than the whole world, for the recouerie of ſome earthly trifle. If wee ſuffer any great croſſe or affliction, hee will perſwade vs that God hath forſaken and hateth vs, or els he would not ſo grieuouſly afflict vs ; and hereby hee moueth vs to deſpaire, murmuring and repining againſt God. Which temptation he findeth ſo forcible, that he confidently preſumed that he could thereby haue cauſed *Iob* to haue blaſphemed God to his face. Yea hee thought it a fit weapon to vſe againſt our Sauiour Chriſt; for, wanting ordinarie meanes to ſuſtaine his hunger, Sathan tempteth him to diſtruſt Gods prouidence, and to ſhift for himſelfe, by turning ſtones into bread, Matth.4.   *Matth. 4.*

Now if wee would withſtand Sathan in this his cunning practiſe, wee alſo are carefully to obſerue our eſtates, and to arme our ſelues againſt thoſe temptations, to which that eſtate wherein we liue is moſt ſubiect. In the time of proſperitie we are continually to meditate, that whatſoeuer wee haue it is the gift of God, beſtowed on vs not for our deſarts, but of his free mercie and goodneſſe, that by the conſideration hereof we may be ſtirred vp to true thankfulnes, and as often as wee looke vpon the gifts may thinke vpon the giuer, and praiſe his name for his benefits, and imploy them to his glorie, and the good of our brethren the poore members of Ieſus Chriſt. Let vs remember that wee are but ſtewards of theſe earthly treaſures, and therefore muſt one day be called to an account, and conſequently the greater our receipts be, the greater will be our reckoning; that theſe earthly things are momentanie and mutable, and we alſo mortall, and therfore there is no reaſon that wee ſhould be proud of them, or contemne

§. *Sect.2.*
How we are to defeat Sathans former policie.

temne our brethren who want them, ſeeing in an inſtant they may abound, and we may be ſtripped of all we poſſeſſe.

So if we be in aduerſitie, wee are to relie our ſelues on the Lords prouidence, who hath promiſed to all that depend vp-on him all things neceſſarie, ſo farre foorth as they tend to the ſaluation of our ſoules : neither are we to beleeue Sathan when he telleth vs that afflictions are ſignes of Gods hatred, ſeeing there are innumerable examples of Gods deare chil-dren grieuouſly afflicted, and plaine teſtimonies of Scriptures which proue the contrarie, as ſhall appeare hereafter.

§. Sect. 3.
How Sathan frameth his temptations in reſpect of our ſpirituall eſtate.

In reſpect of our ſpirituall eſtate Sathan obſerueth whe-ther wee be meere worldlings or profeſſors. If worldlings, then whether we be notoriouſly wicked, or ciuil honeſt men; thoſe that be notoriouſly wicked he plungeth headlong into a gulfe of all wickedneſſe and outragious rebellion againſt God, hee tempteth them to Atheiſme, and to contempt of Gods worſhip and ſeruice, to ſwearing and blaſpheming, to the prophaning of the Sabbaoth, and ſcorning of all religion, to murthers, adulterie, drunkennes, theft, and all diuelliſh practiſes, becauſe they are his ſlaues readie at his appoint-ment to execute all thoſe workes of darknes wherein he will imploy them. For ſuch men it is but loſt labour to ſhew them how they may reſiſt Sathan, ſeeing they take their whole de-light in ſeruing and obeying him ; and therefore before they be taught how to reſiſt him, they muſt be perſwaded to a de-ſire of comming out of his thraldome, of whom they are ta-ken priſoners to doe his will, as it is 2. Tim. 2. 26.

2. Theſſ. 2. 26.

If they be ciuill honeſt men, he perſwadeth them that it is ſufficient if they deale iuſtly and vprightly with their neigh-bours both in their words and actions ; and for Gods ſeruice conſiſting in the duties of pietie, which is commanded in the firſt table , that it is enough if they haue a good meaning, though they be vtterly ignorant of the principles of religion, and that it is onely required of preachers and thoſe that be book-learned, to be able to render an account of their faith; as for them God wil haue them excuſed, ſo they leade an ho-neſt life amongſt their neighbours, and be not tainted with groſſe and outragious ſinnes.

But

But beloued, if we would not be subdued by Sathan, let vs be moſt carefull in withſtanding this dangerous aſſault: for there is not any one temptation wherewith Sathan preuaileth more, than by perſwading men to conteat themſelues with a ciuill kinde of honeſtie, which is deſtitute of religion and the true feare of God. And to this end let vs conſider, that ciuill honeſtie ſeuered from true pietie is but glorious iniquitie: for when wee haue attained to as great a meaſure thereof, as poſſibly we can in this age of corruption, we ſhall come ſhort in diuers duties of many of the Heathens, who haue excelled in theſe morall and ciuill vertues: and conſequently when we are at the beſt we ſhall be but honeſt Infidels and good natured worldlings, if wee doe not ioyne thereunto the duties of pietie. And how goodly a ſhew ſoeuer our workes make in the eyes of men, yet are they odious in Gods ſight, if they be not done in knowledge, and grounded on Gods word and commandement, but in ignorance and according to our own inuentions and the fond conceit of our blind vnderſtanding; if they proceede not from the true loue of God, which is the onely fountaine of all acceptable obedience, but from the loue of our ſelues and other carnall reſpects; if they bee not the fruites of a liuely faith, but done in ignorance and infidelitie; for, *whatſoeuer is not done in faith, is ſinne,* as it is Rom. 14. 23. and therefore cannot pleaſe God, Heb. 11. 6. By which we are not to vnderſtand an hiſtoricall faith, whereby wee know and are aſſured that thoſe workes wee doe are commanded in Gods word; but a true iuſtifying faith which doth applie vnto vs Chriſt Ieſus, and all Gods mercifull promiſes made in him. For, that our workes may be acceptable before God, there is required firſt that our perſons bee acceptable vnto him, neither can any thing we doe pleaſe him, ſo long as we remaine his enemies, in which ſtate we are by nature, till wee are reconciled in Chriſt our Mediatour, as appeareth Rom. 5. 10. Now vnleſſe we haue faith, we cannot apply vnto vs Chriſt nor his merits and righteouſnes, by whom onely wee are reconciled vnto God, and conſequently we remaine Gods enemies, who can doe nothing pleaſing in his ſight.

Secondly, the beſt of our workes are imperfect, and mingled

led with many corruptions, and therefore cannot abide the examination of Gods exact iustice, till their imperfections be couered by Chrifts righteoufnefle, and their corruption wafhed away with his moft precious bloud; now Chrift and his merits cannot by any other meanes be applied vnto vs, but by the hand of a liuely faith.

Laftly, if all our works and honeft dealing be not done in zeale of Gods glorie, & referred to this end that Gods name may be magnified, they are not acceptable before God : for, the caufe why he would haue our light fhine before men, is, *Matth.5.16* that he our heauenly father may be glorified, as it is Matth.5. 16. and the maine end wherefore wee fhould haue our conuerfation honeft amongft the Gentiles and vnbeleeuers, is, that they which fpeake euill of vs, as of euill doers, may, by our good works which they fhall fee, glorifie God in the day *1.Pet.2.12.* of their vifitation, as it is 1.Pet.2.12.

And therefore let not Sathan deceiue vs, in perfwading vs to reft in ciuill honeftie; for if it be feuered from true pietie, from fauing knowledge, from fincere loue of God, iuftifying faith, and a zeale of Gods glorie, it will not be acceptable in Gods fight; as procceding from the loue of our felues, and other carnall refpects, namely to obtaine praife or profit thereby.

§. *Sect.5.*
How Sathan dealeth with professors of religion.

And thus Sathan dealeth with ciuil worldlings. But if thofe which he incountreth be profeffors of religion, then hee feeketh to perfwade them, that if they outwardly perfourme the duties of pietie, as the hearing of Gods word, the publike and priuate calling vpon Gods name, the frequent receiuing of the Sacraments; if they attaine to the knowledge and profeffion of religion, and can tip their tongues with godlinefle; then they may liue how they lift amongft their brethren, neglecting all the duties of the fecond table, fo they outwardly obferue the firft; for though they be barraine of good workes, deftitute of charitie, filled with pride, addicted to couetoufnefle, oppreffion, and all deceitfull dealing, yet they fhall be iuftified by their faith, and approoued of God for their outward profeffion fake. But let fuch men know that this is a notable ftratagem of Sathan, to caufe vs to fall into
his

his secret ambushments to our destruction, which if they *That pietie and* would preuent and auoide, let them consider that pietie and *honestie are in-* charitable honestie are two such twinnes as are borne, liue, *separable.* and dye both together, that they are the life and soule of a Christian which cannot possiblie be seuered; that it is as pos- sible for the good tree to bring foorth bad fruite, for the fire to be without heate, and the Sunne without light, as it is for a liuely faith to be voide of good workes, true profession to be seuered from holie practise, and iustification before God from sanctification and holinesse of life before men; that whosoeuer braggeth of his loue to God and loueth not his brethren is a liar, and there is no truth in him, 1.Ioh.4.20. 1.Ioh.4.20. that though they professe themselues the children of God, yet if they doe not the workes of righteousnes as well as the workes of pietie, and loue their brethren, they are in truth the children of the diuell, as appeareth 1.Ioh.3.10. that not the 1.Ioh.3.10 hearers of the word, but the doers thereof are iustified, Rom. Rom.2.13. 2.13. that *not euery one who saith Lord, Lord, shall enter into the* *kingdome of heauen, but they who doe the will of the father which* Matth.7.21. *is in heauen,* Matth.7.21. that they deceiue themselues who looke to be saued by hearing the word, if they practise not Iam.1.22. that which they heare, Iam.1.22. for in stead thereof they shall plunge themselues into deeper condemnation : *For the* *seruant that knoweth his masters will and doth it not, shall be* Luk.12.47. *beaten with many stripes,* Luk.12.47. And it shall be more easie for Tyre and Sidon, Sodome and Gomorrah, who had not Mat.11.21. the Gospell preached amongst them, nor saw Chrifts mi- racles, than for Corazin and Bethsaida which enioyed both, Matth.11.21. for there as the Lord soweth much, he looketh to reape much, and there as he giueth great meanes of know- ledge, there hee expecteth great fruites in practise, and as hee will be honoured in all, so especially in those that come nigh vnto him; as it is Leuit.10.3. Lastly, that the sentence of sal- Leu.10.3. uation and damnation shall not be giuen according to our words and profession, but according to our deedes and the holie practise of the workes of mercie and Chriftianitie, which are the inseparable fruites and vndoubted signes of Matth 25. true faith. And therefore let not Sathan delude vs, by per-

ſwading vs that pietie without honeſtie, profeſſion without
practiſe, faith without workes are ſufficient for our ſaluation.

§. Sect.6.
How Sathan
dealeth with
ſincere profeſ-
ſors, and firſt
with the weake
Chriſtian.

But if they be ſincere profeſſors, then hee obſerueth whether they be babes or ſtrong men in Chriſt; if he finde them
babes, then he ſeeketh to abuſe their ſimplicitie, by drawing
them either into errours and hereſies, or at leaſt into blinde
zeale and ſuperſtition. If he cannot ſo preuaile, by reaſon that
the bright beames of the Goſpell ſhining in the preaching of
the word doe diſcouer his errours and lies, giuing light to
thoſe that ſit in the darknes of ignorance, and in the ſhadow
of death, whereby their feete are guided into the way of
peace, then he laboureth to ouerwhelme them with the burthen of their ſinnes, and to plunge them into the bottomleſſe
gulfe of horrour and deſpaire, by aggrauating the odiouſnes
of their rebellion, and huge multitudes of their outragious
tranſgreſſions, by ſetting before them the curſe of the law,
the vengeance of God due vnto them, his infinite and exact
iuſtice which muſt be ſatisfied, and the vnſpeakable and endleſſe torments prepared for the damned. But if he cannot aggrauate their ſins, which in truth they haue committed, and
make of them ſuch an huge mountaine as may ſerue to ouerwhelme them, he addeth vnto them his owne ſinnes, by caſting into their minds outragious blaſphemies againſt God,
and ſuch horrible ſuggeſtions of impietie, as it will make
their haires to ſtand on end when they do but think of them,
perſwading them that they are their owne thoughts, and
therefore horrible ſinnes, whereas in truth they are but his
ſuggeſtions, and therefore if wee doe repell and reiect them,
they are not our ſinnes but the ſinnes of the tempter: for as
it is not our fault if a theefe intice vs to ſteale, ſo wee doe not
intertaine his motion, but ſhew our deteſtation of his ſinne;
ſo it is not a ſinne to be tempted, if wee preſently doe repell
the ſuggeſtion, and doe not yeeld vnto the temptation.
And this may appeare by our Sauiour Chriſt himſelfe, who
though he were free from ſinne, yet hee was tempted in all
things like vnto vs, and ſo not free from Sathans ſuggeſtions,
for he was tempted to diffidence, to tempting God, yea to
the worſhipping of the diuell himſelfe; but reſiſting Sathans
ſuggeſtions,

suggestions,he was not guiltie of sinne.Whose example if we imitate,Sathans blasphemous temptations shal neuer be laid to our charge; neither is it possible to be free from temptations, although it be possible by Gods grace to resist them. But more of this hereafter.

If by this meanes he cannot ouerthrow their faith & bring them to despaire,then hee taketh aduantage of their simplicitie, by inticing them to commit sinnes of ignorance. For example, he will tell them that it is lawfull,nay expedient to vse their Christian libertie,when he tempteth them to licentiousnesse; and to the end he may more easily deceiue them, he will set a faire glosse vpon foule sinnes,and seeke to iustifie them by Gods word, apparelling vices in the habite of those vertues which most resemble them. He will tempt to couetousnes,vnder shew of frugalitie, telling them that they who prouide not for their familie are worse than Infidels; and to prodigalitie,vnder the pretence of liberalitie, alleaging that they who sow plentifully shall reape plentifully. He will allure them to tempt God, by neglecting those meanes which he hath graunted them, vnder the colour of affiance in God; and to trust in the meanes,vnder the vizard of carefull prouidence.He will tempt them to propound this end of their good workes,that they may be saued by them,because God hath promised to reward them; or to neglect good workes, as vnnecessarie to saluation, because faith alone iustifieth. Which temptations if wee would withstand,wee must labour after true sauing knowledge that we may discerne betweene vertue and vice,truth and error,that which God hath forbidden as vnlawfull, from that which hee hath commanded as lawfull; to this end vsing diligently all good meanes which tend to this purpose,as hearing,reading,meditating,and conferring of Gods word, that so the clowdes of ignorance being dispelled with the light of knowledge, wee may discouer Sathans delusions and deceits. Otherwise if he depriue vs of knowledge, which is the eye of the soule, he may easily seduce vs out of the right way into the gulfe of perdition.

And thus Sathan dealeth with the weake Christian : but if he finds those whom he assaulteth strong men in Christ, so

§. Sect.7.
How Sathan inticeth the weake Christian to commit sinnes of ignorance.

§. Sect.8.

that

How Sathan dealeth with the ſtrong Chriſtian.

that he cannot take any aduantage of their ignorance, nor o-
uerthrow their faith, then he laboureth to make them wound
their conſcience, by committing ſins of preſumption againſt
their knowledge , vſing the violence of their affections, to a-
buſe their reaſon and miſleade their iudgement ; the daunger
of which temptation *Dauid* well diſcerning by his owne wo-
full experience, doth earneſtly intreat the Lord to preſerue

Pſal.19.13.

him from preſumptuous ſins, Pſal.19.13. And thus hath Sathan
preuailed with ſo many of Gods owne children, that he durſt
therewith aſſault our Sauiour Chriſt himſelfe, by offring him
the whole world and the glory thereof, if he would fall down
and worſhip him ; that his affections tickled with ambition,
might moue him to commit this ſin for the ſatisfying his de-

2.Cor.11.14.

ſires. But if he cannot thus preuaile, he wil transforme himſelf
into an angell of light, and tempt them to the doing of a leſſe
good, that they may neglect a greater ; or that which is in it
ſelfe lawfull and commanded in his due time & place, he will
tempt them to performe it vnſeaſonably, whē as other duties
in reſpect of preſent occaſion are more neceſſary; and ſo vſeth
one vertue or dutie to ſhoulder another, & thruſt it diſorderly
out of it own place and ſtanding. For example, in the hearing
of the word he will caſt into their minds meditations, in their
owne nature good and acceptable to God in their due time
and place, to the end hee may diſtract their mindes and make
them heare without profit : in the time of prayer hee will not
ſtick to recall to their memories ſome profitable inſtructions
which they haue heard at the ſermon, to the end he may diſturbe them in that holy exerciſe, and keep them from lifting
vp their hearts wholy vnto God. Moreouer, in all his temptations he will alleage ſcripture ; but then either hee depraueth
the place by adding or diſtracting, as when he alleageth ſcripture to our Sauiour Chriſt, Matth.4.6. *It is written he will giue
his angels charge ouer thee,&c.* and leaueth out *to keepe thee in
all thy waies,* which is expreſſed in the place he quoteth, Pſal.
90.11. becauſe that made quite againſt him ; or if hee recite
them right, he will wreſt the words vnto another ſenſe, than
the holie Ghoſt hath written them, that ſo he may deceiue vs
and leade vs into error.

CHAP.

Chap. XIX.

How Sathan allureth vs into sinne by degrees, and draweth vs from one extreme to another.

 Nd thus haue I shewed at large Sathans first pol- §. *Sect.*1. liticke stratagem, which he vseth to circumuent vs by fitting his temptations according to our nature and disposition, or our state and condition. A second pollicie which Sathan vseth to circumuent vs, is this; if he cannot at the first intice vs to fall into outragious wickednes, he will seeke to draw vs thereun- *Sathan labo-* to by degrees, beginning at the least, and so bringing vs from *reth to draw* that to a greater, till at last we come to the highest step of *vs into outra-* wickednes: whereby it commeth to passe, that as those who *gious sinnes by* walke to the top of an high hill, whose ascent ariseth by little *degrees.* and little, come to the top without wearines, before they well perceiued that they did ascend; so they who goe forward in the waies of wickednes by degrees, do without any controulment or checke of conscience clime vp to the highest top thereof, whence Sathan casteth them down headlong into the pit of destruction. For example, if he see a professor of religion which maketh conscience of his waies, he doth not vsually seeke at first to draw him into heinous sinnes, vnlesse the cordes of his temptations be exceeding strong; but first he allureth him to come into the companie of wicked men, by offering some pleasure or profit, or by occasion of affinitie and marriage, ioyning him if he can with such a yokefellow as wil draw him faster backe than he can draw her forward in the course of godlines. If he thus farre preuaile, then he tempteth him to winke at their sins which in conscience he condemneth, that he may still inioy his pleasure and profit, or continue in their loue and fauour; then in the next place he moueth him to thinke them tollerable sinnes which they commit, and nothing so outragious as others fall into; and when he hath made this progresse, then he inticeth him to taste of sinne, which he so sweetneth with the sugred delights of this

G 4   vaine

vaine world that he swalloweth it downe without all loath-
somnesse, and neuer tasteth the bitternesse thereof till the
heat of Gods spirit doe cause it worke in his conscience, so as
he is neuer at rest till he haue cast it vp againe by vnfained repentance. Otherwise if he be not preuented thus by Gods spirit, Sathan will by this meanes cause his conscience to swallow and to digest such loathsome sinnes, which in former
times he abhorred to see others commit. And as those who
from their infancie are accustomed to take poysons in small
quantities doe enable their stomackes to digest more, till by
long custome and increasing the quantitie by degrees, it becommeth so familiar to their stomackes, that instead of poy-
soning them they are nourished thereby, as histories doe record of some of the Indian Kings : so Sathan inticeth vs to
swallow downe the poyson of sinne at the first in such small
quantitie, that our consciences may not be sicke thereof: but
hauing well digested the least, he increaseth the measure till
by long custome he hath made it so familiar to our consciences, that those sinnes are euen meate and drinke vnto vs,
which at the first we loathed as deadly poysons.

　　Now if we would defeate this pollicie of Sathan, we must
continually watch ouer our owne hearts and pull them
backe when wee see that they but incline vnto any sinne ;
we must not lightly esteeme of any sinne, nor willingly giue
entertainment to the least wicked thought, for though in it
selfe it be not so hainous, yet it will inlarge our consciences
and make roome for a greater, til at last we keepe open house,
readie to receiue all wickednes which offereth it selfe vnto
vs ; and as we are carefull to auoyde the sinnes themselues, so
with as much diligence we are to shunne the occasions and
meanes by which we might be drawne, or inticed thereunto.
But of this point more hereafter.

§. Sect.2.
Sathans third
pollicie in
drawing men
out of one ex-
treme into
another.

　　A third pollicie which Sathan vseth to circumuent vs, is to
bring vs from one extreme to another. For example, when
we see the vilenesse of prodigalitie, so as we will no longer be
possessed of that vice, then will Sathan make it as odious as he
can, and indeauour to bring vs into extreame hatred thereof,
that so he may the more easily draw vs into the contrarie vice
of

of couetoufnefle. If he cannot any longer keepe vs afleepe in
finne, by rocking vs in the cradell of carnall fecuritie, and finging vnto vs the fweete tunes of Gods mercie and Chrifts merits, the will he labour to plunge vs in defpaire, by fetting before our eyes the heynoufnefle of our finnes, and founding in
our eares the thundring threatnings of the law. If he cannot
any longer nuzzle vs in fuperftition, and caufe vs to place all
our religion in ceremonies, and in reftrayning our felues of
the vfe of things indifferent, he will draw vs to the other extreame by mouing vs to thinke all ceremonies vnlawfull, and
to practife all licencioufnes vnder pretence of chriftian libertie. If he can no longer perfwade vs to feeke for iuftification
by the workes of the law to the end wee may not rely on
Chrifts merits and righteoufnes, he will bring vs into vtter
diflike of this doctrine, by fhewing vs the abfurdities thereof,
that he may draw vs to the other extreme, namely to neglect
good workes, as altogether vnnecefarie to faluation becaufe
faith alone iuftifieth. If he cannot hide out of our fight the
fhining graces of Gods fpirit by cafting before our eyes the
cloude of our finnes and corruptions, then he will caufe vs to
looke on them through the fpectacles of felfe loue and affection to the end we may imagine them much greater than in
truth they are, and fo be puffed vp in pride, and too fecurely
reft in thofe gifts we haue, not feeking for increafe. If he cannot perfwade vs to diffidence and diftruft, he will moue vs to
tempt God vpon no necefarie occafions : and thus he dealt
with our Sauiour Chrift, for firft he tempted him to diftruft
Gods prouidence, and to prouide for himfelfe by turning
ftones into bread; but when he could not fo preuaile, he moued him to make an vnnecefarie experiment of his prouidence and care, by cafting himfelfe downe headlong from the
pinacle of the temple, whereas there were ordinarie meanes
whereby he might defcend.

Now the end why Sathan vfeth this pollicie is, more violently to caft vs into one extreame of finne, when with full
fwinge of will we do auoyde the other: as alfo to make vs beleeue that the latter temptation is the motion of Gods fpirit,
feeing it is cleane contrarie to the former fuggeftion of Sathan,

than, whereas in truth they are but vnlike children of the same father.

§. Sect.3.
That we are to auoyde the former temptation by keeping vs in the golden meane.

The daunger of which tentations if we would auoyde, we must keepe vs in the golden meane auoyding both extreames; and because we are ignorant and vnskilfull in trauayling the straight path which leadeth to Gods kingdome, and euery hower readie to take the bywaies of errour which leade to destruction, let vs vse the word of God for our guide: and as the Israelites trauayling towards the land of promise, were directed by the cloud and piller of fire, going forward when that went before them, and pitching their tents where that stayed; so let vs constantly and boldly trauaile in our christian pilgrimage so long as we haue the word of God for our direction, not staying where it biddeth goe, nor going when it stayeth. Let this be the touchstone to discerne the golden truth from the drossie. extreames on either side; let it be the line to leade vs out of this laborinth of errours; let it be the starre of *Bethlehem* to conduct vs in our tedious iourney vnto the place where our Sauiour Christ is, not now lying in the armes of his mother, but sitting at the right hand of his father in all glorie power and maiestie. And because we are vnskilfull pilots in sailing the daungerous sea of this tempestuous world, readie to fall vpon the rockes while we auoyde the sands; let Gods word be our card, to direct vs to the holy land: otherwise Sathan will raise against vs such stormie tempests, and contrarie blasts of temptations, that our soules will suffer shipwracke vpon the rockes of sinne, and be drowned in a sea of destruction.

CHAP. XX.

Of three other stratagems which Sathan vseth.

§. Sect.1.
How Sathan moueth vs to propound bad ends to good actions.

Fourth pollicie which Sathan vseth to entrap vs in his secret ambushments is this. When by the violence of his tentations he cannot altogether restraine vs from doing that which is good: then he will tempt vs to doe good actions to bad ends. In giuing

of

of almes he will moue men to propound this end that they
may be ſeene of men;in doing of good workes,he will tempt
them to forget Gods glorie, and to ſet before them as their
maine end of all their good actions, the meriting of heauen ;
and if men will needes appeare vertuous and religious, he
will intice them to vſe outward vertues as a cloake to hide
their inward vices,and religion as a faire vizard to couer their
foule impietie. And thus he tempteth men to vſe all outward
ſhewes of humilitie, to the end they may the better diſguiſe
their hidden pride and ambition, as we may ſee in the example of *Abſolon*; and all complements of curteſie and loue,
as a maske to hide their enuie and malice. And thus he allureth men to profeſſe religion,heare ſermons,and vſe glorious
ſpeeches, that they may (ſeeming religious and men of good
conſciences) haue their ſhoppes the better cuſtomed, and
their words credited, and ſo haue the fitter opportunitie of
deceiuing them who for their profeſſion repoſe truſt in them.

A fift pollicie whereby hee ſeeketh to ſurpriſe vs is by
tempting men to vſe wicked meanes for the accompliſhing
of good ends, and to doe euill that good may come thereof ;
and thus he tempted *Saul* to tranſgreſſe Gods commaundement in reſeruing the fat of the cattell to the end he might
ſacrifice therewith vnto the Lord ; and *Iſaac* to ſay that *Re-
becca* was his ſiſter to ſaue his life ; and *Peter* to vſe diſſimulation that he might not offend the Iewes. And thus he tempteth men to tell officious and profitable lies for the auoyding
of greater euils ; he moueth ſeruants to giue their maiſters
goods to the poore without their priuitie or liking, and ſo to
commit theft that they may giue almes ; he tempteth non-
reſidents to poſſeſſe many liuings that they may keepe good
hoſpitalitie, and ſo ſtarue the ſoule to feede the body ; and
citizens to vſe all fraud and deceite that they may prouide
for their familie. Which pollicies of Sathan are exceeding
daungerous ; for hardly can we eſcape them both, namely
doing good things to bad ends, or vſing of euill meanes for
the atchieuing of good purpoſes : but the more difficult the
thing is, the greater muſt be our care ; the more ſecret and
daungerous Sathans ambuſhments are,the more diligent and

§. Sect.2.
*How Sathan
moueth vs to
vſe euill
meanes for the
effecting good
ends.*

Galat.2.

watch-

watchfulnes muſt we vſe in auoyding them.In all our actions
therefore let vs be carefull to propound vnto our ſelues good
ends,and vſe good meanes for the accompliſhing of our honeſt and godly purpoſes ; for if we neglect the firſt, we ſhall
bewray our hypocriſie and impietie,if the latter we ſhall pol-
lute a faire worke with filthie tooles, and ſhew our diffidence
in God in not dairing to vſe thoſe godly and honeſt meanes
which he hath commaunded and commended vs, vnleſſe we
boulſter and prop them vp by our owne fooliſh inuentions,
and wicked practiſes. And whenſoeuer wee are moued to
propound euill ends of our good actions, or to vſe euill
meanes for the accompliſhing of good ends, let vs aſſure our
ſelues that they are not the motions of Gods ſpirit, but the
ſuggeſtions of Sathan, at leaſt ſo farre forth as we are tempted to the euill of the end or meanes; and therefore we are to
purge the wheate from the chaffe, the pure gold from the
droſſe,and to doe the workes of God for thoſe ends, and by
thoſe meanes,which he hath appointed.

§. Sect.3.
How Sathan
tempteth vs to
be proud of our
vertues.
A ſixt pollicie which Sathan vſeth, is to take aduantage of
our vertues to plunge vs headlong into vice ; for example
when we haue mortified our ſinnes, and are plentifull in all
good workes, he taketh occaſion thereby to puffe vs vp with
pride, and a phariſaicall conceite that wee are not as other
men are ; yea if we be ſo humble that hee cannot make vs
proud of any thing elſe, he will labour to make vs proud of
our humilitie. Let vs not therefore be retchleſſe and ſecure,
but haue an eye to our hearts, euen in our good actions: and
when we entertaine any excellent vertue, let vs take heede
leaſt pride thruſt in with it, ſeeing moſt commonly it attendeth vpon vertue, and taketh vp his ſtanding where it lodg-
eth,for we are not quite at libertie, and out of the daunger of
Sathans thraldome, ſo long as pride like a iaylour attendeth
on vs.

CHAP.

CHAP. XXI.

Of the manner of Sathans fight.

Nd fo much concerning Sathans ſtratagems and warlike policies : now let vs confider of the manner of his fight. In which we are firſt to ob-ſerue that it is moſt cruell and cowardly, for he obſerueth no complements of true valour, but then moſt violently aſſaulteth vs when we are leaſt prouided; if he cannot preuaile when we are waking, he will ſet vpon vs while we are ſleeping ; if he cannot hurt vs when we are rea-die in the field armed with the compleat armour of a Chri-ſtian, the girdle of veritie, the breaſt-plate of righteouſnes, the ſhield of faith, the ſword of the ſpirit, &c. he wil watch a time when he can ſpie vs vnarmed, and then he will aſſaile vs ; if he cannot ouercome vs in the time of proſperitie, when God hath hedged vs in with his bleſſings, as it is Iob.1.10. then he will watch till wee be caſt downe with ſome aduerſitie, and then he will lay load on vs whileſt wee are vnder foote ; and whereas all our hope of victorie is in the Lords aſſiſtance, he will perſwade vs to yeeld vnto him, for as much as the Lord is become our enemie.

§. Sect.1.

That Sathan obſerueth no complements of true valour.

Iob.1.10.

Now if wee would reſiſt Sathan, wee muſt ſo prepare our ſelues that he doe not hurt vs by this his daſtardly fight. See-ing therefore he vſeth to ſet vpon vs on all aduantages, wee are alwaies to be ſo prouided as that we giue him no aduan-tage ; being awake, wee are alwaies to ſtand vpon our guard, readie armed with the graces of Gods ſpirit ; being to ſleepe, we are to deſire the Lord to watch ouer vs, and to commaund his angels to pitch their tents about vs, that ſo we may be de-fended from Sathans furie ; ſeeing he is readie to aſſault vs when he ſeeth vs diſarmed, we are alwaies to keepe the coate-armour of a Chriſtian buckled vnto vs : laſtly, ſeeing in the time of proſperitie he is readie to puffe vs vp with pride, and in the time of aduerſitie to plunge vs into deſpaire, let vs humble our ſelues when God exalts vs , by thinking of our vnworthines

vnworthines to receiue the least of Gods mercies; and comfort our selues in the time of our affliction, by remembring that it is the portion of all that will liue godly in Christ Iesus, and that *whosoeuer suffer with Christ, shall also raigne with him*, 2.Tim.3.12.and 2.12.

2.Tim.3.12.
and 2.12.

§. *Sect.2.*
Sathan assaulteth vs when we are most secure.

The second thing to be obserued in his manner of fight, is, that he setteth vpon vs when wee are most secure, and then soundeth the alarum to battaile, when wee most flatter our selues with hope of peace, and that not drowsily and faintly, but with all celeritie and speede, whereby hee ouercommeth oftentimes, or at least foyleth vs, before we can arme or prepare our selues to make any resistance. And thus he assaulted our first parents in paradise, when they securely promised vnto themselues the continuance and increase of their happines; and *Dauid* also after all his troubles when he was retchlesse and idle, sleeping in the day, and after walking on his house top, letting his eyes wander after pleasures.

If therefore we would withstand Sathan, let vs shake off all drowsie and carnall securitie, and continually watch, standing on our guard to resist his encounters whensoeuer he setteth vpon vs : and as in calme weather the carefull Mariner prouideth all things against a tempest, and the valiant souldier doth arme and furnish himselfe with al necessaries before the assault; so when Sathan seemeth to offer vs a time of truce, let vs therein prepare our selues more strongly against the day of battaile; for when this raging lion seemeth to sleepe as though he did not regard vs, then if through retchlesnesse we giue him the least aduantage, hee will suddenly runne vpon vs and deuoure vs, if he get vs within his cruell pawes.

§. *Sect.3.*
Sathan neuer wearie in assaulting vs.
1.Pet.5.8.
Iob.1.7.

The third thing to be obserued, is his indefatigable paines in tempting and assaulting vs, for he neuer taketh rest, but still goeth about like a roring lion seeking whom hee may deuoure; and this is euident by his owne confession, Iob.1.7. where he professeth that he had been compassing the earth to and fro, and walked from place to place. So that he omitteth no paine nor labour in seeking our destruction. And though he ouercome vs not at the first, but retire foyled, yet he will gather his forces againe and againe, and incessantlie

set

set vpon vs. And therefore if we would obtaine victorie,wee
must not thinke much of our labour, but vse all paines, diligence and watchfulnes in repelling his assaults. And seeing
Sathan is so vigilant and painfull in seeking our destruction,
let vs thinke no paines too great in seeking our preseruation;
and considering that Sathan after one , or two, or twentie
foyles is as readie to set vpon vs againe as at the first, let vs
neuer faint, but like valiant souldiers alwaies stand readie in
the field to endure his incounters. But alas, the practise of
most is farre otherwise,for they watch and drudge night and
day to attaine vnto riches and preferment, and in the meane
time little regard this dangerous foe, but to the end they
may attaine vnto their worldly desires, they intangle themselues in the snares which hee hath laid to intrap them to
their vtter destruction.

The fourth thing to be obserued in Sathans fight,is his often changing of his temptations, and taking as it were into
his hand another weapon,when he perceiueth the first woundeth not. For example, he will tempt vs to the contempt of
Gods word ; if he cannot so preuaile, he will intice vs at least
to neglect it ; and if thus he cannot hurt vs,he will, if he can,
choake the seede of Gods word with the thornie cares of the
world,and so make it vnfruitfull. He will moue vs to thinke
that Christ was no Sauiour; if he cannot perswade vs to this,
then he will tell vs he is not our Sauiour. Yea so shamelesse is
this tempter,that he will now tempt vs to beleeue one lie of
his coyning,and presently after when hee seeth wee giue no
credit to that,he wil tell vs the cleane contrarie.For example,
he will sometimes tell vs that wee are such grieuous sinners
that there is no way but damnation : and if we withstand this
assault, hee will soone after perswade vs to an ouerweening
conceit of our owne excellencie,and to a pharisaicall opinion
that wee are not as other men are. Sometimes he will moue
vs to doubt of our election, and if he cannot thus preuaile, he
will presently perswade vs to thinke our election so sure,that
though wee follow our owne lusts, and giue our selues ouer
to all outragious wickednesse, yet in the end wee shall be sa-
ued.In a word,this wicked *Protheus* will transforme himselfe
into

§. *Sect.4.*
That Sathan often changeth his temptations for his better aduantage.

into a thoufand diuers fhapes, and in a fhort fpace will varie many waies his temptations, that if hee cannot preuaile by one meanes, he may ouercome vs by another. And therefore it behooueth vs, if we will withftand him, to arme our felues, not on one fide alone, nor to bee prepared againft two or three affaults of our fpirituall enemie, but wee muft be readie to anfwere all obiections, and not fo wholie incline to one fide and to the defending one part, as that in the meane time wee leaue the other naked to bee wounded with Sathans blowes. And to the end we may the rather be encouraged to ftand conftantly in our defence, wee are to know that when Sathan doth fo often fhift his temptations, and in a fhort diftance of time doth feeke to bring vs into quite contrary vices, it is a manifeft figne that he doth not yet preuaile : for as no enemie is fo foolifh as will after that hee hath made one fufficient breach for entrie, or forced one gate of the citie, go from that to another, but rather enter where the way is made; fo Sathan laying fiege to our foules, would not feeke to make a new battrie with his temptations, if the former had made way for him to enter and furprize vs ; he would not tempt vs to pride and prefumption, if he had ouercome our faith and plunged vs into defpaire ; hee would neuer tranfforme himfelfe into an angell of light, if he could haue ouercome vs in his owne likenes ; he would neuer tell vs of Gods mercie, if hee had alreadie ouerwhelmed vs with the fight of our fins, and confideration of Gods iuftice ; nor yet of Gods iuftice, if he could keepe vs in carnall fecuritie, by fetting before vs his mercie : but that way whereby he perceiues he any whit preuailes, he will follow and continue earneft in the fame purfuite, till he perceiue he cannot catch vs. As therefore when the fit of the ague fhifteth from time to time, it is a good figne that our nature waxing ftrong doth preuaile againft the difeafe ; fo when Sathans temptations in a fhort time often change, and that from one contrarie to another, it is a figne that Gods fpirit being ftrong in vs, doth refift Sathan and putteth him to thefe fhifts, whereas he would hold on a conftant courfe if he preuailed againft vs.

The oft changing of Sathans temptations a probable figne that he doth not preuaile.

§. Sect. 5.

The fift thing to be obferued in the maner of Sathans fight, is, is, that sometimes he setteth vpon vs immediatly in his owne *That Sathan* person, & sometimes mediatly vsing for his instruments the *assaulteth vs sometime him-* world & the flesh. Of the first we haue an example 1.Chr.21. *selfe, and some-* 1. where it is said that Sathan prouoked *Dauid* to number If- *time by his in-* rael. So Ioh.13.2. the Euangelist sheweth that the diuell did *struments.* put in the heart of *Iudas Iscariot* to betray Christ. And the A-postle *Peter* Act.5.3. telleth *Ananias* that Sathan had filled his heart with his suggestions that he should lie vnto the ho-lie Ghost. And thus also he tempted our Sauiour Christ im-mediatly fortie daies together in the wildernes, Mat.4. When he thus fighteth against vs in his owne person, he giueth the assault either in his own likenes, or els transformeth himself into an angell of light. When he incountreth vs in his owne likenes and like a diuell indeede, then he doth as it were pro-claime open warres, tempting vs not onely to those sinnes which, hauing some apparance of good in them, our corrupt conscience doth approue of, or at least can without any great terrour winke at, but also to all outragious wickednesse and hellish impietie, which euen a ciuil worldling would abhorre to thinke of; namely, to Atheisme, Idolatrie, contempt of all religion, blasphemies against God, periurie, sacriledge, perse-cuting the knowne truth, heresie, murther, adulterie, and such like : all which at the first sight may easily be discerned to be the suggestions of Sathan, because this hellish broode do re-semble their wicked father in their very countenance and outward appearance. And therefore Sathan who subdueth more with the serpents wiles than with the lions force, doth seldome vse this fight against any which haue but the ciuill restraining grace of God, vnlesse he intice them thereunto by degrees (as before I haue shewed) or except hee finde them exceeding ignorant, to the end he may make them beleeue that his suggestions are their owne thoughts; but hee practi-seth these temptations, for the most part, against those who haue euen sold themselues to worke wickednes, hauing their hearts hardened and consciences seared with their custo-mable sinning.

And therefore most commonly hee transformeth himselfe §. *Sect.6.* into an angell of light tempting vs to sinne, by vsing friendly
H   perswasions,

perſwaſions, and making liberall offers of pleaſure, profit or preferment, or els minſing thoſe ſinnes to which he tempteth vs as though they were nothing, or masking them vnder the vizard of vertue. Neither doth hee often moue vs to commit thoſe ſins which nature (reſtrained by Gods common grace, or ſanctified by his ſpirit) doth abhorre and tremble to think of; vnleſſe it be either to vexe Gods children with ſuch ſuggeſtions, rather than for any hope of ouercomming them; or els that whileſt their mindes are wholy intent in withſtanding his outward violence, hee may more cunningly intrap them in his ſecret ambuſhments, which they regard not: but otherwiſe hee vſually tempts vs to commit ſuch ſinnes, as through our corruption wee are prone vnto, as not thinking them to be ſinnes, or but ſmall, or rather neuer entring into any conſideration of them at all; as namely, carnall ſecuritie, hardneſſe of heart, infidelitie, impenitencie, neglect of Gods word, prophaning of his Sabbaoths, couetouſnes, ambition, pride, neglect of the generall duties of Chriſtianitie and ſpeciall duties of our callings; all which are not much leſſe hainous in the ſight of the Lord than the other groſſe outward ſinnes, and much more dangerous vnto vs, as being Sathans ſecret ſnares which hee laieth to intrap vs at vnawares; in which when we are caught wee are content to lie bound, becauſe they do not ſo much pinch and torment the conſcience as the other outward ſinnes, they being not ſeene, or not regarded. As therefore thoſe diſeaſes which by diſturbing the braine doe take away all ſenſe of paine, are of all others moſt deſperate, namely, the dead paulſie, the falling ſickneſſe, and ſleepie lethargie, and in other diſeaſes the patient is moſt dangerouſly ſicke when he hath no feeling thereof; ſo there is no ſicknes of the ſoule ſo deſperat and dangerous, as thoſe that afflict not our conſciences with any ſenſe of paine, to wit, carnall ſecuritie, hardneſſe of heart, and the reſt aboue named.

And thus haue I ſhewed Sathans diſguiſed and ſubtill manner of fight, wherein like a Pirate he hangeth out flags of truce, to ſignifie peace and friendſhip, till hee haue gotten vs within his reach and commaund: and then he grapleth with
vs,

vs,and ranfacketh vs of all Gods graces, and cafteth vs ouer
boord into the fea of deftruction. And therefore it behooueth
vs with no lefle care to withftand Sathan when he fawneth,
than when hee frowneth; when hee fighteth by ambufh-
ment,than when he aflaulteth vs by open violence; when he
offreth to ftab vs to the heart, than when hee doth but (as it
were) pricke a vaine, letting vs blood to death without fenfe
of paine; when hee tempteth vs to outragious finnes, than
when he inticeth vs to fecret and hidden finnes; when he allureth vs like a friend to commit finne, by offring pleafure,
riches, or honours, than when like an enemie a roring lion,
or cruell dragon he raungeth about and rageth againft vs;
Nam cum delectabile proponit,moleftum fupponit, & dum vngit
pungit; He propoundeth things delightfull to bring vs to
griefe and miferie, he fawneth on vs that he may bemire vs,
and killeth while he embraceth vs. *Neither doth man know his* | Ecclef.9.12.
time, but as the fifhes which are taken in an euill net, and as the
birds which are caught in the fnare, fo are the children of men
*fnared in the euill time, when it falleth vpon them fuddenly,*as it is
Ecclef.9.12. Nay, feeing this fight is farre more dangerous,
becaufe hee couereth his hooke with an alluring baite; and | *Temptations*
thofe fnares of finne more pernicious which lie hidden, than *vnto fecret fins*
thofe which lie in open view; feeing wee are more eafily *moft dange-*
tempted to thofe finnes which are fecret and difguifed in the *rous.*
habite of vertue, than vnto thofe groffe finnes which haue
their names as it were branded in their foreheads; feeing alfo we can more hardly repent of them, both becaufe they do
not appeare fo horrible and grieuous vnto vs, as the other o-
pen and outward finnes, and alfo becaufe they worke in vs
no fhame after we entertaine and liue in them,neither can a-
ny of our chriftian brethren admonifh or rebuke vs for them,
they being fecret & vnknown: therfore is Sathan made more
audacious to tempt vs, and wee more bold to admit of his
temptation,and after we are fallen wee lacke meanes to raife
vs vp againe by vnfained repentance, for our felues doe ap-
prooue our finnes, and our brethren know them not: which
Bernard well difcerning, vttereth this fpeech fit for this purpofe : *Extimefco magis occulta peccata qua clam committo*

quàm manifesta quæ perpetro palam, clam enim si pecco nemo me redarguit. Vbi autem reprehensio non metuenda est, ibi tentatori patet aditus liberrimus, & peccatum cum voluptate admittitur. I am more affraid (saith he) of my secret, then of my open sinnes ; for if I sinne secretly there is no man to reproue me ; and where reprehension is not feared, there the tempter hath most free accesse and the sinne is entertained with pleasing delight. In a word, seeing we are more easily drawne into these sinnes; and after we are enthralled with them, make no hast to get out of our captiuitie : therefore let vs be much more warie and heedfull in discouering and auoyding these hidden snares and secret sinnes, into which we doe most commonly fall vnwittingly, and being fallen, doe most willingly continue in them.

§. Sect.8.
How Sathan as-
saulteth vs by
his instruments
the world and
the flesh.

Secondly, Sathan assaulteth vs sometimes by his deputies and instruments; especially he employeth in these seruices, the world and the flesh. In the world he doth not onely make choyse of our enemies and prophane irreligious men, which he stirreth vp to afflict and persecute vs, to the end we may be discouraged from the profession and practise of true godlinesse; but also of our deare friends and acquaintance and our neere kindred : sometime our brother or sister, our parents and children, yea sometimes a mans wife which lieth in his boosome, playeth the part of the tempter. As we may see in the example of *Iob*, who was not so much vexed by all his outward afflictions, as by the temptation of his wife, and three friends. The same is euident in the example of *Eue*, whom Sathan vsed as his instrument to intice *Adam* to the breach of Gods commaundement : and *Iesabel* who was the diuels deputie, in prouoking her husband to oppression and horrible murther. Neither doth he onely vse to these ends our carnall friends, but also our spirituall kindred in Christ, who are of the same religion, and make the same profession with vs ; and thus by the old Prophet, he inticed the young Prophet to transgresse Gods commaundement. 1.King.13.

1.King.13.

And thus hee tempted our Sauiour Christ to neglect the worke of our redemption, vsing the Apostle *Peter* as his instrument ; and therefore because he supplied the diuels place,

our

our Sauiour calleth him by his name saying, *Get thee behinde* Matth.16.23.
me Sathan, thou art an offence to me, Matth.16.23. And thus
nowadaies he vseth professors, yea preachers of the Gospell,
as meanes to tempt men to sinne, both by their words and
euill examples : which temptation is farre more daungerous
and of greater force, then if all worldlings should combine
themselues together, and labour both by persuasion and
example to seduce them; for when they can say I am a
professor as well as thou, I am a seruant of God who make 1.King.13.18.
conscience of my waies as well as thou, I am a Prophet as
well as thou, and therefore thou needest not to make any
doubt or scruple in following my councell or example; it is
a most strong temptation to intice vs to sinne: for like sheepe
we are most apt to follow after when any of our owne companie leade vs the way. And therefore if we would resist this
temptation, we must labour after true knowledge, that we
may not depend vpon others for our direction, but vpon the
word of God alone, and not liue by example, but by precept;
for the straightest rule that euer was of the most holy mans
life (our Sauiour Christ excepted) is often and in many places
crooked (for who is it that hath not erred and gone astray?)
and therefore if we alwaies follow their examples in all particulars, we shall erre with them besides all our owne errors.

    So also he vseth the helpe of our owne flesh to betray the §. Sect.9.
spirit, and leade vs captiue into sinne; and that so cunningly, *That Sathan*
that we can hardly discerne between Sathans suggestions *vseth the helpe*
and our owne corrupt motions and desires : for being a spi- *of our owne*
rit, he doth not appeare in a corporall shape and perswade *flesh in temp-*
vs to sinne with reall words, which are conuayed to the heart *ting vs to sin.*
by the eare, but he commeth to vs after a spirituall manner,
and suggesteth secretly his temptations into the heart and
minde directly and immediatly, so as wee can seldome distinguish his motions from our owne thoughts. For as the
spirit of God doth so moue vs to all vertuous and holy actions, as that in the meane time we would thinke his motions 2.Cor.3.5.
to be our owne godly cogitations, but that we are sufficiently
instructed out of Gods word, that we cannot of our selues
so much as thinke a good thought vnlesse it proceede from
God;

God; so much lesse can we discerne betweene the suggestions of Sathan and our owne fleshly thoughts, because they
are both corrupt and alike wicked. By reason whereof it
commeth to passe that Sathan wanteth no opportunitie of
circumuenting vs, because we can put no difference betweene
his temptations and our owne carnall desires : and therefore
he hauing gotten (as it were) our owne watchword, we are
readie to open the gates of our soules when he offereth to
enter, and to yeeld to his temptations as soone as he assaulteth vs ; where as no man almost is so outragiously desperat
that would wittingly and willingly entertaine Sathans suggestions, whom he knoweth to be a common enemie to mankinde, continually seeking their destruction, though hee
should intice him hereunto by offering much riches and
great preferments. Yea hence it is that after Sathan hath many times deceiued and circumuented vs, yet cannot we beware of him, nor auoyde his deceits. For whereas if a man
doe giue vs euill counsell, or any way cousin vs, yet after
once or twice he come vnto vs, we can take heede of him,
and though he make faire shewes of honestie and friendship,
we will notwithstanding be very iealous and suspicious least
againe hee ouerreach vs ; when Sathan commeth to vs this
day and tempteth vs to such grosse wickednes, that we cannot chuse but discerne them to be his suggestions, yet this is
no impediment to him but that he may come againe to morrow, and deceiue vs with some more subtill pollicie, because
we cannot discerne betweene his suggestions and our owne
thoughts, and therefore doe acknowledge no other author
of his temptations but our selues.

Hence also it is that he will not sticke to tempt the most
godly vnto the grossest impietie, and the most learned and
found in iudgement, to entertaine the absurdest heresie or
error. For if he preuaile (which sometime he doth as we may
see in the example of *Dauid* whom he tempted to adulterie
and murther, though hee were a man according to Gods
owne heart; and of *Peter* whom hee tempted to deny and
forsweare Christ, though hee were a most worthie Apostle) then he getteth a great victorie, and giueth them a singular

gular foyle; but if he be repulsed, yet this is no hinderance vnto him, why he may not entrap them in some more secret ambushment. Hence it is that though he begin his fight with cunning pollicie, taking vpon him the person of a friend, and transforming himselfe into an Angell of light, yet this is no impediment but that he may afterwards againe appeare and violently assault vs in his owne likenes; as he assaulted our Sauiour, first with subtill and secret temptations, like a friend and welwiller; and when he could not so preuaile, he doth not sticke to appeare like himselfe, tempting him to outragious grosse idolatrie, saying, all this will I giue thee if thou wilt fall downe and worship me. And contrariwise though he begin his assault like a diuell and professed enemie, this is no hinderance but that he may end it like an Angell of light, and a flattering treacherous friend. So when he hath inticed vs to one extreme and preuaileth not, this is no impediment but that soone after he may allure vs to the cleane contrarie; because though we thinke the first motion to be his suggestion, yet we may imagine the other to be our owne thought, or (as I said) the motion of Gods spirit, because it is quite contrarie to the former.

Seeing therefore the matter standeth thus; how may we resist Sathan, considering that we cannot discerne his suggestions from our owne cogitations? I answere; wee must be skilful in Gods word, and thereby able to iudge what is good and what is euill, to discerne what is vertue and what is vice, what God hath commaunded and what he hath forbidden, which be the motions of Gods spirit, and which the suggestions of Sathan, and the thoughts of our corrupt flesh; and then are we carefully to imbrace that which our conscience approoueth as good, being enformed by Gods word, and to auoyde and reiect those motions which we know to be euill, whether they doe proceede from Sathan or from our selues; for it is not greatly materiall to know who is the author of them, so we are assured that they are euill and wicked; neither is it any dangerous error to ascribe Sathans suggestions to our corrupt flesh; or to attribute the wicked thought of our owne flesh vnto Sathan: for though he be not the next

§. *Sect.* 10.
How we may auoide danger, though we cannot discerne Sathans temptations from our owne lusts.

and

and immediat caufe, yet he is the firſt and principall caufe of all finne and wickednes. And hence it is that in the Scriptures the fame wicked motion and action is fometimes aſcribed to man, and fometimes to Sathan indifferently as appeareth, Act.5.3.5. where firſt *Peter* affirmeth Sathan to be the author of *Ananias* finne, by filling his heart with his fuggeſtions, whereby he was tempted to lie vnto the holy Ghoſt, and after he faith that *Ananias* had conceiued this lie in his owne heart.

Act.5.3.5.

§. *Sect.11.*
How Sathans fuggeſtions may be difcerned from our owne fleſhly luſts.

But though moſt commonly it be very hard to difcerne betweene the fuggeſtions of Sathan, and of our corrupt fleſh, yet fometimes they may be diſtinguiſhed by apparant differences ; as firſt when the temptations are fo cunning and exceeding fubtill, that it is not poſſible they ſhould be the thoughts of a feely ignorant man, but the apparant fuggeſtions of the old wily ferpent.

Secondly, when as the fuggeſtion is vrged with great force and violence, and leaueth behind it a deepe impreſſion, which feemeth to bring a neceſſitie of doing that which is euen contrarie to naturall reafon, whereas the fuggeſtions of the fleſh doe rather leade and intice vs then draw and inforce vs vnto finne.

Thirdly, the temptations of Sathan moue vs oftentimes to fuch outragious wickednes, and helliſh impietie, that euen nature corrupted doth condemne as abhominable, and euen trembleth with feare and horror, when they are firſt fuggeſted.

Fourthly, rhe fleſh taketh occafion of things prefent and fubiect to the fenfes to intice vs vnto finne ; but Sathans fuggeſtions fometimes are farre fetcht and fo ſtrange vnto vs, that before the inſtant they are fuggeſted we neuer thought or fo much as dreamed of them.

Laſtly, the things whereunto we are tempted by the fleſh, are alwaies delightfull and pleaſing vnto vs; but fathan tempteth vs alfo to thofe things which are irkfome and grieuous : as namely to fuperſtitious abſtinence whereby the body is almoſt ſtarued, to puniſhing of our owne bodies, as he tempted the Baalitiſh prieſts, to cut and launce themfelues

before

before their idol ; and the superftitious papifts to whip themfelues before their images, and to take vpon them tedious
and daungerous pilgrimages to idols and reliques of Saints;
and the idolatrous heathen to burne in facrifice their deare
children. So alfo he tempteth fome to defpaire of Gods mercie and fo torment themfelues with horror and feare ; yea
fometimes to lay violent hands vpon themfelues, murthering and taking away their owne life, which by nature is fo
deere and precious vnto them. All which being contrarie to
our naturall inclinations and the defires of the flefh, manifeftly appeare to be the fuggeftions of Sathan.

And thefe are the chiefe differences betweene the temptations of Sathan and the flefh;otherwife they are commonly
fo like one to the other that they can hardly be difcerned:and
therefore let vs not be fo carefull, curioufly to diftinguifh
them,as to auoyde or refift them ; knowing that Sathan is the
captaine generall, and the flefh and the lufts thereof Sathans
chiefe aides and affiftants,which continually fight againft the
fpirit and labour to plunge both bodie and foule into euerlafting deftruction.

Chap. XXII.

Of the generall meanes whereby we may be inabled to with-
ftand our fpirituall enemies.

Nd fo much concerning the manner of Sathans
fight : now we are to fpeake of the conflict it
felfe ; wherein (as I haue fhewed) the parties
affaulting and oppugning are the diuell and his
affiftants the world and the flefh ; the partie
defending and refifting is the chriftian fouldier. The caufe
of the fight is not for lands and dominions,nor for riches and
mines of gold ; for thefe would Sathan be content to giue
if he had them in his poffeffion, if we would renounce Gods
feruice, and fall downe and worfhip him ; but for the euerlafting faluation of our foules which Sathan laboreth by
all meanes poffible to hinder, and to plunge vs into endlefle
deftruction.

§ *Sect.* 1.
The circum-
ftances to be
confidered in
this fpirituall
conflict.

destruction.The weapons which the assailants vse in this fight
are not the sword & speare,or any other carnall furniture,but
spirituall temptations, whereby they seek to intice,draw,and
prouoke man to sin, that consequētly he may receiue the wages therof euerlasting death.The weapons which the Christiā
souldier vseth to defend himself and repell his enemies,is the
spiritual armour before spokē of,namely,the girdle of veritie
the breast-plate of righteousnes,the knowledge & profession
of the Gospel of peace,the shield of faith,the helmet of saluation,the sword of the spirit,and feruent and effectuall prayer.

§. Sect.2.
Of two com-
mon affections
to be considered
of in this spiri-
tuall conflict.

Now in this conflict of temptations, there are first two
common affections or generall properties to be considered
of ; the Christian souldiers manfull resistance, or els his fainting and receiuing the foile ; for either he couragiously standeth vpon his defence, armed with the graces of Gods spirit,
and putteth Sathan to flight by withstanding his temptations ; or els being surprized at vnawares, whilest he is disarmed of these spirituall weapons and Christian armour,hee is
foiled by his spirituall enemies, yeelding vnto their temptations and falling into sinne.

Of the first
meanes to
withstand our
spirituall ene-
mies,to wit,
Gods comman-
dement.

That we may withstand our spirituall enemie valiantly in
all his temptations , and obtaine a finall victorie , there are
certaine general means to be vsed;which may serue as strong
forts and bulworkes,vnto which we may retire our selues as
often as we faint,and be readie to receiue any disaduantage
in the fight.First,we are continually to haue in memorie the
commandement of our chiefe captaine Christ Iesus, whereby
he inciteth vs to a continuall fight without fainting or yeel-

Eph.6.10.11.

1.Pet.5.8.

ding.So Eph.6.10.11.*Be strong in the Lord, and in the power of
his might.Put on the whole armour of God,that ye may be able to
stand against all the assaults of the diuell.*And 1.Pet.5.8.*Your ad-
uersarie the diuell as a roring lion walketh about seeking whom he
may deuoure.Whom resist stedfast in the faith.*

The second
meanes,hope of
victorie.

Secondly, let vs be incouraged to withstand our spirituall
enemies with assured hope of victorie; for we fight the Lords
battailes vnder the standerd of Iesus Christ, whose power is
omnipotent,and therefore able to defend vs,& to ouerthrow
our enemies with a word of his mouth; who also is our head
and

and we his members, and therefore we may affure our felues
that he hath no leffe will than power to fuccour vs. As alfo let
vs alwaies haue in minde the crowne of victorie promifed to
all that ouercome, euen a crowne of glorie and euerlafting
happines in Gods kingdom, Apoc. 2.7. & 3.5.12.21. And this *Apoc. 2.7. and*
will make vs refolue neuer to faint in the battell, nor coward- *3.5.12.21.*
ly yeeld vnto Sathans temptations, though he fhould intice
vs to finne by offring vs the whole world, becaufe we would
not thereby hazard the loffe of this eternall waight of glorie.

Thirdly, we are alwaies to ftand in readines armed with the *The third*
chriftian armour, the graces of Gods fpirit, and to vfe al good *meanes, to be*
meanis that we may be more and more ftrengthened & con- *alwaies in rea-*
firmed in them : but yet when we are at the ftrongeft, we are *dines.*
not to prefume vpon our own ftrength, but to relie our felues
wholy vpon the Lords affiftance, and when wee are tempted
and affaulted, we muft continually implore his help, that being armed with the power of his might, wee may withftand
the temptation and obtaine victorie.

Fourthly, when we are affaulted by our fpirituall enemies *The fourth*
and tempted vnto any finne, we muft not only abftaine from *meanes, to take*
committing thereof, but alfo take occafion thereby of doing *occafion of Sa-*
the contrary vertue. For example, whé we are tempted to vn- *thans tempta-*
lawful pleafures, we muft not only abftaine from thé, but alfo *tion vnto finne.*
we are fomewhat to abridge our felues of thofe that be law- *of doing the*
full, and the more ferioufly and painfully to follow the works *cotrary vertue.*
of our lawfull callings; when we are tempted to couetoufnes,
we muft the more earneftly exercife the works of mercie and
chriftian liberalitie; when we are tépted to ambition, we muft
not only refraine fró vainglorie, but we muft labour after true
humilitie and mortification, refufing not only vnlawfull honours, but thofe alfo which are lawfull, fo oft as we haue iuft
caufe to feare that Sathan wil (taking occafion of our corruption) hereby caufe vs to forget God; when we are tempted to
neglect the hearing of Gods word on the Lords Sabbaoth,
wee are the more diligently to heare it, not only then, being
bound hereunto by Gods commandement, as being one of
the chief means of fanctifying this day confecrated to Gods
feruice ; but alfo on the weeke daies, if the Lord giue vs fit
opportunitie

opportunitie, when as we might lawfully be exercifed in the duties of our callings.In a word,when we are tempted to any vice, wee are to take occafion thereby of doing the contrarie vertue; in the meane time carefully auoiding the policie of Sathan, before fpoken of, whereby hee laboureth to draw vs from one vice to his contrarie extreame. And fo like valiant fouldiers we fhall not onely auoide the daunger and violence of Sathans ftrokes, but alfo wee fhall giue Sathan the foyle with his owne weapon, yea and make him afraide to affault vs againe with his temptations, leaft when hee prouoketh vs vnto finne, we take occafion thereby to ferue God,and more conftantly to imbrace vertue.

§. Sect.3.
The fift meanes to withftand temptations when they are firft fuggefted.

Fiftly, we are moft carefully to withftand Sathans temptations when they are firft fuggefted; and to giue him the repulfe as foone as wee perceiue that he is but beginning to make an entrance.For this gliding ferpent if he can but thruft in his head, will eafily make roome for his whole bodie: and therefore we muft nip and brufe him in the head, and vfe his temptations like the ferpents broode, which if men defire to kill,they doe not tread vpon their tailes, for fo they would turne againe and fting them, but vpon their heads,and then they haue no power to hurt them. So wee are not fondly to thinke that we can without hurt vanquifh Sathans temptations in the end when wee haue long entertained them: for vnleffe they be nipped in the head, and withftood in the beginning,they will mortally poyfon vs with the fting of finne. For as theeues comming to breake into a houfe, if they can but finde roome for the point of their wrench to enter, will eafily by turning and winding about the vice make the doores, though very ftrong, flie open and giue them entrance; fo if this cunning theefe Sathan can finde any entrance for his firft temptations, fo as wee can be content to thinke vpon them, and reuolue them in our mindes with any liking,hee will eafily burft open the gates of our foules, and entring further will rob vs of all Gods graces. Let vs therefore if wee would refift Sathan, follow the aduice of the heathen Poet in a farre different matter : *Principijs obfta:ferò medicina paratur, Cum mala per longas conualuère moras.* Or rather
ther

ther the counfell of the Apoftle giuen vs in this felfefame refpect,Eph.4.27.*Giue no place to the diuell.* And as wife citizens Eph.4.27.
being befieged, doe not let their enemies fcale their walles
and enter the towne,with a purpofe then to repell and beate
them backe againe;but they withftand them as foone as they
giue the firft affault, and keepe them,if they can, from approching neere their walles with fconces and bulwarkes : fo
we are not to fuffer Sathan our enemie and the troupes of
his temptations to enter into our hearts, but to giue them
the repulfe at their firft approching, leaft it be too late afterwards when they haue furprized and wounded vs with finne.
Bleffed are they therefore who take this Babylonifh brood of
Sathans temptations and dafh them euen whileft they are Pfal.137.9:
young againft the ftones, leaft waxing old and ftrong they
furioufly fight againft vs,and leading vs captiue in the chains
of finne,grieuoufly afflict and vex vs.

Sixtly,if we would not be furprized and foiled by Sathan, **§. Sect.4.**
we muft after we haue refifted him in one temptation,be rea- *The fixt means*
die prepared to withftand another,and after we haue once or *is after one*
twice giuen Sathan the repulfe, wee are not fecurely to giue *temptation is*
our felues to reft,as though the warre were at an end: but we *paft to prepare*
muft continually expect his returne with frefh fupplies, and *our felues for*
prepare our felues for a new affault, vfing the time of Sathans *another.*
intermiffion,as a breathing time to recouer ftrength againft
the next encounter. And as fouldiers befieged after they
haue fuftained one affault, and giuen their enemies the repulfe,doe not fecurely giue themfelues to idlenes and fleepe,
but prepare all things readie for the next conflict, mending
the breaches,and repairing thofe places which in the time of
fight they found to be moft weake ; fo when wee haue withftood fome of Sathans temptations , and giuen him the repulfe,we are not to giue our felues to reft, fleeping in retchleffe fecuritie, as though our enemies were quite ouercome,
but rather in the intermiffion of the fpirituall combat, we are
to prepare our felues for the next affault, vfing all meanes to
confirme our felues,where wee difcerned in the time of fight
that wee were moft weake, and more ftrongly to arme our
felues with the fhield of faith and the fword of the fpirit,
                                                    againft

1.Pet.5.8.

againſt thoſe temptations which wee found moſt forcible to preuaile againſt vs. For our enemie like a roring lion continually raungeth about ſeeking whom hee may deuoure; his malice will neuer let him reſt, but euen then when he ſeemeth to entertaine a truce, hee is moſt buſie in plotting meanes whereby he may worke our finall deſtruction : and therefore wee are neuer more carefully to ſtand vpon our guard, than when this enemie ſeemeth to proclaime a peace, or when he fleeth away as though he were vanquiſhed ; for when he talketh of peace, he maketh himſelfe readie for the battaile, and this wicked Parthian doth more hurt in flying than in fighting. Here therefore the Chriſtian ſouldier muſt auoide two dangerous euils : the one, that hee doe not faint or yeeld in the time of the fight ; the other, that he doe not after one victorie waxe inſolent and ſecure : but when he hath once ouercome, he is ſo to behaue himſelfe as though he were preſently againe to be aſſaulted. For, Sathans temptations like the waues of the ſea doe follow one in the necke of the other, and when one is paſt, another is readie to ouerwhelme vs, if like skilfull Pilots we be not readie as well to breake the violence of that which followeth, as of that which went before. Neither muſt we look for any ſound truce or firme peace, till we haue the euerlaſting peace in Gods kingdom ; for as long as wee continue in this life our ſpirituall enemies will continually aſſault vs : and therefore let vs neuer be ſecure, vntill by death we haue obtained a finall victorie.

Reaſons to perſwade vs to perſeuere in fighting this ſpirituall battaile.

And to the end that wee may the rather be perſwaded to continuall care and Chriſtian perſeuerance in this ſpirituall fight vnto the end of our liues ; let vs conſider that Gods promiſes and the crowne of victorie are not promiſed to thoſe that enter into this ſpirituall fight, but vnto thoſe that continue fighting, till they haue obtained a full victorie ouer their enemies. *To him that ouercommeth will I giue to eate of the tree of life,*Reu.2.7. *Be thou faithfull vnto the death, and I will giue thee the crowne of life.* Verſ.10. *He that ouercommeth ſhall not be hurt of the ſecond death.* Verſ.11. *To him that ouercommeth will I giue to eate of the Manna that is hid,&c.* Verſ.17. *He that ouercommeth ſhall be clothed in white aray, and I will not put out*

Apoc.2.7.10. 11.17.and 3. 5.21.

his

his name out of the booke of life. cap.3.5. To him that ouercommeth will I graunt to sit with me in my throne, euen as I ouercame and sit with my father in his throne. As it is verf.21. So that it is not sufficient that we enter the lifts and fuftaine the firft and fecond encounter, if afterwards we fhamefully forfake the ftandard of Chrift and cowardly runne away, or elfe trayteroufly yeeld vnto finne and Sathan : but if we would be made partakers of Gods promifes, we muft ouercome, that is, obtaine a full victorie ouer the flefh, the world, and the diuell. There is none triumpheth for making his enemies once or twice to retire, or for getting the better in fome skirmifh; becaufe they may gather their difperfed forces, and ioyne with them new fupplies, and fo giuing a frefh affault, obtaine victorie : but thofe onely triumph who obtaine a full victorie; neither fhall any triumph in the kingdome of glorie, who refift Sathan in one temptation onely or bridle one luft of the flefh, but they who fubdue them finally and wholy not once alone, but vnto the end of their liues ; for as it falleth out in worldly warres, oftentime the enemie doth retire backe, and counterfeiteth a flight, to the end the other may purfue him fecurely and diforderly with full affurance of victorie ; and then he makes a ftand and reuniting all his forces doth ouercome his retchleffe enemie : fo oftentimes Sathan faineth himfelfe to be put to flight, to the end we may conceiue an opinion of his great weakenes, and our owne inuincible ftrength, and fo be brought to negligence and fecuritie; and then he knits together all his force, and ouerthroweth vs when we are retchlefly fecure fearing no danger. Yea fometimes he is in truth foiled, but yet not fo as that he will furceafe his fight ; for if he cannot preuaile one way, he will try another, fo long as our continuance in this earthly weake tabernacle giueth him any hope of ouercomming or foyling vs: and therefore we are alwaies to ftand vpon our guarde, and to keepe our ftanding continually, watching and preparing our felues againft the frefh affaults of our fpirituall enemies. If *Iob* had been fecure after he had refifted Sathans firft temptation, in taking away his oxen, affes and fheepe, furely thofe which followed would haue made him blaf-

pheme

pheme God as Sathan imagined, but like a good fouldier
after that he had receiued one blow, he did not caft away his
fheild of faith and patience, as though hee had no further
neede of it, but ftill held it vp expecting more, till the combate was ended; whofe example wee muft imitate, if we
would obtaine victorie, and inioy the crowne of victorie e-
uerlafting happines in Gods kingdome. Otherwife if we fleep
in fecuritie after we haue giuen Sathan one ouerthrow, wee
fhall be fure to be affaulted and furprifed before we be aware;
for as one faith, *Diabolus victus quoque vincit*, euen whileft the
diuell is vanquifhed, he obtaineth victorie; and therefore
*non victor magis quàm victus eft extimefcendus. Nam fæpe fe
proftratum afflictumque fimulat, vt acriùs infurgat; fugit vt in
infidias pertrahat & incautos adoriatur; palam cedit vt clàm
vincat :* he is no more to be feared when he ouercommeth,
than when he is ouercome; for oftentimes he faineth himfelfe to be foyled that he may the more fearcely renew the
affault, he flyeth that he may draw vs into his ambufhments,
and affaile vs at vnawares; he retireth openly that he may
fecretly ouercome.

Ioan. Riu. At-
thend. de luct.
Chrift.

§. Sect. 5.
*The feauenth
meanes not to
beleeue Sa-
thans fugge-
ftions.
Ioh. 8. 44.*

Seauenthly, if we would not be circumuented by Sathan,
we muft not giue any credit vnto him whether he lyeth or
fpeaketh true, whether he accufeth or flattereth, whether he
indeauoreth to puffe vs vp with pride and felfe conceite, or
whether he laboreth by aggrauating our finnes to plunge vs
into the gulfe of hellifh defpaire; *for he abode not in the truth
becaufe there is no truth in him. When he fpeaketh a lie he fpeaketh of his owne, for he is a lyer and the father thereof,* as it is,
Ioh. 8. 44. And if at any time he fpeake the truth, it is to the
end he may be the better credited when he lyeth, *Nam verum
dicit vt fallat, blanditur vt noceat, bona promittit vt malum
tribuat, vitam pollicetur vt perimat,* he fpeaketh the truth that
he may deceiue, he flattereth that he may hurt vs, he promifeth good things that he may giue vs euill, he promifeth life
that he may kill vs. And therefore we are not to beleeue the
truth it felfe, becaufe he fpeakes it, but becaufe it is grounded
on Gods word; nor to receiue it from his mouth as his affertion, but from the mouth of God, and his holy Prophets and
Apoftles,

Apoſtles, guided and inſpired with his ſpirit; for either he
ſpeaketh the truth to gaine credit vnto his lies, or propoundeth true promiſes that he may ſophiſtically gather out of
them falſe concluſions. And hence it is that our Sauiour
Chriſt did reiect his teſtimonie though true, and inioyned
him ſilence when he confeſſed him to bee the holy one of Mark.1.24.25
God, Mark.1.24.25. And the Apoſtle *Paul* would not ſuffer
the diuining maide to giue them her approbation though ſhe Act.16.17.18.
ſpake truth, in confeſſing them the ſeruants of the moſt high
God, which did ſhew vnto vs the way of ſaluation. Act.16.
17.18. becauſe Sathan did it, either to this end, that by his
teſtimonie and approbation he might cauſe them the rather
to be ſuſpected and reputed impoſters and deceiuers, who
did their miracles by the helpe of ſome familiar ſpirit; or that
he might afterwards by telling this truth, be the rather credited when he did bely and ſlaunder them.

Eightly, if we would withſtand al Sathans temptations, we §. Sect.6.
muſt auoyde two extreames, the one to deſpiſe them, the *The eight*
other too deepely to apprehend and too greatly to feare *meanes,neither*
them. For if we ſecurely contemne Sathans temptations, we *to deſpiſe Sa-*
will neuer arme and prepare our ſelues to make reſiſtance, *thans tempta-*
and ſo he will ouercome vs before we be aware; if we take *tions,nor tao*
them too much to hart continually meditating vpon their *deeply to ap-*
ſtrength and violence, and vpon our owne infirmitie and *prehend them.*
weakneſſe, they will fill vs with feare, and plunge vs into deſpaire; if we deſpiſe the temptation, Sathan will eaſily ſubdue vs : for there is no enemie ſo weake and feeble which will
not preuaile againſt thoſe who ſecurely contemne them,
though exceeding mightie; becauſe they neglect all meanes
of their preſeruation, and neuer ſtand vpon their guard for
their defence; and therefore much more will Sathan preuaile againſt vs, if wee regard not his temptations, hee being ſtrong and mightie, and we feeble and weake. On the o-
ther ſide if we ſo feare his temptations as that we deſpaire of
victorie, Sathan ſhall not neede to fight againſt vs, for we will
ouercome our ſelues, fainting before the fight, and caſting
away our weapons as ſoone as Sathan doth but muſter his
forces and march againſt vs. And therefore let vs ſo much

feare

feare the temptations, as that we doe not securely contemne them;and not so much feare them as that we should despaire of victorie : let vs feare them so much as that thereby we be stirred vp with more care & diligence to resist and ouercome them ; but not somuch as that we should cowardly faint, distrusting Gods helpe:let vs feare them in respect of our weaknes and their violence, but let vs boldly striue against them, trusting in Gods almightie power & merciful promises of his aide and assistance,being hereby assured of certaine victorie.

§. Sect.7.
The ninth meanes, to obiect Christ against all temptations.
Matth.9.13.
Esa.53.5.

2.Cor.5.21.

Galat.3.13.

Col.1.21.22.

1.Cor.1.30.

Lastly,if we would withstand Sathā,we must obiect our Sauiour Christ against al his temptations:for if we apply him vnto vs by a liuely faith,he will be our sheeld and buckler to defend vs from all Sathans blowes.For example,if Sathan tell vs that we are miserable sinners,and therfore in the state of damnation:we are to answere that our *Sauiour Christ came into the World to saue sinners,& that he was wounded for our transgressions & broken for our iniquities &c.and with his stripes we are healed, and so he which knew no sin, was made sin for vs, that we might be made the righteousnes of God in him.*If he say that we are subiect to the curse of the law; we are to answere that *Christ hath redeemed vs frō the curse of the law when he was made a curse for vs.* If he obiect that we are subiect to Gods wrath, we are to tell him that Christ did beare his fathers displeasure,that he might make our peace:and whereas *we were strangers and enemies,because our minds were set on euill works, he hath now reconciled vs in the body of his flesh through death.* If he tell vs that we are his bondslaues,we are to answere,that we were so indeede in time past,but ourSauiour christ hath paied vnto his father the price of our redemption,& hath set vs free. If he affirme that we are vniust and therefore shall be condemned before Gods iudgment seate ; we are to answere that Christ who was innocent was condemned,that we who are guiltie might be acquitted ; that though we are wicked in our selues,yet we are most iust being clothed with his righteousnes;that he that came to saue vs shall come to iudge vs, and therefore we neede not doubt of mercie, if wee pleade his merits forsaking the plea of our owne righteousnesse and renouncing all selfe confidence. If he say that we shall be held captiue of death and neuer rise

to

to take poffeffion of our heauenly inheritance, we are to anfwere that our Sauiour Chrift hath broken the bonds of
death and led captiuitie captiue ; that he is rifen againe, being the firft fruites of them that flept, and is afcended into Ioh.14.2.
heauen, to prepare vs a place there. If he obiect that Chrift
and all his benefits doe not appertaine vnto vs, for euery
man fhall liue by his owne righteoufnes, and the foule that Ezech.18.
finneth fhall die the death; we are to anfwere that by the
fpirit of God and a liuely faith, Chrift is become our head and
we his members, fo that he is ours and we his, and our fins he
hath taken vpon him, & beftowed on vs his righteoufnes, he
is become our husband and we his fpoufe, and therfore as he
hath cōmunicated himfelf vnto vs, fo likewife al his benefits,
his merits, righteoufnes, fanctificatiō, & euerlafting happines.

But if Sathan will not thus be anfwered, we are not to entertaine any further difputation with him, but to fend him to §. Sect.8.
our Sauiour Chrift who hath taken vpon him to be not onely *That to auoyde*
our redeemer and our mediator and interceffor vnto God *Sathans impor-*
his father, but alfo our aduocate to pleade our caufe and to *tunitie, we muft*
anfwere all fuites made againft vs both by Gods iuftice and *leaue to difpute*
the handwriting of the law, and alfo by Sathan and all his *with him and*
adherents. as it is, 1.Ioh.2.1. Seeing therefore our Sauiour *fend him to our*
Chrift who is the wifedome of his father hath taken vpon *aduocate.*
him the defence of our caufe in all our fuites, let not vs our 1.Ioh.2.1.
felues be ouer bufie in difputing with this wrangling fophi-
fter, but fend him for an anfwere to our Sauiour Chrift who
hath fully fatiffied his fathers iuftice, in all, which it had a-
gainft vs, and cancelled the handwriting of the law, whereby
we were obliged and bound, and therefore much more able is
he to anfwere al accufations which this cauelling accufer hath
againft vs. Neither are we to doubt but that our Sauiour will
be our aduocate to pleade our caufe, efpecially confidering
that it doth principally concerne himfelfe, and his owne glorie and fufficiencie. For the queftions and caufes controuer-
fall betweene vs and Sathan, are not about our owne worthineffe, merits, righteoufnes, and fatiffactions, all which we
renounce and caft away from vs as polluted cloutes, in refpect of being any caufes of our iuftification and faluation:

I 2   but

but concerning Chrifts righteoufnes, merit, and the fufficiencie and efficacie of his death and obedience, for the faluation
of al repentant finners which do apply them vnto themfelues
by a liuely faith: and therefore we may affure our felues he wil
defend his owne caufe againft all Sathans obiections and
imputations.

§. Sect. 9.
If we will a-
uoide Sathaus
importunitie,
we muft imploy
our felues in
holy exercifes.

But if Sathan continue his importunitie, and will admit of
no anfwere, we are as much as in vs lieth to banifh his temptations out of our mindes, and not to thinke and meditate
on them : and to this end we are continually to exercife our
felues in feruent prayer, defiring the Lords gracious affiftance
whereby wee may be enabled to withftand all the affaults of
our enemie, as alfo to heare reade and meditate in Gods
word, and diligently to vfe holy conferences with our chriftian brethren, and painfully to imploy our felues in the
workes of our callings, that fo we may haue no leafure to entertaine Sathans temptations. For as a veffell which is alreadie full can receiue no more, and whatfoeuer is powred there-
into fpilleth vpon the ground : fo when our mindes are re-
plenifhed with holy thoughts, and occupied in godly and
honeft exercifes, there is no roome left for Sathans fuggeftions and therefore as foone as they offer to enter, we prefently reiect them. Whereas on the other fide if we fpend
our times in idlenes, and doe not diligently exercife our felues
in the duties of chriftianitie, and of our feuerall callings; then
are our mindes fit groundes to receiue the feedes of Sathans
temptations, and to nourifh them till they bring forth the
fruites of finne : and if Sathan finde vs like emptie houfes
cleane fwept and voyde of all holy meditations and godly
exercifes, he will eafily enter, and if himfelfe be not ftrong
enough he will take vnto him feuen other fpirits worfe than
himfelfe, that fo he may be more ftrong to keepe poffeffion.
If therefore we would not be ouercome by Sathans temptations, let vs beware of idlenes; for when the minde is emptie
of that which is good, it is moft fit to receiue that which is
euill.

Matth. 12. 45.

But if Sathans temptations be at any time entertained into
our mindes, let vs moft carefully take heede that we doe not
fuffer

suffer them (as it were) to take vp their lodging, by reuol-
uing them in our thoughts, not to meditate too earneftly on
them, but rather on the preferuatiues which may ftrengthen
vs againft their violence; neither are we fo ferioufly to thinke
on Sathans obiections, as that in the meane time we forget
how to anfwere them. For example, when he fetteth before
our eyes the haynoufneffe of our finnes, we are not to bend
all our thoughts to meditate and call to minde all our finnes
both new and old, both which we haue fallen into through
infirmitie, and which we haue willingly committed, for fo
the huge cloude of our finnes being neere our eyes, will hide
from our fight the fhyning beames of Gods mercie and
Chrifts merit, though they are without comparifon greater:
but as foone as we caft one eye vpon our finnes for our humiliation, let vs caft the other prefently vpon Chrift Iefus
who hath payed the price of our redemption, and fuffered all
the punifhment which we by our finnes had deferued. For
if when this fierie ferpent Sathan hath ftung vs with the
fting of finne, we fpend our time in looking vpon the wound,
and neuer thinke vpon the remedie, euen the true brafen ferpent Iefus Chrift hanging on the croffe: the poyfon of finne
will fo inflame our confciences, that the wound will proue
mortall, which at the firft might eafily haue been cured if we
would haue applied thereunto the precious balme of our
Sauiours blood. So when Sathan fetteth before our eyes our
owne wickednes and infirmities, to the end we may defpaire
of victorie, as being neuer able to withftand fuch ftrong
temptations, we are not to fpend our time in thinking hereupon, but prefently to call to minde the almightie power of
God who hath promifed vs his affiftance in this fpirituall
fight. So when he obiecteth vnto vs the iuftice and wrath of
God, in punifhing of finne, and the curfe of the law, and torments of hell prepared for the damned; we are not ouer
ferioufly to reuolue thefe things in our mindes; but prefently to call to minde Gods infinit mercie and Chrifts merits, whereby Gods iuftice is fully fatiffied, his wrath appeafed, the curfe of the law cancelled, and we made of fire brands
of hell heires of heauen. And thus if as foone as Sathan in-

That we muſt not reuolue in our mindes Sathans temptations, but rather meditate on the contrarie preferuatiues.

I 3   flicteth

flicteth the wound we apply the cure, it will neuer be mortall vnto vs ; but if we let the poyfon of his temptations runne in our mindes and neuer thinke of any remedie, though at the firft it feemed but a fmall fcratch, it will fo inflame our confciences with fcorching heate that they will afterwards very hardly admit of any cure. When therefore Sathan doth caft into our mindes his temptations, let vs repell them, and indeuour to quench them whileft they be but fmall fparkes: for our corrupt mindes are like vnto tinder, and Sathans temptations like the fire: and therefore if in ftead of putting them out we blow vpon them, though they be but as a fmall fparke at the firft, within a while they will increafe to an vnquenchable flame which will torment our confciences with fcorching heate : neither is there any thing but the blood of Chrift, and the water of the fpirit which will extinguifh this wilde-fire when once it hath taken deepe hold on vs.

Chap. XXIII.

How the chriftian being foyled by Sathans temptations may be raifed againe.

§. Sect. 1.

A Nd thefe are the meanes whereby the chriftian fouldier may be ftrengthened and encouraged to ftand in the combate of temptations. But fometimes it commeth to paffe that by reafon they neglect thefe meanes, or elfe doe not fo carefully vfe them as they fhould, they are foyled by Sathan, ouercome by his temptations, and led captiue vnto finne. How therefore muft the chriftian thus ouertaken behaue himfelfe ? furely he is not defperatly to caft away all hope of victorie and cowardly to yeelde himfelfe to be the flaue of Sathan, lying contentedly in the chaines of finne, without any defire or indeauour of comming out of his captiuitie: but being fallen he is to labour and ftriue that he may rife againe, and being taken prifoner by finne and Sathan, he is not willingly to remaine in their bonds but earneftly to defire his freedome and libertie.

Now

Now the meanes whereby being fallen he may rife againe, is by vnfained repentance, when as he is hartily forie for his finne, becaufe thereby hee hath difpleafed his louing and gracious father, and ftedfaftly purpofeth for the time to come to leaue and forfake thofe finnes, into which by the malice of Sathan and his owne infirmitie he is fallen; and by a liuely faith, when as he doth apply vnto himfelfe all the mercifull promifes made vnto all repentant finners. For though faith in nature goe before repentance, yet the act and frute of faith, whereby we are affured of Gods mercie in the free forgiuenes of our finnes, alwaies commeth after.

Where by the way we may note a difference betweene the ftate of Gods children and the wicked: both fall into finne very often, both alfo commit heynous and grieuous finnes; yea fometimes the child of God falleth into more fearefull and horrible finnes, than a meere worldling; but herein the chiefe difference betweene them confifteth, that the child of God after his fall is vexed and grieued, and laboreth to rife againe by leauing and forfaking the finne which is odious vnto him; but the wicked man after his fall neuer foroweth nor grieueth, but rather refolueth to liue ftill in his finne, and to commit it againe and againe with greedines and delight when he hath any occafion offered. *A difference betweene the child of God and the wicked.*

But here the weake chriftian whofe foule is oppreffed with the heauie waight of finne will fay vnto me; alas this is fmall comfort vnto me which you fpeake, neither can I hereby haue any affurance that I am the childe of God; for after I am fallen into finne, fuch is the hardnes of my heart that I cannot bewaile nor be forie for it; and whereas euery fmall worldly loffe or croffe maketh me mourne, weepe and waile, when by my finne I haue offended God, I cannot fhed a teare nor fhew any true figne of hartie forrow; and fuch is mine vntowardnes and corruption that in ftead of forfaking my finne, I am readie to fall againe vpon the next occafion: and therefore I cannot haue any faith or full affurance of Gods promifes made in Chrift, feeing they are all limited and reftrained to thofe finners which repent and amend. *§. Sect. 2. The complaint of the weake chriftian.*

I 4   That

That the desire of Gods graces is accepted for the graces which we desire.

That therefore these mourning soules may receiue some comfort, let them know first, that if they haue an earnest desire of repentance, faith, and the rest of Gods graces; if they haue a good purpose to leaue and forsake their sinnes, and to spend their liues in the seruice and worship of God : if they are displeased with their corruptions, and according to the measure of grace giuen, pray vnto God, desiring the assistance of his holy spirit, whereby they may more and more mortifie the old man, and crucifie the flesh, and the lusts thereof : if they hate the sinne they commit, and loue the good which they cannot doe : if they can grieue because they are no more grieued for their sinnes, and be displeased with themselues, becaufe their sinnes doe no more displease them: then may they be assured that they are Gods children, who are acceptable vnto him in Iesus Christ. For he respecteth not so much our actions as our affections; nor our workes, as our desires and indeuours : so that he who desires to be righteous is righteous; he that would repent, doth repent; hee that striueth to leaue and forsake his sinnes, hee reputeth of him, as if he had left and forsaken them; they that would neuer fall, nor bee foiled by their spirituall enemies, God esteemeth as his inuincible souldiers, and valiant worthies, who were neuer vanquished. For the Lord

1. Cor. 8. 12.

accepteth the desire for the deede; and *if there be first a willing minde, it is accepted according to that a man hath, and not according to that a man hath not,* as it is 2. Cor. 8. 12. So he is accounted blessed, not who hath attained vnto perfect in-

Matth. 5. 6.

herent righteousnesse indeede, but he who hungreth after righteousnesse, Matth. 5. 6. that is, who hath a sence and feeling of his wants and imperfections, and withall an earnest desire to haue his wants supplied.

§. *Sect. 3.*
The conditions required vnto that desire which is acceptable.

But yet we must not imagine, that euery flickering and vnconstant desire, proceeding from suddaine passion, and some extraordinary occasion, is pleasing vnto God; for so euery worldling might imagine himselfe to be in the state of grace: but vnto this desire I speake of, there are diuers things required. As first, that this desire be ioyned with an holy indeuour, and earnest striuing and labouring in the vse of the

meanes,

meanes, whereby wee may attaine vnto thoſe graces which we doe deſire : for it is not ſufficient that wee wiſh for faith, repentance, and other graces, vnleſſe we indeuour to attaine vnto them, and to this end carefully vſe all good meanes ordained of God for the obtaining our deſires.

Secondly, this deſire muſt not be ſuddaine like a flaſh of lightening, vaniſhing away as ſoone as it entreth into vs, but we muſt conſtantly perſeuere in it, till it be ſatisfied.

Thirdly, it muſt not bee a ſlight, and indifferent deſire, as though we would haue theſe graces, if we could eaſily attaine vnto them, otherwiſe wee doe not greatly care whether wee haue them or no: but it muſt bee very earneſt, at leaſt ſometime, though not alwayes : So as we may ſay with *Dauid : My ſoule longeth after thee, O Lord , as the thirſtie land.* Pſal. 63.1. And, *As the Hart brayeth for the riuers of water , ſo panteth my ſoule after thee, O God :* as it is Pſal.42.1.

Fourthly, this deſire is true, and pleaſing vnto God, when as it proceedeth from a ſenſe of our owne want and penurie, in regard whereof we are truely humbled. And hereof it is compared to hungering and thirſting; in which two things concurre, firſt, a ſence of want which afflicteth vs , and, a deſire to haue it ſupplied.

Fiftly, it is not ſufficient that we haue a continuall and earneſt deſire of our ſaluation, vnleſſe wee deſire as earneſtly the ſubordinate cauſes and meanes tending thereunto ; namely, vocation, iuſtification, ſanctification, faith, repentance, and the reſt of the graces of Gods ſpirit : for euen *Balaam* himſelfe did wiſh that he might die the death of the righteous, but his deſire was not acceptable to God, becauſe he wiſhed not alſo to liue their life : he deſired to die like them, that he might be ſaued ; but hee deſired not to ſerue the Lord in holineſſe and newneſſe of life, whereby he might haue been aſſured of ſaluation.

If therefore wee would haue our deſires acceptable to God, they muſt be ioyned with an holy indeuour to obtaine thoſe ſpirituall graces which we doe deſire; they muſt be conſtant, earneſt, and proceede from a true ſence and feeling of our owne want, and be referred as well to the meanes, as to

the

the ende, and then the defire of grace is the grace it felfe; the defire of faith is faith; the defire of repentance is repentance; not in it owne nature, but in Gods acceptation, who accepteth the will for the deede.

§ *Sect.4.*
The Chriftians perfection confifteth in defiring and labouring after perfection.

And in truth this is the chiefe perfection of our righteoufnes, when as we feele our imperfections, and labour earneftly after more perfection: for, *Chriftiani fumus potius affectu quàm effectu:* We are Chriftians rather in our affections and defires, than in our workes and abilities: neither doth the Lord beftow vpon his children the full meafure of his fpirit and the graces thereof in this life, but onely the firft fruites, which are as it were but an handfull of corne in refpect of the whole field; and the earneft to affure vs of the reft, which is but as a peny in refpect of many thoufands, which are confirmed vnto vs thereby, as the Apoftle fpeaketh Rom.8.23. 2.Cor.1.22. and 5.5.

Rom.8.23.
2.Cor.1.22.
and 5.5.

True it is indeede that God beftoweth his fpirit and the graces thereof vpon fome of his children in greater meafure, and vpon fome in leffe, euen as the firft fruites may be a greater or leffer handfull, and the earneft is fometimes a peny, and fometimes a fhilling, fometimes more and fometimes leffe; but yet the greateft meafure which any receiue, is but as an handfull of the firft fruites, and an earneft-peny in refpect of the maine fumme and full meafure, which the Lord hath hereby affured vs that he wil beftow vpon vs in his kingdom: and hee that hath receiued the leaft earneft, hath as full and perfect affurance of the whole bargaine, which God hath couenanted to make good vnto vs, as he who hath receiued the greateft, according to the nature of an earneft, to which the meafure of grace here receiued is compared.

But wherein doth this meafure of grace and chiefe perfection of a Chriftian confift in this life? Surely, not in their workes, for they are all imperfect, and fo full of corruptions that they are odious in Gods fight, being confidered in themfelues, and examined by the rule of his exact iuftice; neither in their inherent righteoufnes, and begun fanctification, for when they are at the holieft they are polluted with the reliques of originall corruption, which bring foorth the fruites

of

of actuall tranfgreffions,and make vs vnable to doe the good we would,in that manner and meafure which we fhould,and therefore thofe which are moft righteous are not in this re-fpect acceptable to God : but herein the perfection of a chri-ftian confifteth, when as feeing his imperfections, wants and finnes, he is grieued and truly humbled with the fight and fenfe of his owne miferie and wretchednefle;and difclaiming and reiecting his owne righteoufnes and good workes, doth flee vnto our Sauiour Chrift,hungring after his righteoufnes, and by a liuely faith applying vnto his wounded foule his merit and obedience, doth looke for faluation in him alone; and laftly, when as in obedience to his commandement,and in true thankfulnes for his infinite mercies he hath an earneft defire to glorifie his name, by a godly and Chriftian life, ftri-uing and endeuouring continually to forfake his finnes, to mortifie his corruption, and to attaine vnto more and more perfection in righteoufnes and holines. For, *Maxima pars Chriftianifmi eft toto pectore velle fieri Chriftianum*; It is the greateft part of Chriftianitie to defire with the whole heart to become a Chriftian.

  If therefore we doe keepe the couenant of the Lord,nay,if § *Sect.5.* we but thinke vpon his commandements,to the end we may doe them, the louing kindnes of the Lord fhall endure for euer vpon vs,as it is Pfal.103.17.18 ; if we can from our harts fay with good *Nehemiah*, Nehem.1.11. *O Lord I befeech thee* Nehem.1.11. *let thine eare now hearken to the prayer of thy feruant, and to the prayer of thy feruants who defire to feare thy name,*the Lord will heare vs indeed and graunt our requefts. If with the Prophet *Dauid* we haue but a refpect to Gods commandements, with a care to fulfill them,we fhal not be confounded,as it is Pfal. Pfal. 119.6. 119.6. If wee but defire to obey Gods commandement, the Lord will accomplifh our defire, and quicken vs in his righ- 40. teoufnes,though we be dull, yea dead vnto all goodnefle, as it is verf.40. If with the Apoftle *Paul* wee doe the euill which Rom.7. we would not,and confent to the law that it is good,delight-ing therein in the inner man ; then though we are with him led captiue vnto finne, yet it is not wee that offend, but finne that dwelleth in vs,that is,our old man,our corrupt and vnre-

generate

That neither the name, nor actions of the flesh, can properly be ascribed to the spirituall man.

generate part, which cannot fitly be called by our name, becaufe it is mortified alreadie in fome meafure, and fhall be fully abolifhed by the fpirit of God; neither doth it liue the fame fpirituall life with vs, feeing it is not quickened by the fame fpirit: and therefore as thofe who haue diuers foules, which giue vnto them life and motion, are themfelues diuers and alfo called by diuers names; fo the new and old man liuing as it were by diuers foules, the one being quickned with Gods fpirit, the other by Sathan (whereof it commeth to paffe, that the more the one liueth the other dieth, the more ftrong the fpirit is, the weaker is the flefh; and the actions of both are quite contrarie) therefore they may fitly be called by diuers names: neither can the actions of the flefh bee afcribed to the fpirit properly, feeing they are contrarie the one to the other. For as if a fcience of a crab tree, and another of a pepin tree being grafted into the fame ftocke doe both bring foorth their feuerall fruites, the one crabs, the other pepins, it may fitly be faid this tree bringeth foorth either pepins or crabs, becaufe they grow in the fame ftocke; but yet it cannot bee truly faid that the crab tree fcience bringeth foorth pepins, or the pepin fcience crabs: fo becaufe the flefh and the fpirit are ioyned together in the fame bodie and foule, we may in this refpect fay that this man finneth, or doth that which is good; but yet whē we fpeak of the regenerate or carnall man properly and feuerally, as we cannot truly fay that the flefh doth any good, fo neither can we truly affirme that the fpirit and regenerate man doth commit that which is euill, but (as ȳ Apoftle fpeaketh) fin which dwelleth with him. And though the flefh be the farre greater part, yet doth it not denominate & giue the name to the chriftian & his actions, becaufe it is partly mortified, partly in mortifying, and partly to be mortified, that is, deputed and deftinated to death and deftruction; and alfo becaufe it is the worfe and more vnworthie part without compare, and confequently not to giue the name: for as wine mixt with water is called ftill wine, though the water exceede the wine in quantitie, becaufe it is the more excellent fubftance; fo the flefh being mixt with the fpirit, though it be in greater quantitie, it doth not giue

the

the name to vs and our actions, but the fpirit, as being our moft excellent and worthie part; and of it wee are called fpirituall,regenerate and new men, though the leaft patt be fpirituall,regenerate and renewed.

If therefore we are regenerate, and haue in vs the fpirit of God,and the graces thereof in the leaft meafure , wee may boldly fay with *Paul*,that it is no more we ỹ do offend God, but finne that dwelleth in vs,neither fhall we receiue punifhment but the flefh,that is, our vnregenerate and corrupt part, which fhall be mortified and fully abolifhed by the fpirit of God ; as for the fpirituall and regenerate part, it fhall daily bee more and more ftrengthened and confirmed in the fpirituall life,and the more punifhments,afflictions and torments the flefh hath inflicted on it,the more fhall the fpirituall man grow vp in grace and goodnes, till our corruption being by little and little mortified, and in the end fully abolifhed by death,we fhall be perfect men in Chrift,liuing a fpirituall and euerlafting life in all glorie and happines in his kingdome. When therefore the Lord-fuffreth Sathan to afflict vs in our goods,bodies,and in our foules and confciences as hee did *Iob*,it is not becaufe hee hath forfaken vs and giuen ouer his whole intereft hee hath in vs to this wicked fpirit,but,as the Apoftle fpeaketh in another matter,he deliuereth vs *vnto Sathan* (to be afflicted) *for the deftruction of the flefh, that the fpirit may be faued in the day of the Lord Iefus*,1.Cor.5.5.   1.Cor.5.5.

It may be that the worke of mortification and regeneration doth goe flowly forward, and the Lord may for a time let our corruptions beare great fway in vs, to the end he may hereby truly humble vs with the fight of our infirmities, and take away from vs all felfe-confidence, prefumption and caufe of boafting, and caufe vs wholy to relie vpon his mercie and Chrifts merits: but though it go on flowly,yet it fhall goe furely, becaufe it is not begun and continued by our felues, for we cannot fo much as thinke a good thought ; but all our fufficiencie is of God,as it is 2.Cor.3.5. neither can we   2.Cor.3.5. fo much as will and defire that which is acceptable in Gods fight,for it is he that worketh in vs the will and the deed,euen   Phil.2.13. of his good pleafure, as it is Phil.2.13. And therefore thefe holie

§ *Sect.*5.
Though our fpirituall growth be flow,yet it is certaine.

holie defires, which are the beginnings and firft fruites of regeneration, being the worke of Gods fpirit; he will finifh and
perfect that which he hath begun, till at laft we be fully freed
from our corruption, and indued with vnfpotted holines and

Phil.1.6.
fanctification. According to that Phil.1.6. *I am perfwaded of
this fame thing, that he who hath begun this good worke in you,
will performe it vntill the day of Iefus Chrift.* For as with the

Iam.1.17.
Mal.3.6.
Rom.11.29.
Lord himfelfe *there is neither change nor fhadow of change,*
Iam.1.17. Mal.3.6. fo alfo *are his gifts and calling without re-
pentance:* as it is Rom.11.29.

§. Sect.7.
If we earneftly
defire perfectiō,
the Lord will
perfect vs, and
in the meane
time pardon
our imperfe-
ctions.
If therefore we haue but a defire to forfake our finnes, and
to attaine vnto true fanctification, this defire is Gods worke,
which he wil finifh & accomplifh, according to that Pfal.145
19. *He wil fulfill the defire of them that feare him.*For if the Lord
doe euen preffe vpon vs whileft we doe not defire his companie; if hee ftand waiting and knocking at the doore of our
hearts, calling and crying vnto vs that we will open and giue
him entrance: when his holie fpirit hath inflamed vs with
true loue of him, and opened our hearts with an earneft defire
to haue him enter, will he now thinke you goe away and refufe to come in when wee inuite him? Nay affuredly, for he
hath promifed the contrarie, Reuel.3.20. *Behold* (faith he) *I
ftand at the doore and knocke : if any man heare my voice and o-
pen the doore, I will come in vnto him and fup with him, and he
with me*; that is, I will make him a rich banquet of my heauenly graces, and *giue him to drinke the water of life, of which
whofoeuer drinketh fhall neuer be more a thirft, but it fhall be in
him a well of water fpringing vp into euerlafting life,* as our Sauiour fpeaketh Ioh.4.14. So our Sauiour Chrift calleth fuch as

Ioh.7.38.
Reu.21.6.
thirft vnto him, *If any man thirft, let him come to me and drink:*
And, *I will giue to him that is a thirft of the well of the water
of life freely.*If therefore we haue a thirfting defire after Gods
fpirit and the graces thereof, we fhall in Gods good time
be fatisfied, and filled with the full meafure of them. And in
the meane time though our infirmities be neuer fo great and
manifold, yet in Chrift God wil be well pleafed with vs, when
as our corruptions do difpleafe our felues, fo that we earneftly defire to be freed from them, and to ferue the Lord in righteoufnes

teoufnes and holines of life. For the Lord efteemeth more of
our will than of our deedes, and of our holie endeuour, than
of our beft workes,becaufe this is the feruice and facrifice of
our hearts, wherewith aboue all other things hee is moft delighted : and therefore, *Da cordi Deo & fufficit,*Giue thy hart   Pro.23.26.
to God and it fufficeth,Prou.23.26.

For the Lord is our moft gracious father, whofe loue farre
exceedeth the loue euen of tender mothers,Efa.49.15.Looke   Efa.49 15.
therefore what affection the tender father or mother beareth   and 66.13.
and fheweth towards their childe:and fuch, nay infinit more
will the Lord fhew towards vs, as himfelfe profeffeth Mal.3.
17. *And I will fpare them, as a man fpares his owne fonne that*   Mal.3.17.
ferueth him. Now we know that if a child endeuour to do his
dutie,and ftriue to doe his beft, though through want of power or skill hee is not able to doe as he would, thofe things
which his father inioyned him; there is no louing father but
will winke at his imperfections,and accept his wil;commen-
ding his obedience and dutifull endeuour, though the worke
in it felf deferue no commendations : how much more therefore will our heauenly father,whofe loue is infinite and without all compare,be wel pleafed with vs in the middeft of our
infirmities,if we haue a defire and care to ferue him ?

The Lord is our fhepheard,and we his flock and the fheep   Pfal.23.1.
of his pafture ; as it is Pfal.23.1.and Ioh.10. Now if a fheepe   Ioh.10.
be intangled in the briars, fo as hee cannot follow the fhepheard,though he heare his voyce calling vnto him, yet if hee
ftruggle and ftriue to come out to the vttermoft of his power,and bleat for the fhepheards helpe,when he cannot help
himfelfe,hereby it appeareth that hee is one of his flocke,
which the good fhepheard will not fuffer to be loft; whereas
indeed if he want not power alone, but will alfo to be freed
and to follow after, it is cleere that he belongeth to another
fheepfold : fo if when wee are intangled in the briars of our
corruptions,and fo hindred with our imperfections,that wee
cannot follow the great fhepheard of our foules Iefus Chrift
in the path of righteoufnes,which leadeth to the fheepfold
of euerlafting happines, though wee heare his voyce calling
vnto vs ; yet if with the fillie fheepe we ftruggle and ftriue to
be

be freed from the fnares of finne, and when wee cannot free our felues by our power, doe as it were bleate, and after our fheepifh manner implore the help of our carefull fhepheard; crying out with the Apoftle *Paul*, (that bleffed fheepe of Chrift)*Wretched man that I am, who fhall deliuer me from the bodie of this death*, as it is Rom. 7.24. then will our louing fhepheard Iefus Chrift in his good time come and loofe vs, and if with ftrugling in the briars of finne we are fo difabled that we cannot goe,he will take vs like the ftraied fheepe vpon his fhoulders,and carrie vs by the waies of righteoufneffe into his fheepfold of euerlafting happineffe. Neither can it poffibly be that our heauenly fhepheard, who of purpofe came into the world to feeke vs whileft wee were loft, and fpent three and thirtie yeeres in following and finding vs, who were wandring and ftraied fheepe, crying and calling vnto vs euen till he became hoarce with lowd cries, and paffing thorow the thornie waies of troubles and perfecution, till he had fhed his precious blood,and finally laid down his life for our fakes ; fhould now turne away his eyes and ftop his eares when his fheepe defire to follow him, and earneftly implore his helpe,finding their owne weakneffe and vnabilitie to come fo fwiftly to him as they fhould.

The Lord is our Sauiour and Redeemer,who hath not fpared his owne precious blood, but hath giuen it to his father as the price of our redemption,that wee might bee deliuered out of the captiuitie of the diuell,in which we were detained, as it is 1.Tim.2.6. If therefore we haue a fenfe of our captiuitie,and a defire to be fet at libertie,being wearie of our miferie,and vnwilling to ftay any longer in this cruell bondage; our Sauiour Chrift will redeeme vs, for to this end hee came into the world,as appeareth Luk.4.18. And though like vnto poore captiues who (hauing long time been clogged with heauie bolts, and galled with ftrong chaines) haue their lims fo benummed and fore, that they cannot goe after they are freed out of prifon; fo we after we haue long been detained in Sathans captiuitie,fettred with chaines of finne, and clogged with the heauie bolts of our corruptions, be fo galled and benummed, that wee cannot fwiftly follow Chrift our Redeemer

Rom.7.24.

1.Tim.2.6.

Luk.4.18.

Redeemer in the waïes of righteoufnes vnto his kingdome of glory,but halt and ftumble euery ftep through our infirmitie and weaknes;yet if we haue an earneft defire of côming after him,then furely he that hath giuen this ineftimable price for our redemption,will not now leaue vs in the hands of his and our enemies;but will feede vs with the foode of his word and Sacraments,& ftrengthen and fupport vs with his holy fpirit, inabling vs with the graces thereof to follow his fteps, till hauing obtained full libertie wee arriue at his kingdome of euerlafting glorie.

Laftly, that I may fit the fimilitude to the fpirituall con- §. *Sect.*8.
flict whereof we fpeake. If we haue an earneft defire of ouer- *That thofe are*
comming our fpirituall enemies, and withftanding their *chrifts foul-*
temptations, whereby they labour to draw vs to finne: wee *diers who haue*
may be affured wee are Chrifts fouldiers, how weakly foeuer *a defire of ouer-*
we fight when we come to the encounter. For though a foul- *cumming their*
dier through ficknes be fo infeebled that he cannot weld his *fpirituall ene-*
weapon againft the enemie : yet if hee march forward, and *mies.*
fhew a couragious heart and earneft defire to ouercome, it will hereby plainly appeare that hee is faithfull to his Cap- taine, and therefore hee fhall receiue his pay, though at the firft onfet his lims fhould faint vnder him. And fo if through finne we haue our fpirituall man fo weakned,that he is ready to faint at the firft encounter with our fpirituall enemies, yet if we march vnder Chrifts ftanderd, and fight the battailes of the Lord of hoafts , hauing an earneft defire euen aboue our ftrength to ouercome our enemies , furely Chrift our grand Captaine will acknowledge vs for his fouldiers,and will giue vs our pay, euen a crowne of victorie : and feeing his power is omnipotent and his loue incomprehenfible, we may make fure account that if in the fight wee receiue a foile, hee will ftand ouer vs to defend vs with the fhield of his prouidence and raife vs vp againe; yea if we be taken prifoners and led a- way captiue by finne and Sathan, hee will refcue and deliuer vs. There is no difcredit accreweth to a fouldier by receiuing wounds,or by being by vnrefiftable violence taken prifoner; nay rather it argueth his valour, and fheweth that the inuin- cible courage of his minde doth farre furpaffe the weak force

K   of

of his bodie ; but rather hereby is a fouldier difgraced, if either he dare not march into the field,or being entred the battaile doth fhamefully flee away, or cowardly yeeld vnto the enemie : fo in this fpirituall warfare it is no difhonour to receiue foiles and wounds of our fpirituall enemies, for the moft valiant fouldiers that euer fought the Lords battailes, haue fuftained the like:nay if in the fight they be taken prifoners, yet fo they refift to the vttermoft of their power , and fhew an earneft defire to be out of the captiuitie of finne and Sathan,this is acceptable to their captaine Chrift,and he will in pitie and compaffion reftore them to libertie. But if rather than they would endure the danger of the fight,they profeffe themfelues friends to finne and Sathan;or if hauing profeffed themfelues Chrifts fouldiers , they at the firft encounter of their fpirituall enemies tempting them to any finne,doe forfake Chrifts ftanderd fhamefully, or cowardly yeeld to finne and Sathan,voluntarily liuing in their flauerie without defire of liberty : then either they fhew themfelues notable cowards, worthie to be caffered out of Gods campe ; or traiterous rebels, who though outwardly they made a profeffion that they were Chrifts fouldiers, yet in heart they defired to ferue Sathan.

§ *Sect.9.*   Here therefore is incouragement for the weake Chriftian, who is difcouraged and afhamed to looke his Redeemer Iefus Chrift in the face, becaufe of the manifold foiles which he receiueth in this fpirituall combat ; for howfoeuer before the fight of temptations he refolueth manfully to make refiftance and to ouercome,yet when the diuell ftrongly affaulteth, the world flattreth or frowneth, and the flefh trecheroufly betraieth him,fighting fecretly with whole legions of vnlawful lufts againft the fpirit,then is hee foiled and often taken captiue of finne : But let fuch to their comfort know,that if they continue their earneft defire of fighting ftill the Lords battailes,and ouercomming their fpirituall enemies,they are accepted of Iefus Chrift, and in the end hee will giue them ftrength to obtaine a finall victorie.

And that their manifold foyles and griefly wounds which they receiue of finne and Sathan may not difcourage them ;

let

let them confider that neuer any entred the battaile (our
chiefe captaine Chriſt excepted) but they haue beene ſub-
ieẛ to the like. *Adam* who was the ſtrongeſt champion
in his owne ſtrength that euer entered the liſts, was ouerthrowne at the firſt encounter, and taken captiue of ſinne: in
which bondage he ſhould euer haue remained, had not Chriſt
redeemed him. *Noah* was ouercome with drunkennes; and
Let added thereunto inceſt. *Dauid* a notable ſouldier in fighting the Lords battailes, was made a ſlaue to his owne luſts.
Peter a ſtout champion, ranne away and forſooke his maiſter. In a word there was neuer any that liued, who haue not
been foyled by Sathan, and wounded with ſinne. One perhaps receiueth more and deeper wounds, or is longer held
captiue in the chaines of ſinne than another; but none haue
eſcaped altogether. And thoſe who haue receiued the moſt
grieuous hurts, ſo they haue an earneſt deſire to haue thoſe
wounds healed which ſinne hath made in their conſciences,
to the end they may be enabled to renew the fight againſt
their ſpirituall enemies; may aſſure themſelues that Chriſt
the good Samaritane and their moſt carefull captaine, will
power the oyle of his grace and mercie, and the precious
balme of his blood into their woundes, which will as eaſily
cure them, though they be many and greiſly, as if they were
but few, and (as it were) but ſmall ſcratches.

And ſo much concerning the firſt conſolation which may
ſerue for the comforting and raiſing vp of thoſe who are
fallen. In the ſecond place wee are to conſider that Sathan
foyleth vs and cauſeth vs to fall into ſinne, not at his pleaſure
nor by his owne abſolute power, but becauſe the Lord hath
ſaid, thou ſhalt thus preuaile, for the further manifeſtation
of my glorie : for therefore the Lord doth leaue his children
ſometimes to themſelues, ſo that being aſſaulted by Sathan
they fall into ſinne, and bewray their infirmities and corruption; to the end he may ſhew hereby and declare the riches
of his power, mercie, and goodnes, which otherwiſe would
not ſo manifeſtly appeare. And this the Apoſtle plainly ſheweth, 2.Cor.12.8.9.10. where he ſaith that he beſought the
Lord thrice that he might be deliuered from the pricke in

*That Gods moſt
valiant ſouldi-
ars haue recei-
ued foyles.*

§. *Seẛ.*10.

*That Sathan
preuaileth a-
gainſt vs not by
his abſolute
power, but by
Gods permiſ-
ſion.*

2.Cor.12.8.9.

K 2   the

132

the flefh and the meffenger of Sathan, which did buffet him : but the Lord returned him this anfwere, my grace is fuffici-ent for thee, for my power is made perfect through weake-neffe; after which anfwere receiued, the Apoftle quieteth himfelfe, notwithftanding his infirmities, nay glorieth in them, rather than in his reuelations, as he profeffeth faying, Very gladly therefore will I reioyce rather in mine infirmi-ties, that the power of Chrift may dwell in me.

That the Lord fuffereth vs to fall for the ma-nifeftation of of his owne po-wer, mercy and goodneffe, and for our humi-liation. Though then our infirmities be great and our falles many, yet are we not to be altogether difcouraged thereby, feeing it is the will of God that we fhould thus bewray our infir-mities and corruptions, to the end his power mercie and goodneffe, may be made the more manifeft, and that both vnto our felues, and vnto others. For fuch is our fpirituall blindnes and fecret pride, that if we fhould alwaies alike withftand the temptations of Sathan, without receiuing any foyle, and neuer fall into any finne, we would be readie to thinke that we ftoode by our owne ftrength, and fo afcribe the praife of victorie to our felues, thereby robbing God of the honour due vnto him : and alfo for the time to come, we would rely vpon our felues rather than on the Lords affi-ftance; than the which nothing could bee more difhonora-ble vnto God, nor pernicious vnto our owne foules. But when as in the fpirituall combate of temptations, we fome-times ftand and fometimes fall, fometimes refift thofe affaults which are ftrong and violent, and another time faint and yeeld in the lighteft trials: this maketh it apparant that it is not our owne power, which in it felfe is not much vnlike at all times; but the power of God, which fuftaineth vs fome-times, that we may not be wholy difcouraged; and fome-times withdraweth it felfe, that we may by receiuing foyles learne to know our infirmities, and wholy to rely our felues on the Lords affiftance, returning all the praife of victorie to the Lord, who onely hath fuftained vs. As therefore our in-firmities in refpect of our felues, fhould ferue to abate our pride, and to worke in vs true humiliation and vtter defpare in our owne ftrength: fo in refpect that they fhew vnto vs the Lords power fupporting vs, they fhould the rather incou-

rage

rage vs to fight the fpirituall combate, with affured hope of victorie, feeing it is manifeft that we ftand not by our owne power, which like a broken ftaffe or crackt weapon would faile vs when we did moft truft and rely vpon it, but by the almightie power of God, againft which neither Sathan nor the gates of hell can any iot preuaile. And in this regarde wee may well reioyce in our infirmities with the Apoftle *Paul,* becaufe by reafon of them it more manifeftly appeareth that the power of Chrift dwelleth in vs, which is able to defend vs from Sathans malice and violent rage, not onely when we ftand manfully in the encounter, but alfo when we are foyled and put to the worft.

Yea in this refpect the more weake and full of infirmities the poore chriftian is, the more is the praife of Gods glorious might manifefted and magnified; for when Sathan, who is fo malitious puiffant and pollitike an enemie, hath long time affaulted a feely weake man or woman, and yet cannot wholy preuaile, but returneth away foyled and ouercome; it muft needes be confeffed that they are affifted and ftrengthened by fome fuperior power which farre excelleth Sathan in ftrength and pollicie : whereas it feemeth no fuch wonder when as the ftrong chriftian, who hath obtained a great meafure of knowledge, faith, and other graces, giueth Sathan the repulfe; neither are men fo readie to afcribe the praife of victorie to the Lord, becaufe his immediate power and helping hand doth not fo manifeftly appeare; although in truth their victorie alfo commeth wholy from him, for without his gifts and graces, they were as feeble and vnable to ftand as the weakeft; but yet the weaker and fmaller the meanes are, the more manifeft is the Lords power and wifedome, who hereby doth accomplifh things which are aboue the power of men and Angels. For example; the power and goodneffe of God appeareth great, when as he prouideth for vs foode conuenient, and giueth ftrength thereto to nourifh and fuftaine vs; and yet it is more manifeft, when as he fo ftrengtheneth vs by vertue of one meale that we neede no more in fortie daies, as he did *Elias;* but then it fhineth as it were in his full ftrength, when as he fuftaineth vs without

§. *Sect.* 11.
Gods power moft cleerely appeareth in our weakenes.

K 3　　　　　any

any foode at all, as he did *Mofes* and our Sauiour Chrift. So
it is made manifeft when as he giueth vs victorie ouer our
enemies, though there be fome equalitie in the numbers,
and other preparations, for it is he that *teacheth our hands to
warre and our fingers to fight :* but it is more euident when as
our number is fmall, as when he deliuered the Ifraelites by
Gedeon and his three hundred men, from an innumerable
armie;and ouercame the whole hoft of the Philiftimes,by the
weake meanes of *Ionathan* and his armour-bearer: but then
it is moft cleere and manifeft,when as he ouercommeth our
enemies by his owne immediate power,as he did the Ægyp-
tians in the red fea, and the hoft of *Senacherib* at the fiege of
Ierufalem. And fo when he giueth the ftrong chriftian who
is full of grace, victorie ouer Sathan, his power appeareth ;
for vnleffe he were ftrengthned with his graces, he could not
ftand: but when one who feemeth in his owne eyes deftitute
of grace, and full of finne and corruption(fo,that he plainely
feeth that he is altogether vnable to withftand the leaft affault) is notwithftanding fo fupported by Gods almightie
hand,and immediate power, that he doth not onely ftand in
the battaile, but in the end obtaineth victorie; hereby the
power and goodneffe of God moft cleerely appeares to
themfelues and all the world. Seeing then our finnes and
falles do fhew vnto vs our owne infirmities & weakenes,and
thefe doe declare Gods vnrefiftable power and might,which
notwithftanding our feebleneffe doth vphold vs : therefore
let vs fo defpaire in our felues, as that thereby we may be
mooued to rely wholy vpon the Lord, hauing fo much more
hope of victorie,as the ftrength of God excelleth the ftrength
of man ; let vs be fo humbled with a true fenfe, and forrow
for our owne infirmities and corruption,as that in the meane
time we may receiue more found confolation and true ioy,
becaufe we ftand not by our owne ftrength, which euery
hower would faile vs, but by the power of Gods might: and
therefore though Sathan and all the power of hell confpire
and bande themfelues againft vs, yet fhall they not preuaile;
and though they foyle vs, yet fhall they neuer finally ouercome; for he that is with vs is ftronger than all they who are
againft

Pfal.144.1.

againft vs;and the greater our weakneffe is,the fitter occafion
fhall the Lord haue of fhewing his omnipotent power in
giuing vs victorie.

But if hauing bewrayed thine infirmities, and gotten a
foyle in the fpirituall conflict, thou prefently be difcouraged
and defpaire of victorie, furely it is a manifeft figne that thou
diddeft truft too little in Gods affiftance, and too much in
thine owne ftrength, which becaufe it hath failed, thou haft
caft away all hope : and the greater thy horror and defpaire
is which followeth thy fall, the greater was thy felfe-confidence, and the leffe thy affiance in God. For he that altogether relieth vpon the Lords affiftance, and wholy diftrufteth
his owne ftrength, when he falleth in the time of temptation,
is not much aftonifhed with any great wonder,knowing that
through his owne infirmitie and weakenes, he is moft apt to
fall when God leaueth him to himfelfe ; neither is he vtterly
difcouraged and ouerwhelmed with defpaire,as though now
there were no meanes to ftand in the fpirituall combate, and
to obtaine victorie ; but hating and with a peaceable and
quiet forrow mourning for his finne,becaufe thereby he hath
difhonored his God,and offended his diuine maieftie,he doth
not abate his hope ; but with leffe confidence in himfelfe and
more confidence in God, he renewes the fight againft his
fpirituall enemies, with vndanted courage; knowing that the
Lord in whom he trufteth and wholy relieth will neuer faile
him. And therefore let vs no more reft in our felues, if euer
we would inioy the peace of confcience, or would haue any
affurance of the Lords affiftance ; for he will be all in all, neither can he abide any fharing in the glorie of the victorie:and
therefore fo long as we truft in our owne ftrength, and fight
with our owne forces, he will withdraw his helpe, till our often falles and foyles haue taught vs to know our owne infirmities and corruptions,that fo defpairing wholy in our owne
ftrength, we may peaceably reft wholy vpon his almightie
power,and promifed affiftance.

Laftly, let thofe who are truely humbled in regarde of
thofe foyles which they receiue in the fpirituall conflict,com-
fort themfelues by the experience of Gods loue, care, and

*Horror,feare
and defpaire,
following our
falles, argue
our diffidence
in God,and
felfe-confi-
dence.*

*§. Sect.12.
The laft confo-
lation,taken
from the ex-*

K 4   good-

goodneffe, both in others and in themfelues; for how many haue been caft downe as well as they, and yet haue in the end been raifed vp? how many haue forrowed and mourned, that now reioyce and haue receiued comfort? how many haue taken notable foyles and grieuous falles in the fpirituall conflict, and yet in the end haue obtained victorie? In a word, who hath depended vpon the Lord, and hath been reiected? who hath been truely humbled, and hath not been comforted? who hath fought againft their fpirituall enemies, and hath not by the Lords affiftance ouercome? And is the Lords arme now fhortned, or are his mercies come to an end? hath he forgotten to be gracious, or hath he fhut vp his louing kindnes in difpleafure? Nay rather fay it is thine owne infirmitie, for the Lord is the fame he was, without change or fhadow of change, and therefore as he hath comforted and ftrengthened and giuen victorie vnto others, fo will he comfort and ftrengthen and giue vnto thee a famous victorie ouer thy fpirituall enemies, if thou wilt depend vpon him and waite his leafure.

But if this will not comfort thee when thou heareft of Gods mercie and affiftance in fupporting others, yet at leaft let thine owne experience confirme thee in the affurance of Gods loue and fuccor: for, haft thou not indured many affaults of thy fpirituall enemies, and yet thou ftandeft in the incounter? but I pray thee by whofe ftrength? furely not thine owne, for thou art weake and feeble, and thine enemies ftrong and mightie, and therefore able to deftroy thee euery minute, if the Lord did not fupport thee by his almightie power. Haft thou not alfo receiued many foyles, and bewrayed notable corruptions, and yet thou art not quite ouerthrowne nor fwallowed vp by thy finnes? And who hath preferued thee? furely not thy felfe; for if thou canft not ftand againft Sathan whileft thou art fighting, much leffe couldeft thou rife vp againe when thou art caft downe; but it is the fpirit of the Lord who hath raifed thee vp by vnfained repentance, and hath renewed thy ftrength, fo that againe thou art readie to withftand and refift Sathan and his temptations. Why therefore fhouldeft thou feare leaft Sathan will in the end

end ouercome and destroy thee? why shouldest thou doubt
of the Lords assistance in the time to come, of which thou hast
had sufficient experience in times past? seeing himselfe is vnchangeable and his gifts without repentance, and therefore
those whom he hath defended he will defend, those that he
hath once raised vp, he will euer raise vp, and to whomsoeuer
he hath giuen grace to withstand their spirituall enemies,
to those he will continue and increase his grace, till
in the end they haue a finall victorie, and
the crowne of victorie, euerlasting glorie.

The end of the first booke.

THE SECOND BOOKE,

INTREATING OF SATHANS
ſpeciall and particular temptations, which he
ſuggeſteth againſt the ſeuerall cauſes of our ſaluation ; and of the anſwers whereby they
are to be refuted and repelled.

Chap. I.

*Anſweres to thoſe temptations of Sathan, whereby he perſwa-
deth carnall men of Gods loue.*

§. Sect.1.
*That Sathans
temptations
impugne all the
cauſes and
meanes of our
ſaluation.*

Nd ſo much concerning the common affections of the Chriſtian conflict, namely
his manfull withſtanding Sathans encounters, and alſo his fainting and falling
into ſinne. Now we are to ſpeake of the
ſpeciall temptations themſelues, and the
meanes whereby wee may be ſtrengthe-
ned againſt them. Where firſt wee are to conſider that Sathans temptations are not alwaies one and the ſame, neither
impugne one or two points onely of our faith and religion;
but as the cauſes and the meanes of our ſaluation are manifold, ſo alſo doth he gather manifold obiections againſt euerie one of them, if they truly appertaine vnto vs, that ſo hee
may impugne and race our faith; or els doth fill vs with vaine
preſumption, perſwading vs that all the cauſes and meanes
of ſaluation concurre together in vs, when as in truth wee are
voide and deſtitute of them all.

Let vs therefore conſider of the ſeuerall cauſes of our ſaluation, and obſerue what temptations Sathan ſuggeſteth in
our

our minds againſt euery one of them. The firſt and principall
cauſe of our ſaluation is Gods eternall loue and immutable
goodwill, wherewith he hath loued his creatures from before
the foundations of the world were laid; the which loue and
goodwill in himſelfe did moue him to elect them to ſaluation, whom he ſo loued without any deſerts in themſelues:
for how could they deſerue any thing at Gods hand before
they were? or what good could the Lord foreſee in them,
but that which in his eternall counſaile hee purpoſed to beſtow and impart vnto them?

Firſt therefore we will ſpeake of thoſe temptations which *Sathans temp-*
concerne the loue of God towards vs, which are of two ſorts; *tation whereby*
the firſt leading vs to vaine preſumption and carnall ſecuri- *he perſwadeth*
tie; the other, to horrour and deſperation. For if Sathan ſee *carnall men*
men liuing in carnall ſecuritie, frozen in the dregges of their *beloued of God.*
ſinnes, ſo as in truth there is no ſigne that they are beloued
of God; he will perſwade them that they are highly in his fauour and loue, and therefore though they runne on in their
wicked courſes, yet they ſhall be ſaued. Doeſt thou not perceiue (will he ſay) that God dearely loueth thee? Why, conſider that hee hath made thee one of his chiefeſt creatures,
whereas otherwiſe hee would haue made thee a toade or ſerpent; he hath alſo like a tender father preſerued and nouri-
ſhed thee from thy infancie, and which is more, he hath ſent
his dearely beloued ſonne to die for thee, and hee hath made
choiſe of thee amongſt many others to be a member of his
Church, where thou inioyeſt the preaching of the Goſpell,
and the vſe of the Sacraments, to the end thou maiſt be aſſured of thy ſaluation without all queſtion or doubting. Neuer
therefore take care nor trouble thy ſelfe concerning thy ſaluation, vſe not ſuch ſtrictnes and preciſenes of life, but take
thy pleaſure, and follow thoſe delights which the Lord hath
beſtowed vpon thee as pledges of his loue; for thou art not
now a ſlaue but a ſonne, and therefore maiſt more freely follow thine owne deſire, and vſe thy libertie: caſt away all ſeruile feare, which maketh thee take ſuch paines in vſing all
meanes whereby thou maiſt be aſſured of ſaluation; for thou
art aſſured of the principall, namely of Gods loue, and therefore

fore thou needest not to doubt of the rest, nor to debarre thy selfe of thy pleasures, spending thy time in feare and care, to the end thou maist get the assurance of that which thou needest not to call into question.

And thus doth the diuell fill men with presumption, and lull them asleepe in carnal securitie to their vtter destruction; and therefore it behooueth vs to arme our selues against him, that we be not circumuented. And to this end let vs consider that Gods loue goeth not alone, neither is it idle in those whom he loueth:but as the first linke of a chaine draweth all the rest of the chaine with it, so the loue of God, which is the first cause of our saluation, is accompanied with all the other causes which are subordinate thereunto ; for whom God loueth, them he electeth ; whom he electeth, those in his good time he calleth ; whom hee effectually calleth, them he iusti-fieth ; and whom he iustifieth, those hee sanctifierh : if therefore we be not sanctified, we are not iustified; if wee are not iustified, we are not called ; if we are not called, we can haue no assurance that wee are elected, nor yet of Gods loue and fauour ; and consequently whosoeuer liue in their blind ig-norance,in their infidelitie,and wallow themselues in the fil-thie puddle of their sinnes,without any true sorrow for those which are past,or any good purpose of heart to forsake them in the time to come ; they can haue no assurance of Gods loue,but are rather iustly to feare least they are in the number of those whom the Lord hath eternally reiected,if they con-tinue in this their miserable and desperate estate.

Neither let Sathan bewitch them with that vaine opinion of Gods loue towards them,becaufe of those generall bene-fits,which like the raine and Sunne-shine are bestowed both vpon the good and bad ; for what in this respect can they promise more to themselues than *Esau*, and *Saul?* Were not they created men according to Gods own likenes? were they not preserued and nourished by God,and that more liberal-ly than many of Gods owne children ? For *Esau* had so much that he professed to his brother *Iacob* that he had enough, and was attended vpon by foure hundred men. And was not *Saul* a mightie King,who had all at commaund ? Were not all these

theſe in the Church of God, and outwardly enioyed the word and Sacraments as well as any other; and yet God himſelfe ſaith that he hated *Eſau*, and had reiected *Saul*. And therefore let vs neuer bragge of our aſſurance of Gods loue, becauſe of theſe outward and common benefits which he indifferently beſtoweth both vpon the elect and reprobate; but if we would be aſſured indeed of Gods loue, let vs looke into our ſelues, and conſider if he haue beſtowed vpon vs his ſpirituall graces, faith, hope, patience, loue of him and our brethren, true repentance for our ſinnes, and holineſſe of life and the reſt; and then by the fruites of ſanctification we may be aſſured that we are ſanctified, and conſequently iuſtified, called, elected, and eternally loued of God.

And thus doth Sathan falſely perſwade the carnall man that he is highly in the loue and fauour of God: but contrariwiſe when he aſſaulteth the weake Chriſtian, hee changeth his copie, and goeth about to perſwade him that he is not beloued of God, but ſubiect to his wrath and heauie diſpleaſure. And this he inforceth by two ſorts of arguments: the one drawne from his manifold corruptions, whereby hee is vnworthie of Gods loue; the other from thoſe grieuous afflictions and croſſes which the Lord in this life inflicteth on him; both which he thus vrgeth againſt him. Canſt thou vild wretch conceiue the leaſt hope that thou art beloued of God? Why, doe but take a view of thy ſelfe, and thou ſhalt ſee that originall corruption hath ouerſpread both thy bodie and ſoule like a filthy leproſie; vnto which thou haſt added actuall tranſgreſſions more in number than the haires of thy head, or the ſtarres of heauen; for daily, nay hourely thou omitteſt ſome dutie which thy God hath commanded thee, and committeſt ſome ſinne which hee hath forbidden. Can therefore the Lord, who abhorreth wickedneſſe, loue the wicked? canſt thou obtaine his fauour, and yet doeſt nothing but diſpleaſe him? He that loueth God keepeth his commandements; but thou by tranſgreſſing them all, doeſt ſhew that thou loueſt him not: and will the Lord loue them who hate and rebell againſt him? Can iuſtice it ſelfe loue wickednes, and perfect holineſſe impure corruption? No verely; for in his word hee

§. *Sect. 3.*
How Sathan perſwadeth weake chriſtians that they are not beloued of God.

hath

hath threatned his wrath againſt all ſuch notorious ſinners, and hee is no leſſe true in his threatnings than in his pro-miſes.

But if all this will not perſwade thee that the Lord abhor-reth thee, yet at leaſt bee perſwaded by thine owne expe-rienc. For, hath not thy iuſt God begunne already to make thee taſte the cuppe of his wrath, of which hereafter thou ſhalt drinke in full meaſure; hath hee not ſpoyled thee of thy goods, taken away thy good name, made thee an abieƈt a-mongſt men, afflicted thee in body with grieuous and conti-nuall ſickneſſe, and filled thy ſoule full of horror and de-ſpayre? Is not thy conſcience ſtung with ſinne, and hath not the poyſon thereof drunke vp thy ſpirit? Doeſt thou not plainely apprehend his wrath, and is not thy ſoule as it were ſet vpon the racke, ſo that there is not one part of thee, either of body and ſoule which is not full of miſery and wretchedneſſe? Doe not therefore fondly flatter thy ſelfe with a vaine opinion of Gods loue, but beleeue, if not my words, yet at leaſt thine owne ſenſes; and ſeeing thou haſt no hope of Gods loue, if thou beeſt wiſe loue thy ſelfe, follow thy pleaſures, eate and drinke and cheere vp thine heart, and doe not vainely macerate and turmoyle thy ſelfe in labou-ring after impoſſibilities, and in ſtriuing for the aſſurance of Gods loue, of which, when thou haſt done what thou canſt, yet ſhalt thou neuer be aſſured.

§. *Sect.*4.
*How we may
anſwere the
former temp-
tation.*

And thus you ſee the manner of Sathans temptations, whereby he laboureth to perſwade vs that we are out of the loue and fauour of God; againſt which we muſt moſt care-fully arme our ſelues, as being moſt odious and iniurious vnto God, and moſt pernicious vnto our owne ſoules. It is moſt iniurious vnto God, if we doubt of his loue towards vs, ſeeing he hath giuen vs innumerable pledges and moſt cer-taine teſtimonies thereof, and omitted nothing which might doe vs good. He hath created vs after his owne image, he hath continually preſerued and ſuſtained vs, giuing vs our meate in due ſeaſon, and oft times hath ſuccoured and de-fended vs before we craued his helpe; but which is more, he hath giuen his dearely beloued ſonne to dye a bitter death,

to

to redeeme vs out of the hands of our spirituall enemies:
and to the end we should be made partakers of Christ and
all his benefits, he hath giuen vs his word, and made his couenant with vs, that in Christ he will be our God, and we his
people, he our father, and we his children: And least yet there
should be any place left to doubting, he hath added to his
word, his sacraments, which like seales may assure vs of his
loue and fauour. What iniurie therefore shall we offer vnto
God, if notwithstanding all this we doubt of his good will,
of which he hath assured vs by so many pledges, testimonies
and seales? We know that a kinde friend will take it most
vnkindely, if after he hath heaped vpon a man innumerable
benefits, and shewed all testimonies of true loue, hee notwithstanding doubt of his good will, and suspect his friendship: and so surely the Lord will take it ill at our hands, and
thinke himselfe much abused, if after he hath bestowed such
infinite benefits, euen his dearely beloued sonne to dye for
vs, we now suspect his good will, and growe iealous of his
loue; if we doubt of his loue, who is loue it selfe, as the Apostle speaketh, 1.Iohn 4.8.

But against this which I haue said, there are two obiections, **§. Sect.5.**
the first is made by the worldling, the other by Sathan. The *That carnall*
worldly man will say, that the Lord hath made him also par- *men haue no*
taker of all these benefits, and therefore there is no cause why *assurance of*
he should doubt of his loue; nor any reason why he should *Gods loue*
be censured or condemned for his faith. I answere, that he is *though they*
not reprehended for his perswasion of Gods loue, nor for *boast thereof.*
his assurance of Gods promises in Christ; but for his boasting
of this faith, perswasion, and assurance, whereas there is nothing in him in truth but a dead carcase of faith, carnall secu-
rity, and vaine presumption. For true faith purifieth the heart,
Acts 15.9. and worketh by loue, Gal. 5. 6. it is plentifull in
good workes, and prouoketh vs to performe all good duties
to God and our neighbours : and it is impossible that wee
should be truely perswaded of Gods loue, and not loue him
againe : it cannot be that we loue God, if we shew no care in
glorifying his name, by letting our lights shine before men,
nor any desire to performe obedience to his will. For as our
Sauiour

Sauiour ſaith, *He that loueth me keepeth my Commaundements,
and he that loueth me not, keepeth not my words,* as it is Iohn 14.
23,24. If therefore we liue in our ſinnes without repentance,
if we make no conſcience of our waies,and ſhew no zeale in
glorifying Gods name ; if our faith be deſtitute of the fruites
of good workes, then is our perſwaſion but fond preſumption;our aſſurance, carnall ſecuritie; our faith dead, and like
a carcaſe which breatheth not,as *Iames* ſpeaketh, chap.2.26.
Wee doe not then reprehend any for being perſwaded of
Gods loue, gathering his aſſurance out of Gods manifolde
mercies,and innumerable benefits beſtowed on his Church :
nay, contrariwiſe wee affirme that notwithſtanding all our
ſinnes and vnworthineſſe, we are to be perſwaded of Gods
loue in Chriſt, yea, and to beleeue againſt beleefe, and to
hope againſt hope, when as there is no ground or reaſon of
either in our ſelues: but this we maintaine, that whoſoeuer
hath this aſſurance and faith, in the leaſt meaſure begunne in
him,doth truly loue God againe, and earneſtly laboureth after mortification and newneſſe of life; and whoſoeuer is deſtitute of Gods loue, and liueth in his ſinnes, without any
ſorrowe for thoſe which are paſt, or purpoſe to leaue them
for the time to come,he may well brag of his faith and aſſurance of Gods loue, but in very trueth there is as yet nothing in him but carnall ſecuritie and vaine preſumption.

§. Sect.6.
*That euery
particular
Chriſtian may
aſſure himſelfe
of Gods loue.*

Secondly, the tempter will obiect that the Lord hath giuen all theſe teſtimonies and pledges of his loue vnto his
Church, and that it therefore may well be aſſured thereof;
but as for particular men, they notwithſtanding may iuſtly
doubt of his loue, ſeeing they haue no ſpeciall reaſons to
perſwade them that theſe teſtimonies and pledges were giuen vnto them. But I anſwere that this is a fond obiection.
For what is the Church, but the whole company of Gods
ſaints ? What is it but a body conſiſting of many members,
which are particular chriſtians ? how therefore can the
whole Church be perſwaded of Gods loue,if all the ſeuerall
members doubt thereof? How can any thing belong to the
whole, which belongeth not to the particular parts ? as
though a whole citie could be aſſured of the Princes fauour,
and

and yet all the particular men in the citie ſhould thinke
themſelues in his diſpleaſure. Saint *Paul* teacheth vs another leſſon in his owne perſon, ſaying; Gal.2.20. *Who hath* Gal.2.20.
loued me and giuen his life for me : he ſaith not,who hath loued
and giuen his life for the Church, but for himſelfe. Neither
doth the Apoſtle here ſpeake this by reuelation, whereby he
might extraordinarily be aſſured of Gods loue: but he vſeth
for his argument a reaſon common to all Chriſtians ; namely, that God loued him, becauſe hee had giuen himſelfe to
death for him : whoſoeuer therefore beleeueth with *Paul*
that Chriſt dyed for him, may bee aſſured alſo with him of
Gods loue.

Secondly, if we doe not beleeue that God loueth vs,wee §. *Sect.7.*
make him a lyar, for he hath profeſſed his loue, and giuen vs *That doubting*
many teſtimonies thereof in his word, neither doth he re- *of Gods loue, is*
quire any condition at our hands but that we beleeue him. *iniurious vnto*
For his mercifull promiſes doe not exclude any for their vn- *him.*
worthineſſe,but for their vnbeleefe : according to that, Iohn
3.16. *So God loued the world, that hee gaue his onely begotten* Ioh.3.16.
ſonne, that whoſoeuer beleeueth in him,ſhould not periſh,but haue
euerlaſting life. Seeing then there is no other condition required but faith,for the aſſurance of Gods loue. and euerlaſting life; ſurely moſt deſperately doe we ſinne againſt our
owne ſoules,and moſt blaſphemouſly againſt God,if we will
not beleeue his word confirmed by his ſeale,no not his oath
whereby he hath ratified his couenant betweene him and vs,
but make him,who is truth it ſelfe, a liar,a couenant breaker,
yea, a periured perſon. For ſo the Apoſtle ſpeaketh, 1.Iohn
5.10. *He that beleeueth not God, hath made him a lyar, becauſe* 1.Ioh.5.10
hee beleeued not the record, that God witneſſed of his Sonne.
Though therefore we ſinne, yet let vs not thus blaſpheme ;
though we be grieuous ſinners, and vnworthy Gods loue,
yet let vs not adde this to all our other ſinnes and vnworthineſſe, to diſtruſt Gods trueth in his gracious promiſes : for
if we put all our other ſinnes into the one ſcole, and this a-
lone into the other, yet will it weigh downe all the reſt; neither are we damned for our other ſinnes, if we doe not adde
vnto them infidelitie. For whereas the precious baulme of
                           L   our

our Sauiours blood is a soueraigne salue to cure all other sores of sinne ; yet this it cannot helpe, because it doth refuse the cure, and as it were pulleth off this precious plaister when it is laid on it.

But as this distrusting and doubting of Gods loue is iniurious vnto him, so also it is pernitious vnto our owne soules. For first, it tormenteth our mindes, and setteth our consciences vpon the racke, when as we haue no other assurance of Gods loue, but onely so farre foorth as we finde our selues worthy of it : for so often as wee fall, and the sight of our sinnes commeth before our eyes, hauing no other ground of Gods loue but our owne deserts, wee doubt and stagger like a ship tossed with the billowes of the sea, and in the end sinke into the gulfe of despaire, being ouer balanced and too heauily laden with the vnsupportable waight of our sinnes; whereas if we were throughly perswaded of Gods free loue and goodwill, grounded on his owne good pleasure, and not on our worthinesse, if we did fall we would be grieued in deede euen at the very heart, because wee had displeased our gracious God and louing Father; but yet our sinnes would not make vs despaire or doubt of his loue towards vs, because it hath not it ground on our worthinesse, but vpon Gods owne free mercie, grace, and goodwill.

Secondly, if we doubt and distrust of Gods loue towards vs, we shall neuer loue him from our hearts : for who loueth him intirely, of whose loue he is not perswaded? or who can performe the dueties of loue to such an one as hateth and abhorreth him? *Cos amoris amor,* Loue is the whetstone of loue. And if this be true amongst men, then much more be-

tweene God and vs : for *we loue him because he loued vs first,* as the Apostle sayth, 1.Ioh.4.19. As therefore the cold stone can of it selfe cast foorth no heate, till it be first warmed by the Sunne beames, and then it reflectsth againe some of the heate which it receiued : so no more can our cold hearts cast any beames of hearty loue towards God, till they be warmed with the apprehension of his loue towards vs, and then they begin to returne some sparkes of loue towards God, after they are inflamed with the beames of his loue cleerely

shining

ſhining in them. Vnleſſe therefore wee be aſſured of Gods Rom. 13.8.
loue we cannot loue him, and conſequently cannot performe any duetie of loue in obedience to his will: for as loue
is the fulfilling of the Law, as it is, Rom.13.8. ſo the want
of loue is the tranſgreſſing of all the commandements : for
all conſiſt in the loue of God, which is the fountaine of all
true obedience; and in the loue of our neighbour, which as
a ſpring iſſueth from it. Nay, when we diſpaire of Gods loue,
then doe we deſpaire of our ſaluation, and therefore hauing
no hope of happineſſe in the life to come, wee are ready to
ſeeke al the pleaſures and delights which this life wil affoord
vnto vs, giuing our ſelues ouer to the ſatisfying of all the filthy luſts of the fleſh, and ſpending our times in all Epicuriſme and ſenſuality.

Laſtly, our doubting and diſtruſting of Gods loue doeth §. Sect.9.
ouerthrow our patience in the time of affliction, and cauſeth *The manifold*
vs to murmure and repine againſt God, blaſpheming him to *euils which ac-*
his face; it hindereth all Chriſtian reſolution in ſuffering any *companie, our*
thing for the Name of Chriſt; for how ſhould we ſuffer any *doubting of*
thing patiently for his ſake of whoſe loue we are not aſſured? *Gods loue, and*
It maketh the day of death horrible, when as we are not per- *which follow*
ſwaded that we ſhall render vp our ſoules into the hands of *our perſwaſion*
a gracious father, but into the hands of a ſeuere iudge: where- *thereof.*
as on the other ſide, when we are throughly perſwaded of
Gods loue, then may we patiently, yea, ioyfully ſuffer all afflictions, becauſe wee know that they are but gentle trials,
and fatherly chaſtiſements, which our gracious God doth inflict on vs for our euerlaſting good : when we are perſecuted
for our profeſſion of the Goſpel, we will triumph with ioy,
becauſe we are thought worthy to ſuffer any miſerie for the
Name of Chriſt, who hath laid downe his life for our ſake : Act.5.14.
when the day of our departing approacheth we reioice, becauſe we deſire nothing more than to be diſſolued, and to be Phil.1.23.
with Chriſt, who ſo tenderly loueth vs. In a word, come proſperitie, come aduerſitie, come affliction, come perſecution,
come fire, come ſword, come life, come death, nothing can
come amiſſe, nothing can diſmay or diſcourage vs, if wee be
once fully aſſured of Gods loue in Chriſt, both becauſe our

loue

loue of God, which by his loue is wrought in vs, will make
the heauiest and most tedious burthen seeme light and momentanie, which it shall please our heauenly father to lay vpon vs: and also because *we know that all things* (euen miseries,
afflictions, persecutions, yea death it selfe) *worke together for
the best vnto them that loue God.* As it is Rom.8.28.

Rom.8,28.

CHAP. II.

*That our sinnes and vnworthinesse should not make vs doubt
of Gods loue.*

§. *Sect.1.*

Eeing therefore that our doubting and distrusting of Gods loue towards vs, is both iniurious
vnto God and pernicious vnto our selues; let
vs in no case admit of Sathans temptations
whereby he laboureth to perswade vs that the
Lord hateth vs. But forasmuch as there is no perswasiō without knowledge and faith, neither can we know and beleeue
that we are in Gods fauour, vnlesse we haue some ground and
warrant out of Gods word, whereupon we may cast our wauering mindes, and confirme our fainting faith against the
boysterous blasts of Sathans temptations : therefore let vs
examine Sathans reasons, whereby he goeth about to perswade vs that we are not beloued of God, by the touchstone
of Gods word; and waigh his obiections in the scoles of
the sanctuarie, to see if they be of any waight or substance, or
els but frauthie, light, and of no sound consequence.

*Answere to
Sathans temp-
ta·ions groun-
ded vpon our
vnworthines.*

First therefore whereas Sathan obiecteth that we are miserable sinners, vnworthie altogether of Gods loue, and most
worthie of his wrath and heauie displeasure; that God is infinitly iust, and therefore cannot nor will not loue vs being
notoriously wicked : we are to answere, that indeede we are
in our selues vnworthie the least dram of Gods loue, by reason of our originall corruption, and actuall transgression;
and therefore if our assurance of Gods fauour, had no other
foundation but our owne deserts, we had great reason not
onely to doubt, but also vtterly to despaire of Gods loue
towards

towards vs. But the loue of God is not grounded vpon our Gods loue not grounded on our worthines. worthines which is nothing, but vpon his owne good will and pleasure,which is infinit as himselfe is infinit; and therefore though in our selues we are most miserable and wretched,yet this is no reason why we should distrust or in the least degree doubt of Gods loue, seeing it ariseth not from any thing in vs,but from himselfe who is vnchangeable.

The truth hereof manifestly appeareth by the scriptures, where it is said that the Lord hath loued vs not for our excellencie and worthinesse,but of his free grace and louing kindnesse. So Hof.14.5. *I will heale their rebellion ; I will loue them* Hof.14.5. *freely,&c.* And the Apostle *Iohn* telleth vs that herein Gods loue appeareth,in that when we loued not him, he so deerely 1.Ioh.4.10. loued vs, that he sent his sonne to be a reconciliation for our sinnes; 1.Ioh.4.10. And *Paul* saith, that hereby *God setteth* Rom.5.8.10. *out his loue towards vs,seeing that whilest we were yet sinners, Christ died for vs, and when we were enemies God reconciled vs vnto himselfe by the death of his sonne.* Rom.5.8.10. If therefore the Lord loued vs when we were enemies vnto him and dead in our sinnes ; how much more will he loue vs now being reconciled in Christ, and in some measure purged from our corruption, and quickned by his spirit to newnesse of life ? If when we were most vnworthie, he freely shewed such exceeding fauour towards vs : how much more hauing by his spirit and the graces thereof made vs more worthie, will he continue his loue vnto vs ? If he hath hetherto loued vs not for any deserts of ours, but of his free mercie, because he is loue it selfe, as *Iohn* calleth him, 1.Ioh.4.8. and the God 1.Ioh.4.8. of grace, as *Peter* maketh him, 1.Pet.5.10: why should we 1.Pet.5.10. doubt of Gods loue in respect of our vnworthinesse, seeing his loue hath not his ground vpon our worthinesse, but vpon his owne nature which is immutable, and therefore whom he once loueth,he loueth them vnto the end,though in themselues they are miserable and wretched.Ioh.13.1. Ioh.13.1.

But as the Scriptures shew that God hath loued vs freely §. Sect.2. from all eternitie; so also doe they as plainely declare, that God hath manifested this loue in the worke of our saluation freely,and without any respect of our worthines : as may appeare

peare

Gods election
not grounded
on our works
and worthines.
Rom.11.5,6.

peare in the seuerall causes thereof. As first he hath elected vs of his owne free loue and good will, and not for any of our deserts; and therefore it is called the election not of vertue and works but of grace. Rom.11.5. Nay it is flatly opposed to workes in the verse following. *And if* (saith the Apostle)*it be of grace it is no more of works, or els were grace no more grace: but if it be of works it is no more grace, or els were worke no more worke.* So that our election is not grounded vpon our worthinesse,but on Gods grace and goodwill : and therefore it cannot be ouerthrowne by our vnworthinesse, so we wholy rely vpon Gods free mercie in Christ.

Our worthi-
nesse is not
the condition
of Gods coue-
nant.

Secondly the couenant betweene God and vs, wherein he professeth himselfe our God, and taketh vs for his people and heires of his promises , is not the couenant of workes, but the couenant of grace : in which hee offereth freely in Christ,his grace and mercy to all who will receiue it,by the hand of a liuely faith. And this the Lord himselfe expresseth Ierem.31.31. *Beholde the dayes come saith the Lord, that I will make a new couenant with the house of Israel* (that is, my Church.) 32. *Not according to the couenant which I made with their fathers* (that is, the couenant of workes) *the which my couenant they breake,&c. but this shall be my couenant that I will make with the house of Israel, after those daies saith the Lord; I will put my law in their inward parts, and write it in their hearts, and will be their God,and they shall be my people.* So the Apostle *Paul* saith,that the promise made to *Abraham* and his seede, *was not giuen through the lawe, but through the righteousnesse of faith,*Rom.4.13. *and that it was therefore by faith that it might come by grace, and the promise might be sure to all the seede.* For if the couenant were of workes and not of faith, of deserts and not of grace,we should continually disanull and make it of no effect

Ierem.31.31.

Rom.4.13.

§.Sect.3.
Our redempti-
on not caused
by our worthi-
nesse.
Eph.1.7,8.

Thirdly, as we are elected before all times, so were we in time redeemed freely,and without respect of our owne worthinesse,of the meere mercy and loue of God; although our Sauiour Christ payed the full price of our redemption vnto God his father for vs : and this appeareth,Ephes.1.7. *By whom we haue redemption through his blood, euen the forgiuenesse of* sinnes;

sinnes, according to his rich grace. 8. *Whereby he hath been abun-*
dant towards vs in all wisedome and vnderstanding. So that our
redemption was not free vnto our Sauiour Christ, for it cost
him the inestimable price of his most precious bloud; but it
was free vnto vs, without any respect of our workes and worthinesse. For we were like desperate debters, deeply ingaged
vnto God, and not able to pay the least farthing; and therefore were cast into the prison of euerlasting death, there to be
detained till we had discharged the whole debt: which being
impossible vnto vs, it pleased our Sauiour Christ of his meere
pitie and free goodwill to become our suretie, and to make
full satisfaction to his father, euen to the least mite, that so
we might be released and set free. We were all of vs miserable
captiues, held in the thraldome of sinne, Sathan and death,
vnable to deserue in any measure to be set at libertie; for wee
were the children of wrath, who were not sick only, but euen
dead in our sinnes, as it is Eph.2.1.5. But our Sauiour Christ of   Eph.2.1.5.
his vndeserued loue did pay the price of our redemption, and
set vs out of our captiuitie, quickning and raising vs vp from
sinne to newnesse of life; as the Apostle setteth it downe Eph.
2.3. *And you were by nature the children of wrath as well as o-*   Eph.2.3.4
thers. 4. But God which is rich in mercie, through his great loue
wherewith he loued vs, 5. Euen when we were dead by sinnes, hath
quickened vs together in Christ, by whose grace ye are saued,
6. And hath raised vs vp together in heauenly places in Christ Ie-
sus. 7. That he might shew in ages to come the exceeding riches
of his grace, through his kindnesse towards vs in Christ Iesus. So
that there is no worthinesse in our selues which the Lord respected, for we were all alike the children of wrath, and dead
in our sinnes; but onely of his free mercie and great loue, he
hath redeemed vs by Christ.

    Fourthly, as the Lord hath freely redeemed vs, so also hee   §. Sect.4.
hath freely called vs to the knowledge of the mysterie of our   *Our worthines*
redemption wrought by Iesus Christ, and chosen vs amongst   *no cause of our*
all nations to be his Church and peculiar people, and that of   *calling.*
his meere grace and free goodwill, without any respect of
our worthines, as appeareth 2.Tim.1.9. *Who hath saued vs, and*   2.Tim.1.9.
called vs with an holy calling, not according to our workes, but ac-
                          L 4   *cording*

cording to his owne purpose of grace which was giuen vs through
Christ Iesus before the world was. So *Moses* telleth the children of Israel, that the Lord had called and made choise of
them aboue all other nations to bee his Church and people,
not for any respect of themselues, or their owne worthinesse,
but of his free loue and vndeserued mercie, as it is Deut.7.7.8.
Psal.44.3.

Our works and worthinesse no causes of our iustification. Fiftly, as the Lord hath freely called vs, so being called he
hath freely iustified vs: not for any inherent righteousnesse in
our selues, but of his owne grace and goodwill, through the
righteousnesse and obedience of Iesus Christ which he imputeth vnto vs. And this is euident Rom.3.24. where it is said,
that *we are iustified freely by Gods grace, through the redemption
which is in Christ Iesus.* And Tit.3.7. where the Apostle saith,
that we are iustified by his grace. And least wee should ioyne
with Gods grace our owne workes and worthines, he telleth
vs that *Abraham* himselfe, though a most righteous and holy
man in respect of his sinceritie and integritie of heart, was
notwithstanding not iustified by his workes, *but Abraham
beleeued God, and that was imputed vnto him for righteousnesse,*
Rom.4.3 : & ver.5. he flatly excludeth works from being any
causes of our iustification ; *To him* (saith he) *that worketh not,
but beleeueth in him that iustifieth the vngodly, his faith is counted for righteousnesse.* So that wee are freely iustified of Gods
grace and goodwill, without any respect of our owne works
and worthinesse, as being any causes of our iustification, although they are necessarie and inseparable fruites thereof.
For the same death and bloudshed of Christ, whereby we are
freed from the guilt and punishment of sinne and euerlasting
death, doth free vs also from the death of sin to newnesse of
life, and doth not onely iustifie but also sanctifie vs, as the A-
postle plainly sheweth, Tit.2.14. *Who gaue himselfe for vs, that
he might redeeme vs from all iniquitie,* (that is, free vs from the
guilt and punishment of sinne to which we were subiect) *and
purge vs to be a peculiar people vnto himselfe, zealous of good
workes.*

Sixtly, our sanctification and inherent righteousnesse it
selfe, what is it els but the free gift of God, begun, increased,

and

Margin notes:
Deut.7.7.8.
Rom.3.24.
Tit.3.7.
Rom.4.3.5.
Tit.2.14.

and finished by his gracious spirit? what are the graces in vs
but Gods free and vndeserued gifts? what are our best works
but the fruites of his spirit working in vs? for by nature wee
are dead in our sinnes, and the children of wrath as well as
the vnbeleeuing heathen or most prophane worldling, Eph. Eph. 2. 1. 3.
2. 1. 3. By nature we are not able so much as to thinke a good
thought, or to will that which is good, no more than those
who remaine in the state of condemnation, as appeareth
2. Cor. 3. 5. Phil. 2. 13. but it is our Sauiour Christ, *who so loued* 2. Cor. 3. 5.
his Church, that he gaue himselfe for it, that he might sanctifie it Phil.. 2. 13.
and cleanse it, by the washing of water through the word, &c. as it Eph. 5. 25. 26.
is Eph. 5. 25. 26. So that when we haue attained to the highest
measure of sanctification that wee can possibly attaine vnto,
we must in all humilitie confesse with *Paul*, that by the grace 1. Cor. 15. 10.
of God we are that we are, as it is 1. Cor. 15. 10. Neither must
wee attribute any thing in the worke of our saluation, vnto
our sanctification and good workes, but ascribe all to the free
grace and vndeserued loue of God in Christ, whereby we are
sanctified and stirred vp to new obedience, who were altogether polluted, yea dead in our sinnes; so that our sanctification and worthinesse is not the cause of Gods loue and mercie towards vs, but his loue and free goodwill is the cause of
our sanctification, and maketh vs, who were vnworthie in our
selues, worthie in Christ of his loue and fauour. And therefore
we must not measure Gods loue by our worthines and abundance of grace as being a cause thereof; nor despaire of his
fauour and mercie, when wee see our vnworthines and weaknes in sanctifying graces; for these are no causes of his loue
but effects, and consequently when wee want them altogether, though there be no cause of hope whilest we remaine in
this state, yet wee are not vtterly to despaire for the time to
come, seeing the Lord in his good time may begin his good
worke in vs; and when it is begun, and we haue receiued the
least measure of sanctification, euen a desire and holie endeuour to liue in holinesse and righteousnesse, wee may be assured that it is Gods worke, which he hauing begun will finish
and accomplish, according to that Phil. 1. 6. In the meane Phil. 1. 6.
time let vs possesse our soules with patience, and with a quiet

and.

and peaceable minde labour after the increase of grace, vsing
all good meanes ordained of God for this purpose, submitting our selues, in regard of the measure of grace which wee
doe desire, to his good will and pleasure, who will dispose of
all so, as shall be most for his glory and our good. And in any
case let vs beware that wee doe not so impatiently and violently desire encrease of more grace, as that in the meane
time we forget to be thankfull to God for that wee haue, turning our songs of praise for Gods great benefits, into murmuring and repining. Let vs not be like vnto rich misers, who
haue their mindes so intent vpon the getting of that riches
they haue not, as that they forget to enioy and take comfort
of that they haue ; let vs not resemble those vnthankful men,
who when they haue receiued many benefits, doe still desire
more, and when their desires are not presently satisfied, vngratefully murmure against their benefactors, as though they
had receiued nothing : but let vs make vse of those graces
which we haue receiued, to Gods glory & our comfort; let vs
desire more, ÿ we may more glorifie him with his own gifts;
and though our desires be not presently satisfied, let vs not
fall into impatiencie, but submit our selues vnto his goodwill
and pleasure, and be truly thankfull for that portion of grace,
which it hath pleased him of his abundant mercie to bestow
vpon vs.

§ *Sect.6.*
*Our owne wor-
thinesse no
cause of our
saluation.*
Rom.6.23.
Eph.2.8.
Tit.2.11.

Lastly, our saluation it selfe dependeth not vpon our owne
worthinesse, but vpon Gods free mercy and vndeserued loue;
for saluation is the free gift of God, and not the wages of our
owne worthinesse, as death is the wages of sinne, as appeareth Rom.6.23. And *wee are saued by grace through faith, and
that not of our selues ; it is the gift of God*, as it is Eph.2.8. And
the Apostle telleth vs, Tit.2.11. that *the grace of God bringeth
saluation, and teacheth vs to denie vngodlinesse and worldly lusts,
and that wee should liue soberly and righteously and godly in this
present world* : so that our forsaking sinne and imbracing holinesse and righteousnesse is not the cause of our saluation,
but the grace of God, by which all these effects are also
wrought in vs. But most plaine is that of the Apostle 2.Tim.

2.Tim 1.9. 1.9. where he excludeth our owne workes and worthinesse, to
the

the end he might afcribe the whole worke of our faluation to Gods grace and goodwill. *Who hath faued vs* (faith he) *not according to our workes, but according to his own purpose and grace.* So Tit.3.5. *Not by the works of righteousnesse which we had done,* Tit.3.5. *but according to his mercie he faued vs, by the washing of the new birth, and renuing of the holy Ghost.*

Seeing therefore Gods loue is not grounded vpon our owne worthinesse, seeing he electeth, redeemeth, calleth, iustifieth, sanctifieth, and finally faueth vs of his meere mercie and free goodwill, without any respect of our owne merits or good workes, let vs not restraine the infinite loue of God to our deferts, nor meafure his vnmeafurable goodwill by the short ell of our owne merits; but as the Lord hath freely loued vs, fo let vs acknowledge his free and vndeferued loue, and relie wholy thereupon, notwithstanding our vnworthinesse, seeing our worthinesse is no caufe of his loue, but it is his loue which maketh vs, and will furely make vs worthie to be beloued, if we rest wholy vpon him in Christ by a true and liuely faith. For, fo much as we defpaire in respect of our own vnworthinesse, fo much would wee afcribe to our owne worthinesse; and looke how much we attribute vnto our felues in the worke of our faluation, fo much wee detract from Gods free mercie and Christs merit: and therefore let vs humbly acknowledge our owne vnworthinesse, and become nothing in our own eyes, that we may wholy rely vpon God, that hee may bee all in all. For well worthie are we to thirst if wee leaue the fountaine of living waters, and dig vnto our felues broken cefternes which will hold no water; well wor- Iere.2.13. thie are we to fall into the gulfe of defpaire, if we forfake the firme pillar of our faluation Gods mercie and Christs merit, relying and resting vpon the broken staffe of our owne righteousnesse; well worthie are we to be damned, if wee enuie the Lord the praife and glorie of our faluation, defiring rather to afcribe it vnto our felues.

But here the tempter wil obiect that God is iust, and ther- §. *Sect.*7. fore in his iustice cannot loue, elect, iustifie and faue vs who are vnworthie his loue, polluted with finne, and destitute of righteousnesse. I anfwere, that God doth not loue, elect, iustifie

That being vn-worthie in our selues, we are loued, elected, and saued in Christ.

fie and saue vs in our selues, but in our sauiour Christ, in whom being vnworthie of our selues wee are made worthie; being vniust in our selues, wee are made iust, after wee are adorned with the rich robe of his righteousnesse; being in our selues the children of wrath and firebrands of hell, wee are made children of God and heires of heauen. For *he is made vnto vs*

1.Cor.1.30.31   *of God, wisedome, righteousnesse, sanctification and redemption, that he who reioyceth might reioyce in the Lord,* as it is 1.Cor.1. 30.31. And therefore the Apostle teacheth vs, that God hath giuen his grace, not simply vnto vs, who were altogether vn-worthie thereof, but in Iesus Christ, 1.Cor.1.1.4. *and that in all*

1.Cor.1.4.   *things we are made rich in him,* as it is vers.5. So he telleth vs,
verf.5.   that *grace doth raigne by righteousnesse vnto eternall life, through*
Rom.5.21.   *Iesus Christ our Lord,* Rom.5.21. And *that he hath shewed the exceeding riches of his grace, through his kindnesse towards vs in*

Eph.2.7.   *Christ Iesus,* Eph.2.7. And as God is gracious to vs in Christ, so hath he declared this his loue towards vs in Christ onely, as may appeare in the seuerall causes and meanes of our salua-tion. For in him God hath elected vs to saluation, as appea-

Eph.1.5.   reth Eph.1.5. In him is made the couenant of grace, as being that seede of *Abraham* in whom all the nations of the earth

Galat.3.16.   are blessed, and to whom all the promises were made, as it is
Eph.1.9.10.   Gal.3.16. In him are wee called and gathered together into
2.Tim.1.9.   one bodie, whereof he is the head, as it is Eph.1.9.10. 2.Tim.
Rom.5.18.19.   1.9. In him are wee iustified, as appeareth Rom. 5.18.19. Esa.
Esa.53.5.   53.5. 1.Cor.1.30. In him we are reconciled vnto God, Col.1.
1.Cor.1.30.   20.21. Eph.1.6.and 2.12.13.14.&c. In him we are adopted to
Col.1.20.21.   be the sonnes of God, Gal.4.4.5.6.7. Eph.1.5. In him we are
Eph.1.6.and   sanctified, 1.Cor.1.30. In a word, in him wee are saued, as ap-
2.12.13.&c.   peareth 1.Ioh.5.11. *God hath giuen vs eternall life, and this life*
Gal.4.4.5.&c.   *is in his sonne.* Though therefore the Lord could not in his iu-
Eph.1.5.   stice bestow vpon vs these his benefits, because wee were vn-
1.Cor.1.30.   worthie of the least of them, and most worthie of al his iudg-
1.Ioh.5.11.   ments and punishments: yet in Christ wee haue fully satisfied his iustice, & performed perfect obedience, and therfore euen in his iustice he could not but bestow these his mercies and graces vpon vs, because in him we deserued his loue, though in our selues we haue deserued eternall shame and confusion.

And

And therefore not trufting in our owne worthineffe, nor yet diftrufting in Gods mercie and free loue in regard of our vnworthineffe, let vs caft off all felfe-conceit and opinion of our owne righteoufneffe, fo that wee may put on the righte-oufneffe of Chrift; and acknowledging our owne weakneffe, yea our nothing, let vs neuertheleffe be ftrong in the grace which is in Chrift Iefus, as the Apoftle exhorteth 2.Tim.2.1. 2.Tim.2.1. In his name let vs goe boldly vnto the throne of grace, that Heb.4.16. we may receiue mercie, and finde helpe in time of neede : for though in our felues we are the childre of wrath, *yet are we re-conciled and accepted of God, as his beloued in his beft beloued,* as Eph.1.6. it is Eph.1.6.

CHAP. III.

That temporall afflictions are rather fignes of Gods loue, than of his hatred.

THe fecond argument whereby Sathan feeketh to perfwade vs that we are out of the fauour of God, is taken from the manifold afflictions which are laid vpon many of Gods children , whileft they remaine in this vale of miferie. But it is eafie to anfwere this obiection, if we be but a little couerfant in the book of God; for there we may learne that afflictions and croffes are rather fignes of Gods loue than of his hatred; and markes rather of our elec-tion and adoption, than of reprobation and eternall damna-tion. For the Lord hath forefhewed vs that his childré fhould mourne when the world fhall reioyce ; that they fhould be hated and perfecuted for his name fake ; that *all who will liue godly in Chrift Iefus, fhall fuffer perfecution and affliction,* 2.Tim. 3.12. That they who will be conformable to him in glorie, muft alfo be conformable vnto him in his fuffrings Rom.8. 29. That *this fhort and momentanie affliction fhall caufe vnto vs a farre moft excellent and eternall waight of glorie,* 2.Cor.4.17. That *if we fuffer with Chrift, we fhall alfo raigne with him,* 2.Tim. 2.12. That *whom the Lord loueth he chafteneth: and fcourgeth euery fon that he receiueth,* as it is Heb.12.6. That thofe whom he

§. *Sect.*1. *Afflictions markes rather of our adop-tion than of our reproba-tion.*

2.Tim.3.12.

Rom.8.29.

2.Cor.4.17.

2.Tim 2.12.

Heb.12.6,8.

he doth not thus correct, *are bastards and no sonnes,* verf.8.
And to thefe wee may adde the examples of Gods children
from time to time, as of *Abraham, Iacob, Iofeph, Mofes, Dauid,*
Iob, the Apoftles, but efpecially our Sauiour Chrift himfelfe,
who was hungrie, harbourleffe, defpifed, fcoffed, reuiled, buffeted, fpit vpon, crowned with thorne, and laftly crucified; and
yet euen whileft he fuffered al thefe afflictions, he was the only begotten and beft beloued fonne of his heauenly father.

§. Sect.2.
That afflicti-
ons, though in
their owne na-
ture euill,
turne to the
good of Gods
children.

So that both by teftimonies and examples it is manifeft,
that afflictions are figues rather of Gods loue, than of his hatred; and markes of the children of God, rather than of the
children of wrath. But here the tempter will demaund how
this can be, confidering that the Lord promifeth to his children all good things; whereas afflictions are euils, and punifhments inflicted on the wicked. To this we may anfwere,
that though in their owne nature they be euill, yet through
the wifedome and gracious prouidence of our God, they
turne to the good of his children; and though 'to the wicked
they are plagues and punifhments, yet to the godly they are
but trials and fatherly chaftifements; for all their finnes are
punifhed in Chrift, neither will it ftand with Gods iuftice
to punifh them againe in the faithful: and therfore there is no
other end of them but the manifeftation of Gods glory, and
our fpiritual good and euerlafting faluation. For as they are
trials they ferue to fhew vnto all the world, and efpecially to
our felues, our faith, hope, patience, obedience, conftancie,
and the reft of the graces of Gods fpirit, to the praife of his
glory who hath beftowed them, and to the comfort of our
owne foules who haue receiued them. And as they are chaftifements they ferue for fharpe eye-falues to cleere our
dimme fight, fo as we may fee our finnes, and truely repent
of them. They ferue for fowre fauces, to bring vs out of loue
with our fweete finnes, and for fire and files, whereby wee are
purged and fcoured from the droffe and ruft of our corruptions. They are fharpe pruning kniues, to lop and trimme vs,
that we may bring forth plentifull fruits in godlineffe. They
are fpurres to pricke vs forward in the Chriftian race, and
hedges to keepe vs from wandering out of the way. They
are

are sharp salues to draw out our secret corruptions, and bitter potions to cure our desperate diseases. They are that wormewood, wherby the Lord weaneth vs frō the loue of the world, whose pleasing delights we would euer sucke without wearinesse, if our mouthes were not distasted with some afflictions. They are roddes, wherewith being scourged, wee are made more circumspect in our wayes, and more carefull to performe obedience vnto all the commandements of our heauenly Father. In a word, they are the straight path which leadeth to euerlasting happinesse, and a bridle to restraine vs from running headlong in the broade way, which leadeth to endlesse wo and miserie. And therfore seeing our momentany afflictions do serue for the manifesting of Gods glorie, for the increasing of spirituall graces, and the furthering of our eternall saluation, let not Sathan perswade vs that wee are out of Gods loue and fauour because of our afflictions, but rather let vs repute them as they are indeede signes of his gracious prouidence and fatherly care which he hath ouer vs.

But here the tempter will obiect that this I speake is true §. *Sect. 3.* of the outward afflictions of the bodie, for thereby the flesh *Sathans temp-* is mortified and subdued, and the spirituall graces of Gods *tations groun-* spirit exercised and increased in vs; but thy afflictions (will *ded vpon our* he say) are farre different, for thy soule is filled with horrour *spirituall afflic-* and feare, thy conscience is mortally stung with sinne, and *tions.* the waight thereof ouerwhelmeth thee; thou seest thy selfe subiect to the curse of the law, and art alreadie tormented with the paines of hell; thy God who looketh vpon his children with an amiable countenance, frowneth vpon thee like a seuere Iudge, and thou tastest of nothing but of his heauie wrath and displeasure; in a word, thou hast not one sparke of true consolation wrought in thee by Gods spirit, with which those that are Gods children are fully replenished, and wherby they are incouraged patiently to abide all afflictions, but thy inward vexations are the torments of an euill conscience, and the flashings of hell fire wherewith hereafter thou shalt eternally be burned.

To this temptation we must answere, that it cannot be denied but that the afflictions of the minde are farre more grieuous

That our spiri- uous than the afflictions of the bodie; and that the torments
tuall afflictions of conscience caused by the waight of sinne, and the appre-
are no signes of hension of Gods fearefull wrath,are as it were Gods three-
Gods hatred. stringed whip,in respect of the gentle rod of outward afflic-
Pro.17.12. tions; for *a sorrowfull mind drieth vp the bones,* as it is Pro.17.
Pro,18.14. 12.and *the spirit of a man may sustaine his* other *infirmities, but
a wounded spirit who can beare,*as the wise man speaketh,Prou.
18.14.Neuerthelesse,though these corrections are more sharp
and grieuous,than the outward afflictions of the bodie, yet it
cannot be denied but that these also are the chastisements
which our heauenly Father inflicteth vpon his children: somtimes for his owne glorie, and sometime for their triall or
chastisement,when more light correction will not reclaime
them. For first those places of scripture before quoted, are
spoken generally of all afflictions whatsoeuer, and therefore
are not to be restrained to the outward afflictions of the bodie, seeing they extend themselues also to the afflictions of
the minde; neither doth our heauenly Father correct all a-
like,but some he rebuketh onely by his word, and goeth no
further when as this reclaimeth them; but if this will not
preuaile,hee goeth a step further, and chastizeth them with
gentle correction,as with outward crosses and afflictions;but
if this will not reforme them, he taketh his whippe into his
hand, wherewith hee grieuously scourgeth them, to the end
they may more sensibly taste of his displeasure, and amend
that which is amisse; and this he doth by making them feele
Reu.3.19. the waight of sinne, and apprehend his wrath and heauie dis-
Heb,12.6. pleasure, which by their sinnes they haue iustly incurred; and
yet notwithstanding all this he still remaineth their gracious
Father, who seeketh not their destruction but their reforma-
tion.Neither need this dealing of our heauenly Father seeme
strange vnto vs, seeing earthly parents take the same courses
with their children whom they tenderly loue; for when they
offend them,they first seeke their amendment by words and
fatherly admonitions;and when this will doe no good they
proceed to blowes,and in a gentle manner do correct them;
and if this preuaile not with them, then they vse more sharpe
and seuere chastizement; but if all this be to no purpose,
                                                        then

then will they difguife their fatherly affection vnder the vizard of wrath and heauie difpleafure;they banifh out of their countenance all fignes of loue, and affume terrible looks and bitter frownes; yea they will fometimes thruft them out of doores, and reiect them a while, leauing them to fhift for themfelues, and to endure all miferie. And whence proceedeth all this? furely not from hatred, but from loue and tender care which they haue ouer them for their good. And this maketh them vfe the bridle of correction, to reftraine them from running into all licentioufneffe; this caufeth them to pretend wrath in the countenance, that they be not by their lewdneffe forced to entertaine it into their hearts; this mooueth them to reiect them for a time, that they may reclaime and retaine them for euer. Neither doth our heauenly Father, who is infinite in loue, deale otherwife with his difobedient children; hee vfeth but his word if his word will fuffice; hee goeth no further then gentle chaftizement if that be inough; but if hee fharply fcourge vs, yea if hee looke vpon vs with a frowning countenance,and fhew nothing in outward appearance but his wrath and heauie difpleafure; if he feeme to reiect vs for a time,and to giue vs ouer to be tormented by Sathan: yet vndoubtedly all this proceedeth from his loue and that fatherly care hee hath ouer vs, for our euerlafting good and faluation; hee feeketh not our deftruction, but amendment; he frowneth on vs for a time, that hee may looke gracioufly on vs for euer; he feemeth to reiect vs for a while,that like the prodigall fonne we may returne againe,and be received into his euerlafting loue and fauour.

Secondly, the Lord fendeth afflictions to mortifie in vs the old man,the flefh and vnregenerate part: now the flefh is not onely in our bodie, but alfo in our foule and euery part and facultie thereof, and therefore the Lord doth not afflict the bodie alone with outward calamities, but euen the foule alfo with griefe of minde and horrour of confcience, with the waight of finne and fenfe of his wrath, to the end that our corruptions both in bodie and foule may be mortified, the old man with the lufts thereof crucified, and in the end fullie abolifhed.And therefore doth the Lord breake our hard and

§. Sect.4.
That spirituall afflictions tend to our mortification.

Iere.4.4.

M ftonie

ſtonie hearts, therefore doth he plowe and teare them vp
like fallow ground, to the end that the ſeede of his grace being ſowne in them may take roote, fructifie and bring forth
a plentifull harueſt of godlineſſe, to his glorie and our com-
fort.It is not therefore for want of loue, that our heauenly
father doth thus bruſe vs and euen cruſh vs in peeces;it is not
becauſe he will reiect vs and caſt vs of:but when we are truely
humbled, when our hard hearts are ſoftned, and our ſpirits
broken and made contrite, then will he regard vs and ſhew
his tender loue and mercifull kindneſſe vnto vs as he hath
graciouſly promiſed.Matth.12.20. *The bruſed reede will he not*

Matth.12.20.
Pſa.51.17.

breake, and ſmoking flax ſhall he not quench. So Pſal.51.17.
*The ſacrifices of God are a contrite ſpirit, a contrite and broken
heart O God thou wilt not deſpiſe.* And the Prophet telleth vs
that our Sauiour Chriſt was ſent into the world *to preach
glad tidings vnto the poore, to binde vp the broken harted,&c.*

Eſa.61. 1,2,3.

*to comfort all that mourne, to giue them beautie for aſhes, the
oyle of ioy for mourning, the garment of gladnes for the ſpirit of
heauines &c.* as it is Eſa.61.1.2.3.Luk.4.18.

§. Sect.5.
Gods deareſt
children ſub-
iect to ſpiritu-
all affliction.

Laſtly, that the afflictions of the minde, the apprehenſion
of Gods wrath, the ſting of ſinne, and torments of conſcience, are not any true and certaine ſignes of Gods hatred,
hereby it plainely appeareth : in that the moſt deare children
of God haue been ſubiect to them,and that in great meaſure.
For example, *Iob* who by Gods own teſtimony was the iuſteſt

Iob.1.8.

man that liued on the earth, Iob.1.8. notwithſtanding was ſo
grieuouſly afflicted both in body and minde , that he bur-

Iob.6.4.&9.
17,18.& 13.
24.26.& 16.
9.& 19.11.

ſteth out into theſe grieuous complaints,Iob.6.4.*The arrowes
of the almightie are in me, the venime whereof doth drinke vp
my ſpirit, and the terrors of God fight againſt me.* And chap.9.
verſ.17. *He deſtroyeth me with a tempeſt and woundeth me without cauſe.*18. *He will not ſuffer me to take my breath, but filleth
me with bitterneſſe.* So, c.13.24. *Wherefore hideſt thou thy face
and takeſt me for thine enemie?* And v.26. *Thou writeſt bitter
things againſt me, and makeſt me to poſſeſſe the iniquities of my
youth.* And c.16.9. *His wrath hath torne me,and he hateth me
and gnaſheth vpon me with his teeth; mine enemie hath ſharpned
his eyes againſt me.* And, c.19.11. *He hath kindled his wrath*
againſt

against mee and counteth mee as one of his enemies.

Looke alſo vpon the example of the Prophet *Dauid*, who
though he were a man according to Gods own heart, yet was
he made to drinke a deep draught in this cup of inward afflictions, and was vexed not only outwardly in his eſtate, goods,
and body, but alſo in his ſoule, with the ſenſe of Gods wrath,
with the waight of ſinne, and the terrors and torments of conſcience, which make him to vtter theſe and ſuch like pittifull
complaints in the booke of the Pſalmes. Pſal.6.3. *My ſoule is* **Pſal.6.3.**
alſo ſore troubled: but Lord how long wilt thou delay? And v.6.
I fainted in my mourning: I cauſe my bed euery night to ſwim,
and water my couch with my teares. So Pſal.38.2. *Thine arrowes* **Pſal.38.2.3.**
haue light vpon me, and thine hand lieth vpon me. 3. *There is*
nothing ſound in my fleſh, becauſe of thine anger: neither is there
any reſt in my bones becauſe of my ſinne. 4. *For mine iniquities are*
gone ouer mine head, and as a waightie burthen they are too hea-
uie for me. &c. And Pſal.88.7. *Thine indignation lieth vpon me,* **Pſal.88.7.14.**
and thou haſt vexed me with all thy waues. And v.14. *Lord, why* **15,16.**
doſt thou reiect my ſoule, and hideſt thy face from me? 15. *I am*
afflicted and at the point of death: from my youth I ſuffer thy ter-
rors, doubting of my life. 16. *Thine indignations goe ouer me,*
and thy feare hath cut me off. So in the 77 Pſalme he taketh vp **Pſal.77.7,8,9,**
this lamentable complaint. verſ.7. *Will the Lord abſent him-* **10.**
ſelfe for euer? and will he ſhew no more fauour? 8. *Is his mercie*
cleane gone for euer? doth his promiſe faile for euermore? 9. *Hath*
God forgotten to be mercifull? hath he ſhut vp his tender mer-
cies in diſpleaſure? 10. *And I ſaid, this is my death.* Looke
alſo vpon the Apoſtle *Paul*, who though he were a choſen
veſſel, whom God had ſeperated from his mothers wombe
to carrie his name before the Gentils, as is is Act.9.15. **Act.9.15.**
Gal.1.15.
Gallat.1.15; yet was hee afflicted grieuouſly, not onely **2.Cor.6.4,5,**
outwardly in body, as hee profeſſeth 2.Corinth. 6. 4. 5. **6,7,8.**
6.7.8. &c. but alſo in minde; for the meſſenger of Sathan was
ſent to buffet him, and hee had a long time a pricke in the **2.Cor.12.7,8.**
fleſh, from which hee could not be freed, though he often
begged this fauour at Gods hand, as appeareth, 2.Cor.
12.7.8. And the burthen of ſinne grieuouſly afflicting his
conſcience, forced him to cry out Rom.7.24, *O wretched* **Rom.7.24.**
man

man that I am, who shall deliuer me from the body of his death?

§.Sect.6.
That Christ himselfe indured these spirituall afflictions.
1.Cor. 10.13
1.Pet.5.9.

Esa.53.3.

So that by these and many such like examples, that is manifest vnto our comforts which the Apostle speaketh, 1.Cor. 10.13. *There hath no temptation taken you but such as appertaineth to man; for the same afflictions (which we suffer) are accomplished in our brethren which are in the world,* as it is, 1. Pet.5.9. Yea the same and farre greater were indured by our head Iesus Christ himselfe, who receiued deepe and grisly woundes, in respect of those small scratches which we suffer, and drunke the full cupe of Gods heauie displeasure, of which we onely sip or taste; for he was not onely in his outward state deiected and reputed as an abiect amongst men, nor persecuted by his cruell enemies alone, euen to the taking away of his precious life, by a cruell and shamefull death; but also inwardly in his soule he sustained farre more heauie crosses thē that which he outwardly carried on his shoulders, though the waight thereof caused him to faint for wearines. For to say nothing of Sathans temptations and the power of hell which was set against him, let vs consider of that bitter agonie which he sustained in the garden, where the burthen of Gods anger, for our sinnes was so heauie vpon him, that it pressed out of his blessed body a sweate of water and blood; neither was he presently eased of this vnsupportable waight, but he was faine to beare it euen vnto his crosse; neither was he comforted in minde when the panges of death had taken hold of his body, but euen then he was so vexed with the sense of his fathers displeasure, that in bitternesse of soule he crieth out my God, My God why hast thou forsaken me: Not that he despaired vtterly of Gods loue and assistance, or thought himselfe a reprobate and castaway, for he calleth him stil his God: but the deitie hauing for a time withdrawne it selfe, to the end the humane nature might suffer that punishment which we had deserued euen vnto death it selfe, which otherwise it could not haue been subiect vnto, he vttereth this speech truely according to his present sense and apprehension. Now if we consider who it is that was thus grieuously afflicted both in body and minde, we shall finde that it was not one hated of God, but his onely begotten

and

and beſt beloued ſonne, in whom he profeſſeth himſelfe to be
well pleaſed.Matth.3.17. Seeing therefore our Sauiour Chriſt Matth.3.17.
who was the natural ſonne and heyre of God, and ſo tenderly
beloued of his heauenly father that in him hee loueth all his
children, did notwithſtanding indure not only grieuous afflictions of body, but the intollerable burthen of his fathers diſpleaſure in his ſoule alſo: why ſhould we imagine ỹ either our
outward or inward afflictions are any ſignes or argumẽts that
God hateth or hath reiected vs?eſpecially conſidering that he
hath predeſtinated vs to be made like to the image of his ſonne, not
only in his glory, but alſo in his afflictiõs: ſo that firſt we muſt ſuffer Rom.8.29.
with him, & after raigne with him, as it is Ro.8.29.2.Tim.2.12. 2.Tim.2.12.
    But it may be obiected that our Sauiour Chriſt ſuffered all Obiection.
this, not for any ſinne that was in himſelfe, for he *did no ſinne,* 1.Pet.2.22.
neither was there guile found in his mouth. 1.Pet.2.22. *but he*
was wounded for our tranſgreſſions, he was broken for our iniqui-
ties, as it is Eſa.53.5. And therefore conſidering that the Eſa.53.5.
Lord did thus hate ſinne, euen when his dearely beloued
ſonne did take it vpon him; how much more will he hate it in
vs? if he ſo ſeuerely puniſhed his deare darling when he had Anſwere.
taken the ſinnes of others vpon him, how fearefull puniſh- 1.Pet.3.18.
ments are prepared for the ſinners themſelues? I anſwere,
that indeede *Chriſt who was iuſt did ſuffer for vs who were vn-*
iuſt, as it is 1.Pet.3.18. and that ſinne is ſo odious to Gods
eyes, that rather then it ſhould not be puniſhed, he would
puniſh it in his deerely beloued ſonne; the conſideration
whereof ſhould make vs alſo to hate and fly from it as the
greateſt euill : but yet this ſhould be ſo farre of from diſcou-
raging vs, or from making vs doubt of Gods loue, that nothing in the world doth more aſſure vs thereof; no conſolation can be imagined more comfortable: for what greater teſtimonie of Gods loue can be imagined, then that whẽ we were
ſtrangers yea enemies to God, he ſhould ſend his deare belo- Rom.5.10.
ued ſon to die for vs, to the end that by this meanes his iuſtice
might be ſatiſſied, his wrath appeaſed, and we being receiued
into grace & fauour, might be made heires of euerlaſting life?
what greater aſſurance can we haue that our ſins are forgiuen
vs, then that they are alreadie puniſhed in Chriſt? it being a-

gainſt the iuſtice of God to puniſh the ſame ſinnes twice?
What ſtronger argument can be brought, to proue that we
ſhall neuer be ſubiect to Gods wrath, nor be caſt away in his
heauie diſpleaſure; than that our Sauiour hath borne his fathers anger, to the end hee might reconcile vs vnto him?
and therefore though our Sauiour ſuffered theſe outward and
inward afflictions, not as he was the dearely beloued ſonne
of God who was free from ſinne, but as he was our mediator,
who had taken vpon him our ſinnes, to the end he might
ſatiſſie his fathers iuſtice; yet ſeeing he indured theſe things
in our ſtead, to the end we might be freed from them, hence
ariſeth vnto every true chriſtian ſound comfort, and certaine
aſſurance of Gods loue and goodnes towards him.

§. Sect.7.
A daungerous temptation grounded vpon our not-profi-ting by afflicti-on.

But the tempter will further vrge his obiection after this
manner; let it be graunted (will he ſay) that God doth cha-
ſtiſe ſometime his children whom he loueth, both with outward and inward afflictions, and that they ſuffer euen the
ſame miſeries which thou indureſt; yet ſeeing they are ſometimes puniſhments alſo which he inflicteth vpon the wicked, hence thou canſt not gather that they are fatherly chaſtiſements and ſignes of his loue to thee : nay contrariwiſe
thou maieſt aſſure thy ſelfe, that they are fearefull puniſhments and ſignes of Gods hatred, which God in iuſtice inflicteth on thee for thy ſinnes, that others may bee warned
by thine example. For if they were chaſtiſements and fatherly corrections, then would they indeede correct thee,
that is, reforme and amend thee; for this is the end why
God inflicteth them on his children, and his end cannot be
fruſtrate : but in thee there is no reformation wrought, nor
any increaſe of patience, whereas in the faithfull, *tribulation*

Rom.5.3.
bringeth forth patience, as euen by the Scriptures it is manifeſt. Nay contrariwiſe when the hand of God is vpon thee,
thou bewraieſt great impatiencie, and vttereſt inconſiderate
ſpeeches, which tend to Gods diſhonor, giue offence to the
world and wounde thine owne conſcience. And therefore
howſoeuer to other theſe are fatherly chaſtizements, yet to
thee they are ſeuere puniſhments, which mooue thee rather
to deſpare, than aſſure thee of Gods loue.

To

To this we anſwer, that it cannot be denied, but that Gods corrections doe correct and amend his children, and that afflictions ſerue to the encreaſing of their patience, faith and other graces; but yet let vs know that Sathan playeth the falſe deceauer, when he moueth vs to looke for the aſſurance of Gods loue, and for our amendment & increaſe of Gods grace, in the very time when the hand of God is vpon vs, whileſt the conflict laſteth, and the temptation grieuouſly ſhaketh and battereth vs : as if he ſhould come to a man who hath endured much and tedious ſickneſſe and ſhould ſay vnto him, thou diddeſt imagine thy ſelfe awhile agoe very beautifull and exceeding ſtrong, but thou waſt much decei- ued, for if thou lookeſt in a glaſſe thou ſhalt preſently per- ceaue that thou art leane, pale, and deformed, and if thou makeſt triall of thy ſtrength, thou ſhalt finde that it is ſcarce ſufficient to ſuſtaine the waight of thine owne body. Now who would not deride ſuch fond reaſoning? who could not eaſily anſwere, that iudgement is not to be taken of the beautie and ſtrength of the bodie in the time of ſicknes, but in the time of health ? but this is the very like caſe, and thus ſottiſhly doth Sathan conclude, or rather delude Gods chil- dren in the time of temptation; for he ſayeth thus vnto them, thou diddeſt perſwade thy ſelfe that thou art the childe of God, and in his loue aud fauour, that thou art indued with faith, patience, and other graces, and daily increaſeſt in them ; but now thou art come to the triall it proueth farre otherwiſe; for thy faith is turned into doubting or infidelitie, and thy patience to impatiencie, and therefore there is no likely- hoode that thou art beloued of God, for then thou wouldeſt profit by afflictions, and increaſe in grace and ſtrength, where- as thou bewrayeſt nothing but thy manifould corruptions. But we are to know that we are not to iudge of our grace and ſtrength, in the time of temptation, and of the ſpirituall con- flict, when as our ſoules are grieuouſly ſicke with the ſenſe of ſinne and apprehenſion of Gods heauie diſpleaſure in- curred thereby, when as the fire of Gods ſpirit is couered with the aſhes of our corruptions, and the fruites and graces thereof nipped with the coulde winter and boyſterous blaſts

of

of temptations, but we are to looke into our selues when the
fit is paſt and the confliƈt ended, and then ſhall we finde our
patience by experience of Gods loue confirmed, our faith
renewed, all other graces ſtrengthened and increaſed; and
then ſhall we clearely diſcerne the bright beames of Gods
loue and fauour, ſhining vpon vs, when the cloudes of temptation are paſt away which did hide them from vs.

§. Seƈt.8.
*That Gods
deare children
in greiuous
temptations
ſhew impati-
encie, and vtter
ſometime in-
conſiderate
ſpeeches.*

But if in the time of triall and temptation we iudge according to our preſent ſenſe and feeling, we muſt needes be deceiued : for it cannot be denied but that euen the deare children of God who haue recciued a great meaſure of grace,
when the hand of God is vpon them doe doubt of his loue
and fauour, and when they are grieuouſly affliƈted doe bewray their corruption, and ſhew their impatience by vttering inconſiderate ſpeeches; for while we continue in this
life, we haue the reliques of ſinne hanging on vs, and we are
partly fleſh and partly ſpirit, yea the fleſh is the ſtronger part,
and therefore it is no maruaile if the fleſh being pinched in
the time of temptation doth complaine, and being launced
deepely with the raſor of ſharpe affliƈtions doth cry out for
paine, complaining of the Surgeon that he dealeth too rigo-
rouſly with him. And if men through bodily ſicknes haue
their iudgements blinded, their vnderſtanding daſled and
miſled, their memorie ouerthrowne, ſo that they can put no
difference betweene their friends and their enemies, but euen
raile vpon thoſe whom in the time of their health they
dearely loued, and thinke none ſo much their enemie as their
phyſition, rauing and inconſiderately ſpeaking they know
not what; what wonder is it if the like effeƈts follow the
ſickneſſe of the ſoule, when it is as it were ſet vpon the racke,
preſſed with the burthen of ſinne, and tormented with the
apprehenſion of Gods anger, conſidering that theſe kinde
of affliƈtions are farre more grieuous and without compariſon more intollerable, *for a man may ſuſtaine his infirmities,*
but a wounded ſpirit who can beare? as it is Pro.28.14. What
meruaile then is it, if they take God for their enemie, when
they feele his ſharpe medicines, though in truth he be their
louing Phiſition, who by this meanes cureth them of their
diſeaſes

difeafes of finne and corruption? what wonder is it if they
vtter rauing fpeeches when the fenfe of paine preffeth them
fo fore? how is it poffible but that they fhould doubt of
Gods gracious loue and fauour, when as they prefently tafte
of nothing but his rigor and iuftice?

We muft not therefore iudge of our ftate while the croffe
is vpon vs, for fo fhould we condemne the generation of the
iuft to be moft wicked, then fhould we imagine thofe who
haue excelled in patience to be moft wayward and impatient. Looke vpon *Iob* who is renowned for patience, and you
fhall finde that while the hand of God was vpon him, he be-
wrayeth the corruption of the flefh and fheweth notable impatiencie, curfing the day of his natiuitie, and wifhing that
he had neuer been borne, or elfe that he had prefently after
his birth been fwallowed vp in the iawes of death, Iob.3. So
chap.6.8.9. he thus crieth out like a man vtterly defperat. *O
that I might haue my defire, and that God would graunt me the
thing that I long for.9. That is, that God would deftroy me: that he
would let his hand goe and cut me off. 10. Then fhould I yet haue
fome comfort, though I burne with forrow, let him not fpare &c.*
Where *Iob* feemeth to deale with God as a condemned malefactor with a iuft & feuere iudge, who feeing the anger of the
iudge incenfed againft him for his crime, hath no hope that
he can by intreatie and perfwafions mooue him to reuoke
his fentence of death, and therefore onely defireth a mitiga-
tion of the tortures, and that he may quickly be difpatched
and ridde out of his paine; *nam mifericordia genus eft citò
occidere,* it is a kinde of mercie to be fpeedie in execution:
So *Iob* hauing no hope to be freed from his miferies, defireth
onely this fauour at Gods hands, that he would not (as it
were) torment him peecemeale, but make a quicke difpatch
of him by laying on a greater waight of afflictions, till by
their vnfupportable burthen the breath were preffed out of
his body. And chap.10.18. *Wherefore haft thou brought me out
of the wombe? Oh that I had perifhed, and that none eye had
feene me! 19. And that I were as I had not been, but brought
from the wombe to the graue.* Looke vpon the Prophet *Dauid*
who was a man according to Gods owne heart, endued

with

§. Sect.9.
*Example to
cleere the for-
mer point.*
Iam.5.11.

Iob.3 & 6.8.
9.10.

Iob.10.18.

with a ſtedfaſt faith and conſtant patience; and you ſhall perceiue that Gods loue, and the graces of Gods ſpirit in him,
were ſo ſhadowed with the grieuouſneſſe of his preſent afflictions,that he could not diſcerne them.For he complaineth
like a man vtterly caſt off and reiected of God. Pſal.88.14.

Pſal. 88.14   *Lord why doſt thou reiect my ſoule, and hideſt thy face from me ?*
                  16. Thine indignation is gone ouer me, and thy feare hath cut me
& 77.8.9.   *off.* The like complaint he taketh vp. Pſal.77.8.9.10. Neither
had the Prophet in theſe times alwaies the ſpirit of ſupplication and prayer, but ſometime the grieuouſneſſe of his paine
Pſal.32.3.4.   did ſhut his mouth ſo as he could not confeſſe his ſinne, nor
humble himſelfe before his God ; though through the
waight of affliction, his bones were conſumed, and he roared
for griefe all the day long, as appeareth Pſalm.32.3.4. So
Ierem.20.14.   *Ieremie* ſeeing the word of God contemned, and himſelfe
15.18.   who was Gods ambaſſador deſpiſed, could not beare it but
burſteth out into great impaciencie, curſing the day of his
birth, and euen the man that brought newes thereof to his
father, becauſe he was borne to ſee labour and ſorrow, and
that his daies ſhould be conſumed with ſhame. Ierem.20.14,
15.18. If therefore we iudge of *Iob, Dauid,* and *Ieremie,*a-
cording to their outward behauiour, and their owne inward
feeling in the time of afflictions,and in the combate of temptations; wee ſhould thinke them voyde of faith, impatient,
and deſtitute of all aſſurance and hope of Gods loue and fauour : but the Scriptures teach vs otherwiſe, propounding
them vnto vs as patternes of patience and true godlineſſe;
and themſelues alſo at other times doe ſhew their ſingular
faith, patience, and the reſt of the graces of Gods ſpirit. Seeing then this is not our caſe alone,but the ſtate of Gods deareſt children, let vs not beleeue the tempter telling vs that
we are not Gods children becauſe we ſee not Gods graces
ſo plainely in the time of temptation and triall, but contrariwiſe bewray our impatiencie and other corruptions : but let
vs be truely humbled in the ſight of our infirmities,laboring
and ſtriuing to reforme them;and iudge of our ſtate, not as
we finde it in the time of the conflict, but as it was or is before or after the combate is ended.

                                                          Laſtly,

Laſtly, the tempter obiecteth, and hath ſtirred vp his wicked inſtruments the enemies of Gods truth to defend, that
though wee are not wholy to deſpaire of Gods loue, yet wee
muſt doubt thereof: and to this purpoſe they alleadge that
ſaying Eccleſ.9.1. which they reade thus : *I haue handled all
theſe things in my heart that I might curiouſly vnderſtand: Iuſt
and wiſe men and their workes are in the hand of God ; and notwithſtanding, a man knoweth not whether he be worthie of loue or
hatred, but all things are kept vncertain for the time to come &c.*
I anſwere, that if Gods loue or hatred did depend vpon our
owne vnworthineſſe, wee might well doubt; nay I will ſay
more, wee might iuſtly deſpaire of his grace and goodwill,
and certainly aſſure our ſelues that we were hated and abhorred of God; for this, if any thing, wee haue deſerued. But the
truth is, that as Sathan tempting our Sauiour, and quoting
ſcripture for his purpoſe, left out that which made againſt
him; ſo here by his inſtruments aſſaulting his members, he
addeth to the ſcriptures that which maketh for him : for neither in the Hebrew, which is the originall, nor in the Greeke
tranſlation is there any one word of our worthineſſe or vnworthineſſe; but thus it is in the text as it is truly tranſlated in
our Bibles ; *No man knoweth either loue or hatred of all that is
before them :* and whereas they reade the words following
thus ; *But all things are kept vncertain for the time to come,* they
moſt groſly depraue the text, which is thus to be read as wee
haue it tranſlated ; *All things come alike to all, and the ſame condition is to the iuſt and the wicked* ; and thus alſo doth *Arias
Montanus* one of the moſt learned amongſt themſelues
tranſlate it.

Neither wil their corrupt tranſlatiō ſtand with the ſenſe and
truth of the place : for, as he ſaith, no man knoweth whether
he be worthie of loue, ſo alſo, that no man knoweth whether
he be worthie of hatred : but this is vtterly falſe; for ſo ſhould
wee ſay that wee could not know whether the Sodomites for
their filthineſſe, the Canaanites for their idolatrie, *Iulian*
for his apoſtaſie were worthie to be hated of God; whereas
the ſcriptures witneſſe the cleane contrarie, and euen they
themſelues doe confeſſe, that they who deſperatly giue ouer
themſelues

themfelues into all finne and wickednefle, are not to doubt but that they are worthie of Gods anger and heauie difpleafure; why therefore on the other fide may not thofe who are truly conucrted vnto God, and indued with a liuely faith which worketh by loue, be affured of Gods loue and fauour, feeing he hath affured them hereof in his word? Nay in the fame chapter verf.7.their corrupt expofition is ouerthrowne; for there he biddeth vs to *eate our bread with ioy,and to drinke our wine with a cheereful heart,for God now accepteth our works.* Now, though God did indeede accept our workes, yet wee could not be moued to ioy and cheerefulnefle of heart hereby,vnlefle alfo we might be affured of his acceptation.

The expofition of Ecclef.9.1. But let vs examine thefe words and fhew the true fenfe of them.There are two expofitions giuen,which may ftand with the analogie of faith and the circumftances of the text. For fome vnderftand thefe words not of Gods loue or hatred, but of mans loue towards thofe things he defires, and of his hatred towards thofe things he flieth; and then this is the fenfe of the place; A man knoweth not whether thofe things which he loueth, as pleafures, honours and riches, or thofe things which hee hateth,namely croffes and afflictions fhall happen vnto him,becaufe they are not difpofed by his owne power,but by the prouidence of God who giueth thefe outward things indifferently to all both iuft and vniuft.So that if the words are thus to be vnderftood, there is no fhew of reafon in the Papifts expofition.

Secondly,let it be granted that it is to be vnderftood of Gods loue towards vs,yet it will make nothing for their purpofe: for then this is the plaine fenfe of the words; no man can know whether hee bee loued or hated of God by thefe common outward things which happen alike to al,and in refpect whereof there is the fame condition to the iuft and the wicked,and to the pure and polluted, to thofe that worfhip God and thofe that worfhip him not: there is no iudgement that can bee giuen, either of our felues or others in refpect of our outward ftate, for fometime the iuft are poore, the vniuft rich, the wicked aduanced to honour,and the godly afflicted and perfecuted. For example, *Efau* enioyed his
delights

delights and plentie of all things, *Iacob* like a poore pilgrime
went into a ftrange countrie, hauing no other riches but his
clothes on his backe and his ftaffe in his hand, & when he was
come amongft his friends he endured tedious labours,& many miferies; and fo *Dauid* was perfecuted,whileft *Saul* did fit
on the throne;yea our Sauiour Chrift himfelfe was arraigned
at the barre and condemned, whileft *Pilate* and the chiefe
Priefts and Pharifies fate in the feate of iuftice, ouerfwaying
all at their owne pleafures: and yet at the fame time, *Iacob*
was beloued,*Efau* hated; *Dauid* chofen of God, *Saul* reiected ; our Sauiour Chrift the deare fonne of his heauenly father, and his enemies the inftruments and limmes of Sathan.
So that it is moft true that *Salomon* fpeaketh, namely,no man
ean haue affurance of Gods loue and fauour by thefe outward
benefits beftowed both vpon the godly and wicked; neither
by his aduerfities and afflictions can gather that the Lord hateth him: for thefe befall all indifferently, as it pleafeth God
to punifh the reprobate,or to chaftize his owne children.

But though we can gather no found argument from thefe
outward things of Gods loue, yet it followeth not that there
is no other meanes to affure vs hereof:for by the fame reafon
wee may conclude that man is no better than brute beafts,
and that there is no immortalitie of the foule , becaufe it is Ecclef.3.19.
faid, Ecclef.3.19. that the condition of the children of men
and the condition of beafts is the fame. But as the Wifeman
fpeaketh there of their outward mortalitie alone,and not ab-
folutely in all refpects ; and therefore he faith that they are a-
like to fee to, that is, in outward appearance,verf.18.and ex-
plaineth himfelfe in the words following ; for (faith hee) as
one dieth fo dieth the other : fo he doth not meane here fimply that there is no affurance of Gods loue, but onely in refpect of thefe outward things, and therefore he addeth, that
in thefe outward refpects all things come alike to all,and the
fame condition is to the iuft and the wicked.

Though then there is no affurance of Gods loue to be gathered out of our worldly eftate, yet it cannot hence be concluded that therefore there is no meanes whereby we may be
affured hereof : for the Lord hath giuen vnto vs his word and
mercifull

mercifull promifes, he hath giuen vnto vs his holy fpirit *cry-*
ing in our harts Abba father, and witneffing to our fpirits that we
*are the fonnes of God,*Rom.8. He hath manifefted his loue by

Rom.8.

giuing vs his onely fonne, and begetting in vs by his word
and fpirit a liuely faith, whereby wee may apply him and all
his benefits vnto vs. Whofoeuer therefore beleeueth truly in
Iefus Chrift, he may be affured of Gods loue and euerlafting
life, according to that Ioh.3.16. *So God loued the world, that he*
gaue his onely begotten fonne, that whofoeuer beleeneth in him
fhould not perifh, but haue euerlafting life.

Ioh.3.16.

If therefore we beleeue in Iefus Chrift, we need not to defpaire, no nor to doubt of Gods loue and fauour towards vs;
notwithftanding our vnworthineffe, nor yet in regard of the
manifold afflictions which God inflicteth on vs, neither in
refpect of thofe manifold infirmities which we bewray whileft the hand of God is vpon vs: but wee may foundly and affuredly conclude with the Apoftle *Paul,*Rom.8.38. *I am per-*
fwaded that neither death nor life, nor Angels, nor principalities,
nor powers, nor things prefent, nor things to come, 39. Nor height
nor depth, nor any other creature fhall be able to feparate vs from
the loue of God which is in Chrift Iefus our Lord.

Rom.8.38.

And fo much concerning the firft caufe of our faluation,
namely Gods loue and goodwill, and alfo the temptations
of Sathan, whereby hee laboureth to impugne our affurance
thereof : the fecond caufe is Gods free election, which proceedeth from the other ; for whom he loueth, thofe hee electeth vnto euerlafting life and happineffe, it being an infepa-
rable fruite of loue to feeke the good and felicitie of the partie beloued.

Election therefore is that part of Gods eternal and immutable decree, whereby of his free loue and vndeferued grace
he hath preordained fome in Chrift vnto faluation, and to the
vfe of the meanes tending thereunto, for the praife of the
glorie of his grace.

CHAP. IIII.

Of Gods election,the causes, subiect,obiect, and properties thereof.

IN this definition is set downe first the efficient cause or author of our election, namely God himselfe, the Father, the Sonne and the holy Ghost; and this appeareth Eph.1.4. *He hath chosen vs in him before the foundation of the world, that we should be holy &c.* And Ioh.15.16. *Ye haue not chosen me, but I haue chosen you, and ordained you that ye goe and bring foorth fruite,&c.*

Secondly, the motiue or impulsiue cause of Gods election is expressed,namely,Gods free loue,meere goodwill and vndeserued grace.And this also is manifest Luk.12.32. *Feare not little flocke, for it is your fathers pleasure to giue you a kingdome.* And Eph.1.5. who *hath predestinated vs to be adopted through Iesus Christ vnto himselfe, according to the good pleasure of his will.*

Here therefore are excluded all other causes,wherewith diuers haue imagined God was moued to elect vs ; as namely our owne will, the foreseeing of our workes worthinesse or faith, and the merits of our Sauiour Christ. And that these were not the causes which mooued the Lord to elect vs, it may be prooued by manifest testimonies of scripture. First, our owne will is expressely excluded,Rom.9.16. *It is not in him that willeth or runneth,but in God that sheweth mercie.* Secondly,not the foresight of our owne workes,for the Apostle plainly affirmeth Rom.9.11.12. that *before the children were borne,and when they had neither done good or euill, that the purpose of God might remaine according to election,not by workes,but by him that calleth.* 12. *It was said vnto her, the elder shall serue the younger,* 13. *As it is written, I haue loued Iacob and hated Esau.* And chap.11.5.6. he saith, that *Gods election is of grace, and if it be of grace it is no more of workes, or els were grace no more grace.* Thirdly, not the foresight of any worthinesse in vs more than in others ; *For there is no difference, for all haue*
sinned

finned and are depriued of the glorie of God: as it is Rom.3.23.
And the Apoftle affirmeth both of himfelfe and others, *that*
they were all dead in their finnes, and by nature the children of
*wrath as well as others,*Eph.2.1.3. Fourthly, the Lord refpec-
ted not our faith as an impulfiue caufe mouing him to elect
vs,but only as an effect of our election ; neither was the Lord
mercifull vnto vs in making choife of vs to bee partakers of
euerlafting happineffe,becaufe we were faithfull, but,that we
might be faithfull, as *Paul* profeffeth of himfelfe 1.Cor.7.25.
And the holy Ghoft affirmeth,Act.13.46. that as many of the
Gentiles as were ordained vnto eternall life beleeued. Laftly, although the merit of Chrift was the onely meritorious caufe
of our faluation,yet it was not the caufe of Gods election,for
Gods election was from all eternitie,and the caufe of Chrifts
merits, which were in time and the effects of Gods election,
and therefore that which came after could not be the caufe
of that which was from all eternitie, neither can the effect
produce the caufe,but the caufe the effect. Moreouer, we are
not faid in the fcriptures to be chofen for Chrift,but in Chrift,
Eph.1.4. And the Apoftle *Iohn* affirmeth, that Gods eternall
loue was the caufe which moued the Lord to fend his fonne
to redeeme vs by his death, and not that his death was the
caufe of his loue,Ioh.3.16. And fo much concerning the efficient caufe of our election. The materiall caufe thereof was
the purpofe or counfaile of God himfelfe, whereby hee determined to elect vs.

§. Sect.2.   The formall caufe was the feuering and fetting apart of
certaine men which were to bee faued, felected from the reft
who were reiected.

     The end of Gods election was two-fold : the firft and chief
end was the glorie of God,fet forth by manifefting his grace
and mercie in the faluation of the faithfull. And this the A-
poftle plainly expreffeth Rom.9.23.namely, that the end of
Gods election is, *that he might declare the riches of his glorie*
in the veffels of mercie, which he hath prepared vnto glorie. And
Eph.1.4,5,6.he faith,that *he hath chofen vs in Chrift,and prede-*
ftinated vs,to the praife of the glorie of his grace.
     The fecond end which is inferiour and fubordinate to the
                                                             other,

other, is the saluation of the elect, and this also is expressed
by the Apostle Rom.9.23. where hee saith, that the elect *are
prepared vnto glorie.* And Act.13.48. the holy Ghost saith,*as
many as were ordained to eternal life:*thereby implying that the
saluation of the elect is the end of Gods election. And these
are the causes of Gods election. The effects which inseparably follow hereupon, are Christ the Mediatour, and the
whole worke of his mediation and our redemption wrought
by him, our adoption, effectuall calling, iustification, sanctification, and glorification; and these are the degrees and
meanes of our election, which are as well contained in Gods
decree as our saluation it selfe.

The subiect in which we are elected, is Christ Iesus our Mediatour and head; not in regard of his deitie alone, for so he is
the efficient cause ; nor in respect of his humanitie alone, but
as he is God and man. And wee are therefore elected in him,
both because in our selues we were not capable of such glorious dignitie, as also because hee alone is a fit Mediatour in
whom we should be elected, seeing with our election there is
an vnion & coniunction of vs with God who hath elected vs.

The obiect of Gods election are all those who are preordained vnto euerlasting life, and whom the Lord will eternally saue; which being considered in themselues are a great
number, but yet in respect of the number of the reprobates
but a small and little flocke ; for *though many be called, yet few
are chosen,*as Christ himselfe affirmeth, Matth.22.14.

The last thing, which also is expressed in the definition, are
certaine properties attributed to Gods election; namely, that
it is eternall, free and immutable. That this decree is eternall,
it appeareth Eph.1.4. *He hath chosen vs in him before the foundation of the world.* So Rom.9.11.

Secondly, that it is free and of his meere grace, it is manifest Rom.9.18. *He hath mercie on whom he will, and whom he will
he hardneth.* So Eph.1.11. *In whom we are chosen when wee were
predestinate, according to the purpose of him which worketh all
things after the counsaile of his owne will.*

Lastly, that it is immutable and most firme and certaine, it
plainly appeareth 2.Tim.2.19. *The foundation of God remai-*
N   *neth*

neth sure, and hath this seale, the Lord knoweth who are his.
Where we may obserue, that this immutabilitie and certaintie of Gods decree, doth not depend vpon vs or our perseuerance, but vpon Gods good pleasure and foreknowledge, for
it is a foundation in it selfe firme and stable, and hath not the
seale of our worthinesse or perseuerance in grace, but of
Gods foreknowledge whereby he knoweth who are his.

CHAP. V.

*Sathans temptations concerning Gods election answered, and
first those wherewith he assaulteth carnall worldlings.*

§. Sect. 1.
Sathans temp-
tation whereby
he perswadeth
worldlings that
all in the end
shall be saued,
answered.

NOw concerning this decree of election and the af-
surance thereof, there are two sorts of Sathans
temptations: the first he suggesteth into the minds
of carnall worldlings, to nourish in them fond presumption
and carnall securitie: the other, into the minds of weak christians, whereby he moueth them to doubt & despaire of their
electiō to euerlasting life. The worldly man he assaulteth with
two principal temptations: first, he perswadeth him that there
is no election at al or reprobation, but that all in the end shall
be saued. Which grosse absurditie that hee may make more
plausible and probable, hee setteth before them the infinite
mercie of God, and the generall promises and consolations

Ezech. 13.
and 18.
1. Tim. 2. 4.

in the Gospell: as, *that he will not the death of a sinner,* and that
he will *that all men shall be saued,* in both places cunningly dis-
sembling that which followeth; for to the first place is added, but *that he repent,* and in the latter, that they *who shall be
saued must also come to the knowledge of the truth.*

But this temptation is so palpably absurd, that it becommeth not Sathans policie to vse it to any, but those onely
whose hearts are hardned, their eyes blinded, their consciences seared, and who hauing not beleeued and loued the truth,
are giuen ouer of God to beleeue strong delusions; and therfore I will not spend much time in answering this temptation: onely let such men as are seduced with Sathans lyes
know thus much, that Gods mercie is a iust mercie, as his iustice

stice is a mercifull iustice; that God is infinite in both, and no lesse glorified in the manifestation of the one than of the other. Let them know that there are no promises of the Gospell so generall, which are not limited with the condition of faith, and the fruite thereof vnfained repentance. Let them know, that God who is not onely mercifull but also true, yea truth it selfe, hath in his word reuealed his will, as well concerning the eternall death and destruction of the wicked, as the saluation of the godly : he hath said, that *many are called* Matth. 22. 14. *and few chosen*; that the gate of heauen is so straight, that and 7. 13. there are few who finde it ; that he will say to the workers of iniquitie, *Goe your waies I know you not*; that hee will make 23. a separation betweene the sheepe and the goates, and as hee saith to the one, *Come ye blessed of my father, inherit ye the kingdome prepared for you from the foundations of the world*, so hee Mat. 25. 34. 41. will say to the other, *Depart from me ye cursed into euerlasting fire, which is prepared for the diuell and his angels.* Let them know that neither *fornicators, nor idolaters, nor adulterers, nor wantons, nor buggerers, not theeues, nor couetous, nor drunkards,* 1. Cor. 6. 9. 10. *nor railers, nor extortioners*, nor any that liue in the like sinnes, without repentance, *shall inherit the kingdome of God*, for truth it selfe hath spoken it, 1. Cor. 6. 9. 10. but they shall haue *their part in the lake which burneth with fire and brimstone, which is* Reu. 21. 8. *the second death*, as it is Reucl. 21. 8. And therefore let not Sathan bewitch them, by setting before their eyes Gods mercie ; for as sure as God is iust and true of his word, so surely shall such as continue in their sinnes, without repentance, bee eternally condemned ; neither is it any impeachment to Gods mercie, if hee exercise his iustice in inflicting due punishment vpon obstinate and rebellious sinners, seeing it is sufficiently manifested in the saluation of those who repent and beleeue.

The second temptation which Sathan suggesteth into the §. Sect. 2. minds of carnall men, to the end they may runne on in their desperate courses, and wallow still in the pleasing filth of their corruptions, hee thus frameth ; Why enioyest thou not (saith he) thy pleasures ? why art thou afraid to satisfie all thy desires ? what needest thou to take any paines in perfour-

ming

ming Gods worſhip and ſeruice, and to what purpoſe ſhouldeſt thou forſake thy pleaſing ſinnes, ſtudying and ſtriuing after mortification and newneſſe of life, which is ſo bitter and vnpleaſant vnto thee? for Gods decree of predeſtination is ſure and moſt vnchangeable as himſelfe is without change, and therefore if thou art elected of God thou maieſt follow thy delights, goe on in thy ſinnes, liue as thou liſt, yet ſurely thou ſhalt be ſaued, and he will giue thee repentance, though it be deferred to the laſt gaſpe. But if on the other ſide thou art a reprobate, reiected of God in his eternall councell, then take what paines thou wilt, make thy throte horce with praying, and thy bagges emptie with giuing almes, be neuer ſo diligent in Gods ſeruice, neuer ſo carefull in mortifying thy ſins, yet all is in vaine, for thoſe whom he hath reprobated ſhall be condemned. And therefore much better were it to take thy pleaſure and to follow thine owne deſires whileſt thou art in this life: for the puniſhments of the life to come will be enough, though thou addeſt no torments of this life vnto them.

And thus doth Sathan reaſon in the minde of a carnall man, partly to continue and increaſe his ſecuritie in the courſe of ſinne, and partly to diſcredit the holy doctrine of Gods eternall predeſtination, as though it opened a dore to all licentiouſneſſe. But if we conſider of this temptation aright, and ſound it to the bottome, we ſhall finde firſt that it is moſt fooliſh and ridiculous, ſecondly that it is moſt falſe and impious. That it is moſt fooliſh it will eaſily appeare, if we vſe the like manner of reaſoning in worldly matters; for it is all one as if a man ſhould thus ſay: thy time is appointed, and the Lord in his counſaile hath ſet downe how long thou ſhalt liue; if therefore it be ordained that thy time ſhall be ſhort, vſe what meanes thou wilt of phiſicke and good diet, yet ſhalt thou not prolong it one day; but if God hath decreed that thou ſhalt liue to olde age, take what courſes thou wilt, runne into all deſperate daungers, vſe ſurfetting and all diſorder of diet, nay eate no meate at all, and yet thou ſhalt liue till thou art an old man. Or as if he ſhould ſay; God hath decreed alreadie whether thou ſhalt be rich or poore, and if

he

he hath appointed thee to be poore, take neuer so much paines, follow thy calling as diligently as thou wilt, abstaine from all wastfulnesse and prodigalitie, yet shalt thou neuer get any wealth: but if thou art preordained to be rich, sell all thou hast and scatter it abroade in the streetes, spend thy time in gaming, drinking and whoring, neuer troubling thy head with care, nor thy hands with worke, yet shalt thou be a welthie man. Now who would not laugh at such absurd manner of reasoning if any should vse it? because euery man knoweth, that as God hath decreed the time of our life, so he hath decreed also that we should vse the meanes, whereby our liues may be preserued so long as he hath ordained that we should liue, namely auoyding of daungers, good diet, and phisicke; and as he hath decreed that a man should be rich, so he hath decreed also that he should vse all good meanes of attaining vnto riches, namely prouidence and paines in getting, and care and frugalitie in keeping that he hath gotten; and whosoeuer vse not the meanes, doe make it manifest that they were not ordained vnto the end. Although indeede, because the Lord would shew his absolute and almightie power, he doth not alwaies tie himselfe vnto meanes, but sometimes crosseth and maketh them vneffectuall to their ends, and sometime he effecteth what he will, without or contrarie to all meanes; and hence it is that some quickly die who vse all meanes to preserue health, and some become poore who vse al meanes of obtaining riches, whereas others being depriued of the meanes attaine vnto long life and riches by the immediate blessing of God. But ordinarily the meanes and end goe together, and therefore it is fond presumption to imagine or hope, without the vse of the meanes, to attaine vnto the end. And thus it is also in spirituall matters appertaining to euerlasting life; those whom God hath elected, he hath ordained also that they should attaine vnto and vse all good meanes tending thereunto, namely faith, repentance, sanctification, and newnesse of life: and therefore it is as absurd for any to imagine, that they shall be saued continuing in their ignorance, infidelitie, vnrepentancie, and filthie corruptions, as it is for a man to thinke that

N 3   he he shall liue to be old, and yet runneth into all daungers, for-saketh phisicke yea and foode also whereby his life should be sustained. For the spirituall meanes of saluation are as well (nay much more) contained in Gods decree, as the corpo-rall meanes of preseruing life: for it hath been heard-of, that some haue liued in the middest of daungers, and in the ab-sence of meate, for a long time; but it was neuer heard that any haue attained vnto euerlasting life without faith, repen-tance, and sanctification : for euen the thiefe vpon the crosse beleeued in Christ, and shewed the fruites of his faith in ac-knowledging his owne sinne reprooving his fellow, in con-fessing our Sauiour Christ euen then when his Apostles de-nied and forsooke him, in calling vpon his name and desiring by his meanes euerlasting life.

§. Sect.3.
Sathans temp-tation groun-ded vpon the vnchangeable-nesse of Gods decree false and impious.

But as this temptation is foolish, so also it is false; for whereas he saith that though we liue in our sinnes without repentance, yet we may be elected and therefore shall be saued; and though we take neuer so great paines in Gods seruice, and most carefully indeauour to spend our liues in holinesse and righteousnesse, yet we may be reprobates and therefore shall bee condemned; this is vtterly vntrue : for, whomsoeuer the Lord hath ordained to euerlasting life, those also he hath ordained to vse the meanes whereby they may be saued, and consequently whosoeuer carefully vse these meanes may be assured of their saluation, whosoeuer neglect and despise these meanes they manifestly declare that they are not in the number of the elect, so long as they continue in their neglect and contempt: for the end and the meanes tending to the end, are inseparably ioyned in Gods decree; so that they who vse the one shall obtaine the other, they who neglect and contemne the meanes shall neuer attaine vnto the end.

The end of Gods election twofold.
Eph. 1.5.6.

Now the end of Gods election is two fould. The chiefe and principall is his owne glorie, as appeareth Ephes.1.5.6. *Who hath predestinate vs to bee adopted through Iesus Christ vnto himselfe, according to the good pleasure of his will; to the praise of the glorie of his grace.* And this end the Lord will not suffer to be frustrate: for his glorie shall shine in all his elect, and

therefore

therefore we also are most carefully to labour that we may further this end; for the more that the praise of Gods mercie doth shine in vs, the better assurance we haue of our election. And seeing God is most glorified when as our lights shine brightest before men in a godly and christian life, therefore let vs be most carefull to spend our time in holinesse and righteousnesse, that thereby we may glorifie our heauenly father, and also make our owne election sure; for he hath chosen vs that we should be holy, and therefore if we be holy it is a most certaine signe that he hath chosen vs.

Mat.6.16.
1.Pet.2.21.

Eph.1.4.

The second end of Gods election is the saluation of his elect; for the iust accomplishing whereof, he hath preordained diuers subordinate causes or meanes, which are the inseparable effects and fruites of his election; all which are so linked one with another, as that the precedent meanes is the cause of that which next in order followeth, and Gods decree the cause of all. The effects of Gods election, which are the subordinate causes or meanes of our saluation, are principally three; Vocation, Iustification, and Sanctification. By vocation we are separated from the world, made members of the Church, & ingrafted in to the body of Christ; and this is ordinarily done by the preaching of the word being made effectual by the inward operation of Gods spirit, or extraordinarily by some other meanes, or immdiately by the illumination of the holy Ghost. In our iustification we haue the pardon and remission of all our sinnes by vertue of Christs merit, and are adorned with his righteousnesse imputed vnto vs: and this is done, principally by God himselfe, & instrumentally by a liuely faith. Our sanctification consisteth in our dying to sin, and rising vp to newnes of life; which is begun, increafed, and finished in vs by Gods spirit. Whosoeuer therefore are predestinate to saluation, they also are effectually called, that is separate from the world, and ingrafted into the body of Christ; and this they attaine vnto by diligent and attentiue hearing of the word. Whosoeuer are effectually called, are also iustified; and therefore haue obtained a true and liuely faith. Whosoeuer are iustified are also sanctified, that is, die vnto their sinnes, and rise againe to newnes of life,

The second end of Gods election.

and

and confequently whofoeuer are ftill meere worldlings and no true members of Chrifts bodie (as all thofe are who make no confcience of hearing Gods word diligently, reuerently, and attentiuely, nor of treafuring it vp in their hearts) they are not truly called; whofoeuer haue not Chrifts righteouf-neffe and obedience imputed and applied vnto them (which none haue that are deftitute of a true and fruitfull faith)are not iuftified; whofoeuer liue in their finnes, without repentance, without any earneft defire and hartie endeuour of fer-uing the Lord in holineffe and righteoufneffe of life are not fanctified; and whofoeuer are not called, iuftified and fancti-fied, fhall neuer be faued; for the end and the meanes ten-ding thereunto are ioyned together in Gods predeftination. So that where the one is, there the other is; where the one neuer is, there the other fhall euer be wanting. And therefore as by our fanctification, iuftification, and vocation, wee may certainly conclude that we are elected and fhall be faued; fo if we be without thefe, wee may as certainly inferre that wee are reiected, and fhall be condemned if wee liue and die in this ftate.

Seeing then this is Gods truth, let not Sathan lull vs in fe-curitie with that fophifticall cauill; if wee be elected we fhall be faued liue how wee lift; if we be reprobates wee fhall be condemned, be we neuer fo earneft in labouring after godli-neffe: for thefe principles may well ftand together, it is im-poffible that the elect fhould perifh, and as impoffible alfo that any who beleeue not in Chrift, and bring not foorth the fruites of their faith in a godly and Chriftian life fhould bee faued; it cannot bee that the reprobate fhould attaine vnto euerlafting happineffe, and that any fhould not attaine there-unto, who defireth and endeuoureth to ferue and feare the Lord: becaufe predeftination and faluation are fo coupled together with the meanes that come betweene them, that they cannot poffibly be feuered from one another, nor the meanes from either of them, nor yet amongft themfelues; euen as the firft lincke of a chaine is ioyned with the laft by thofe which are betweene them, and thefe which are in the middle one with another.

CHAP.

CHAP. VI.

Sathans temptations whereby he moueth the weake Chriſtian
to doubt of his election, anſwered.

Nd theſe are the temptations wherewith Sathan
aſſaulteth the worldling : but if he haue to deale
with a true Chriſtian, who is indeede elected of
God, and ſheweth the fruites of his election, by
deſiring and endeuouring to ſerue the Lord in
holineſſe and righteouſnes, then he perſwadeth him to doubt
of his election, and to hang as it were wauering in the ayre,
ſometime lifted vp with hope, ſometime deiected and caſt
downe with feare, till at laſt he being wearie and tired with
his doubtful thoughts, and hauing no where to reſt himſelfe,
is ſwallowed vp of deſperation : like vnto a ſillie bird which
flieth ouer the maine Ocean, and one while hopeth to attaine
vnto the land, another while feareth ſeeing no place where to
light, till at laſt being ſo weary that ſhe can flie no further, ſhe
falleth downe and is drowned in the ſea. So theſe one while
hope, and ſoone after finding their owne infirmities, and not
ſeeing where they may reſt their wauering minds, doubt and
feare, till at laſt through wearineſſe they ſinke downe and are
ſwallowed vp in the gulfe of deſperation, where they are
drowned and deſtroyed, if it doe not pleaſe the Lord to lift
them vp again, and to ſhew them the firme Rock Ieſus Chriſt,
whereupon they may reſt their wearie mindes and refreſh
their fainting ſoules ; which hee alwaies doth perfourme to
thoſe that belong to his election; for it is impoſſible that any
of them ſhould periſh, though Sathan and all the power of
hell ſeeke their ruine and deſtruction.

§. Sect. 1.
The cauſes
which moue Sa-
than and his
inſtruments to
perſwade the
weake chriſtian
to doubt of his
election.

But at this marke Sathan aimeth though hee neuer hitteth
it, and though he neuer finally preuaile, yet to this doubting,
and in the end deſpairing, he laboureth to perſwade the true
Chriſtian ; neither doth hee content himſelfe with the forces
of his owne temptations, but he ioyneth with him the world,
which is as readie as Sathan himſelfe to oppugne the certaintie.

tie of our election, and our owne traytcrous flesh which is
easily moued to doubting and despaire, when as it seeth nothing in it selfe whereupon it may rest. In the world he maketh his choise not of sillie ignorant men, but of the most
subtill Sophisters and learned Doctors, the true successors of
the Scribes and Pharisies, euen the whole rabble of the Popish clergie; who stand on Sathans part stoutly fighting his
battailes, being perswaded and ouercome by that temptation which our Sauiour Christ withstood, *All this will I giue
thee.* For to what end (I pray you) doe these great Doctors
so stifly stand in the defence of Sathans cause, perswading
men might and maine to doubt of their election, and consequently of their saluation? Surely that by emptying mens
minds of all true comfort, they may fill their own chests, and
get the treasures of the earth into their possessions. For when
the weake conscience wauereth and doubteth of his election,
and not finding any true consolation whereupon it may rest,
commeth vnto them for some comfort and better assurance;
they behaue themselues like vnto vngracious Surgeons, who
intending to make a pray of their patients, and to get their
gains out of their pains and tortures, do one day heale, and
the next day hinder the cure, making the wound worse than
it was whē they took it in hand, til at last they haue so poysoned the sore that it is past their cure, whereas they could easily haue healed it, if they had not regarded their profit more
than their own credit, or their patients health: or like vnto deceitfull Lawyers, who somtimes speake in their clients cause,
and sometimes betray it, going about in a tedious circuit,
whereas the direct way lieth open before them, that so their
clients cause being made more doubtfull & tedious, & themselues impatient of delaies, are faine to double and trebble
their fees, and yet oftentimes to no purpose, becaufe the
more they receiue, the fitter they thinke them to be their perpetuall Clients. So doe these Popish Chirurgeons and Ro-
mish counsailers deale with their Pacient and Client; for shewing his wounded conscience, and desiring some comfort at
their hands, they will not make any soueraigne salue of the
simples which they might gather out of Gods word, whereby
he

he might soone be healed, for then their cure, and consequently their gaines were at an ende : but they holde him in
suspense, and increase his disease of doubting, applying
thereunto poysons in stead of salues, whereby at last his
wound is made desperate. Thou canst not (will they say) attaine vnto any certaine assurance of thine election, for that
were fond presumption; but thou art to hope well : and that
thou maist confirme thy hope, thou must make vowes and
goe on pilgrimage,to inuocate and offer vnto these and these
saints,thou must doe these workes of supererogation, build
such a Monastery,repaire such a Church,giue so much money
to such a Cloister,buie these Indulgences,whereby thou maist
recciue pardon for thy sinnes ; and for more surety sake, thou
shalt at thy death bequeath so much money to the Priests,
for Masses,Trentals and Dirges,that if it happen thou goe into Purgatorie, thou maist speedely be deliuered : but all this
while they speake not a word of Gods vndeserued grace and
free election, not a syllable of Christs death and satisfaction
for our sinnes; no,this were too soueraigne a salue,and would
too soone heale the wounded conscience, and so marre the
market of these mount-bankes,making their Vowes, Pilgrimages,Masses,Dirges,Indulgences,and other trumpery-ware
not worth the cheapning.

But let vs consider the state of the question betweene vs
and Sathan,with his Doctors and Proctors, whom he seeth
with worldly riches to pleade his cause. We hold that a man
truly conuerted,indued with a liuely faith and sanctified,may
ordinarily be assured that he is the child of God, elected to
saluation: but they affirme that it is presumption for such to
haue any certaine assurance hereof,vnlesse it be by extraordinary reuelation ; he may hope indeede that he is elected and
shall be saued, but this hope must he tempered with feare,
and mixt with doubting ; and this doubting they call humilitie, which they doe not account an infirmitie, but rather a
vertue which doth commend their faith, esteeming firme assurance to be but hereticall confidence and damnable presumption,and pronouncing him accursed in their councell of
*Trent,*who affimeth that we are to beleeue without doubting
the

§. *Sect.2.*
*The state of this
question be-
tweene the
Christian and
Sathan with his
assistants.*

the remission of our owne sinne and euerlasting life in particular.

And becaufe they cannot but confesse, that doubting and beleeuing, in themselues are oppoſed one againſt another; they teach, that their faith is affured of Gods mercy and Chriſts merits, as in themselues infinite and sufficient; but it doubteth (in respect of our vnworthinesse and manifold imperfections) to apply them particularly vnto our selues: so that when we looke vpon God and Chriſt, there is cauſe of firme affurance, but when we looke vpon our selues, there is nothing but matter of doubting, there is in deed some place left to their ſtaggering hope, but none to affurance of faith : as though our faith were grounded on our owne worthinesse, and not vpon Gods free mercy and Chriſts merits; and as though reſting vpon these alone, it could not haue certaine affurance of our election and saluation, notwithſtanding our vnworthinesse and corruptions. But let vs arme our selues a-gainſt this their doctrine, which containeth nothing elſe but principles whereupon ſathan may ground his temptations, whereby he perſwadeth vs firſt to doubting, and afterwards to deſpairing of our election and saluation; for when the troubled conscience hath no other affurance of Gods loue and his owne election, but that which is gathered from his owne worthinesse and workes, he ſtill doubteth whether yet he be worthy, or haue fulfilled the measure of workes requi-red; and then further examining himſelfe to cleare his doubt, and finding his beſt workes exceeding imperfect, and that his ſinnes and corruptions are innumerable, then is his conscience ſet vpon the racke, and his soule plunged into deepe deſpaire, hauing no other ſtay but the broken ſtaffe of his owne righ-teouſnesse, which moſt deceiueth him when he moſt truſteth to it.

§. Sect. 3.
The points to be considered of in this controuersie.

And that we may be confirmed againſt ſathans tempta-tions, and the ſubtill ſophiſtrie of these his Doctors, I will handle this poynt at large, and will plainely proue, firſt, that the childe of God being conuerted, iuſtified and ſanctified, may be certainely affured of his particular election, and that without any ſpeciall reuelation after an ordinarie manner.
. Secondly,

Secondly, I will shew the meanes whereby we may attaine
vnto this assurance; and the infallible signes of our election.
Lastly, I will answere such obiections as are made against it
by sathan and his adherents.

Concerning the first, namely, that we may be certainely assured of our election and saluation, it may be proued by testimonies of Scriptures, and also by infallible reasons grounded vpon them. For we must not thinke that we can haue this
assurance, by ascending into heauen, and there searching into
Gods secret decree, but we must gather it out of Gods word,
wherein the Lord hath reuealed his will vnto vs: and in regard
hereof, though Gods will in it selfe be secret, so that we may
aske *who hath knowne the will of the Lord?* yet seeing the Lord
hath reuealed his hidden will in his word, we may say with
Paul, that we haue knowne the minde of Christ. Now this knowledge of Gods will concerning our election, is not to be gathered out of the lawe, as the Papists would haue it; for by
reason of the condition annexed to the promise of euerlasting life (*Doe this and liue*) it leaueth our consciences in perpetuall doubting, nay, rather in vtter desperation, because we
knowe that we are farre from the exact obedience thereof: but
out of the gracious promises of the Gospell, freely made to
euery one who beleeueth, without any condition of our owne
workes and worthinesse. And therefore if wee beleeue the
promises of the Gospell made in Christ, we may be assured of
our election and saluation, though in our selues we are miserable sinners, who haue transgressed all Gods commaundements: for the couenant and promises of God made to *Abraham* and his seede, was not *through the lawe, but through the
righteousnesse of faith,* as it is Rom 4.13. and therefore it is by
faith, that it might come by grace, and the promise might be
sure, not in selfe onely, and in respect of the sufficiencie of
Gods mercie and Christs merits, as the Papists dreame; but to
all the seede, that is, to all that beleeue, and be the children of
Abraham, who was the father of the faithfull both Iew and
Gentill. For otherwise we should haue no better assurance of
saluation by the Gospell than by the Law; for euen the promise of the Law was most sure in it selfe and on Gods part,

*That we may
be certainly
assured of our
election, proued
by the testimo-
nies of the
Scriptures.*

1.Cor.2.16.

*The couenant
of grace made
to assure vs of
our election.*

Rom.4.13.

yet

yet not sure to vs who could not perfourme the condition: and therefore the Lord made a new couenant, not of workes but of grace, onely on the condition of faith; that so the promise might be sure, not onely in it selfe and on Gods behalf, but also vnto vs who are *Abrahams* seede, that is, true beleeuers, as appeareth Rom.4.16. And this also notably appeareth Heb.6.17.18. where the Apostle saith, that God *willing more abundantly to shew vnto the heires of promise the stablenes of his counsaile, bound himselfe by an oath,* 18. *That by two immutable things wherein it is impossible that God should lie, wee might haue strong consolation, which haue our refuge to hold fast the hope that is set before vs,* 19. *Which we haue as an anchor of the soule both sure and stedfast.* In which words the Apostle plainly sheweth, that the Lord hath added his oath to his promise, not to the end that in it self it should be confirmed, or needed any confirmation on Gods part (for his bare word is yea and Amen, so infallible and sure, that though *heauen and earth passe away and perish, yet not one iot or title of his word shall faile till all things be fulfilled*) but to the end that we to whom the promises are made, might be assured of the stablenesse of his counsaile, and thereby receiue strong consolation, and might rest our soules in the tempests of temptations vpon firme hope, as it were vpon a stedfast and sure anchor. Now what stabilitie, what strong consolation, what stedfastnesse of hope, if wee are still vncertaine of our election, sometimes hoping, as when wee looke vpon Gods mercie and Christs merits, and sometimes doubting, as when wee looke vpon our owne sinnes and vnworthinesse? For what is this but to be shaken from our anchor hold, and to be tossed vp and downe with the waues of doubting, till at last wee dash against the rockes of despaire, and so make shipwrack of our soules?

§. Sect.4.
Particular testimonies proouing this point.

And thus you see that the couenant of grace was therefore made with vs, that wee might be assured of our election, and that the whole Gospell is nothing els but Gods ambassage, whereby he certifieth vs of his free and vndeserued loue in Iesus Christ: but let vs further consider of some speciall testimonies whereby this assurance is confirmed. Rom.5.1. it is said, that being *iustified by faith, wee haue peace towards God through*

(margin: Rom.4.16. Heb.6.17.18. Mat.5.18. Rom.5.1.)

torough our Lord Iesus Christ. But what peace can we haue, if wee be not assured of our election, but haue our mindes distracted and racked betweene faith and doubting, hope and despaire? Rom.8.38.the Apostle professeth, that *he is perswa-* Rom.8.38.
ded that neither death nor life, nor angels, nor principalities, &c. nor any other creature should be able to separate vs from the loue of God which is in Christ Iesus our Lord. It is true (wil the tempter say) that *Paul* had this assurance of his election and saluation, but it was by some speciall reuelation, and nor ordinarily; and therefore it followeth not hereof that euery particular Christian can haue this assurance. I answere, that the Apostle groundeth not his faith on reuelations in that place, but on a foundation common to him with all true Christians, namely on the death of Christ, verf.32. on Gods free iustifi- Verf.23.
cation, ver.33.and vpon Chrifts interceffion, ver.34.and from 33.
hence hee confirmeth his and our refolution, that nothing 34.
should feparate vs from the loue of Christ, verf.35.from the 35.
loue of God in him. Whofoeuer therefore with *Paul* beleeueth that Christ died for him, that God freely iustifieth him through Chrifts merits, and that our Sauiour fitteth at the right hand of his Father to make interceffion for him, he may be aflured of Gods loue, and confequently of his election. Secondly, *Paul* fpeaketh this not of himfelfe alone, but alfo of all the faithfull, and therefore he vfeth the plurall number, *I am perfwaded that nothing fhall be able to feparate vs*. So Eph. 3.12.the Apoftle faith, that wee haue through Christ *boldnefse* Eph.3.12.
and entrance with confidence by faith in him. And Heb.4.16. he Heb.4.16.
exhorteth vs to goe boldly vnto the throne of grace, that wee may and 10.22.
receiue mercie &c. And chap.10.22. *Let vs draw neere with a true heart in aflurance of faith, &c*. But I would faine know what entrance with confidence, what boldnefle and aflurance of faith, when we draw neere vnto God, and prefent our felues before his throne of maieftie, if we remaine doubtfull of his loue and our election? So Heb.6.19. he faith that *our* Heb.6.19.
hope is a fure and ftedfaft anchor of the foule; but what certaintie or ftedfaftnes is there in it, if it wauer and ftagger through doubtfulnes, fo often as wee looke vpon our finnes and vnworthineffe? The Apoftle *Peter* alfo doth tell vs, that the

truft.

1.Pet.1.13.

trust which we haue through Iesus Christ must *be perfect*, that is, *entire and perpetuall, till we enioy the thing which we hope for,* 1.Pet.1.13.And 2.Pet.1.10,he exhorteth vs *to vse all diligence that we may make our calling and election sure :* which if we could not doe, he should perswade vs to the vndertaking of a needelesse labour. Nay he plainely assureth vs, that *if we doe these things (to wit if we ioyne vertue with our faith, and with vertue knowledge, and with knowledge temperance, and with temperance patience, and with patience godlinesse, and with godlinesse brotherly kindnesse, and with brotherly kindnesse loue)we shall neuer fall*; becaufe thefe are effects and vndoubted fignes of our election. And the Apostle *Iohn* would not haue it a matter doubtfull, whether we are elected and shall be saued or no; but certainely knowne and vndoubtedly beleeued : and therefore he aimeth principally at this marke, and propoundeth this as the chiefe end of his epistle, namely to shew how we might know ordinarily, and be fully assured that we are

1.Ioh.3.14.

beloued of God, elected, and shall be saued. So 1.Ioh.3.14. *We know that we are translated from death to life, becaufe we loue the brethren.* And therefore in the latter end of his epistle he saith, that he had written it to this end, that *we might know that we haue eternall life.*

and 5.13.

chap.5.13. Seeing then the Scriptures doe commend vnto vs a stedfast and assured faith, whereby we particularly are assured and perswaded of our election and saluation, notwithstanding our sinnes and vnworthinesse: therefore let not the tempter perswade vs to cast away this certaine perswasion, and to wauer in doubting; but let vs

2.Tim.1.12.

say with the Apostle *Paul* 2.Tim.1.12, Though I am vnworthie *yet I know whom I haue beleeued, and I am perswaded that he is able to keepe that which I haue committed to him.*

§. *Sect.5.*
An obiection grounded vpon the indefinitnesse of Gods promifes anfwered.

But against that which hath been said the tempter obiecteth, that the promifes of the Gofpell are generall and indefinit, and therefore no man can gather out of them any certaine assurance of his particular election. I answere that this confequence is falfe: for out of a generall and indefinit propofition, we may truely and by the lawes of reafon gather and inferre a particular conclufion, though not contrariwife. For example, if I thus conclude ; all men are reafonable creatures.

tures: but I am a man; therefore I am a reasonable creature:
it is rightly and truely inferred. Though therefore the promifes of the Gofpell be contained in generall propofitions,
yet may euery faithfull man as certainely conclude, that they
belong vnto him, as if they were particularly applied vnto
him by name. For when the Lord by his ambaffadors maketh Ioh.3.16.
this generall propofition in the preaching of the word; whofoeuer truely beleeue in Chrift, they are all elected vnto e-
uerlafting life; the faithfull hearer maketh this affumption in
his minde, but I by the grace of God, and by the preaching
of his word made effectuall by his fpirit, haue a true faith
begotten in me, whereby I beleeue in Chrift my Sauiour;
and therefore Gods promife of life and faluation belongeth
vnto me. And thus alfo doth the confcience of man out of
the generall curfes of the law conclude that he is accurfed;
for when the law deliuereth this propofition in generall,
Curfed is euery one who abideth not in all things which are writ- Deut.27.26.
ten in the booke of the law to doe them; euery particular man Gal.3.10.
maketh this affumption in his owne confcience, but I haue
not continued in all to doe it, nay in ftead of doing all, I haue
neglected all, in fted of continuing in obedience, I haue
been continually difobedient, in fted of doing the duties
commaunded, I haue committed the finnes forbidden, and
therefore by the fentence of the law I am accurfed. So that
though both the threatnings of the law, and the promifes of
the Gofpell be generall and indefinit, yet doth euery mans
confcience truely informed by Gods word, gather out of
them moft certaine particular conclufions.

But here the tempter will obiect further; it is true indeede §. Sect.6.
that euery faithfull man, may apply the generall promifes of *That we may*
the Gofpell vnto himfelfe, but all the queftion is whether *be affured that*
thou canft know that thou haft faith or no, feeing many who *we are the*
continue in their infidelitie, bragge moft of their faith. I an- *faithfull,vnto*
fwere that it cannot be denied but that many are deceiued, *whom the pro-*
by contenting themfelues with their carnall fecuritie,in ftead *mifes of the*
of a liuely faith; but hence it followeth not, that becaufe *Gofpell are*
many are deceiued with an opinion of faith, therefore thofe *made.*
that beleeue indeede cannot be affured that they haue faith;

O   no

no more then this followeth, some men dreame that they
are rich, and are not so indeede when they awake, therefore
no man knoweth whether he be rich or no ; for what is their
secure opinion, but an idle dreame of their owne braines,
which hath no warrant out of Gods word? where as faith certainely and euidently perswadeth, and like a candle doth
not only manifest other things, but also it selfe appeareth by
his owne light. So that as a man who seeth and feeleth the fier
and the heate thereof, doth certainely know that hee seeth
and feeleth it, so he that beleeueth in Christ doth know that
he beleeueth indeede : yea as much more certaine is this
knowledge, as the knowledge of faith grounded vpon Gods
word which is infallible, is more certaine than the knowledge of the senses, which are often deceiued. Furthermore if
we could not be assured that we haue faith, then to what pur-
2.Cor.13.5. pose serues the admonition of the Apostle 2.Cor.13.5. *Try*
your selues whether you are in the faith, examine your selues :
know you not your owne selues, how that Iesus Christ is in you
except ye be reprobates? In which words the Apostle plainely
implieth, that we may know that we haue a true and liuely
faith, or els this triall and examination were vaine: nay hee
plainely saith that we may know that Christ is in vs, except
we be reprobates, and consequently that we haue faith; for
this onely is the hand whereby we apply Christ vnto vs and
1.Cor.11.28. all his benefits. So 1.Cor.11.28. the Apostle willeth vs to
examine our selues before we come to the Lords table, that
so we be not vnworthie guests; in which examination the
chiefe thing which we are to respect, is whether we haue a
true faith; for this is the mouth of the soule, whereby we
feede vpon the body and blood of our Sauiour Christ; and
therefore vnlesse we can know whether we haue faith when
we are truely indued therewith, this admonition of the Apostle were to no purpose; neither can we haue any assurance
to our owne soules, that we are worthie guests of the Lords
table, and consequently we rest doubtfull whether we receiue the Sacrament to our spirituall good and saluation, or
to our iudgement and condemnation. Thirdly, we are as-
Rom.14.23. sured of this by Gods word that *whatsoeuer is not done of*
faith

faith is ſinne. Rom.14.23. And *without faith it is impoſſible to* Heb.11.6.
pleaſe God Heb.11.6. If therefore we cannot be aſſured that
we haue faith, we can haue no aſſurance that our beſt actions,
our calling vpon Gods name, our hearing of his word, and
all other duties of pietie and iuſtice, are any better than
ſinnes and odious in Gods ſight : whereof it muſt needes follow that theſe actions, how good ſo euer in themſelues, will
be done of vs in doubting, becauſe we know not whether
they be done in faith; and being done doubtingly they become ſinnes indeede , and therefore diſpleaſing in Gods
ſight. Laſtly, if I can know whether I beleeue a man vpon his
word, and whether I truſt and rely my ſelfe vpon his promiſe
or no ; why may I not much more know whether I beleeue
Gods gracious promiſes made vnto all repentant ſinners,
and amongſt the reſt vnto my ſelfe, namely, that for the obedience and merits of Chriſt, I ſhall haue remiſſion of my
ſinnes and euerlaſting life ? ſeeing this faith is not out of our
ſelues, but a gift of God wrought in vs by his holy ſpirit,
which is not idle in vs, for it purifieth the heart, and worketh
by loue ; it mooueth vs to hate and flie from thoſe ſinnes we
haue loued, and to imbrace and loue that holineſſe and righteouſneſſe of life, which heretofore hath been loathſome vnto
vs. As therefore the fier is knowne by his heate, the ſunne
by the light, the good tree by his fruites, ſo when our cold
hearts are inflamed with the loue of God, and a feruent zeale
of his glorie, when our blinde vnderſtandings are inlightned
with the knowledge of God, and of the true religion, when
we bring forth the fruites of our profeſſion in a godly and
chriſtian life, then may we certainely know that we are indued with a true and liuely faith.

But here the tempter will take occaſion to perſwade the §. *Sect.7.*
weake chriſtian and the troubled conſcience, that he hath no *A temptation*
faith, ſeeing he doth not certainely know that he hath it, nor *grounded vpon*
diſcerneth theſe ſignes and fruites of faith in himſelfe. To *our aſſurance*
this ſuggeſtion we are to anſwere, that we doe not ſay that *of faith, anſwe-*
the weake chriſtian may be aſſured at all times, that he hath *red.*
faith by his preſent ſenſe; for firſt when we are newly conuerted, and the ſeedes of faith are ſowne in our hearts, we doe

not

not presently discerne it; but as the corne which is cast into the ground, is for a time couered and after springeth vp the blade, and then the eare; so faith being sowen in our hearts, which first like fallow grounds are plowed vp, and as it were harrowed and broken with the threatnings of the law, and apprehension of Gods anger due vnto our sinnes, doth in the time of our humiliation and contrition, lie couered so as we cannot discerne it, till being more and more watered with the water of the spirit, and the heauenly promises of the Gospell, which in the preaching of the word, like sweete dewes and pleasant showers distill vpon it, it sendeth forth the blade, namely an holy desire and earnest indeauour to serue God, and afterwards the fruite, euen a plentifull haruest in godlinesse and righteousnesse of life.

And secondly, sometime after that faith is begun in vs, and we haue seene the frutes thereof to our comfort, it is after hid from vs againe, as when either we wounde our conscience by committing some grieuous sinne against knowledge wittingly and willingly, or when it pleaseth the Lord to exercise vs in the spirituall conflict of temptations; for then sometimes it commeth to passe that our faith for a time lieth hid vnder the ashes of our corruptions; and the cloude of our sinnes, and the apprehension of Gods anger, doth so ouershadow the eyes of our vnderstanding that we cannot discerne the beames of Gods loue and fauour shining vpon vs; although when the conflict is ended, our faith againe flameth out in the loue of God, and zeale of his glorie, and the louing countenance of the Lord shineth gracioufly vpon vs when these cloudes of temptations are ouerpast. And therefore though we do not certainely know our faith by the fruites therof, either soone after our conuersion, or in the time of temptation, yet this must not discourage vs, because these are no fit times to iudge thereof: onely when we want this knowledge and full assurance, let vs vse all good meanes ordained of God that we may attaine thereunto if we neuer had it; or recouer and againe renew it, if after we haue once had it, we lose the sense and feeling thereof, either by falling into hainous sinnes, or by the violence of Sathans temptations.

CHAP.

Chap. VII.

That we may be assured of our election,prooued by diuers argu-
ments.

Nd thus haue I shewed by plaine testimonies of §. *Sect*.1.
scriptures,that we may infallibly be assured of *First,because*
our election ; now I will also prooue the same *the Gospell ma-*
by strong arguments, drawne from the same *nifestly sheweth*
fountaine. First therefore we may thus reason ; *that we are ele-*
cted. Whatsoeuer is manifestly shewed vnto vs in the Gospel, that
we are bound to beleeue,and of that we may be assured : but
it is manifestly declared in the Gospel, that wee are elected
vnto euerlasting life: and therefore we are bound to beleeue
it,and may be assured that we are elected.The proposition or
first part of this reason containeth two branches : the first is,
that we are bound to beleeue whatsoeuer the Gospell reuealeth ; the second,that we may be assured of it;both which are
euident truths. For that which Christ commandeth,that wee
are bound to perfourme : but he commandeth vs to beleeue
the Gospell,Mar.1.15.*Repent and beleeue the Gospell.* So *this is* Mark.1.15.
*his commandement that we beleeue &c.*1.Ioh.3.23. The breach 1.Ioh.3.23.
of which commandement is punished with euerlasting death.
For he that will not beleeue shall be damned, as it is Mar.16.16. Mar.16.16.
And as we are bound to beleeue it, so wee may also come to
be assured thereof; seeing the Gospell commandeth vs nothing, which it doth not also by the inward and ordinarie
cooperation of Gods spirit enable vs to perfourme. For this
difference is betweene the commandements of the Law and
the commandements of the Gospell: the Law sheweth vs
the duties which we should perfourme, but ministers vnto vs
no power whereby wee may be enabled to perfourme them;
but the Gospell being assisted with the operation of Gods
spirit, doth command and withall giueth vs abilitie to perfourme the commandement, for the words of the Gospell
are spirit and life, as our Sauiour speaketh,Ioh.6.63. and with Ioh.6.63.
the preaching thereof the spirit inwardly worketh,quickning

and ftrengthening vs to perfourme that which it enioyneth.
The affumption or fecond part of the reafon is alfo cleere,
namely, that the Gofpell manifefteth vnto vs our election;
for what els is the whole Gofpell but a declaration of Gods
loue, and of our election and redemption in and by Iefus
Chrift? what is it els but the ambaffage whereby God recon-
cileth vs vnto himfelfe? what els is contained therein, but
Gods mercifull promifes of life and faluation, made on no
other condition but on the condition of faith, which we need
not feare to perfourme, feeing it is commanded vs of God?
and therefore though we had no other reafon to beleeue, yet
wee fhould beleeue in obedience to Gods commandement,
feeing he commandeth nothing which is not good in it felfe,
tending to his owne glorie and our faluation; and if we doe
beleeue, though our vnworthineffe bee neuer fo great, yea
though our faith bee neuer fo weake and fmall, yet may wee
thereby be affured of our election and faluation; for this is
Gods will, *that whofoeuer beleeueth in his fonne fhall haue euerlafting life*, as it is Ioh.6.40. So Ioh.3.36. *He that beleeueth in
the fonne hath euerlafting life*. But moft notable is that place
1.Ioh.5.10. *He that beleeueth in the fonne of God, hath the witneffe in himfelfe:* that is, they neede no other reafons to perfwade them, that the teftimonie which God hath giuen of his
fonne (namely, that whofoeuer beleeue in him fhall haue
euerlafting life) is true; for they haue full and fufficient affurance hereof by their faith. Whofoeuer therefore can be affured that they beleeue in Iefus Chrift (as all may who bring
forth the fruits of faith in fanctification and holines of life, or
at leaft defire and endeuour to ferue the Lord in the duties of
pietie and righteoufneffe) they may be affured, nay they are
bound by Gods expreffe commandement, vndoubtedly to
beleeue that they are elected and fhall be faued, becaufe all
the promifes of the Gofpell are made vnto them without any
other condition.

§. *Sect.2.*
*Secondly, we
are affured that
we are redee-*

Secondly, whofoeuer are bound to beleeue that Iefus
Chrift is their Sauiour and Redeemer, they are alfo vndoubtedly to beleeue and may alfo be affured of their election;
but euery Chriftian is bound by Gods expreffe commandement

Ioh.6.40.
and 3.36.

1.Ioh.5.10.

ment to beleeue that Iesus Chriſt is their Sauiour and Redee- *mid, and conse-*
mer, as appeareth 1.Ioh.3.23. and therefore they are vndoub- *quently that we*
tedly to beleeue and may bee aſſured of their election. The *are elected.*
propoſition is manifeſt, ſeeing all thoſe and thoſe onely are
ſaued and redeemed by Chriſt, who are elected to ſaluation Rom.8.30.
in Gods eternall decree. The aſſumption is moſt certaine, for Matth.25.34.
whereas God commaunds vs to beleeue in Iesus Chriſt, hee Act.13.48.
doth not onely enioyne vs to beleeue that he is a Sauiour of
his Church in generall, or of the Patriarchs, Prophets, and A-
poſtles alone, for this alſo the diuels beleeue as well as wee;
but wee are to beleeue that he is our Sauiour and Redeemer,
and to applie all the promiſes of life and ſaluation made in
him, particularly vnto our ſelues; for otherwiſe how ſhould
wee haue that aſſurance of fàith and that bold confidence Heb.4.16.
when we approach vnto the throne of grace, which the A- and 10.22.
poſtle requireth of vs, Heb.4.16.and 10.22. if wee cannot be
aſſured that he is our Sauiour and Redeemer, in whom God
loueth and hath elected vs?

Neither muſt this faith and aſſurance of our election and §. Sect.3.
ſaluation be mixt with doubting, as the Papiſts would beare *That our aſſu-*
vs in hand, who make doubting not an infirmitie, but a com- *rance should*
mendable vertue of their faith : for faith & doubting though *not be mixt*
they are often mixt in Gods children, yet in reſpect of their *with doubting.*
owne natures they are oppoſed in the ſcriptures one againſt
the other. So it is ſaid of *Abraham, that he doubted not of Gods* Rom.4.20.
promiſe through vnbeleefe, but was ſtrengthened in the faith,
Rom.4.20. where the Apoſtle ſheweth, that doubting is a
fruite of vnbeleefe and not a commendable vertue; nay, hee
oppoſeth it to faith, ſaying, that hee doubted not of the promiſe, but was ſtrengthened in the faith. So the Apoſtle *Iames*
chap.1.5. ſaith, *If any man lacke wiſedome, let him aske in faith* Iam.1,5.
and wauer not; where he oppoſeth faith to wauering or doubting. And our Sauiour Chriſt alſo maketh this oppoſition,
Matth,21.21. ſaying, *If ye haue faith and doubt not.* So that Matth.21.21.
though faith and doubting are not oppoſed in reſpect of the
ſubiect wherein they are, for euen the moſt deare children of
God haue their faith often mixt with doubting, they being
partly fleſh and partly ſpirit; yet theſe two in their owne na-

tures

tures are opposed one against the other; and euen in respect of their subiect they thus far disagree, that though they haue their subsistance in the same subiect, yet not in the same part; that is, though they be in the same man, yet not in the same part, for faith is in the regenerate and spirituall part, doubting in the vnregenerate or fleshly part.

Doubting a fruite of vnbe-leefe opposed vnto faith.

Doubting then is no vertue of faith, but opposed thereunto as a fruite of vnbeleefe; it proceedeth not from the spirit but from the flesh, and as a fruite of the flesh it is condemned in Gods word, though the Papists highly commend it. So

Matth. 14. 31.

Matth. 14. 31. our Sauiour reprehendeth *Peter* for his doubting; *O thou of little faith, wherefore diddest thou doubt?* And

Luk. 12. 29.

Luk. 12. 29. he telleth vs that wee must not stand in doubt, or (as the word μὴ μετεωρίζεσθε signifieth) *be not like vnto meteors* which are carried about in the ayre with euery winde. And

Iam. 1. 7.

the Apostle *Iames* chap. 1. 7. compareth him that wauereth or doubteth, to a waue of the sea tost of the winde and carried away. And *Paul* is so farre from commending doubting for a vertue, that hee doth not onely condemne it as a sinne in it selfe, but also as a cause which maketh our actions which are indifferent or good in themselues to become sinnes. So the eating of this or that meate is a thing indifferent and lawfull if it be recciued with prayer and thankisgiuing, but yet the Apostle telleth vs Rom. 14. 23. that he *who doubteth is condemned*

Rom. 14. 23.

if he eate ; and he rendreth this reason, *because he eateth not of faith, and whatsoeuer is not of faith is sinne.* So that by this hee sheweth, that he who doubteth, eateth not of faith; and that whatsoeuer is not done of faith is sinne. Seeing therefore doubting is opposed vnto faith, and is in it selfe not onely a sinne, but also a cause of sinne; let vs not intertaine it though it bring letters commendatorie from the Pope and all his shauelings; but labour to banish it out of our harts, and striue after faith and full assurance of our election and saluation in Christ Iesus ; and though we finde our great vnworthinesse of the least of Gods mercies, and cannot see any reason in our selues why we should beleeue that wee are elected and shall be saued, yet let vs hope against hope, and beleeue against beleefe, for it is not a thing left to our choise but inioyned vs

by

by God, as the chiefe and maine dutie required in the Gospell : and therefore laying aside all reasoning and disputing, let vs resolue to beleeue in obedience to Gods commandement; and then though we are neuer so full of corruptions, yet will this faith purifie vs ; though wee are most backward in perfourming any good worke, yet will it be fruitfull in vs, and will worke by loue ; though wee be most vnworthie, it will make vs more worthie, by applying vnto vs the righteousnesse of Christ and the merits of his death and bloudshed, which will not onely free vs from the guilt and punishment of sinne, but wil also purge vs from the vices and corruptions themselues.

Thirdly, the certaintie of our election may be prooued, by an argument drawne from the nature of faith: which is not a doubtfull opinion, but a certaine perswasion ; not a generall notion, but a particular assurance, whereby we do applie and appropriate vnto our selues those things which wee doe beleeue. Whosoeuer therefore hath true faith, he doth certainly beleeue and is particularly assured of his election, iustification and saluation. That faith is a certaine perswasion, it may appeare first by those properties and names which are giuen vnto it in the word. Heb.11.1. faith is said to be ὑπόστασις, that is, a subsistance or present being of things hoped for; so that hope waiteth for them in time to come, but faith enioyeth them as being present, namely in respect of the certaine assurance and particular application of the promises vnto our selues : and therefore the Apostle saith, that *hereby we may know* (not that wee shall haue, but) *that we haue eternall life*, 1.Ioh.5.13. not in possession but in assurance of faith. It is called ἔλεγχος in the same place, which word is quite contrarie to doubting, as signifying a manifest demonstration which doth not only shew a thing probably, but also doth conuince with strong arguments, and make that truth cleere and manifest, which was otherwise obscure and secret, and therefore in the text it is called a demonstration of things not seene. So there is ascribed vnto it fulnesse of perswasion, Heb.10.22. *Let vs draw neere with a true heart,* ἐν πληροφορία πίστεως, *in full assurance of faith:* and also boldnesse with confident trust, Eph.3.12. by whom

we

Side notes: Act.15.9. Galat.5 6.

§. Sect.4. *Thirdly, faith is a certaine and particular perswasion, and not a doubtfull opinion or generall notion.*

Heb.11.1.

Heb.11.1. 1.Ioh.5.13.

Heb.10.22. Eph.3.12.

we haue boldnesse and entrance with confidence (not by extraordinarie reuelations,but)by faith in Christ : which full affurance,boldnesse and confidence wee could not haue,if wee
were not assured of Gods loue and our election; but remained doubtfull whether we were beloued of God and elected
or no.

    To these names and properties of faith,we may adde some
plaine testimonies of Scriptures, which cleerely shew that
faith is not a doubtfull hope, but a certaine perswasion.

1.Ioh.3.14. 1.Iohn 3.14. The Apostle saith, that *we knowe that we are tran-*
slated from death to life (not by reuelation but) *becanse we loue*
the brethren ; he doth not say that we knowe that we shall be,
but that we are translated from death to life, to note the certainty of this knowledge and perswasion. Rom.3.2. the A-

Rom.5,2. postle saith, that *by Christ we haue accesse through faith vnto*
Gods grace, wherein we stand and reioyce vnder hope, or,as the
word signifieth, glory and triumph with ioy : so that we doe
not wauer and stagger, but stand firmely through faith, we
doe not feare and timorously hope, but euen glory and tri-
umphe in our reioycing : saying with the Apostle, Rom.8.33.

Rom.8.33,34. *Who shall lay any thing to the charge of Gods chosen? it is God that*
35,38. *iustifieth.* 34. *Who shall condemne? it is Christ which is dead :*
yea,or rather which is risen againe,who is also at the right hand of
God, and maketh request also for vs. 35. *Who shall separate vs*
from the loue of Christ,&c. So, that though our sinnes be manifold,our vnworthinesse great, and our faith weake ; yet if it
be true, it may also be certaine in the assurance of Gods loue
and our election : because it is not grounded on our worthinesse, but vpon Gods free iustifying and accepting of vs, as

Heb.6.18. righteous in Christ,and vpon Christs death, resurrection, and
intercession for vs vnto God his father; which is a most sure
foundation that cannot faile. In deede if our faith and the
anchor of our hope,did pitch,rest,and fasten it selfe,vpon the
light and hollow sands of our owne merits and worthinesse;
the surging waues and boysterous blasts of Sathans temptations, would disanchor and tosse vs too and fro, till at length
we should make shipwracke of our faith,against the rockes of
despaire:but seeing we take holde and rest vpon the firme and
sure

fure anchor-hold Chriſt Ieſus his merits and righteouſneſſe;
well may the tempeſts of Sathans temptations ſhake vs, but
they ſhall neuer remoue vs from our firme hold and certaine
aſſurance which wee haue in Chriſt; becauſe wee apprehend
him,nay rather, *are apprehended or taken hold of by him,* as the
Apoſtle ſpeaketh, Phil.3.12. *And no man* (no not the whole
power of hell) *is able to plucke vs out of his hands,* as our Sauiour ſpeaketh, Iohn 10.28. For though they be mighty to deſtroy, *yet Chriſt is almightie to ſaue,* as it is Eſa.63.1. and therefore let vs not ſuffer our ſoules to be racked betweene hope
and feare; but let vs *truſt perfectly on the grace that is brought
vnto vs by the reuelation of Ieſus Chriſt,* as the Apoſtle exhorteth, 1.Pet.1.13.

Phil.3.12.

Ioh 10.28.
Eſa.63.1.

1.Pet.1.13.

Laſtly, that we may be moſt certaine of this certainty of
faith,we will adde to theſe teſtimonies,ſome examples of beleeuers mentioned in Gods word. And firſt let vs conſider
the faith of *Abraham:*which was not wauering and doubtfull,
but moſt certaine and aſſured; for aboue hope he beleeued
vnder hope, and hee was not weake in faith, neither did hee
doubt of the promiſe of God through vnbeleefe, but was
ſtrengthened in the faith, and gaue glory vnto God, being
fully aſſured that hee which had promiſed was able to performe it; and therefore it was imputed vnto him for righteouſneſſe ; as the Apoſtle ſetteth it downe, Rom.4. 18,19,20,
21,22. Now,*Abraham* was not onely a bare beleeuer,but the
father of the faithfull; neither was his faith propounded vnto
vs as a worder to admire at, but as an example for all his
ſonnes to imitate. And therefore it is ſaid, verſ.23. *That this
is not written for him onely that* his faith *was imputed to him for
righteouſneſſe.* 24. *But alſo for vs to whom it ſhall be imputed for
righteouſneſſe,which beleeue in him, who hath raiſed vp Ieſus our
Lord from the dead.* But it may be obiected,that *Abraham* is
not ſaid here to beleeue thus certainely his owne election or
ſaluation, but that he ſhould haue a ſonne, and become a father of many nations : I anſwere, though this were the next
and immediat obiect of his faith, yet this was not the chiefe
and principall; but the promiſe of bleſſedneſſe and happineſſe,which was made to him and all the nations of the earth,

§. Sect.5.
*The certainty
of faith,pro-
ued by the ex-
amples of belee-
uers.*

Rom.4.18,19,
20,21,22,23,

in

in his feede Chrift. For *Abraham* could not bee iuftified by beleeuing that he fhould haue a fonne, but by beleeuing in the Meffias which fhould come out of his loynes, by whofe rightcoufneffe and obedience he fhould be faued. And there-fore the Apoftle Gal.3.16. doth appropriate that promife made vnto *Abraham*, Gen.22.18. *In thy feede shall all the nations of the earth bee blessed,* vnto the promifed feede Iefus Chrift.

Looke alfo vpon the prophet *Dauid,*and you fhall fee,that though his faith was often fhaken with doubting, yet in it felfe it remayned certaine:like a tree fhaken with the windes, which is not ouerthrowne, but taketh more firme and deepe roote: Pfalm.23.4. *Though I walke through the valley of the shadow of death, I will feare no euill, for thou art with mee.* So Pfalm.27.1. *The Lord is my light and my faluation, whom shall I feare? The Lord is the strength of my life, of whom shall I be afraide?* Neither had he onely this affurance in himfelfe, but fheweth that it is alfo the ftate of all the faithfull, Pfal.125.1. *They that trust in the Lord shall be as mount Sion, which cannot be remoued, but remaineth for euer.* So *Iob* in the middeft of his afflictions fheweth his certaine affurance and faith, faying, Iob.13.15. *Loe, though hee slay mee yet will I trust in him :* And chap.19.25. *I am fure that my redeemer liueth, and he shall stand the last on the earth.* 26. *And though after this skinne, wormes destroy this body, yet shall I fee God in my flesh, &c.* And *Paul* fpeaking not onely of his owne affurance of Gods loue, and euerlafting life, but of all the faithfull,faith,that he is perfwaded *that nothing in the world should be able to feparate vs from Gods loue in Christ,*Rom.8.38.

§. Sect.6.

And thus haue I fhewed, that faith is a certaine affurance of Gods loue and fauour in Chrift. Now I will alfo proue that it particularly perfwadeth vs of our owne election and life euerlafting. For firft; fuch a faith is begot now in our hearts, by the Preaching of the word, as was begot in the hearts of men,by our Sauiour Chrift himfelfe; for as there is but one God, fo there is but one true and iuftifying faith, Ephef.4.5: but by that faith they were particularly perfwaded of the remiffion of their finnes, and confequently of their

their iustification and saluation, as appeareth Luke. 7.42.50.
where our Sauiour saith thus to the woman: *Thy sinnes are for-* Luk.7.48.50.
giuen thee, thy faith hath saued thee, goe in peace. So Matth.9.2.
he saith to the sicke of the Paulsie, *Be of good comfort, thy sinnes* Matth.9.2.
are forgiuen thee. And therefore the faith which is now begot
in vs by the Preaching of the word, doth also particularly
perswade vs of the remission of our sinnes and eternall saluation. For as our Sauiour Christ by his owne absolute authoritie, did remit the sinnes of those that did beleeue; so he
hath left this authoritie to his ministers (not absolutely by
their owne power to remit sinnes, which the man of sinne
doth chalenge vnto himselfe, but) to declare and pronounce
their sinnes forgiuen who truly beleeue in the sonne of God,
and repent them of their sinnes: the which their sentence is
ratified in Heauen, according to that Matth.16.19. *I will giue* Matth.16.19.
vnto thee the keyes of the kingdome of Heauen, and whatsoeuer
thou shalt binde in earth shall be bound in Heauen, and whatsoeuer
thou shalt loose in earth shall be loosed in Heauen ; which authoritie is not giuen to *Peter* alone and his successors, as the Papists dreame; but as *Peter* answered, not onely for himselfe,
but also in the behalfe of all the rest, so he receiueth this power both for himselfe and for all the Apostles ; yea, for all
Gods true Ministers, the vndoubted successors of the Apostles, as our Sauiour expoundeth himselfe, Iohn 20.23. where
hee giueth this authoritie to all the Apostles ; saying, *Whose*
sinnes so euer yee remit, they are remitted vnto them, and whose Ioh.20.23.
sinnes so euer yee retaine, they are retained. So that, the Ministers
of Gods word by the Preaching thereof, may assure men particularly of the remission of their sinnes : for when he maketh this generall proposition, whosoeuer beleeueth and repenteth him of his sinnes shall haue them remitted, and bee
made an heyre of euerlasting life; and the particular hearer
doth truely assume that he beleeueth and repenteth, the Minister hath authoritie giuen him of God to make this conclusion : therefore bee thou assured that thy sinnes are forgiuen
thee in Christ, and that thou art an vndoubted heyre of euerlasting life.

Secondly, as the Lord doth offer vnto vs his gracious promises

mises of life and saluation, so doe we receiue them by faith; but the Lord doth not only generally in the word offer these his gratious promises to all that will receiue them, but also particularly in the right vse of the Sacraments to euery faithfull receiuer : for in the Sacraments wee must consider a relation and correspondencie betweene the outward signes and things signified : as therfore the Minister doth offer and giue, and I receiue and eate the outward signes of bread and wine; so am I as certainly to beleeue that God doth offer and giue, and that I doe receiue and feede vpon Christ Iesus and all his benefits, with the hand and mouth of faith, vnto the nourishing of my particular soule to euerlasting life, as my bodie is nourished with these outward elements of bread and wine.

Lastly, the Apostle saith, that through faith wee *haue entrance vnto God with boldnesse and confidence,* and therefore by faith the beleeuer is particularly perswaded of the remission of his sinnes and of his reconciliation with God : for with what boldnesse or confidence can the poore sinner come before God, who is terrified with the threatnings of the Law, with the temptations of Sathan, and with the consideration of his owne vnworthinesse and selfe-guiltinesse; if hee bee not particularly assured that his curse is borne by Christ, that hee is forgiuen the whole debt of his sins, and reconciled vnto God? What assured comfort can hee receiue, if hee beleeue that God hath elected *Peter* and *Paul* and all his Church, if hee be not also assured that he is in this number? If a whole Citie should rebel and commit high treason against a Prince, and the Prince should send out a proclamatiō, declaring that vpon some conditions he would receiue them to mercie; with what boldnesse or confidence can any in this citie come before him, if he be not assured that he hath perfourmed these conditions? But this is our case, wee haue rebelled against God, and hee hath proclaimed in his Gospell the pardon of our sinnes, so wee lay hold vpon Christ by a true and liuely faith, and repent vs of our sinnes: If therefore we could not be assured that wee haue a liuely faith and true repentance, and consequently that Gods mercifull promises belong particularly vnto vs; with what boldnesse or confidence can we come

before

Eph. 3. 12.

before him? But the Apostle saith, that by faith we haue this boldnesse and confidence, and therefore it followeth that we may be assured that we haue faith and repentance, and thereby may certainly be perswaded of Gods loue and of our particular election.

Fourthly, that we may certainly be assured of our election, it may be proued by an argument drawne from the doctrine and vse of the Sacraments; for the Lord hath added to the couenant of grace, his Sacraments as seales, not to confirme Gods promises in themselues, which are so vndoubtedly true that they neede no confirmation, but to strengthen our faith in this full assurance that they belong particularly vnto vs. For whereas in the word the promises of grace and saluation are generally propounded to all beleeuers; in the vse of the Sacraments, they are particularly applied to euery worthie receiuer; to the end that all doubting being remooued, they may certainly bee assured that all the promises of the Gospell doe belong particularly vnto themselues. Now if the Lord would haue vs doubt of our election and saluation, and if this doubting were a vertue of faith, as the Papists teach, then surely there were no vse of the Sacraments; for the word is sufficient to beget that generall faith which is mixt with doubting, and the Sacraments which doe further assure vs and applie vnto vs Gods promises, would be rather hurtfull than profitable, because they take away doubting, which is a vertue of their faith. But we are otherwise instructed by Gods truth, namely, that the Lord would not haue vs doubt of his promises : and therefore he hath not onely written his couenant, but also hath confirmed it by his seale, and hath thereby particularly applied it to the vse and benefit of euery one who receiueth it by the hand of a liuely faith, that there may be no place left to doubting. And hence it is that the Sacrament of Circumcision is called *the seale of the righteousnesse of faith*, Rom.4.11. because thereby as by a seale *Abraham* was confirmed in the trueth of Gods promises, and assured that the righteousnesse of faith, that is, the righteousnes of Christ, who was the promised seede, did belong vnto him. And answerable to this Sacrament is Baptisme, wherein Christ and

all

§.Sect.7.

The fourth argument, drawne from the doctrine and vse of the Sacraments.

Rom.4.11.

all the gratious promises of life and saluation made in him, are particularly applied to the partie baptized; and therefore the Apostle saith, that all that are baptized into Christ haue

Gal.3.27.

put on Christ, Gal.3.27. where the Apostle compareth Christ to a garment, which by the hand of faith is put on by euery particular beleeuer. So in the administration of the Lords Supper, the bread and wine is particularly deliuered vnto all the communicants, to signifie vnto them, that euery one who stretcheth foorth the hand of faith doth receiue Christ and all his benefits, whereby his soule is nourished vnto euerlasting life. Whosoeuer therefore hath faith, he may be assured that he receiueth Christ; and whosoeuer receiueth Christ, he may be assured of his election and saluation; for *to as many as receiue him, to them he giueth power to be the sonnes of God:* and

Ioh.1.12.

who are those? *euen those that beleeue in his name,* as it is Ioh.

Ioh.6.54.47.

1.12. *And whosoeuer eates his flesh and drinkes his bloud hath eternall life,* as our Sauiour saith Ioh.6.54. Now if wee would know how we feede vpon him, it is by the mouth of faith, as he expoundeth himselfe verf.47.

§. Sect.8.
The fift argument taken from prayer.
1.Ioh.5.14.15.

Fiftly, whatsoeuer we are bound to pray for; that wee may be assured of, nay we ought stedfastly to beleeue that we shall receiue it: and this is euident 1.Ioh.5.14. *This is the assurance that wee haue in him, that if wee aske any thing according to his will he heareth vs. 15. And if we know that he heareth vs whatsoeuer we aske, we know that wee haue the petitions that wee haue desired of him.* And the Apostle *Iames* would haue vs to *aske in*

Iam.1.5.
Mat.6.12.

faith without wauering, that is, not doubting *to receiue that we aske.* But we are taught to pray for the remission of our sins: and therefore we are certainly to beleeue that our sinnes are remitted, and consequently that we are iustified, called, elected, and shall be saued; for *whom he did predestinate, them also*

Rom.8.30.

he called, and whom he called, them also he iustified, and whom he iustified, them also he glorified, as it is Rom.8.30.

§. Sect.9.
The fixt argument taken from the confession of our faith.

Sixtly, whatsoeuer we professe in the Articles of our faith, that we should beleeue, and of that we may and ought particularly to be assured: but euery man professeth that he beleeueth the remission of sinnes and life euerlasting, that is, that the Lord doth not onely forgiue sinne, and granteth vnto
some

some the fruition of euerlasting life, for this the diuels beleeue as well as we, but also that he doth particularly forgiue
me my sinnes, and that he will make me an heire of eternall
happinesse : for this is the nature of faith, to assure vs certain-
lie and particularlie of that which wee beleeue, as wee haue
shewed; and therefore we ought particularly to be assured of
the remission of our sinnes, and that wee shall attaine vnto e-
uerlasting life, and consequently that wee are elected, seeing
none enioy it but Gods chosen. But it may be obiected, that
if euery one be bound to beleeue as an article of his faith
that his sinnes are forgiuen, and that hee is an heire of euerlasting life, then some are bound to beleeue that which is false,
for those who liue and die in their sinnes without repentance,
shall neuer obtaine either the one or the other. I answere,
that wee are not bound to beleeue, being destitute of a true
and a liuely faith, for this were rather fondly to presume,
than surely to bee perswaded of the promises of the Gospell,
but wee are first bound to haue a true liuely and iustifying
faith, and so to beleeue and applie vnto our selues the promises of the Gospell; but those that liue in their sinnes without
repentance, they are altogether destitute of true faith, which
wheresoeuer it is purifieth the heart, and worketh by loue,
mooning the beleeuer to endeuour and striue to mortifie his
corruptions, and to rise from the death of sinne to newnesse
of life : and therefore well may they securely presume, but it
is impossible that they should truly beleeue, because they are
vtterly destitute of a liuely faith, and where the cause is not
the effect cannot follow: and consequently for their infidelitie they are subiect to eternall plagues and punishments, because they doe not that which they are bound to performe.
Neither must we thinke that euery kind of faith, or rather euery fond perswasion of faith is enioyned vs, but such a faith as
is grounded vpon Gods word; but the word of God doth
teach vs, that *whosoeuer liue in the flesh cannot please God, and if* Rom.8.8.13.
we liue after the flesh we shall dye, Rom.8.8.13. *That the vnrigh-* 1.Cor.6.9.
teous shall not inherit the kingdome of God, 1.Cor.6.9. That the
workers of iniquitie shall be reiected of Christ, Matth.7.23. And Mat.7.23.
that *no vncleane thing, nor whatsoeuer worketh abomination and* Reuel.21.27.

lies shall enter into the kingdome of heauen, Reuel.21.27. And therefore those who liue in the flesh, those who are workers of iniquitie, vnrighteous and vncleane, in which ranke are all those who liue in their sins without repentance, fulfilling the lusts of the flesh, and falling continually into sinne with plea-sure and delight, are not bound simply and absolutely to be-leeue, so long as they resolue to continue in this state, for so should they be bound to beleeue that which is false and re-pugnant to Gods word; but they are bound to haue a true faith, which being wrought in their hearts will moue them to forsake their sinnes by vnfained repentance, to hunger after righteousnes, to endeuour to serue the Lord in holinesse and newnesse of life, and so to beleeue in Christ as their Sauiour and Redeemer, which fruites if our faith bring not foorth, we cannot be assured that we haue true faith, or do truly beleeue. For though in nature faith be before repentance, yet in our sense and feeling it alwaies followeth it : neither doth faith euer soundly and truly perswade vs of Gods loue, till we haue sorrowed for our sinnes, and at least in purpose of heart haue forsaken them. So that whosoeuer liueth still in his sins with pleasure and delight, and yet beleeueth that he is elected to saluation, and that he is in Gods fauour, and shall continuing in this state be made an heire of eternall life, he is not indued with true faith, but with fond presumption and carnall secu-ritie, which maketh him to beleeue that which is false and re-pugnant to Gods word. Though then all men, euen carnall worldlings and reprobates are bound to beleeue, and because they doe not, are subiect to condemnation, as committing a great and fearefull sinne; as appeareth Ioh.3.18. and 16.8.9.

Ioh.3.18.
and 16.8.9.

where our Sauiour saith, that the holy Ghost *should reproue the world of sinne, because they beleeue not in him:* yet they are not bound to beleeue continuing in their worldlinesse, and resol-uing to goe on in their sinnes, for such a faith were but fond presumption; but they are bound so to beleeue as that their faith may be grounded vpon Gods word, which it can neuer possibly be if it be seuered from true repentance, and for want of this faith they are condemned.

CHAP.

CHAP. VIII.

*The laſt argument grounded vpon the teſtimo-
nie of Gods ſpirit.*

Aſtly, whatſoeuer the ſpirit of God doth teſtifie in **§. Sect.1.**
the heart and conſcience of a man, and doth fully
aſſure him thereof, that he is to beleeue, and of that
he ought vndoubtedly to be aſſured: but the ſpirit of God
doth teſtifie to the faithfull, and doth fully aſſure them that
they are the ſonnes of God by adoption and grace, and conſequently that they are elected; for none are the ſonnes of
God but thoſe who are predeſtinate to be adopted through
Ieſus Chriſt, as it is Epheſ.1.5: and therefore the faithfull are **Eph.1.5.**
to beleeue, and ought vndoubtedly to be aſſured that they
are the ſonnes of God elected to euerlaſting life. The pro-
ſition is manifeſt; for, what more certaine truth can be imagined, than that which the ſpirit of God witneſſeth vnto our
ſpirits, and confirmeth vnto vs, ſeeing all the properties required in a true witneſſe, doe concurre in him in the higheſt
degree, namely knowledge, truth, and faithfulneſſe? for
knowledge, he is infinit and knoweth all things, euen the e-
ternall councell, and decree of God concerning our election,
as appeareth 1.Cor.2.10. *The ſpirit ſearcheth all things euen* **1.Cor.2.10.12**
the deepe things of God; and this ſpirit doe we receiue that we
may know the things that are giuen to vs of God. As it is verſ.12.
What fitter witneſſe therefore can be imagined in this reſpect than Gods ſpirit, who wholy and onely knoweth all his
ſecret counſailes? In reſpect of truth hee is moſt true, yea
truth it ſelfe, and in regarde hereof hee is called *the ſpirit*
of truth which leadeth vs into all truth. Ioh.16.13. And there- **Ioh.16.13.**
fore as in reſpect of his knowledge he cannot bee decei-
ued, ſo in reſpect of his truth he cannot deceiue. In reſpect of
faithfulneſſe he is moſt *faithfull and iuſt in all his waies* Pſal. **Pſal.145.17.**
145.17. 1.Cor.1.9. eſpecially in his word; for *his teſtimonie* **1.Cor.1.9.**
is ſure as it is, Pſal.19.7. and therefore he cannot lie, neither **Pſal.19.7.**
will he conceale the truth for any reſpect of perſons; and
conſequently

consequently whatsoeuer this al-knowing true and faithfull witnesse testifieth, we are vndoubtedly to beleeue as being most sure and certaine. If an Angell sent from heauen should assure vs from God that wee are elected, euen the Papists themselues could not deny, but that we might be assured thereof by such a reuelation without any manner of doubting : but the testimonie of Gods spirit witnessing to our spirits that we are the sonnes of God, is so much more certaine and without exception than the testimonie of Angels, as the spirit of God better knoweth the counsels of God than Angels, as it excelleth them in truth and faith, as the testimonie which is imprinted in the heart is more firme then that which is spoken in the eare, which may easily be forgotten. And therefore if by their doctrine we might be assured of our election by the extraordinarie reuelation of an Angell ; then much more certainely may wee be assured hereof by the ordinarie testimonie of Gods spirit which he witnesseth in the hearts and consciences of the faithfull.

§. *Sect.*2.

That Gods spirit testifieth that we are the sonnes of God.

The proposition being manifest, let vs proue the assumption; which containeth two branches, first that the spirit of God testifieth to our spirits, that we are the sonnes of God; and secondly doth fully assure vs of this testimonie that it is most vndoubted true ; both which are manifest by Gods word. First that Gods spirit giueth this testimonie in the hearts of the faithfull, it is euident Rom.8.15.16. *For ye haue not receiued the spirit of bondage to feare againe ; but ye haue receiued the spirit of adoption whereby we crie abba father:the same spirit beareth witnesse with our spirit, that we are the children of God.* So Gal.4.6. *Because ye are sonnes, God hath sent forth the spirit of his son into your hearts which crieth abba father.* Which places doe so euidently proue this point,that there needes no more reasons or allegations ; for first he excludeth the spirit of bondage, which like the Papists faith causeth vs to feare and doubte of our election and saluation ; and then hee telleth vs that wee haue receiued the spirit of adoption which beareth witnesse vnto our spirit that wee are the children of God.

Rom.8.15.16.

Gal.4.6.

§. *Sect.*3.

Secondly, because we are exceeding weake and the graces in,

in vs shadowed with imperfections and our faith mixt with
doubting, because *we are saued as yet but by hope*, as it is Rom.
8.24. And *we walke by faith and not by sight*, as it is 2.Cor.5.
7.and this our faith is continually shaken with manifold
temptations, therefore least we should doubt of Gods loue
and our election adoption and saluation, the Lord hath
giuen vs his spirit to seale, and further to confirme this assurance in our hearts; and that it might be an earnest and a sure
pledge vnto vs, whereby he might secure vs concerning the
couenant which he hath made with vs. The truth hereof appeareth in many places of the Scripture. 2.Cor.1.22. *Who* 2.Cor.1.22.
*hath sealed vs and hath giuen the earnest of the spirit in our
hearts.* So Ephes.1.13. *In whom also ye haue trusted, after that* Eph.1.13.
*ye heard the word of truth, euen the Gospel of our saluation, where-
in also after that ye beleeued, ye were sealed with the holy spirit of
promise.* 14.*Which is the earnest of our inheritance, vntill the redemption of the possession purchased vnto the praise of his glorie.*
And Ephes.4.30. The Apostle exhorteth vs not to *grieue the* Eph.4.30.
*holy spirit of God, by whom we are sealed vnto the day of our re-
demption.* And 2.Cor.5.5. he saith that *God hath giuen vnto vs* 2.Cor.5.5.
the earnest of his spirit.

Which wordes doe minister vnto euery faithfull man no
small consolation, if they bee rightly waied; for first wee
vse to seale those things which we would haue most certaine
and out of all controuersie; as when a man hath made a promise or couenant with another, for his better securitie he
doth commit it to writing, and least yet there should any
scruple or doubt rest in his minde, he doth confirme it by
adding his seale, to put the matter out of all question; so the
Lord hath added to the written couenant of his word, whereby he hath assured vs of our election adoption and saluation, the outward seale of the sacraments, and the inward
seale of his spirit, whereby he hath ratified it, not in it selfe,
but in our hearts, that so all cause of doubting being taken
away, we might certainely be assured of his promises, that
they belong vnto vs not after a generall manner as the Papists teach, but particularly euen as this assurance is particularly sealed by Gods spirit in the heart of euery true be-

leeuer,

Rom.4.11. leeuer, Rom.4.11. The end therefore why we are fealed to faluation by Gods fpirit, is not that we fhould doubt thereof, but that it might be out of all queftion fully ratified and confirmed vnto vs: for this is fignified by this metaphor here vfed of fealing, as may appeare not onely by the ordinarie cuftome amongft vs, but alfo by the vfe thereof in former times. So when *Ahafhuerofh* would haue letters written in the Kings name, which no man might reuoke, he commaundeth Heft.8.8. that they fhould be fealed with the Kings ring. Heft.8.8. And Ioh.6.27. Ioh.6.27. it is faid that God the *father had fealed our Sauiour Chrift,* that is, confirmed him in his office of mediation, by giuing euident teftimonies and manifeft fignes that the people might not doubt of his calling and anoynting. Matth.3. 17.and 17.5.and Ioh.1.32.

So, whereas the holy Ghoft in the faithfull is called the earneft of our inheritance, this miniftreth vnto euery true beleeuer no fmall confolation, nor doubtfull affurance of their faluation ; for we know that an earneft is giuen amongft men to ratifie and binde a bargaine, fo as they cannot goe from their agreement after earneft is giuen and receiued.The word *arrhabo* which is here tranflated earneft,hath alfo other fignifications which minifter vnto Gods faithfull, the fame Gen.38.17.18 affurance and the like true comfort. Genef.38.17.18. this word is vfed to fignifie a pledge or pawne, than the which there can bee no better affurance of performing promife : 2.King.14.14. and 2.King.14.14. it fignifieth a hoftage giuen in warres which is giuen for affurance to confirme couenants agreed vpon. Whereas therefore Gods fpirit in the faithfull is called *arrhabo,* which fignifieth an earneft pawne and hoftage: we are hereby affured that the Lord will performe his couenant betweene vs and him; that he will not miffe a day in the performing of his promife; that howfoeuer we were enemies, yet now being reconciled by the death of his fonne, he hath giuen vs an hoftage to affure vs of eternall peace, euen his holy fpirit. And therefore let not Sathan nor all his affiftants caufe vs to doubt of Gods couenant, wherein he hath affured vs of our election, adoption, and faluation; feeing he hath fealed this couenant with his fpirit, and hath giuen vnto vs
this

this earneſt and pawne, to aſſure vs that he will performe his promiſe and bargaine.

But here the tempter obiecteth, that we cannot know and diſcerne whether we haue the ſpirit of God, vnleſſe it ſhould bring forth in vs ſome extraordinarie effects: and though it ſhould be granted that we were indued therewith, yet we cannot diſcerne the teſtimonie thereof from our owne thoughts, vnleſſe it be by ſome ſpeciall reuelation. To the firſt I anſwere, that though many lulled aſleepe with carnall ſecuritie, doe vainely dreame that they haue Gods ſpirit, and ſo are deluded with their owne phantaſies; yet this hindereth not, but that he who hath the ſpirit of God indeede, may certainely be aſſured that it dwelleth in him; for it ſealeth in vs the aſſurance of Gods couenant, and who can receiue this ſeale and not feele the impreſſion? it is an earneſt, and who receiuing an earneſt cannot know whether he hath receiued it? for otherwiſe how can it aſſure vs of our bargaine, if of it ſelfe we haue no aſſurance? it is a pawne of Gods loue and our ſaluation, and who hauing a pawne in his cuſtodie cannot know that he poſſeſſeth it? it is a heauenly light which doth illuminate our vnderſtandings, which were blinde and ignorant in the knowledge of Gods truth, and who cannot diſcerne betweene blindneſſe and ſight, light and darkneſſe? it is a water which purgeth vs from our corruption, and who that is thus waſhed and clenſed, can doubt that this water hath touched him? it is a fire which inflameth our cold froſen hearts with a zeale of Gods glorie, and loue of our brethren, and how can fire which is caried in our breſts be hidden from vs? it is a precious oyle which mollifieth our hard ſtonie hearts, and maketh them flexible and pliable able to Gods will, which before were ſo ſtiffe and obdurate that they would rather haue broken then bowed to obedience; it ſuppleth alſo our ſtiffe ioynts and maketh them actiue and nimble in the workes of holineſſe, and righteouſneſſe, and who finding thoſe ſtrange alterations in himſelfe, may not be aſſured that he is annoynted with this oyle? it is the Lords champion fighting in vs againſt the fleſh, and ſubduing the luſts thereof, and who feeling this inteſtine warre

§. Sect.4.
That we may diſcerne Gods ſpirit by the effects thereof.

2.Cor.1.22.

Eph.1.17.18.

Eſa.44.3.
Ezech.16.9.

Matth.3.11.
Act.2.3.

1.Ioh.2.20.27

Gal.5.17.

in

in his owne bowels can doubt that the combatants haue
their residence in him? in a word it is onely this spirit which
restrained vs from the euill, which naturally we loue, and
prouoketh vs to imbrace that good, which through naturall
corruption we loth and abhorre: if therefore sinne growe vnpleasant vnto vs, and vertue and true godlinesse delightfull,
we may be assured that this is the worke of Gods spirit dwelling in vs. Would we then be assured that we are indued with
the spirit of God? why then let vs consider if our eyes blinded with ignorance are inlightned in any good measure,
with the knowledge of Gods truth; if our soules polluted
with the filth of sinne, are purged in some sort from our corruptions; if our cold hearts are inflamed with the zeale of
Gods glorie and the loue of our brethren; if our hearts more
hard than adamant, and more inflexible than steele, are softened and made obsequious to Gods will; and if the other
members of our body, which were benummed and as it were
taken with a dead paulsie, be made nimble and actiue in the
workes of holinesse and righteousnesse; if we feele a fight and
combate betweene the flesh and the spirit, the one striuing
to leade vs captiue vnto sinne, the other resisting and drawing
vs out of this captiuitie; if the sins which heretofore we haue
loued, be now lothsome vnto vs, and the vertues which we
haue abhorred be delightfull and pleasant; and then we may
assure our selues that it is the light of Gods spirit which hath
shined vpon vs, it is this heauenly water which hath washed
vs, it is this diuine fire which hath inflamed vs, it is this precious oyle that hath mollified and softned vs, it is this champion of the Lord of hosts which maketh warre against our
trayterous flesh, and subdueth the lusts thereof; in a word
it can be nothing but Gods spirit, which makes vs hate that
sinne which naturally we so dearely loue, and to loue vertue
and godlinesse which by nature is lothsome and bitter vnto vs.

§. *Sect.5.*   And thus it is manifest that wee may be assured that we
haue Gods spirit, by the ordinarie fruites thereof in euery
faithfull man. Now let vs consider how we may know the
testimonie of Gods spirit, witnessing in our hearts that we are
elected,

electded adopted and shall be saued, from our owne phantasies caused through carnall securitie and vaine presumption.
And to this end we are to know, that the preaching of the
Gospell is *the ministerie of the spirit*, whereby wee are sealed
and confirmed in the assurance of our saluation, as appeareth
2.Cor.3.6. And hence it is that the preachers of the Gospell
are called *the ministers by whom the people beleeue,* 1.Cor.3.5.
And the words of the Gospell are called by our Sauiour
Christ *spirit and life*, because it is the ministery of the spirit
which quickneth vs, as it is Ioh.6.63. And Gal.3.2. the Apostle saith that we haue receiued the spirit by the hearing of
faith, that is, the doctrine of faith preached in the ministery
of the Gospell. If therefore the testimonie of saluation in the
mindes of the faithfull, be conceiued by the preaching of the
Gospell applied vnto them by faith, then is it most certainly
the testimonie of Gods spirit; for the inward testimonie of
Gods spirit is not different from the outward testimonie of
the word: but if this perswasion be not grounded vpon Gods
word, as theirs is not who perswade themselues that they are
electded, adopted, and shall be saued, notwithstanding that
they liue in their sinnes without repentance, making no conscience of their waies, nor indeauoring to serue the Lord in
holinesse and righteousnesse of life; then is it not the testimonie of Gods spirit, but a presumptuous phantasie, and a
secure and carnall imagination: for the testimonie of Gods
spirit in the conscience, is the same with the testimonie
of the word, and therefore it doth not beare witnesse nor
giue any assurance that they are saued, which Gods word
pronounceth to bee in the state of damnation. When
therefore this testimonie is giuen in a faithfull man and,
agreeable to Gods word; it is the testimonie of the spirit
which sealeth vs in the full assurance of that wee beleeue:
according to that Ephesians.1.13. where the Apostle saith,
that after the faithfull *had receiued the word of truth, euen the
Gospell of their saluation, and beleeued therein, they were sealed with the holy spirit of promise.* But those who make no conscience of hearing the Gospell preached, and when they
heare it, doe not beleeue it, nor apply it to themselues by a
true

true and liuely faith, nor bring foorth any fruites thereof in a holie and Christian life, they haue neither faith nor Gods spirit: and therefore if they haue any perswasion of their election and saluation, it is not the testimonie of Gods spirit, but their owne phantasie, and a vaine opinion arising from carnall securitie and presumption.

§. Sect.6.
Another means to discerne the testimonie of the spirit.

Secondly, the testimony of Gods spirit may hereby bee knowne: first, in that it throughly perswadeth the faithfull of their election and saluation; secondly, by the manner of perswading them; thirdly, by the effects of this testimonie and perswasion. For the first, the spirit of God doth not only giue this bare testimonie that wee are elected, adopted, and shall be saued: but also doth fully perswade vs hereof, as being a thing most certaine and without question. So 1.Cor.2.12. the

2.Cor.2.12.
Apostle saith that *wee haue receiued the spirit of God, that wee might know the things that are giuen to vs of God.* And Eph.1.

Eph. 1,17,18.
17,18. Gods spirit is called *the spirit of wisedom and reuelation, which doth inlighten the eyes of our vnderstanding, that we might know what the hope is of his calling, and what the riches of his glorious inheritance is in the Saints; and what is the exceeding greatnesse of his power,* particularly *towards vs that beleeue, according to the working of his mightie power.* So the Apostle *Iohn*

1.Ioh.3.24.
saith, *hereby we know that Christ abideth in vs, euen by the spirit which he hath giuen vs,* 1.Ioh.3.24. So that wee may be assured that we haue Gods spirit, & therby be throughly perswaded that Christ dwelleth in vs, and consequently that wee are elected and shall be saued. And chap.4.13. *Hereby know wee that*

and 4.13.
we dwell in him and he in vs, because he hath giuen vs of his spirit. And the Apostle *Paul* by the spirit of God was so stedfastly assured of Gods loue, that he professeth that he was firmly perswaded that nothing could separate him from it, Rom.8.38,

Rom.8,38,39.
39. So that the spirit of God throughly perswadeth the faithfull that they are elected and shall be saued; whereas the wicked who are destitute of Gods spirit, may wel haue a fond opinion and a foolish conceit, that they are highly in Gods loue and elected to saluation, through carnall securitie and vaine presumption; but they are neuer throughly perswaded hereof: for when any affliction of bodie or minde is inflicted

on

on them, their vaine perswasion vanisheth away, and nothing remaineth but doubting, which in the end bringeth them to vtter desperation.

But here the tempter will take occasion to discourage the weake Christian, and to perswade him that he hath not Gods spirit, seeing he doth not feele in himselfe this firme perswa- *The perswasion* sion of Gods loue and his election and saluation. To which *of the spirit not* we are to answere, that Gods spirit doth throughly perswade, *alwaies discer-* although not at all times, neither in our present sense and *ned in our sense* feeling; for immediatly after our conuersion when wee are *and feeling.* newly regenerate, and like new borne babes in Christ, the motions of the spirit are but weake in vs, and we are not skil-full in vnderstanding this heauenly language of the spirit, wherewith we haue been altogether vnacquainted; but the spirit waxing stronger in vs, and we growing to a ripe age in Christ, doth crie in our hearts, Abba father, and testifieth to our spirits that we are the sonnes of God; which we then be-ing better acquainted with this heauenly speech, do well vn-derstand, and are throughly perswaded thereby. And second-ly, when the poore Christian who hath receiued a great mea-sure of the spirit is exercised in the spirituall conflict, the hi-deous noise of Sathans temptations which like Cannon-shot sound in his eares, and the tumultuous outcries of his owne passions doe so disturbe and wholie possesse him, that he can not heare the voyce of the spirit perswading him that hee is the child of God; till the skirmish bee past and the noise of temptations ceased, and then againe as in former times hee heareth to his comfort the spirit of God perswading him of Gods loue, and hereby hee is againe assured thereof. So that wee are not to iudge of the hauing of Gods spirit in the time of our Christian infancie and spirituall nonage, nor yet ac-cording to our present sense in the time of temptation, but when wee are come to perfect age, and when the conflict of temptations is ceased.

Secondly, the testimonie of Gods spirit perswading vs of his loue and our election, is knowne by the manner whereby it perswadeth vs: namely, it perswadeth vs hereof with argu-ments grounded vpon Gods word, and drawne not from

any

any worthineſſe in our ſelues, but from Gods free grace and vndeſerued mercie, and from the righteouſneſſe and merits of Chriſt; whereas Sathan and our owne fleſh neuer vſe ſuch reaſons, but either mooue vs to a bare and vaine opinion which hath no ground at all but ſelfe-loue, which maketh men eaſily beleeue that which they deſire; or els with ſome arguments drawne from ſome outward common benefits, beſtowed indifferently vpon the good and bad; or laſtly from a phariſaicall conceit and falſe opinion of our owne worthi-neſſe and deſerts.

Laſtly, the teſtimonie of Gods ſpirit is knowne and diſ-cerned by the effects thereof; for after that it hath effectual-ly perſwaded vs, that we are elected and the deare children of God, we are mooued thereby to truſt wholie in God, and to loue him as our gratious father: from which loue proceedeth a zeale of his glorie, and a true hatred of ſinne, becauſe there-by our heauenlie father is diſhonored & diſpleaſed with vs; and a true loue and heartie endeuour of imbracing holineſſe and righteouſneſſe, becauſe thereby our gratious father is glorified and well pleaſed with vs. If therefore theſe effects and fruites follow this perſwaſion of Gods loue and our ele-ction, wee may bee aſſured that it is the ſpirit of God which doth perſwade vs; but if wee haue no ſuch truſt and affiance, no ſuch loue of God, no zeale of his glorie, no hatred of ſinne, no loue nor deſire of embracing righteouſneſſe, but remaine as carnall, worldly, and prophane as euer we were, then let vs bragge as much as wee will of our perſwaſion of Gods loue and our election, yet it is moſt certaine that this perſwaſion is not wrought in vs by Gods ſpirit, but that it is a vaine conceit and fond opinion which proceedeth from ſelfe-loue, carnall ſecuritie, and fond preſumption, which in the end vaniſhing away will leaue vs in deſpaire.

CHAP.

CHAP. IX.

*Of the meanes whereby we may be assured
of our election.*

Nd thus haue I proued that those who are conuerted vnto God, iustified, and in some measure sanctified, may ordinarily attaine vnto the assurance
of their election: Now I will shew the meanes
and signes whereby wee may bee thus assured. The first and
principall meanes which assureth vs of our election, is the inward testimonie of Gods spirit which *crieth in our hearts Ab-*
ba father, and witnesseth vnto our spirits that we are the children
of God, as it is Rom.8.15,16. Which testimonie it doth not
giue by extraordinarie reuelation, but by a secret application
of the promises of the Gospell vnto vs, and by an inward cooperation whereby it maketh the outward ministerie of the
word effectuall for the begetting of faith in vs, whereby as
with an hand wee doe appropriate the generall promises of
the word vnto our owne selues. And when the Ministers vse
reasons to perswade vs of Gods loue in Christ, the holy ghost
openeth our deafe eares, and inlighteneth our blinde vnderstandings, and powerfully inclineth our wils, so that we may
attentiuely heare, truly vnderstand, and bee fully assured of
that truth which is deliuered, not only in respect of the whole
Church, but also in respect of our selues particularly, so as we
can say, I beleeue that these promises of God are true, and
that they belong to all the faithfull, and consequently vnto
me who doe beleeue and am assured of them, seeing they are
promised on no other condition.

But the tempter will obiect, that many through carnall
presumption doe perswade themselues, that al the promises
of the Gospell doe belong vnto them, and therefore we may
easily be deceiued, not being able to discerne betweene the
testimonie of the spirit and presumptuous securitie. I answer,
that those who are indued with Gods spirit, may easily discerne the testimonie of the spirit from the carnall language
of

§. Sect.1.
The first means
the testimonie
of the holie
Ghost.

Rom.8.15,16.

Diuers diffe-
rences betweene
the testimonie
of the spirit
and presump-
tuous securitie.

of presumption, as is euident by that which before I haue deliuered, and also may more plainly appeare by manifeft differences, if the one bee compared with the other.For prefumption is a fruite of originall corruption which accompanieth vs from our mothers wombe, till it bee beaten downe with Gods sanctifying spirit; but the teftimonie of the spirit is a thing fupernaturall,which no man euer feeleth before his conuerfion vnto God,when as by the preaching of the word he is humbled vnder the burthen of finne, forrowing and grieuing for his finnes paft,and detefting them from his hart, and purpofing to leaue and forfake them in the time to come. If therefore wee haue had alwaies this teftimonie in our mindes that wee are in Gods fauour and elected,and neuer felt our conuerfion, nor difcerned any fruites thereof; then doth this teftimonie proceede from carnall prefumption and not from Gods spirit. Secondly,thofe who haue the teftimonie of the spirit, make confcience of the diligent and carefull vfe of the outward meanes of faluation, as the hearing and reading of the word, the receiuing of the Sacraments, and other holie duties of Gods feruice,becaufe they know that the inward teftimonie of the spirit is not ordinarily feuered from the outward teftimonie of the word; and the affurance of Gods loue and our election is not wrought immediatly in vs by reuelation of the spirit, but by the preaing of the word and vfe of the Sacraments,made effectuall by the inward cooperation of the holy Ghoft. But prefumption as it arifeth not from the vfe of thefe meanes made thus effectuall,but from carnall fecuritie,fo is it not confirmed thereby : for the leffe that the prefumptuous man heareth the word and perfourmeth the duties of pietie and Gods feruice, the more confidently doth he boaft of his faith and full affurance,and therefore hee maketh no confcience of vfing thefe meanes ordained of God; nay contrariwife he will not fticke to affirme, that the hearing of the word too often is the caufe that troubleth mens mindes and afflicteth their confciences, moouing them to doubt of Gods mercie, which before they neuer called into queftion: and why is this,but becaufe hereby men are rouzed out of their fleepe of fecuritie, and haue
their

their confident presumption beaten downe. If then wee are
carefull to vse all holie meanes ordained of God to assure vs
of our saluation;that assurance and testimonie which followeth is the testimonie of Gods spirit : otherwise it is nothing
els but fond presumption.Thirdly,presumption is most confident, and neuer doubteth nor maketh any question of his
election & saluation who thus presumeth; but this testimony
of the spirit is much assaulted with doubting,and oftentimes
thereby so exceedingly weakened that wee cannot heare the
voyce thereof:as wee may see in the example of *Iob,Dauid,*
the father of the possessed child,the two Disciples who iour-
neyed to Emaus, and in all Gods children who haue not yet
attained vnto fulnesse of perswasion, vnto which none can
come but by degrees. And therefore if wee can bragge with
secure worldlings, and say with the proud Pharisie,I neuer
was troubled I thanke God with any doubting of mine election & saluation, as many are;but alwaies haue had a strong
beleefe that I am in Gods loue and shall vndoubtedly be sa-
ued:wee may assure our selues that this is the voyce of presumption, and not the testimonie of Gods spirit. Fourthly,
presumption is ioyned with worldlinesse and prophanesse,
but the testimonie of Gods spirit is neuer seuered from sanctification, or at least from an earnest desire and holie endeuour of seruing the Lord in holinesse and righteousnesse: for
(as I said) the testimonie of the spirit in the conscience is neuer contrarie to the testimonie of the spirit in the word, neither doth it beare witnesse that those are in Gods loue and
elected to saluation, which the Scriptures witnesse to bee in
Gods displeasure and in the state of condemnation, namely,
all vnrepentant sinners continuing in their vnrepentancie :
and therefore if the assurance which we haue of our election
and saluation be not ioyned with a desire to leaue our sinnes,
and with an earnest endeuour of seruing God in the duties of
holines and righteousnes,then it doth not proceed from the
testimonie of Gods spirit,but from carnall securitie and fond
presumption. Lastly , presumption no longer perswadeth
men of Gods loue and fauour, than they enioy the outward
benefits of this life; but when the Lord laieth vpon them any

grieuous

grieuous affliction, either outwardly in bodie and state, or inwardly in mind; then this perswasion vanisheth, and nothing remaineth but doubting, which commonly endeth in vtter despaire : but the testimonie of the spirit is constant and permanent; and howsoeuer wee cannot by reason of the grieuousnesse of afflictions, and the violent noise of our own passions heare the voyce thereof at some times, yet afterwards againe it crieth alowd in our hearts Abba father, and witnesseth vnto our spirits that we are the sonnes of God : So that the chiefe meanes whereby wee are assured of our election is the spirit of God. But seeing we haue it not naturally in our selues, how may we attaine vnto it? Surely we are to haue our recourse vnto the Father of lights by earnest prayer, *from whom descendeth euery good and perfect gift,* hauing our faith grounded vpon Gods gratious promise, namely, that if we aske we shall receiue, and more especially, that hee will giue his holie spirit to them that aske it, as it is Luk.11.13.

Iam.1.17.
Matth.7.7.
Luk.11.13.

§. Sect.2.
The second meanes, the hearing of the word.

The second meanes whereby wee may attaine to the certaintie of our election, is the hearing of the word, wherein the Lord manifesteth his grace and goodwill to all beleeuing and repentant sinners, and whereby also he ordinarily begetteth this faith and repentance in all his children. For howsoeuer *Paul* may plant and *Apollos* may water, but God alone giueth the encrease; yet Gods blessing ordinarily accompanieth his owne ordinance, making it effectuall by the inward operation of his spirit for those ends for which he hath ordained it. And though the word may long sound in our eares before it pearce the heart, or beget any sauing grace in vs, vnlesse the Lord open our hearts and make the seed of his word fruitfull: yet those who make conscience of hearing the word, with diligence reuerence and attention, and pray for the assistance of Gods spirit, whereby it may become profitable to their saluation, may constantly expect the blessing of God vpon his owne ordinance, which they carefully vse in obedience to his will; whereas those who neglect and contemne Gods word haue no such assurance, because it is the meanes and instrument which is ordained of God for this purpose, without which the spirit of God doth not ordinarily beget
faith,

faith or any sauing grace in vs. Though therefore we doe not after long hearing of the word, feele this assurance of Gods loue and our election, yet let vs not giue it ouer but expect Gods blessing vpon it, and waite his leasure assuring our selues that in the end, hee will make this his owne ordinance effectuall for those ends, for which he hath ordained it.

The third meanes whereby we may attaine to the assurance of our election, is the frequent and religious vse of the Sacrament of the Lords supper, whereby our faith is more and more confirmed the in truth of Gods promises. For the Lord to the preaching of his word which is the couenant of grace, hath added these seales that we might be the more throughly assured of his loue and fauour; and therefore if we conscionably frequent this holy Sacrament, the Lord will blesse also this his owne ordinance. Moreouer they who worthily receiue these holy misteries, doe receiue Christ Iesus, and haue the vnion and communion which is betweene him and them, more and more strengthned and confirmed, for *hee that eateth his flesh and drinketh his blood, dwelleth in Christ, and Christ in him,* As it is Ioh.6.56. *Now there is no condemnation to those that are in Christ Iesus* Rom 8.1; and therefore they neede not doubt of their election and saluation. §. *Sect.3.* *The third meanes, the vse of the Sacraments.* Ioh.6.56. Rom.8.1.

The fourth meanes whereby we may be assured of our election, are the effects of Gods predestination, which are the vndoubted signes thereof; for the effects argue the cause, as the cause the effects, and that not onely in naturall things, but also in those which are supernaturall and spirituall: and therefore as certainely as we know that there is fire because it casteth forth heate, and the sonne by his casting forth of bright raies whereby the world is lightned, and that a tree is good by the good fruits which it bringeth forth, so also may wee as certainely be assured that we are elected of God, when wee finde in our selues the effects and vndoubted signes of our election. §. *Sect.4.* *The fourth meanes, the effects of our election.* Zanch.de Attrib.l.5.c.2.

Neither are these effects bare signes onely of our election, but also manifest seales which by their plaine impression, doe euidently assure vs thereof: so that though we do not directly and immediatly know Gods election, predestination, and eternall decree of our saluation in God himselfe, electing predestinating,

Q ftinating,

ſtinating, and decreeing that we ſhall be ſaued, yet we may
plainely ſee apparant ſcales and impreſſions hereof in our
ſelues, liuely reſembling that which is ſecret in Gods hidden
councell ; and as we not ſeeing the ſeale which maketh the impreſſion, doe eaſily diſcerne the forme, faſhion, and quantitie
thereof by the print which it hath made; ſo wee not ſeeing
Gods ſecret decree of predeſtination, may notwithſtanding
attaine to the euedent knowledge thereof, by that impreſſion
which it maketh in vs.

This alſo may further be illuſtrated by a familiar ſimilitude;
namely, as the ſunne ſhining vpon vs with his bright beames,
doth imprint as it were in our eyes the image of his light,
whereby we ſee the ſunne and the light thereof (the beames
of the ſunne which are caſt vpon vs, being reflected backe a-
gaine to the ſunne it ſelfe;) ſo the foreknowledge of God
whereby he hath decreed that we ſhall be ſaued before all e-
ternitie,is ſecret in it ſelfe,ſo that we cannot ſee not vnderſtand
it directly, but yet whileſt God doth acknowledge vs for his
elect, he doth expreſſe the image and forme of this his foreknowledge in thoſe whom he hath elected, whereby we doe
alſo acknowledge him our gracious God who hath elected vs;
and ſo it commeth to paſſe that by the true knowledge of
God, which is communicated vnto vs, whereby we acknowledge him for our God and father, wee alſo know his foreknowledge, whereby he knoweth and acknowledgeth vs for
his ſonnes and children. For firſt God knoweth vs, and then
by the light of this knowledge communicated vnto vs, he inlightneth our hearts with the true knowledge of himſelfe, as
the ſunne firſt inlightneth our eyes,and by this light we ſee the
ſunne it ſelfe. And this our Sauiour Chriſt intimateth, Ioh.10.
14. where firſt he ſaith he *knoweth his ſheepe,*and then he addeth
that he *is alſo knowne of them.* As though he ſhould ſay,whileſt
I know and acknowledge them for my ſheepe, hereby I bring
to paſſe that they in like manner by the participatiõ of this my
light and knowledge, doe acknowledge me for their true pa-
ſtor.If therefore we know and acknowledge God,for our gracious God & louing father in Chriſt,it is a moſt certaine ſigne,
that he alſo by his foreknowledge, doth know and acknowledge vs for his people and children. But if we remaine in our
ignorance,

Ioh,10.14.

ignorance, without the knowledge of God, and his sonne Chrift, we can gather no affurance vnto our felues of our election; for if the foreknowledge of God had fhined vpon vs, the beames thereof would haue illuminated our hearts, fo as wee fhould by their light haue knowne God alfo.

The like may be faid of Gods eternall loue, wherewith he hath loued vs in Chrift; for God louing vs, hath imprinted the image of his loue in our hearts, whereby wee loue him a-gaine: and when this heauenly heate of Gods loue hath de-fcended on vs, and warmeth our cold hearts, frozen in the dregges of finne, then doe we reflect fome of thofe beames of Gods loue towards him againe. And this the Apoftle *Iohn* plainely fheweth 1.Ioh.4.19. where he faith *that we loue God becaufe he loued vs firft*; that is, by that eternall loue where-with God loued vs in Chrift, there is imprinted in our hearts the loue of God. And hence it is that he faith verf.7. that loue commeth from God: becaufe we can neither loue God, nor our neighbours aright, till his loue towards vs hauing fhined vpon vs, hath inflamed our hearts. So the Apoftle *Paul* faith, Rom 5.5. that *the loue of God is fhed abrode in our hearts, by the holy Ghoft which is giuen vnto vs*, whereby loue towards God is begotten in vs. If therefore the loue of God be in our hearts, we may be affured that it is but an impreffion which is made in vs, by the feale of his loue towards vs, but a little fparke kindled by this heauenly flame, and a fmall modell or little counterfaite refembling the infinit loue of God, wherewith from all eternitie he hath loued vs in Chrift. Thus alfo Gods eternall election, whereby before all worlds he hath chofen vs in Chrift, doth make an impreffion, and fealeth in our hearts the form or image thereof, whereby we make choyfe of the true God Iehouah, amongft all the Gods of the nations to be our onely God, whom we will ferue and worfhip. And there-fore if we haue made this election, and dedicated our felues wholy to Gods worfhip and feruice alone, it is a moft cer-taine figne of our election, whereby God hath chofen vs: fot our choofing of God is an effect of his choofing of vs, and an impreffion or print wherewith by his election hee hath fea-led vs.

And thus it appeareth that the effects of Gods election doe

Gods loue caufe of our loue.

1.Ioh.4.19.

Verf.7.

Rom.5.8.

§. Sect.5.

not

The first effect of our election is our sauiour Christ, by whom we are assured that we are elected.

not onely as signes signifie, but also as seales confirme vnto vs the assurance thereof: but let vs further consider the special effects of our election, whereby we may be assured that we are chosen of God. The first effect, is our Sauiour Christ himself, set apart of God to be the mediator to reconcile all Gods elect vnto him, dwelling in vs by his spirit; who may iustly be called the first effect of Gods election, because all the other, namely our vocation, iustification, sanctification, and saluation, are by him and through him alone. Whosoeuer therefore are assured that Christ dwelleth in them and they in him, they haue a most vndoubted signe of their election: and whosoeuer haue not Christ dwelling in them by his spirit, can haue no assurance that they are chosen, as the Apostle plainely sheweth 2.Cor.13.

2.Cor.13.5.

5. *know you not* (saith he) *that Iesus Christ is in you except you be reprobates?* but how shall we know whether Christ dwelleth thus in vs and we in him? the Apostle telleth vs Rom.8.1.

Rom.8.1.

that those who are in Christ Iesus walke not after the flesh but after the spirit, that is, those who doe not willingly submit themselues to be ruled and led by the lusts of the flesh, but labour and striue to resist and subdue them, studying and indeauoring to liue a spirituall life, in holinesse and righteousnesse. For in whomsoeuer Christ dwelleth by his spirit, those he regenerateth and raiseth from the death of sinne, to newnesse of life; and his blood is effectuall, not only to purge them from the guilt of sinne, but also to cleanse them in some measure from the corruptions themselues.

§. Sect.6.
The second effect of our election, is our effectuall calling.

The second effect of our election, is our effectuall calling; whereby we are separated from the world, and ingrafted into Christ, and made liuely members of his body: and this is done ordinarily by the diligent and attentiue hearing of the word, ioyned with the inward operation of Gods spirit. If therefore we haue heard Gods word preached, diligently and attentiuely; if thereby wee haue attained vnto the knowledge of the worke of our redemption wrought by Iesus Christ, and are delighted therewith; if by this meanes wee haue our hearts somewhat weaned from the world, and fixed vpon our Sauiour and heauenly things; and thinking it sufficient to haue

1.Pet.4.2.3.

spent the rest of our liues past in the lusts of the Gentiles, doe liue hence forward after the wil of God: then are we truely and

effectually

effe&ually called, for thofe are Chrifts fheepe that heare his
voyce and follow him Ioh.10.4. Thofe are ingrafted into
his body, who bring forth the fruites of godlineffe: for as the
branch can bring forth no fruite except it abide in the vine,
fo neither can we bring forth any fruites of pietie and righteoufneffe except wee abide in Chrift; and therefore if we doe
bring forth thefe fruites, it manifeftly appeareth that we are in
Chrift, and confequently truely called and ele&ed, *for without
him we could doe nothing*, as it is Ioh.15.4.5.

Ioh. 10.4.

Ioh. 15.4.5.

The third effe& of Gods ele&ion, is our iuftification, con-
fifting in the remiffion of our finnes, and the imputation of
Chrifts righteoufneffe : and to this is required a true and liuely
faith, which affureth vs of the remiffion of our finnes, and applieth vnto vs Chrifts righteoufneffe. If therefore we beleeue
that our finnes are forgiuen, if we doe by faith apply vnto vs
Chrift and his righteoufneffe, we may be affured that we are
iuftiffed, and confequently ele&ed: now this perfwafion and
liuely faith, is difcerned by the fruites thereof; for it purifieth
our hearts, and worketh by loue ; and it worketh in vs an hatred of finne, and loue of righteoufneffe, which is our fan&ifi-
cation.

§. Se&.7.
*The third effe&
is our iuftifica-
tion.*

So that our fan&ification which is the laft effe& of Gods
ele&ion wrought in vs in this life, is the true touchftone of all
the reft: whereby wee may certainely know whether we be
effe&ually called, that is, feparated from the world, and ingrafted as liuely members into the body of Chrift; and whether we be truely iuftified, that is, purged from the guilt and
punifhment of our finnes by Chrifts blood, and adorned with
his righteoufneffe imputed vnto vs. For if we be feparated
from the world, then doe we not fet our mindes vpon worldly things, but haue *our conuerfation in heauen from whence we
looke for a fauiour, euen the Lord Iefus Chrift*; if we are ingrafted
into the body of Chrift who is the true vine, then doe we bring
forth the fweete grapes of holineffe and righteoufneffe in our
liues and conuerfations, as it is Ioh.15.5; if we haue by a true
faith the affurance of the remiffion of our finnes, then will we
loue God who hath forgiuen vs fo great a debt, and labour to
expreffe our loue by glorifying his name, in caufing our light
to fhine before men ; and if the blood of Chrift be effe&uall

§. Se&.8.
*The fourth ef-
fe& is our fan-
&ification,
which is the
touchftone of
all the reft.*

Phil.32.a.

Ioh.15.5.

vnto vs for the purging away of the guilt and punishment of sinne, then will it also in some measure purge away the corruptions themselues. For *we are grafted with him into the similitude of his death and resurrection, and our olde man is crucified with him and the body of sinne destroyed, that from henceforth we should not serue sinne,* as it is Rom.6.5.6. And as our sanctification is the onely vndoubted signe of our vocation and iustification; so also of our election; for the Lord hath chosen vs that wee should bee holy, Ephes.1.4. And therefore if wee be holy wee haue a manifest effect and inseparable fruite of our election, if we be not holy nor make conscience of seruing the Lord in the duties of pietie and christianitie, we haue no assurance that we are elected : for though the foundation of God remaineth sure on Gods part being sealed and confirmed in his eternall counsell, yet it is not sealed in our hearts vntill we depart from iniquitie, as it is, 2.Tim.2.19.

Though then there be no place vnto our sanctification in Gods decree, as being any cause thereof; and therefore when the question is asked why we are elected, we must answere not for any deserts or holinesse in our selues, but because of Gods good pleasure and vndeserued grace; and when it is demaunded in whom we are elected, wee must reply in Christ Iesus only: yet there is chiefe place vnto our sanctification in the assurance of our election, so that when the question is asked who are elected, answere is to be made, those onely who are also sanctified in Gods good time by his gracious spirit ; for *without this holinesse no man shall euer see God,* as it is, Heb.12.14.

Now our sanctification doth principally consist in a loue of righteousnesse, and a true hatred of sinne ; from whence proceedeth an earnest desire, and hartie indeauour of forsaking that which is euill, and of cleauing vnto that which is good; and for the better effecting hereof, a carefull studie of mortifying the flesh and the lusts thereof, and painefull diligence in vsing all good meanes whereby the spirit may be strengthened, and the gifts and graces thereof encreased, that so wee may not be so prone to fall into that sinne which we hate, nor so backward in imbracing and following that righteousnesse and holinesse which wee loue. And this is the sanctification which is an inseparable fruite and effect of Gods election in

all

Margin notes:

Rom.6.5.6.

Eph.1.4.

2.Tim.2.19.

Heb.12.14

§. Sect.9.
Wherein our sanctification consisteth.

all his children, which though it be the last in nature and next *That those who* vnto saluation it selfe, for first God electeth, and those whom *will be assured* he hath elected,in his good time he calleth, and whom he cal- *of their electi-* leth those he iustifieth, and lastly, whom he iustifieth those he *their assurance* sanctifieth and saueth; yet when we are to gather assurance of *at their sancti-* our election, we are not to obserue this order, but to begin *fication.* where the Lord endeth, and so ascend from the lowest degree till we come to the highest. For as it is a foolish thing for a man, to thinke that he can leap to the top of an high ladder at the first step, and therefore euery one beginneth with the low- est,and so ascendeth step by step till he come to the highest : so it is a foolish thing for a man to imagine,that he can leape into heauen, and there search the vnsearchable councels of God, and so know whether he is elected or no ; but we must begin at the lowest step, namely our sanctification which being at- tained vnto, we may ascend a step higher in our assurance, namely that we are iustified, and so to the next, that we are effectually called, and lastly to the highest that we are elected. Otherwise if we curiously diue into the bottomlesse secrets of Gods councels, we shall be drowned and ouerwhelmed; if we approach vnto this vnapproachable light, the eye of our vnderstanding wil be dazled,yea starke blinded;if we presume to vnderstand beyond sobrietie, we shall by the iust iudge- ment of God be infatuated, and thrust our selues into an end- lesse laborinth, out of which we shall neuer finde way,wanting the line of Gods word to guide vs. And therefore if we would haue any true assurance of our election, we must examine our selues whether we be sanctified ; and if we finde in our selues sanctification by the fruites thereof, wee may vndoubtedly conclude that we are iustified, called,elected, and shall be sa- ued. If we walke not after the flesh but after the spirit,we may be assured that we are in Christ Iesus, and therefore there is no condemnation belonging vnto vs,Rom.8.1. If we bring forth *Rom.8.1.* the fruites of righteousnesse and holinesse, we may be assured that we are good trees of Gods owne planting, Matth.7.17. *Matth.7.17.* If we be fruitfull braunches we may assuredly know, that we are ingrafted into the true vine Iesus Christ,Ioh.15.4.5. *Ioh.15.4.5.*

Seeing then our sanctification assureth vs of our election *§. Sect.10.* and saluation,and without it there is no assurance; what stron-

ger

ger argument can be imagined to make vs flee sinne, and labour after mortification and newnesse of life; what keener
knife can be vsed to cut insunder the cordes of vanitie, wherein naturally we are fettered and intangled; what sharper spur
to pricke vs forward in the course of godlinesse;than to know
and consider that by our sanctification and holinesse of life,
we are certainely assured that God hath elected vs,to be heires
of the vnspeakable ioyes of his kingdome, and that by our
wickednesse and profanesse wee haue no lesse certaine assurance that we shall haue our portion for euer in the lake that
burneth with fire and brimstone? for if wee liue holily like
true christians on earth, we shall liue happily like glorious
Angels in heauen; but if here we lie frozen in the dregges of
our sins,without any sense of sorrow for those which are past,
or any desire and purpose of heart to forsake them in the time
to come, we shall be thrust from the Lord amongst the workers of iniquitie, and the wrath of God shall pursue, ouertake
and consume vs. What sinne therefore can be so pleasant to
our taste, which this consideration will not make more bitter
than wormewood? what dutie of holinesse and righteousnesse
so displeasant and grieuous, which this will not make sweete
and delightfull?

§. Sect.11.
*Diuers kinds of
counterfait ho-
linesse which
giue no assu-
rance of our e-
lection.*

Now that we may not deceiue our selues with a counterfait
holinesse, in sted of true sanctification,we are to know that this
assurance of saluation,doth not proceede from euery kinde of
holinesse, but from that which is true and vnfained : for there
is an holinesse of the tongue,seuered from the holinesse of the
heart,in shew but not in deede, in profession but not in practise;
there is an holinesse in performing outward duties of Gods
seruice,seuered frō righteousnes towards our brethrē; there is
an holines in leauing some or ỹ most sins,without any desire or
purpose to forsake some one or two sins by which we receiue
greatest pleasure or profit ; there is an holines in tything mint
and cummin,which neglecteth the waightie things of the law,
and which maketh cleane the outside of the platter & cup,lea-
uing the inside full of rapine and excesse; and outwardly maketh a glorious golden shew, when as within there is nothing
but putrefaction and rottennes: there is an holines which consisteth in the pharisaicall censuring of poore publicanes, and

in

in extolling our owne vertues. The first kinde is of those whom
the prophet reproueth Esa.29.13. who drew neere vnto God Esa.29.13.
with their lips when as their hearts were farre from him : and
of those whom the Apostle brandeth 2.Tim.3.5. who *make* 2.Tim.3.5.
a shew of godlinesse, but in their liues deny the power thereof: in
which ranke many professors also in these daies may fitly
march. The second kinde is of those who are content to serue
God in the outward duties of his worship, because they finde
them good cheape, yea often gainefull; but cannot away with
righteousnesse, because that is sometimes painefull and sometimes requireth cost. And these men in stead of making godlinesse their gaine, make a gaine of godlinesse. The third kinde
is *Herods* holinesse, who heard *Iohn* gladly and did many
things, yet could not abide to leaue his incest : and such holinesse is in some now adaies, who will be content to leaue all
grosse outward sinnes, so they may continue in their couetousnesse or voluptuousnesse. The fourth is the holinesse of those
pharisies which are most zealous in ceremonies and their
owne traditions, but keycolde in those duties which most concerne Gods glorie and their neighbours good. The last kinde
was the holinesse of the auncient pharisies, and is the holinesse
of our new Brownists, who place the most of their religion in
censuring and condemning the corruptions of the Church,
and misdemeanors of priuate men, not looking into their
owne sinnes of hellish pride, bitternesse, enuie, and want of
charitie.

But none of these, no nor yet all these ioyned together, will §. *Sect.*12.
euer giue vnto vs any sound assurance of our election; but it *The fruites*
is that true sanctification indeede, which beginneth not in the *and properties*
mouth but in the heart, and sanctifieth our will and affecti- *of true sancti-*
ons, making vs to loue and to imbrace to our vttermost power *fication.*
vertue and godlinesse, and to abhorre and flee from sinne and
iniquitie: and from the heart it proceedeth to the tongue and
hands, making the word of God and all holy conferences
honie in the mouth, and inciting vs to the practise of that
which we professe. It alwaies approueth golden pietie to be
pure, and without mixture of the drosse of hipocrisie, by the
touchstone of righteousnesse; it is as carefull in approuing the
heart and secret actions vnto God, as the outward actions vnto
men;

men; it caufeth vs to hate as well one finne as another, and
that finne moft of all into which we are moft prone by nature
to fall, though it bring neuer fo much pleafure and profit; it
embraceth afflicted godlineffe when it is attended with loffe
pouertie and fhame, as well as when it is waited vpon with
gaine, pleafure, and the praife of men; it is very charitable in
cenfuring the faults of others, but moft feuere and ftrict in
iudging and condemning the finnes which our felues haue
committed. And therefore if our fanctification haue thefe properties, we may moft certainly be affured thereby that wee are
elected and fhall be faued; but if thefe be wanting, it is but a
counterfeit holineffe which affoordeth no fuch affurance.

The miferable
eftate of thofe
who haue not
fo much as a
fhew of godli-
neffe.

Now if this be true, what hope can they haue who haue not
fo much as a fhew of godlineffe? how defperate is their ftate,
who euen in outward apparance fhew nothing but wickedneffe and prophaneffe? If the figge tree which beareth faire
greene leaues be accurfed, what curfes, what miferie and wretchedneffe are they to beare and fuffer, who haue not fo much
as leaues, that is, an outward profeffion of godlineffe? If *Herod*
be a damned wretch in hell, who heard *Iohn* the Baptift willingly, and did many things according to his doctrine, becaufe
he nourifhed one finne in his bofome; what fearefull condemnation are they to expect, who contemne and neglect Gods
word, not thinking it worth the hearing, and cannot finde in
their hearts to fubmit themfelues to the obedience of any part
thereof, neither will be brought to forfake any one fin wherewith they are delighted, till it leaue them? And yet fuch is the
blind ignorance, carnall fecuritie, and vaine prefumption of
fuch men, that they will not fticke to bragge that they are fure
of Gods loue, and that they are elected to faluation, though
there bee no fhew of reafon whereupon they may probably
ground their foolifh perfwafion. But the truth is, that whileft
they continue in this damnable eftate, confolation it felfe can
not giue vnto them any true comfort, for without fanctifica-

Ephef.4.14.

tion there is no hope of election or faluation: and feeing the
Lord hath elected vs that wee fhould be holie, therefore without holineffe there is no affurance that we are elected: feeing
he hath fworne that all thofe whom he hath redeemed and faued, out of the hands of their fpiritual enemies hell, death and
the

the diuell, *shall worship him in holinesse and righteousnesse all the* Luk.1.74 75. *daies of their life;* what hope of redemption and saluation can they conceiue, who liue in impietie and vnrighteousnesse, seeing by Gods oath they are excluded from both, whilest they continue in this state?

Chap. X.

Of the signes and infallible notes of our election.

§.*Sect*.1.
*The first signe,
an earnest desire after the meanes of our saluation.*

And thus haue I set down the meanes whereby we may be assured of our election : now let vs consider of some speciall signes which are infallible notes of those that are elected. The first signe is an earnest desire after the meanes of our saluation, and a conscionable endeuour in vsing them after we enioy them. For the end and the meanes are neuer separated in Gods decree, and therefore those that carefully vse the meanes may be assured that they shall attaine vnto the end. For example, the hearing of Gods word is the chiefe meanes of our conuersion, being made effectuall by the inward operation of Gods spirit ; and as thereby we are begotten vnto God, so also it is that bread of life, wherewith our soules are nourished and strengthened in all spirituall graces. So that whomsoeuer God hath elected, those he hath decreed to call ordinarily by these meanes ; and by the same also to furnish w   graces being called. Whosoeuer therefore labour to purchase this precious pearle, whosoeuer hunger after this heauenly Manna, and are content to enioy it not only when it is good cheap, but also when it is very chargeable, whosoeuer enioying it do attentiuely and diligently heare it and receiue it with delight, they vse the meanes of their saluation, and therefore may bee assured that they are elected, for the meanes & the end go together. And that this is a note of Gods child, it appeareth Ioh. 10.3.4. where our Sauiour saith that his sheep heare his voyce. And Matth.13.45. he compareth the true member of the kingdome of grace to a Merchant, who rather then he would want the precious pearle of Gods word, selleth all he hath to buy it. Those therefore who make this precious account of Gods

Ioh.10.3.4.

Matth.13.45.

word,

word, and carefully diligently and attentiuely heare it when they enioy it,may to their comfort assure themselues that they haue an vndoubted signe of their election. And on the other side, those who had rather bee without it than enioy it,those who wil bestow no cost to obtaine it, nor forgoe any pleasure or commoditie that they may heare it,nor when they do heare it are affected with any delight, but are glutted with loathing satietie,hearing no part of the sermon with any pleasure but the conclusion onely; they can haue no assurance of their election,because they neglect the means of their saluation,which are ioyned with the end in Gods eternall decree. The like also may bee said of other meanes, as the receiuing of the Sacraments,meditating in Gods word,the workes of holinesse and righteousnesse,and the rest.

§. Sect.2.
The second signe,the spirit of supplication.

The second signe of those that are elected, is the spirit of supplication, when as they can powre foorth their soules in feruent and effectuall prayer vnto the Lord, confessing their sinnes,and imploring his grace and mercie:for this is a notable fruit of Gods spirit working in vs,which we cannot by any naturall meanes attaine vnto ; *for of our selues wee know not what to pray as we ought, but the spirit helpeth our infirmities,and maketh request for vs with sighes which cannot be expressed,*as it is Rom.8. 26.

Rom.8.26.

Prayer therefore is a most inseparable fruite and vndoubted signe of Gods spirit, and Gods spirit certainly assureth vs of our election and adoption, for *it beareth witnesse with our spirits that we are the sonnes of God,* as it is vers.16. So Rom.10. 13.it is said,that *whosoeuer call vpon the name of the Lord shall be saued.*

Vers.16.

Rom.10.13.

But this prayer must proceede from faith; for, as it followeth,*How shall they call on him in whom they haue not beleeued?* and must be perfourmed in spirit and truth, and not with deceitfull lips ; for it is to no purpose to draw neere vnto God with our mouthes,if our hearts be farre from him,Esa.29.13.

Esa.29.13.

§. Sect.3.
The third signe is,when we are weaned from the loue of the world,and minde heauenly things.

The third signe of those who are elected and adopted to be the children of God,is,when as their hearts are somwhat weaned from the world, and seated in heauen minding the things that are aboue ; and when their tongues being set a worke by the heart, doe gladly entertaine godly and religious conferences ; for there as the treasure is, there will the heart be also, and with whatsoeuer the heart is affected,the tongue is delighted.

lighted. Now that thefe holie meditations and religious difcourfes are fignes of the child of God,hereby it plainly appeareth; in that they cannot poffibly proceede from our corrupt
nature, to which they are irkfome and tedious, but from the
fpirit of God dwelling in vs, and guiding and directing vs in
our thoughts and words; and whofoeuer are thus *led with the
fpirit of God,they are the fonnes of God*,as it is Rom.8.14. He that　Rom.8.14.
is right heire to a roiall kingdome and not yet poffeffed thereof,is neuer wearie of thinking on it,nor glutted with fuch difcourfes as tend to the extolling the riches and glorie which
there attend him,or fhew the meanes whereby he may be affured to come into fpeedie and peaceable poffeffion of his right:
and fo thofe who are elected by God,and adopted to bee the
heires of his euerlafting kingdome of glorie, are neuer fatiffied in meditating and fpeaking of the riches and ioyes of this
heauenly inheritance,or of the meanes whereby they may bee
affured vndoubtedly to obtaine it;whereas thofe who haue no
fuch intereft nor hopes, thinke and talke of thefe things with
loathfome wearineffe, as being matters not concerning them;
and therefore when fuch thoughts come into their mindes,
they vanifh as fuddenly as a flafh of lightning,and when they
are prefent at any fpirituall difcourfes the time feemeth long,
and they fit vpon thornes vntill they bee ended ; and they remaine dumbe as though they were tongue-tyed, vnleffe they
take occafion to interrupt fuch holie conferences, and to di-
uert them to fome worldly affaires.

　　The fourth figne of the childe of God who is elected to fal-　§ *Sect.*4.
uation,is,when he feeth his finnes and imperfections, and tru-　*The fourth*
ly repenteth of them, that is, bewaileth thofe which are paft,　*figne,is the*
and endeuoureth to forfake them in the time to come. For na-　*fight of finne*
turally we are blinde,and yet doe not perceiue our blindneffe,　*and forrow*
we are moft finfull and miferable,and yet doe not fee our fins　*for it.*
and miferie, but with the proud Pharifie and iufticiarie Papift
wee thinke our felues righteous, and with the Church of the
Laodiceans we imagine that we are rich and haue need of nothing, not knowing that wee are wretched, miferable, pour-　Reuel.3.17.
blind,and naked,vntill it pleafe the Lord to annoynt our eyes
with the eye-falue of his fpirit,whereby we are enabled to difcerne the pure gold of Chrifts merits,which only maketh rich,
　　　　　　　　　　　　　　　　　　　　　　from

from the droſſe of our owne workes, and the white raiment of
Chriſts obedience from the polluted ragges of our owne righteouſneſſe. And though wee ſee our ſinnes, yet naturally wee
are not ſorie for them, nay we delight our ſelues with their remembrance; or if we ſuſtaine any griefe, it is not for the ſinne,
but for the puniſhment which either wee feele preſently infli-
ɛted, or feare as being hereafter threatned, vntill it pleaſe the
Lord to adopt vs for his ſonnes, and to giue vs the ſpirit of adoption, which moooueth vs to grieue and ſorrow for our ſinnes,
not ſo much for feare of puniſhment, as for ſon-like affeɛtion,
becauſe by our ſinnes we haue diſhonoured and diſpleaſed our
gratious and louing father : and becauſe wee cannot wholie
mortifie them ſo long as wee continue in this life, we lamentably crie out with *Paul, Wretched man that I am who ſhall deliuer
me from this bodie of death ?* And becauſe we know that we ſhal
be neuer freed from it altogether ſo long as wee liue, wee wiſh
earneſtly with the Apoſtle that we may be ſpeedily diſſolued,
being contented to part with our liues, becauſe wee can no o-
therwiſe part with our ſinnes. Whoſoeuer therefore hath this
ſorrow for ſinne, hee may be aſſured of his eleɛtion and ſaluation : for, as it is 2.Cor.7.10. *this godly ſorrow cauſeth repentance
vnto ſaluation not to be repented of, whereas worldly ſorrow cauſeth
death* ; and all the promiſes of life and eternall happineſſe, are
made onely to ſuch repentant ſinners, and to them onely they
appertaine. And as Gods children are grieued for their ſinnes
paſt, ſo doe they hate and deteſt them, as in all others ſo eſpecially in themſelues, which hatred cauſeth them to flee from
them, and auoide all occaſions which might cauſe them to fall
into the like wickednes, ſtriuing and endeuouring to mortifie
their luſts and euill concupiſcences, and to leade their liues in
holineſſe and righteouſneſſe, becauſe herewith their heauenly
father is well pleaſed. Whereas the wicked man, if hee bee not
reſtrained with a ſeruile feare of Gods iudgements, or of temporarie puniſhments, goeth on in his ſinnes with pleaſure and
delight, adding drunkenneſſe vnto thirſt, and drawing iniquitie vnto him with the cords of vanitie. Whoſoeuer therefore
haue this ſon-like care, and holie endeuour of forſaking their
ſinnes, and betaking themſelues to ſerue the Lord in the duties of holineſſe and righteouſneſſe, they may bee aſſured that
                                                                  they

2.Cor.7.10.

they are elected and adopted to be the sonnes of God; but those who haue no such purpose can neuer haue this assurance; for if they were the sonnes of God, they would be affected like louing children to such a gratious father.

The fift signe of the childe of God elected to saluation, is, when as feeling his owne miserie and wretchednesse, he carnestly desireth and euen as it were hungreth and thirsteth after Christs righteousnesse, looking for life and saluation in him alone; for such as these our Sauiour Christ calleth vnto him: Ioh.7.37. *If any man thirst let him come vnto me and drinke*; and to such he promiseth euerlasting happinesse. Reuel.21.6. *I will giue to him that is a thirst, of the well of the water of life freely, of which whosoeuer drinketh shall neuer be more a thirst, but it shall be in him a well of water springing vp vnto euerlasting life.* And to this we may adde also, an high and incomparable estimation of Christ and his righteousnesse, after that wee are assured of them, whereby wee prise and value them so much aboue all worldly things, that with *Paul* we esteeme them all but drosse and dung in respect of gaining Christ, Phil.3.8. and are content not onely with the Merchant to sell all wee haue that we may buy these precious pearles, but also to suffer tribulation, anguish, persecution, famine, nakednesse, perill, sword, yea death it selfe, rather than wee would be separated from the loue of Christ, as the Apostle speaketh Rom.8.35.

§. *Sect.5.*
The fift signe, is an hungring desire after Christs righteousnesse.
Ioh.7.37.
Reuel.21.6.
Ioh.4.
Phil.3.8.
Rom.8.35.

The sixt signe of the childe of God, is the inward combat which they feele, betweene the flesh and the spirit, whereby on the one side they are drawne vnto sinne, and on the other side incited vnto holy obedience; now delighted in the lawe of God, and yet soone after led captiue vnto sinne; one while rowing against the tide of their carnall affections, and another while carried violently downe the streame, by reason of their weakenesse, and the strength of their in-bred corruption. For naturally we goe al one way, without any stop, opposition or resistance, euen the broad way which leadeth to hell and destruction: naturally we serue sinne, and willingly subiect our selues to liue in the bondage of our spiritual enemies, vntil the Lord doe with his holy spirit renew our will, and sanctifie our affections, working in vs an earnest desire to come out of this miserable captiuitie, that we may attaine vnto the glorious liberty

§. *Sect.6.*
The sixt signe, is the inward fight betweene the flesh and the spirit.

berty of the fonnes of God : which renewing and fanctification, becaufe it is done but in part, therefore is it oppofed by
the contrary corruption which wee haue by nature, fo that
what the fpirit loueth the flefh hateth, what the fpirit imbraceth the flefh abhorreth, what the fpirit would haue vs doe,
the flefh hindreth and inforceth vs to leaue vndone, with
whatfoeuer the fpirit is delighted, with that the flefh is vexed
and difpleafed ; and this fpirituall fight is in all Gods children

Rom.7.23.
Gal.5.17.

as appeareth Rom.7.23. Gal.5.17. which fhould bee fo farre
from difcouraging vs, that nothing more can affure vs of our
election ; for naturally we are all flefh, wholy fubmitting our
felues to be ruled by Sathan, neither is there any fight or oppofition in vs, for Sathans kingdome is not deuided againft it
felfe, and whileft the ftrong man wholy keepeth the houfe, all
that he poffeffeth is in peace, vntill our Sauiour Chrift, by the
operation of his fpirit, thrufteth him out of his poffeffion, and
feeketh to rule in vs by the fcepter of his word ; and then the
diuell rageth and ftriueth to keepe his hold, and the flefh ftor-
meth, defiring ftill to ferue his old maifter. When therefore
we feele this inward fight within our felues, we may be affured
that Chrift is come to dwell in our hearts by his holy fpirit,
and confequently, that we are the children of God, and heires
of euerlafting life, for *as many as receiue him, to them he giues*

Ioh.1.12.

power to be the fonnes of God, euen to them that beleeue in his name,
as it is Iohn 1.12.

§. Sect.7.
The feuenth
figne, is new
obedience.
1.Ioh.2.5.

    The feuenth figne of the childe of God is new obedience,
when as he applies his heart to the keeping of Gods comman-
maundements, defiring and indeauouring to ferue the Lord in
holineffe and newneffe of life; for *if any man keepeth Gods word,*
in him is the loue of God perfect in deede, and hereby we know that
we are in him, as it is 1.Iohn 2.5. *And whofoeuer abideth in him*
finneth not, whofoeuer finneth hath not feene him, neither hath

chap.3.v.6.10

knowne him, as it is chap.3.ver.6. So verf.10. *In this are the chil-*
dren of God knowne and the children of the diuell, whofoeuer doth
not righteoufneffe is not of God,&c. So that our new obedience
is a figne of the child of God, and the neglect thereof a marke
of the child of darkneffe. But wee are not to vnderftand this of
that exact obedience which is required in the Law ; for thereby none liuing can haue any affurance of their election and
                                                            faluation,

saluation, but rather of reprobation and damnation; but it is
to be vnderstood of an euangelicall obedience, which consisteth in an holie desire and earnest endeuour of keeping all
Gods commandements; with which the children of God are
so wholy possessed, that after their true conuersion it is impossible that they should fall into any knowne sinne, with full
consent of will and with their whole hearts. And this is the o-
bedience which the Gospell requireth, and of which the A-
postle speaketh, and thus wee neuer sinne but keepe all Gods
commandements, namely, in respect of our desire and earnest
endeuour. This is that righteousnesse which is accepted, as
though it were perfect before God, who spareth vs as a man
spares his sonne whom hee tenderly loueth, as hee professeth
Mal.3.17. and therefore measureth our obedience not according to our actions, but according to our affections, and accepteth of the will for the deed, as before I haue shewed.

Mal.3.17.

But yet that we may not deceiue our selues with a counterfeite shew, wee are to know that this euangelicall obedience
hath these properties; first, it must be totall, and that both in
respect of the subiect and of the obiect; that is, wee must not
share our selues betweene God and the world, giuing one the
tongue, the other the heart; one our outward actions, and the
other our inward affections; but we must performe our obedience with our whole hearts, yea with the whole man bodie
soule and spirit: for though wee be regenerated and sanctified
but in part, yet is there no part of the whole man vnregenerate
and vnsanctified, howsoeuer the flesh and the corruption of
nature be spread likewise and mixed therewith throughout the
whole bodie & soule. And therfore though all our obedience
sauour of the flesh, and is mingled with manifold imperfections, yet it doth proceede from the whole man bodie and
soule, because regeneration from which it proceedeth is not of
any part alone, but of the whole man. So also it must be totall
in respect of the obiect; for it is not sufficient that with *Herod*
we obserue many things, if we nourish willingly any one sinne
taking therein pleasure and delight, but wee must desire and
endeuour to forsake all our sinnes, and to performe obedience
vnto all Gods commandements; for if we nourish one sinne in
our hearts, it will open a doore to let in more when wee are

§. *Sect.*8.
*The properties
of true obedi-
ence: first, that
it must be to-
tall and entire.*

tempted

tempted vnto them; as wee may see in the example of *Herod* and *Iudas*, the one harbouring incest, the other couetousnesse; if we neglect willingly, obedience to one precept of Gods law, it wil so harden our harts and seare our consciences, that soone after we shall neglect all. If therefore we would haue our obedience acceptable vnto God, we must with the Prophet *Dauid*

Psal.119.6.
Iam.2.10.
The second propertie, that it must be perpetuall and constant.

Psal.119.6. haue *respect vnto all Gods commandements*; for, *he that faileth in one, is guiltie of all*, as it is Iam.2.10.

Secondly, this obedience must be perpetuall, continuing in a constant course from the time of our conuersion to the end of our liues; for we are not to iudge of our selues or others, by one or two or many actions whether they be good or euil, but by the whole tenour and course of our liues, so that he who in this respect is holie and righteous, hee is so accepted before God, notwithstanding his many falles and great infirmities; he that in the course of his life is wicked and prophane, is so esteemed of God, although hee seeme to himselfe and others religious by fits, and perfourmeth many excellent duties and good workes. It is therefore not sufficient that we begin in the

Galat.3.3.

spirit, if we end in the flesh, Gal.3.3. It is not sufficient to professe and practise godlinesse in our youth, if wee breake off in our age; it is not enough that we enter into the Christian race and runne well in the beginning, if wee stand still in the midst, or before we come to the goale; *for he only that endureth to the*

Matth.24.13
Luk.9.62.

end shall be saued, as it is Matth.24.13. As for him *that laieth his hand on the plough and looketh backe, hee is not fit for Gods kingdome*, as our Sauiour affirmeth Luk.9.62.

The third propertie, that it must be grounded on Gods word, and referred to his glorie.

Lastly, our obedience must be grounded vpon Gods word, and therefore perfourmed because the Lord hath enioyned such duties vnto vs; it must proceed from faith, which first purifieth the heart, and then worketh by loue; it must not bee done for any worldly respect, but of a conscionable care of perfourming our duties, and in a feruent zeale of Gods glorie, which is magnified when as our lights shine before men; which zeale will make vs goe forward in our course of godli-

2.Cor.6.8.

nesse, *through euill report, and good report, honour and dishonour*. And if our obedience spring from these fountaines, and be referred to this end that God thereby may bee glorified; then will we make no lesse conscience of secret, than of open sinnes;
then

then will wee be no lesse readie to serue God in the duties of pietie and righteousnesse when there is no witnesse of our actions, than if all the world should looke vpon vs ; then will we be as fearefull to offend God in the breach of any of his commandements in our secret chambers in the darke night, as in the Church or market place at noone day.

The eight signe of the childe of God, is the loue of our brethren in obedience to Gods commandement; when as a man loues intirely a Christian, because he is a Christian, and ingrafted into the same bodie of Christ whereof he is a member : for as it is impossible that one member of the bodie should not loue, cherish, and defend another, because they are quickened by the same soule and gouerned by the same head ; so it is not possible but that one true Christian should loue, cherish, and defend another, because they are quickned by the same spirit, and ruled by the same head Iesus Christ. And this is made a marke of Gods child by the Apostle *Iohn*, 1.Ioh.3.14. *We know that we are translated from death to life, because wee loue the brethren:* as the want of this loue is a sure note of the childe of wrath, for as it followeth in the same verse, *he that loueth not his brother abideth in death.*

Now the vndoubted signes of loue and christian charitie are two ; giuing to those that want, and forgiuing those that offend : for it is a propertie of true loue to bee bountifull, 1.Cor. 13.4. as to all, so especially to those that are of the houshold of faith, as it is Gal.6.10 ; and on the other side, *He that hath this worlds good, and seeth his brother haue neede, and shutteth vp his compassion from him, he is destitute of the loue of God*, and consequently of the loue of his brethren, which is but a streame issuing from this fountaine, 1.Ioh.3.17. And this Christian liberalitie as it is a signe of true loue, so also of our election and saluation ; for our Sauiour Christ hath shewed vs, that according to these fruites of charity, and actions of Christian liberalitie, hee will pronounce the sentence of euerlasting ioy and happinesse at the day of iudgement, Matth.25.34,35,36. and on the other side, that he will pronounce the sentence of condemnation against the neglectors of these duties of Christian charitie, vers.41,42,43.

The second signe of true loue is forgiuing, when as wee are

readie

readie for Gods sake and in obedience to his commandement to remit and pardon those iniuries which are offered vs; for, *loue is not prouoked to anger,* and therefore much lesse to reuenge; *it suffreth all things, it indureth all things,* as it is 1.Cor. 13.5,7. Nay, it doth not onely not render euill for euill, but it ouercommeth euill with goodnes, leauing reuenge vnto God, and to his deputies and vicegerents the Magistrates, as we may see in the example of our Sauiour Christ, and the blessed Martyr *Steuen,* who prayed for their persecutors; whose example wee are to imitate, as the Apostle exhorteth Rom.12.14. *Blesse them that persecute you; blesse ! say and curse not.* And so shall wee haue a certaine signe of true loue, and an vndoubted note of Gods spirit dwelling in vs, of the remission of our sinnes, and consequently of our election and saluation. For naturallie we are Wolues, Leopards, Lions, yea Cockatrices who kil with their lookes, as the Prophet speaketh Esa.11.6,8. and like bruit and sauage beasts willing to offer all iniuries, but impatient of suffring any : and therefore when our sauage crueltie is turned into charitie, and wee become as meeke and harmelesse, as the lambe, calfe, or little childe, it is a manifest signe that our stoute courages are abated and beaten downe with the rod of Christs. mouth, that wee are borne anew and quickened by his spirit, and that now wee are seated in the mountaine of his holinesse, and shall be heires of his kingdome of glorie. So also hereby we are assured of the remission of our sinnes, when we find our selues readie and willing to forgiue our neighbours; for our Sauiour Christ hath promised, that if we *doe forgiue men their trespasses, our heauenly father will also forgiue vs,* Matth.6.14. and consequently wee may assuredly gather, that wee are iustified, called, elected, and shal be glorified.

§. *Sect.*10. The ninth signe of the child of God elected to saluation, is, the loue of Gods true Ministers and ambassadours, not onely because they are Christians, but also because they are sent of God to execute these holie functions, for the gathering together of Gods elect. And this our Sauiour Christ declareth, Matth.10.41. *He that receiueth a Prophet in the name of a Prophet, shall haue a Prophets reward*; that is, euerlasting ioy and vnspeakable happinesse in Gods kingdom ; for, *they that turne many vnto righteousnes, shall shine as the starres for euer and euer.*
And

Marginal notes (left column):

1.Cor.13.5.7

Rom.12.19. 21.

Rom.12.14.

Esa.11.6.8.

Matth.6.14.

§. *Sect.*10.
The ninth signe, is the loue of Gods ministers.

Matth.10.41.

Dan.12.3.

And becaufe none fhould pretend that by reafon of their pouertie they cannot fhew their loue to Gods Minifters, therefore the Lord encourageth euen the pooreft, to fhew their
goodwill and affection vnto them,Matth 10.43. faying, *Who-* Matth.10.43.
foeuer fhall giue to any of thefe little ones to drinke,a cup of cold wa-
ter onely, in the name of a difciple, verely I fay vnto you he fhall not
lofe his reward, namely in Gods kingdome. Moreouer, thofe
that loue Gods ambaffadours, doe prooue vnto themfelues
and fhew vnto the world, that they haue receiued good by
their ambaffage,euen reconciliation with God, peace of confcience and affurance of faluation , which maketh them to
thinke no worldly benefit fufficient to requite thefe fpirituall
graces, which by their meanes and minifterie they haue recei-
ued:and therefore with the Galatians they could bee content,
if it were poffible to doe them good hereby, to pull out their Gal.4.15
owne eyes and to giue them vnto them,feeing by their means
the blind eyes of their vnderftandings, are inlightened with
the knowledge of God and Chrift their Sauiour. And becaufe
they haue receiued from them to their comfort,the glad tidings of peace and good things; therefore their feet, that is,
their approaching and comming vnto them, feeme beautiful Rom.10.15.
and delightfull,as the Apoftle fpeaketh Rom.10.15. If an am-
baffadour were fent from a mightie Prince,who was our enemie in time paft,and able at his pleafure to deftroy vs and our
countrey,to the end he might conclude a peace; and not only
fo,but to offer vs the free vfe of al the riches and commodities
of his kingdome ; who would not receiue him with ioy,and
giue him royall entertainment,if they were perfwaded of the
truth of his ambaffage?But wee by our finnes had made the
glorious King of heauen and earth our enemie, who is able e-
uery minute to deftroy vs with the breath of his noftrels;and
it hath pleafed the Lord to fend his ambaffadours,not only to
offer peace,but alfo to befeech vs that wee would be reconci- 2.Cor.5.20.
led vnto him, as the Apoftle fpeaketh 2.Cor.5.20 ; and vpon
this reconciliation, hee affureth vs of the riches of his kingdome: who therefore recciuing and beleeuing this ambaffage,
will not loue the Ambaffadours that bring thefe bleffed tidings vnto them? Who can bee affured of fuch ineftimable
benefits,and yet fhew no token of rhankfulnes towards them,

who are the meanes whereby they are deriued vnto them.

Where by the way we may note, how few the number is in thefe daies, who receiue the Lords ambaffage to their fpiritual comfort; how few they are to whome it is effectuall for the begetting in them the graces of Gods fpirit; how few hereby come to the true affurance of the remiffion of their finnes and euerlafting happineffe: feeing the number is fo exceeding fmall who loue and refpect the Lords ambaffadors in regarde of their ambaffage. Nay rather the moft, euen for their minifterie fake doe contemne thofe, whom otherwife in refpect of their learning, wifedome, and other excellent gifts of bodie and minde, they would refpect and highly efteeme if they were not of the minifterie. So that their honorable calling, which aboue al things fhould commend them, doth aboue all things make them bafe & contemptible: and no maruell, feeing the moft are flefh and not fpirit, the children of *Mammon* and not the children of God: and therefore, fauoring onely the things of the flefh & not perceauing the things of the fpirit of God, they feeme foolifhneffe vnto them, and the preachers of them fooles, and men of fhallow conceites. But let fuch know, that *God hath chofen the foolifh things of the world to confound the wife, and weake things to confound mightie things; & vile things of the world, and things that are defpifed hath God chofen, and things that are not, to bring to nought things that are, that no flefh fhould reioyce in his prefence*, as it is 1.Cor 1.27.28. Let them know that this their contempt, or at leaft fmall regarde of Gods ambaffadors, is a moft manifeft figne that they neuer receiued good by their ambaffage: for had they receiued from them fpirituall things, they would neuer grudge to beftowe vpon them their worldly things, which in the true chriftians eftimation are not to be compared with them; and much leffe would they againft their owne confcience defraud them of their owne right, which by the lawes of God and man is due vnto them, whereby it commeth to paffe that whereas all men being induftrious and frugall, may liue plentifully euen of their meaneft trades, onely the Lords ambaffadors, though neuer fo painefull in their callings, liue in want and miferie.

1.Cor.2.14.

1.Cor.1.27.28.

§. Sect.11.   The laft figne of Gods childe elected to faluation, which I will

will speake of, is their earnest desire that our Sauiour Christ
should come to iudgement: whence proceedeth that patheti-
call prayer, *Come Lord Iesus come quicklie,* Reuel.22.20; and
that prayer which our Sauiour hath taught all the faithfull to
pray daily,*let thy kingdome come,* Matth.6.10. Now that this is
a note of those that are elected to saluation, it appeareth
plainely 2.Tim 4.8. Where the Apostle saith that *a crowne of*
righteousnesse is laide vp for all those that loue his appearing. And
Rom.8.23, he telleth vs, that those who haue the first fruites
of the spirit,doe euen sigh in themselues,waiting for the adoption euen the redemption of their body, when as their corruption shall put on incorruption, and the mortall body immortalitie,as he speaketh 1.Cor.15.53. So our Sauiour Christ
hath tolde vs, that his faithfull children should at his comming, *looke vp and lift vp their heads,because their redemption*
draweth neere, Luk.21.28; and on the otherside *that the king-*
dome of the earth shall mourne, and that the prophane worldlings and reprobates *shall say to the mountaines and rockes, fall*
on vs and hide vs from the presence of him that sitteth on the
throne,and from the wrath of the lambe ; Reuel.6.16. So that by
these places it is manifest,that if we loue the appearing of the
Lord Iesus, and desire his comming to iudgement; we are the
children of God indued with his spirit, which assureth vs of
our saluation. For naturally we abhorre to thinke of this fearefull day,and tremble with feare when mention is made of the
appearing of our iudge, because by our sinnes we haue deserued euerlasting damnation: but when the spirit of God by the
ministerie of the word,hath begot faith in vs, whereby we apply vnto our selues Christ Iesus, and all his merits,by whom
we are reconciled vnto God and made friends who before
were enemies, and sonnes of God and heyres of euerlasting
happinesse who before were the children of wrath and firebrands of hell, then doe we earnestly desire the companie of
our heauenly father ; when we are assured that our iudge shall
be our Sauiour, then can wee goe boldly to his iudgement
seate without feare of condemnation;when we are assured that
we are the beloued spouse of Christ, then we long for nothing
more then for the comming of our bridegroome ; when we
are certainely perswaded that by Gods spirit we are ingrafted

into

into the bodie of Chriſt, and are become liuely members of
his body; then doe we hartily wiſh with the Apoſtle to be diſſolued, that we may be with Chriſt our head in his kingdome
of glorie, where together with him wee ſhall receiue, and be
fully ſatisfied with ſuch incomparable ioyes, as *neither eye hath*
ſeene nor eare heard nor the heart of man conceiued.

1.Cor.2.9.

CHAP. XI.

The obiections alleadged againſt the aſſurance of
our election, anſwered.

§. Sect.1.
Anſwers vnto
teſtimonies al-
ledged.

Nd thus much concerning the ſignes whereby we
may be aſſured of our election: now I will anſwere ſuch obiections as are brought againſt this
doctrine by the enemies of Gods truth. And
theſe are of two ſortes, firſt teſtimonies of Gods
word, and ſecondly reaſons. The teſtimonies of ſcriptures are
diuers: firſt they obiect ſuch places as theſe; 1.Cor.10.12. *Let*
him that thinketh he ſtandeth, take heede leaſt he fall. Pro.28.14.
Bleſſed is the man that feareth alwaies, Rom.11.20. *Be not high*
minded but feare. Phil.2.12. *Make an end of your ſaluation with*
feare and trembling. 1.Pet.1.17. *Paſſe the time of your dwelling*
here in feare: to all which and many other ſuch like places, we
may anſwere generally, that the holy Ghoſt would not hereby take away our certaintie of faith, but carnall ſecuritie; he
would not depriue vs of the aſſurance of the remiſſion of our
ſinnes and our election, but rather by theſe admonitions as
with a bridle he curbeth in our vnrulie affections, and reſtrai-
neth vs from running into all licentiouſneſſe vnder this pretence that we are aſſured of our election; he would not haue
vs doubt of Gods grace, but he would not haue vs too much
truſt and rely on thoſe graces which wee haue receiued; and
therefore he putteth vs in minde of our owne weakeneſſe and
infirmitie, not to the end we ſhould doubt of our election,
and deſpaire or feare our perſeuerance, but to the end that diſtruſting our owne ſtrength wee may wholy rely vpon the
power loue and promiſes of God, and thereby gather ſo much
more certaine aſſurance of our election and perſeuerance, as
the

1.Cor.10.12.
Pro.28.14.
Rom.11.20.

Phil.2.12.
1 Pet.1.17.

the power of God is aboue the power of man ; laſtly he giueth vs not theſe admonitions to bring vs into doubting, but would hereby ſtirre vp our faith vnto the exerciſe of holineſſe and righteouſneſſe, that it may not through idleneſſe faint and waxe ſtiffe and benummed, and vnable to performe theſe holy actions, whereby this aſſurance and certaintie of our election, would bee infeebled and not ſo ſenſibly diſcerned : and therefore theſe and ſuch like ſpeeches tend not to this end that wee ſhould doubt of our election, but rather that wee ſhould be preſerued from doubting;to which,carnall ſecuritie, ſelfe confidence,negligence in the duties of holineſſe and righteouſneſſe, and continuance in ſinne would in the end bring vs ; all which the ſpirit of God by theſe admonitions and exhortations preuenteth.

Secondly, I anſwere that theſe and ſuch like admonitions, **2** are not directed onely to the faithfull, who may and ought to be aſſured of their election, but in generall to the whole Church, wherein there are many hypocrites who content themſelues with a bare ſhew of godlineſſe, and many worldly men who pleaſe themſelues with carnall ſecuritie, and a carcaſe of faith, which neuer ſo much as breatheth, and muchleſſe performeth any actions of holineſſe and righteouſneſſe: and therefore as it was neceſſarie that the faithfull ſhould be more and more confirmed with the promiſes of the Goſpell, ſo was it requiſit that hypocrits and ſecure worldlings ſhould be rouzed out of their ſecuritie,with theſe and ſuch like admonitions and comminations.

Neither were they neceſſarie for hypocrits and worldlings alone, but euen for the deere children of God : who becauſe they are partly fleſh and partly ſpirit, therefore as they haue neede that the ſpirituall man ſhould be comforted and their faith confirmed againſt diffidence and doubting, with the ſweete promiſes of the Goſpell; ſo had they neede to haue their vnruly fleſh curbed in, and reſtrained from falling into retchleſſe ſecuritie, by theſe admonitions and comminations. And becauſe by reaſon of this diuiſion which is in our ſelues, we are readie as it were to mutinie, one part of our forces being readie to march cheerefully to the land of promiſe, the other to forſake the way, ſometimes on the one ſide being

§. Sect.2. **3**
Admonitions and comminations profitable for Gods children.

readie

readie to turne backe againe, as vtterly despairing of attaining
to the end of our iorney, when wee consider the sonnes of
Anakim our spirituall enemies, in respect of whose stature
and strength we are but as grashoppers, and the mightie op-
positions which are made against our weake force; and sometimes to goe on in a way which God hath not appointed,
presuming vpon our owne strength and abilities. Therefore
that wee may keepe the straight way without declining on
either hand, God doth as it were hedge vs in on both sides, to
restraine vs from wandring; on the one side with sweete promises, that we may not despaire, but rely our selues on his
strength and assistance; on the otherside with sweete admonitions and fearefull comminations, that we may not trust too
much vnto our owne power, nor presume vpon our owne a-
bilities: and by the meanes of the one, he doth as it were pricke
vs forward in our iourney, keeping vs from once thinking of
standing still, or returning againe into Ægypt; and by the
other as with an hand he doth vphold vs, when we are wearie
and readie to faint, hauing an eye to the crowne of glorie, and
the garland of happinesse, which is prepared for vs at the end
of our course, and race of christianitie. And as a skilfull pilot,
when his ship is in a tempestuous and straite sea, in daunger
to runne on the rockes or to sinke in the sandes, doth cast out
ancor on both sides, or most carefully looke vnto the sterne
to keepe it in an euen course; so we sailing in the tempestuous
sea of this miserable world, are in daunger on the one side to
dash vpon the rockes of presumptuous securitie, and on the
otherside to sinke in the sands and to plunge into the gulfe
of desperation: and therefore the Lord doth stay vs from both,
as it were with two strong cables; the first is legall comminations and strict admonitions, to keepe vs from carnall securitie and hypocriticall presumption, the other is sweete promises whereby he keepeth vs from falling into doubting and
desperation; neither doth one of these hinder another, but
both stay vs from falling into these extremes.

§. Sect. 3.
True true mea-
ning of the se-
uerall places
obiected.

So that these admonitions are not giuen to make vs doubtfull of our election, but partly to take away the presumption
and securitie of hypocrites and carnall worldlings, and partly
to bridle and restraine the flesh from running headlong into
sinne,

sinne, and from growing insolent ouer the spirit euen in Gods
children, whereby in deede their assurance of saluation would
be abated and languish. The truth whereof appeareth if wee
examine the seuerall places. For first, whereas the Apostle,
1.Cor.10.12. saith, *Let him that thinketh he standeth, take heede* ⟨1.Cor.10.12.⟩
least he fall; he doth not moue those that are faithfull, to doubt
of their perseuerance, but those that want true faith, not to deceiue themselues with vaine presumption, and with an opinion
of faith in stead of true faith in deede: and therefore hee saith
not simply, let him that standeth, but let him that thinketh he
standeth, that is, he that doth not stand in deede but in his
owne fond opinion. Neither can it necessarily be proued, that
this falling is to bee vnderstood of finall falling away from
God; but rather as the coherence of the text sheweth, of falling
into those sinnes which the Israelites fell into: and though it
were, yet is it but an admonition to take away carnall securitie,
not giuen to make vs doubt of our standing, but to preserue vs
from falling.

Secondly, whereas the wise man saith, Pro.28.14, *Blessed is* ⟨Prou.28.14.⟩
the man that feareth allwaies: he doth not vnderstand thereby
a doubtfull feare of our election, but a feare to sinne, and a
conscionable care of auoiding those things which are displeasing in Gods sight; which feare is opposed to carnall securitie
and hardnesse of heart, as appeareth in the same place where
this is added, *But he that hardneth his heart shall fall into euill:*
as though hee should say, that man is blessed which feareth
the Lord, for this will worke in him a conscionable care of a-
uoiding sinne, which is odious in the eyes of God, and of imbracing holinesse and righteousnesse, which being acceptable
vnto God, hee will reward with eternall blessednesse; but hee
that hardneth his heart and continueth in carnall securitie, runneth headlong into the euill of sinne, and consequently the
euill of punishment, euen euerlasting condemnation.

Thirdly, whereas the Apostle, Rom.11.20, exhorteth, vs *not* ⟨Rom.11.20.⟩
to bee high minded but feare; hee doth not meane that wee
should doubt of our election and saluation, but doth hereby
beate downe our spirituall pride, and opinion of our owne
righteousnesse and holinesse, whereby we are ready to insult
ouer the Iewes, as though we were chosen and preferred before

fore them, for some excellencie or worthinesse in our selues, and so derogate from the free grace and goodnesse of God, whereby he hath chosen vs without any respect of our deserts. And that this is the meaning of these words, appeareth in the eighteenth verse, where he willeth the Gentiles not to boast themselues against the Iewes who were the naturall branches. Neither doth the Apostle write this to the faithfull onely, but to the whole Church of the Gentiles, in which were many hypocrites and carnall men, who contenting themselues with a bare name of Christians, would insult ouer the Iewes, whom God had cast off from being his Church and people; whom he warneth, not to be puft vp in pride, as though in this respect their state were most secure and out of all danger; for as (saith he) they were cast off for their infidelitie, euen when they were naturall branches, so shall you much more be reiected, who being wilde branches were grafted in their places (that is, called to be the members of the visible Church) if you continue in the like infidelity, contenting your selues with vaine confidence and fond presumption, in stead of a liuely faith.

§. *Sect.*4.
Phil.2.12.

Fourthly, whereas the Apostle, Phil.2.12. doth exhort vs to worke out *our saluation with feare and trembling*; he doth not hereby take away from vs assurance of our election and saluation, but carnall securitie and selfe confidence; that so despairing of our owne strength, as being vnable of our selues to thinke a good thought, or to will that which is good, we may in all humilitie rest and rely our selues, wholy vpon the Lord. And that this is his meaning, appeareth by the reason which he adioyneth in the verse following: for saith hee, *it is God which worketh in you both the will and the deede.* As though hee should say, there is no reason why you should bee secure, as though you were able to stand by your owne strength; there is no cause why you should be lifted vp with fond presumption, or be carried away with selfe confidence, for of your selues, you are not able so much as to will that which is good, or to performe it though you should will it, vnlesse it please the Lord of his owne good pleasure and free will to worke both in you, and therefore respecting your owne infirmities and imperfections, you should bee so farre from carnall securitie or selfe confidence, that contrariwise you should continually
feare,

feare, leaſt through your corruption you ſhould be ouertaken
of ſinne, and ſo diſpleaſe the Lord which is your ſoueraigne
King and gracious Father. So that the Apoſtle doth not here
exhort vs to doubt of our election and ſaluation, but to a
godly feare that we doe not fall into ſinne : he would not haue
vs to doubt of Gods grace and free promiſes, but of our own
ſtrength, by which wee are altogether vnable to ſtand if hee
leaue vs to our ſelues : hee would not haue vs feare leaſt wee
ſhould be reiected and damned, after we are truely conuerted
vnto God, but leaſt we fall into ſinne, and neglect that duety
which we owe to our heauenly father.

Theſe two therefore may well ſtand together : for the more *Feare and di-*
we diſtruſt our owne weakeneſſe, the more firmely we reſt vp- *ſtruſt in our*
on the power and aſſiſtance of God, and the more we rely vp- *owne weake-*
on him, the more ſure we are of ſtanding vnto the end: the ſu- *neſſe, and aſſu-*
rer we are of Gods loue and fauour, the more we loue him a- *rance of our e-*
gaine; and the more we loue him, the more fearefull we are to *lection, may*
diſpleaſe him : the more we ſee our proneneſſe to ſinne, the *well ſtand to-*
more we feare leaſt we ſhould fall into it; and the more we ſuſ- *gether.*
pect our ſelues, the more earneſtly we implore the aſſiſtance of
Gods ſpirit, whereby wee are inabled to withſtand temptations. And therefore *Dauid* ioyneth theſe together, Pſal.2.11.
Serue the Lord in feare, and reioyce in trembling ; noting thereby *Pſal.2.11.*
that Gods children feare, yea, euen tremble in regard of their
owne infirmities and corruptions, and yet at the ſame time
they reioyce and are filled with conſolation, in reſpect of that
full aſſurance which they haue of Gods loue and fauour, and
their election and ſaluation. And as he ioyneth them in pre-
cept, ſo alſo in his owne practiſe, Pſalm.5.7. *I will* (ſaith he) *Pſalm.5.7.*
come into thine houſe in the multitude of thy mercy ; and in thy
feare will I worſhip towards thy holy temple : ſo that at the ſame
time, when as hee was incouraged by the conſideration of
Gods great mercy, to goe boldly and with a liuely faith vnto
the throne of grace ; he was alſo touched with a godly feare
in regard of his vnworthineſſe and imperfections ; not that he
doubted leaſt hee ſhould not bee accepted of God, but leaſt
in worſhipping of God hee ſhould bewray his corruption,
and not doe it in that manner and meaſure which God requireth.

But.

But againſt this it may be obiected that *Iohn* ſaith, 1.Epiſt. 4.18. *There is no feare in loue, but perfect loue caſteth out feare, &c.* I anſwere, that there is a twofold feare mentioned in the ſcriptures ; the firſt is a ſeruile feare proceeding from incredulitie, whereby men feare God as a ſeuere iudge, who is ready to inflict on them thoſe iuſt puniſhments which by their ſinnes they haue deſerued, which feare is expelled when as we are aſſured of Gods loue and loue him againe. The other is a ſonne-like feare, which is a fruite of faith, whereby we doe not feare God as an enemy or an angry iudge, but as a gracious Father, whoſe diſpleaſure we would by no meanes incurre ; not that we feare his wrath and vengeance, as though it were ready to fall vpon vs, but becauſe we would not thus abuſe his mercy and goodneſſe towards vs, nor doe any thing which might cauſe him to looke vpon vs with a frowning countenance : or if we doe feare Gods iudgements, it is as they are inflicted on another ſubiect, and not as being ready to fall vpon vs : for this difference is betweene the feare of the wicked and Gods children, they like malefactors which are led out to puniſhment, are filled with horror and feare when they thinke of the torments which they are to indure, but yet did neuer feare to commit ſuch crimes as deſerued the puniſhments, and though they ſhould eſcape, yet this would be no warning for the time to come ; but Gods children ſeeing the iudgements which are exerciſed vpon the wicked, doe feare, not leaſt they ſhould be inflicted vpon them preſently, but leaſt they ſhould ſo offend and deſerue the like puniſhments, firſt auoyding ſinne, that they may not recciue the wages thereof. And this ſonne-like feare is commended vnto vs in the ſcriptures, as being a part of the honour and ſeruice which we owe vnto God, as appeareth Mal.1.6. *A ſonne honoureth his father, and a ſeruant his maiſter, if I be a father where is mine honour, if I be a maiſter where is my feare ſaith the Lord?* So Pſalm.34.9. *Feare the Lord yee his ſaints, for nothing wanteth to them that feare him.* And Pſalme 112.1. *Bleſſed is the man that feareth the Lord and delighteth greatly in his commaundements.* In which places we are not to vnderſtand a ſeruile and ſlauiſh feare, but an ingenuous and ſonne-like feare, which drawes vs backe from falling into ſinne, and incites vs to performe all good duties of holineſſe

and

Mal.1.6.

Pſalm.34.9.
and 112.1.

and righteousnes to God and our brethren, becaufe we would not incurre the difpleafure of our heauenly father, but do thofe things which are acceptable in his fight.

Laftly, whereas the Apoftle *Peter* 1.epift.1.17. exhorteth vs *to paffe the time of our dwelling here in feare*, hee doth not vnder- I.Pet.1.17. ftand fuch a feare as maketh vs to doubt of our election and faluation, but fuch an one as prouoketh vs to obey Gods commandements, and reftraineth vs from wallowing and defiling our felues in finne : for with this feare in the verfe following he ioyneth certaine knowledge of our redemption, and confequently of our election and faluation, *knowing* (faith he) *that ye were not redeemed with corruptible things, as filuer and gold from your vaine conuerfation, &c. but with the pretious blond of Chrift.* So that this feare doth not take away the certaine knowledge of our election and redemption, but this knowledge caufeth vs to feare leaft we fall into finne after we are affured of this great benefit of our redemption, and thereby difpleafe our gracious God, and defile our foules after they are purged with the pretious bloud of Iefus Chrift.

Befides thefe places, there are others alfo obiected, as that §. Sect.6. Iob.9.21. *Though I were perfect, yet I know not my foule ; therefore* Other places *I abhorre my life.* To which I anfwere, that *Iobs* fcope and drift obiected an- in this place is to fhew, that euen the moft iuft and holie man fwered. cannot ftand before Gods iudgement feate in his owne righ- Iob.9.21. teoufneffe and holineffe, which is polluted and imperfect, and that therefore it behooueth euery one to defpaire in himfelfe and his legall righteoufneffe, as not being able to iuftifie him in Gods fight, in refpect of whofe puritie euen the very heauens are vncleane, that fo he may wholy rely vpó Gods mercy and Chrifts merits ; and this appeareth verf.2.3. I know verely (faith he) that it is fo (that is, that God is iuft and all men are Iob.9.2. finners, who are righteoufly punifhed for their demerits, as *Bildad* had reafoned in the former chapter) and therefore how fhould man compared vnto God be iuftified ? 3. If he would Verfe 3. difpute with him, hee could not anfwere him one thing of a thoufand. And verf.20. If I would iuftifie my felfe, mine owne Verfe 20. mouth fhould condemne me ; if I would bee perfect, hee fhall iudge me wicked. 21. And though I were innocent or perfect, (that is, though I feemed iuft in mine own eyes, and knew nothing

thing by my selfe) yet I know not mine owne soule, nor what secret corruptions may lurke in it, and therfore I will not hereby looke to be iustified, nay in this respect I abhorre my life, and cast mine owne righteousnesse from me as a polluted cloute. By which manner of reasoning hee confuteth *Bildads* obiection, who affirmed that *Iob* and his sonnes were punished of God for their sinnes and that iustly, and therefore they were not so iust and innocent as they had seemed : to this *Iob* answereth, that it is true indeede he could not iustifie himselfe in respect of his owne righteousnesse, if hee compared himselfe with Gods exact iustice, but must needes condemne himselfe for a wretched sinner; yet hence it followed not that therfore God thus afflicted him, seeing this was the state not of him onely but of all men whatsoeuer: and therefore this could not be the onely cause of his extraordinarie afflictions. So that this place makes nothing against the assurance of our saluation, which is grounded vpon Gods free mercy and Chrifts merits; but against that presumption which relieth it selfe in whole or in part, vpon our owne legall righteousnesse.

§. *Sect.* 7.
1. Cor. 4. 3 4.

The like place to this is that saying of *Paul* which they obiect, 1. Cor. 4. 3, 4. *I iudge not mine own selfe, for I know nothing by my selfe, yet am I not thereby iustified, but he that iudgeth me is the Lord.* For answering whereof, we are to know, that there were diuers in the Church of Corinth, who censured *Pauls* ministerie and disgraced his gifts; against which detractations he bendeth his speech and maketh an apologie for himselfe, saying, that hee would not take vpon him to iudge himselfe, concerning the excellencie and worth of his ministerie and gifts, but would leaue the iudgement and approbation thereof vnto God, whose ambassadour hee was; and though he knew nothing which might bee obiected against him in regard of his ministerie, yet hereby hee would not looke to bee iustified in Gods presence: So that if this be the sense of the words, as appeareth by the coherence and the drift of the place, it maketh nothing for popish doubting. But let it bee granted that *Paul* speakes not of his ministerie, but of his righteousnesse and obedience to the law, yet this maketh nothing against the certaintie of our election; for the Apostle speaking of his owne righteousnesse and innocencie, doth disclaime it from being

any

any cauſe of his iuſtification: neither doth he ſay that in regard
therof he doubteth, as the Papiſts would expound him, but he
affirmeth directly that he is not thereby iuſtified, and rendreth
this as a reaſon, that it is God who iudgeth him : and therfore
though he were vnblameable before men, yea though he knew
nothing by himſelfe, yet hee could not hereby be iuſtified before the iuſt iudgement ſeate of God, who requires ſuch perfection and exact obedience as can be found in no man liuing;
for he that but once breaketh but one commandement, is guil- Iam.2.10.
tie of all, as it is Iam.2.10. And therefore it behooued the A-
poſtle and al others, not to ſeeke for iuſtification in themſelues
and their owne righteouſneſſe, but in the righteouſneſſe and
obedience of Chriſt, which wee may boldly preſent before
Gods exact iudgement ſeate, and there bee accepted as righteous. And of this iuſtificatiō the Apoſtle ſpeaketh, not doubtfully or timorouſly, but boldly and certainly, Rom.5.1. *Being*
iuſtified by faith, we haue peace towards God through our Lord Ie- Rom.5.1.2.
ſus Chriſt. 2. *By whom alſo we haue acceſſe through faith vnto his*
grace wherein we ſtand, and reioyce vnder the hope of the glorie of
God. So Rom.8.33. *Who ſhall lay any thing to the charge of Gods* Rom.8.33.
choſen? it is God that iuſtifieth. 34. *Who ſhall condemne? it is*
Chriſt who is dead, yea rather which is riſen againe,&c.

Moreouer, they obiect theſe places to moue vs to doubt of §. Sect.8.
our election and ſaluation. Ioel 2.14. *Who knoweth if he will re-* Ioel 2.14.
turne and repent ; and Amos 5.15. *It may be that the Lord God* Amos 5.15.
of hoaſts will be mercifull vnto the remnant of Ioſeph. And Ion.3.9.
Who can tell if God will turne and repent, and turne away from his Ionas 3.9.
ſcarce wrath that wee periſh not? To which I anſwere, that the
Prophets in theſe places doe not ſpeake of the election or e-
ternall ſaluation of thoſe that truly repent, but of their deliuerie from outward afflictions, and temporarie calamities threatned againſt them for their ſinnes : which ſometimes the Lord
doth inflict on his children after their true repentance, either
for their chaſtizement, that they may therby hate ſinne for the
time to come, when they feele the ſmart of it ; or els for their
triall: and ſometimes alſo the Lord after hee hath threatned
them againſt the wicked, doth notwithſtanding hold backe his
hand, and as it were put vp his ſword of iuſtice againe into the
ſcabberd, which he had drawne out to puniſh their ſinnes, vp-

S   pon

on their outward humiliation and fained repentance, that hee may shew hereby how highly hee esteemeth the true repentance of his children, as appeareth in the example of the Nineuits and of *Ahab*, 1.King.21.29. And therefore seeing the Lord keepeth no certaine course in these temporarie chastizements, but sometimes inflicteth them vpon the repentant whom hee dearely loueth, and sometime spareth the wicked when they but outwardly humble themselues before him; therfore the Prophets speak doubtfully and exhort to repentance, referring the euent to Gods wise and gracious prouidence. And thus doubtfully doth *Dauid* speake in this respect 2.Sam. 12.22. *Who can tell* (said he) *whether God will haue mercie on me that the child may liue?* and chap.16.12. *It may be the Lord will looke vpon mine affliction*; and yet though hee were doubtfull whether hee should be freed from these temporall crosses, hee was notwithstanding certainly perswaded of his election and saluation; as hee professeth Psal.16.11. So that these places speaking of temporarie chastizements, make nothing against the certaintie of our election.

§. *Sect*.9. And like vnto these, is that which they alledge to the same purpose, Act.8.22. where *Peter* exhorteth *Simon Magus to repent of his wickednesse, and to pray vnto God, that if peraduenture the wicked thought of his heart might be forgiuen him.* To which I answere, first, that the originall word α *δεα*, which is translated, *if peraduenture*, and in our Bibles, *if it be possible*, somtimes also signifieth, *that truly*, and in this sense it maketh nothing for doubting. Secondly, though wee vnderstand it as a speech of doubting, yet it maketh not for their purpose; for it is not to bee referred vnto God, as though it were doubtfull whether he would forgiue the sinnes of the Magician, if he did truly repent and call vpon him; for hee hath certainly assured vs by his gracious promise, that whosoeuer truly repenteth him of his wicked waies, he will receiue him to mercie, Ezech. 33.11. But it is to be referred to *Simon Magus*, of whose repentance and liuely faith *Peter* might well doubt, least either they would be none at all, or els fained and hypocriticall, seeing his heart was not right in the sight of God, but in the gall of bitternesse and bond of iniquitie. Lastly, though it should be a doubtfull speech and bee referred also to God, yet it maketh

Marginal notes:

1.King.21.29.

2.Sam. 12.22. and 16.12.

Psal.16.11.

§. *Sect*.9.
Act.8.22.

Ezech. 33.11.

keth

keth nothing against the certaintie of faith; for the Apostle
seeing him in the gall of bitternesse and bond of iniquitie,
thought it not fit to raise him vp suddenly, by applying vnto
him the sweete promises of the Gospell, nor to cast those pretious pearles before such a filthie swine, vnlesse first hee preserued them as it were in the casket of a doubtfull and perplexed
speech, from being trampled vnder his bemired feete, till hee
had washed them in the teares of vnfained repentance. Moreouer, he thus doubtfully speaketh to giue him a more cleere in-
sight of the hainousnesse of his sinne, as though it might bee
well doubted of, whether the Lord would forgiue it or no, that
so his minde hereby being least perplexed, might by the consideration of his horrible sinne bee beaten downe and truly
humbled; and because those things which are hardly obtained are more earnestly sought, therefore *Peter* intimateth vnto him by this doubtfull speech, that it was no easie matter to
obtaine forgiuenesse for such outragious wickednesse, that hee
might hereby work in the Magician more earnest & hearty repentance, & incite him to call vpon the Lord for mercie with
more vehemencie and feruencie of spirit. It is not therfore the
Apostles meaning to ouerthrow the certaintie of faith, or to
call into question Gods mercie, whether hee will extend it or
no to hainous offenders who truly repent of their sinnes and
beleeue, for this were contrary to the whole course of the Gospell; but he vseth this doubtfull speech to this desperate sinner, that he might not make the soueraigne salue of Gods gratious promises base and contemptible, by applying it to the
festred sores of a filthy dogge, which were neuer cleansed with
the sharpe corrasiues of the law; and also for the good of this
malitious sinner, for he doth not absolutely assure him of mercie and forgiuenes, that hee might be stirred vp with more earnestnesse and care to seeke it; for the easinesse of obtaining
maketh the suiter carelesse and negligent in seeking and suing;
neither doth hee absolutely exclude him frō all hope of grace,
least hee should neuer labour after it, but desperately run on in
his wickednes; for when hope is cut off, the desire also fainteth,
and therefore he vseth a perplexed and wise tempered speech,
which on the one side might preserue him frō secure presumption, and on the other side from falling into hellish desperatiō.

Lastly,

§. *Sect.*10.
Eccles.5.5.

Lastly, they object that saying Eccles.5.5. which they thus reade : *De propitiato peccato noli esse sine metu,neque adijcias peccatum super peccatum.* That is,be not without feare concerning sinnes forgiuen, neither adde sinne vnto sinne. To which,first I answer,that this book is not canonicall scripture, and therfore not to bee alledged for the determining of questions in controuersie,nor for the confirming of doctrines of faith. Secondly, I answere that they haue corruptly translated the originall text,for hee willeth vs not to feare concerning our sinnes forgiuen, but concerning the forgiuenesse of them before they are remitted,least wee should securely adde sinne vnto sinne, because forgiuenesse is promised whensoeuer wee repent,and so abuse the mercie and long suffring of God to our iust condemnation.So that he forbiddeth not to beleeue certainly,that our sinnes are remitted when God hath pardoned them, but he forbiddeth vs to runne on in sinne securely, presuming vpon forgiuenes, as plainly appeareth by the originall text and the whole drift and scope of the place. For in the verse going before he vseth this speech : *Say not I haue sinned,and what euill hath happened vnto me,for the Lord is long suffring,but yet he will not dismisse or acquit thee* ; and in this verse hee biddeth vs not to be without feare concerning the forgiuenesse of sinne, adding sinne vnto sinne,that is, we must not goe on in sinne presuming vpon forgiuenesse : and vers.6.*Doe not say that his mercie is great, he will forgiue my manifold sinnes* : 7. *For mercie and wrath are swift with him* ; *but vpon sinners his indignation shall rest.* 8.*Doe not deferre to turne vnto the Lord, neither put it off from day to day* ; *for suddenly the wrath of the Lord shall breake foorth, and in thy securitie thou shalt be destroyed, and thou shalt perish in the time of vengeance.* In all which words hee doth not take away the assurance of the forgiuenesse of our sinnes after we haue truly repented of them, but carnall securitie and vaine presumption , whereby men deferre their repentance vpon hope of mercie and forgiuenes whensoeuer they repent. Lastly,though this place were to be vnderstood concerning sinnes forgiuen, yet the scope thereof is not to hinder our assurance of forgiuenesse when we haue truly repented,but only that we doe not after wee haue obtained remission of our sinnes, take occasion thereby of falling into sinne againe,and so abuse the

mercie

mercie and goodnesse of God, vsing it as an argument to mooue vs to goe on in sinne, because the Lord vpon our repentance is alwaies readie to receiue vs to mercie.

CHAP. XII.
The reasons alledged against the assurance of our saluation, answered.

Nd so much concerning the testimonies of scripture, which are alledged against the certaintie of faith : now let vs consider their reasons. First, they obiect that it is proud arrogancie and hereticall presumption for a miserable sinner, without all doubting to assure himselfe that he is elected and shall be saued. To which I answere, that if with the pharisaicall papists and proud iusticiaries, we did build our assurance vpon our owne merits and worthinesse, it were indeede intollerable arragancie and proud presumption, not onely certainely to beleeue, but euen to doubt whether we are elected and shall be saued(for where as doubting is there is some hope also) whereas the scriptures peremptorily conclude, that they who *looke for righteousnesse and saluation by the law, are vnder the curse,* Gal.3.10 ; and that *by the workes of the law shall no flesh be iustified in Gods sight,* Rom.3.20 ; and that *we are iustified not by our deserts,* in whole or in part, *but freely by Gods grace through the redemption which is in Christ Iesus,* as it is, vers.24. But seeing we wholy disclaime our owne righteousnesse, and humbly acknowledging our owne miserie and wretchednesse, doe wholy rely our selues vpon the gracious promises of God, and the merits of Christ Iesus, seeing we become nothing in our selues in the worke of our saluation that God may be all in all, seeing we cast away all glorie from our selues, that we may wholy glorie in the Lord according to that Ierem.9.24. *Let him that glorieth, glorie in this that hee vnderstandeth and knoweth me :* This is not proud arrogancie nor hereticall presumption, but christian humilitie which giueth all glorie vnto God, leauing nothing to our selues but the comfort which is wrought in our hearts, by the assurance we haue of Gods promises. Nay the more vndoubtedly we trust in Gods promises,

§. *Sect*.I.
That it is not arrogancie or presumption to be assured of our saluation.

Galat.3.10.
Rom.3.20.

Ier.9.24.

the

the greater is our humilitie; for the more wretched we are in our owne eyes, the more we fee our imperfections, yea our nothing in Gods fight; and hereby we are moued to goe out of our felues, to feeke for faluation onely in Gods free grace and Chrifts merits, and to reft in them with full affurance, as being in themfelues all fufficient without our workes and worthineffe. On the otherfide the more we doubt of our faluation, in refpect of our vnworthineffe, the more is our pride and arrogancie; for we would not doubt in regarde of our vnworthineffe, vnleffe we looked for faluation by our worthineffe, and therefore we come fo farre fhort in faith and hope, as we finde our felues fhort in merits; and whence can this proceede but from arrogancie and pride, which maketh men to looke for faluation in themfelues, and to doubt of Gods mercie and Chrifts merits, vnleffe they finde that they haue deferued them by their owne workes and worthineffe? Let vs therefore abhorre this proud humilitie of the papifts which maketh them doubt of Gods mercifull promifes, and confequently of his truth; for as it is 1.Ioh.5.10. *He that beleeueth not God,hath made him a lyer;* and alfo of the fufficiencie and valew of that ineftimable price which Chrift Iefus hath giuen for our redemption, as though it were imperfect in it felfe, vnleffe it be eitched and patched vp with our owne merits and worthineffe: and though we are moft abiect, wretched, and in a defperate cafe in refpect of our felues, yet let vs haue affured truft and confident bouldneffe, yea a triumphant boafting and glorying in refpect of our Sauiour Chrift, as the Apoftle fpeaketh Ephef.3.12. Rom.5.2. Notable is the faying of *Auftine* to this purpofe, *Ideo præfume non de operatione tua fed de chrifti gratia,* prefume therefore (faith he) not of thine owne working but of Chrifts grace, for ye are faued by grace faith the Apoftle; therefore here is no arrogancie but faith, to fhew what thou haft receiued; it is not pride but deuotion. So in another place, *Hoc dixit deus, hoc promifit,fi parum eft hoc,iurauit.* The Lord hath faid this, he hath promifed it,and if this be not enough he hath fworne it. Becaufe therefore the promife is fure and confirmed, not according to our merits but according to his mercie,let no man profeffe that with feare,of which he cannot doubt.

1.Ioh.5.10.

Eph.3.12.
Rom.5.2.
Serm.28.deuerbis domini.
Omnia tibi peccata tua dimiffa funt.

In Pfal.88.

But

But they further vrge, that humble doubting is better than *Doubting pro-* presumptuous assurance; I answere, first that their doubting *ceedeth from* is full of pride, which maketh them looke for saluation in their *pride and arro-* owne worthinesse, rather than in Gods free mercie and Christs *gancie.* merits: secondly that our faith and certaine assurance is full of humilitie; for wee freely confesse our owne vnworthinesse, and dare not offer before the seate of Gods iustice any righteousnesse that is in vs, as desiring in whole or in part to be iustified thereby; nay rather we pray with the Prophet Psal. 143.2. *Enter not into iudgement with thy seruant, for in thy sight* Psal.143.2. *shall none that liueth be iustified*; and *though we know nothing by our selues* yet doe we plainely affirme with the Apostle, that *we are not hereby iustified.* 1.Cor.4. 4. But this humilitie doth 1.Cor.4.4 not abate our faith and certaine assurance, nay rather it doth confirme and increase it, for it maketh vs to goe out of our selues, as finding no hope of saluation whereupon we may rest, and moueth vs to seeke for saluation in Christ, who is such a sure ancorhold that whosoeuer pitch the ancor of their hope on him, shall finde it sure and steadfast, and whosoeuer build their faith on this foundation and corner stone, the power of hell shall neuer preuaile against them.

Secondly, they obiect that we are vnworthie of Gods loue, §. Sect.2. or to be elected, and therefore we cannot be assured thereof. *Our vnworthi-* I answere, this were true if Gods election depended vpon our *nesse no cause* worthinesse and deserts; but seeing the Lord respecteth not *why we should* any thing in vs, but elected vs freely of his vndeserued grace *doubt of our e-* and meere goodwill; our vnworthinesse in our selues may well *lection.* stand with the assurance of our election: for those who are most vnworthie neede not to doubt of Gods loue and their election and saluation, so that they wholy rely vpon Gods mercie and Christs merits by a true and liuely faith; forasmuch as they are not grounded vpon their worthinesse, and therefore cannot be ouerthrowne by their vnworthinesse. Notable is the saying of *Austine* to this purpose . *Tria (inquit) sunt quæ sic roborant & confirmant cor meum, vt nulla me penuria meritorum &c.* There are three things (saith he) which so strengthen and confirme my heart, that no want of merits, no consideration of mine owne vilenesse, no estimation of the heauenly blessednesse, can deiect me from the height of my hope: vpon them

my

my foule is furely fetled. Wilt thou know what they are?I confider three things vpon which my hope wholy relieth, to wit,
the loue of adoption, the truth of the promife, the abilitie of
performance. Let now my foolifh cogitation murmur as
much as it will, faying, but who art thou, or how great is that
glorie; or with what merits doeft thou hope to obtaine it?
And I will boldly anfwere, I know whom I haue beleeued,
and I am affured, becaufe God hath adopted me in great loue,
becaufe he is true in his promife, becaufe hee is powerfull in
performance,for he may doe what he will.

§.Sect.3.
*Weakenes of
faith and cer-
taintie may
well stand to-
gether.*

Thirdly,they obiect that our faith is weake and feeble, and
by reafon thereof the faithfull (as appeareth by continuall experience) are affaulted with doubting, and grieuoufly fhaken
with Sathans temptations,fo as there can be no fuch certaintie
of faith as we fpeake of. To which I anfwere, that weakeneffe
of faith is not oppofed as contrarie to certaintie,but to ftrong-
neffe and full perfwafion, and therefore weakeneffe and certaintie may well ftand together. Neither doe we imagine fuch
a certaintie of faith which is neuer fhaken with doubting, nor
affaulted with temptations; nay rather we teach that thofe
whom God indueth with moft faith, he moft exercifeth in the
conflict of temptations, like a wife captaine who fetteth that
fouldier which is beft armed and ftrongeft,to beare the brunt
in the forefront of the battaile: and the diuell is moft readie
to affault thofe who moft refift him, and moft violently to
ftrike where he feeth the fhield of faith held vp to defend; and
therefore our Sauiour hath taught all his faithfull children to
pray, leade vs not into temptation, but deliuer vs from euill.
But withall we affirme that though this weake faith be affaulted with Sathans temptations,yet is it neuer ouercome;though
it bee oppofed with doubting yet it neuer falleth from affurance and certaine perfwafion; though it bee fometimes fhadowed,and the fhining light thereof dimmed,yea though it be
for a time hid and couered, yet in it owne nature it remaineth
firme and ftedfaft;like the funne which alwaies fhineth,though
oftentimes by reafon of the interpofition of the cloudes or the
earth,we cannot difcerne the beames thereof; or like vnto the
fire which being hid vnder the afhes doth retaine his naturall
heate,although we feele it not ; So our faith retaineth in it felfe
his

his certaintie and assurance as it were his light and heate,when
as it is shadowed with the cloudes of doubting, and couered
vnder the ashes of Sathans temptations.

But it may be demaunded how a weake faith assaulted with *A weake faith*
Sathans temptations can cótinue certaine, seeing the strongest *doth as truely*
faith can doe no more but certainely persvade? I answere,that *assure vs of our*
our certaintie respecteth not our faith it selfe but the obiect *election as a*
thereof,namely Gods mercie and Chrifts merits:and therefore *stronger.*
seeing a weake faith doth as well apply vnto vs the mercies of
God & merits of Christ as a stronger,therefore also it certainely persvadeth vs as well & truely, though not so strongly and
fully of our election and saluation, as a stronger doth. So that
when we haue the least sparke of faith, it doth illuminate our
mindes, so as we can truely discerne the louing countenance
of the Lord shining vpon vs though some what dimly,and as it
were a farre of; euen as he that is pore-blind doth as certainely see the sunne, as he who is most sharpe sighted, though not
so cleerely; and as he who is in a darke dungeon doth discerne
the light as surely at a little hole, though he be compassed a-
bout with blacke darkenesse, as he who is in the open fieldes;
so when we are as it were pore-blind, and compassed about
with the darke miste of ignorance, yet by the dimme sight of
faith we certainely discerne Gods loue and fauour shining vpon vs, though the more we encrease in knowledge and faith,
the more cleerely we perceiue it,till at last hauing attained vnto fulnesse of faith,we see him neere at hand and as it were face
to face.

True it is that our faith which is in it selfe weake and feeble,
and compassed about with the darkenesse of ignorance,is mixt
and turmoyled with much feare and doubting, by reason of
our naturall inclination vnto diffidence and incredulitie, the
manifold temptations of Sathan,and the burthen of our sinnes
lying heauie vpon our consciences : which maketh Gods deere
children to grone and complaine, yea sometime to murmur
and repine against God himselfe, as though he were their enemie, because he suffereth them thus to be vexed ; but still it riseth after it hath receiued a foyle,and gathereth new strength
against all new assaults,vntill in the end it obtaineth full victorie, so as all the faithfull may say with the Apostle 2.Cor.4.8.

We

*We are afflicted on euery side, yet are we not in distresse ; in pouer-
tie but not ouercome of pouertie. 9. We are persecuted but not forsaken, cast downe but we perish not.* For though their faith be
weake, and their temptations vehement and violent, yet this
brused reede is not broken, this smoking flax is not quenched;
for as the reede in a boysterous tempest is blowne downe euen
to the ground, but when the tempest is past riseth vp againe
to his former estate ; so though the boysterous blasts of Sathans temptations beate vs downe euen to earth, yet by faith
we rise againe when the storme is ouerblowne.

§. *Sect.*4.   Secondly, it may bee demaunded how the faith of Gods
How our faith   children can be said to be certaine, seeing it is continually af-
though assalted saulted and often foyled with doubting, which is opposed to
with doubting   the certaintie of faith. To which we may easily answere, if we
may be cer-   know and remember that euery christian is divided into two
taine.   parts, the flesh and the spirit, which continually fight and striue
the one against the other ; and as they themselues are thus op-
posed, so are their qualities and fruites, for in the spirit is faith,
loue, hope, zeale, ioy in the holy Ghost, and such other sanctifying graces ; in the flesh is doubting, and infidelitie, hatred
of God, presumption and desperation, coldnesse, dulnesse, yea
deadnesse in religion, feare, horror, and such like corruptions,
so as we may say with the Apostle, *I know that in my flesh,* that is,
Rom.7.18.   in my vnregenerate part *dwelleth no good thing,* Rom.7.18. Now
as there is a continuall warre betweene the flesh and the spirit,
so also betweene their qualities and fruites ; for faith is continually assaulted with doubting and infidelitie, loue of God
with the hatred of God, hope with presumption and desperation, zeale with coldnesse and dulnes in religion, the ioy in the
holy Ghost with horror and feare of Gods anger, the curse of
the law and condemnation; and sometimes the one sometimes
the other hath the vpper hand, both in the meane time retaining their nature and properties, although (as we say) *remis-
sis gradibus,* not exercising them in that measure and degree,
as they doe when they haue victorie and giue the other the
foyle. For example, when in some grieuous affliction, the hatred
of God doth assault the loue of God in our hearts, and doth
so foyle and wound it, that wee can scarce discerne that it
breatheth or retaineth life, yet notwithstanding the loue of
                                                              God

God euen at that inftant is not turned into hatred, nor receiueth any properties thereof, but ftill retaineth his owne nature and properties, which againe cleerely appeare and fhew
themfelues when the conflict is ended. The like may be faid
of our hope, zeale, ioy in the holy Ghoft, and other graces,
when they are moft foyled by the corruption of the flefh
which fight againft them, fo as they cannot poffibly exercife
their owne actions and functions, yet doe they not receiue any
carnall properties, nor loofe any of their owne, but retaine
ftill their owne nature, which againe manifefteth it felfe when
the affault is ended. Euen as fire couered ouer with afhes retaineth ftill his owne nature of light and heate, though then
by reafon of the afhes the light be not feene, nor the heate felt;
but when the afhes are remooued and new matter added vnto
it, then it fhineth and burneth and heateth as much as it did
before: fo when the graces of Gods fpirit are couered (as it
were) vnder the afhes of our corruption, they are not difcerned
by their properties and effects ; but when the corruptions are
remooued by vertue of Gods fpirit, and the graces nourifhed
with hearing of the word, prayer, holy conferences, and fuch
like fpirituall exercifes , as it were with new matter added
vnto them, then doe they againe fhine in their brightneffe, and
exercife their wonted ftrength in all good duties to God and
our neighbour.

And as it is with all other graces, fo alfo with faith, which is §. *Sect.5.*
often affaulted with doubting and infidelitie, and fometimes *Faith affalted*
alfo fo foyled that we can hardly difcerne any breath or life in *with doubting,*
it; but yet euen then it retaineth it owne nature and proper- *retaineth his*
ties, and doth not receiue the nature and properties of doubt- *owne nature*
ing ; but as the tree which is fhaken with boyfterous blafts of *and properties.*
winde and is not ouerthrowne, doth in the middeft of the
tempeft liue and fucke nourifhment out of the earth, and ftill
retaines his owne nature and properties ; fo when our faith is
fhaken with the boyfterous blafts of Sathans temptations, and
with our owne naturall doubting and infidelitie, yet it ftill
liueth and fucketh nourifhment out of Gods gracious promifes, and ftill it retaineth his owne propertie of certaine perfwafion, though then it doe not exercife it in action, fo manifeftly as before and after the conflict of temptations, and as
the

the shaking of the tree is not of the nature thereof, for of it selfe it standeth firme and steadie, but by outward accident, namely the winde blowing vpon it: so is not vncertaine waue-ring and vnconstant doubting of the nature of faith, for of it selfe it is firme and certaine; but it commeth by outward acci-dent from the boysterous blasts of infidelitie, and the temp-tations of Sathan which (as it were) violently blow vpon it, which being past, it remaineth like the tree firme and constant. And as the graces of Gods spirit, and the flesh and the corrup-tions thereof doe still retaine in themselues their owne nature and properties, so also doe they most commonly shew them-selues in their diuers fruites and effects, and that oftentimes in the conflict and time of temptation, so that the regenerate man may at the same time feele in himselfe contrarie affections and actions ; for the spirit acknowledging Gods goodnes mercie and truth in his promises, is replenished with ioy, being in hope to inioy them, on the otherside the flesh feeling present miserie, and the sharpnes of afflictions, sorroweth and grieueth. The spirit apprehending and applying vnto it the sweete pro-mises of the Gospell, doth quietly rest vpon them; the flesh see-ing it owne corruption, and the huge waight of sinne that pres-seth it downe, feareth and doubteth: the spirit being assured of euerlasting happines, triumpheth with ioy, desiring nothing more than to be dissolued and to be with Christ ; the flesh fin-ding it selfe guiltie of sinne, and in this respect subiect to the anger of God and condemnation, feareth and trembleth to thinke vpon death : The spirit conceiueth of God as of a mer-cifull father in Christ, and in all necessities flyeth vnto him by heartie prayer; the flesh conceiueth of him as of an angrie and seuere iudge, and therefore flyeth from him, desiring rather to seeke for helpe any where else than of the Lord : so that the christian by reason hereof, at the same time findeth in himselfe opposition betweene action and action, affection and affection. For at the same instant, while the flesh, hauing in it the consci-ence of sinne and sense of guiltinesse, doth murmur repine and complaine vpon God, as an enemie which is readie to destroy vs; the spirit doth flie vnto God by a liuely faith, and commit-teth it selfe to his prouidence, will and protection, expecting saluation from him onely ; which it could neuer doe, if it were
not

not aſſured that we were in his loue and fauour. And in this the chriſtian may not vnfitly be compared to a childe, who hauing been ſharpely corrected by his father, doth auoyde his preſence as though hee were his enemie; but if at the ſame time ſome ſuddaine danger affright him, before al other he runneth to his father for ſafegard and protection: ſo when our heauenly father hath ſharpely corrected vs, either with ſome outward or inward afflictions, we flee from his preſence as though he were our enemy; but when an imminent danger ouertaketh vs, and we be in perill to be ſupplanted with ſathan and his aſſiſtants, who are our enemies in deed, then the ſonne-like affection which is wrought in our hearts by Gods ſpirit, doth moue vs to runne vnto him before all other, deſiring and crauing his ayde and aſſiſtance.

And thus it appeareth, that though the fleſh and the ſpirit be mixt together, yet they retaine their owne natures, properties and effects; and though faith which is a grace of the ſpirit, be mingled with doubting, yet this doubting is not of the nature of faith, which in it ſelfe is certaine and aſſured, nay, it is not an infirmity of faith, as lameneſſe is an infirmity of the ioynts, and dimneſſe of the ſight, for it is not any way incident to the nature thereof: and therefore much leſſe is it a commendable virtue of faith, as the Papiſts teach, but it is a fruite of vnbeleefe, which is in the part vnregenerate, and is oppoſed vnto faith, as appeareth Rom.4.20. and conſequently, though faith be aſ-ſaulted with doubting, yet in it owne nature it may and doth remaine certaine and aſſured. Rom.4.20.

Fourthly, they obiect that it is raſh preſumption, and proud boldneſſe for any man to ſearch into the myſtery of Gods ſecret counſailes, or to take vpon him peremptorily to determine that hee is one whom God hath elected. *For who hath knowne the minde of the Lord?* as it is 1.Cor.2.16. I anſwere that it is true indeede, whoſoeuer prieth into Gods hidden counſailes and ſecret decree of predeſtination, is proude and preſumptious, and ſhall in the end receiue the puniſhment of both, being giuen ouer of God to fall into many errors, and in the end vtter deſperation: and therefore it is very dangerous, yea, pernicious to our ſoules, if we labour after the aſſurance of our election by vſing theſe meanes, and iudge of Gods decree,

§. *Sect.6.*
That it is no preſumption to labour for the aſſurance of our election.
1.Cor.2.16.

decree,according to the conceite of our own reason & doubtfull speculations. But yet though the will of God be in it selfe
secret and not to be searched into;this must not hinder vs from
looking into his will reuealed , though we can gather no certainty of our election by searching into his secret decree, yet
this is no impediment why wee may not gather it out of his
word, where hee hath reuealed his decree and the execution
thereof: though we can haue no assurance by our owne speculations, yet we may attaine vnto it by the testimony of Gods

Rom.8.16.   spirit,*which witnesseth to our spirits that we are the sonnes of God,*
which also searcheth all things,euen the deepe things of God,and is
giuen vnto vs that we also might know the things which God hath
1.Cor.2.10.12 *giuen vs,* as the Apostle teacheth vs, 1.Cor.2.10.12. and therefore it is no pride or presumption to be certaine and assured of
that which the Lord hath reuealed in his word,to this end that
we might be certainely assured thereof. But it may be deman-
ded how this certainty can be gathered out of the Scriptures.
I answere,that if we would attaine vnto it,we must not seeke it
in the law, where the promises of life and saluation are made
vpon the condition of our own works and worthinesse, which
condition we can neuer performe, and therefore can neuer be
assured of the promise:But out of the Gospell,which doth not
only shew that some are predestinated to life, and some reiected,neither doth it only speake of our election,as it was ordained in Gods secret decree in it selfe, or reuealed in his word,
but also it setteth out vnto vs the execution of the decree,with
the causes,meanes,signes and effects of our election, and how
it is accomplished for the bringing vs to those ioyes to which
God hath chosen vs. First therefore it sheweth the decree of
God concerning our election. Secondly,Gods decree concerning our redemption by the death and obedience of Christ our
mediator. Thirdly ,the decree of God concerning the calling
of his Church by the ministery of the word, that they may be
ingrafted into the body of Christ,and so participate with him
in all his benefits to their saluation. Fourthly, the decree concerning the sending of his spirit into the hearts of his chosen,
by the inward operation whereof the word is made effectuall
for the begetting of faith and repentance. Fiftly and lastly,his
decree concerning the iustifying and sauing of those who re-
                                                        pent

pent truely of their fins, and apprehending and applying vnto themfelues by a liuely faith, Chrift and his merits & obedience, doe approach vnto the throne of grace to receiue mercy and forgiuenefle. And all thefe are fo linked together that they can neuer poffibly be feuered, fo that he who is affured of one, may be affured of all ; whofoeuer is certaine that he hath faith and repentance, may be certaine alfo of his election, though he neuer prefumptuoufly fearch into Gods fecret counfaile.

Fiftly, they obiect that there is no certainty of faith, which is not grounded vpon Gods word: but there is no place of Gods word which affureth vs of our particular election and faluation: and therefore we can haue no certainty of faith concerning our particular election & faluation. I anfwer; though the Lord giue vs no particular promife in his word, yet he giueth vs that which is equally effectuall, and of like force; namely his generall promife without any limitation, exception or condition, but the condition of faith and repentance, with a commaundement to applie the fame. And becaufe naturally we are vnable in our felues to performe this, therefore he hath ordained the miniftery of the word, and the vfe of the facraments, which he maketh effectuall by the inward operation of his fpirit, for the begetting and confirming of our faith, and ftirring vs vp to repentance; which being wrought in vs, we may as certainely be perfwaded that the generall promifes belong vnto vs, as if they were made vnto vs particularly and by name.

§. Sect. 7.
That the Lord particularly affureth vs of our election.

Sixtly, they obiect that we cannot be affured of the fufficiencie of our faith and repentance, and therefore we can haue no certaine affurance of our election and faluation. I anfwere; this reafon were good if our election and faluation depended vpon the worthines or meafure of our faith and repentance; but feeing that they depend not thereupon, but vpon Gods free mercy, and the worthinefle and fufficiency of Chrifts merits and obedience, therfore though our faith be neuer fo weake, and our repentance but in fmall meafure, yet fo they be true and vnfained, not diffembled and hypocritical, we may certainely be affured of our election and faluation, for a weake faith doth apply Chrift & all his benefits vnto vs as well as a ftrong, though not in fo ftrong and perfect a manner, as fhal appeare hereafter. But yet we muft not content our felues with a fmall and

§. Sect. 8.
That our affurance of election dependeth not vpon the fufficiency of our faith and repentance.

weake

weake meafure, but labour to growe vp from faith to faith, till
we become perfect men in Chrift.

§. Sect.9.
*The fight of our
imperfections
no caufe why
we fhould
doubt of our
election.*

Seuenthly, they obiect that though there were no caufe of
doubting, fo long as we looke vpon Gods mercy and truth in
his promifes, and Chrifts obedience and merits, yet at leaft
there is caufe of doubting when we looke vpon our felues, and
finde our great indifpofition to perfourme the condition of
faith and repentance, which God requireth of all who fhall be
partakers of his promifes, and our manifolde imperfections
and great vnworthines of the leaft of Gods mercies. And thus
thefe iugglers play faft and loofe, making their faith like vnto
the *ignis fatuus,* or going fire, which interchangeably fometimes fhineth cleerely, and fometimes vanifheth and leaueth
behind it nothing but blacke darkneffe. But let vs conftantly
oppofe our felues againft fuch inconftancie, and in no wife admit of fuch mutable variety in our faith, which maketh it more
changeable than the Moone, which one while fhineth with full
brightneffe, and in fmall diftance of time cannot be difcerned;
and to this end let vs know, firft, that though in our felues wee
be not worthy of the leaft of Gods mercies, yet our vnworthines maketh vs not vncapable of the greateft, for al Gods benefits are his free gifts, which he promifeth and beftoweth without any refpect of our worthines or deferts, of his meere grace
and vndeferued loue: and therfore as when we are moft worthy
in our own conceit, there is no reafon why we fhould prefume
the more; fo when wee finde our felues vnworthie, there is no
caufe why wee fhould hope the leffe, or be more weakly affured of Gods promifes; for as they are not made vpon the condition of our worthineffe, fo they are not difanulled and made
voide by our vnworthineffe, otherwife no man liuing could
haue affurance of them, feeing all men liuing are vnworthie of
them. But the Lord hath made al his promifes vnto vs in Chrift,
who was fent to bee our Mediatour, to the end that wee who
were altogether vnworthie in our felues, might be made worthie in him of all Gods mercies and benefits. And therefore
whofoeuer lay hold vpon Chrift, with a true though a weake
faith, and bring foorth the fruites thereof in repentance, they
may certainly bee affured of their election and faluation, notwithftanding their vnworthineffe. Secondly, wee are to know
that

that our faith doth not respect our selues in our selues, neither
are wee the obiect thereof, but Christ and his merits and obedience; whom our faith doth not behold standing aloofe of (as
the Papists dreame) but as hee is vnited vnto vs, and become
our head and we his members; so as now we cannot look vpon our selues but we must looke vpon Christ, because hee is in
vs and we in him. And therefore when wee consider the greatnesse of our sinnes we despaire not, because now we look vpon
them as they are translated from vs and laid vpon Christ, who
hath fully satisfied his fathers iustice by his alone and al-sufficient sacrifice vpon the crosse; when we consider our imperfections we doubt not of Gods promises, because they are couered with his perfect righteousnesse; when we consider our vnworthinesse wee are not discouraged, seeing by communicating of Christs worthinesse wee are made worthie; when wee
consider that in our selues wee are subiect to the curse of the
law, the anger of God and eternall condemnation, wee are neuerthelesse assured of euerlasting life and saluation, because we
are vnited to Christ our head, who hath taken away our curse
and nailed it to his crosse, borne his fathers displeasure to reconcile vs vnto him, and was condemned and suffred death to
free vs from death and condemnation, and to make vs heires
of life and saluation. So that now we behold the huge debt of
our sinnes, as it is discharged and cancelled with his merits
and full satisfaction; we behold our imperfections, but as perfected by his perfections; wee looke vpon our vnworthinesse,
but as it is ennobled with his worthinesse; when we set before
vs the curse of the law, the anger of God and sentence of condemnation, wee consider them as taken away and swallowed
vp of Christs death and full obedience; because now wee are
vnited vnto Christ, and hee is become ours that wee might become his; hee hath taken vpon him our sinnes and vnworthinesse, that hee might make vs partakers of his righteousnesse
and worthinesse. And therefore that which God hath wisely
ioyned together let not our faith fondly separate; for if it bee
vnlawfull in carnall mariages, then much more in the spirituall
mariage betweene Christ and his Church. But let vs looke vpon our selues, not in our selues, but as wee are vnited vnto
Christ, and then our selfe-worthinesse of hell and destruction

T

will

will not abate our assurance of life and saluation.

§. *Sect*.10.
Heretikes and worldlings boasting of faith, no cause why those should doubt who truly beleeue.

Eightly, they obiect that euery heretike, epicure and worldling, continuing in their sinnes and wickednesse, may faine vnto themselues such a perswasion of the certaintie of election: but this is nothing to the purpose; for the question is not of epicures and worldlings, who haue no faith or a dead faith, but of true beleeuers, who bring foorth the fruites of their faith, at least in an holie desire and endeuour of seruing the Lord in holinesse and righteousnesse. For they that cannot be assured that they haue faith, cannot haue any certaintie of their election; but none can haue any assurance of faith, vnlesse they bring foorth the fruites of their faith in dying to sinne and rising againe to newnesse of life, for faith purifieth the heart and worketh by loue: and therefore such as liue in their sinnes without repentance hauing no faith, can haue no certaintie of their election, though they may delude themselues with a fond perswasion which hath no other ground but carnall securitie and fond presumption: but hence it followeth not, that because a dead faith affoordeth no true certaintie, therefore a liuely faith doth it not; because a prophane epicure or carnal worldling, deceiueth himselfe with a vaine opinion, therefore those that are truly conuerted, mortified vnto sinne and raised vp to newnesse of life, can haue no certaintie of their election and saluation. For what similitude is there betweene light and darknes, righteousnesse and vnrighteousnesse, the children of God and the children of Belial, the repentant and vnrepentant, faith and no faith?

§. *Sect*.11.
That this doctrine openeth no way to securitie and presumption.

Lastly, they obiect that if we teach this doctrine of the certaintie of election, men will abuse it to nourish in them carnall securitie and presumption. To which I answere, that wicked men abuse the whole doctrine of the Gospell to their destruction; for when they are taught that God is most gratious and mercifull, that Christ hath died for vs, and giuen himselfe as a sufficient price to redeeme vs out of the power of sinne, Sathan, death and damnation, and maketh intercession for vs to God his father; that the Lord is slow to wrath and ready to forgiue, they take occasion hereby of continuing in their sins, and deferring their repentance, till God take them away and consume them in his heauie displeasure: but hence it followeth

eth not that the Gospell must not bee taught, becaufe carnall
men abuse it to their iust condemnation ; for though to thefe
it be the fauour of death vnto death , yet to those who are faued it is the fauour of life vnto life,as it is 2.Cor.2.16. Though
it be foolifhnes to those that perifh,yet it is the power of God
to those whom God hath ordained to faluation, and God is
no leffe glorified in the one by fhewing his mercie, than in the
other by fhewing his iuftice. Though worldly men abufe it to
carnall fecuritie,yet the godly are the more incited thereby to
ferue the Lord in holineffe and newneffe of life:for like louing
children,the more they are affured of the loue of their heauenly father,and fecured of his mercie and bountifull benefits, the
more they loue him againe, the more they loue him the more
zealous they are of his glorie,and the greater their zeale is, the
greater is their care in making the light of their godly and
Chriftian liues to fhine before men, that their heauenly father
may bee glorified. So that it is not the fault of this precious
feede,but the barrenneffe of the ground which maketh it fruit-
leffe, or els for good wheate fendeth tares cockle and darnell;
it is not any defect or ill difpofition in this fweet fmelling flower,but the venemous nature of thefe fpiders which turne honey into poyfon : and therefore the feed muft be caft vpon the
earth, though there bee ftones with the good ground which
will neuer bring foorth fruite; the flowers of fweete confolation muft not be pulled vp by the rootes and caft away. For
though the fpider gathereth poyfon,yet the profitable Bee wil
gather honey out of them. Secondly,when wee teach the certaintie of election, wee doe not teach that men muft gather it
out of Gods fecret counfaile, but from their owne fanctification, by which they may be affured that they are iuftified, called and elected : and therefore whofoeuer are not fanctified
but continue in their finnes without repentance, can haue no
affurance by our doctrine that they are elected or fhall be faued; nay contrariwife,we teach out of Gods word,that *whofoeuer liue in the flefh fhal die*,Rom.8.13.that they which performe
the lufts thereof fhall neuer inherit the kingdome of God,Gal.5.19.
20,21. that none who continue in their vnrighteoufneffe and
vncleanneffe fnall enter into the heauenly Ierufalem, 1.Cor.6.
9.10.Reu.21.27;but fhall haue their portion in the lake which

2.Cor.2.16.
1.Cor.1.18.

burneth with fire and brimſtone; as it is verſ.8. Now what ſtronger bridle to curbe in our vnruly fleſh when it is ready to runne into ſinne,than to be aſſured that if wee liue in ſinne and fulfill our carnall luſts, wee are in the ſtate of condemnation? what ſharper ſpurre to pricke vs forward when wee are readie to faint, or ſlacke our pace in the Chriſtian race of holineſſe and righteouſneſſe,than to conſider that our ſanctification and newneſſe of life,is the onely meanes whereby wee may come to the aſſurance of our election and ſaluation?

CHAP. XIII.
Of our Redemption.

§. Sect. 1.

Nd thus much concerning our election and the certaintie thereof. The next cauſe of our ſalua-tion is our redemption by Ieſus Chriſt:for as the Lord hath from all eternitie elected vs to ſalua-tion, of his meere mercie without any reſpect of our works or worthines; ſo he hath ordained in this his eternal decree, our Sauiour Chriſt to bee the Mediatour who ſhould worke the worke of our ſaluation, and as it were the conduit whereby hee would conuey his grace, mercie and euerlaſting ſaluation vnto vs; and hath ſet him apart to be our Sauiour and Redeemer, who ſhould ſaue and deliuer vs out of the captiui-tie and bondage of our ſpirituall enemies, and reſtore vs to the glorious libertie of the ſonnes of God.

*Redemption
what it is.*

    This our redemption is an effect of Gods election,whereby our Sauiour Chriſt (being ſet apart of his father for this pur-poſe)hath freed and deliuered all Gods elect out of the capti-uitie of their ſpirituall enemies, ſinne death and the diuell; by offring himſelfe for the price of their redemption,and a ſuffi-cient ſacrifice for ſinne,for the appeaſing of his fathers diſplea-ſure and ſatisfying of his iuſtice; to the end that being deliue-red, they may ſerue him in holineſſe and righteouſneſſe all the daies of this life, and afterwards may inherit the kingdome of glorie, and the crowne of eternall happineſſe which is purcha-ſed for them.

*The definition
explained.*

    Firſt I ſay,that it is an effect of Gods election; for whom he had choſen to euerlaſting life in Chriſt, thoſe by Chriſt he hath
ſaued

faued and redeemed,and thofe only as we fhall fee afterwards.

Secondly,I fhew who is our Sauiour and Redeemer,namely Chrift Iefus,who only faueth vs from our finnes,as it is Matth. 1.21;*Neither is there faluation in any other*, as it is Act.4.12.For *as there is but one God,fo there is but one Mediatour between God and man,which is the man Iefus Chrift*,as it is 1.Tim.2.5. *And by him alone we haue redemption through his bloud,euen the forgiue-neffe of finnes*,and that without any refpect of our worthineffe, but *according to his rich grace*,Eph.1.7. And though we do not exclude God the Father,from the worke of our redemption,for he is the author and firft caufe, who hath fo loued vs that hee fent his fonne to faue and redeeme vs;nor the holy Ghoft who applieth vnto vs the merits and efficacie of Chrifts death, ma-king them effectuall for our faluation;yet if we fpeake proper-ly, our Sauiour Chrift onely can be called our Redeemer,and that in thefe refpects; firft, becaufe he alone was ordained and deputed to perfect the worke of our redemption ; fecondly, becaufe he onely was God and man,both which were necefla-rily required in our Mediatour and Redeemer, that hee might haue full right and abilitie to redeeme vs ; thirdly, becaufe hee alone gaue himfelfe to bee the price of our redemption ; and laftly, becaufe in him onely there is perfect redemption as be-ing our head,who not only hath faluation in himfelfe,but alfo deriueth it to all the members of his bodie.

Thirdly, I fet downe the captiuitie it felfe out of which wee were redeemed; namely, not the captiuitie of Egypt or Baby-lon,nor out of the flauerie of the Turke, Spaniard,or any other earthly Tyrant,whofe thraldome might well be bitter but not long, becaufe our liues are fhort ; and grieuous to the bodie, but extendeth not to the foule : but Chrift hath deliuered vs out of the bondage of finne, Sathan, hell and death, in which we fhould haue been enthralled and fearefully tormented for euer and euer,not in bodie alone but in foule alfo.

Fourthly, I fhew the price which hee hath giuen for our re-demption, namely, not filuer and gold , or any corruptible thing,but himfelf;euen his bodie to be crucified and his bloud to bee fhed,that fo his fathers iuftice being fatisfied and his wrath appeafed, wee might be fet free out of the thraldome of our fpirituall enemies. But it may be demaunded,how it can

Matth.1.21.
Act.4.12.

1.Tim.2.5.

Eph.1.7.
Luk.1.68.

§. *Sect*.2.
1.Pet.1.18.
How Chrift is faid to haue bought vs with a price.

T 3 truly

truly be said that Chrift hath redeemed vs by paying the price of our redemption, feeing the fcriptures teftifie that by his power hee hath forcibly deliuered vs out of the hands of our fpirituall enemies. So Heb.2.14. it is faid, *that Chrift destroyed him who had the power of death, that is the diuell.* And Col.2.15. the Apoftle fheweth, that hee *hath fpoyled principalities and powers, and hath led them openly and triumphed ouer them.* And Luk.11.22. hee is compared to a valiant champion who hath thruft the ftrong man Sathan out of his poffeffion : by which it may appeare, that our Sauiour hath not redeemed vs by giuing a price after a legall manner, but by force, and as it were by conqueft. I anfwere, that Chrift hath both paid the price of our redemption, and alfo hath deliuered vs forcibly by his power; for hee paid the price vnto God to whom hee offered the facrifice of himfelfe, that it might be a full fatisfaction for finne, and a fufficient price to redeeme vs out of the captiuitie of our fpirituall enemies, and to purchafe the fauour of God, and our heauenlie inheritance in his kingdome : and therefore in refpect of God the Father, to whom our Sauiour offred himfelfe, hee is faid to haue redeemed vs by giuing a ranfome for vs. But when Gods iuftice was fully fatisfied, Chrift dealt not with our fpirituall enemies by intreatie (much leffe offred hee this price of our redemption to Sathan ; for if no facrifice might lawfully bee offered vnto any faue God alone, much more vnlawfull was it that this facrifice of Chrifts bodie, fhould be offred vnto the diuell) but by his almightie power hee ouercame the power of darkneffe, vanquifhed Sathan, fubdued death, and broke open the prifon of the graue, and fo by ftrong hand fet all Gods elect at libertie. For after that the debt of our finnes was difcharged, our ranfome paid, and the handwriting of ordinances cancelled and nailed vnto the croffe, thefe our fpirituall enemies had no iuft intereft vnto vs, nor any thing to alledge why they fhould longer hold vs in their captiuitie ; but yet the ftrong man who had taken poffeffion would not willingly lofe it, vnleffe hee were ouercome with a greater ftrength : and therefore our Sauiour Chrift hauing bought vs of his father, and fo become our true owner, buckled with our fpirituall enemies, ouercame thefe principalities and powers, triumphed glorioufly ouer them, and freed

vs

vs out of their tyrannicall iurifdiction.

But it may bee obiected that wee were captiues vnto Sathan, and therefore the price of redemption was to be paied vnto him, and not vnto God the father who held vs not in his captiuitie. I anfwere that though Sathan held vs in his captiuitie, yet not in his owne right, for wee had not finned againft him to whom we were not bound to performe obedience, nor were indebted vnto him; but wee had finned against God, whofe feruants wee were by right of creation, and had infinitly runne into his debt, which we were altogether vnable to pay; and therefore like a iuft iudge he condemned vs to the perpetuall prifon of death, and committed vs to the cuftodie of Sathan, as vnto a iaylor, to be kept in his bondage, till we had fatiffied for our finnes and difcharged our debt: which being impoffible to vs, our Sauiour Chrift hauing affumed our nature and become our furetie and mediator, payed that we owed, and fuffered that which we had deferued, and fo fully fatiffying his fathers iuftice, hath purchafed our redemption; fo as now Sathan had no more anthoritie to retaine vs in his captiuitie, then the iaylor hath of holding him in prifon who by the iudge is releafed, or the executioner of hanging him whom the iudge hath acquitted or pardoned. And therefore tyrannically exercifing ftill his iurifdiction, our Sauiour by ftrong hand ouercame him and all the power of hell, that fo he might fet vs at libertie whom his fathers iuft fentence had acquitted and his mercie pardoned.

The laft thing to be confidered is the end of our redemption, namely that we fhould no longer ferue finne and Sathan, out of whofe bondage wee are releafed; but become the feruants of Chrift, who hath redeemed vs, feruing him in holines and righteoufnes all the daies of our liues; that fo glorifying him here on earth, he may glorifie vs in heauen, and make vs partakers of thofe euerlafting ioyes, which by his death and bloodfhed he hath purchafed for vs.

Chap. XIIII.

Sathans temptations concerning our redemption, wherewith he moueth the worldling to presumption, answered.

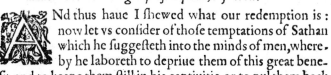 Nd thus haue I shewed what our redemption is : now let vs consider of those temptations of Sathan which he suggesteth into the minds of men,where by he laboreth to depriue them of this great benefit,and to keepe them still in his captiuitie,or to pul them back againe when they are escaped. And these are of two sortes,the first leading to securitie and presumption, the other to doubting and desperation.For if he haue to deale with worldlie men; who were neuer truely conuerted vnto God, hee laboreth to perswade them that they are redeemed by Christ, and therfore though they liue in their sinnes, yet they shall bee saued, for Christ came into the world to saue sinners:but when he assaulteth the true christian, who is indeede the redeemed of the Lord; then he moueth him to doubt and despaire,either of the sufficiencie or of the efficacie, of the worke of our redemption wrought by Iesus Christ.

That he may continue the worldly man in his carnall securitie, and fond presumption, he vseth two principall reasons; the first,that the redemption wrought by Christ is vniuersall, and effectuall for the saluation of al the world,out of which he frameth this temptation. Christ hath shed his precious blood, and suffered death for all the world ; and hath redeemed all mankinde which were lost in *Adam*,out of the bondage of Sathan death and hell ; why therefore shouldest thou be so strict in flying sinne, with which thou art so much delighted ? why dost thou striue against the streame of thy corruptions ? and wherefore shouldest thou take any great paines in the workes of holines and righteousnes,which are so bitter and vnpleasant to thy taste and appetite?for Christ came into the world to saue all men,and not those onely who are so strict in their waies; he came to redeeme the whole world, & gaue himselfe as a sufficient ransome for all men:and therefore doubtlesse he will not lose his labour,nor spill his blood in vaine;he wil not willingly let any perish, whom he hath purchased at so high a rate, and
redeemed

redeemed with fo deare a price:he is alfo fo powrefull that nothing fhall be able to pull them out of his hand, as himfelfe af- Ioh.10.28.
firmeth, Ioh.10.28; and fo wife that hee would not fhed his
blood,for thofe whom he would not faue. And who can imagine that God who is moft iuft,will impute thofe finnes vnto
thee for which Chrift hath fuffered, inflict death on thee for
whom Chrift died,and require that debt againe which is alreadie difcharged?Or who can imagine that God,who is immutable,fhould fhew fuch inconftancie as to fend his fonne into the
world,to fuffer death for the redemption of thofe whom hee
now will not faue; for if he would who could refift his will or
withftand his power? And therefore if he hath redeemed all,
furely he will faue all,and confequently thee amongft the reft,
though thou liue as thou lift and follow the lufts of thine owne
heart: for thy finnes and vnbeliefe cannot make his purpofe
voyde, nor annihilate the worke of thy redemption; nay the
more thy finnes abound, the more his grace will abound alfo.

For the anfwering of which temptation,we are to know,that §.*Sect.*2.
vniuerfall redemption which is the ground and foundation *The anfwere to*
thereof, is an idle dreame of mans braine,which cannot be iu- *the former*
ftified by the word of God which is the touchftone of al truth; *temptation.*
neither hath our Sauiour Chrift redeemed any other,than thofe
whom hee effectually calleth vnto the fauing knowledge of
their redemption, indueth with true faith and vnfained repentance, iuftifieth, fanctifieth, and laftly faueth,if we refpect the
purpofe of God,and the will of our bleffed Sauiour; although
indeede the price he gaue for our redemption,was of fufficient
value for the finnes of all the world,if it were applied by a liuely faith.

But becaufe this doctrine hath many enemies, it is not fuf- *Teftimonies of*
ficient to propound it vnlefle I proue it: and therefore I will *Scripture al-*
fhew firft by teftimonies of fcriptures, and after by ftrong rea- *ledged againft*
fons,that our Sauiour Chrift hath died for,and by his death re- *vniuerfall re-*
deemed, thofe onely whom hee indueth with true faith and *demption.*
vnfained repentance,and not for al the world as they imagine.
Matth.20.28. it is faid,that *he came into the world to giue his life* Matth.20.2
a ranfome for many. and 26.28. that his blood *was fhed for many* and 26.28.
for the remiffion of finnes. And Efa.53.11. that Chrift *fhould iu-*
ftifie many by bearing their iniquities. So that he hath not giuen

uen his life a ranfome and fhed his blood, and by bearing their iniquities iuftified all, but many, that is, part of all. Luk.2.34. *Simeon* faith, that Chrift *was appointed by Gods decree, for the fall and rifing againe of many,* that is for the fall of many reprobates, and the rifing againe of many who are elected, and therefore not for the redemptió of all. So Chrift faith that *he layeth downe his life for his fheepe,* Ioh.10.15.and therefore not for wolues and goates, *for his friends,* Ioh.15.14. & therfore not for his wicked enemies ; *for vs,* that is, for the companie of the faithfull beleeuers, Rom.8.32.33. and therefore not for the finagogue of Sathan and wicked vnbeleeuers.So Matth.1.21.he is faid to be the Sauiour of *his people,* and not of aliants and ftrangers;and to haue giuen himfelfe for *his Church,* Eph.5.25,and not for thofe who haue no fellowfhip in the communion of faints ; that he *fhould die for the nation,* that is as *Iohn* faith for al Gods childrē Iewes and Gentils,Ioh.11.52.and therfore not for the wicked, and the children of Sathan. So the Apoftle Rom.3.22.faith that *the righteoufnes of God* (that is, the righteoufnes of Iefus Chrift imputed vnto vs by God, or the righteoufnes of Chrift God and man) *is manifefted vpon all and vnto all that beleeue* ; and verf.23. that God hath fet *forth Chrift to be a reconciliation through faith in his blood,* and verfe 26. *That he is the iuftifier of him, which is of the faith of Iefus.* Where the imputation of Chrifts righteoufneffe, reconciliation with God,and iuftification,is reftrained to the beleeuers onely. And to the fame purpofe is that of the Apoftle,Heb.5.9. where Chrift is faid *to be the author of eternall faluation vnto all that obey him,* and therefore not vnto them who continue in their rebellion not obferuing his will, nor fubmitting themfelues to bee ruled by the fcepter of his word.

And as by thefe places it is apparant,that Chrift and his benefits are reftrained to the faithfull, fo alfo in other places the vnbeleeuers and fuch as continue in their wickednes,are flatly excluded from the participation of them. Ioh.3.18. *He that beleeueth in him fhall not be condemned, but he that beleeueth not is condemned alreadie.* And verf.36. *He that beleeueth in the fonne hath euerlafting life, and he that obeyeth not the fonne fhall not fee life,but the wrath of God abideth on him.* So Rom.8.9. *If any man haue not the fpirit of Chrift, the fame is not his* ; and confequent-

ly

Luk.2.34.

Ioh.10.15.
and 15.14.

Rom.8.32.33.
Matth.1.21.

Eph.5.25.

Ioh.11.52.
Rom.3.22.
25.26.

Heb.5.9.

Ioh.3.18

verf.36.

Rom.2.9.

ly it folioweth that if he be not Chrifts, then Chrift and his benefits belong not vnto him. And the Apoftle 1.Ioh.3.8. plaine- 1.Ioh.3.8.
ly affirmeth *that he who committeth finne* (that is, he who liueth
in finne without repentance) *is of the diuell, and that he who is
borne of God* (that is, regenerate by his fpirit) *finneth not,* that is,
liueth not in his fins, neither committeth them with full confent of will. And *Paul* willeth *Timothie* to inftruct his hearers, 2.Tim.2.26.
that they *might come to amendment out of the fnare of the diuell*;
whereby it is manifeft that thofe in whom finne raineth, are not
of Chrift but of Sathan, and that notwithftanding Chrifts
death they are ftill in the fnare of the diuell til they come to a-
mendment of life; becaufe the blood of Chrift is not effectuall
to free any out of their fpirituall bondage, till it be applied vnto them by a liuely faith.

And thus it appeareth by plaine teftimonies, that the re- §. Sect.3.
demption wrought by Chrift belongeth onely to the faithfull; *Reafons to*
which alfo by vertue of Chrifts death & bloodfhed, haue their *proue that re-*
finnes and corruptions in fome meafure mortified; and not vn- *demption is*
to the wicked, who liue and die in their finnes without repen- *not vniuerfall.*
tance. Now I will alfo confirme this truth by ftrong reafons.
Firft, thofe who were neuer knowne of Chrift (that, is acknowledged for his) were neuer redeemed by his precious bloodfhed; neither is it probable that the father would giue his welbeloued fonne, and that the fonne would giue himfelfe for the
redemption of thofe, whom in his eternall councell he had decreed to reiect, or (as all confeffe) whom he forefaw fhould perifh: but our Sauiour will *profeffe to the workers of iniquitie that* Matth.7.23.
he neuer knew them, Matth.7.23: and therefore he neuer gaue
himfelfe for their redemption.

Secondly, for whomfoeuer Chrift hath offered a facrifice vnto
his father, for them alfo he maketh interceffion and is become
their aduocate; neither is it probable that Chrift would die for
thofe for whome he will not intreate, and that he would offer
the facrifice of his body for thofe for whom he would not offer
the facrifice of his lips. Befides it was the office of the fame
high prieft to offer facrifice and to pray for the people, and
confequently of our Sauiour Chrift, as appeareth 1.Ioh.2.1.2. 1.Ioh.2.1.2.
where he is faid as well to be our aduocate, as the propiciatory
facrifice for our finnes; and the Apoftle *Paul* Rom.8.35. faith, Rom.8.35.
that

that as Chrift died for vs,fo he maketh interceffion for vs; but our Sauiour Chrift flatly excludeth, from all participation of the fruite of his interceffion,all thofe who are of the world,that is,all meere worldlings. Ioh.17.9. *I pray not for the world but for them which thou haft giuen me*; and the Apoftle faith, that as he perfectly faueth, fo alfo he maketh interceffion for thofe who come vnto God by him, that is, true beleeuers onely: and therefore for them alone he hath offered himfelfe, a facrifice vnto his father.

Ioh.17.9.

Heb.7.25.

Thirdly, Chrift hath died for thofe alone in whom he hath attained vnto the end of his death; for whatfoeuer attaineth not his end is done in vaine,which argueth want of wifedome, or power,in the agent and efficient, neither of which without blafphemie can be afcribed vnto Chrift, who is in both infinit: but the end of Chrifts death (that is, the eternall faluation of thofe for whom he died)is attained vnto onely in the elect and faithfull;for as it is Mark.16.16. *He that fhall beleeue, fhall be fa-ued; but he that will not beleeue, fhall be damned.* And Ioh.3.36. *He that beleeueth in the fonne hath euerlafting life, and he that obeyeth not the fonne fhall not fee life,but the wrath of God abideth on him*: And therefore,Chrift hath died for thofe alone, who beleeue and bring forth the fruites of their faith in obedience, and not for the vnbeleeuers and difobedient.

Mark.16.16.
Ioh.3.36.

Forthly, if all were redeemed by the death of Chrift, then fhould they alfo be faued: for what fhould hinder them from faluation, who are redeemed, feeing they haue receiued the pardon and remiffion of their finnes, as appeareth Ephef.1.7. *In whom we haue redemption through his blood,euen the remiffion of our finnes.* Col.1.14. And confequently whofoeuer are re-deemed are iuftified, and alfo heires of eternall bleffednes; for *bleffed are thofe whofe iniquitie is forgiuen, and whofe finne is couered*,as it is Pfal.32.1.Seeing alfo Chrift who hath redeemed vs,is ftronger than Sathan and all the power of hell,and there-fore al their fpiritual enemies conioyned together,cānot pluck thofe whom he hath redeemed out of his hand violently and againft his will, neither can we with any probable fhew of reafon imagine that he would willingly lofe thofe whom he hath redeemed with the ineftimable price of himfelfe, neither will it ftand with the iuftice of God to impute the finnes of

Eph.1.7.
Col.1.14.

Pfal.32.1.

any

any to their condemnation, for which Christ hath fully satisfied, nor to exact that debt againe which hee hath paid : and therefore if Christ had died for all, God in his iustice could not chuse but saue all : and Christ might well say to his father, to what purpose haue I died if thou destroyest those whom I haue saued? what profit is in my bloud, if thou condemnest those whom I haue redeemed?

Lastly, if hee died and by his death redeemed all; then also he died for and redeemed the Pagans, Turkes, Atheists and Epicures, who were out of the Church and couenant of grace; and so iustification, redemption and saluation should be out of the Church, and be extended to those whom God neuer receiued into his couenant; which is quite contrarie to the whole course of the scriptures, where it is said, that all who are saued are also added vnto the Church, Act.2.47. and that Christ *hath* Act.2.47. *giuen himselfe onely for his Church,* Eph.5.25. Yea if Christ died Eph.5.25. for all, and by his death redeemed them, then it must necessarily follow that hee had redeemed euen those damned soules who were in hell before his comming, which is most absurd to be imagined ; for if they were redeemed, how did they againe fall into condemnation , seeing they being once become Christs can neuer perish, neither is any able to pull them out of his hands, as it is Ioh.10.28.

But against this it is obiected, that in the scriptures Christ §. *Sect.4.* is said to haue died and to haue giuen himselfe a ransome for *In what sense* all men. 1.Tim.2.6. *Who gaue himselfe a ransome for all men.* And *Christ is said to* Heb.2.9. he is said to haue *tasted death for all men* ; and 1.Ioh. *haue died for* 2.2. he is said to be *a reconciliation for the sinnes of the whole* *all men.* *world.* To which I answere; first, that these speeches are not to 1.Tim.2.6. be vnderstood of all and singular men, but of all the faithfull Heb.2.9. which are gathered out of the whole world; for the drift of 1.Ioh.2.2. the Apostles is to shew that our Sauiour Christ died not onely for the beleeuing Iewes, but for the Gentils also, of what countrie, nation or condition soeuer they were. And so these generall speeches are expounded Ioh.11.52. where our Sauiour Ioh.11.52. Christ is said to haue died, not onely for the Iewish nation, but that also he might gather together in one, the children of God which were scattered. So also hee is said Reu.5.9, to *haue redee-* Reuel.5.9. *med vs* (that is all the faithfull) *vnto God by his bloud, out of euery*
kinred,

kinred, tongue, people and nation : and Galat.3.26.that *all are the*
Gal.3.26.28. *sonnes of God by faith in Christ Iesus*; and verf.28. *That there
is neither Iew nor Grecian,bond,nor free, male nor female, but all
are one in Chrift Iesus.* So that these places are not to be vnderstood of all and singular men, but of al beleeuers, of what nation or condition soeuer they be. For all the promises and benefits promised in the Gospel, which is the couenant of grace,
are to be restrained to the condition of the couenant, be they
neuer so generall and vniuersall; and this condition is sometimes expressed and sometimes vnderstood, but neuer exclu-
Ioh.3.16. ded. So Ioh.3.16. *So God loued the world, that he hath giuen his
onely begotten sonne,that whosoeuer beleeueth in him should not pe-
Rom.3.22. rish,but haue life euerlafting.*Rom.3.22.it is said, that *the righteousnesse of God by faith in Iesus Chrift,is giuen to all that beleeue.*
Gal.3.22. So Gal.3.22. *The scripture hath concluded all vnder fin, that the
promise by the faith of Iesu: Chrift should, be giuen to them that
Act.10.43. beleeue.*As also Act.10.43.

Secondly I answere, that Chrift in some sense may be truly
said to haue died for all the world, namely in respect of the
sufficiencie of his death,though not in respect of the efficacie ;
for by his death hee paid a sufficient price for the finnes of all
the world,and a full ransome for all mankinde, if all would or
could applie his merits and obedience vnto themselues by a
liuely faith ; but in respect of Gods counsaile, Chrifts wil, and
the euent, his death was not effectuall for the redemption of
all,but the faithful only. Euen as a soueraigne salue, may haue
sufficient vertue in it selfe to cure innumerable wounds and
sores, but yet it is effectuall for the healing of those onely to
which it is applied; so the precious baulme of Chrifts bloud,is
of sufficient vertue to heale the wounds of all finners whatsoeuer,but notwithstanding it is effectuall to those only,to whom
it is applied by a true and liuely faith.

§. Sect.5.
The former ob-
iection vrged
and answered.
Mar.1.5. But it is further vrged that it is plainly said in the scriptures,
that hee died for all without exception. I answere,that it is an
vsuall thing in Gods word,to put this word (all) for many,or
for all those which are of one kinde. So it is said Mar.1.5.that
*all the countrey of Iudea and they of Ierusalem,went out vnto Iohn
the Baptift and were baptized of him* ; that is, not euery man
without exception,but great multitudes.So it is said Mat.4.23.
that

that our Sauiour *Christ healed euery disease and sicknesse amongst* Matth.4.23. *the people,* that is, many that were diseased, or diseases of all kindes. And Act.10.38.it is said,that *Christ healed all that Were* Act.10.38. *oppressed by the diuell,* that is, very many, for otherwise great numbers oppressed of the diuell neuer came into our Sauiours presence. Thus also it is said ver.12.that there was in the sheete which *Peter* saw in his vision (πάντα τὰ τετράποδα) *all fourefooted beasts,*that is,beasts of all kinds. And thus somtimes, by all, we are to vnderstand all the elect and them onely, and sometimes all the reprobate and them alone. In the first sense are these places to bee vnderstood. Ioh.12.32.our Sauiour saith,that af- Ioh.12.32. ter he *is crucified he will draw all men vnto him,* that is, all the faithfull and elect, for they only are conuerted vnto God and drawne vnto Christ. So it is said Esa.54.13.*that al shall be taught* Esa.54.13. *of God.*And Iere.31.34.that *all shall know him from the least to the* Iere.31.34. *greatest.*And Ioel 2.28.the Lord saith,that in *the latter times he* Ioel.2.28. *will powre out his spirit vpon all flesh* ; which places cannot be vn- derstood of the reprobates and wicked, but of all Gods elect and faithfull. Sometimes also we are hereby to vnderstand all the reprobate and wicked. So Phil.2.21.the Apostle saith,*that all seeke their owne, and not that which is Iesus Christs,* that is, all Phil.2.21. worldlings and wicked men. And Ioh.3.32. the Baptist saith, *that no man hath receiued Christs testimonie,*that is,none of the Ioh.3.32. wicked and reprobate,for all the faithfull and elect receiue it and beleeue. By all which places it is euident that this word (all)sometime signifieth many, and sometime all of one kind; and therefore in those places where it is said that Christ hath died for al men,we may vnderstand it of many,as it is expoun- ded Matth.26.28. or of all the faithfull, as in many places it is Matth.26.28. restrained.

Secondly,it is obiected that Christ died euen for the wicked and damned ; for it is said that some shall denie the Lord who hath bought them,2.Pet.2.1. that some who are purged after- 2.Pet.2.1. wards become blind and forgetfull,2.Pet.1.9.that he may be chap.1.2.9. destroyed for whom Christ died,Rom.14.15.that they who are Rom.14.15. sanctified may count the bloud of the Testament an vnholie Heb.10.29. thing and tread it vnder their feete,Heb.10.29. To which I an- swere, that these and such like places are to be vnderstood of men,not as they are in truth and in Gods sight,but as they are

in

in outward ſhew,profeſſion,and in the eſtimation of men,who according to the rule of charitie iudge the beſt, when they ſee not euident reaſon to the contrarie ; or it may bee vnderſtood of hypocrites as they are in their owne opinion, or according to their vaine boaſting ; and ſo thoſe that are in ſhew, or in their owne opinion redeemed by Chriſts death, may bee reprobates and condemned, but not any who are redeemed in truth. Secondly, thoſe hypocrites that are in the outward viſible Church are ſaid to be redeemed, in reſpect that they are numbred for a time amongſt the faithfull, till they bewray their hypocriſie,and depart from the communion and fellowſhip which they haue outwardly with the Saints, though they are not in truth redeemed, vnleſſe they be of the Church and members of Chriſts bodie.

§. Sect.6.
That al are not redeemed by Chriſt, who periſhed in Adam.
1.Cor. 15.22.

Laſtly, it is obiected that *as in Adam all die,euen ſo in Chriſt ſhall all be made aliue,* as the Apoſtle ſpeaketh 1.Cor.15.22.but all died in *Adam,* and therefore all are made aliue in Chriſt. I anſwere, that the Apoſtle here vnderſtandeth all the faithfull, of whoſe reſurrection he here diſputeth ; and it is as much as if he had ſaid,as al the faithfull died in *Adam,*ſo al ſhall be made aliue in Chriſt : or though it bee vnderſtood of all, that they died in *Adam,* yet it prooueth not that all are redeemed by Chriſt,for then the ſenſe is thus much ; as *Adam* deriued death vnto all his, by natural propagation,ſo Chriſt hath deriued life to all his by grace : and this appeareth in the verſe following, where hee ſaith, that firſt Chriſt roſe, and afterwards they that are of Chriſt ſhall riſe at his comming : now they onely are Chriſts who are led by his ſpirit, and therefore they who haue not their part in the firſt reſurrection,whereby being ſanctified they riſe againe, from the death of ſinne to newneſſe of life, ſhall not haue their part of the ſecond reſurrection, whereby they riſe to inherite thoſe ioyes which Chriſt hath purchaſed for them.

But it may bee further vrged,that if all doe not liue in Chriſt who died in *Adam, Adams* ſinne ſhall bee of more force than Chriſts death and ſatisfaction,and *Adam* ſhall be more ſtrong to deſtroy than Chriſt to ſaue. I anſwere,that their power and ſtrength is not to bee meaſured by the number of thoſe who are deſtroyed and ſaued ; but according to the manner whereby
by

by they were deſtroyed and ſaued, or according to the vertue
and force required to ſauing and deſtroying ; for it is far more
eaſie to hurt many than to helpe a few, to kil a multitude than
to reſtore one to life ; for euen bruite beaſts can kill and deſtroy, but neither man ,angel, nor other creature can giue life
ſaue God alone ; and ſo it was no hard matter for *Adam* to
plunge al mankind into the gulfe of perdition, but to ſaue and
deliuer vs out of this wretched eſtate, neither he nor any other
could perfourme ſaue Chriſt alone : and therefore though our
Sauiour had freed and reſtored to life but only one, and *Adam*
by his ſinne deſtroyed all, yet Chriſts death was ſtronger and
of more vertue in ſauing, than *Adams* ſinne in deſtroying. Secondly I anſwere, that Chriſts death is as ſufficient for the redemption of all the world, as *Adams* ſinne for their condemnation, in reſpect of the infinite value and price thereof; if, as
Adams ſinne was deriued vnto all by naturall propagation, ſo
Chriſts death and merits were applied vnto them by faith ; for
there is no want of vertue in this precious ſalue to heale, but
the cauſe why it healeth not, is becauſe it is reiected and caſt a-
way through incredulitie. Thirdly, Chriſts death is of far more
vertue and force than *Adams* ſinne, in that it bringeth vnto vs
farre better things than we loſt in *Adam*; for we loſt by *Adam*
but earthly benefits, but wee haue deriued vnto vs by Chriſt
heauenly glorie and euerlaſting happineſſe; *Adam* caſt vs out
of the poſſeſſion of the earthly paradize , but Chriſt giues vs
poſſeſſion of the heauenly Ieruſalem ; *Adam* made vs of the
ſeruants of God the bondſlaues of Sathan, but Chriſt made vs
of the bondſlaues of Sathan , the ſonnes of God and heires of
his kingdome.

CHAP. XV.

That all who are redeemed are alſo ſanctified.

Nd thus I haue taken away the ground of Sathans
firſt temptations, whereby hee mooueth carnall
men ſecurely to continue in their ſinnes, becauſe
Chriſt hath redeemed and will ſaue the wicked
as well as the godly, by prouing that Chriſt hath
redeemed the faithfull onely.

§. *Sect.* 1.
Sathans temp-
tation to per-
ſwade men to
all licentiouſ-
neſſe.

V   The

The second temptation which he vseth to the same purpose, he thus frameth ; Christ hath redeemed all, at least who beleeue in him,be their sinnes neuer so many and grieuous : and therefore thou maist continue in thy sinnes with pleasure and delight,and satisfie the lusts of thine owne flesh;only beleeue and thou shalt be saued, for Christ requireth no other condition. Neither is there any other end of Chrifts comming,but that he should by his suffring take away thy sinnes ; and therefore why shouldest thou vexe and torment thy selfe,in embracing bitter mortification and newnesse of life,and in shunning thy sweete and pleasing sinnes, seeing Christ redeemeth the greatest sinners as well as the least?

The answere.   To this we are to answere, that there are no sins so innumerable in multitude, and so hainous in their qualitie and nature, which will exclude vs from the benefit of our redemption wrought by Christ, so we applie his death and merits vnto vs, by a true and liuely faith : but yet notwithstanding,this can be no encouragement for any to continue in their sinnes;for first, we are to know,that none haue part in this redéption wrought by Christ,but those onely who are made partakers thereof by a true and liuely faith; which is neuer separated from the fruites thereof,true repentance and holinesse of life ; neither is it possible that any should bee assured of Gods loue,but this assurance will make them to loue God againe, and this loue will worke in their hearts a zeale of his glorie,and a care to glorifie his name,by causing the light of their godly liues to shine before men ; it is not possible that any who truly beleeue that that they are redeemed with the precious bloud of Christ, should not highly esteeme and bee exceedingly thankfull to Christ for this inestimable benefit , which none can doe who tread the bloud of Christ vnder their feete,and voluntarily cast themselues into the bondage of sinne, out of which we are redeemed with so precious a price , and so scorne this benefit and despite our Sauiour who hath bestowed it ; it cannot bee that any should bee so foolish as to sell their soules vnto sinne for euery vaine pleasure and trifling commoditie , if they bee assured that Christ redeemed them with the price of his precious bloud, which was of more value than many worlds ; and therefore whosoeuer make no conscience of sinne haue no

true

true faith, and conſequently the worke of our redemption
wrought by Chriſt, doth not appertaine vnto them.

Secondly, whomſoeuer Chriſt redeemeth with his bloud, §.*Sect.2.*
thoſe hee ſanctifieth with his ſpirit; and in whomſoeuer his *That whom*
death is effectuall for the taking away of the guilt and puniſh- *Chriſt redee-*
ment of ſinne, in them it is effectuall for the mortifying of their *meth thoſe he*
corruptions and the ſinne it ſelfe; for, being the members of *ſanctifieth.*
Chriſt, *we are grafted with him into the ſimilitude of his death and* Rom.6.5.6.
reſurrection, and our old man is crucified with him, that the body of
ſinne might be deſtroyed, that henceſoorth we ſhould not ſerue ſin, as
it is Rom.6.5.6. And as our Sauiour Chriſt *is our wiſedom, righ-*
teouſneſſe and redemption, ſo hee is our *ſanctification alſo,* as it is 1.Cor.1.30.
1.Cor.1.30. So that whomſoeuer he redeemeth and iuſtifieth,
thoſe alſo he ſanctifieth, as it may further appeare by many &
euident teſtimonies. Tit.2.14. he is ſaid to haue giuen *himſelfe* Tit.2.14.
for vs, that he might redeeme vs from all iniquitie, and purge vs to
be a peculiar people vnto himſelfe zealous of good workes. Luk.1.
74.75. the Lord bindeth it with an oath, that *whomſoeuer hee re-* Luk.1.74.75.
deemeth out of the hands of their ſpirituall enemies, they ſhall wor-
ſhip him in holineſſe and righteouſneſſe all the daies of their life.
1.Pet.2.24. the Apoſtle ſaith, that our Sauiour *bare our ſinnes in* 1.Pet.2.24.
his bodie on the tree, that we being deliuered from ſinne ſhould liue
in righteouſneſſe. And *Paul* ſheweth Rom.6.18. that as ſoone as Rom.6.18.
we are freed from the bondage *of ſinne, we are made the ſeruants*
of righteouſneſſe. So Heb.9.14. it is ſaid, that the *bloud of Chriſt* Heb.9.14.
doth purge our conſciences from dead workes, that we may ſerue the
liuing God; neither are we onely iuſtified, but alſo ſanctified by
the offring of the bodie of Chriſt once made, as it is chap.10. Heb.10.10.14
ver.10.14. and as hee is appointed of God to be a prince and
Sauiour to giue remiſſion of ſinnes, ſo alſo to giue repentance,
as appeareth Act.5.31. So the Apoſtle ſaith, that Chriſt gaue Act.5.31.
himſelfe for his Church, not that it might continue ſtill in pollution and the filthineſſe of ſinne, but that he might ſanctifie it Eph.5.25.26.
and cleanſe it by the waſhing of water through the word,
Eph.5.25.26. If therefore wee walke in the light as hee is in the 1.Ioh.1.7.
light, then his bloud purgeth vs from all our ſinnes, 1.Ioh.1.7.
If we are ſprinkled in our hearts from an euill conſcience, then
we may draw neere with a true heart in aſſurance of faith, Heb. Heb.10.22.
10.22. But if wee continue in our ſinnes without repentance,
and

and commit them with delight and greedineſſe, then let vs
brag as much as we will that wee are redeemed by Chriſt, yet
wee are ſtill in the bondage of the diuell; for *Chriſt appeared*
not onely to free vs out of his captiuitie, but alſo that he might
*looſe the workes of the diuell,*as appeareth 1.Ioh.3.8. He hath redeemed vs out of the thraldome of Sathan,that wee might become his owne ſeruants, whom he wil rule and gouerne by his
word and ſpirit; and therfore if we haue not this ſpirit to leade
vs, we are none of his,as it is Rom.8.9.if we wil not ſubmit our
ſelues to the ſcepter of his word, we are none of his ſubiects,
but continue ſtill the ſeruants of ſinne and Sathan.Seeing then
it is manifeſt by Gods word, that whoſoeuer are redeemed are
alſo ſanctified, and whomſoeuer Chriſt hath waſhed with his
bloud, from the guilt and puniſhment of ſinne, he doth alſo
purge and cleanſe them by vertue of the ſame bloud, from the
ſinnes and corruptions themſelues ; and ſeeing he hath redeemed vs out of the hands of our ſpirituall enemies, to the end
we ſhould become his ſeruants, worſhipping him in holineſſe
and righteouſneſſe all the daies of our life:let vs neuer bee perſwaded by Sathans temptations,fooliſhly to imagine that wee
may the more ſecurely liue in our ſinnes, becauſe Chriſt Ieſus
hath paid a ſufficient price of our redemption : for, firſt,what
horrible ingratitude is this vnto God, to take occaſion by this
ineſtimable benefit the more to offend him? what a blaſphe-
mous imagination is this againſt Ieſus Chriſt,to thinke that he
came into the world, to be a bolſter whereupon we may more
ſecurely ſleepe in ſinne; and that he ſhed his precious bloud to
purchaſe libertie for vs,that we may liue in all wickednes;that
hee reconciled vs vnto his father by his death that wee might
the more freely offend him ; that hee hath redeemed vs out of
the bondage of Sathan, that wee may more diligently ſerue
him ; that hee hath with his bloud waſhed vs from the filth of
ſin,that we may more ſecurely wallow in this ſtinking puddle
againe?for,what were this but to make Chriſt another *Siſiphus,*
who aſſoone as he hath ended his labor is new to begin again?
what is it but euery day to crucifie the Lord of life afreſh, and
to tread his precious bloud vnder our feet as an vnholy thing?
what is it but to contemne and baſely to eſteeme of,the ineſtimable price of our redemption, if wee will not ſticke to ſell
                                                                            againe

1.Ioh.3.8.

Rom.8.9.

againe our ſoules vnto ſin, for euery beaſtly pleaſure and baſe
commoditie, which Chriſt hath purchaſed at ſo high a rate?
Secondly as hereby we ſhall ſhew horrible ingratitude againſt
God & our Sauiour Chriſt, ſo alſo ſhall we be moſt iniurious to
our own ſoules, ſeeing we can neuer attaine vnto any true aſſurance of our redemption, till we finde our ſelues freed in ſome
meaſure from the power of ſin, & ſanctified by Gods ſpirit, for
the Lord who is truth it ſelf hath ſaid it, & if this be not enough
he hath ſolemnly ſworne it, ẙ all *thoſe who he hath redeemed out
of the hands of their ſpirituall enemies, ſhall worſhip and ſerue him
in holines and righteouſnes all the daies of their life*; and therefore
as well may God ſpeake, nay ſweare an vntruth, as thoſe may
be redeemed who liue in their ſinnes, deſtitute of all holines
towards God, and righteouſnes towards their neighbour.

§. Sect. 3.

Thirdly, we are to conſider that the Lord hath redeemed vs
to a twofold end: the firſt and principall is his owne glorie,
the ſecond which is ſubordinate vnto the other, is our ſaluation
and euerlaſting happines: both which concurre in all thoſe, to
whom the redemption of Chriſt is made effectuall. Now God
is not glorified by redeeming ſuch as continue in their rebellion towards him, and will not by any meanes leaue the ſeruice
of ſin and Sathan, but rather in ſhewing his iuſtice and power,
in puniſhing their ſinnes which they commit with greedines:
but he is glorified when hee mercifully deliuereth repentant
ſinners, out of the bondage of ſinne and Sathan, who are wearie of their captiuitie, and deſire nothing more then freedome,
that they may in the reſt of their liues ſerue him their redeemer
in the duties of holines and righteouſnes. And therefore they
who liue in their ſinnes without repentance, continuing ſtill
traytors to God & ſeruants of Sathan, can haue no aſſurance of
their redemption, for the Lord hath therefore bought vs; *with
a price that we ſhould glorifie him both in our bodies and ſoules:* and
therfore thoſe who in ſted of letting their lights of holines and
righteouſnes ſhine cleerly before men, ẙ their heauenly father
may be glorified, doe nothing els but diſhonor him by their
ſins and wicked conuerſation, ſhew plainely that the redemption wrought by Chriſt doth not as yet appertaine vnto them.

A twofold end of our redemption, Gods glory and our happineſſe.

1. Cor. 6. 20.

Fourthly, we are to know that the worke of our redemption
wrought by Chriſt, conſiſteth of three parts or degrees; for

§. Sect. 7.

firſt

Three degrees of our redemption which alwaies concurre.

firſt Chriſt redeemed vs by paying the price of our redemption, and thus he is ſaid in the Scriptures to haue redeemed vs with his blood. Secondly, he redeemeth vs when as he applieth this benefit of our redemption vnto vs in particular, and doth thereby free and deliuer vs from the diuell ſin and death, ſo as we are no longer in their bondage ſubiect to their power and gouernment, although we be continually aſſaulted and often foyled by them; thirdly, he redeemeth vs when as he perfectly freeth vs, not onely from the power and gouernment, but alſo from the aſſaults and moleſtations of all our ſpirituall enemies, and giueth vs eternall peace in his kingdome. The firſt was wrought immediatly by himſelfe, when as he paied a ſufficient price for our redemption, and thereby fully ſatiſſied his fathers iuſtice; the ſecond he worketh by his owne ſpirit, whereby he doth diſpell out of our minds and hearts the darke miſts of ignorance and infidelitie, and by the glorious light thereof doth illuminate our vnderſtandings, with the beames of true knowledge and a liuely faith, ſo that we know acknowledge and beleeue that Chriſt is our ſauiour and redeemer, and are aſſured that he hath freed vs from the bondage of our ſpirituall enemies: after which aſſurance hee begetteth in vs an earneſt deſire, of beeing more and more freed from them actually, and an holy indeauour of withſtanding all their aſſaults and temptations, whereby they labour againe to bring vs into their captiuitie, and withall enableth vs with ſome meaſure of ſtrength, to withſtand and ouercome them; and reneweth and confirmeth this ſtrength recciued, when in the conflict of temptation we are weakned, and haue receiued the foyle, that we may riſe vp againe and afreſh maintaine the fight. Laſtly, our Sauiour Chriſt redeemeth vs, when as he perfectly freeth and deliuereth vs from our ſpirituall enemies at his ſecond comming, when as we ſhall not onely not be ouercome nor foyled of them, but alſo not ſo much as once aſſaulted. And of this redemption our Sauiour ſpeaketh Luk.21.28. *When* (ſaith he) *theſe things begin to come to paſſe, then looke vp & lift vp your heads; for your redemption draweth neere.* And theſe are the three degrees of our redemptiō, which alwaies follow one another, for, for whomſoeuer Chriſt hath giuen himſelfe as the price of their redemption, to thoſe alſo hee giueth his holy ſpirit,

Luk.21.28.

which

which doth illuminate the eyes of their vnderſtanding blinded
with ignorance, and ſanctifieth their will and affections, working in them a deſire and holy indeauour of ſeruing the Lord
in holines and righteouſnes, and of withſtanding the temptations of the fleſh, the world and the diuell. And whomſoeuer
he thus redeemeth out of the power and gouernment of their
ſpirituall enemies, thoſe he will perfectly redeeme and deliuer
from all their malicious attempts, and giue them the eternall
peace of his kingdome. But thoſe who haue not their part in
the ſecond degree, that is, thoſe who continue in their blind ignorance, and in the naturall pollution of their will and affections, willingly ſubiecting themſelues to the ſeruice of ſinne and
Sathan, and ſtubbornly withdrawing their ſtiffe neckes out of
the yoke of holy obedience vnto Gods commaundements;
they can neuer haue any aſſurance that Chriſt hath redeemed
them by paying the price of his blood, nor will deliuer them
at his ſecond comming out of the bondage of Sathan, in which
they haue liued all their life time, with pleaſure and delight;
for, whomſoeuer hee ranſometh with the price of his blood,
thoſe he freeth out of the gouernment of their ſpirituall enemies, ſinne, death, and the diuell; and therefore they that ſtill
liue in ſinne with pleaſure and delight, they are ſtill the ſeruants of ſinne, as our Sauiour ſaith Ioh.8.34, yea the ſeruants   Ioh.8.34.
of Sathan alſo, as the Apoſtle teacheth, 1.Ioh.3.8. *For their ſer-*   1.Ioh.3.8.
uants we are to whom we obey, whether it be of ſinne vnto death, or   Rom.6.16.
of obedience vnto righteouſnes, as it is Rom.6.16 : and thoſe who
ſtill remaine in the ſeruice and ſlauerie of ſinne and ſathan, haue
no part in the firſt redemption, wrought by the ſhedding of
his blood, nor ſhall haue any part in the laſt redemption, at his
ſecond comming to iudgement.

Laſtly, we are to know that Chriſt hath redeemed the whole   §. *Sect.*5.
man, body, and ſoule, and hath freed and deliuered euery part   *That Chriſt*
and facultie of them, out of the bondage of our ſpirituall ene-   *hath redeemed*
mies, that all and euery of them may performe ſeruice vnto   *the whole man.*
God. For example, our vnderſtandings were captiued in the
darke priſon of ignorance and blindnes, as appeareth Epheſ.   Eph.4.17.18.
4.17.18 : but our Sauiour Chriſt redeemed vs, and hath diſpel-
led theſe miſts of darkenes with the preaching of the Goſpell,
which like a glorious ſunſhine hath appeared vnto vs, and by

the

the operation of his holy ſpirit, he hath cauſed the ſcales of ignorance to fall from the eyes of our vnderſtanding, ſo that we can ſee the miſterie of our redemption,and worke of our ſaluation

Luk.1.77.78. tion wrought by him, as it is Luk.1.77.78.79. Our wils which were ſo inthralled that wee could not ſo much as deſire any

Phil.2.13. thing pleaſing and acceptable vnto God, as appeareth Phil.2.13, hath our Sauiour redeemed and freed out of this ſpirituall bondage, and by the good motions of his holy ſpirit doth ſo rule and incline them,that to will is preſent with vs,and we are

Rom.7.18.22. delighted in the law of God concerning the inner man; as the Apoſtle ſpeaketh of himſelfe Rom.7.18.22. And though the law of our members and corruptions of the fleſh,doe rebell againſt the law of our minde, leading vs captiue to the law of ſinne, yet doe we abhorre this ſinne, and earneſtly deſire to be freed from it, and to ſerue the Lord in holines and righteouſnes, indeauoring and ſtriuing to mortifie the fleſh and the corruptions thereof, and to riſe againe to newnes of life. Our affections alſo were wholy corrupted and diſordered, ſo that we hated God,and loued the world,feared man,and not the Lord, truſted vpon the inferior meanes, neuer regarding the fountaine of all goodnes; in a word wee were giuen ouer to our

Rom.1.24.26. owne harts luſts,and vnto vile affections, as it is Rom.1.24.26: but by the redemption wrought by Chriſt becomming his, and being quickned and ſtrengthened by his holy ſpirit, wee

Gal.5.24. haue crucified the fleſh with the affections and luſts thereof, as the Apoſtle ſpeaketh,Gal.5.24. Laſtly,the members of our bodie were *ſeruants to vncleanes and iniquitie,to commit iniquitie,*

Rom.6.19. Rom.6.19. our eyes full of adulterie, our tongues forges of lies, our feete ſwift to ſhed blood: but our Sauiour Chriſt redeeming vs hath deliuered our bodies alſo from the thraldome of ſinne and Sathan, ſo as though ſinne dwell,yet it ſhall no

Rom.6.12. longer raigne in our mortall bodies, that we ſhould obey the luſts thereof,as appeareth Rom.6.12.In a word,both body and ſoule were in miſerable captiuitie to our ſpirituall enemies:but

1.Cor.6.20. our *Sauiour hath bought vs with a price,to the end we may glorifie God in our bodies and in our ſpirits,for they are Gods,*as it is 1.Cor 6.20. And *hath redeemed vs not with corruptible things, as ſiluer*

1.Pet.1.18.19 *and gold, from our vaine conuerſation, but with his owne moſt precious blood,*as *Peter* teacheth vs 1.Pet.1.18.19.

If

If therefore we are redeemed by Chrilt, then our blind vnderstandings are inlightened by the preaching of the Gospell, and we freed from our former ignorance : our willes which were rebellious are inclined to obedience, so as we earneslly desire to leaue our sinnes, and to serue the Lord in the duties of sanctification, and haue an endeauor of mortifying our sins, and rising againe to newnes of life ; our affections also are purged from their corruptions, so that we loue, feare, trust in, hope, and expect all good from him, who is the fountaine of all goodnes; our bodies *which were giuen as seruants vnto sinne, are now become the seruants of righteousnes vnto holines* ; In a word both in bodie and soule we are freed from sinne, and made seruants vnto God. But if our vnderstandings are still blinde and ignorant, our willes backward to imbrace any goodnes, and moll prone vnto all euill, our affections as corrupt as euer they were, and our bodies the readie instruments to act all sinne and wickednes, then haue we as yet no fruite of the redemption wrought by Christ, for it is not a titularie but a powerfull redemption, which indeed and truth deliuereth vs, euen in this life, from our spirituall enemies: so that though they may assault, and grieuously vexe vs, yet they shall neuer gouerne and raigne ouer vs; and therefore whosoeuer feele not the redemption wrought by Christ, powerfull in this life to free them in some measure, from the rule and iurisdiction of sinne, Sathan, the world and the flesh, shall neuer finde it fruitfull and effectuall to free and deliuer them, from condemnation hell and destruction in the life to come.

Rom.6.19.
verf.22.

Chap. XVI.
Of those temptations which Sathan vseth against the faithfull concerning their redemption.

Nd thus much concerning those temptations which Sathan suggesteth into mens mindes to nourish in them carnall securitie : now we are to confider of those which he vfeth to moue men to doubting and desperation. Firlt therefore he obiecteth that it is a thing vnreasonable, and vtterly repugnant to Gods iustice, that Christ who was innocent should be punished

§. Sect.1.
That it is not repugnant to Gods iuftice to punish Christ for vs.

shed for vs who are guiltie, that we should deserue the blame, and he suffereth the stripes, that the righteous should be condemned, and the wicked acquitted, that wee who like *Barrabas* were cruell murtherers and wicked sinners should be let lose, and the immaculate lambe of God in whom there was no fault should be deliuered vp to be crucified; for what were this but to make the iust God like vniust *Pilate?* what were this but to deny his owne word, hauing said that the righteous

Ezech. 18.20. should liue in his righteousnes, and the sinner die in his iniquitie? To which I answere, first, that it would not indeede haue stoode with Gods iustice, to haue punished Christ as he was innocent and righteous, nor to haue acquitted and absolued vs who were vnrighteous and wicked ; but he punished Christ in respect that he had taken vpon him the sins of all the faithfull, and absolueth vs as we are freed from our sins, & clothed with his righteousnes and obedience. He punished Christ, not as he was most iust and free from sin, but as he was our suretie who had taken vpon him to discharge our debt, and to satisfie for our sinnes; and thus the creditor may iustly require his debt of the suretie though in respect of himselfe he owed him nothing, and thus he may, nay ought to release the principall, when the suretie hath allreadie discharged the debt. Secondly I answere that it had bin iniustice in God, if he had forced our Sauiour Christ, who was iust and innocent, to vndergoe the punishments which were due vnto vs, who were malefactors and offenders ; for this were to condemne the righteous, and to iustifie the wicked : but our Sauiour Christ of his owne free accord, did voluntarily offer himselfe to stand in our place, and to discharge that debt which we owed, and to make satisfaction to his father, by suffering that punishment which wee had

Ioh. 10.18. deserued. And this appeareth, Ioh.10.18. where our Sauiour saith, that *no man tooke his life from him, but that hee laied it downe of himselfe.* And the Apostle telleth vs that *he humbled*

Phil. 2.8. *himselfe, and became obedient vnto death,* Phil.2.8. In which respect, his death is called a sacrifice or free oblation, which he

Heb. 9.14. voluntarily offered vnto his father, Heb.9.14: and therefore the Lord might iustly take that which Christ freely gaue, nay it had been crueltie and iniustice if he should haue refused, the paiment of such a sufficient suretie, when he voluntarily offered

it

it for our difcharge, choofing rather ftill to haue kept vs in prifon, bound in the chaines of euerlafting death. Laftly, there
might haue been fome fhew of rigor and iniuftice, if Chrift the
innocent had been ouerwhelmed, in fuffering the punifhments
which were due vnto vs, who were the offendors; but being
not onely man which fuffered but God alfo, and therefore of
infinit power and maieftie, he was able to pay our great debt,
and yet is neuer the poorer; to fuffer death and ouercome it
by fuffering: and by yeelding a while to the malice of our fpirituall enemies, he finally vanquifhed and glorioufly triumphed ouer them all; and therefore it was not iniuftice in God to
fuffer our Sauiour Chrift, to vndergoe that which he was fure to
ouercome; but vnfpeakable mercie towards vs, in fending his
fonne to pay that debt which we could neuer haue difcharged,
and to fuffer punifhments for a time, which otherwife wee
fhould haue endured for euer.

By this then it appeareth, that God might iuftly receiue the
price of our redemption, which Chrift freely offered. But feeing by the lawes of redemption there is required, not onely
that the redeemer pay a price or ranfome, but alfo that he haue
right to that which he doth redeeme, it may be demaunded
what right our Sauiour had ouer vs, that hee fhould pay this
price for vs. I anfwere, that as our Sauiour Chrift confifteth of
two natures, fo alfo he had a twofold right vnto vs; for as he
was God, he had the right of proprietie, & was our true owner;
he was our Lord and therefore had right to redeeme his owne
feruants; he was our King, and therefore had right to redeeme
vs who were his fubiects; yea he was our creator, and therefore
he had more right then any Lord or King to redeeme vs who
were his creaturs; as he was a man he was our kinfeman, flefh
of our flefh, and bone of our bone; yea he was our brother, as
it is Heb.2.11.12. and Ioh.20.17; and therefore had alfo the Heb. 2. 11. 12.
Ioh. 20. 17.
right of propinquitie, which was required by the law of re- Leuit.25.25.
demption. Leuit.25.25.

Secondly, Sathan may obiect that the death of Chrift is not §. Sect. 2.
a fufficient price for our redemption; for how could the death *That Chrift*
of one, be a fufficient fatisfaction for the finne of al the faithful, *hath offered a*
feeing euery one by their innumerable finnes, had deferued in- *fufficient price*
numerable deaths? and how could the temporary and fhort *for our redemp-*
                                                         punifhment *tion.*

Act.20 18.

punishment which Christ indured,free vs all that beleeue from the euerlasting punishments of hell fire, seeing the iustice of God requireth that there should be some proportiô, betwen the punishment which we deserued,and the satisfaction which Christ made and offred? I answere,that Christ who suffered for vs, was not man only but God also; in which respect it is said, that God purchased his Church with his blood; not that God hath blood, but because he that shed his blood, was not onely man but also God; and therefore his short sufferings were of more worth,vertue and valew,than the euerlasting suffrings of al the world;for they should euer haue suffred,but could therby neuer haue satisfied, because our sins deserued infinite punish-ments, in that we had by them offended the infinit iustice and maiesty of God;which because finit creatures could not beare, Gods iustice required that they should be infinit in time and euerlasting, seeing they could not be infinite in measure ; but the suffrings of Christ,though short in time,yet were they infi-nit in valew, worth and merit, because he was not man alone, but God also,and therfore at once he put away sin by the sacri-fice of himself, & *by his one oblation he took away the sins of many,* as it is Heb.9.26,28. As therefore *Adams* sinne,which in it selfe was finit, as proceeding from a finit creature,notwithstanding deserued infinit punishment,because God whom by his sin he offended was infinit; so contrariwise Chrifts suffrings were but of short continuance in respect of time,but yet of infinit merit and worth,because he that suffered was not man alone, but al-so God,and therefore infinite.

Heb.9.26.

§. Sect.3.
That Chrifts death and me-rits belong to euery particu-lar beleeuer.

Lastly, the tempter will obiect that Chrifts death and me-rits,though they be in themselues a sufficient price for our re-demption,yet they do not belong vnto vs,neither wil be effec-tuall for our saluation. Let it be graunted (will he say) that the death and merits of Christ are sufficient for the saluation of all: yet what comfort canst thou receiue hereby, seeing thou canst haue no assurance that they belong vnto thee, or will be effec-tuall for thy redemption ? for either he hath redeemed all or but some only ; if all,then some who are redeemed may perish notwithstanding, seeing the scriptures shew that the greater part of the world are the children of destruction, and it is not vnlikely but that thou art in the greatest number.But if he haue
redeemed

redeemed some only, how canst thou conclude that thou art one of these whom he hath redeemed, seeing out of mere particular propositions thou canst not inferre any sound consequence? For example, if thou dost thus conclude, some men are redeemed by Christ, but I am a man, therefore I am redeemed: thou mightest as wel reason thus, some men are kings, but I am a man, therefore I am a king. To this wee must answere, that though Christ hath only redeemed some, yet wee may after a more sound manner conclude that we are in this number, not vsing the helpe of sathans absurd fallacions; but inferring our conclusion out of generall propositions grounded vpon Gods word after this manner; whosoeuer beleeue in Christ, those he hath redeemed and will saue; for this is the voyce and promise of Christ in the Gospell: but I (may euery faithfull man say) doe truely beleeue in Christ: and therefore I am redeemed and shall eternally be saued.

But against this particular application of Christ & his merits vnto vs, the tempter vrgeth diuers obiections; first, that Christ only saueth and redeemeth his own body which is his Church, and that this his Church is glorious without spot or wrinkle, holy and vnblameable, as it is Ephes.5.25.27. and therfore (wil he say) what hope of redemption or saluation canst thou haue, who art defiled not onely with originall corruption, but also with innumerable actuall transgressions? To this we must answere that the Apostle saith not, that the Church which Christ redeemeth and saueth, is now already without spot or wrinkle; but ỹ he hath by giuing himself for it, redeemed it, that hereby he might wash and clense it from all spots, and might make it holy and without blame; either by his merits and righteousnes imputed vnto it which is done in this life; or by freeing it altogether from corruptions and the filthy spots of sinne, wherewith naturally it is defiled, which is begunne in this life, but shall not be perfected vntill the life to come.

Secondly, he obiecteth, that if Christ had redeemed vs out of the thraldome of sinne, then wee should not still be ouercome therby, nor so often, will we nill we, transgres Gods commandements. To which we are to answere, that our Sauiour Christ hath deliuered vs from our sins, first in regard that for his merits and satisfaction sake, the Lord hath pardoned and remitted them,

§. Sect.4.
Sathans temptations against the particular application of Christs merits, answered.
Eph.5.25.27.

Our falling into sinne, no reason to proue that we are not redeemed.
Col.1.14.

them,

them,so as they shall neuer be imputed vnto vs, nor arise vp in iudgement to our condemnation,neither in this world nor the world to come : secondly, he doth deliuer vs from our sinnes, whilest he doth giue vnto vs his holy spirit,whereby our sinnes are in some measure mortified,& the strength of them abated, so that they do not raigne and rule in vs as in former times,although we cannot wholy expell them from dwelling in vs,according to that Rom.6.12, *Sinne shall not raigne in your mortall bodie that you should obey it in the lusts thereof.* And though we cannot vtterly subdue this Cananitish brood of our corruptions, but that still whilest we continue in this life, they are as thornes in our sides,alwaies vexing and grieuing vs:yet by the helpe of Gods spirit assisting vs,we weaken their force, abate their courage,and make them become tributaries;and if at any time they rebel,we curbe them in,& giue them the ouerthrow; yea,though sometimes they gaine ground, & giue vs the foile, yet wee rise againe by vnfained repentance, and recouer our selues,being assisted with the fresh supply of Gods spirit,till at last by death we obtaine a finall victory.

§. Sect.5.
That our obedience to the Lawe,proueth not that we are not redeemed.
Gal.3.13.

Thirdly,he obiecteth that we are still vnder the law,and tied to the obedience thereof,and therefore Christ hath not freed vs from it: I answer,that though Christ hath not freed vs from the obedience of the lawe, yet he hath freed vs from the curse and malediction,as it is Gal.3.13.so as though we do not performe it in that exact manner and measure which God requireth, yet our transgression shall not be imputed vnto vs;for he hath perfectly fulfilled the law for vs,that his righteousnesse might become our righteousnesse,and he hath suffred death,that by his blood he might wash away our sins.And thus *when the law was impossible to be performed,by reason of the weaknes and corruptions of our flesh,the Lord sent his Son in the similitude of sinfull flesh,and for sin condemned sin in the flesh, that the righteousnesse of the lawe might be fulfilled in vs,* as it is Rom.8.3,4. Moreouer,we are not now tied to performe obedience to the lawe, to the end that thereby we may be iustified,nor yet shall we for the imperfections of this our obedience be in danger of condemnation,but now onely it is a meanes before our conuersion to bring vs to Christ, by shewing vnto vs our sinnes and insufficiency in our selues, and after our conuersion it serueth for a rule or square,

according

according to which we are to frame our liues in holinesse and righteousnesse, that so we may shew our thankfulnes vnto our heauenly father for his inestimable benefits, by glorifying his name in a godly life. And because this also is bitter and vnpleasant to flesh and blood, therefore the Lord hath also granted and giuen vnto vs his holy spirit, which mortifieth our corruptions, whereby we are made lesse prone vnto sinne; and quickneth vs in the inner man, inabling vs to performe obedience in some measure to the law of God, with alacrity and cheerefulnes, so that now *his commandements are not grieuous vnto vs,* as 1.Iohn 5.3. the Apostle speaketh, 1.Ioh.5.3, but his yoke which so much galled vs while we were rebellious, and like vntamed oxen, is now become easie, and his burthen which heretofore was so heauy and irkesome, is now become light, as our Sauiour telleth vs, Matth.11.30. ░Matth.11.30.

Fourthly, the tempter may obiect to the weake conscience which laboureth vnder the burthen of sinne, that our Sauiour Christ hath not redeemed vs from the anger of God due for sin, seeing we still see his frowning countenance, and apprehend the scorching heate of his wrath inflamed against vs: but let all know, that if they truly beleeue in Christ, and onely rely themselues vpon this their mediator, if their sins past grieue them, and they purpose for the time to come, to labor that they may forsake them; then they are reconciled vnto God by Christ, and in him hee is become their louing and gracious father, as the Col.1.20.21. Apostle telleth vs, Col.1.20.21. Let not such therefore be discouraged, if God seeme to frowne vpon them for a time, for hee will not frowne for euer, nor alwaies retaine his anger, as the Psalmist speaketh, Psalm.103.9. Nay, in truth he is not Psalm.103.9. angry with vs at all as a Iudge to punish, but as a Father to correct and amend vs : and if we will speake properly, he alwaies loueth and delighteth in vs ; for as hee is well pleased with Christ our head, so is he alwaies well pleased with vs in him, as being members of his body : notwithstanding as a tender Father when his Sonne offendeth, maketh semblance as though his wrath were kindled, to the ende that hee may bee carefull in the time to come, to auoyde the like fault, and to amend ; so the Lord who is our gracious Father, seemeth oftentimes to bee grieuously displeased with his

§. *Sect.6.*
That God is not angry with the faithfull, though he seemeth to frowne vpon them.

his

his children when they haue ſinned againſt him, hiding from them his amiable louing countenance, and ſhewing nothing but ſignes of wrath, not that hee hath in truth caſt them out of his loue and fauour; for he neuer falleth out with thoſe whom Chriſt hath reconciled vnto him, neither can hee ceaſe to loue the members of Chriſt, nor Chriſts members ceaſe to bee his members after they are once ingrafted into his bodie by his holie ſpirit and a liuely faith: onely like a wiſe father he frowneth vpon them and ſeemeth angrie, to make them in the time to come forſake their ſinnes, whereby they haue incurred his diſpleaſure.

§. *Sect.7.*
That though Sathan tempt vs, yet we may be aſſured that we are redeemed.
Heb.2.14.

Col.1.13.

Col.2.15.

Ioh.12.31.

Luk.11.21.

1.Pet.5.9.

Fiftly, the tempter will obiect that we are not freed and deliuered out of his power and iuriſdiction, ſeeing he doth often aſſault and ouercome vs with his temptations, and leadeth vs captiue faſt bound in the fetters of ſinne. To which wee muſt anſwere, that our Sauiour Chriſt by his *death hath deſtroyed him that had the power of death, that is the diuell; that he might deliuer all them which for feare of death were all their life time ſubiect to bondage,* as the Apoſtle ſheweth Heb.2.14.15. That God *hath deliuered vs from the power of darkneſſe, and hath tranſlated vs into the kingdome of his deare ſonne,* as it is Col.1.13.That our redeemer Ieſus Chriſt *hath ſpoiled the principalities and powers, and hath made a ſhew of them openly, and hath triumphed ouer them vpon his croſſe, and that not onely for himſelfe, but for all his members,* Col.2.15. That hee hath now broken the Serpents head, ſo that well may hee hiſſe againſt vs, but yet hee cannot ſting vs. And whereas heretofore hee was the prince of the world, who did rule and gouerne vs at his pleaſure and according to his will, now he is caſt out by the prince of princes, as it is Ioh.12. 31.and our Sauiour Chriſt hath eſtabliſhed his kingdom in vs, ruling and gouerning vs with the ſcepter of his word and holy ſpirit. Whereas hee was the ſtrong man who quietly kept his poſſeſſion in vs, Luk.11.21; our Sauiour Chriſt who is ſtronger than he, hath ſpoyled him of his armour wherein hee truſted, and hath thruſt him out of his poſſeſſion. Whereas hee was a cruell tyrant who held vs faſt bound in his captiuitie, our Sauiour Chriſt hath redeemed vs out of his thraldome, ſo as now he cannot hurt vs though hee neuer ceaſeth to aſſault vs; and though hee goeth about like a roring lion ſeeking whom hee

may

may deuoure, yet now we are enabled by Gods ſpirit to reſiſt him ſtedfaſtly in the faith, and ſo armed with the coat-armour of Gods ſpiritual graces, that though he may with the violence of his aſſaults foyle vs, yet ſhall hee neuer be able to ouercome vs. God doth indeed ſuffer this wicked enemie to make warre againſt euen his deareſt children, and that ſometimes after a ſtrange and extraordinarie manner, not that he will giue them ouer againe vnto his thraldome, out of which he hath purcha-ſed them with ſo deare a price, but partly to driue them hereby to flie vnto him by earneſt and effectuall prayer, imploring his aide againſt Sathans crueltie, and that hauing receiued it they may aſcribe the whole glorie of the victorie to him alone, by whoſe ſtrength they haue ouercome; and partly to ſhew vnto them their owne weakeneſſe, that they may not relie nor reſt vpon it. Sometimes hee ſuffreth them to be thus aſſaulted, that his power may be magnified in their weakeneſſe; and ſome-times that the graces which he hath beſtowed vpon them, may ſhine glorioũſly to all the world. Sometimes for the confirma-tion of others who ſhall hereafter be tried with the like temp-tations, when they haue in their brethren often experience of Gods loue power and fatherly aſſiſtance; and ſometimes the more to ſtrengthen themſelues in his ſpirituall graces, and to confirme them more fully in the aſſurance of his loue and their ſaluation. For as a citie which hath once bin beſieged and not ſacked, wil euer after be more ſtrong to hold out if it be aſſaul-ted by the like danger, becauſe the citizens will carefully for-tifie their walles and increaſe their bulwarkes; and as he who hath been once robbed by theeues, will euer after ride better prouided to make reſiſtance, that hee doe not againe fall into their hands; ſo thoſe who are beſieged and aſſaulted by their ſpirituall enemies, will euer after more carefully arme them-ſelues againſt them with the graces of Gods ſpirit, that they may not be ouercome nor foiled by them. We know that whi-leſt men quietly enioy their poſſeſſions and inheritance they reſt ſecure, keeping their writings in a boxe without euer loo-king on them from yere to yere, but when their title and right is called into queſtion, and ſome man labours to thruſt them out of their poſſeſſion, then they peruſe their writings and deeds with al diligence; &, not ſatisfied with their own iudge-

That God tur-neth Sathans temptations to the good of his children.

X   ment

ment they reſort to skilfull Lawyers, crauing their counſaile
how they may maintaine their right, and anſwere the plea
which their aduerſarie makes againſt them; whereby oftentimes it commeth to paſſe that they make their title not onely
much more ſtrong in it ſelfe, but alſo more cleere and euident
vnto al others, ſo that afterwards none dare once aduenture to
trouble them againe, or call their right into queſtion : ſo whileſt we neuer doubt of our heauenly inheritance we reſt ſecure,
and let the book of God which is our beſt deed and euidence,
lie vnder our cupbords till it mould for want of vſe; but when
ſathan by his temptations doth call our title into queſtion, and
pleades that we haue no right to Gods kingdome, then do we
moſt carefully and diligently peruſe the booke of God, then
doe we goe vnto Gods Miniſters, deſiring their counſaile how
we may anſwere Sathans plea and cleere our title, then doe we
moſt carefully vſe all good means to increaſe our knowledge,
that thereby wee may throughly infourme our ſelues of our
right, and confirme our aſſurance againſt all cauils and obiections. And hereby it commeth to paſſe, that thoſe who before
had very weak titles to their heauenly inheritance, whileſt they
remained retchleſſe and ſecure, and but ſlender aſſurance euer
to enioy it; now, by their care, paines and diligence, haue ſo
confirmed it vnto themſelues, and ſo cleered it to al the world,
that Sathan dare neuer after call it into queſtion, vnleſſe he doe
it (like many contentious men in theſe daies) rather that he
may trouble and vexe them with a tedious ſuite, than for any
hope of preuailing in the end. And thus you ſee that Chriſt
hath redeemed all the faithfull out of Sathans thraldome, notwithſtanding that he ſtil aſſaulteth them with his temptations;
neither doth hee hereby ouercome them and againe inthrall
them in his captiuitie, but rather by Gods bleſſing they ſerue
to ſtrengthen them in the ſpirituall graces of Gods ſpirit, and
to confirme them in the full aſſurance of their ſaluation.

§. *Sect.8.*
That though
we die, yet we
are redeemed
from death.
Gen.3.19.
Heb.9.27.

Sixtly, the tempter will obieſt that wee ſtill die, and therefore are not redeemed and deliuered out of the bondage of
death. To which we may anſwer, that Gods iuſt ſentence once
denounced could not be reuoked, Gen.3.19, *Duſt thou art, and*
into duſt thou ſhalt returne; and therefore the Apoſtle ſaith Heb.
9.27, *It is appointed vnto all men that they ſhall once die.* But as
Abaſhuerus,

*Abashuerus,*though he could not reuoke the sentence of death
againſt the Iewes after it was once pronounced, becauſe it was
a decree of the Medes and Perſians which might not be altred;yet at *Heſters* ſuite ſent out another decree, whereby hee
armed and ſtrengthened the Iewes againſt their enemies, to
the end they might reſiſt, ouercome, and deſtroy them : ſo the
Lord hauing pronounced the ſentence of death againſt all the
ſonnes of *Adam*,could not reuoke his decree and ſentence,as
being farre more vnchangeable than the decree of the Medes
and Perſians, yet at the ſuite of our Sauiour Chriſt hee made
another decree,whereby wee might be armed againſt our enemie death,and ouercome him. So that now though we die, yet
are we not ſubiect vnto death,neither ſhall wee be held vnder
the dominion thereof; though wee are not wholy exempted
from death,yet now the nature therof is quite altred ; for heretofore it was vnconquerable, but now eaſily ouercome ; heretofore it was a curſe for ſinne, but now turned into an exceeding bleſſing,as deriuing vnto vs many benefits : for firſt it
freeth vs from all our afflictions, with which in this life wee are
ſo much moleſted ; it deliuereth vs from the irkſome company
of prophane wicked men, who grieue the very ſoules of the
righteous, and make them to crie out with *Dauid*; *Woe is me*
that I remaine in Meſhech, and dwell in the tents of Kedar ; it
wholy freeth vs from ſinne, and purgeth away thoſe corruptions which in this life cleaue ſo faſt vnto vs ; ſo that though
heretofore there was great amitie betweene ſinne and death,
for ſin was the only cauſe which inlarged deaths dominions,
and made al the world to become his tributaries,yet now they
are at oddes,and death now is the means,to free vs out of ſins
thraldome and vtterly to deſtroy it. And thus hath the Viper
ſinne, bred a yong one which eateth out it own belly;for ſinne
brought foorth death, and death deſtroyed ſinne : had it not
bin for ſinne, death had neuer entred into the world, and were
it not for death, ſinne would neuer go out of the world. Moreouer, by death wee obtaine a full and perfect victorie ouer the
fleſh, the world,and the diuell ; for whereas in this life we are
in a continual fight,and ſometimes *Ameleck*, ſometime *Iſrael*
hath the vpper hand:death puts an end to this battaile, and giueth vs full victorie ouer the fleſh,the world, and the diuell;ſo

as

as they fhall neuer afterwards not only not preuaile, but not fo much as affault or trouble vs : and thus doth euery Chriftian, with *Dauid* cut off *Goliahs* head with his own fword; for death was the weapon which Sathan vfed to deftroy vs, and with this weapon we giue Sathan a finall ouerthrow. Laftly, death which heretofore was the high way to hell and deftruction , is now become the readie entrance into Gods kingdome, and like a foule gate whereby we enter into a faire palace ; heretofore it was a firie ferpent which by ftinging killed & deftroyed vs, but, now our Sauiour hath pulled out the fting, it is become fo harmeleffe that we may fafely put it into our bofoms, without receiuing any hurt: and in this refpect it may not vnfitly be compared to the brafen Serpent, which looked like other Serpents, but in fteed of wounding it prefently cured, in fteede of killing it preferued life ; fo though death retaine his former fhape, fo that wee are afraid and readie to flee from it, yet it is but in outward appearance; for in fteed of an euer dying life, it giueth vs poffeffion of a neuer dying life and endleffe happineffe. Heretofore it was the diuels fergeant to arreft and carrie vs without baile, into the perpetual prifon of vtter darkneffe, but now it is the Lords gentleman-vfher to conduct and place vs in the kingdome of heauen. Heretofore it was like the diuels cart wherein we were carried to execution, now it is like *Elias* firie chariot whereby we mount vp into heauen. And this *Paul*

2.Cor.5.1. fheweth 2.Cor.5.1.*We know* (faith he)*that if the earthly houfe of this tabernacle be deftroyed, we haue a building giuen vs of God, a houfe not made with hands, but eternall in the heauens.* Why therfore fhuld we feare, nay why fhould we not defire death, feeing

Phil. 1.23. now it is vnto vs aduantage ? as it is Phil.1.23. why fhould we
verf.21. not defire to be diffolued and to be with Chrift, feeing that is beft of all ? as it is verf.21. for now we may fay, not that we die,
Ioh.8.21. but that we depart and goe to our father, as our Sauiour fpeaketh Ioh.8.21.

But yet wee muft take heede that wee doe not imagine, that death in it owne nature worketh and procureth for vs thefe great benefits; for in it felfe this temporarie death is but a ftep to euerlafting death, and as it were a fearefull prologue to a more fearefull tragedie : but our Sauiour Chrift it is alone who hath gathered holefome honey out of this pernitious poyfon,

and

and by mingling the flefh of this venemous ferpent with his owne moft precious bloud, hee hath made thereof a holefome Triacle.

And thus haue I prooued, notwithftanding Sathans temptations and obiections, that Chrift hath perfectly redeemed vs, out of the hands of all our fpirituall enemies; now in the laft place Sathan fuggefteth, that though Chrift hath once redeemed vs, yet we may come into their bondage againe, and then there is no hope of a fecond redemption. But wee are to know that our Redeemer is God omnipotent, whofe power all the power of hell cannot withftand; and therefore nothing *is able to pluck vs out of his hand,* as himfelfe fpeaketh Ioh.10.28; neither are we to think, that he will eafily & willingly lofe them, which hee fo intirely loues that hee fpared not his precious bloud, but freely gaue it as a price of their redemption. And therefore, as hee *is able, perfectly to faue all thofe who come vnto God by him*; *becaufe he euer liueth to make interceffion for them,* as it is Heb.7.25. fo we neede not doubt of his will, feeing hee hath redeemed vs with fo deare a price: for if hee would not lofe vs when we were his enemies, much leffe will hee fuffer vs to perifh when we are become his fubiects, yea his fpoufe, nay members of his owne bodie: and therefore we may affure our felues that if our Sauiour, our fpoufe and head hath once redeemed vs, then he hath alfo *obtained eternall redemption for vs,* as the Apoftle affirmeth Heb.9.12. So that though the diuell rage like a roring lion, and the flefh betray vs and harbour whole legions of vnlawfull lufts which fight againft our foules, and the world fometime frowne, and fometime faune, and all of them by all meanes labour to deftroy vs; yet our omnipotent redeemer, our louing and careful fpoufe and head, will not fuffer vs to be loft whom hee hath fo dearely bought, but will giue vs the poffeffion and fruition of that heauenly inheritance, and thofe vnfpeakable ioyes which hee with his owne moft precious bloud hath purchafed for vs.

§. *Sect.9.*
That thofe who are once redeemed cannot againe be brought into bondage.

Ioh.10.28.

Heb.7.25.

Heb.9.12.

CHAP.

CHAP. XVII.
Of our Vocation.

§. *Sect.*1

And thus much concerning our redemption; the next cause of our saluation is our vocation: for, whomsoeuer the Lord hath elected vnto euerlasting life, those also he hath redeemed out of the hands of their spirituall enemies; and whom he hath redeemed, those in his good time he effectually calleth, and applieth this great benefit of their redemption vnto them, by separating them from the world, and ingrafting them into the body of Christ, whereby they become his, and he with all his benefits becometh theirs.

VVhat our calling is.

In speaking hereof, I will shew first what this calling is, and afterwards answere Sathans temptations, whereby he laboreth to make it frustrate and vnprofitable vnto vs. For the first, our vocation or calling is an effect of Gods election, whereby our Sauiour Christ, God and man, doth by his kingly authoritie call and inuite vs whilst we liue here, vnto the participation and imbracing of the inestimable benefit of our redemption, that thereby we may attaine vnto euerlasting life.

And thus are we called sometimes sooner, and sometimes later, when it seemeth good vnto the Lord: as appeareth in the parable of the housholder, who hired laborers into his vineyard, some at the dawning of the day, others at the third, sixt, and ninth howre, others at the eleuenth howre, not long before the sunne setting, as it is Matth.20.

Matth.20.

A twofold calling, generall and effectuall.

Moreouer, this our calling, is either commune and generall, or els speciall and effectuall. The general calling is, whereby all indifferently, good and bad, elect and reprobate, are outwardly inuited by the ministerie of the Gospell, to imbrace the benefit of our redemption wrought by Christ : which outward calling is vneffectuall to the wicked and reprobates, because being inuited to the supper of the King they refuse to come, that is, they either altogether neglect the hearing of the heauenly ambassage of the Gospell, or els contemne those inestimable benefits which are therein offered, preferring before them the honors, riches, and pleasures of this life ; whereby it commeth

commeth to paffe, th it the word of God findeth no place in their hearts, but vanisheth away, leauing nothing behinde it but the fauour of death, to their more deepe condemnation.

The fpeciall and effectuall calling is, that which is proper to Gods elect, when as with the outward minifterie of the word, wherein grace and faluation is offered to all beleeuers, our Sauiour Chrift ioyneth the inward operation of his holy fpirit; which openeth our deafe eares, inlighteneth our blind vnderftandings, and foftneth and fanctifieth our hard and corrupt hearts, fo as we attentiuely heare, truely vnderftand, and by a liuely faith apply, the doctrine of grace and faluation which is preached vnto vs: whereby alfo we are feparated from the world, giuen to Chrift and he to vs, whereupon followeth that neere vnion, whereby we being ingrafted into his body, miftically doe become his members, and he our head.

That this effectuall calling is proper to thofe that are elected and fhall be faued, it appeareth by the parable of the fupper, where many, outwardly inuited to the great fupper of the king, refufe to come, & therefore are excluded from the mariage, Mat.22.3. And Rom.8 30, the Apoftle faith *that whom he did predeftinate, them alfo he called, and thefe alfo he iuftifieth.* So Act.13.48. it is faid *that as many as were ordained to euerlafting life, beleeued* at the preaching of *Paul* and *Barnabas*, and therefore thefe onely were effectually called. And Ioh.6 45. our Sauiour faith, that *euery one who hath heard and hath learned of the father, commeth vnto him.* So that, outward hearing is not fufficient to bring vs to Chrift, vnleffe the father alfo inwardly inftruct vs with his holy fpirit, opening our deafe eares, inlightening our blynd vnderftandings, inclining our willes, and fanctifying our affections, that we may attentiuely heare, truely vnderftand, and heartily imbrace the Gofpell preached vnto vs. And this appeareth in the example of *Lydia*, Act.16.14. whofe heart the Lord is faid to haue opened, that fhe might attend vnto the things which *Paul* fpake, and bee conuerted: by which fpeech the holy Ghoft implyeth thus much, that her heart was (as it were) clofe fhut, and faft locked vp, fo as fhe could not receiue the word preached, till the Lord had opened it by the inward operation of his holy fpirit. Which matter neede not feeme ftrange vnto vs, feeing it is continually con-

§. Sect.2.
VVhat our effectuall calling is.

Effectuall calling proper to the elect.
Matth.22.3.8.
Rom.8.30.
Act.13.48.
Ioh.6.45.
Act.16.14.

X 4　　　　firmed

firmed by our owne experience: for how comes it to paffe that
many amongft vs, heare the word preached from day to day
and yeere to yeere, and yet are neuer the nearer, but still remaine as ignorant in their mindes, as peruerfe in their willes, as
corrupt in their affe-ctions, as prophane in their liues as euer
they were? On the other fide how hapneth it that fome attentiuely heare Gods word, treafure it vp in their memories, and
thereby haue their minds inlightned with the knowledge of
God, their wils inclined to holines and righteoufnes, their affe-ctions fan-ctified, their liues reformed? furely becaufe the
Lord doth ioyne in thefe, the inward operation of his fpirit
with the outward minifterie of his word, making it effe-ctuall
for their true conuerfion; whereas he leaueth the other to their
owne corrupt affe-ctions and hardnes of heart.

And thus it appeareth that the elect onely are effe-ctually
called: as for the wicked and reprobate, though they heare the
outward preaching of the word, by which they are inuited vnto Chrift; yet they ftubbornly refufe to come vnto him, and re-
ie-ct all the gracious promifes of the Gofpell, to their eternall
perdition; becaufe the Lord leaueth them to their owne lufts
and corruption, not opening their hard hearts, nor inclining
their peruerfe willes nor fan-ctifying their corrupt affe-ctions.

§. Sect.3.
Of the parts of
effe-ctuall cal-
ling, and firft
of our fepara-
tion from the
world.

In the next place let vs confider, the parts of our effe-ctuall
calling; the firft is our feparation from the world, of which in
former time wee were citizens and true members, that from
henceforth we fhould be of Gods houfehold and family: for
naturally we are meere worldlings, dead in our finnes, and to
euery good worke reprobate, liuing without God and feruing Sathan, the world and the corrupt lufts of our flefh, vntill
it pleafe the Lord to make choyfe of vs among many other,
calling and feparating vs from this corrupt maffe of mankind,
that he may make vs fubie-cts, firft of his kingdome of grace,
and afterwards of his kingdome of glorie. Of this our Sauiour

Ioh.15.19.

fpeaketh Ioh.15.19.*If you were of the world, the world would loue
his owne; but becaufe you are not of the world, but I haue chofen you
out of the world, therefore the world hateth you.* And the Apoftle

Eph.2.19.

faith that after our calling and conuerfion, we are *no more ftrangers and forreners, but citizens with the faints, and of the houfehold
of God.* Now the Lord maketh this choyfe of vs before others,

not

not for any respect of worthines or excellencie in vs more then *That the Lord* in them, but of his meere mercie, vndeserued grace, and free *calleth vs, not* good will; neither doth he therefore intertaine vs into his *for any respect,* Church and family, becaufe wee are alreadie, or becaufe hee *of our own wor-* knoweth we will bee hereafter holy and righteous; but ha- *thines.* uing freely called vs without any our deferts,he doth alfo of his owne vndeferued loue giue vs his holy fpirit, whereby we are purged from our corruptions,fanctified and raifed vp from the death of finne to newnes of life; fo that our holines is not a caufe of our calling,but Gods election and calling is a caufe of our holines. And this appeareth both by teftimonies of Scrip- ture and examples. For the firft, the Lord profeffeth, Efa.65.1. *Efa.65.1.* that he offered himfelfe *to thofe that asked not after him, and was found of them that fought him not &c.* The Apoftle Ephef.2.1. affirmeth that euen thofe who are the Church and people of God,were before their calling and conuerfion, not ficke only, but euen *dead in their fins, in which they walked according to the course of the world; that they were by nature the children of wrath* *Eph.2.1.3.12.* *as well as others,* as it is verf.3. *and that they were without Chrift, aliants from the common-wealth of Ifraell, ftrangers from the co- uenant of promife, and had no hope, and were without God in the world,* as it is verf.12. So 1.Cor.6.11. he faith, that thofe who were now fanctified and iuftified,were in time paft fornicators, *1.Cor.6.11.* idolators,adulterers, wantons, buggerers &c. The Apoftle *Pe- ter* likewife writing to the Church of Chrift, faith both of him- felfe and them alfo, that they had fpent the time paft before their conuerfiõ,after *the luft of the gentiles,walking in wantonnes,* *1.Pet.4.3.* *luft,drunkennes,gluttonie,and in abominable idolatries,* 1.Pet.4.3. And the Prophet *Efay* faith,that we al were wandering fheepe, *Efa.53.6.* vntill the Lord gathered vs into his fheepefold. So that it was fo far of, that we fhould deferue any grace or mercie at Gods hand that in his iuftice he might rather haue confumed vs as his enemies, than called vs to be his Church and people.

This alfo is plaine in the examples fpecified in the booke of God: for,what excellencie or worthines was in *Abraham* who before his calling was an idolater? or in *Rahab* who had fpent her time in luft and filthines? or in *Manaffes* who was a cruell idolater, a murtherer, a forcerer? or in *Matthew* who was a publicane? or in *Paul* who was a bloodie perfecutor? or in the thiefe

thiefe, who had spent his life in al outrage and wickednes? what
excellencie or defert was in any of vs, who haue not fo much
as a thought, or inclination to any good thing, or any power
to performe it? and therefore we muft conclude with the Apoftle, that *we are called with an holy calling, not according to our*
workes, but according to his owne purpofe of grace, &c. 2.Tim.1.9.

2.Tim 1.9.

§. *Sect.*4.
Of the fecond
part of our ef-
fectuall calling,
to wit, our reci-
procall donati-
on.

  The fecond part of effectuall calling, is that reciprocall donation whereby God the father giueth Chrift Iefus his onely
begotten fonne, truely and effectually to al his elect, to be their
head, redeemer, and Sauiour; and alfo whereby he giueth his
elect vnto Chrift to become his members, that fo they may be
faued and redeemed by him: whereupon all Gods elect may
truly fay, that this Chrift Iefus, God and man, is mine head, my
Sauiour and redeemer; and all his merits obedience and benefits, purchafed by both, are become mine by this right, as being a member of his bodie; and our Sauiour alfo, may as truely
fay of Gods elect, that they are his whom he hath right to redeeme and faue, becaufe hee is their head and they his members. Of this mutuall donation and gift, the Scriptures fpeake
euidently; and firft that Chrift is giuen vnto vs; *Efa.9.6. Vnto*
vs a childe is borne, and vnto vs a fonne is giuen. Ioh.3.16. So God
loued the world, that he gaue his onely begotten fonne, that whofo-
euer beleeueth in him fhould not perifh, but haue euerlafting life.
Rom.8.32. Secondly, that we are giuen vnto Chrift, it is manifeft, *Ioh.17.6. I haue declared thy name vnto the men which thou*
gaueft me out of the world, thine they were and thou gaueft them
me, &c. So. *Ioh.10.29. My father which gaue them me is greater*
then all, and none is able to take them out of my fathers hand. By
which places it plainely appeareth, that Chrift is giuen vnto vs
by God his father, and we vnto Chrift. But in what manner is
this mutuall donation made? furely not grofely and corporally; but fpiritually & after a celeftiall manner: for the meanes
whereby it is brought to paffe on Gods part, is his diuine and
holy fpirit, and on our part a true and liuely faith.

Efa 9.6.
Ioh.3.16.

Rom.8.32.
Ioh.17.6.

Ioh.10.29.

§. *Sect.*5.
Of the third
part viz. our
vnion with
Chrift.

  The third part of effectuall calling, is the vnion and communion which is betwixt Chrift and Gods elect: which followeth
vpon the donation before fpoken of, whereby Chrift Iefus and
they are miftically coupled together into one body, hee becomming their head and they becomming his members. Of
this

this the Apostle speaketh Ephes.4.15.16.where hee exhorteth
the faithful, *to grow vp into him which is the head, that is Christ,* Eph.4.15.
by whom all the bodie being coupled together by euery ioynt &c.re-
ceiueth increase. And chap.5.30. *We are members of his bodie, of* and 5.30.
*his flesh, and of his bones.*And of this our Sauiour Christ speaketh
in the parable of the vine Ioh.15.1.where he copareth himselfe Ioh.15.1.
to the stock & root, and al the faithful to the branches; and the
Apostle expresseth it by a metaphoricall speech taken from a
building, comparing Christ to the foundation, and the Church
to the rest of the building, Eph.2.20.21.22. Now wee must not Eph.2.20.21.
conceiue of this vnion, that it is either natural, as the three persons in Trinitie are vnited in the same diuine nature, or perso-
nall as the bodie and soule being vnited make one man, or
corporall as the parts of a building are coupled one with another: but this coniunction and vnion is made by the spirit of
God, which dwelling in the manhood of christ aboue measure,
filling it with the graces thereof, is from it deriued vnto all the
faithfull and true members of Christs bodie, filling them with
the like graces in measure; and on our part by a true and liuely faith, whereby we doe applie vnto vs Christ Iesus and all his
benefits.And this appeareth Eph.2.22.where the Apostle saith
that *wee are the habitation of God by the spirit.* And 1.Ioh 4.13. Eph.2.22.
Hereby we know that we dwell in him and he in vs,because he hath 1.Ioh.4.13.
*giuen vs of his spirit.*So that by the spirit of God dwelling in vs,
we are made one with Christ and Christ with vs.Now the manner whereby this vnion is made is this; the faithful man, body
and soule, is vnited vnto whole Christ God and man; but first
and immediatly to the humane nature, and mediatly thereby
to the diuine nature, both which are most necessarie; for life
and saluation is wrought for vs by vertue and power of the
Deitie, but it is deriued and communicated vnto vs by the humane nature of Christ. According to that Ioh.6.54. *Whosoeuer* Ioh.6.54.
eateth my flesh and drinketh my bloud, hath eternall life, and I will
raise him vp at the last day. And this is the vnion which is betweene Christ our head and vs his members, by vertue whereof we haue sure interest and iust title, both to Christ and all his
benefits, his obedience death and merits, by which we are iustified, sanctified and saued.

  And so much concerning the parts of our effectuall calling;
             the §. Sect.6.

the meanes whereby the Lord thus calleth vs, are firſt on Gods part the preaching of the word, which is made effectuall by the inward operation of his ſpirit; firſt to mollifie our hard hearts, and truly to humble vs, by ſetting before vs our ſinnes and corruptions, and this is done by the preaching of the law: and after wee ſee our inabilitie and inſufficiencie of working our owne ſaluation, we are thereby brought out of our ſelues, to ſeeke for ſaluation in Chriſt Ieſus, applying him and his merits vnto vs by a true and a liuely faith, and this is done by the preaching of the Goſpell.

The meanes on our part is the ſauing hearing of the word, whereby our hard hearts are mollified, and we truly humbled, and brought out of our ſelues to ſeeke for ſaluation in Chriſt, whereby alſo true faith is begot in vs, wherewith wee applie Chriſt vnto vs, and relie vpon him alone for our ſaluation.

And thus haue I ſhewed what our vocation is, and the means therof. Now let vs conſider of thoſe temptations, which Sathan ſuggeſteth into mens minds in reſpect of their vocation, to the end hee may hinder them from the participation and fruition of Chriſt and his benefits, whereunto in the preaching of the word they are called and inuited. And theſe are of two ſorts, firſt thoſe wherewith he aſſaulteth them who are not called: ſecondly, thoſe wherewith he aſſaulteth them who are truly called and conuerted.

CHAP. XVIII.

Sathans temptations whereby he ſeeketh to make our calling vneffectuall, anſwered.

THoſe who are not called hee tempteth diuers waies, that he may hinder their effectuall calling; and firſt he laboureth to perſwade them, to neglect this their calling as a thing not neceſſarie, and to contemne the miniſterie of the word, which is the meanes whereby we are effectuallie called.

But we are to withſtand theſe temptations: and to this end wee are firſt to know, that before our effectuall calling wee are not true members of the Church, though wee may outwardly thruſt our ſelues into this ſocietie; for what els is the Church but

but that companie or congregation which is truly called and
felected out of the world ? and from hence it hath it name, for
it is called *Ecclefia* ἀπὸ τῦ καλεῖν, from the calling thereof: vnleffe
therefore we be called we are not members of the Church, and
if wee bee out of the Church there is no faluation; for our Sauiour gaue himfelfe for his Church alone, and he is the *Sauiour*
of his owne bodie, as it is Eph. 5.23.25. and he addeth *daily vnto*   Eph. 5.23.25.
the Church fuch as fhall be faued, as it is Act. 2.47.   Act. 2. 47.

Moreouer, vnleffe we be truly called we fhall neuer be truly
iuftified, and without iuftification there is no glorification: for   Rom. 8.30.
this is the goldē chaine of our faluatiō, as appeareth Rom. 8. 30.

Laftly, wee can neuer come vnto Chrift, nor communicate
with him in any of his benefits, nor receiue any fanctifying and
fauing grace of Gods fpirit, till by the grace of God wee are
made partakers of this holie calling ; for naturally wee are
meere worldlings, deftitute of all grace and goodneffe, and fo
we remaine till by this holy calling we are feparated from the
world, and ingrafted into the bodie of Chrift, by whofe fpirit
we are quickened who were dead in our finnes, and haue fanctifying graces begotten nourifhed and increafed in vs.

Seeing therefore this our effectuall calling is fo neceffarie,
let not Sathan perfwade vs to neglect it, neither let vs when
the Lord inuiteth vs to this royall feaft pretend excufes, one
that he muft goe fee his farme, another that hee muft goe trie   Matth. 22.
his oxen, a third that he muft goe about his merchandize, and   Luk. 14.
a fourth that he is hindred by a carnall mariage : for if we will
not come when the Lord inuiteth vs, like vnworthie guefts we
fhall be fhut out of the doores, and not fuffred to be partakers
of this banquet of eternall bleffedneffe. *Whileft to day we heare*   Pfal. 95.7.8.
his voyce let vs not harden our hearts, for hee hath not promifed
that he will call againe to morrow, whileft now he ftandeth at
the doore and knocketh and calleth for entrance, let vs hearing his voyce open the doore of our hearts, that he may come
in and fup with vs and we with him ; for if vnkindly wee denie   Reuel. 3.20.
him entertainment, we can haue no affurance that hee will returne againe to fuch churlifh and vngratefull hoafts. In a word,
feeing the Lord pafsing by many other in the world maketh
choife of vs, calling and inuiting vs to the participation and
fruition of eternall bleffedneffe and happineffe, let no worldly
bufineffe,

Matth.8.21.

buſineſſe,though it ſeeme as neceſſarie as the burying of our deare father, hinder vs from harkening and obeying this heauenly call; let no tranſitorie trifle ſtay vs from comming to God,when hee offreth to make vs good aſſurance of his royall kingdome : for though many things bee conuenient, yet one thing is neceſſarie , and thrice happie are they which make choiſe of the better part.

§. Sect.2.

Sathans temptations where-by he moueth vs to neglect the meanes of our effectuall calling.

But it is impoſſible that euer we ſhould be truly called, vnles we carefully vſe the meanes when the Lord offreth them vnto vs,and attentiuely liſten vnto the Lords voyce when hee inuiteth vs to come vnto him : and therfore Sathan laboureth,not ſo much to perſwade vs that our vocation is a thing vnneceſſarie vnto ſaluation,ſeeing this is manifeſtly repugnant to plaine teſtimonies of ſcriptures,as to mooue vs to neglect the meanes whereby we are called, namely the miniſterie of Gods word : partly working vpon our inbred corruption, which not conceiuing the things of God condemneth them of fooliſhnes, and not being delighted with thoſe things which it vnderſtandeth not, they ſeeme irkſome and tedious; and partly inticing vs with the commodities and pleaſures of the world, which are more pleaſant to carnall men than their meate and drinke, hee cauſeth vs to ſpend that time in our earthly buſineſſes or vain delights,which we ſhould beſtow in the hearing of Gods word,whereby we ſhould be effectually called, that is, ſeparated from the world, and ingrafted as liuely members into the bodie of Chriſt Ieſus.

Motiues to per-ſwade to the diligent hea-ring of Gods word.
The firſt mo-tiue.

Let vs therefore ſtrongly arme our ſelues againſt this temption, as being moſt pernitious vnto our owne ſoules : and to this end let vs briefly conſider of ſome reaſons, whereby wee may be ſtirred vp diligētly to frequent Gods holy aſſemblies, to be made partakers of this heauenly ambaſſage. Firſt therefore wee are to know, that the miniſterie of the word is Gods owne ordinance,which he hath inſtituted and ordained *for the gathering together of the Saints, and building the bodie of his*

Eph.4.11.12.

*Church,*as appeareth Eph.4.11.12.Neither doth he vſe ordinarily any other meanes (eſpecially where this is to bee had) for the true conuerſion of his children,and for the working of the ſanctifying graces of his ſpirit in them. And therefore though he could by extraordinary meanes,haue ſufficiently inſtructed the

the Eunuch in the waies of ſaluation, yet he would not, but rather vſeth his owne ordinance, and ſendeth *Philip* to preach
vnto him, Act.8. Though hee could haue illuminated the eyes
and vnderſtanding of *Paul*, by the immediat worke of his ſpi- | Act.8.
rit, yet hee choſe rather to ſend him to *Ananias*, Act.9.6.17. | Act.9 6.17.
Though hee could by the miniſterie of his Angel, haue ſufficiently infourmed *Cornelius* in things neceſſarie to ſaluation,
yet he would not offer ſo great diſparagement to his owne or-
dinance, and therefore he cauſeth him to ſend for the Apoſtle | Act.10.5.6.
Peter, Act.10.5.6. And therefore if wee would haue any aſſurance, of our effectual calling and true conuerſion vnto God,
let vs with all care and diligence heare the word of God preached vnto vs.

Secondly, let vs conſider that it is euen God himſelfe, who | *The ſecond*
ſpeaketh by the mouthes of his Ambaſſadours, and that they | *motiue.*
come not in their owne names but in Chriſts ſtead, to intreate
vs that we would be reconciled vnto God, as it is 2.Cor.5.20; | 2.Cor.5.20.
that though they bee but earthen veſſels, yet they bring from
God a heauenly treaſure, which heretofore hath been hid from
the world, and is yet hid to thoſe that periſh, 2.Cor.4.7. And | 2.Cor.4.7.
héce it is that the Prophets, being to pronounce their prophecies, ſtill begin with, *The Word of the Lord*, and, *Thus ſaith the
Lord*; and God himſelfe ſending *Ieremie* to preach, ſaith, that
he had put *his words into his mouth*, Iere.1.9. Whoſoeuer there- | Iere.1 9.
fore refuſe to heare the word of God preached, refuſe to heare
the Lord himſelfe, as our Sauiour plainly affirmeth Luk.10.16. | Luk.10.16.
*He that heareth you heareth me, and he that deſpiſeth you deſpi-
ſeth me*; and what hope can they haue of comming vnto God,
who cannot endure to heare his voyce calling them vnto him?

Thirdly, the titles which are giuen vnto the word in the | §. Sect.3.
Scriptures, may ſerue as ſtrong arguments to moue vs careful- | *The third*
ly to heare the ſame: for it is called the miniſterie of reconci- | *motiue.*
liation, whereby we are reconciled vnto God, 2.Cor.5.18. and | 2.Cor.5.18.
therfore without it, there being no other ordinarie meanes of
reconciliation, we remaine ſtill Gods enemies. It is called the
Goſpell of peace, Eph.6.15. without which wee haue neither | Eph.6.15.
peace with God, nor the peace of conſcience; It is called the
word of grace, Act.14.3, and 18.32, becauſe it is the meanes | Act.14.3.
whereby the Lord deriueth vnto vs his grace and mercie, and
all

all the fpirituall graces of his fanctifying fpirit; It is called the word of life, Phil.2.16. and the word of faluation, Act.13.26. becaufe it is the meanes wherby we are faued out of the hands of fpirituall enemies, and are certainly affured of euerlafting life and happineffe; It is called the kingdome of God, Matth. 13.44.becaufe thereby we are brought, firft into the kingdom of grace, and afterwards into the kingdome of glorie; It is that heauenly feede whereby we are begotten vnto God, in which refpect the minifters thereof are called fpiritual fathers,1.Cor. 4.15. and therefore without it wee can neuer be regenerated and borne vnto God; It is the foode of our foules, euen milke for babes, and ftrong meate for men of ripe yeares,1.Cor.3.2. Heb.5.12.whereby we are nourifhed vnto euerlafting life :and therefore let vs not refufe this heauenly foode like waiward children when our heauenly father offreth it vnto vs, for fo our foules being hunger-ftarued, nothing can follow but eternall death and deftruction; It is the phificke of our foules, whereby being ficke in finne they are cured and reftored : for as Chrift is our heauenly phyfition, fo is his word the potion which hee giueth to purge vs from our corruptions, and the preferuatiue which confirmeth vs in health, and preferueth vs from the leprous infection of finne, yea this phyfick is fo foueraigne, that though with *Lazarus* wee haue lien dead in our graues foure daies, that is, continued long in our naturall corruptions, yet this phyficke being applied will raife vs vp to newneffe of life; and therefore thofe who neglect this diuine phyficke, are fubiect to all infection of finne, and being infected can neuer attaine to their health againe. It is the fquare and rule of our liues, from which wee muft not decline neither on the right hand nor on the left, Deut.5.32. and therefore without it our workes muft needs be crooked in Gods fight. It is a lanthorne to our feete, and a light vnto our paths, Pfal.119.105, whereby wee are guided in the waies of holineffe and righteoufneffe which leade vs to euerlafting happineffe, which being taken away we fhall walk in darkneffe, and be euery ftep readie to fall into fin and eternall deftruction. It is the fword of the fpirit, wherewith we defend our felues and offend our fpirituall enemies,Eph.6.17; which being neglected, or not skilfully vfed, we fhall lie open to all thrufts and blowes, and be eafily ouercome.

Marginal references:
- Phil.2.16.
- Act.13.26.
- Matth.13.44.
- 1.Cor.4.15.
- 1.Cor.3.2.
- Heb.5.12.
- Deut 5.32.
- Pfal.119.105.
- Eph.6.17.

come. In a word, it is profitable for all vses, as being the onely ordinarie meanes ordained to conuey vnto vs all good, and to preserue vs from all euill : and therefore great folly it is for any man to contemne it, or to preferre before it vaine pleasures, or trifling commodities, which also are momentanie and vncertaine.

Fourthly, the manifold benefits which by the word of God are deriued vnto vs, may serue as a strong argument to stirre vs vp to the diligent and carefull hearing thereof; for first thereby we become true members of the Church, out of which there is no saluation, and being ingrafted into the body of Christ, are made partakers of all his benefits. And this appeareth Eph. 4.11.12, where the Apostle sheweth that the end of the ministerie is *for the gathering together of the saints, and for the edification of the body of Christ.* A notable example whereof wee haue Act.2.41.where, by one sermon three thousand soules were added to the Church. Secondly, hereby we are regenerated and begotten vnto God, and therefore in this respect *Paul* professeth himselfe, the father of the Corinthians 1.Cor.4.15. and without this regeneration and new birth, none shall euer enter into the kingdome of God, as our Sauiour sheweth vs, Ioh.3.5. Thirdly, vnlesse the blinde eyes of our vnderstandings be illuminated, we shall fall into a laborinth of errors, and neuer finde the hard way which leadeth to Gods kingdome ; but the word of God is that heauenly light, which shineth vnto vs *who sit in darkenes, and in the shadow of death, guiding our feete into the way of peace,* as it is Luk.1.79. and in this respect, Gods ministers ars called the light of the world, Math.5.14. Act.13. 47. because, as lights, they guide and direct men in the waies of saluation, and reueale vnto them the great light, euen the Sunne of righteousnes, Christ Iesus. Fourthly, *through faith we are saued,* Ephes.2.8. Neither is it possible, that without faith wee should euer attaine vnto saluation, for this is the condition of all the promises of the Gospell, without which wee cannot haue any assurance of them, Ioh.1.12. and 3.16.18. Moreouer, *whatsoeuer is not done of faith is sinne,* Rom.14.23. *And without faith it is impossible to please God,* Heb.11.6. But the preaching of the word is the ordinarie meanes of begetting faith in vs, as appeareth Rom.10.17. *Faith commeth by hearing,*

§. Sect.4.
The fourth motiue.

Eph.4.11.12.

Act.2.41.

1.Cor.4.15.

Ioh.3.5.

Luk.1.79.
Matth.5.14.
Act.13.47.

Eph.2.8.

Ioh.1 12.
and 3 16.18.
Rom.14.23.
Heb.11.6.

Rom.10.17.

Y   and

and hearing by the word of God. And therefore whofoeuer contemne or neglect the hearing of Gods word, they refufe the
meanes of faith; and being without faith, all they doe is finne,
and cannot pleafe God, neither can they euer haue any affurance of Gods promifes, or their owne faluation. Laftly, by the
hearing of Gods word we are faued, and therefore Gods minifters in this refpect are called Sauers of the people, 1.Tim.

1.Tim.4.16.

4.16. *Take heede vnto thy felfe and vnto learning*; *continue therein,for in fo doing thou fhalt both faue thy felfe and them that heare
thee*; becaufe they are the minifters of God, whom he vfeth as
meanes, and inftruments in working the faluation of the elect:
and therfore feeing by the preaching of the word, we are made
members of the body of Chrift, regenerated & inlightned; feeing therby we attaine vnto faith, & euerlafting faluation, let vs
as we loue our owne foules, diligently heare the word, and not
fuffer our felues to be hindred from frequenting the holy af-
femblies of Gods faints, with euery vaine pleafure and bafe
commoditie.

§. *Sect.5.*
*Sathans temp-
tations, where-
by he with-
draweth men
from the di-
ligent hea-
ring of Gods
word, anfwe-
red.*

But here the tempter wil be readie to object, that though the
word preached be thus neceffarie and profitable at fometimes
when we are at leafure, yet this fhould be no reafon to moue
vs to neglect our bufines, or abandon our pleafures ; for when
once by the hearing thereof we are conuerted, inlightned with
the knowledge of Gods true religion, and indued with faith, it
is fufficient if we but feldome heare it; for what in fubftance can
we learne, which we haue not alreadie learned, or what can the
preacher teach vs, which we doe not know as well as he ? A-
gainft which temptation, which is fo common and pernicious,
it behooueth euery chriftian moft carefully to arme himfelfe;
and to this end let vs know, firft that this neglect of Gods
word is a manifeft figne that fuch are not as yet truely conuerted, nor indued with any meafure of fauing knowledge and

Ioh.8.47.
and 10.27.

true faith ; for *Whofoeuer are of God heare his Word*, Ioh.8.47;
and all Chrifts *fheepe heare his voyce and follow him*, as it is Ioh.
10.3.4.27. Whofoeuer haue attained vnto knowledge, faith,
and the reft of the graces of Gods fanctifying fpirit, they will
be fo rauifhed with the excellencie of them, that it is not poffible for them to content themfelues with a fmall meafure, but
ftill they will labour to grow from knowledge to knowledge,
from

from faith to faith, from one grace to another, till they become perfect men in Chrift. And as thofe who haue but once tafted of fome delicious meate, are not fatiffied therewith, but againe and againe feede vpon it if eafily they may come by it, becaufe their tafte is exceedingly delighted therewith; fo if euer we did but truely tafte of this heauenly Manna, and fpirituall foode of our foules, the word of God, we would not reft fo contented, but when oportunitie is offered, we would often feede vpon it, vntill our foules were fully fatiffied, and nourifhed vnto perfect ftrength; and forafmuch as fo long as we continue here, our knowledge is but in part and our faith weake, and Gods graces but in fmall meafure, therefore we would continually feede on this heauenly nourifhment, to the end of our liues, that thereby our knowledge may be increafed, our faith ftrengthned, and all other graces confirmed and multiplied in vs. But if on the otherfide we loath this heauenly Manna, it is a manifeft figne, we neuer tafted thereof in truth, or that our foules are exceeding ficke in finne, which maketh them that they cannot rellifh this daintie and delicious foode, and that we haue not knowledge, faith, or any grace begotten in vs, neither that our felues are begotten vnto God. For as the childe being begotten and conceiued, doth prefently draw nourifhment from the mother; and the bigger it waxeth, the more it defireth till it come vnto perfect age and ftrength : fo as foone as the graces of Gods fpirit are begotten in vs by the preaching of the word, they draw nourifhment from their fpiritual mother, the Church; and the ftronger they waxe in grace, the more earneftly they defire a greater pittance till they become perfect men in Chrift. And therefore where there is no defire of this foode, there is no regeneration nor new birth.

1. Cor. 11.13.

Moreouer the word of God is the foode of our foules, whereby we are nourifhed, and the graces of Gods fpirit confirmed and increafed in vs ; and therefore it is not fufficient to eate of this foode once or twice, but continually, euen as often as the Lord calleth vs to this fpirituall banquet. For as the body will waxe faint, and quickly perifh, vnleffe that which wafteth away be continually fupplied by nourifhment: fo will the foule languifh and waxe faint in fpirituall graces, vnleffe it be often nourifhed with this heauenly Manna. Let not therefore

Gods word, the food of our foules, often to be receiued.

fore

fore Sathan perſwade vs, that ſeldome hearing of Gods word
is ſufficient,whereas this banquet is often prouided;for though
in the time of ſcarcitie by the extraordinarie bleſſing of God,
wee may goe with *Elias* fortie daies in the ſtrength of one
meale,yet if we feede no oftner when the Lord graunteth vnto
vs plentifull prouiſion of the ſpirituall foode, our ſoules will
be hungerſtarued. Neither let our often receiuing of this heauenly nouriſhment, cauſe vs with the vnthankfull Iſraelits to
loath it,or like wayward children, or impacient ſicke patients,
ſpit it out of our mouthes againe; for if our appetites be thus
cloyed through a ſurfet of ſatietie, ſurely we are to feare, leaſt
the Lord who is a cunning phyſition, will preſcribe vs a long
faſt, till we haue recouered our ſtomackes, as he threatneth

Amos.8.11. Amos 8.11. *I will ſend a famine in the land, not a famine of bread
nor a thirſt of water, but of hearing the word of the Lord. And
then we ſhall wander from ſea to ſea, and from the North euen to
the Eaſt ſhall we runne to and fro to ſeeke the word of the Lord and
ſhall not finde it.*

§. Sect.6.
*That we ſhould
often heare,
though we had
ſufficient know-
ledge.*

Laſtly, though it ſhould be graunted that we had attained
vnto ſuch a meaſure of knowledge, that we ſhould neede no
more, yet are there many reaſons why we ſhould continually
heare Gods word with as great diligence as euer we did; for
the end of our hearing is not onely to know, but alſo to practiſe;not only to informe our iudgements, but alſo to reforme
our affections; not onely to beget the graces of Gods ſpirit in
vs,but alſo to nouriſh and increaſe them ; not onely to teach vs
what we ſhould doe,but alſo to ſtirre vs vp to the doing thereof ; and the word of God is not onely a light for our feete to
ſhew vs the way, but alſo a pricke in our ſides to make vs goe
in the way,and a bridle in our mouthes to keepe vs from wandering; it is not onely *profitable to teach,but to improue,to correct and inſtruct in righteouſnes. That the man of God may be abſolute,being made perfect vnto all good workes,* as it is,2.Tim.3.16.
2.Tim.3.16. it is not onely profitable for doctrine, but for edification, exhortation and conſolation, as appeareth, 1.Cor. 14.3. And
1.Cor.14.3. therefore it is not ſufficient to come once or twice to the aſſemblies of Gods ſaints, but we muſt aboue all things deſire
with the prophet *Dauid,* that we may dwell in the houſe *of the*
Pſal.27.4. *Lord all the daies of our life, to behold the beautie of the Lord, and*

tc

to viſit his temple, Pſal.27.4. For though our knowledge be neuer ſo great, yet ſo long as we haue any ſinne hanging on, or
any grace imperfeƈt in vs, we had neede to be continuall hearers of Gods word, for the ſuppreſſing of the one and perfeƈt-
ing of the other.

CHAP. XIX.

*Sathans temptation, ℣hereby hee perſwadeth men that the
Scriptures are not Gods word, anſwered.*

He ſecond temptation which Sathan ſuggeſteth into   §. Seƈt. 1.
mens mindes, to the end he may moue them to neg- *The temptati-*
leƈt the hearing of Gods word, or though they doe *on.*
heare it, to reieƈt it through vnbeliefe, he thus frameth. What
folly is it to take ſuch paines in hearing the ſcripture, and what
madnes is it ſo ſtedfaſtly to beleeue it, ſeeing thou knoweſt not
whether it be Gods word, or the ſubtill deuiſe of mans braine,
to keepe the people in awe, and to reſtraine them from ſuch
ſecret faults, as other humane lawes ratified and confirmed
with temporall and outward puniſhments and rewards cannot keepe them from; becauſe the lawes of princes cannot (no
more than the lawgiuers themſelues) either foreſee, preuent or
puniſh any faults and offences, which are not open and manifeſt? why ſhouldeſt thou thereby be moued to forſake thy delightfull ſinnes, and to imbrace vnpleaſant godlines, to abandon thy pleaſures, and to vndertake an auſtere and ſtriƈt courſe
of life, ſeeing thou knoweſt not whether the ſcriptures be true
or falſe, the word of the euerlaſting God or the inuention of
mortall man.

   Againſt which temptation it behoueth euery man moſt *The anſuvere:*
carefully to arme himſelfe, as vndermining the very foundati- *that all religi-*
on of all true religion; for take away the authoritie of the *on dependeth*
ſcriptures and you ſhall open a wide dore to all carnall world- *vpon the autho-*
lines, beaſtly epicuriſme, and diueliſh atheiſme; they being the *ritie of the*
onely true rule of vertue, whereby we are direƈted to chuſe the *Scriptures.*
good and refuſe the euill; the ſcepter of God whereby he ruleth all the ſubieƈts of his kingdome, which being reieƈted we
giue ouer our ſelues to be ruled by the diuell, and the luſts of
our owne fleſh; the light of our eyes without which wee are

blind and walke in darkenes;the foode of our foules which being taken away, they languifh in all fpirituall graces, and fall into miferable death and deftruction; and the fworde of the fpirit whereby wee defend our felues, and beate backe our fpirituall enemies, which being plucked out of our hand, we are eafily vanquifhed and led captiue vnto all finne and wickednes.

And that we may be the better prouided againft this temptation, let vs propound fome reafons whereby gainefayers may be conuinced, and Gods children perfwaded of the truth and authoritie of the fcripture. The firft argument to proue the fcriptures to be written by the motion and reuelation of Gods fpirit,is the antiquitie thereof; for whatfoeuer religion is moft auncient, that proceedeth from God: but the religion contained in the fcriptures, is of all other moft auncient: and therefore God was the author thereof. The firft part of this reafon is cleere and manifeft; for feeing man was created for Gods glorie,to the end he fhould worfhip and ferue him,and could not performe acceptable worfhip and feruice vnto God,vnleffe he reuealed his wil vnto him;therfore, that man might attaine vnto the end of his creation,it was neceffarie that the Lord fhould from the beginning reueale vnto him his true religion, whereby he might know how to worfhip and ferue him, according to his will. And confequently, the firft and moft auncient religion is the true religion, which proceeded from God; and all other are falfe and counterfait, which are difagreeing and repugnant hereunto, feeing Gods will is one and the fame,conftant and immutable. The fecond part of this reafon, namely that the religion deliuered in the fcriptures is of all others moft auncient, is of vndoubted truth; for it is within a few daies as auncient as the world it felfe, taking it beginning from mans creation, and fo continuing in a conftant and vnchangeable courfe vnto this day. Now all other religions are but new and vpftart in comparifon hereof, taking their beginnings diuers thoufand yeares fince the creation; yea euen the Gods themfelues which they worfhip (which intruth were men like themfelues) had their beginning for the moft part, long fince the time of *Abraham*, as their owne hiftories manifeftly declare. Neither did any other religion of the heathen continue one
and

and the ſame; for that which one receiued another reiected, that which one confirmed another changed, and time hath worne them all out, leauing ſcarce any ſmall remnants or reliques of them. And therefore all other religions, ſauing that which is deliuered in the ſcriptures, are falſe and counterfet; and this only the truth of God.

Secondly, the puritie and perfection of the ſcriptures, doe euidently ſhew that they are the word of God, indited by his holy ſpirit; for they manifeſt vnto vs the onely true God, and propound him alone vnto vs, to be worſhipped, expreſſing alſo the manner and meanes of his ſeruice, from which we muſt not decline on the right hand, or on the left: but all other religions teach vs either to worſhip many Gods, which is a thing abſurd in reaſon, and contrarie to the light of nature, as diuers of the wiſeſt philoſophers well diſcerned; or to worſhip the true God not according to his reuealed will, but according to their falſe imaginations, & erroneous ſuperſtitions. Now, nature, reaſon, and experience it ſelfe teach vs, that there is no wiſe King but will ſet downe rules and lawes, according to which he will be ſerued and obeyed, and not leaue it to euery ones fantaſie and vaine imagination; and ſhall we thinke God leſſe wiſe then man, that he ſhould not haue a perfect law for the gouernment of his people, but ſuffer euery man to follow his owne blind conceite and ignorant ſuperſtition?

§. Sect.3. 2. Reaſons taken from the puritie and perfection of the Scriptures.

Thirdly, the ſinceritie and vprightnes of the writers of the holy ſcriptures, is a manifeſt argument that they were guided and directed by Gods ſpirit; for they deliuer nothing in their owne name, but in the name of the Lord, not arrogating any praiſe vnto themſelues, but aſcribing all glorie vnto God; neither did they in their preachings or writings ſeeke themſelues, or ayme at any worldly benefit; nay rather they were content to be contemptible, ſubiect to ſcoffes and taunts, yea to offer themſelues to death, and depriuation of all worldly felicitie, for the truth of God which they had deliuered. And whereas diuers of them might haue liued in all pompe, if they would haue followed the times, winked at the ſinnes of rulers, and ſuppreſſed the word of the Lord, which they had receiued of him; they choſe rather to ſuffer perſecution, yea death it ſelfe, then they would keepe backe any of the counſell of God, as

§. Sect.4. 3. Reaſons taken from the ſinceritie of the writers of the Scriptures.

appeareth

appeareth in the example of *Esay, Ieremie, Ezechiel, Michæas, Zacharias, Amos,* and many others of the Prophets, and Apostles. Neither doe they in their writings abstaine onely from seeking their owne glorie and praise, but also set downe those things which might tend to their discredit, to the end God might be glorified in their infirmities, the truth confessed and preserued, and the Church of God benefited, when by seeing the weakenes of the most strong, they are kept from presuming on their owne strength, and from desparing in Gods mercie. And thus *Moses* concealeth not the fall of our grand parents, the drunkennes of *Noah,* the incest of *Lot,* the lie of *Isaack,* the whoredome of *Iudas*; nay which more neerely concerned him, he plainely reuealeth the horrible and bloodie sin of his grandfather *Leuy,* and *Simeon,* in murthering the Sichemites, and the curse of their father *Iacob* pronounced against them for this their outrage, Genes.49.5.6. which could not in humane reason but be dishonorable to his stocke & progenie, and offensiue to all who were of that tribe : furthermore he displayeth the corruptions, imperfections, and often rebellions of that people whose saluation hee preferred before his owne soule; he spareth not to set downe the Idolatrie of his own brothnr *Aaron,* nor the sinne of his sister *Miriam* in murmuring against him, nor of *Aarons* sonnes in offering with strange fire. Nay hee leaueth the remembrance of his owne sinne of impatiencie and vnbeliefe, for which hee was debarred from entring into the land of promise, vnto all posterities, as a perpetuall note of his owne weaknesse and infirmitie. Neither sought he at al his own glorie, and the aduancement of his posterity, but the glory of God & the good of the church, as may hereby appeare in that when the gouerment was established in his hand, he doth not make his owne sonnes his successours, but *Iosua* his seruant, because God had so appointed it. The like may be said of *Ieremie,* who hath in his prophecie left recorde of his murmuring and impatiencie, Iere. 20; Of *Ionas* who hath set downe his owne rebellion, punishment, and repining against God; Of the apostle *Paul* who hath not spared to call himselfe a cruell persecuter and chiefe of al sinners. Now we know that naturally, we desire to conceale the faults of our friendes and kindred, and we count him an euill bird that defileth

Gen.49.5.6.

Ierem.20.

fileth his owne neſt;naturally we ſeeke our own praiſe and the
aduancement of our children, and can brooke nothing leſſe
than that our faults ſhould bee diuulged and become table
talke : and therefore this detection of their owne and their
friends falles and faults could not proceed from nature,or any
worldly policie, but from the direction of Gods ſpirit which
ouerruled their affections,and tooke away all partialitie.

Fourthly, the wonderfull concent which is amongſt the diuers writers of the Scriptures, doth euidently ſhew that they
were guided and directed,by one and the ſame ſpirit of God :
for whereas it is truly ſaid of other men, *Quot homines tot ſen-*
tentiæ, Looke how many men there be, and ſo many mindes
there be ; wherof it commeth to paſſe that euery writer almoſt
varieth from another, gainſaying and confuting that which
another hath deliuered, that ſo out of the aſhes of their credit
and reputation they may build a monument of their owne
fame: the quite contrarie is to be obſerued in the writers of the
ſcriptures,who ſucceſſiuely writing one after another the ſpace
of diuers thouſand yeeres,doe notwithſtanding conſent together in the ſame truth, the later ratifying and confirming that
which the former had deliuered without any alteration,oppo-
ſition or emulation, as though they were diuers hands ſet on
worke by the ſame ſoule, which could not poſſibly come to
paſſe vnleſſe they were ouerruled by Gods ſpirit.

§. Sect.5.
The fourth
reaſon,taken
from the con-
cent of the di-
uers writers of
the Scriptures.

Fiftly, the mightie oppoſitions which haue been made by
the diuell and his wicked impes againſt this doctrine of the
ſcriptures,and yet al in vaine, doe euidently ſhew that they are
Gods word and truth, the patronage and protection whereof
he hath himſelfe vndertaken, aboue al humane reaſon and po-
wer.For hath not the diuell in former times, and doth hee not
ſtill at this day oppoſe himſelfe againſt the word of God ? and
doe not his curſed inſtruments,vngodly men,the more they
exceed in wickedneſſe the more bend their whole power malitiouſly to oppugne this truth, perſecuting the children of
God, for this cauſe onely that they are profeſſors and practi-
zers of Gods true religion ?And whence proceedeth this malitious oppoſition but from this, that the ſcriptures are the
word of God ? and therefore as they hate and oppoſe themſelues againſt God himſelfe, ſo alſo againſt his word ; and becauſe

§. Sect.6.
The fift reaſon,
taken from the
wonderfull
preſeruation of
the Scriptures
againſt all op-
poſitions.

caufe they know that by this light their workes of darkneſſe
are difcouered, therefore they labour to put it cleane out, that
their wickedneſſe may not be defcried; becauſe it is pure and
holie they cannot endure it, they themſelues being corrupt
and wicked; becauſe it is the rule of iuſtice which ſheweth the
crookednes of their waies, they would, if they were able, burne
it or cut it in peeces; becauſe it is the word by which they are
condemned, therefore they loathe as much to heare it, as the
priſoner doth abhorre to heare the ſentence of the iuſt Iudge.
And hence proceedeth their oppoſition and oppugning of the
holie ſcriptures with all their force and might; but all in vaine,
for the more the diuell and wicked men rage againſt the word
of God, the more by the almightie power of God ſupporting
it, the glorie thereof appeareth and ſpreadeth it ſelfe ouer the
face of the earth; the more they labour to keepe it downe, the
more it floriſheth. And as they who goe about to ſtop the current of a mightie riuer, doe but make it to ſwell the higher and
ouerflow all the countrey, whereas before it was contained
within the compaſſe of his owne bankes: ſo when Sathan and
his wicked impes, do feeke to ſtay this heauenly ſtreame which
floweth from Gods Sanctuarie, and labour might and maine
to hinder the paſſage & propagation of Gods truth; the more
it ſpreadeth it ſelfe, maugre their malice, and ouerfloweth the
whole earth. And whence can the defeating and fruſtrating of
this powerful violence proceede, but from a greater power,
euen the power of God? for though all men ſhould combine
themſelues together, they were vnable to reſiſt Sathans rage, or
protect the word of God from vtter ruine: onely the Lord
whoſe power is omnipotent could thus vphold it, and make it
preuaile againſt all the power of hell.

And as the Lord by preferuing and defending the ſcriptures,
from the beginning vnto this day, doth euidently ſhew that
they are his own word and reuealed wil: ſo alſo by puniſhing,
euen in this life, with vtter ruine and deſtruction, al thoſe who
haue moſt violently and malitiouſly oppoſed themſelues a-
gainſt it, and perſecuted the Saints of God for the profeſſion
hereof; as may appeare notably in the examples of *Antiochus
Epiphanes, Herod, Nero, Domitian, Dioclefian, Iulian* the apoſtata and many others; who by their ſhamefull and horrible
deaths

deaths teſtified and prooued the ſcriptures to bee the truth of God, which they had oppugned and perſecuted the whole courſe of their wicked liues.

Sixtly, the Lord hath approoued the ſcriptures to bee his truth by wonderfull miracles, which Sathan himſelfe cannot ſo much as imitate; as by giuing the blind their ſight, raiſing the dead to life, turning backe the courſe of the Sunne in the firmament, diuiding the ſea in two parts, and ſuch like; which miracles were wrought by the almightie power of God, to this end that the faithfull might be confirmed in the aſſurance of Gods truth, and the wicked conuinced. But againſt this, Sathan will be readie to ſuggeſt, that there were neuer any ſuch miracles as are recorded in the ſcriptures. To which I anſwere, that theſe miracles were not done in a corner, or in hugger mugger, but in the preſence of great multitudes; otherwiſe the Prophets and Apoſtles who were but meane and ſimple men, ſhould haue laboured in vaine to haue perſwaded men, to haue embraced their doctrine and religion (eſpecially being ſo contrarie to humane wiſedom, and our natural diſpoſition and affections) if they had onely themſelues reported, or brought ſome few witneſſes of their miracles wrought, and not publikly ſhewed them to all the people. Moreouer, ſeeing this doctrine hath had ſo many enemies from the beginning, it is not probable but that they would haue exclamed, and written againſt the writings of the Prophets and Apoſtles, as ſoone as they were publiſhed, for writing ſuch things as were neuer done: but amongſt all thoſe who haue oppoſed themſelues againſt the ſcriptures, there is no man ſo impudent as to denie that ſuch miracles were done, of which ſo many were eye-witneſſes: nay contrariwiſe the Heathen themſelues, who neither knew God nor his true religion, haue made mention of them in their writings; and the Iewes who to this day withſtand the worke of redemption wrought by Chriſt, doe notwithſtanding confeſſe that ſuch miracles were wrought by Chriſt and his Apoſtles; neither in truth are they able to gainſay them, ſeeing they haue receiued this truth by tradition from their fathers: and therfore they are driuen to confeſſe, that Chriſt was a great Prophet, though not the promiſed Meſſias.

Seuenthly, the conſtant teſtimonie of innumerable Martyrs,

§. *Sect.7.*
The ſixt reaſon taken from miracles.

§. *Sect.8.*

tyrs, who haue sealed this truth with their dearest bloud, is a notable argument to assure vs that it is indeede the word of God : for it is not likely that so many would so constantly and cheerefully haue suffred for their profession, the most exquisite torments that wit and malice could inuent, if the spirit of God had not certainly assured them that it was the truth of God, and if it had not supported them in suffring these torments a-boue all humane power and strength. And whereas it may bee obiected, that wicked men haue suffred also for their sects, opi-nions and heresies, we are to know that there is great differēce betweene them ; first, because the number hath been few who haue suffred for their seuerall sects and heresies, but the Mar-tyrs almost innumerable who haue suffred for the same truth ; secondly, the same cheerefulnesse, constancie and reioycing in their suffrings hath not bin in them who haue suffred for their errors, which hath alwaies been obserued in Gods Saints. And lastly, these heretikes haue alwaies been confuted and conuin-ced of their errors and heresies before their suffrings, whereas Gods Saints directed by his holie spirit, haue stopped the mouthes of their aduersaries with the wisedom of Gods word, which Sathan himselfe cannot resist, and through violent rage being vnconuicted haue been led to the slaughter.

Chap. XX.
Other reasons to proue that the Scriptures were indited by Gods spirit, taken from the Scriptures themselues.

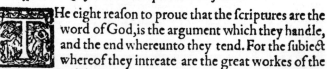

He eight reason to proue that the scriptures are the word of God, is the argument which they handle, and the end whereunto they tend. For the subiect whereof they intreate are the great workes of the euerliuing God, how hee exerciseth his mercie towards his children in sustaining, defending, and sauing them from all their enemies, and his iustice towards the wicked in turning their counsailes to foolishnes, in ouerthrowing their designes and purposes, curbing in their rage and violence, and in pu-nishing and destroying them. Now if you consider and peruse all other writings in the world besides, you shall finde no such matter contained in them ; for some labour in polishing humane

mane Arts ; some set out large histories of the actions, counsailes, successe, policies, enterprises and perturbations of men
like themselues.: so that at the first sight wee may know that
they are indited by the spirit of man , seeing they are wholie
spent in humane affaires, neuer intermedling with any spirituall matter appertaining vnto God. Moreouer,the scriptures
attribute the gouerning and wise disposing of all things to
Gods al-ruling prouidence,that he may haue the whole praise
of his owne workes ; as when they speake of some famous victorie,they doe ascribe it neither to the wisedome of the Captaine, nor to the valour of the common souldier, but vnto the
Lord of hoasts alone ; neither doe they make poems in the
praise of *Moses, Iosua, Dauid, Ezechias,* or any other of the
Kings and Leaders, but in the praise of the Lord, who by his
owne strong arme hath giuen his children victorie ouer their
enemies. Now whence can this proceed but from the spirit of
God inditing them,who contrarie to the nature of man which
desireth rather all praise himselfe, doth moue him to refuse all
glorie attributed to himselfe, that all the praise may bee ascribed vnto God ? So when they speake of any benefit receiued
by the Church,they doe not attribute it to worldly friends,
their good fortune, or their owne industrie and labour, but to
the blessing of God proceeding of his meere mercie & goodnesse towards them. And contrariwise, when they set downe
the destruction of the wicked, they doe not ascribe it to any
want of their owne care and prouidence, nor to the malice or
power of their enemies,nor to blind chance,or other outward
accident, but to the hand of God exercising his iudgements
vpon them, and punishing them for their sinnes. Now if you
peruse all other writings, you shall finde that they aime at nothing lesse than Gods glorie ; for some write to shew their eloquence, others to extoll their wits and deepe learning, others
to aduance the praise of mortall men aboue the clowdes,some
for one end, and some for another , all aiming at their owne
praise, pleasure or profit, neuer so much as once respecting
Gods glorie in their least thought ; and hence it is that setting
downe any victorie they ascribe it to the weaknesse or want of
wit,prouidence or courage of the aduerse part,or to the fortitude of the Captains, the resolutenesse of the souldiers,the ad-

uantages of the place, Sunne, winde, and such like circumstances, in the meane time excluding y̆ God of battailes, as though
he had no stroke in this busines. So likewise when they speake
of any other affaires or accidents which fall out in the gouernment of the world, they ascribe all to outward circumstances,
inferiour meanes and subordinate causes, as though God had
giuen ouer the gouernment of the earth, and had committed
the ruling of the sterne to blind fortune. Now whence can this
exceeding difference proceede, that they should altogether
aime at the glorie of God, and these wholie at the praise, pleasure, & profit of man? that they should alwaies ascribe the gouernment and disposing of all things to the wise prouidence
of God, and these to outward accidents, naturall causes and inferiour meanes? Surely because they were indited by the spirit
of God, and therefore themselues are diuine, sauouring wholie
of the author of them: and these by the spirit of man, and therfore al contained in them is meerly humane carnall & natural.

§. Sect. 2.
The ninth rea-
son, taken from
the stile of the
Scriptures.

The ninth reason may be taken from the stile and manner of
penning the Scriptures, in which they much differ from all o-
ther writings whatsoeuer: for whereas men in their writings
affect the praise of flowing eloquence and loftinesse of phrase,
the holie Ghost in penning the Scriptures hath vsed great simplicitie and wonderfull plainnesse, applying himselfe to the
capacitie of the most vnlearned: in which low and humble maner of speech, he doth notwithstanding set foorth the deepe
wisedome of God, and the profound mysteries of religion, the
bottome whereof the most wise and learned in the world can
not search into: and vnder the vaile of simple and plain speech,
there shineth such diuine wisedom and glorious maiestie, that
all the humane writings in the world, though neuer so adorned with the flowers of eloquence, and sharpe conceits of wit
and learning, cannot so deeply pearce the heart of man, nor so
forcibly worke vpon his affections, nor so powerfully incline
his will either to the imbracing of that which is good, or auoiding of that which is euill, as the word of God: and whence
can this proceed but from the vertue, power and wisedome of
the spirit of God who is the author of them?

Moreouer, wee may obserue in the stile of the Scriptures, a
maiesticall authoritie aboue all other witings, which onely beseemeth

seemeth the glorious King and soueraigne commander of heauen and earth: for they speake in the same manner, and inioyne the like obedience, to prince and people, rich and poore, learned and vnlearned, without any difference or respect of person; not vsing any arguments, reasons, or perswasions, but absolutely commanding that dutie which is to be done, and forbidding that sinne which should be left vndone, and that vnder the promise of euerlasting life and blessednesse, and the paine not of the gallowes, racke, or wheele, but of eternall death and damnation; and whom beseemeth it to promise euerlasting life, or to threaten euerlasting death, but him only who is himselfe eternall and euerlasting? and who hath this absolute authoritie of commanding all without any difference, but he who is Lord, Creator and gouernour of the prince as well as the people? Lastly, this word of God doth not only extend it selfe to the outward actions and conuersation, requiring onely the externall obedience which is in fact and outward behauiour, which is the vttermost that humane lawes respect, because the lawgiuers can see no further; but the law of God requireth especially the obedience of the heart, and forbiddeth not only consent to any euill, but euen concupiscence and lust? now who can make lawes for the heart and conscience, or though he should be so fond to make them, who could either reward the obedient, or punish the disobedient, but God alone who searcheth the heart and reines? The stile therefore of the scriptures being peculiar vnto themselues, shewing maiestie in lowlinesse & meanesse, an ouerruling power in perswading, without rendring reason or bringing any argument besides absolute authoritie, and an vniuersall iurisdiction ouer all without difference or respect, and that as well in regard of the secret thoughts as the outward actions, doth manifestly shew that they are not the inuention of man, but the word of God indited by his holy spirit.

But it may bee obiected, that if the Lord who is infinite in wisedome were the author of the Scriptures, they would haue excelled all humane writings in conceit of wit, and excellencie of phrase and stile, as farre as God excelleth man, whereas wee see that they are penned after a most simple plaine and vnpolished manner. To which I answere, that it doth not become a

§. Sect. 3.
Why the Scriptures were penned in a simple lowly and plain stile.

Prince

Prince to play the Oratour when he setteth out an edict,nor to vse Rhetoricall figures and alluring perswasions when he hath to deale with his subiects, but rather peremptorie commandements and plaine phrases, full of grauitie and authoritie without all affectation; and how much lesse should the chiefe com. mander of King and subiect, vse such a stile as sauoured any whit of humane eloquence, seeing, it better beseemeth his maiestie plainly to commaund, than to perswade, or allure with inticing speeches? Secondly, the Scriptures were penned by the holy Ghost, not onely for the wise and learned, but also for the simple and ignorant : and therefore howsoeuer the Lord in the profunditie of his wisedome, could haue written in such a loftie stile as would haue filled euen the most learned with admiration,yet hee vseth a simple easie stile fit for the capacitie of all, because it was for the vse of all, and necessarie to saluation to be vnderstood of all sorts and conditions. As therefore he frameth himselfe to our shallow capacitie in the penning of the Scriptures,and speaketh not according to his vnsearchable wisedome,but after the manner of men, or els no man, no not the most wise and learned could vnderstand him:so he thought it fit to speake aswell to the capacitie of the simple as the wise, because the knowledge of his word was no lesse necessarie to saluation to these than to the other ; and in his mercie and goodnesse hee vouchsafed as well milke to the babe, as strong meate to those who were come to more ripe yeeres in knowledge and spirituall wisedome. At which the wise and learned haue no reason to be offended,seeing the saluation of one is as deare to God as of another,and they may with greater facilicy vnderstand the Scriptures being plaine and easie, which could not be vnderstood of the simple,if they were penned in a lofty eloquent phrase. And yet if they examine the Scriptures in the balance of a true iudgement,they may finde food therein contained fit for their owne pallat and taste ; for vnder this humilitie they shall discerne more maiestie, vnder this simplicitie more deepe wisedome,vnder this vnpolished plainnesse more powerful perswasions to work vpon and incline the affections, than in all humane writings whatsoeuer. Thirdly,humane eloquence and wittie sharpe conceits,are not onely vnfitting the graue maiestie of our heauenly King, but also needlesse in re-
speĉt

spect of the Scriptures themselues; for what are they but Gods truth, and what is more agreeable and beseeming truth, than plainnesse and simplicitie? For what needes beautie the helpe of painting, or a precious Diamond much art to polish it, seeing they are glorious in their own nature? And what needs the truth of God, which in it selfe shineth cleerely like the Sunne in his chiefest brightnes, the goodly ornaments of humane eloquence which would but darken the beames thereof? Or what needes that which is heauenly and diuine, any helpe from that which is earthly and carnall to commend it to mans iudgement? No, no, the flowers of Rhetoricke and helpe of wittie Sophistrie, is more fit for *Tullies* orations, whereby oft times a good cause is made bad, and a bad one good, right wrong, and wrong right, than for Gods diuine truth, which like the Sunne shineth most gloriously when it is bare & naked. Lastly, it is to be obserued that the Lord in his wisedome doth manifest his power in weaknesse, his maiestie in basenes, and his wisedome in foolishnes, to the end that weaknes, basenes, and follie, may serue as foiles to make his power, maiestie, and wisedom appeare to vs more glorious, though in truth in themselues they are infinite, and nothing can be added to their excellencie. But because wee lie groueling on the earth, and are readie to ascribe al to the inferiour means, and nothing vnto God : therefore the Lord chuseth weake and simple meanes, that his own power and wisedome may be in them more manifest. For example, if the Lord had penned the Scriptures in such an eloquent stile as would haue rauished the readers with delight, we would like fooles haue stood admiring at the curious worke of the casket, and neuer opened it to looke vpon the precious iewel therin contained; & haue bin so much affected with the words, that in the meane time we would haue neglected the matter; but when this treasure is brought vnto vs but in an earthen vessell, when this beautifull feature is cloathed in meane attire, and the diuine wisedome of God set foorth in an humble and simple stile, wee leaue shadowes and behold the substance, neither doe we rest in the outward letter, but search after the inward truth. So also if the Lord had in the penning of the Scriptures vsed inticing eloquence, or affected humane learning, men would haue been readie to haue said, that by the force thereof so many were drawne or inticed, to embrace religion and to spend

Z   their

their liues in Gods feruice; but when as in outward fhew there is nothing but vnpolifhed plainneffe and fimple rudeneffe, by which neuerthelefle the hearers vnderftanding is more inlightened, his wil more powerfully inclined, his affectiós more ftrongly ruled, than by all the eloquent perfwafions which wit and learning can inuent, they are driuen to confeffe that the wifedome of God is hidden vnder this fimplicitie, his power vnder this outward weaknes, and that the Scriptures haue their vertue and force, not from the inticing fpeech of mans wifedome and excellencie of words, but from the power and plaine euidence of Gods fpirit, who was the author and inditer of them.

§. Sect.4.
The tenth reafon, taken from the Contents of the Scriptures, which in many things are a-boue the reach of humane reafon.

The tenth reafon, to proue that the Scriptures are not the inuention of man, but the word of God indited by his fpirit, is, that many things contained therein are aboue the reach of humane vnderftanding, and fo deepe that mans wifedome and reafon cannot conceiue them nor fearch them to the bottome. For example, though all men know by the light of nature that there is a God, feeing this truth is written in large characters in the faire volume of the creatures, fo as none can behold them but he muft needes know and acknowledge it; yet that this God being one in nature fhould be diftinguifhed into three perfons, the Father, Sonne, and holy Ghoft, without any diuifion of fubftance or confufion of perfons, mans reafon cannot conceiue, though the Lord hath reuealed it, and much leffe could inuent it feeing now it cannot comprehend it. So, that the world and the creatures therein contained were created, the light of nature fufficiently teacheth vs, feeing they haue an end and therefore had a beginning, a time of corruption and therefore a time of generation alfo, and as is the nature of euery feuerall part, fo is the nature of the whole vniuerfall; feeing alfo one effect brings vs to his caufe, and that caufe to a fuperiour caufe, and that to another vntill we come to the higheft and fupreame caufe which is God, who hauing his being of himfelfe giueth being to all things: but that all this goodly order fhould bee brought out of confufion, this light out of darknes, that al thefe excellent creatures fhould be created of nothing, by the alone word of their omnipotent Creator, it paffeth the conceit of humane reafon, & therefore his inuention alfo. So, that we are wretched and full of miferie, not only our reafon but euen our fenfes can teach vs; but how wee

fhould

should be freed out of this miserie and attaine vnto euerlasting
happinesse, is a thing aboue the reach of mans wisedome. And
that we are vnable to performe those duties we ought, and leaue
those sinnes vndone which we snould omit, and by both offend
God, the law of nature written in our hearts, and the checks and
feares which euery one feele in their owne consciences doe sufficiently teach vs : but the meanes whereby wee should be reconciled vnto God whom we haue offended, as they are set down in
his word, namely, that the second person in Trinitie should take
vpon him mans nature and be borne of a pure virgin, that in this
nature hee should for vs performe perfect obedience to Gods
law, and suffer affliction, miserie, yea death it selfe to reconcile vs
to his Father and procure his loue, to free vs from euerlasting
death and damnation, and to purchase for vs euerlasting life and
happinesse , and that his obedience and merits should become
ours, by reason of that vnion whereby hee becommeth our head
and wee his members, which vnion is made principally by his
spirit, and instrumentally by faith, doe all seeme strange, yea absurd to humane reason ; and therefore the Apostle saith, that the
natural man perceiueth not the things which are of the spirit of God,   1.Cor.2.14.
for they are foolishnes vnto him, neither can hee know them, because
they are spiritually discerned; as it is 1.Cor.2.14. And if he cannot
know and conceiue them when in the preaching of the Gospell
they are reuealed vnto him; how much lesse could hee inuent
them hauing neuer heard of them? or who can imagine that in
policie he would haue deuised such a religion to keep the world
in awe and obedience, as to euery worldly man seemeth foolish
and absurd, yea contrary to his nature ? For what can be more a-
gainst the haire, than to deny our selues and to take vp our crosse
and follow Christ? than to reiect our owne workes and worthinesse, and to seek for iustification in Christs death and obedience
alone? than to imagine that manifold afflictions and great miserie, is the high way that leadeth to glorie and endlesse felicitie?
and that pleasures, honours, and riches, make vs vnfit to enter into Gods kingdome ? And therefore seeing the doctrine of the
Scriptures are not onely aboue the reach of humane reason, but
also flat contrary to naturall wisedome, it plainly prooueth that
they are not the inuention of mortall man (for then the effect
would bee like the cause) but the word of the euerliuing God,

which

which fauoureth of his hidden and fpirituall wifedome.

§. Sect.5.
The eleuenth
reafon,taken
from the pro-
phecies of holy
Scriptures.

The eleuenth argument, to proue that the Scriptures were indited not by man but by Gods fpirit, are the prophecies therein
contained, which were fulfilled in their due time ; as that there
fhould be enmitie betweene the feed of the woman and the feed
of the Serpent, and that the promifed feede Chrift Iefus fhould
vanquifh the diuell;that the pofteritie of *Cham* fhould be accurfed;that *Abraham* fhould haue a fonne by his wife *Sarah*, when
they were both old,and fhe paft the time of child-bearing; that
his pofterity fhould be bond men in Egypt foure hundred yeres,
foretold before hee had *Ifaac* of whom they came ; that *Iudaes*
pofteritie who was but the fourth fonne,fhould haue foueraigntie and dominion ouer the reft; that the fcepter fhould not be taken from him till the Meffias fhould come ; that the tribe of *E-
phraim* fhould excell the tribe of *Manaffes* ; that hee who fhould

Iofh.6.26.

reedifie Iericho after it was deftroyed, fhould be punifhed with
the death of his fonnes, as appeareth Iofh.6.26, which was fiue

1.King.16.34.

hundred yeeres after fulfilled in *Hiel* the Bethelite,as it is 1.King.
16.34 ; that *Iofias* by name fhould deftroy idolatrie and the ido-

1.King.13.1.2.
2.King.22.
and 23.

laters,and reftore the true religion,foretold almoft 300 yeeres
before he was borne, 1.King.13.1,2. 2.King.22.and 23 ; that the
people of Ifrael fhould bee led captiue into Babylon, and be fet

Efa.44.26.
27.28.

free by *Cyrus* by name, prophecied of aboue an hundred yeeres
before *Cyrus* was borne, Efa.44.26,27,28. And to thefe we may
adde the prophecies of *Ieremy*,concerning the taking of Ierufalem and their captiuitie into Babylon , and the time of feuentie
yeeres limited for their abiding there ; the prophecies of *Daniel*
concerning the foure Monarchies, which are fo cleere and perfpicuous as if hee had feene them in his time ; the prophecie of
Chrift concerning the deftruction of Ierufalem ; the prophecies
contained in the Reuelation of S.*Iohn*,many of which we fee fulfilled in our time, efpecially that concerning the Antichrift of
Rome,his manner of comming, his increafing, his workes,feate
and place of refidence ; all which are fo manifeftly and plainly
defcribed, as if the Apoftle had written an hiftorie and not a
prophecie. Which plainly proueth that the Scriptures were not
deuifed by man, but penned by the infpiration of Gods fpirit,
who by his prouident wifedome forefeeth all things, and by his
wife prouidence ruleth all things.

But

But here Sathan will be readie to obiect, that we are not able
to prooue that these prophecies were written by any such Prophets and holy men as are mentioned in the Scriptures, so long
before the things contained in them were done, and that for
ought wee know they might be forged and foysted in by some
cunning fellow after the things were come to passe. The like obiections also he maketh against the rest of the Scriptures, as that
either there was not any such *Moses*, or if he were, that he was
but some cunning fellow who writ of miracles and wonders neuer done, to gaine credit to his law which he had published ; or
if he wrote nothing but truth in his time, yet we know not whether these books which goe vnder his name are perfect as he left
them, or depraued and corrupted, hauing many things altred,
added, & detracted, according to the pleasure of those who haue
had the keeping of them. And so also hee obiecteth against the
other parts of holy Scriptures. To this I answere, that as it were
great absurditie to call in question the writings of *Cicero*, *Sene-*
ca, *Plutarch* and other Heathen men whether they were penned
by any such men or no, because the next age receiued them from
the authors themselues, and deliuered them to the next insuing,
and so by tradition from hand to hand they are come vnto vs ;
so it is no lesse absurditie to call into question whether the scriptures were written by the Prophets and Apostles who liued in
their seuerall times, seeing the Church hath receiued them from
time to time, and deliuered them to their successors to this day.
Moreouer, the law published by *Moses* was not in secret or in a
corner before some few witnesses, but in the presence of sixe
hundred thousand men, besides women and children, and the
strange miracles and workes of God full of wonder, which hee
wrought for the better confirmation of his law giuen, were done
and perfourmed in the presence of many thousands, who made
relation of them to their posteritie, and they to theirs to this
day. Neither was it easie to be corrupted, altred or changed, seeing the lawgiuer did straightly charge all men that they should
not adde, detract, or alter any thing vpon paine of present death
in this world, and euerlasting death in the life to come ; who
therefore would incurre the danger of such fearfull punishment
for the satisfying of his fruitlesse phantasie? Moreouer, this book
of the law was safely kept in the Tabernacle, and after in the

§. *Sect.6.*
That the Scrip-
tures were pen-
ned by the holi
men of God
which are in
them mentio-
ned, and not
forged in their
names by some
polititian.

Temple

Temple in the Arke which was placed in the holy of holieſt, and diuers authenticall copies written out of it for euery one of the twelue tribes, which were euery Sabbaoth day read and expounded in their Sinagogues; yea ſo familiar were theſe writings with the Iewes, that they were written in their houſes, and vpon their garments, ſo as it was not poſſible for any man to falſifie them but it would preſently bee eſpied. Yea (will the tempter ſay) but though they could not be deprauced or corrupted, yet they might at firſt bee inuented by ſome more ſubtill than the reſt, and ſo thruſt vpon men vnder the authority of God himſelfe, as being the writings of his Prophets and Apoſtles. To which I anſwere, that there is no probabilitie of truth in this obiection; for I would faine know in what age this man ſhould write. In the time of *Moſes?* how then could he write the hiſtorie of the Iudges who ſucceeded him? In the time of the Iudges? how then could he write the hiſtorie of the Kings? What then? could he write theſe things in the time of the Kings, and ſo faine a relation of ſuch things as went before? why then it is neceſſarie that hee ſhould haue liued in the time of the laſt Kings, or els he could not haue penned their hiſtorie alſo: but before this time, there were many copies abroad of the Scriptures in diuers nations, by reaſon that the Iewes were ſcattered abroad through their captiuitie, where they as conſtantly profeſſed their religion as in their owne countrey. Beſides, if theſe writings had been fained, in what age could they come to light but men diligently inquiring into them, as being matters importing no leſſe than their eternall ſaluation or condemnation, would haue found them counterfeit? For if they had been penned in the ſame age wherein the things were done, who would haue beleeued them, if they did not aſſuredly know that they contained nothing but certaine truth? If in an after age, who would haue ſtraight ſubſcribed vnto them, vnleſſe they had by tradition from their anceſtors bin aſſured that ſuch things were done in former times? Furthermore, it is not probable but that the Iewes would haue made mentió of ſuch an author if they had known him; or if they had by ſome accident found them written in this forme, it is not likely that they would haue been ſo ſimple as to haue built their faith ſo firmely vpon them, that they would rather chuſe to ſuffer all torments than be brought to denie any one part of them.

Laſtly,

Laftly,it is obiected that in the time of *Antiochus*,the books of the Scriptures were by his tyrannie and extreame crueltie wholy abolifhed,and thefe which we haue, afterwards inuented by the Iewes to grace their religion. To which I anfwere, that this obiection is fo fottifhly foolifh, that it fauoureth not of common fenfe,much leffe of any force of reafon; for feeing now there were extant almoft innumerable copies of the Scriptures, what meanes could be inuented by wit and rage vtterly to fup-preffe them, efpecially feeing the Iewes made farre more pre-cious account of them than of their liues, fo that for the profef-fion of this truth they were content to fuffer euen in this tyrants time cruell deaths? Befides, if they had been all deftroyed and a-bolifhed in his time, how came it to paffe that prefently after his death they were againe (as it were) pulled out of the afhes and reuiued ? Or how could others be put in their place, feeing in-numerable men liued before and after his perfecution,who had the fight and perufing of the fame bookes before they were fup-preffed,and afterwards againe when they came to light? Laftly, though it fhould be granted that all the bookes of holy Scrip-tures had bin vtterly defaced in al the dominions of *Antiochus*, yet this were nothing for the tempters purpofe: for the Iewes were now fcattered far and wide, and had their Sinagogues and fchooles in fundrie nations where he had no authoritie; & ther-fore though he had deftroyed all the copies of the Scriptures in all places of his kingdome, yet there were many in other places where hee bare no fway. Neither were they now in the Hebrew tongue alone, but alfo tranflated into the Greeke by the 70 In-terpreters,at the requeft of *Ptolomey Philadelphus*, and the tran-flation carefully kept in his Librarie long before the time of this *Antiochus*. By al which it is more then manifeft, that the Scrip-tures are the fame which were penned by the Prophets and holy men of God, infpired with his diuine fpirit, confirmed with fo many and wonderfull miracles, and fealed with the bloud of in-numerable Martyrs.

To this which hath been faid, I might adde the teftimony of heathen writers,who in their feueral times haue in their writings made mention of the moft principal things which are contained in the ftory of the Bible : but as we neede not the helpe of a can-dle to fee the funne, which more fufficiently fheweth it felfe by

his

his own light: so this glorious light of Gods truth is in it selfe so cleere and manifest,that it needeth not the testimony of Infidels to confirme it, vnlesse it be to those who farre exceede them in infidelitie. And that noble learned and religious Gentleman, *Philip Mornay* in his bookes of the Trunesse of Christian Religion, hath eased me of this labour, from whose neuer wasting candle I haue borrowed the chiefest part of my light in the handling of this question.

Chap. XXI.

That the testimony of Gods spirit,doth onely perswade vs,that the Scriptures are the Word of God.

Nd these are the arguments whereby all gainesaiers may be conuinced, who deny the Scriptures to be the word of God, and his infallible trueth ; but though they are sufficient for the conuiction of all opposers, and for stopping the mouthes of all Atheists,Epicures and meere naturals ; yet notwithstanding,not any of these,nor al these are in themselues sufficient, to beget faith in the heart of any,or to perswade him with full assurance, to beleeue that the Scriptures are the word of God, vnlesse there be adioyned vnto the the testimony of Gods spirit, which doth not only conuince,but also throughly perswade vs of this truth ; and this alone in it selfe is al-sufficient, though we neuer heard any other of the former reasons, for the working of faith in vs, and a full perswasion of this truth.

§. *Sect.1.*
That all other arguments are without this vnsufficient.

Matth.11.25.

That all other arguments are insufficient without the testimony of Gods spirit,hereby it is more then manifest,in that not many wise, nor many learned in the world doe beleeue the Scriptures,which is the cause why they doe not submit themselues to the obedience thereof;whereas if faith might be wrought in men by force of arguments or naturall reason, they who best conceiue them would most easily be perswaded by them: but contrariwise, we see that these things are hid from the wise and prudent,and are reuealed vnto babes,not by meanes of naturall reason,but by the testimony of Gods spirit. For naturally we are all blind in spirituall things, neither can the *naturall man discerne the things*

things of the spirit of God, neither can he know them, because they are 1.Cor.2.14.
spiritually discerned, as it is 1.Cor.2.14. and therefore, though the
Scriptures be the glorious light of Gods truth, shining as bright
as the sunne in the firmament, to those whose eyes are inlightened with Gods spirit ; yet to those who continue in their naturall blindnesse, and were neuer annoynted with the precious eye-
salue of Gods spirit, this glorious light appeareth not, no more
than the sunshine to those who want their sight, and hence it is
that they grope at noone dayes. And as the poore woman, of
whom *Seneca* speaketh, being suddainely in the night stricken
with blindnesse, desired the next day to vndraw the curtaines and
open the windoes that shee might see, whereas the cause of her
not seeing was not want of light, but want of eyes: So these men
who are stricken with naturall blindnesse, complaine that they
cannot see the glorious light of Gods truth shining in his word,
and therefore desire to haue it cleered by taking away the clouds
of obiections which seeme to shadow it, and by adding vnto it
the light of humane reason ; but the truth is, the fault is not in
this glorious light, which alwaies shineth, but in their blindnesse
who cannot discerne it; and yet such is the pride, selfe loue, and
vaine opinion, which euery one hath of his owne gifts, that they
will sooner imagine that the sunne wanteth light, than they eyes
to looke vpon it.

True it is, that by the former reasons they may be conuinced, §. *Sect.2.*
so that they haue nothing to obiect, and perhaps they may bee *Other argu-*
brought to haue a good opinion of the Scriptures, & to a doubt- *ments con-*
full conceite that they are the word of God in deede ; they may *uince, but not*
with the two Disciples which trauailed to *Emaus,* when they *perswade.*
heare the Scriptures interpreted, haue their harts burne and throb
within thē, imagining that which they heare, to be more than the
word of mortall man; and as the blind man in the Gospell, when
his eyes were a little illuminated by our Sauiour, discerned men,
not as men, but as moouing trees, so they may in some confused
manner know and acknowledge the Scriptures to be the word
of God; but before Christ hath fully opened their eyes, and by
the precious eye-salue of his spirit hath dispelled their naturall
blindnesse, they wil neuer certainely be perswaded nor assuredly
beleeue, that the Scriptures are not the word of man, but the infallible truth of God. For it is not in mans power to beget faith
                                                                    in

in any, neither is it grounded vpon any natural reasons or perswasions, but it is the supernaturall gift of Gods spirit, who illuminates our vnderstanding, and inclines our will, so that we see, and stedfastly beleeue that trueth which it deliuereth, as appeareth Ephes.2.8. 2.Thess.1.11.

Ephes.2.8.
2.Thes.1.11.

Gods spirit fully perswadeth vs of this truth.
1.Cor.2.15.

And when we haue this testimony of Gods spirit in our hearts, it will certainely perswade vs of this truth, though we had no other reason: as appeareth by testimonies of Scripture, and by our owne experience. For the first it is said, 1.Cor.2.15. *That the spirituall man*, that is, he who is indued with Gods spirit, *iudgeth all things, and yet himselfe is iudged of no man.* So 1.Iohn 2.27. *But the*

1.Ioh.2.27.

annoynting which ye receiued of him, dwelleth in you, and ye neede not that any man teach you, but as the annointing teacheth you all things,

Vers.20.

and verse 20. *But ye haue an oyntment from him that is holy, and ye haue knowne all things.* Whereby hee vnderstandeth the spirit of

1.Cor.2.10.12

God, *which searcheth all things, euen the deepe things of God, which spirit is giuen vnto vs that we might know the things which are giuen vnto vs of God:* as it is 1.Cor.2.10.12. So our Sauiour promiseth

Ioh.16 7.13.

to send a *comforter vnto vs, euen the spirit of truth, who shall leade vs in all truth,* as it is Iohn 16.7.13. And in deede who is more fit then the spirit of God to confirme vs in the assurance of that truth, which he himselfe hath indited and inspired? or who can better iudge of the things of God then the spirit of God? who can better informe vs in this truth then hee who is the spirit of truth? And therefore if we haue the testimony of Gods spirit in vs, we shall neede no other witnesse, nor any reasons inuented by mans wit, to confirme vs in this truth, that the Scriptures are the word of the euerliuing God.

Gods spirit perswadeth vs of this truth by our owne feeling and experience.

For whosoeuer are indued with Gods spirit, doe also by their owne experience sensibly feele by the effects and operation of the scriptures in themselues, that they are not the word or inuention of mortall man, but the word of the almightie and most wise God: for when they perceiue that the eyes of their vnderstanding are illuminated, which before were blind and full of darkenes; that their will is inclined to the obedience of Gods commaundements, which before was stubborne and rebellious; that their heart is become soft and tender, so as like the heart of *Iosias* it melteth at the preaching of the law, which before was obdurate and more hard then the Adamant; that their conscience

which

which was dead and feared, is now readie to checke & controule them when they commit any sinne, and to allow and approue all good actions; that their affections are cast in a new mould, so that whereas heretofore they loued nothing but the world and worldly things, now their loue is fixed on the Lord and those things that are aboue; and whereas nothing was more odious in former times then vertue and godlines, nothing more pleasing then sinne and the delights thereof, now contrariwise, nothing is more lothsome then sinne, nothing more sweete and delight-full, then obedience to Gods commaundements; and when they further consider, that this great alteration is made in them onely by the hearing of Gods word preached, they neede no further perswasions, nor other instructor to teach them, that the scriptures were penned by the diuine operation of Gods spirit, seeing the word of mortall man could neuer make such a change in them, nor any thing else but the word of the e-uerliuing God; which at the first was alone sufficient for their creation and generation, and now onely is of power sufficient for their regeneration, and new birth. As therefore the blind Ioh.9. man reasoned with the Pharisies, Iohn. 9, not with any farre fetcht reason, but from his owne experience, to proue that our Sauiour was not a notorious sinner, as the Pharisies accused him, but some great Prophet sent from God; saying, doubtles this is a maruelous thing that ye know not whence he is, and yet he hath opened mine eyes; and, if this man were not of God he could haue done nothing : so may we reason with those who affirme that it cannot be knowne whence the scriptures came, from God or man; vsing this argument taken from our owne experience, saying, doubtles this is a meruelous thing that ye doe not know whence the scriptures are, seeing they haue opened mine eyes which were blinde from my birth, inclined my wil to obedience which before was rebellious, softned my heart and sanctified and quite changed mine affections, so that I now loue that good which before I hated, and hate that euill which before I loued ; and am delighted with those holy exercises which heretofore did most displease me ; and am displeased with those vaine plea-sures and filthie sinnes, which in times past did most delight me ; and therefore if it were not of God it could haue done no such thing, if it were not inspired and indited by his holy spirit, and

made

made effectuall by the vertue and power thereof, it could neuer haue wrought in me such strange alterations.

Chap. XXII.

Sathans temptations suggested against the translations of holy Scriptures answered.

§. Sect. 1.
That the Scriptures are truly translated.

Nd somuch for answering Sathans second tempta-tion whereby he laboreth to make men neglect the hearing of Gods word, that so they may neuer be effectually called. Now thirdly, if he cannot per-swade men that the Scriptures are not the word of God, that so he may take away all the authority thereof, then he will take exceptions against the translation; suggesting into their minds, that though the Scriptures bee the word of God as they were penned in their own proper languages, by men inspired by his spirit, yet for ought they know being vnlearned, the Scrip-tures may be corruptly translated, altered from their first origi-nall, and things added and detracted at the translators pleasure. To this I answere, that not onely professors of religion, but also Pagans, Infidels, Epicures and Atheists, who are euen the very limmes of the diuell, haue been skilfull and learned in these lan-guages ; and therefore if the translations were not neere the ori-ginall, who could stop their mouthes from inueighing against such falsehood ? Who could restraine them from declaiming a-gainst such corruption, seeing they so hate and abhor this truth, as that they wish the vtter extirpation thereof, and with ex-treame malice oppose themselues against it, persecuting and murthering to their vttermost power, whosoeuer imbrace and professe it? Moreouer, we knowe that the Iewes who more mali-tiously maligne Christians and christianity than the Turkes and Pagans, doe notwithstanding agree with vs in the translation of the old Testament, and can take no exception against the new. Thirdly, there hath been euer since Christs comming many sec-taries and heretikes, who for the maintenance of their opinions haue but sought to corrupt some few places of the Scriptures, but still God hath raised vp some godly learned in the originall tongues, who haue confuted them and cleered the text; how
therefore

therefore in ſuch diuiſion and vehement diſcord ſhould ſuch a thing be concealed. How ſhould any corrupt the whole Scriptures, or any principall places; ſeeing there is ſuch controuerſies from time to time about euery letter and ſyllable ? Laſtly, this truth of the Scriptures hath been ſealed and confirmed with the blood of many Martyrs, who haue been excellently learned in the originall tongues : and who can imagine that they would haue been ſo fooliſh, as to haue giuen their liues for the maintaining that truth which is contained in the Scriptures as we haue them tranſlated, if they thought them corrupted and falſified in the tranſlation?

But the tempter will obiect that the tranſlations exceedingly differ one from another, and therefore ſome of them muſt needs bee falſe, and who would ground his faith vpon any, vntill hee know which is the beſt and trueſt ? I anſwere, that though there be diuers tranſlations, and one better than another; yet euen that which is moſt corrupt and imperfect is ſufficient to inſtruct vs in the knowledge of God, and in the principles of Chriſtian religion ; neither is there amongſt them all, many errors which concerne the articles of our faith, or come neere the ſubſtance of doctrine which we are bound to beleeue, for all the tranſlatours haue laboured to conforme their tranſlations according to the analogy of faith ; and though they haue not in all places deliuered the proper ſenſe, yet they haue endeauored to come as neere it as they can, and where they haue fayled, it is rather in circumſtances than in ſubſtance, in the proper and ſpeciall truth, than in the common and generall ; and though in one place they do not ſo cleere the truth as they ſhould, yet they doe it in many other. And therefore let not Sathan perſwade vs to neglect the Scriptures, becauſe there are wants and imperfections in the tranſlations; for if we ſtudie and meditate euen in the meaneſt, and conforme and frame our liues according to that trueth which wee learne out of them, wee ſhall attaine vnto euerlaſting life and happineſſe. Men doe not vſe to neglect their buſineſſe, becauſe by reaſon of ſome cloude the ſunne doth not ſhine vpon them in his full brightneſſe ; for that light which they inioy is ſufficient, though not ſo gloriouſly bright as when it ſhineth in his full cleereneſſe: ſo we muſt not neglect the conforming of our ſelues to the Scriptures, becauſe we cannot ſee them ſhine in their own
glorious

§. *Sect.2.*
Of the diffe-
rence of tranſ-
lations.

glorious brightneffe, as they were penned by the infpiration of the holy Ghoft in the originall language (for as well may a painter expreffe in his table with artificiall colours the glory of the Sunne, as any man liuing can expreffe that perfect beautie and diuine glory which fhineth in the naturall phrafe of holy Scriptures in a tranflation) but rather wee are to inioy the benefit of this glorious fhining Sunne of Gods word, though the brightneffe bee as it were vayled and fomewhat fhadowed with the cloude of another language; for notwithftanding, through it they fhine and afford vs fuch light, as may be fufficient to guide and direct vs in the waies of holineffe and righteoufneffe, which will bring vs in the end to eternall glory and endleffe felicity.

CHAP. XXIII.

Sathans temptations taken from the euill liues of the Minifters, anfwered.

ANd fo much concerning the obiections which Sathan maketh againft the Scriptures themfelues, to the end hee may make men neglect to heare and reade them. But if this will not preuaile, then hee leaueth to difgrace the word it felfe, and feeketh by difcrediting the Minifters thereof, to make them to contemne their Minifterie; and to this ende hee vfeth all his skill to draw them into fome groffe and fcandalous finne, and to neglect that doctrine themfelues which they teach vnto others, fhewing in their liues and conuerfations, neither zeale of Gods glorie, nor defire of their neighbors good; and when he hath attained vnto his purpofe in fome, he thinketh it a fufficient ground for the flaunder of all, and a notable foundation whereupon he may builde a moft pernicious temptation. Art thou fo foolifh (will he fay) as to thinke all Gofpell which the minifters teach, that all truth commeth from their mouthes, & that there is not a more eafie way of attaining to euerlafting life, then that which they fhew vnto thee? why, do but looke vpon themfelues and thou fhalt finde their liues farre diffonant from their words, that whileft they exhort thee to ftricktnes, they take their libertie, whileft they diffwade thee from taking thy pleafure, affecting honors,

honors, setting thy heart vpon riches, themselues in the meane time are as voluptuous, ambitious, and couetous as any other; and whilest they indeauour to make sinne to appeare vnto thee as blacke as hell, themselues imbrace it with pleasure and delight as though it were the ioy of heauen. Who therefore can imagine that they thinke as they speake, or that they are perswaded that heauen gate is so straight, and the way so troublesome and hard to finde, as they goe about to perswade thee, seeing themselues take the least paines in walking in this way which they prescribe vnto others? Or if it be the truth which they teach, then surely they are not worth the hearing who in their liues deny this truth which in their words they professe; for what hope canst thou haue that it will be powerfull to worke grace in thee, seeing it hath no power to worke it in themselues? or that they can perswade thee to that holines, to which themselues are not perswaded?

And thus doth Sathan seeke to keepe men from hearing of Gods word, that so being weakned and hungerstarued for want of this heauenly Manna, he may vanquish them at the first onset, and leade them captiue vnto all sinne; and being still hudwinckt with the thicke vaile of ignorance, he may leade them the direct way to hell and vtter destruction: and therefore it behoueth euery one to arme themselues, that so they may beate backe the violence of this temptation. First therefore, whereas he saith that the ministers speak not as they think, becaufe they do not as the speak; we are to know for the answering of this temptation, that ministers are subiect to the same corruptions and infirmities which are incident vnto other men, and though they are called in the scriptures Angels in respect that they are Gods messengers to bring and publish the glad tidings of the Gospell, yet are they not Angels in respect of their puritie and perfection: but as they are flesh and blood, subiect to all humane frailtie; as they are borne in sinne and defiled with originall corruption, so are they as prone as others to fall into al actuall transgressions, if the Lord restraine them not. Neither must we imagine that learning and knowledge doe indue men with sanctification and the sauing graces of Gods spirit, for then we might attaine vnto them by our studie, labour and industrie; whereas the Scriptures teach vs that they are Gods free gifts which hee bestoweth on whom

§. Sect.2.
The answere to the former temptation.

Ministers subiect to all humaine imperfection.

he

he will; then it would follow that hee who is indued with moſt knowledge and learning, ſhould alſo haue moſt grace and ſanctification, whereas our owne experience teacheth vs, that many of the greateſt Doctors of the world ſpend their liues in all voluptuous pleaſures and licentiouſneſſe. What then ? doe theſe men teach one thing and beleeue another. Surely it may be the caſe of many, for faith commeth not by varietie of knowledge, neither is it tied to learning; but it is the free gift of God beſtowed as well, yea and as often alſo, vpon the ſimple fiſherman as vpon the learned Phariſie ; and therefore though they haue ſuch great learning and knowledge, that they are able to inſtruct others and defend the truth againſt all oppoſers, yet may they be as hard hearted and full of infidelitie, as the moſt ignorant and ſottiſh in the world. Shall then their hardneſſe of heart and infidelitie moue vs to call the truth of God which they deliuer into queſtion, as though it were a matter doubtfull whether it is the word of God or no ? God forbid. Nay, let God be true and euerie man a liar. For their owne conſciences are conuinced of this truth though not perſwaded, and the Lord hath giuen them eies to ſee it , though not hearts to beleeue it; to the end that the praiſe of our ſaluation may wholy be aſcribed to his owne free grace, who calleth and iuſtifieth, ſanctifieth and ſaueth whom he will, and not vnto humane learning or knowledge, which may be attained vnto by mans induſtrie and labour.

§. *Sect.*3.
That not learning, but Gods ſpirit freeth vs from our naturall corruptions.

    It may bee alſo that theſe who teach one thing and practiſe the cleane contrarie, doe notwithſtanding beleeue, that is know and giue their aſſent to that which they deliuer ; but this generall faith is incident as well to the diuels themſelues as vnto men, and therefore thoſe who haue it may neuertheleſſe be as worldly, carnal, and prophane as euer they were ; for before we attaine vnto a true iuſtifying faith, and be ſanctified by Gods ſpirit, our knowledge and learning wil not free vs from our corruption of nature, wherein wee are conceiued borne and bred; and therefore though wee ſee the truth, yea know and acknowledge it to be the word of God, which ſhall one day either iuſtifie or condemne vs, yet if the Lord doe not ioyne with this knowledge the inward operation of his ſpirit , making it effectuall for our ſanctification, and for the purging of vs from our corruptions, wee are as readie to fall into all ſinne, being inticed

and

and carried away with the riches, honours and pleasures of the
world, as if we were still most sottishly ignorant. A notable example hereof we haue in *Salomon*, who though hee had receiued
such a measure of wisedome and diuine knowledge, as neuer *That neglect of*
meere man attained vnto the like, yea though he were a penman *dutie doth not*
of an excellent portion of holie Scriptures, yet the Lord leauing *alwaies argue*
him to the corruption of his owne heart, he fell most grieuously *incredulitie.*
into all abominable wickednesse: and yet who will dare to say,
that *Salomon* did not write as he thought, and not rather that he
was carried away through the violence of his corruptions, to
commit that sinne which his conscience condemned, and to
neglect obedience to Gods vndoubted truth? So *Dauid* who
was indued with notable knowledge and no lesse grace, fel notwithstanding most fearfully into adulterie and murther; but
shall we therefore thinke that he was not perswaded that these
were horrible sinnes, or that when he commended mercie, innocencie and chastitie, he spake not as he thought? And *Peter* likewise denied and forswore his master, whom before hee had acknowledged to be the sonne of God; but shall wee hence conclude that *Peter* dissembled when he made that notable confession, because when hee came to the triall hee vtterly disclai-
med it? Nay rather we may certainly be perswaded, that *Dauid*
was carried away with his lust and concupiscence, and *Peter* o-
uercome with feare and frailtie, and both drawne, through their
corruption, to commit those sinnes which their consciences condemned. But leauing such farre fetcht instances, let euery man,
yea euen he who hath attained vnto the greatest measure of faith
and sanctification, enter into a strict and due consideration with
himselfe, and examine his owne conscience before Gods tribunall seate; and then let him tell me whether hee perfourme obedience to all that truth which hee knoweth and beleeueth, or
whether he may not iustly complaine, that our corruption takes
occasion by the knowledge of Gods commandement, to work
in vs all manner of concupiscence; that hee doth those things
which he alloweth not, nay which he hateth and abhorreth; that
though hee doe not onely know the law of God, but also is delighted therewith in the inner man, yet that there is another law
in his members which rebelleth against the law of his mind, and Rom.7.8.15.
leadeth him captiue vnto the law of sinne, as it is Rom.7.8.15.23. 23.

A a And

And if this be the cafe of *Salomon, Dauid, Peter,* and of all Gods children, who haue attained to the greateſt meaſure of knowledge and ſanctification; let not Sathan perſwade vs that wee may ſafely neglect the miniſterie of the word, becauſe the miniſters thereof ſeeme not perſwaded that the doctrine which they deliuer is true, in that they do not practiſe it in their own liues: for many knowing and beleeuing that truth which they deliuer, are notwithſtanding deſtitute of the ſanctifying graces of Gods ſpirit, and therefore wholy carried away into all licentious wickedneſſe; and many alſo who are ſanctified, being not wholy purged from their naturall corruptions, are readie to ſhew their frailtie and infirmities to all the world, though they know, acknowledge, beleeue, and from their hearts embrace, that truth which they teach and profeſſe.

§. Sect. 4.
The ſecond temptation taken from the euill liues of Miniſters, anſwered.

But if Sathan cannot thus preuaile, nor cauſe vs to doubt of Gods truth, becauſe the miniſters liue not according to that doctrine which they teach; then he will perſwade them at leaſt to refuſe to heare ſuch whoſe liues are ſcandalous, as being vnworthie to take the word into their mouthes, and vnable to conuert or amend others, ſeeing the word is not powerfull which they deliuer for the conuerting and reforming of their owne liues. Which temptation of Sathan is moſt dangerous and pernicious vnto many; for what greater diſcouragement can there be to a ſicke patient, than to take phyſicke of ſuch a Phyſition who can not cure himſelf of the ſame diſeaſe? Or who will willingly eate of that foode, which he who giueth it vnto him ſo loatheth and abhorreth, that he will not ſo much as taſte of it? Or who taketh delight in hearing him diſcourſe of mercie, chaſtitie, and liberalitie, whom he knoweth wholy poſſeſſed of crueltie, luſt, and couetouſneſſe? And therefore it were to be wiſhed that Gods miniſters ſhould be Phyſitions to themſelues, before they take vpon them the cure of others; that they ſhould not ſtand like Images by the high way ſides, directing others in their iourneys, themſelues neuer mouing foot, but that they ſhould like guides goe before them, and inſtruct them not only by their word, but alſo moue them to receiue their inſtructiō by their example. But yet let vs take heed, that Sathan doe not take occaſion vpon the neglect of their dutie to make vs neglect ours; & that he do not robbe vs of the ineſtimable treaſure of Gods word, and depriue

vs of this heauenly Manna and foode of our soules, whereby all
the graces of Gods spirit are begotten, nourished and increased
in vs, because the minister who offreth it vnto vs doth not feede
vpon it himselfe. And to this end we are to know that the ministerie of the word is Gods ordinance, which dependeth not vpon the worthinesse of him who deliuereth it, neither is it made
voide and vneffectuall by his vnworthinesse; but it hath it vertue
force and power from the blessing of God, and from the inward
operation of his spirit, who applieth it to the hearts and consciences of men, and thereby illuminates their vnderstandings, begetteth faith in them and all sanctifying and sauing graces. And
hence it is, that the minister himself, findeth not the word which
he deliuereth, effectual for the begetting of faith or any grace in
him, which notwithstanding is powerfull in many of the hearers for these purposes, because the Lord vouchsafeth not the assistance and inward cooperation of his holy spirit with the outward ministerie of the word vnto him, which notwithstanding
he mercifully granteth vnto others. Seeing then the ministerie
of the word is Gods owne ordinance, which he maketh effectuall to whom hee will by the inward operation of his holy spirit,
by whomsoeuer it is deliuered; and seeing those ministers which
are most holy and vertuous cannot at their pleasure infuse grace
into their hearers; for *Paul may plant, and Apollos may water, but* 1. Cor. 3. 5.
God giueth the increase; so that neither the one nor the other are
any thing in themselues without Gods blessing; seeing also
those who are loose and vicious, if they truly preach the truth it
selfe, cannot by their badnesse hinder Gods ordinance, but that
comming from their mouthes it will be effectuall for the conuersion of men vnto God, and the eternal saluation of those that
beleeue: for though vnto himselfe it be but a dead letter, yet the
spirit of God may giue life vnto it in those who receiue it; and
though he preacheth for glorie or gaine, or for enuie and strife,
yet we must with the Apostle *reioyce that Christ is preached any* Phil. 1. 15. 18.
manner of way, and reape the fruite thereof to our eternal comfort. Lastly, seeing the wisedome of God thinketh it good to
send ambassadours of both sorts, sanctified and vnsanctified, and
oftentimes maketh the word in the mouth of a faithfull and
godly minister the sauour of death vnto death, and the same
word in the mouth of one who is voide of grace and sanctifica-

That the Mini-
sters wicked-
nesse or vnwor-
thinesse should
not make vs
neglect hea-
ring.

tion

tion the fauour of life vnto life, to the end that we fhould not depend vpon man, but wholy reft and relie our felues vpon Gods
owne ordinance, giuing and afcribing vnto him the whole glory
and praife of our conuerfion and faluation; let not Sathan perfwade vs to thinke the worfe of the pure word of God, becaufe
of his corruption who deliuereth it : for what were this but to
refufe a comfortable ambaffage from a gracious prince, becaufe
we diflike the qualities of the ambaffadours? what were this but
to fcorne to receiue a kind letter from a louing father, becaufe
the carrier doth difpleafe vs? what is this but to refufe a rich
treafure, becaufe it is brought vnto vs in an earthen veffell which
is fraile and brittle? what is it but like proud beggers to refufe
the bountifull almes of a mercifull prince, becaufe it is deliuered vnto vs by an Amner who is couetous and hard harted? Yea
what is it but to croffe our Sauiour Chrifts expreffe commandement, who commanded all to heare euen the Scribes and Pharifies who fate in *Mofes* chaire, and to do after their words though
not after their workes? In a word, what is it els than to pin Gods
ordinance vpon mans fleeue, and to make the preaching of the
Gofpell, *which is the power of God to faluation vnto euery one who*
beleeueth, to depend vpon the weake ftrength of fraile flefh, either to bee made effectuall by his worthineffe, or to bee made
vaine and vnprofitable by his vnworthineffe?

Matth.23.

Rom.1.16.

Chap. XXIIII.
Sathans temptations taken from fundrie opinions, fects, and reli-
gions, anfwered.

§.Sect.1.
Sathans temp-
tations perfwa-
ding vs to pro-
feffe no reli-
gion.

ANd thus Sathan may be anfwered, when he taketh occafion of difcrediting the Gofpell and hindring the courfe
thereof, by obiecting the wickedneffe and worldly pro-
phaneneffe, or the infirmities and fraile weakneffe of the Minifters thereof. But if he cannot thus preuaile, he leaueth their liues
and commeth to their doctrine. Doeft thou not fee (will he fay)
that there are innumerable fects and contrary factions amongft
thofe who profeffe Chriftianitie? fome Papifts, fome Proteftants,
fome Arians, fome Anabaptifts, fome Pelagians, fome Liber-
tines, fome Familifts, fome Donatifts, & many other who all cite
and alledge Scriptures for the defending of their contrarie opinions,

nions,& confidently affirme ẏ they only haue the truth amongſt
them?how therfore canſt thou know which is truth and which is
falſehood;who interpret the ſcriptures aright,and who wreſt and
miſconſter them ? or if thou wert diſpoſed to be religious, what
religion wilt thou profeſſe in this great confuſion ? to what
Church wilt thou adioyne thy ſelfe ſeeing one is contrarie to
another,and thou knoweſt not which is in the truth?If thou beeſt
wiſe therefore keepe thy ſelfe quiet and let all alone, harken not
to any of them, or if thou doſt, beleeue them not ouer haſtily,
be of that religion which will beſt ſtand with thine aduantage ;
or if thou wilt needes ſerue God,follow thine owne conſcience,
haue a good intention in that thou doeſt, and it is enough ; but
profeſſe not one religion more than another,till thou ſeeſt thoſe
who are learned agree amongſt themſelues, for vntill then thou
canſt haue no aſſurance that thou profeſſeſt the truth. For the anſwering of which temptation we are to know,that the ſcriptures
haue foretould vnto vs that there ſhould *be ſects, diuiſions,hereſies* I.Cor.11.19.
& falſe teachers,euen vnto the end of the world;as appeareth 1.Cor. 1.Tim.4.1.
11.19.1.Tim.4.1.2.Pet.2.1.And the experience of al times both 2.Pet.2.1.
vnder the law,& vnder the Goſpel,may ſufficiently teach vs that
whereſoeuer the truth of God is publiſhed and preached, there
it is oppoſed by innumerable ſectaries and heretikes, which by
the malice and ſubtiltie of Sathan,are ſtirred vp to impugne and
diſcredit the true religion:and therefore if Sathan can ſtill keepe
vs blindfoulded in ignorance, and reſtraine vs from the confeſſion and profeſſion of our faith,till there be a generall vnitie and
agreement in the true religion, without all oppoſition or gaine-
ſaying, then he hath attained his deſire ; for ſo ſhall we neuer
ioyne our ſelues in the communion of the ſaints, nor bee true
members of the Church, profeſſing & practizing the religion of
Ieſus Chriſt, ſeeing the diuell will not ceaſe to ſtir vp his wicked
inſtruments, falſe Prophets, ſectaries and heretikes, to the end
they may oppugne and contradict the truth when it is ſincerely
preached, and make it fruteleſſe in the hearts of vnbeleeuers ;
ſeeing alſo our Sauiour hath taught vs that his Church is but a
little flocke, which is aſſaulted and grieuouſly vexed, not onely
with Lyons, Tigers and open enemies,but alſo with Foxes,and
Wolues in ſheepes clothing, and ſecret enemies who vnder the
ſhew and profeſſion of religion, ſeeke to vndermine and bring

1.Cor.11.19.

it to ruine. And the Apoſtle alſo hath forewarned vs that *there muſt be hereſies among vs, that they who are approoued might be knowne.*1.Cor.11.19. Though therefore there be many ſects,and hereſies, many falſe religions, and but one truth, this muſt not make vs to neglect all, till there be an vniuerſall agreement,for as well may we reconcile light and darkenes, the children of God with the children of the diuell,grace & naturall corruption, truth and error, as the true religion with thoſe which are falſe, or the profeſſors of the one with the profeſſors of the other.

Thoſe who haue important buſineſſes abroad, doe not ſtay at home and refuſe to trauaile becauſe ſome goe out of the way; but therefore they are more carefull to informe themſelues of e-uery turning in their iourney,becauſe they would not erre with others : thoſe that haue a deſire to liue, doe not refuſe all meate becauſe ſome ſurfet & die, by eating that which is vnwholſome; but rather hereby they are made more warie in making good choyſe of ſuch diet as is fit for the preſeruation of their health: thoſe alſo who are ſicke, doe not neglect all phiſicke, becauſe there are many couſening Impoſters and vnlearned Emperickes who kil in ſted of curing;but this maketh thē with more circum-ſpection to find out a skilful and learned phiſition. Let vs there-fore follow the like practiſe in theſe ſpirituall things:and ſeeing there is but one direct way which leadeth vnto heauen,and ma-ny bywaies which leade to deſtruction, let not this keepe vs from trauayling this heauenly iourney, but rather moue vs with more diligence to inquire the right and perfect way : ſeeing alſo there are many which offer vs poyſon in ſted of the wholeſome foode and phiſicke of our ſoules, let vs learne with more care to make choyſe and to put a difference betweene the one and the other.

§.Sect.2.
How the vn-learned may diſcerne the true religion from that which is falſe.

But here it will be demaunded how thoſe who are ſimple and ignorant can iudge which is the true religion, and which is the falſe,who teacheth the truth and who falſehood?To which I an-ſwere, that euery one muſt labour to informe himſelfe of the truth, by ſtudying and meditating in Gods word: this muſt be his light to guide him,his counſaylor to informe him, his touch-ſtone whereby he may diſcerne the ſtubble and ſtraw of mens inuentions, from the pure gold of Gods true religion. Neither are we to receiue all doctrines hand ouer head, but as the Apoſtle

ftle exhorteth vs, we *muft trie the fpirits whether they be of God or* 1.Ioh.4.1.
*no:*and with the men of Berea, we muft fearch the fcriptures, to A&.17.
fee ifthofe things be fo as they are deliuered, and accordingly
either receiue them if they are confonant with Gods word, or
reiect them if they be diffonant thereunto. Yea (will fome fay)
this were a direct courfe if thofe onely who haue the truth on
their fide had fcripture to alledge,but feeing euery heretike is as
readie to quote fcripture, for the vpholding and defending of
his herefie, as the profeffors of Gods truth for the maintenance
thereof;all the queftion is,whofe interpretation is to be receiued
as good, and whofe to be reiected as falfe and erroneous ? To
this I anfwere,that though there be fome places in the fcripture
hard and fomewhat doubtful,and therefore the more eafie to be
wrefted vnto a wrong fenfe, yet are there others cleare end euident,for the confuting of all fects, herefies, and errors whatfoeuer: and therefore we muft expound thofe places which are
darke and ambiguous,by thofe which are perfpicuous and manifeft. For example, if we would know whether Poperie be the
true religion or no, we muft examine the doctrines thereof by
Gods word, not making choyfe of thofe places which feeme
any way hard and doubtfull, but of thofe which are cleere and
manifeft ; and fo we fhall finde that their doctrines are as contrarie to Gods truth,as light to darkenes. For whereas they teach
that we are able to fulfill the law,and to merit heauen, the fcriptures affirme the cleane contrarie, namely that *in many things we* Iam.3.2.
*finne all,*Iam.3.2.*and whofoeuer fhall keepe the whole law and yet fai-* and 2. 10.
leth in one point is guiltie of all, Iam.2.10.*that there is no man who*
finneth not, 1.King.8.46. *that in Gods fight none that liueth can be* 1.King.8.46.
iuftified, Pfalm,143.2. *that when we haue done all thofe things that* Pfal.143.2.
are commaunded vs,we are vnprofitable feruants,and haue done but Luk.17 10.
*our dutie,and therefore merit nothing.*Luk.17.10.So whereas they
teach that wee muft pray to Saints and Angels, becaufe they
make interceffion for vs, the Apoftle flatly excludeth all other
from this office, but Chrift alone . 1.Tim.2.5. *there is one media-* 1.Tim.2.5.
tor betweene God and man. Where as they teach that marriage is
vnlawfull for fome men at all times, and fome meates vnlawfull
for all men at fome times,the holy Ghoft telleth vs plainely that
this is *erroneous and a doctrine of diuels ;* and *that euery creature of* 1.Tim.4.1.3.4
God is good, and nothing ought to be refufed, if it be receiued with

thankefgiuing. 1.Tim.4.1.3.4. And *that marriage is honorable for*
all men and the bed vndefiled. Heb.13.4.that *to auoyde fornication*
*euery man muſt haue his wife,and euery woman her owne husband.*1.
Cor.7.2.and that *better it is to marrie then to burne.*v.9. Whereas
they teach that our Sauiour Chriſt is carnally and corporally
preſent in the ſacrament, the ſcriptures teach vs the contrarie,
namely that he is aſcended into heauen,and therefore not vpon
the earth. Matth.28.6. That when *he was taken into heauen he was*
*taken from vs,*Act.1.11. *That the heauens muſt containe him vntill*
*the time that all things be reſtored,*Act.3.21. Whereas they teach
that we muſt make and worſhip images, both are expreſly forbidden in the ſecond commaundement, and in many other places of ſcripture. Whereas they teach that the ſcriptures ſhould
be kept from the common people, in an vnknowne language ;
the Apoſtle plainely affirmeth that he had rather in the Church
ſpeake fiue words with his vnderſtanding, that he might alſo
inſtruct others,than ten thouſand words in a ſtrange tongue;and
flatly inioyneth that the Prophets ſhould keepe ſilence in the
Church, rather than ſpeake ſtrange languages, where there is
no interpreter, 1.Cor.14.19.27.28. Whereas they hold that the
cup in the adminiſtration of the Lords ſupper, is to be withheld
from the common people, and giuen onely to the Prieſts, the
quite contrarie is to be obſerued in the inſtitution, whereas our
Sauiour ſaith, *Drinke ye all of it, becauſe it is his blood of the new*
teſtament that is ſhed for many, for the remiſſion of ſinnes: plainely
thereby inferring,that this ſigne and ſacrament of his blood belongeth to as many as were redeemed by it, Matth.26.28. And
whereas they ſay that here the diſciples were onely,and that to
them alone this ſpeech was directed, the Apoſtle plainely
taketh away this cauill: for ſetting downe the words of inſtitution for the vſe of the whole Church of Corinth, hee willeth euery one indefinitly to examine himſelfe and ſo to eate
of this breade and drinke of this cuppe. 1.Corinth.11.28. And
thus if wee ſtudie and meditate in Gods word, wee ſhall find
moſt cleere & manifeſt places for the confirmation of the truth,
and confutation of all ſects errors and hereſies. But what if this
meanes be taken away from vs,of reading & ſtudying the ſcriptures, either becauſe they are onely to bee had in an vnknowne
language,as in the time of popery, or becauſe we cannot reade
and

(marginal references, left column:)

Heb.13.4.

1.Cor.7.2.

Matth.28.6.
Act.1.11.

Acts 3.21.

1.Cor.14.19.

Matth.26.28.

1.Cor.11.28.

and haue no body to teach vs? What if both reading and ſtudying them,we finde many doubts and difficulties, and diuers places which ſeeme to fauour diuers and oppoſite opinions and religions? how then muſt we quit our ſelues out of this laberinth
of ambiguitie and doubtfulneſſe, ſeeing it is preiudiciall to appeale to the iudgement of either faction? I anſwere,that in theſe
dayes the meanes of knowledge are not ſo ſcant,but ẏ they may
inioy them that labour for them;for either they may obtaine the
vſe of the Scriptures in their owne language where they dwel,or
elſe in ſome other place by remouing their habitation;& though
they cānot reade, yet it is no hard matter to learne,to thoſe who
will vſe paines and diligence,or at leaſt to get the helpe of others
to ſupplie their want and defect in this behalfe. But let it bee
granted that we were abandoned of all theſe meanes, or that v-
ſing them,there were ſome doubt remaining of which we cannot be reſolued; are we therefore deſtitute of helpe,and forſaken of all meanes, whereby wee might attaine vnto the knowledge of the truth? No ſurely. For,if when all other meanes faile
vs,we haue our recourſe vnto God by earneſt & effectual prayer,
inſtantly crauing his holy ſpirit to guide and direct vs, we haue
a mercifull promiſe that he will heare our requeſt and graunt vn- Luke 11.13.
to vs his holy ſpirit,as it is Luke 11.13 : and that thereby he will
illuminate the blinde eyes of our vnderſtanding, inlighten our
minds with the knowledge of the truth, and take away from vs
all preiudice of opinion and foreſtalled iudgement,ſo as we ſhal
diſcerne truth from falſehood,and Gods true religion, from er-
rors and lies,ſects and hereſies. For *this ſpirit of truth will leade vs* Iohn 16.13.
into al truth,as it is Ioh.16 13.*He ſearcheth al things,euen the deepe* 1.Cor.2.10.12
things of God; *and to this end we receiue him,that we may knowe the*
things which are giuen vnto vs of God,as it is 1.Cor.2.10.12: He is
that precious eye-ſalue,wherewith being annointed we ſee,who Reuel.3.18.
before were blinde, Reuel.3.18. And if once wee haue receiued
this annoynting,*we neede not that any man ſhould teach vs, for this* 1.Ioh.2.27.
annoynting teacheth vs all things,as it is 1.Ioh.2.27.Though therefore we were abandoned of all other meanes, yet let not Sathan
perſwade vs to neglect all religion, becauſe we cannot diſcerne
the true religion from that which is falſe: for if we earneſtly and
ſincerely labour after the knowledge of the truth,and with good
Cornelius continually implore the aſſiſtance and direction of
Gods,

Gods ſpirit, wee ſhall bee ſure to obtaine our deſire, for the Lord hath promiſed it, and hee will vndoubtedly be as good as his word.

CHAP. XXV.

Sathans temptations taken from our vnworthineſſe and vnfitneſſe to heare, arſwered.

§. Sect.1.
That our ſins and vnworthi-neſſe ſhould not hinder vs from hearing Gods word.

And ſo much concerning the temptations of Sathan, which he draweth from the Miniſters, to diſcredit the Goſpel, and to diſwade men from ŷ hearing thereof; but if he cannot thus preuaile, he will leaue the Mini-ſters, and come to the parties themſelues, ſuggeſting into their minds that they are vnworthy, in reſpect of the innumerable number of their ſinnes, to be hearers of the Goſpell, which is ſo pure and excellent; and that their corruptions are ſo great, their vnderſtandings ſo blind, their memories ſo ſlippery, their wils ſo peruerſe, their heart and affections ſo wicked and prophane, that it is to be feared in regard of this their vnfitnes to heare, that the word of God, which in it ſelfe is the ſauour of life vnto life, will become vnto them the ſauour of death to their more deepe con-demnation. For the anſwering of which temptation, wee are to know, firſt, that our ſinnes and vnworthineſſe ſhould be ſo farre from hindring vs frō the hearing of Gods word, that they ſhould rather ſerue as forcible arguments to moue vs more attentiuely and diligently to heare it : becauſe it is the meanes ordayned of God to pull vs out of our ſins, to purge vs from our corruptions, to worke in vs true ſanctification, and to make vs of the ſonnes of wrath the children of God. Moreouer, though we want faith and all other ſanctifying graces, yet we are to heare the word of God : for therefore the Lord hath ordained the miniſtery of the word, not onely to increaſe grace where it is begun, but alſo to beget and begin it where it is wanting; ſo that we muſt not only heare becauſe we are fit, but alſo that we may be made fit, who before were vnfit. Neither are we to imagine that faith and other graces goe before hearing, but follow after as fruits and effects thereof; as the Apoſtle plainely ſheweth, Rom.10.14. *But how ſhall they call on him in whom they haue not beleeued? And how ſhall they beleeue*

Rom.10.14.17

beleeue in him of whom they haue not heard? And how shall they heare without a Preacher? And verse 17. *Faith commeth by hearing, and hearing by the word of God.* If then there be no faith without hearing, nor no grace without faith, it must needs follow, that before we heare, we are destitute of faith & all sauing grace, and that by hearing they are wrought in vs, God preuenting vs with his grace, and calling vs vnto himselfe, not only when we had no deferts to merit his mercy, but also not so much as any grace to defire it. And hence it is that the Apostle saith, 2. Tim. 1. 9. That *God hath called vs with an holy calling, not according to our works, but according to his own purpose and grace, which was giuen vnto vs through Christ Iesus before the world was.* The truth hereof may appeare in all the examples of Gods saints, who before their calling were so far from deseruing any grace at Gods hand, that rather they deserued confusion & vtter destruction. For example, what worthines was in *Abraham* before his conuersion who liued in grosse idolatry? what worthines in *Rahab* ȳ harlot? in *Manasses* a cruell tirant, a wicked sorcerer, an horrible idolater? what worthines in *Marie Magdalene* possessed by seuen diuels? or in *Matthew* and *Zacheus* the Publicanes? or in *Paul* who persecuted the Church of God? In a word, what worthines is in any of Gods saints, before the Lord by the preaching of his word, made effectuall by the inward operation of his spirit, hath called and conuerted, and pulled them out of their sins and corruptions in which they wallowed, and indued them with some measure of his sanctifying and sauing graces?

Secondly, whereas he obiecteth our vnfitnes to heare, because our eares are dull, our eyes blind, our hearts hard, and our wils, affections, and all the powers and faculties of our bodies and soules wholy corrupted and disordered; this must not moue vs to neglect the hearing of Gods word, but to become hearers thereof with more care and diligence : for it is the two-edged sword of the spirit, which will pearce and make way for it selfe to enter, and will builde a lodging for it selfe to dwell in ; it is not onely a light to guide those that see, but a precious eye-falue to giue sight vnto those who were borne blinde ; it is not onely the heauenly deaw which maketh Gods graces to spring in vs, but also that diuine seede which giueth them being and rooting in our hearts ; it is not onely the foode of our soules to

preserue

2. Tim. 1. 9.

§. *Sect. 2.*
That our vnfit-
nesse to heare,
should not
make vs neg-
lect hearing.

preferue and increafe that ftrength which wee alreadie haue, but alfo that immortall feede by which wee are firft begotten vnto God and borne againe, who before were dead in our finnes, and that excellent phyficke of our foules by which they are purged from their corruptions and reftored vnto health, which before were deadly ficke in finne; it maketh **vs** firft to will that which is good, and then further to defire it; it giueth vs life who before were dead in our finnes, and then preferues this life; it begets and begins faith & fanctification and all other graces in vs, and being begotten and begun it ftrengtheneth & increafeth them : and therefore let not Sathan diffwade vs from the hearing of Gods word, becaufe of our finnes, vnworthineffe and vnfitneffe; for as it is a notable meanes ordained of God for the increafing of grace where it alreadie is, fo is it no leffe effectuall for the begetting of grace where it neuer was. There is no wife man that will neglect his trade and liue idely becaufe he is poore, but rather this will moue him to be more painfull therein, as being the meanes whereby hee may become rich; neither doe men refufe all nourifhment, becaufe they haue emptie and hungrie ftomackes, but doe more earneftly defire meate that they may be filled and fatisfied; yea euen thofe whofe ftomackes are weake doe not altogether refufe their foode, but eate fomething to fharpen their appetite, and fo by little and little in vfing their ftomackes they get ftomacks : let vs follow the like practife, and when we perceiue our beggerlineffe in Gods graces, let vs more earneftly labour after this heauenly treafure and precious pearle, that we may be made rich; whē we feele our emptines of all vertue and goodneffe, let vs more eagerly hunger after this fpirituall Manna that we may be filled and fatisfied; when we finde our appetite weake and our ftomacks indifpofed to eate of this heauenly foode, let vs a little force our felues againft the appetite, or vfe all good meanes to quicken and fharpen it, and fo wee fhall finde that the oftner we eate, the oftner we fhall defire, the more wee heare the word of God, the more wee fhall defire to heare, and the greater benefit wee fhall receiue by it. Whereas neglect of hearing will make vs euery day more vnfit to heare, euen as long abftinence doth quite fpoyle the ftomack.

CHAP.

CHAP. XXVI.

How wee must arme our selues against Sathans temptations, whereby he laboureth to make the word of God fruitlesse.

Nd these are the temptations which Sathan vseth to disswade vs from hearing the word ; but if we breake these snares and cannot bee withheld from frequenting Gods holie assemblies ; then hee will labour by all meanes to make the word of God which we heare, fruitlesse and vneffectuall for our conuersion and saluation; and to this end hee will labour to work in vs a negligent carelesnesse in hearkening to those things which are deliuered ; and this is vsually accompanied with dulnesse of spirit, drowsinesse and sleepinesse : or if wee set our selues to heare the word, with any care and conscience to profit thereby, then he wil seeke to distract our mindes with wandring thoughts, either by offring and suggesting to our consideration and memorie the world and the vanities thereof, as our affaires and businesse and those pleasures wherewith wee are most delighted ; or if this will not preuaile, by casting into our mindes things in their owne nature good and religious, if they were thought vpon in time conuenient, to the end that wee may be distracted, and be made vnfit to heare the word with profit.

§. Sect. 1.

That Sathan tempteth vs to carelesse negligence in hearing.

Which temptations we are to withstand as being most dangerous and pernicious: and to this purpose there is something required at our hands to be perfourmed before our comming to Gods assemblies, and something afterwards. Before wee come to the hearing of the word, there is required due preparation, whereby our mindes are made fit vessels to receiue the spirituall treasure and foode of our soules. For if we come into the congregation of the faithfull, without any premeditation, reuerence, or regard of the action which we are to take in hand ; if we present our selues rashly and vnaduisedly, as if we went to a play, or to dispatch some worldly businesse: we shall hardly keepe our minds from negligent wandring and world-

That to resist Sathan we must prepare our selues before we heare.

ly

ly diſtractions, which will make the word of God fruitleſſe and vnprofitable.

§. *Sect.2.*
VVherein this preparation conſiſteth.
Eccl.4.17.

Now this preparation doth principally conſiſt, firſt in the purging of our corrupt affections, to which duty the wiſe man exhorteth vs; Eccl.4.17. *Take heed to thy feete when thou entreſt into the houſe of God,* that is, be carefull to purge thine affections which are the feete of thy ſoule. And this was typically ſignified by the outward waſhing of the Iſraelites before the promulgation of the law, Exod.19.10. where by the waſhing of their clothes and bodies, the purging of the ſecret corruptions of the heart was ſignified and repreſented. Which dutie is neceſſarily to be performed, of al thoſe who will heare the word with profit: for as the moſt pure liquor is defiled and made vnprofitable for vſe, if it bee put into a polluted and ſtinking veſſell; ſo the pure liquor of Gods word is defiled and made fruitleſſe, vnto al thoſe who receiue it into an heart polluted with vncleane affections: As therefore *Moſes* was enioyned by God to put off his ſhooes from his feete, before he might tread on that ground made holy by Gods preſence, or receiue the Lords ambaſſage to his people; ſo hee requireth of vs that we put off the ſhooes, that is, the corruption of our affections, before we tread vpon the holy ground of his Church, there to heare the glad tidings of the Goſpell, concerning our euerlaſting deliuerie out of the bondage of our ſpirituall enemies. What theſe affections are the Apoſtle *Iames* partly ſheweth, Iam.1.19. namely wrath, filthineſſe, malitiouſneſſe, to which *Peter* addeth diſſimulation and hypocriſie, enuie and euil ſpeaking, 1.Pet.2.1. And to theſe alſo wee may adde all other like vnto them.

Exod.19.10.

Iam.1.19.
1.Pet.2.1.

§. *Sect.3.*
VVe muſt baniſh all foreſtalled opinions of the miniſter.

Secondly, wee muſt baniſh out of our mindes all preiudice, foreſtalled opinions, and ſiniſter conceits, of the miniſter of Gods word whom wee are to heare; whereby men are either carried away with a vaine admiration of his gifts, and in the meane time make no conſcience of feeding vpon that foode which is offred; like vnto them who in ſteede of drinking of the wine, ſtand wondring at the curious workmanſhip of the cup; or els with a preiudicate opinion of his inſufficiencie in gifts, or imperfections of life, whereby they are ſo foreſtalled
                                                              that

that they thinke nothing which hee can deliuer will be worth
the hearing.

Thirdly,we muſt expell out of our cogitations, the remem- *VVe muſt ex-*
brance of all worldly buſineſes,pleaſures & delights,leaſt they *pell all worldly*
diſtract our mindes in the hearing of the word, and ſo choak- *cogitations.*
ing this heauenly ſeede make it fruitleſſe; for as the veſſell
which is alreadie full, will receiue no more, and whatſoeuer
is powered into it, ſpilleth vpon the ground : ſo the minde
that is full of worldly meditations, is not fit to receiue the
word of God, but as ſoone as it offereth to enter, it is kept
backe and ſo periſheth; for God and Mammon, the holy word
of God and the cares and vanities of the world, can neuer dwel
at the ſame time together,but as ſoone as one entreth it expelleth the other. As therefore men purpoſing to write a ſermon,
doe make cleane their writing tables, by blotting out ẙ which
was written in them before, for otherwiſe there would be ſuch
a mixture & confuſion,that nothing would be legible ; ſo whē
we purpoſe to carry away a ſermon faire writtē in the tables of
our memories, we muſt firſt blot out all worldly affaires and
buſineſſes,otherwiſe there will be nothing but confuſion, and
we ſhall not be able to recall any thing to our remembrance.

Fourthly, before the hearing of the word wee muſt ſearch §. *Sect.4.*
and examine our hearts both concerning our ſinnes and cor- *We muſt ex-*
ruptions, as alſo concerning our wants and imperfections; *amine our ſins*
for the firſt we muſt conſider to what ſins we are moſt addic- *and wants.*
ted, and with what temptations we are moſt eaſily ſubdued,
to the end wee may bring our ſinnes to bee ſlaughtered and
mortified with the ſword of Gods ſpirit, being otherwiſe vnable to ouercome them our ſelues; and that we may alſo thereby ſo ſtrongly arme all parts,both of our bodies and ſoules,ſo
as they ſhall not in time to come, bring vs againe vnder their
dominion. And as citizens being beſieged with their enemies,
doe learne by their aſſaulting which part of the citie is moſt
weake, and ſo with more care and labour fortifie it, with men
and munition, trenches and bulworkes ; ſo when we who are
continually beſieged by our ſpirituall enemies, doe learne by
their aſſaulting of vs where we are weakeſt, and the enemie
moſt like to enter, then we muſt goe into Gods armorie and
prouide ſufficient weapons and munition, whereby we may be
enabled

enabled to hold out and make refiftance. So alfo we are to
confider of our wants and imperfections, that fo we may be
ftirred vp with an earneft defire, to haue them fupplied, and
hereby may be moued with more care to apply vnto our felues
fuch foode as fhall be moft fit to fupply thefe our wants, and
amend our imperfections; for as men who hunger earneftly
defire to be fatiffied with wholefome foode, neither will they
willingly without any difference eate of all meates, efpecially
if they haue weake ftomackes,but of that which is moft fit and
beft agreeth with them;fo thofe who finde their fpiritual wants
earneftly defire to be fatiffied, and to haue their defects fupplyed : and for as much as all foode contained in Gods word,
is not fit for this purpofe, nor agreeable to their ftomackes, to
the end that Gods graces may be nourifhed in them, therefore
they will wifely make choyfe of that which beft agreeth to
their prefent ftate, and apply it vnto themfelues accordingly.
For example, he who findeth his heart hard and fecure, muft
feede vpon the threatnings of the law, to the end he may be
humbled, and his heart molified, and refolued into teares of
vnfained repentance; he that is of a broken heart and contrite
fpirit,muft feede vpon the fweete and gracious promifes of the
Gofpell ; he that is ignorant, muft hunger after milke,and defire to be inftructed in the principles of religion; he that hath a
good meafure of knowledge, may defire ftronger meate, that
is, attend vnto the more deepe poynts of diuinitie; in a word,
euery man is to examine his particular ftate, and to fearch out
his greateft wants, that fo comming to heare the word,he may
more diligently apply fuch doctrines,inftructions, and exhortations as fhall bee moft fit for his vfe and benefit; for that
which is foode to one is poyfon to another, and that falue
which is fit to heale one fore, doth make another to fefter and
ranckell, and one part of the word of God being applied to
men of diuers eftates,doth worke diuers effects,one it feedeth,
another it poyfoneth, one it healeth another it woundeth, to
one it is the fauour of life vnto life, and to another it is the
fauour of death vnto death : and therefore before we come to
the hearing thereof, we are to examine our ftates that we may
apply and make profitable vfe to our felues of that which is
moft fit to nourifh and ftrengthen vs in Gods graces.

Laftly,

Laſtly and moſt eſpecially we are to vſe earneſt and harty prayer vnto the Lord that he may *open our blind eyes, ſo as we may ſee the wonderfull things of his law,* that he will take away our ſtonie harts, and giue vs fleſhly hearts in which his word may more eaſily be imprinted; that hee will with the oyle of his grace bow our ſtubborne willes, and make them flexible and inclinable to perfourme obedience to his wil, reuealed in his word, that he wil ſanctifie our affections and purge them from their naturall corruptions, that hee will diſtill the heauenly dew of his holy ſpirit into our mindes and barraigne harts, that ſo the ſeede of his worde being watred there by may yeeld a plentifull harueſt in grace and godlineſſe.

We are to vſe earneſt praier Pſ.119.18.

And theſe are the duties which we muſt perfourme in the time of our preparation: now after we are thus prepared and haue preſented our ſelues into Gods holy aſſemblies, there are alſo other duties to be performed to the end that Sathan may not diſtract our minds and ſo make the word which we heare fruitleſſe: firſt wee are to ſet our ſelues in the preſence of God who looketh vpon vs, & beholdeth all our behauiour in this action, according to the example of good *Cornelius.* Act.10.33. *Here* (ſaith hee) *wee are all preſent before God to heare all things that are commanded thee of God.* And if we thus doe we ſhall not careleſly and negligently heare the word of the Lord, but with feare and trembling as in his preſence, before *whom the earth trembleth, and the foundations of the mountaines moue and ſhake as it is Pſal.18.7.*

§. Sect.5.
Of the duties which we muſt perfourme in hearing it, to ſet our ſelues in Gods preſence.

Secondly, wee are to heare the word preached not as the word of a mortal man, but as it is in truth the word of the euerliuing God, according to the example of the *Theſſalonians.* 1.Theſ.2,13. when (ſaith the Apoſtle) yee receiued the word of God which ye heard of vs, yee receiued it not as the word of men, but as it is indeed the word of God. For the miniſter is not his owne ſpokeſman but the ambaſſadour of the Lord, it is not his owne meſſage which he bringeth, but the Lords embaſſage, & hence it is that the Prophets and Apoſtles prefixe before their writings; theſe & ſuch like ſpeaches, The word of the Lord, the burthen of the Lord, thus

2. *Wee muſt heare it as the word of God.*

B b ſaith

saith the Lord; so also the Apostle professeth in his owne name, and in the behalfe of all Gods true ministers, that they are the Lords ambassadours who in Christes stead beseech their hearers that they will be reconciled vnto God. 2. Cor. 5. 20. We must not therefore looke vpon the man but on God who sendeth him, nor on the earthen vessell, but on the heauenly treasure which it bringeth, nor on the simplenesse of the casket, but on the precious pearle which is contayned in it, nor vpon the meanesse of the ambassadour, but vpon the glorious royalty of the prince who sent him: and on his ambassage which is the glad tidings of the gospel, the word of saluation and life; which is able to saue our soules and then his feete will seeme beautifull and none shall be better wel-come, then shall we not contemne or neglect their ministe-rie but receiue ioyfully, reuerently, and attentiuely the word preached by them, remembring what our Sauiour Christ hath said, Luk. 10. 16. *Hee that heareth you heareth mee, and he that despiseth you despiseth me, and he that despiseth me despi-seth him that sent me.*

§ *Sect. 6.*
3. We must stirre vp our selues with meditation of the benefite of hearing.

Thirdly let vs stirre vp our selues to reuerent attention by the consideration of those inestimable benefites which are deriued vnto vs by the hearing of the word, as that it is the liuely seede whereby we are begotten vnto God, the foode of our soules wherby we are nourished vnto euerlasting life, that spirituall physicke wherby we are purged from our cor-ruptions, that light which guideth vs in the waies of holines and righteousnesse, in a word that it is the cheife meanes to worke in vs all Gods graces in this life, and to assure vs of euerlasting happinesse in the life to come. And if these and such like meditations come to our remembrance, they will serue to stirre us vp from our drowsie dulnesse and to heare Gods word with alacritie and chearefulnesse, fastening our eyes on Gods ministers according to the example of Christs hearers. Luke 4. 20. and euen hanging vpon them (like the child on the mothers brest) to sucke our soules nourishment, as the people hanged on our Sauiour. Luke 19. 48.

Fourthly wee must heare the word as if wee were neuer-
more

more to heare it, for who can tell whither hee shall liue till the next sabboth? or though he doe, yet how knoweth hee whether hee shall haue his senses, vnderstanding, and memorie, seeing hee will not vse them to Gods glorie and his owne good? or though hee haue, yet may the word of God bee taken from him and such a famine bee of this heauenly foode that hee may wander from sea to sea, and from North *Am. 8. 11.* to East seeking it and shall not find it, and therfore whilst the Lord speaketh vnto vs, to day let vs harken and not harden our hearts, for he hath not promised vs to morrow that we shall heare it, whilst wee inioy this heauenly light let vs looke vpon it and be directed by it to doe the workes of holynesse, for it may be it will shortly set and neuer rise againe vnto vs, and then what will follow but eternall darkenesse?

Lastly let vs be stirred vp to attention by the consideration of Gods iudgments which he inflicteth on the contemners and neglectours of his word which he may iustly euery minute poure vpon vs whilst our minds are a wandringe not regarding that which hee sayth vnto vs, hee may suddenly strike vs with frenzie and madnes, or with death it selfe, and then how fearefull and lamentable were our state if such a iudgement should seafe vppon vs. Let vs remember what *Actes 20.* hapned to drowsie *Eutichus,* and consider with our selues that that which befalleth vnto one may happen vnto another.

§ Sect. 7.

And thus are wee to stirre vp our selues to the diligent and attentiue hearing of Gods word that so it may bee fruitful in our heartes and effectual for our conuersion and calling vnto God; but when wee haue gone thus farre we must not heere rest, for if our enemie sathan can not hinder the seed of Gods word from falling into our heartes then hee will labour to steale it away as soone as it is sowed that it may neuer take roote nor bring forth any fruite, as appeareth by lamentable experience; for how many are there who receiue the word of God with their approbation, and are somewhat affected with that which is spoken and yet soone after it vanisheth away; and nothing remaineth but their old corruptions? and whence doth this proceed but from the malice

How we are to behaue our selues after we haue heard the word.

of Sathan who when hee findeth the feed of the word not throughly entred into the ground of the heart and therein couered like a rauinous bird deuoureth it, or if it haue a little rooting, yet hee choaketh it with the thornie cares of the world fo as it neuer springeth vp no not fo much as into a blade of profeffion, or if it be fo farre growne vp, yet he in-deauoureth to keepe it from euer thriuing further, by cau-fing the hot funne of perfecution to arife and with the heate thereof to make it wither, and perifhe, though for a time it haue made a flourifhing fhewe; as our Sauiour Chrift hath taught vs in the parable of the Sower. Mat, 13. And there-fore it behoueth euery one of vs to take no leffe paines after the hearing of the word to keep it from deuouring and to preferue and nourifh it, that it may take deep roote and bring forth much fruit, then we did in the time of pre-paration, and in the time when we receiued it; for as the care-full hufbandman taketh great paines in ftirring vp his fallow grounds; and preparing it for the feed, as alfo in the feed time in fowing it in the ground thus prepared, and yet all this were to no purpofe if hee did not afterwards harrowe it and couer it in the ground; fo though we take greate paines in breaking vp and preparing the fallowe grounds of our hearts, and alfo in receiuing the feed of Gods word yet if we be not as carefull after all this to couer and hide this feed in the furrowes of our heartes that it may take deepe rooting it will neuer bring forth any fruite of true godlineffe. Now the meanes to preferue and nourifh this heauenly feed of Gods word is firft ferious meditation; wherby wee call to mind that which wee haue heard, in which it it is very re-quifite that wee examine the doctrines which were deliue-red according to the touchftone of Gods word, and turne ouer the bible to thofe proofes which we remember alledg-ed as moft principall for the confirmation of the doctrines which were deliuered : a notable example whereof we haue in the noble men of *Berea*. Actes. 17.10.11. Who though with great readineffe they receiued that doctrine which Paul had deliuered yet when they came home they fearched the

scriptures

ſcriptures to ſee if thoſe things which they hard were conſo-
nant and agreeable with them or no.

Secondly, we muſt vſe holy and Chriſtian conference one
with another, about thoſe matters which we haue heard, for
hereby it will come to paſſe that what one did not obſerue or
hath forgotten, the other remembreth and repenteth, and ſo
likewiſe the other helpeth out in another point where his
neighbour faileth, till at laſt they recall al the material points
to their remembrance, euen as many meeting together at a
feaſt do euery one caſt in his ſhot til the reckoning be made,
ſo many ioyning their heads together for the recalling of a
ſermon to mind, one repeateth a little and another as much
more, till at laſt all be repeated. And ſecondly, this benefit
redoundeth hereof that all which euery one remembreth by
this repetition is more ſurely imprinted in his memorie and
is not afterwards eaſily forgotten.

Laſtly, the beſt and ſureſt way to imprint things in our
memorie neuer after to be blotted out, is vpon all occaſions
to practiſe it in our liues and conuerſation, for as we only truly
know that in chriſtianitie that which we practiſe, ſo likewiſe
that is onely well remembred which is well practiſed.

CHAP. XXVII.

*Sathans tentations whereby he perſwadeth men to delay their
repentance anſwered.*

Nd ſo much concerning the ſubtill tentations of §. Sect.1.
Sathan, whereby he laboureth to make the word *The tentation*
of God fruitleſſe and vneffectuall for our con- *alluring to*
uerſion, wherewith if he cannot preuaile being *deferre re-*
repelled by the meanes before ſpoken of, & if men by their *pentance.*
hearing of the word haue learned thus much knowledge
that their conuerſion and turning to God is neceſſarie to ſaluation ; then he will in the next place labour to perſwade
them to deferre their repentance for a time, till they haue
better opportunitie and are more fit for this purpoſe. Let it

be

be graunted(will he say)that it is necessarie that thou shouldest repent & turne vnto God, yet thou mayest deferre thy
repentance vntill thine old age, or at least till the time of
sicknesse, for then thou wilt be more fitte to perfourme this
dutie, then in the flowrishing prime of thy youth, when as
the exercises of religion are so tedious and vnpleasant, and
the pleasures of the world so sweet and delightfull; neither
needest thou to feare any in conuenience which will come
hereby, for God is so gratious that whensoeuer thou retur-
nest vnto him he will receiue thee to mercy, for he hath promised in his word, that whensoeuer a sinner repenteth him
of his sinnes he will blot all his wickednes out of his remembrance : And therfore thou mayest inioy both the pleasures
of this life and the life to come, thou mayest repent time
inough hereafter and liue a strict and religious life, when the
heate of youth is past and old age drawes on, which is farre
more fit for these exercises : for what folly is it so to dote
vpon the heauenly ioyes to come, as that thou shouldest depriue thy selfe of those worldly pleasures which are present
seeing thou maiest inioy both?

This tentati-
on most dan-
gerous.

Against which tentation it behoueth euery man most
carefully to arme himselfe as being in it selfe most daungerous and pernicious to great multitudes, as may appeare by
too too lamentable experience; for when as Sathan can no
longer hudwinke their eyes with the vayle of ignorance but
that they plainly see, that it concerneth their eternall saluation to harken vnto the Lord calling them to repentance,
then notwithstanding thus farre he preuaileth with them
that they are content to delay their conuersion and turning
vnto God, either vntill the time of sicknesse, or till their old
age. And therefore it shall not be amisse to set downe briefly
some waighty arguments, whereby euery Christian may be
moued to speedy repentance, and not to deferre their conuersion from day to day, but to turne vnto the Lord when
he first calleth them.

§. Sect. 2.
Motiues to
perswade vs
to hasten our
repentance.

The first motiue to perswade vs to the hastening of our
conuersion is Gods commandement, whereby he inioyneth

vs

vs speedily to turne vnto him, that we may doe him seruice
all the daies of our life, to which end he hath created and redeemed vs and doth continuall preserue vs. Psal.95.7.8. *To
day if you shall heare his voyce harden not your hearts,* so as he
chargeth vs not to resist his calling no not till to morowe, for
if to day we will not harken vnto him, he hath not promised
to call vs againe vnlesse it be to iudgment. So Eccl. 12.1.*Remember now thy creatour in the dayes of thy youth whiles the e-
uill dayes come not, nor the yeeres approch, wherein thou shalt say
I haue no pleasure in them,* that is their old age, as afterwards
he expoundeth himselfe. And Esa.55.6. *Seeke yee the Lord
whilest he may be found, call yee vpon him whilest he is neere.*
Matth.3.2. *Repent; for the kingdome of heauen is at hand.*Act.
3.19.And our sauiour Christ doth inioyne vs,*first to seeke the
kingdome of God and the righteousnesse thereof.* Matth.6.33. If
therefore we wil not wittingly and wilfully breake Gods co-
maundement, let vs offer vnto him the seruice of our youth
as well as the seruice of our old age, for he requireth this as
well as the other, nay before the other, and this was signified
vnder the types of the old law, where the Lord requireth
that they should offer vnto him the principall of the flocke,
and such beasts as were whole and found yong and without
blemish. So Leuit.3.1. the Lord requireth that the sacrifice
which they offered should be with out blemish, and 22.20.
*Ye shall not offer any thing that hath a blemish for that shall not
be acceptable for you.* And Deut.15.21. *if there be any blemish
therein as if it be lame or blind, or haue any euill fault thou shalt
not offer it vnto the Lord thy God.* And for transgressing this
law the Lord reprehendeth the people by his Prophet. Mal.
1.8. *And if ye offer the blind for sacrifice is it not euill? and if ye
offer the lame and sicke is it not euill? offer it now to thy Prince;
will he be content with thee or accept thy person saith the Lord of
hoastes.* And verse.14. *Cursed be the deceiuer which hath in his
flocke a male and voweth, and sacrificeth to the Lord a corrupt
thing.* Now did the Lord regard the beasts, and hath he made
so many lawes that he might haue the best of them? surely
this is not Gods mayne end, but hee would thereby teach vs

to offer and dedicate vnto his ſeruice euen our beſt things as the prime of our youth & our flouriſhing age, for was the Lord greatly offended when as men reſerued the beſt of the flocke to themſelues and offred the old, blind and lame vnto him; and will he be well pleaſed that we ſhould dedicate our youth and the ſtrength of body and ſoule vnto Sathan, and our owne luſtes and reſerue for him onely our old decrepit lame and withered age, when as our bodies are full of diſeaſes and our mindes of infirmities? will any Prince accept of vs if we ſpend the whole time of our youth and ſtrength in the ſeruice of his enemies, and when we are ſicke, old, lame & blind, offer him our ſeruice, and will the Prince of Princes thinke hee be well pleaſed if he be thus vſed? if Sathan and the world haue all the pure wine will he be contented with the lees and dregs, if they haue the ripe fruite, will God haue that which is rotten and putrified. If they haue our health wil he haue our ſickneſſe? ſurely it is not likely; for the Lord who hath created vs redeemed vs and doth preſerue vs, doth looke to be ſerued with our youth health and ſtrength which he hath beſtowed on vs.

§ *Sect. 3.*
2. *Motiue ta-ken from the momentany ſhortneſſe of mans life.*

The ſecond argument to mooue vs to haſten our repentance and turning vnto God is taken from the momentanie ſhortneſſe and the mutable vncertainty of our liues; in reſpect of the ſhortneſſe of our liues they are compared to a pilgrimage, to the flower and graſſe of the field, to the wind, a cloud, ſmoke, vapour, to a dreame, a tale tould, a ſpanne ſhadow, and the paſſage of the weauers ſhuttle, yea it is called vanitie it ſelfe. And therefore ſeeing our liues are ſo ſhort ſurely they are al to little though they were wholy ſpent in Gods ſeruice; but ſeeing wee haue ſpent a great part of this ſhort time euen our whole life before our conuerſion after the luſts of the gentiles, let vs thinke that inough yea farre too much to be ſo ill beſtowed, *and from hence for ward let vs liue* (*as much time as remaineth in the fleſh*) *not after the luſts of men but after the will of God,* as the apoſtle admoniſheth vs. 1. Pet. 4. 2. 3. But though our life were ſhort yet if this ſhort time were certain there were ſome more ſhew of reaſon why we

we ſhould defer our conuerſion; but as it is ſhort ſo is it moſt
vncertaine, for wee haue not aſſurance that wee ſhall liue
one hower, wee are tenants at will in theſe earthly taberna-
cles, neither doe wee know how ſoone our great landlord
will turne vs out of them; wee are the Lords ſtewards here
on earth and we know not how ſoone our Lord and maſter
will call vs to a reckoninge and therefore it behoueth vs to
haue our accompts alwayes perfect and the bookes of our
conſciences made vp in readineſſe. We are vncertaine when
death will arreſt vs and carry vs to iudgment and therefore
we ſhould be prepared for it all times; when wee goe to bed
we are ſo to lay vs downe as though we were neuer to riſe til
we riſe to receiue our laſt ſentence, when we riſe vp in the
morning wee are ſo to ſpend that day as though it were the
laſt of our liues, for how many haue gone well to bed who
haue beene dead before the morning ? how many haue riſen
(as they thought in perfect health) and yet haue beene at-
tached by death before the euening ? and therefore it behooueth euery one who hath any regarde of the eternall ſaluation of his ſoule to turne ſpeedily vnto God, and while to
day they heare his voice not to harden their heartes. Men
vſually delaie matters of leaſt waight and in the firſt place
diſpatch buſineſſe of greateſt importance, and therefore vnleſſe we thinke the preſeruing of our bodies and ſoules from
the eternall torments of hell fire and the aſſurance of euerlaſting happineſſe and bleſſedneſſe in Gods kingdome to be
matters of leſſe importance, then the obtaining of ſome vain
pleaſures, vnconſtant honours or baſe commodities, let vs
turne vnto the Lord betimes by vnfained repentance and
according to our ſauiours aduiſe. Matth. 6. 33. *Let vs firſt
ſeeke the kingdome of God and the righteouſneſſe therof, and then
worldly neceſſaries ſhalbe caſt vnto vs as a vantage in this maine
bargaine.* If our houſes were on fire we would ſeeke firſt to
preſerue thoſe things which are moſt deare and pretious vnto vs good houſhould ſtuffe before lumber, Iewels before
ſtuffe, and children before Iewels, but our liues are dayly in
a conſumption *et dum creſcimus vita, decreſcit,* whilſt wee
grow

grow and increase,our liues decrease, and therefore in the first place let vs seek to preserue our soule,which is,our chiefe Iewel and not suffer it to perish through impenitencie, whilst we gaine some earthly vanities. But most lamentable is the practise of most who liue as though they were neuer to die, or as though they had taken of God a long lease of their liues which is to expire at a certaine appointed time; and this makes them deferre their repentance and to put the euill day far from thē,til at last death attacheth them & carrieth them to iudgment; and this appeareth by the scripturs and continual experience.Iob speaking of earnal secure men saith,*that they take the tabret & harpe & reioyce in the sound of the organs, they spend their days in wealth & suddainly they go downe to the graue. Iob* 21.12.13.So.*Eccl.*9.12.*man doth not know his time but as the fishes which are taken in an euill nette and as the birds that are caught in the snare, so are the children of men snared in the euill time when it falleth vpon them suddainly. when the euill seruant shal say in his heart my maister doth deferre his comming and shall beginne to smite his fellowes and to eate and drinke and to be drunken; that seruants maister will come in a day when he loketh not for him and in an howre that he is not aware of,and will cut him off and giue him his portion with the vnbeleeuers. as our sauiour hath taught vs.* Luke 12.45.46. *And we know what hapned to the rich man who saide vnto his soule, soule thou hast much goods laid vp for many yeeres, liue at ease, eate drinke and take thy pastime, euen the same night God said vnto him, O foole this night will they fetch thy soule from thee, and then whose shall those things be which thou hast prouided.* Luke 12.19.20.

§.*Sect.* 4.
That many purposing to repent in old age are cut of in the meane time by Gods iudgment.

Moreouer how many may we obseruein our owne experiencewho haue deferred their repetance frō day to day thinking to repent either in their old age or in the time of their sickenesse, and haue beene preuented and cut of by Godes iudgment? doe we not see that many haue beene taken away with suddaine and violent deaths, many depriued of the vse of their sences,memorie,and vnderstanding, in the time of their sickenesse and haue so dyed mad,franticke, and sensles, many who come totheir old age and yet are further from repentance

repentance then in the time of their youth. And this cōmeth to paſſe by the iuſt iudgment of God for what can be more righteous then that the Lorde ſhould contemne them at the houre of death who haue contemned him their whole life? that they ſhould looſe their memorie and vnderſtanding in the time of ſickenes, who haue continually abuſed them to the diſhonour of God in the time of their health; that they ſhould dye impenitent who haue liued in impenitencie, that they ſhould forget God when they are readie to goe out of the worlde, who would neuer remember him whilſt they were in the worlde; that God ſhould withdraw his grace when they are ſicke, which being often offered they deſpiſed when they were in health. And this the Lord threatneth Pro.1.24. *Becauſe I haue called and yee haue refuſed, I haue ſtretched out mine hand & none would regard.* v.25. *but ye haue deſpiſed all my counſayle and would none of my correction.* v.26. *I will alſo laugh at your deſtruction & mocke when your feare cō-meth.* v.27. *when your feare commeth like ſuddaine deſolation, and your deſtruction ſhall come like a whirlewind, &c.* and v.28. *then ſhall they call vpon me, but I will not anſwere, they ſhall ſeeke me early but they ſhall not find mee.* v.29. *becauſe they hated knowledge and did not chooſe the feare of the Lorde.* So Za-char.7.11.12.13. the prophet ſaith, that *becauſe the people re-fuſed to harken, pulled backe their ſhoulder, and ſtopped their eares that they ſhould not heare, but made their hearts as an A-damant ſtone leaſt they ſhould heare the words of the lord, ſent in his ſpirit by the miniſterie of the former prophets, therfore came a great wrath from the Lord of hoſtes, whereof it came to paſſe that as hee cried and they woulde not heare, ſo they cried and the Lord would not heare their crie.* And therefore when the Lord calleth, let vs anſwere Lorde I come, let vs not delay our con-uerſion from day to day, but *ſeeke the Lord whileſt he may be found, and call vpon him whileſt he is neere, let the wicked (now) forſake his wayes, and the vnrighteous his owne imaginations and returne vnto the Lord, and he will haue mercy vpon him, and to our God, for he is very ready to forgiue,* as it is. Eſay 55.6.7. But if we contemne the miniſterie of his worde, and when God
calleth

calleth to refuſe anſwere, if wee harden our hearts againſt
the meanes of our conuerſion, & quench the good motions
of his ſpirit when he putteth them into our mindes, ſurely it
will come to paſſe, that as we neglect the Lord, ſo he will neglect vs ; and though hee call vs to day yet he will not call a-
gaine to morrow, but will let vs die in our ſinnes without repentance. Let vs remēber the fearefull example of *Eſau* who
contemning his bleſſing and birthright, *afterwards when he
would haue inherited the bleſſing was reiected, for he found no
place to repentance though he ſought it with teares,* as it is, Hebr.
12.16.17. And of the 5. fooliſh virgins who neglecting the
opportune time of prouiding oile for their lamps, afterwards
went to buy when it was too late, for the bridegrome paſſed
by and they were ſhut out of dores. Call to mind the fearefull example of *Pharaoh,* who ſtill hardening his hart againſt
Gods word ſent vnto him and confirmed by many miracles
and wonders, at laſt was deſtroyed with his whole armie. So
Herode hauing hard *Iohn Baptiſt* willingly, and perfourmed
obedience to ſome things which he had learned, yet becauſe
he did not turne to the Lord with his whole heart nor repented of his inceſt, was neuer after called againe but left of God
to his owne hardneſſe of hart; the like may be ſaid of *Pilate,
Agrippa, Fœlix, Iudas, Demas Iulian* the *Apoſtata,* who hauing not harkened to the Lords call, but quenched the good
motions of his ſpirit, afterwards were giuen ouer of God to a
reprobate ſenſe to their euerlaſting ruine and deſtruction.
So likewiſe when as the Lord gaue the falſe propheteſſe *Ieſa-
bel* a time to repent, and ſhee repented not, he threatneth his
heauie iudgements againſt her; in a word this is manifeſt in
the examples of carnall ſecure men in theſe dayes, who hauing abuſed Gods mercy and long ſuffering, and deferred
their conuerſion from day to day, at laſt they are taken away
in Gods heauie diſpleaſure, and as they liued like beaſtes ſo
commonly they die like beaſtes : and therefore as wee loue
the ſaluation of our ſoules let vs harken when the Lord calleth, and not harden our hearts againſt the good motions of
his ſpirit, for if we be like theſe men in our wicked practiſe
there

Matth.25.

Apoc.2.21.
22.

there is no hope we ſhould be vnlike them in fearefull puniſhments.

Thirdly, we are to conſider that our conuerſion and turning vnto godly,vnfained,and true repentance: is the gift of God from whom euery good and perfect gift deſcendeth,as it is,Iam.1.17.And therfore we are to accept of this gift whē he offereth it vnto vs ; for God doth not promiſe his giftes and graces,with condition that we may receiue them when we liſt,but when he offereth them, Pſal.95.7. *To day if yee will heare his voice harden not your hearts,* he doth not giue vs reſpite till to morrow : now God calleth and inuiteth vs to to come vnto him,now he knocketh at the dore of our harts, deſiring to enter that he may dwell in vs by his holy ſpirit, and if we refuſe to let him enter, how know we whether he will euer knocke againe ? if he doe not;what gaineſt thou, but the pleaſures of ſinne for a ſeaſon,and in the end eternall death ? and what looſeſt thou, no leſſe a thing then euerlaſting life and an eternal waight of glory in Gods kingdome? well, yet Chriſt knocketh at the dore of our hearts,and if we will open he wilbe our gueſt and ſuppe with vs, bringing his cheere with him,euen an heauenly banquet of all his ſpirituall graces, but if wee rudely ſhut the dores againſt him,what hope can we haue that he will come againe when he findeth ſuch rude and vnciuill entertainement ? and then what will follow but that eyther wee ſhall neuer ſeeke after him, and then our caſe wilbe moſt miſerable, or with his ſpouſe in the Canticles we ſhall long ſeeke him but not find him without great difficultie, yea perhaps wee may ſeeke him as *Eſau* ſought his bleſſing with teares and neuer find him?

§. *Sect.*5.
The 3 motiue becauſe repentance is Gods gift.

Apoc.3.20.

Cant.5.

CHAP. XXVIII.
Of the fourth motiue taken from difficultie of repenting, cauſed by delayes.

§. *Sect.*I.

THe fourth motiue to perſwade vs to ſpeedy repentance and turning vnto God, is that the longer we deferre it the harder wee ſhall find it, for the difficultie thereof wilbe much increaſed by delay,

That the longer we defer repentance, the more hardly weſhal repent.

delay, and our ſelues alſo who are vnfit to day will be more
vnfit to morrow, the reaſons hereof are many, firſt becauſe
by continuall ſinning wee get a cuſtome and habite of ſinning, and if a cuſtome which is but affected be hardly left,
what ſhall we ſay of a cuſtome which is confirmed by nature
or what is nature ſtrengthened by cuſtome? who knoweth
not that the drunkard is more eaſily reclaimed frō his drunkenneſſe when he firſt falleth to this vice then when he hath
long liued in it, that the ſwearer the longer hee vſeth and
inureth his tongue to ſwearing, the more hardly can hee
forbeare it, and the couetous man as he increaſeth in yeeres
increaſeth alſo in couetouſneſſe, and the like may be ſayd of
all other vices. Neyther neede this ſeeme ſtrange vnto vs ſeeing it is a thing apparent in reaſon and in experience; for the
longer the diſeaſe hath poſſeſſed the body the more hardly it
is cured, and therfore that counſaile is good, *Venienti occurrite
morbo,* preuent the diſeaſe before it hath ſeaſed on thee or
preſently after it hath taken place remoue it. The longer the
ſore is neglected the more it feſtreth & the greater difficultie
there is to heale it, the lōger the tree groweth the deeper root
it taketh and the more harde it is to pull it vpp; the enemie is
more eaſily kept from ſcaling the walls, then beaten backe
when he is entred into the middeſt of the citie; & ſo it is with
ſins and vices, *facilius repelluntur quam expelluntur,* they are
more eaſily kept from entrance then beaten out : as therfore
you would condemne him of extreame folly who would not
regard his ſickeneſſe till it had ouerthrowne nature and then
thinke to cure it, or who would neglect to applie any ſalue
to a greiſly wound till it were feſtred and then thinke the
better to heale it; or that ſhould aſſay to pull vp a young plant
and being vnable ſhould deferre it till it were growne to a
great tree, thinking then more eaſily to plucke it vp by the
rootes, or that would let the enemie quietly enter into the citie with a purpoſe then to expell him with more facilitie and
leſſe loſſe; ſo alike nay much more fooliſh is hee, who finding
it nowe a hard matter to turne vnto God and to forſake his
ſinnes deferreth it for many yeares togither, till the corrupti-
tion

tion of nature haue receiued double ftrength by long cuftōe imagining that then hee can very eafily attaine vnto his pur-pofe, let vs therefore breake of our finnes by vnfained repen-tance, and take heed of confirming our naturall corruptions by long cuftome, for as one fayth *Dum confuetudini non* **Auguft.** *refiftitur fit neceffitas,* whilft cuftome is not broken it becom-meth neceffitie, and as another, *Sicut non poteft aliquis dedif-* **Bafil.** *cere maternam linguam, fic vix longam peccati confuetudinem,* as a man cannot eafily forget his mother tongue, fo neither can he leaue cuftomable finne. So it is faid Iob 20. 11. *that the wicked mans bones are full of the finnes of his youth and that they fhall lie downe with him in the duft;* whereby it is implied that as difeafes after they are entred into the marrow & bones are incurable in fo much as they goe with mē to their graues; fo finnes and vices which are the ficknefles of the foule ha-uing feafed and taken faft hold of a man by long and conti-nuall cuftome from his youth;will moft hardly leaue him in his age but will hang faft on till the day of his death. And hence it is that the Lord by his Prophet doth note it to bee a thing impoffible in refpeЄt of humaine power to leaue thofe finnes which are cuftomablely committed. Ier. 13 23. *Can the blacke more change his fkin;or the leopard his fpotts? then may yee alfo doe good that are accuftomed to doe euill.* and therefore if euer we meane to leaue our finnes & to turne vnto God it is beft to beginne before the corruptions of nature bee con-firmed by cuftome.

Secondly while wee liue in our finnes wee continue in Sa- §. *Sect.3.* thans thraldome and he hath full poffeffion of vs; which pof- *2. Becaufe* feffion the longer he holdeth the more hardly will he be caft *Sathan will* out; for as thofe who haue a long time quietly inioyed their *more hardly* houfes and lands though their title be but weake yet are more *be caft out of* hardly difpoffeffed then if at their firft entrance their right *his poffeffion* had bene called into queftiō,both becaufe long cuftome hath *when he hath* in it the nature of a law, and the parties themfelues will bee *long held it.* more earneft in vfing all meanes to retaine their poffeffions which they haue long held,time hauing worne out al doubt-ing of their right : fo fathan is more hardly thruft out of his
poffeffion

poſſeſſion when he hath long kept it, becauſe his long houl-
ding of vs in his thraldom maketh him imagine that he hath
right to hould vs ſtill, and hee is moſt earneſt in vſing all his
ſtrength and pollicie; to hould that which he hath already
gotten and long kept in his poſſeſſion. We know that when
a ſouldier in fight hath taken another captiue, at firſt he vſeth
al meanes to breake from him as hauing better opportunitie
when they are ſtill in the field, then he can hope for after whē
he is carried away and clapt vp in priſon : and as he hath leſſe
meanes, ſo alſo he hath leſſe deſire to eſcape; after that by cō-
tinuance of time his captiuitie is made more familiar vnto
him; and we commonly ſee that a bird as ſoone as ſhee is taken, fluttereth and ſtriueth to get away, but after ſhee hath
beene a while in the cage ſhee is content to ſtay there ſtill
though the doore be open; and ſo it is in our ſpirituall thraldome, at the firſt wee haue beſt meanes to eſcape and moſt
deſire alſo , for after wee are inured to ſathans captiuitie
wee are content to remaine his bondſlaues ſtill. And if wee
deſire to eſcape hee would more diſdaine that wee ſhould
ſtriue and oppoſe our ſelues againſt him, after he hath long
time had vs at commaund, and ruled vs at his becke, then
when at the firſt we fell into this cruell ſlauerie.

§ Sect. 4.
3. By conti-
nuance the
ſtrength of
ſinne increa-
ſeth.

Thirdly the longer that ſinne hath dominion ouer vs the
more it increaſeth in ſtrength, and the more hardly it is ſubdued, for it is the nature of ſinne as ſoone as it is entertained
to make way and roome for more and thoſe worſe then it ſelf
as wee may ſee in the example of *Dauid*, for when hee was
ouercome of idleneſſe, it made way for adulterie, and adulterie for murther. So *Herod* entertained inceſt; and that o-
pened a doore in his heart to let in murther, and both theſe
made open way for all helliſh impietie; ſo *Iudas* retayninge
ſtill his couetouſneſſe was mooued thereby to betray his
maiſter; and this ſinne brought him firſt to deſperation, &
then to hange himſelfe; yea the Apoſtle *Peter* after that he
ioyned himſelfe in companie with the wicked ſeruantes of
the more wicked high Prieſt; at firſt was mooued hereby to
denie his maiſter, and when hee had gone thus farre, then

Matth. 26.

hee

hee denieth him againe with an oath, and when hee had thus farre proceeded in the courſe of ſinne, hee maketh no conſcience of redoubling his oathes, curſing himſelfe if hee knew the man; ſo that the longer wee let ſinne haue dominion in vs, the more it will increaſe it ſelfe in ſtrength and number, till our heartes bee full of ſinne and wickedneſſe. As therefore thoſe citizens were to bee accounted moſt fooliſh, who when they ſaw an hundred enemies entred into the citie, ſhould deferre the beating of them out or killing of them, till they had opened the gate to let in ten thouſand more better armed and more ſtrongly prouided, thinking then to haue better opportunitie, and more abilitie to giue them the repulſe, ſo alike fooliſh are thoſe who finding it hard and defficult to ſubdue ſome few ſinnes, to which they are now giuen, doe deferre it till the time to come, when as they are increaſed in huge multituds imagining then to doe it with more eaſe. Sinne, it is the poyſon of the ſoule, as therfore poyſons being drunke are preſently to be caſt vp againe, otherwiſe they diſperſe themſelues in the vaines and ſo going to the hart cauſe death; ſo this poyſon of ſinne if it be long kept in vs, it will diſperſe it ſelfe ouer the whole bodie and ſoule, and ſeaſing vpon the heart, wil plung vs into euerlaſting death and deſtruction. Sinne it is an heauie burthen and vpon whomſoeuer it lieth it will preſſe them downe vnto hell; as therefore the way to eaſe a man of his burthen is not to adde more vnto it but to caſt it of, ſo the way to eaſe vs of the heauie burthen of ſinne, is not to increaſe the waight by adding ſtill more and more vnto it but by caſting it of ſpeedily, for when by this continuall addition our ſinnes are growne to an vnſupportable wayght, they will ſooner preſſe vs downe then we ſhall caſt them of.

Fourthly, the longer wee liue in ſinne the more vnpleaſant will vertue and godlineſſe be vnto vs; and the more wee are delighted in the fulfilling the luſtes of the fleſh, the more bitter it wilbe to mortifie them, and to imbrace any ſtrict courſe of ſanctification, ſeing theſe are contrary the one to the other; he that hath long continued in darkneſſe cannot indure the light of the sunne; hee that neuer tasted any thing but sweet and pleasant meats, cannot abide to feed vpon those which are sowre and bitter; hee that was borne and bred in hote countries, is not able to brooke those which are cold; and so those who haue accustomed themselues to sinne wil hardly be euer brought to imbrace vertue and godlinesse, these being as contrarie one to another, as light and darkenesse, sweet and sower, hote and cold, especially considering that sinne is as delightful to the tast of a natural man, as drink when hee is extreamely thirstie, or meat when he is ready to pine for hunger.

§ *Sect. 5.*
5. Because the longer we delay the more we are disabled.

Fiftly, the longer we liue in our sins and deferre our conuersion vnto God, the more are our vnderstandings darkned, our wils peruerted, our affections more corrupted, our harts hardned, and our consciences seared, & all the powers and faculties of our bodies and soules are more and more disabled; for as the longer that sicknesse hath continued, the more it weakneth the body & maketh it vnfit for any worke or actiō, so the longer sinne which is the sicknesse of the soule hath seased on vs, the more vnable we are to shake it off, and the weaker it maketh vs to performe any good actions. When men at first fall into vnusuall sinnes, their consciences checke them, and they feare least the Lord will poure vpon them his heauie iudgements, but when they haue committed the same sinnes againe and againe, and yet are not punished, then like theeues who hauing escaped after one robberie committed, are ready to commit another, so they hauing not tasted of Gods iudgements threatned, thinke that they shall neuer be inflicted on them, and therefore are readie to sinne againe; vntill by long custome in sinning their hearts are hardned and their consciences seared as it were with a hote iron, so as none without any checke or remorse, yea with all pleasure and delight they cannot commit those sinnes, which in former times they would haue trembled, to haue entertained into their secrets thoughts.

§. *Sect. 6.*
6. Because the meanes

Sixtly, the longer wee deferre our repentance the more vneffectuall will the meanes be of our conuersion; for the
word

word of God, will either soften our hearts like waxe,or grew vneffe-ctuall by delayes.
harden them like clay, either it wilbe the fauour of life vnto
life,or the fauour of death to our deeper condemnation,as it
2 Cor.2.16. *If it once goe out of Gods mouth it shall not returne*
vnto him voyde,but it shall accomplish that which he will, and it
shall prosper in the thing whereto he sendeth it, (whether it be for
the conuersion or hardening of those who heare it) as it is
Efa.55.11. we know if a falue be applied vnto a wound eyther it healeth it, or els the fore ouercoming the vertue therof doth more fefter and ranckle, and fo this fpiritual falue,
being applied vnto our foules wounded with finne, doth either cure them, or elfe becomming vneffectuall they waxe
worfe and worfe. When men fleepe & are fuddainly wake-
ned with fome ftrange and vnufual found, they prefently
ftart vp and are amafed,but after a long time they haue bene
acquainted with the noyfe they can fleepe fecurely and not
be much difquieted; fo when men fleeping in carnall fecuritie are awaked with the threatnings of the law preached vnto them,which like Canon fhot thudreth in their eares,they
are at firft fomewhat rouzed vp and beginne to looke about
them,but giuing themfelues to fleepe againe in their finnes,
after they haue bene many times awakened, at laft this fearfull found nothing moues nor difquietts them neither wil
any thing waken them out of this fpirituall lethargie, but
the voyce of the Archangell commanding them to arife and
to come vnto iudgement.

Seuenthly,if we deferre our conuerfion vntil our old age, §. Sect.7.
it will then be more harde and difficult then in the time of *7. Becaufe*
youth,becaufe old men are more indocible & vnfit to learn, *old age is*
then they were in their youthfull dayes, and therefore who- *more vnfitt*
foeuer meane to attaine vnto learning, or to knowledge of *for repentáce*
any fcience, trade or occupation they doe not deferre it to *then youth.*
their old daies, but giue themfelues vnto it in the time of
their youth,when as their wits are moft frefh, & their capacitie moft quicke to receaue inftruction. Seing then there is
much knowledge neceffarily required to the making of a
true Chriftian (for without knowledge we can haue no faith,

and

and without faith there is no ſaluation) therefore for the attaining hereunto it is very needfull that we beginne betimes
and ſet our ſelues to learne Gods true religion in the time
of our youth, when as wee are moſt fit for this purpoſe. And
this counſayle the wiſe man giues vs Prou.22.6. *Teach a*
child in the trade of his way and when he is old he ſhall not depart
from it. Secondly, as old men are more vnfit to learne, ſo alſo
they are more forgetfull to remember that which is taught
them, and therefore if they doe not ſet their whole mindes
vpon Gods word, and continually call to mind that which
hath beene deliuered vnto them in the preaching thereof,
meditating therein with the prophet *Dauid* day and night,
all they haue learned, will eaſily ſlip out of their weake and
decayed memories. Which thing is moſt hard for them to
perfourme by reaſon of manifold diſtractions, which that
age is ſubiect vnto, as the infirmities of the body, ſickneſſe,
aches, and innumerable griefes, and alſo the manifold troubles and cares of mind, not onely in reſpect of their owne
ſtate, but alſo in the behalf of their children, yong nephewes
& neere friends, whoſe welfare is as deere vnto thē as their
owne : now if a ſingle man hath cares inow to diſtract
him from Gods ſeruice, how many are their diſtractions
whoſe cares are doubled and redoubled : and therefore if
we would make choiſe of the fitteſt time for our conuerſiō
we muſt not deferre it till our old age, but turne vnto God
in our youth, when as our wittes are moſt fit to receyue,
and our memories to retaine inſtruction.

§. Sect.8.
8. *Becauſe*
the hour of
death is the
moſt vnfit
time for re-
pentance.
Laſtly if wee deferre our conuerſion vnto God till our old
age, or till we lye on our death bed, we ſhall find it more
difficult in that our enemie ſathan who alwayes goeth a-
bout like a roaring lion, ſeeking to deuoure vs, doth then
redouble his malicious diligence in working our deſtruction when as hee ſeeth the time drawe neere wherein hee
muſt attaine his purpoſe, or elſe for euer faile of his deſire,
what, therefore will now our malicious powerfull and moſt
ſubtill enemie leaue vnattempted ? what violence will hee
not now offer ? what pollicy will hee not aſſay to drawe
vs

vs from God, to his kingdome of darkeneſſe ? wee knowe
that when enemies beſeidging a citie doe heare that their
ſeidge is ſhortly to be rayſed by the approaching of mighty
ſuccours; or within a while will become vaine and boote-
leſſe, by reaſon that the citie well bee more ſtrongly man-
ned and better victualed, howe they will bend all their
ordinance againſt the wall to make a breach, how furi-
ouſly they will giue the aſſault, and how deſperately they
will fight that they may not bee diſapointed of their hope
and looſe all their former labour; and ſhall wee thinke
that ſathan who hath longe beſeidged vs, deſiring nothing
more then to ſacke our ſouls, and to ſpoile them of al Gods
graces and to lead them captiue to hell and deſtruction,
will vſe leſſe politicke furie in aſſaulting vs with all his engines of battrie when hee ſeeth the time approach when as
now or neuer he is to accompliſh his deſire ? But let vs
conſider moreouer how able wee are to indure his aſſaults
if wee doe not prepare our ſelues before the time of ſickneſſe, arming our ſelues with the whole armour of God;
ſurely wee are naked and lie open to all his violence, being
deſtitute of the girdle of veritie; the knowledge of Gods
truth, neither armed with the breſtplate of righteouſneſſe,
nor hauing our feete ſhod with the preparation of the
goſpell of peace, whereby wee might bee inabled chearefully to march in the afflicted way which is full of the
thornes and briars of tribulation and afflictions, wherin
we muſt trauaile if we will goe to Gods kingdome; neither
yet hauing the ſhield of faith whereby wee might quench
the firie dartes of the wicked one, nor the helmet of ſaluation, nor yet any ſkill to vſe the ſword of the ſpirit, the
word of God : eyther for the defending of our ſoules; or
the offending of our enemie. And whereas wee may hope
that God will at that time ſupply all our wantes and giue
vnto vs all his ſpirituall armour whereby wee may bee defended and ſathan repulſed, wee are to knowe that God v-
ſeth not to giue his heauenly and ſpirituall graces at the
houre of death to thoſe, who haue contemned them al their

life,

life, or if hee doe beſtowe them vpon any it is ordinarily by meanes which hee hath ordayned for this purpoſe, as the hearing of the word, harty prayer, holy conferences, and ſuch like ſpirituall excerciſes : now let it bee graunted that wee may haue at ſuch times of our mortall ſickneſſes, Gods miniſters and all other outward helpes to further vs, in performing of theſe duties (which yet notwithſtanding no man can promiſe to himſelfe) yet howe vnfit is any man in this caſe for the effectuall doing of theſe holy exerciſes, when as his bodie is full of paine, and his minde full of anguiſhe, partly fearing Gods iudgments and eternall damnation, partly being greeued with the loſſe of all his delights, and becauſe hee is to parte with his friendes, partly being troubled and diſtracted with diſpoſing of his worldly eſtate and ſetting all things in order; and when to all theſe incumbrances there is added ſathans dangerous temptations, who then moſt violently aſſaulteth, and moſt ſubtilely vndermineth vs that hee may worke our finall deſtruction ? And therefore ſeeing our conuerſion in the time of our ſickneſſe is ſo hard and difficult, (I had almoſt ſayd deſperate,) let vs whileſt the Lord giueth vs the outward meanes of our conuerſion, and withall the vſe of our ſenſes, vnderſtandings, and memories, (all which when wee are grieuouſly ſicke, are alwaies exceedingly weakened, and ſometime quite ouerthrowne) let vs (I ſay) vnfaynedly turne vnto the Lorde by vnfained repentance in the time of our health, and ſtrengh, and not by our delayes, hazard and deſperately indanger the eternall ſaluation of our ſoules for the inioying of the tranſitory trifles and vaine delightes of this miſerable world.

CHAP. XXIX.

Of the fift Motiue which is that our delay will bringe more ſorrowe or vtter deſtruction.

The

He fifth argument to perſwade vs to ſpeedy repentance and turning vnto God, is that by our
delay eyther wee prepare more matter for our
owne ſorrow and griefe, or elſe treaſure vp for
our ſelues a more fearefull meaſure of wrath againſt the day
of wrath; for if the beſt happen that wee canne hope for, or
imagine, it is that wee truely repent vs of our ſinnes without which, there is no forgiueneſſe, and what is this repentance, but an harty ſorrowe, and bitter greefe, for our ſinnes
paſt, and an earneſt deſire and indeuoure of forſaking
them in time to come ? and therefore ſeeing whatſoeuer
pleaſure wee haue taken in ſinninge wee muſt after looſe it
in ſorrowing for ſinne, ſeeing our laughing muſt ende in
weeping, and our hony bee turned into gall, and worme-
woode, let vs breake off our ſinnes betimes, by vnfained
repentance, and not heape vp matter of more greefe, let
not our mindes ſo much dote to taſte of the honie which
ſinne bringeth in the mouth, as that we forgette the poyſon
which it carrieth in the tayle; let vs not be ſo eager in drinking of this poiſon of ſinne, though it be ſweete and pleaſant
to the taſt, remembring that it is deadly in opperation if it
bee not (as it were) caſt vp againe by vnfained repentance;
let not our gluttonous appetites cauſe vs to ſurfet on the
pleaſures of ſinne, ſeeing the preſent delight will not coun-
tervaile the future paine, when as being ſicke in ſinne, and
tormented in conſcience, wee ſhall vomit that with greefe,
which wee haue eaten with pleaſure, finding more bitterneſſe in the caſting vp, then ſweeteneſſe when we ſwallowed
it downe. But this is the beſt which can befall vs, for if we
doe not thus hartely ſorrowe for our ſinnes, but ſtill liue
in them with pleaſure and delight, then doe wee nothing
elſe but heape vp iudgement, and puniſhments, which ſhall
one day bee powred vpon vs in full meaſure, and fill vp
the vialls of Gods wrath, till being filled vp to the brimme,
hee will powre them out vpon our one heades. And this
the Apoſtle plainely ſheweth. Rom. 2 . 5. *But thou (ſaith
hee) after thine hardneſſe and heart that cannot repent, heapeſt*

vnto thy selfe wrath against the day of wrath, and of the decla-ration of the iust iudgment of God. 6. *Who will rewarde euery man according to his workes.* &c. And this is all the treasure which sinners, by deferring their repentance heape vp vnto themselues for the last daies; as *Iames* speaketh. Iame. 5. 3. The longer therefore wee deferre our repentance the more wee increase the bills of accoumpts, of which wee shall ne-uer bee able to giue a reckoning, at the great, and generall audit, the more wee heape vp our sinnes, the more wee heape vp Gods wrath; and increase the measure of our con-demnation, and hellish tormentes euery day, (as it were) pyling vp wood, in which we shall eternally be burned.

§. *Sect.* 2.   The sixt motiue to perswade vs to hasten our conuersion
The sixt mo-   vnto God with all speed, is the consideration of the dange-
tiue our dan- rousnesse of our estate before our conuersion; for wee are
gerous estate dead in our sinnes, the children of wrath and enemies vnto
before con- God, who euery minute lye open to his iudgements and pu-
uersion. nishments. And this the Lord implieth in his speach to *Cain,* Gen. 4. 7. *If thou doest not well* (saith he) *sinne lieth at the dore,* that is the punishment due to thy sinne, like a cruell wilde beast still watcheth and waiteth for thee, so as thou canst not stirre any way but it is ready to seafe vpon and destroy thee. Now in what a fearefull state are those who euery minute liue in this daunger, of which if they be surprised what can remaine vnto them but euerlasting death and destruction; *For as the tree falleth so shall it lie,* as it is Eccl. 11. 3. that is; as the day of death leaueth vs, so shall the day of iudgment find vs, and therefore if wee be taken away in our impænitencie whilest we are dead in our sins, children of wrath, and ene-mies vnto God, such shall we be presented before the tribu-nal seate of iudgement in the presence of the great iudge of

§. *Sect.* 3.   heauen and earth.
The seuenth   The seuenth motiue may be drawne from the manifold
motiue taken benefits which will accompanie our speedie conuersion, for
from the be- first vertue and goodnesse being sowne in vs in the time of
nefites which youth, will take more deepe roote in vs, so as it cannot easily
accompanie be left or lost, for as the vessell doth longest retaine the smell
our conuer-
sion.   and

and tast of that liquor which was put into it whilest it was new and vnseasoned, so they will longest retaine vertue and goodnesse who haue it planted in them in their youth, according to that Pro. 22. 6, teach a child in the trade of his way, and when he is old he will not depart from it. Secondly if we turne to God betimes the exercises of religion, and workes of sanctification, will be farre more pleasant and easie then if we deferre them till our old age, for often vse will bringe vs to a custome, and long custome will worke in vs an habite of vertue, which will be easie and familiar, if children from their youth be brought vp in trades and occupations which are exceeding hard and difficult, they do attaine to the skill and practise of them with exceeding dexteritie and quicknesse, but if the learning of them be deferred till old age they cā neuer attaine vnto them, or at least performe them slowly and with great difficultie, and so if from our childhood wee accustome our selues to the learning and practise of the workes of holinesse and righteousnesse, they will growe exceeding easie and pleasant, whereas being deferred they wilbe difficult and tedious. If the oxe whilest he is yong be accustomed to the yoke hee draweth in it quietly and with no great paine, but if he runne long in the pasture vnbroken and vntamed, when he is brought to the yoke he strugleth and striueth, and therewith gaulling his necke draweth with exceeding payne and irksomenesse; and so if in our youth we accustome our selues to beare the yoke of obedience, it wilbe easie and pleasant, but if we vse delayes we shall grow stubborne and stifnecked like vntamed oxen, and the bearing of Christs yoke through our impaciencie, and the rebellion of our nature will gaule and vexe vs. Thirdly, the sooner wee turne vnto God, the more ioy, peace and comfort shall we haue in the whole course of our liues, for what ioy may bee compared with the ioy in the holy Ghost, what peace is like the peace with God; & the peace of conscience, when as we are sure that we are now friends, who before we were enemies and children of God and heires of his euerlasting kingdome of glory, who in time past were children of

Pro. 15. 13.

wrath

wrath and fire brands of hell? what comfort in the world
can be imagined like vnto the confolation of Gods fpirit,
which is able to make all afflictions light; and euen death it
felfe fweet and pleafant vnto vs, but this ioy, peace, & comfort doe all companie our true conuerfion vnto God, and
therefore who would deferre it for one day, feeing it bringeth fuch ineftimable benefits and fuch furpafling pleafures
as none fufficiently vnderftand them, but they who feele &
inioy them. Whereas on the other fide if we deferre our cō-
uerfion, in the meane while wee are continually fubiect to
the checkes and terrours of an euill confcience, in feare of
Gods iudgements and eternall damnation: and though in
outward fhewe wee may bee exceeding merie and pleafant, yet our mirth is ful of forrow, and our ioy of bitternes,
and of *fuch laughter wee may fay, thou art madde, and of this ioy
what is that wh ch thou doeft*? as the Wife man fpeaketh, Ec-
cle.2.2, for it is but *Sardonicus rifus* laughter from the teeth
outward, which is ftraight controuled with fome inward
pange or checke of confcience. Fourthly, the fooner wee
turne vnto the Lord; the longer time we fhall fpend in his
feruice, which in truth is perfect liberty, now what can bee
more delightful vnto any Chriftian heart, then to ferue our
creatour from the daies of our youth, & to fhew our thank-
fulnefle to God our redeemer for all the ineftimable benefits which he hath beftowed vpon vs, by caufing our lights
to fhine before men, and by glorifying his name in our godly & Chriftian liues? what can be more pleafing to a thankfull mind then to take all occafions of expreffing thankful-
fulnefle to him vnto whom we are fo much bounden? Laftly, as by our fpeedy conuerfion vnto God we liue in fweete
comfort and ioyfull peace, fo alfo wee fecurely expect death
and giue it entertainement when it commeth with cheerefull countenance, for being conuerted vnto God we are at
peace with him and in his loue and fauour, wee are affured
that the curfe of the law is nayled to Chriftes croffe, that he
was condemned that we might be iuftified and put to death
that wee might liue eternally, that he is gone before vs into
heauen

heauen to prepare vs a place there, and now sitteth at the right hand of his father to giue vs ioyfull entertainement when we come vnto him, that he hath taken away the sting of death which is sinne, and hath made a soueraigne medicine against this poyson with his precious bloud, and therefore being conuerted vnto God we need not to feare death, nay rather wee may wishe with the Apostle to be speedily *dissolued that we may be with Christ seeing that is best of all.* As it is Phil. 1. 23. neyther need wee to feare the destruction of this earthly tabernacle, seeing *wee are assured that we haue a building giuen vs of God, a house not made with hands but eternall in the heauens.* as it is 2. Cor. 5. 1. Moreouer we shall not need to feare either suddaine death; or an euill death, for it cannot be suddaine to them who are alwaies prepared, *Nec potest male mori qui bene vixit,* neither can he die ill who hath *August.* liued well. On the other side those who deferre their repentance and turning vnto God, when death approcheth are filled with horrour & feare when as they see that they are still subiect to the curse of the law and euery minute in danger of Gods fearfull iudgements; when as the waight of sin presseth them, Sathan and their owne conscience accuseth them, death waiteth on them to bring them to euerlasting death, hell, and destruction. And therefore seeing so many benefits accompanie our speedy conuersion both in life and death, and so many euils follow our delayes: let vs not be moued by Sathans tentations, the sweetenesse of sinne, nor with the alluring vanities of this deceitfull world to deferre our repentance from day to day, but let vs now harken whilest God, yet calleth vs, and take the good and acceptable time when he offereth it vnto vs.

The eight motiue to perswade vs to speedy conuersion, is that our turning vnto God being deferred to our olde age, or till the time wee lie sicke on our deathbeddes, is not so excellent in it one nature, nor so acceptable vnto God, as if it were performed in the time of our youth; for what great matter is it if wee leaue our sinnes, when they are readie to leaue vs, to renounce the world with the riches

§ Sect. 4.
The 8. motiue because repentance deferred to olde age is not so excellent or acceptable.

honoures,

honoures, and pleasures thereof, when they are readie to a-
bandon vs; to imbrace mortification, when as our bodies
are mortified with sickenesse, and brought to the gates of
death; to giue to the pore when wee can keepe our goods
no longer, to forgiue our enemies, when as we can not offer
them any further wrong, or violence, to comend our wiues,
and children, into the hands of God, when as we our selues
can no longer defend and prouide for them ? to cease to
sweare and blaspheme Godes name, when as soone after
wee shall cease to speake? moreouer how can wee thinke
that this will be acceptable vnto God when as wee doe not
come vnto him before all the world forsakes vs, nor craue
his helpe till wee are abandoned of all other succour,
nor offer to come into his seruice before wee are ready to
goe out of the worlde, and that rather for feare of punishment; and hope of reward, then for any loue we beare to our
Lord and maister. But let it be granted (as in trueth it cannot bee denied) that whensoeuer wee truely repent vs of
our sinnes and turne vnto God he wil receiue vs to mercy,
should wee take occasion hereof to deferre our conuersion
and to continue in our sinnes ? should his loue and mercy towardes vs mooue vs to rebellion, and impietie, towards him, and becaufe hee is gratious and long suffering
shall we therfore the more offend him, and as it were whet
the edge of his wrath against vs ? be it farre from vs. Nay rather if God be gratious and mercifull, let vs bee ashamed to
offend so gratious and mercifull a God, and though wee
shoulde bee so hard harted as not to feare his iustice, and
fearefull iudgementes, yet euen in common humanitie
let vs blush for shame to offende him in confideration of his infinite loue, and mercie. If wee had a friende
who by reason of the loue hee beareth vs, would hardly
bee displeafed, or mooued to anger against vs, would wee
make this vse of his loue and patience, still to prouoke him
with new iniuries ? Nay if their bee any good nature and
ciuilitie in vs, would not his loue towardes vs, mooue vs to
loue him againe, and woulde not this loue worke in vs a
                                                    care

care and feare not to diſpleaſe him ? yes aſſuredly. O let not then the Lordes loue, patience, and long ſuffering, who is our friend of frindes, make vs to take occaſion of offending, and diſpleaſing him, but rather let the conſideration thereof bee a forcible and ſtronge motiue to mooue vs to repentance.

Laſtly though the Lorde bee ſo gratious, and mercifull, that he is ready to receiue vs into his loue, and fauour whenſoeuer wee vnfainedly repent, and truely turne vnto him; yet foraſmuch as hee extendeth his mercy to thoſe onely, who are truely penitent, & ſeing the repentance of the moſt is fained, and hypocriticall, which then onely beginneth when death or ſome extreame daunger approacheth, this ſhould bee a ſtronge motiue to perſwade vs to repent, and turne vnto the Lorde, when wee are in our perfect health, ſtrength, and proſperite that ſo wee may haue aſſurance that our conuerſiō is ſincere and vnfained, and not forced or diſſembled. Wee knowe that *Pharaoh* himſelfe when hee was vexed with Gods fearefull plagues, could ſay I haue ſinned, and promiſe amendment, And *Saul*, when God threatned to cut him off, and to take the kingdome from him, could acknowledge his wickedneſſe, and pretend a deſire to worſhip the Lord. And *Ieroboam* could ſhewe more contrition for the loſſe of his hand, then he euer ſhewed for the loſſe of his ſoule. And wicked *Achab* when he heard heauie iudgments denounced againſt him, could outwardly humble himſelfe, put on ſackcloth, faſt and goe demurely. And who may not obſerue in his owne experience, how many there are who in the time of their ſickeneſſe, make godly ſhewes of repentance, promiſing goulden mountaynes and vowing if they recouer, that they will leade a newe life, forſaking their ſinnes, and indeuouring to ſerue the Lorde in the duties of holineſſe, and righteouſneſſe, and yet the ſame men being reſtored to their heath, with the dogge returne to their vomit, and with the ſowe to wallowe againe in the filthie puddle of ſinne, becomming as prophaine, wicked, irreligious, and negligent in all duties of chriſtianitie, as euer they were,

Rom. 2. 4.
§. Sect. 5.
The laſt motiue becauſe repentance in time of ſicknes is often vnſound.

Exod.9.27.
& 10.16.17.

Sam.15.24.
25.

1.King.13.6
& 21.27.

were; which is a moſt vndoubted ſigne, that there repentance was but faigned, and diſſembled, and that they were
mooued thereunto not for any loue of God, or hatred of
ſinne, but for feare of Gods iudgmentes, and eternal condemnation, and therefore as ſoone as the cauſe of their feare
is a little remooued, their repentance alſo ceaſeth. Moreouer wee knowe that true repentance is the gifte of God,
and that we haue it not at our owne beck and call, but when
he offereth and vouchſaueth it vnto vs, and therefore it is no
maruaile if they who haue ſcorned this gratious gift all the
whole courſe to ther liues, ſhould be denied it at the time of
death, & left ſo to the hardnes of their harts, that though with
Eſau they ſeeke repentance with teares, yet they ſhall neuer
find it. And though with the fiue fooliſh virgins they deſire
to buy oyle for their lamps yet the time of grace being paſt
they ſhall be ſhut out of doores and excluded from the mariage. Neither doth the Lord ordinarily beget faith, repentance and other ſanctifying graces in any man, but by the vſe
of the meanes which he hath ordayned for this purpoſe; now
the meanes ordained of God are not ſickneſſe or the infirmities of old age, but the miniſterie of his word, made effectuall by the inward operation of his ſpirit for our conuerſion &
ſanctification; and therefore if the Lord hath oftentimes
grauted vs this meanes, and they haue not beene effectuall for our conuerſion if hee haue often called vs in the
preaching of the word and wee haue refuſed to come, what
hope can we haue that wee ſhould turne vnto God, without
this meanes in the time of ſickneſſe, who by the continuall
hearing of the word haue not beene conuerted in the time of
our health, ſeeing not any come vnto Chriſt but whom the
father draweth, and the meanes whereby he draweth vs vnto
him, is not ſickneſſe or the approching of death ordinarily,
but the miniſterie of his word; for when the ſheepe heare
Chriſts voyce and thereby knowe him to bee the true ſhee-
pheard. then (and not before) they follow him as it is Iohn.
10.27. So that though we were ſicke and certainely aſſured
wee ſhould die to morrow, yet for all this, wee are neuer the
neerer our conuerſion, faith, and repentance then we were

Eph 4.11.12

Iohn 6. 44.

before; as appeareth in the example of the Epicures. 1. Cor. 15
32. *Let vs eate and drinke* (fay they) *for to morrow we fhall die*
a man would thinke they fhould rather haue fayd, let vs faft
and pray for to morrow we fhall die; but this plainly fheweth
that we are neuer the neerer our conuerfion vnto God, and
true repétance though we are certaine that death approcheth; it is onely the worke of Gods fpirite which ordinarily
worketh not by the means of ficknefle or feare of death, but
by the minifterie of the word which is Gods owne ordináce, Eph. 4. 11. 12
infituted of God for the gathering together of the Saints, and for
the edification of the body of Chrift. And therefore while ft the
Lord calleth vs in the preaching of the word, let vs harken
vnto his voice, and turne vnto him by vnfained repentance,
for if Gods owne ordinance is not effectuall for our conuerfion, affuredly there is no hope that euer we will be conuerted by ficknes or any other extraordinarie meanes whatfoeuer. It is an admirable miracle wrought by the infinite
wifedome and almighty power of God, that a poore finner
fhould be conuerted vnto him by the preaching of the word,
for hereby we who were dead in finne, are raifed vp to newneffe of life, we who were borne blind, are indued with fight,
our hearts more hard then the Adamant are made flexible,
and foft as waxe to receaue any impreffion, which the Lord
wil imprint in them, and wee are moued to denie our felues,
and to caft away our owne righteoufnefle, and to reft and relye vpon Chrift Iefus alone for our iuftification and faluation, which is quite contrarie to our naturall difpofition: but
it were a miracle of miracles that all thefe things fhould be
wrought in vs by ficknefle, which the Lord hath not ordayned for this purpofe, when as the meanes appointed by God
himfelfe the minifterie of his word, which is Gods owne ordinance could neuer worke them in vs. It may bee indeed
that Gods hand lying heauy vpó vs in the time of ficknefle,
and fearing worfe iudgements in the life to come, we may be
moued hereby to make a goodly fhew, and to vowe great reformation if we might bee reftored to our health: It may be
that with *Pharaoh* we may make a fained confeffion of our
finnes, and promife to amend if this iudgement may be re-

moued, or that we may with *Achab* outwardly humble our selues before God, to the end we may escape those fearefull punishments which are threatned in his word; but it is a thousand to one if we then truly repent who haue liued our whole time in impænitency, or then turne vnto God if wee were not before that time effectually called and conuerted; for as wee liue so wee commonly die, neither is it likely that hauing led our liues like wicked *Balaam* we should die the death of the righteous, that hauing alwaies hitherto been thornes and thistles we should now bring forth sweet figges and pleasant grapes when wee are ready to be cut downe and to be cast into the fire, that hauing all our life sowed the seedes of wickednesse we should at our death reape the fruit of godlinesse; *And therefore* (as the Apostle exhorteth) *let vs not be deceiued : God is not mocked; for whatsoeuer a man soweth that shall he also reape; for he that soweth to his flesh, shall of the flesh reape corruption, but he that soweth to the spirit, shall of the spirite reape life euerlasting.* as it is Gal.6.7.8.Let vs now turne vnto God while he calleth vs and graunteth vs the meanes of our conuersion the ministerie of his word; now is the acceptable time, now is the day of our saluation; and if wee will now turne vnto God and truly repent whilest we might continue in our sinnes, we may be assured our repentance is true and vnfained, and not pressed out of vs with sence of present paine, nor forced with feare of future punishment, and that turning to God wee shalbe receaued to grace and mercy, seeing we then offer to serue him, when wee might haue serued Sathan, the world and our owne corrupt flesh.

CHAP. XXX.

Two letts which hinder worldlings from speedy repentance re-mooued.

§. Sect. 1.

The first let, is the misa-plying of

Nd so much concerning these Motiues, whereby wee may bee perswaded to speedie repentance, all which the worldly secure man wardeth and beareth of with a double fence, so as

they

they can neuer beate him downe with true humilitie Gods mercy nor pearce his heart with vnfained sorrow for sinne; the one and gratiou promises. is by alleadging Gods mercy manifestly declared vnto vs in the sweet promises of the Gospel; the other by obiecting the example of the conuerted thiefe, who though hee had spent his whole life in sinne and wickednesse, yet at the last hower was receiued to mercy.

For the first, hath not the Lord (will they say) protested in Ezech.13. his word that he desireth not the death of a sinner, but that 32.& 33.11. he turne from his way and liue? hath not our Sauiour tould Math.9. 13. Math.11.28 vs that he came not to cal the righteous; but sinners to repentance? and doth he not inuite such vnto him as labour vnder the heauie burthen of sinne promising that hee will ease them? And hath not the Apostle *Paul* taught vs, that 1.Tim.2.4. Gods will *is that all men should be saued, and come to the knowledge of his trueth.* Seeing therefore God is so mercifull why should we doubt of our saluation? Why should we feare to deferre our repentance & follow our pleasures and delights for a time, seeing the Lord will receiue vs to mercy whensoeuer we turne vnto him?

I answere first, that though al this were certaine, true, and The first let not to bee doubted of, yet it is a most vnthankefull part remoued. and horrible ingratitude against our gracious God and louing father to take occasion of his mercie the more to offend him, as before I haue shewed. Secondly I answere, that as God hath shewed his mercy in the gratious promises of the Gospell, so also he hath as plainely declared his iustice in the seuere threatnings of the law, and he is as true in the one as in the other: And therefore all the question is who shal tast of his mercy, and who of his iustice, seing that is promised to some, and this threatned against others; or rather in truth it is without all question, for the Lord hath plainely shewed in his word that hee will extend his mercy to all repentant sinners and to them onely; and that he will declare his iustice in powring out his iust iudgements vpon the wicked who liue in their sinnes, and especially vpon those who take occasion of Gods mercie to continue in their vnrepentancie,

tancie,despising the riches of his bountifulnes,his patience &
long suffering;for hereby they heape vnto themselues *wrath
against the day of wrath and the declaration of the iust iudgmēt
of God,* as the Apostle speaketh, Rom. 2.4.5. Though then
there be neuer so many sweet promises in the gospel,yet they
who continue in their sinnes without repentance can reape
no true comfort by them,because they are not made to them
but to repentant sinners; and on the other side though there
be neuer so many terrible threatnings denounced in the law,
yet the pænitent sinner need not to feare them, seeing they
are threatned onely against those who continue in their impænitencie;though God be of infinit mercy let not the wicked man who liueth in his sinnes presume,seeing it is sufficiently declared in pardoning the sinnes of repentant sinners.
Neither let him who is truly pænitent despaire because God
is of infinite iustice, seeing it is sufficiently manifested in punishing the sinnes of those who continue in their vnrepentancie ; let not him who is turned vnto God from his wicked waies feare Gods iustice, for it is fully satisfied in Christ
and therefore it shall neuer attach him, neither let him who
continueth in his sinnes without repentance hope in Gods
mercy for it doth not belong vnto him, nor yet in the sweet
promises of the Gospell which though they be neuer so generall,yet are they alwaies to be restrained to the condition
of the couenant of grace, faith, and repentance. And this is
manifest in the places before alleaged which worldly men so
much abuse to nourish in them carnall securitie;for whereas
the Lord saith Ezech.33.11.*That he will not the death of a sinner,* he addeth in the next wordes, *but that he turne from his
way and liue,* so that the Lord speaketh not of all sinners but
of those who turne vnto him from their wicked waies.So our
sauiour Christ saith Math.9.13, that *hee came not to call the
righteous,* that is those who are iust & righteous in their owne
conceipts, *but sinners to repentance,* so that whosoeuer are called vnto Christ that in him they may haue saluation are
called also to repentance. And Math.11.28.our sauiour doth
not call all sinners vnto him without difference, but those
onely

onely who *are wearie and heauy laden,* that is who find their
sinnes irksome and grieuous vnto them, and desire nothing
more then to be freed of this vnsupportable burthen. And
the Apostle *Paule* likewise 1.Tim.2.4. doth not say simply
that God would haue all men to be saued, but that he would
also to haue them come to the knowledge of the truth, that
is to the knowing, acknowledging, & beleeuing of the principles of Christian religion cōcerning God, themselues, and
the worke of redemption wrought by Christ. Let therefore
no carnall secure man take occasion to presume vpon Gods
mercy in regard of the sweet and gratious promises of the
Gospell, for vnlesse they turne vnto God from their euill
waies and truely repent them of their sinnes, vnlesse they are
wearie and heauie laden, desiring nothing more then to be
eased of their heauie burthen; vnlesse they come out of their
blind ignorance and attaine to the knowledge of the truth,
the gratious promises of the Gospell do not appertaine vnto
them.

Secondly, whereas they alleadge the example of the thiefe
conuerted at the hower of death we are to know that this is
but one particular act of Gods mercy, and therefore we can
make thereof no generall rule, especialy seeing to this one
we may oppose many thousands of those who hauing deferred their repētance to the last hower, haue beene taken away
in their sinns and impænitencie. It is true indeed that if with
this thiefe we truely turne vnto the Lord by vnfained repentance, and shew our faith by the like liuely fruites he wil pardon our sinnes and receaue vs to mercy according to his
gratious promises, but this faith and repentance are not in
our owne power, but the free gifts of God which hee very
seldome bestoweth on those at the hower of death who
haue neglected & contemned them their whole liues: sometimes indeed hee calleth and conuerteth some at the last
hower to shew the infinite riches of his mercy, but most
commonly he leaueth those who haue deferred their repentance to die in their impænitencie that they may be examples of his iustice. And to this purpose *Austine* speaketh

well;

§. *Sect.*2.

The 2. *let is presumption vpon the example of the conuerted thiefe.*

well; there is(faith hee) mention made in the Scriptures of
one whome the Lord receaued to mercy that none might
despaire, and but of one that none might presume. It is the
maner of princes to send their gratious pardon sometimes
to those who are led out to execution, but if any will wilfully
offend in hope hereof, or hauing offended wil deferre to sue
for his pardon to the last hower, surely he is well worthy to
be hanged, both for his offence; and also for his presumption, so the Lord mercifully pardoneth some few when death
is ready to cease vpon them, and to transport them into the
eternall torments of hell fire, to shew the riches of his grace,
but if any shall take occasion hereby the more to offend a-
gainst his maiestie, or hauing offended deferreth to sue for
pardon by powring out the teares of vnfained repentance
vntill his last hower, hee is vndoubtedly vnworthy of any
grace and mercy, and in all likelihood he shall be deliuered
vp to suffer eternal torments. Moreouer as this act of mercy
in receiuing this thiefe to grace was very extraordinary, so
was it reserued as being most fit for the time of Christes passion; for as great Princes at the time of their coronation pardon such notorious offences, the like whereof they wil hardly euer after remit, to the end that their clemencie and mercy may appeare to all, so our Sauiour Christ the glorious
king of heauen and earth, being ready to lay downe the
forme of a seruant and to take vpon him the crowne of endlesse glory and maiesty, gaue his gratious pardon to this
greeuous offender, that his infinite mercy and goodnesse
might be manifested vnto al men, that so they might breake
of their sinnes by vnfained repentance, and by a liuely faith
come vnto him, looking and expecting for life and saluation onely in this their sauiour and redeemer; and as cunning
Surgeons hauing made a soueraigne salue, do vpon the next
occasion make experiment thereof by curing some griesly
and desperate wound, that so they may commend it to all
who shal haue need to vse it, so the Lord hauing made a pretious plaister and soueraigne salue to cure all soules; who being wounded with sinne, will apply it vnto them by a liuely
                                                    faith

faith, prefetly tooke occafion of curing there with this poore
theefe grieuoufly wounded with finne, that all others in his
ftate, feing the vertue thereof, might more earneftly defire it
and more carefully feeke after, and apply it to their wounded foules. And therefore feeing the occafion of this cure
was altogether extraordinary, the action is not like to bee
ordinarie, the occafion being remooued, and the mercy of
God and vertue of Chriftes death and bloodfhed being fufficiently manifefted to al the world. Thirdly, we are to know
that the eftate of thefe men, is farre vnlike and much more
defperate then the ftate of the conuerted theefe; for hee was
in all likelihood neuer before this time called, and prefently he harkeneth vnto the voyce of Chrift, and willingly intertaineth the good motions of his fpirit, but thefe men
being often called, haue refufed to come, and haue quenched the good motions of Gods fpirit; he perfifted in his fin
ignorantly, hauing not heard the doctrine of the Gofpell,
whereby he might be inuited to come vnto Chrift by a liuely
faith, and might turne vnto God by vnfained repentance,
thefe haue often heard thefe glad tidings, and haue neglected
and contemned them; hee continued in his finnes through
ignorance, neither did hee vngratefully refolue to ferue the
diuell his whole life, referuing the time of his old age and
ficknefle for the feruice of God, only for his own aduantage,
but thefe men hauing bin ofte inftructed in the law of God,
and wayes of godlinefle, notwithftanding wittingly and wil
fully perfift in their finns, prefuming vppon repentance and
hope of mercy at the laft houre, intending then to turne vnto God, not for any loue they beare him, but for feare of hel
torments and eternall damnation, laftly his repentance was
moft vnfayned and exceeding earneft, and his faith brightly
fhined prefently after his conuerfion in fingular fruits thereof. For he made a notable confeffion of his fauiour and redeemer, euen when all his difciples for feare forfooke him.
He iuftifieth Chrift when all men condemned him, and euen
his Apoftles doubted of him. He praieth feruently vnto him,
when the multitude mocked and reuiled him, hee humbly

confeffeth

confeſſeth his owne ſinns, and louingly admoniſheth his fellow of his wickedneſſe, deſiring earneſtly that as they had bin
fellowes, and copartners in ſinne, ſo they might be partakers
in pardon, and in the benefitte of redemption wrought by
Chriſt. Whereas moſt commonly their repentance is forced and diſſembled for feare of puniſhment, rather then for
hatred of ſinne, or loue of God: as they vſually make it manifeſt if they recouer of their ſickeneſſe. And therefore ſeing
there is ſuch great diſſimilitude; and difference in their purpoſes, liues, and courſes, it is not probable that they wil euer
bee like in their conuerſion, death, and ſaluation.

CHAP. XXXI.

Sathans tentations mouing men to reſt in a counterfait repen-
tance, anſwered.

§ *Sect.* I.
That the pro-
miſes of the
goſpell are
made onely to
thoſe who re-
pent ſeriouſly.

And ſomuch for the anſwering of thoſe tentations wherby Sathan laboreth to make vs delay
and deferre our repentance from day to day:
with which, if he cannot preuaile both becauſe
we ſee the neceſſitie of repentance vnto ſaluation, and alſo plainly perceiue by the former reaſons that delayes are moſt dangerous, then hee will laboure in the next
place to perſwade vs to content our ſelues with a ſmale meaſure of repentance, or rather in truth with a coūterfait worke-
repentance, which is only in outward ſhew and neuer pear-
ceth the heart; making vs beleeue that if when wee ſee our
ſinns, hauing our conſciences conuinced out of Gods word
we doe in ſome generall tearmes confeſſe that we are all ſinners, and deſire God after a formall manner to haue mercie
vppon vs, if we can ſometime ſtraine from vs a broken ſighe
and be content to leaue ſome of our leaſtpleaſing ſinnes, our
repentance wilbe very acceptable to God, and ſuffitient for
our ſaluation.

And with this tentation Sathan deludeth, and deſtroyeth,
innumerable men in theſe our dayes, and therefore it behooueth

ueth euery man, to prepare himfelfe for this incounter. And
to this ende we are to know that the mercy of God, and merits of Chrift, doth not belong vnto thofe who thus flubber
ouer their repentance; neither doth Chrift Iefus call vnto
him fuch as flightly forrow for their finnes, and thinke the
burthen of them light, and eafie to bee borne, but fuch as
labour, and are heauie loaden. as appeareth Matth. 11. 28.
Come vnto me all ye who are wearie and heauie loaden, and I will
eafe you. In which wordes our fauiour Chrift plainely fheweth whom hee calleth to the participation of the worke of
redemption wrought by him, and what meafure of repentance hee requireth of them; for the firft worde κοπιῶντες
fignifieth fuch as labour vntill they bee wearie, and the other
worde πεφορτισμένοι fignifieth fuch as are heauie laden with
a burthen vnfupportable and therefore, being grieuoufly
preffed therewith, they defire nothing more, then to bee
eafed of it , for φορτος from which this worde is deriued
properly fignifieth the burthen of a fhippe, and is taken
metaphorically for any thing which is very troublefome and
grieuous. So that by ioyning thefe two together our fauiour
euidently declareth whom hee calleth, and inuiteth vnto
him. Namely thofe onely who knowe, acknowledge, and
feele , that their finnes are an intollerable heauie burthen,
and being exceedingly vexed with them, moft earneftly
defire to bee eafed, and releafed of them, and to this purpofe flee vnto Chrift by a true and liuely faith finding themfelues deftitute of all meanes whereby they may otherwife
be eafed and releeued.

If then wee would haue any affurance that wee are in
the number of thofe whom Chrift calleth and inuiteth vnto
him, wee muft haue firft a fight, and fenfe, of our finnes,
and a true and feeling knowledge of our miferable, and
wretched eftate, in which we are, by reafon of them, and the
punifhment due vnto them. Secondly we muft be wearie
in bearing this heauie burthen, as being moft irkefome
and grieuous vnto vs. Thirdly wee muft haue an earneft
defire to be eafed and freed from it. Laftly we muft come

§. *Sect.* 2.
What things
are required
in thofe who
truly repent.

vnto

vnto Chriſt by a true and liuely faith, to the ende that hee may eaſe and releaſe vs.

For the firſt Wee muſt come to the knowledge of our ſinnes, before wee can truely repent of them, for we cannot ſorrowe for them, vntill wee ſee them; neither is it ſufficient that wee ſee, and know, that wee are greeuous and hainous ſinners, vnleſſe we alſo feele the waight of this intollerable burthen, preſſing vs downe, and vexing, and grieuing vs euen to the verie heart; for wicked and prophane men may ſee their ſinnes, (for what can hide them from their eyes being ſo innumerable in multitude, and ſo grieuous and hainous in reſpect of their quantitie, and quallitie, but yet they feele not their waight, neither are troubled with them; nay it is a paſtime to a foole to doe wickedly, as it is Prou. 10, 23. and the abhominable filthie ſinner drinketh iniquitie like water, as it is Iob. 15. 16. and there are ſome ſo delighted with vngodlineſſe, and all lewd prophaneſſe that they euen *drawe vnto them iniquitie with the cordes of vanitie, and ſinne as with cart-ropes,* as the prophet ſpeaketh Eſa. 5. 18. and though they bee laden with their ſinnes as it were with an intollerable burthen, yet they feele them not, neither are they any thing vexed with their waight, and though the iniquitie of ſinners bee ſo heauie *that the earth cannot beare it but reeleth too and fro like a drunken man, and is remooued like a tent,* as it is Eſay 24. 20. though it make all the creatures grone and trauaile in paine together, as the Apoſtle ſheweth Rom. 8. 22. yea though it euen wearieth God himſelfe in ſuffering and bearing with it, as it is Eſa. 43. 24. yet doe they walke bolt vpright, and with ſtretched out neckes, neuer ſo much as ſtooping vnder this vnſupportable burthen, till at laſt it growe ſo heauie, that it ouerwhelmeth them, and preſſeth them downe to the bottome of hel.

The reaſon here of is becauſe they are wholy plunged yea drowned and dead in their ſinns, and therefore as thoſe who being diued to the bottome of ſome deepe water, doe not feele the waight of that which is aboue them, whereas if they were pulled out of the waters, they would be ouerwhelmed

with

with the burthen of one tunne, so those who are deeply plū-
ged into the gulph of sinne and wickednesse, doe not feele
the waight of this intollerable burthen, but if once they
come out of their sinns by vnfained repentance, the waight
of some few of them woulde presse them downe vnto the
gates of hell, if they bee not supported and freed from this
burthen by our sauiour Iesus Christ.

But such as these, are not called by our sauiour, neither
will he ease them, though their burthen be neuer so intollerable; but he inuiteth those onely who are heauie laden, and
finding their burthen irkesome are wearie of it and desire to
be eased; he harkeneth only vnto those who from their harts
cry out with Dauid. psal. 38. 4. *mine iniquities are gone ouer
my head, and as a waighty burthen they are to heauie for me. 6.
I am bowed and crooked very sore, I goe mourning all the day.*
He respecteth only those who are of a broken heart and con- Psal. 51. 17.
trite spirit, for these only perfourme the condition of the co- Esay 66.2.
uenant and consequently to them alone the promises contayned in the couenant doe appertaine.

The condition of the couenant is faith and repentance, §. *Sect.*3.
neither of which doth hee performe who doth not see nor *That hee who*
feele the burthen of his sinnes; for wee will neuer rest vpon *feeleth not his*
Christ for our saluation, vnlesse wee see that wee haue no *sinnes hath*
meanes of our owne to escape condemnation, wee will ne- *nor repētance.*
uer seeke vnto Christ to be our redeemer vnlesse wee perceiue that we are the bondslaues of sinne and Sathan, wee
will neuer labour to obtaine the riches of his righteousnesse,
vnlesse we discerne our owne nakednesse and beggerie, we
will neuer come vnto Christ to be washed and purged from
the pollution of our sinnes and corruptions with his bloud,
vnlesse we see our naturall filthinesse, wee will neuer desire
to be eased of the heauy burthen of our sinnes, vnlesse wee
feele the waight of them, we will neuer intreat Christ to be
our Physition, vnlesse wee find that our soules are sicke in
sinne; we will neuer goe vnto him who is the author of life,
vnlesse we see that we are dead in our sinnes, in a word we
will neuer intreat Gods mercy, vntill wee feele our owne
miserie

miferie.

If therefore without this fenfe of finne we will neuer come vnto Chrift, then confequently without it we fhall neuer be eafed, for he forceth thofe onely from condemnation who relie themfelues wholy vpon him for their faluatiõ, he came to be their redeemer alone who feele their miferable captiuity, and earneftly defire to be releafed, he wil not inrich any but thofe who perceiue their owne beggery, and craue reliefe, he will not wafh any with his precious bloud; but thofe who fee their pollution and filthineffe, and come vnto him intreating him to purge and cleanfe them, he will not eafe any but thofe who finding their finnes to be a heauie burthen, are wearie and come vnto him to be freed from them; he came into the world to be a phyfition, not to thofe who feele no infirmitie, but to thofe who are ficke and difeafed; he came to giue life to thofe alone who are dead in their fins and trefpaffes; neither will the Lord fhew mercy vnto any, but vnto thofe alone who perceiue their eftate to bee moft wretched and miferable.

For who can imagine that the Lord who is moft infinite in wifedome, fhould vnaduifedly beftow his benefits vpon fuch, as finding no want of them, do not defire them; when they are without them, nor efteeme them though they had them, and confequently will neuer be truely thankefull for that which they neither want, defire, nor efteeme; who can in reafon conceiue that he will offer himfelfe to bee a Sauiour, to fuch as doe not thinke themfelues loft and condemned, or to be their redeemer who will not acknowledge that they are in captiuitie, or that he will beftow the riches of his righteoufneffe vpon fuch proud beggers, as find no need thereof, being righteous inough themfelues in their owne conceipts, that hee will vainely fpend his precious bloud in wafhing of thofe who thinke themfelues cleane already, and need no fuch purging, that he will in compaffion eafe thofe of the burthen of their finnes who were neuer troubled with bearing of them; that hee will offer them any phyficke who will not acknowledge themfelues ficke; or to giue life to
thofe

thofe who will not confeffe that they are dead in finne; and who can imagine that the Lord will euer fhewe to thofe his mercy, who will neuer fhew to the Lord their wretched mi-ferie.

Whofoeuer therfore haue not a true fenfe and feeling of the heauie burthen of their finnes; they wil neuer come vnto Chrift, neither can they euer haue any affurance that he will eafe thē, & confequently they are deftitute of a true faith which is the chiefe condition of the couenant of grace; but as they want faith, fo alfo they can neuer attaine vnto true repentance. For fo long as they haue not the fenfe of their finnes they are not grieued with them, neither doe they de-fire to leaue and forfake them, and as thofe who bearing a burthen and are not vexed with the waight, they are not wearie of bearing it, nor defirous to leaue it; fo thofe who be-ing loaded with the vnfupportable burthen of their finnes and haue no fenfe of the waight they are not grieued with wearineffe nor defirous to be freed from it, and confequent-ly they are deftitute of true repentance which is nothing els but an harty griefe and a true forrow for our finnes paft and an earneft defire and indeuour to leaue and forfake them in the time to come.

So that whofoeuer haue not a true fenfe and feeling of the vnfupportable waight of finne, they are deftitute of true faith and repentance, and therefore the promifes of the gof-pell being made, onely to the faithfull & repentant finners, doe not appertaine vnto them. Which may more euidently appeare if wee confider fome of the particulars; Efay 61. 1. It is faid that our fauiour Chrift was fent to *preach glad tidings vnto the poore, to bind vp the broken harted, to preach libertie to the captiues, and to them that are bound, the opening of the prifon.* 2. *To comfort all that mourne, and to giue vnto them beautie for afhes, the oyle of ioy for mourning, and the garment of gladneffe for the fpirit of heauineffe.* Math.9.13. our fauiour faith that he *came not to call the righteous, but finners to repentance,* and the apoftle witneffeth of him, that he came into *the world to faue finners.* 1.Tim.1.15. If therfore we be not poore in fpirit and

§ *Sect. 4.*
The former point prooued by particular teftimonies.

brokē

broken harted, if we be not miferable captiues, heauie mour-
ners, & wretched finners, our fauiour Chrift was not fent to
preach the glad tidings of the gofpell vnto vs, hee will not
giue vs libertie nor affoord vs any comfort, hee came not to
call vs neither will hee faue vs. So our Sauiour profeffeth,
Math.18.11. that he *came to faue that which was loft, and to
fetch home the wandring fheepe.* If therefore wee bee not
loft in our felues wee fhall neuer bee found of Chrift, if wee
doe not confeffe with the Prophet Efay, that wee haue
gone aftray like wadring fheepe, he will neuer feeke vs, nor
cary vs on his bleffed fhoulders to the fheepfould of eternall
happineffe. In a word as without the fenfe of finne, we can
neuer attaine vnto faith and repentance, fo without faith
and repentance, we can neuer haue any affurance of any of
the promifes of the Gofpell.

Efay 53.6.

§. *Sett.5.*
*The meanes
whereby wee
may attaine
to a true fight
of our liues.
2.King.22.
19.
Att.2.37.*

And therefore it behooueth vs as we tender our faluation, that wee labour after the fight and fenfe of our finnes,
that with good *Iofias* our hearts melt within vs, and euen refolue themfelues into the teares of vnfained repentance;
that we euen rent our hearts with true compunction, as the
Prophet exhorteth. Ioel.2.13. and that with the Iewes wee
haue our hearts prickt within vs, when we come to the fight
of our finnes, and all this not fo much in regard of the punifhment we haue deferued, as that by our finnes wee haue
difpleafed our good God and gratious father, and haue caufed our fauiour Chrift who is the Lord of life, to be put to a
fhamefull and painefull death.

Zach.12.10

1. *Meanes
prayers.*

*Reuel.3.17.
18.*

And that wee may attaine vnto this fenfe and feeling of
our finnes, there are diuers meanes to be vfed effectuall for
this purpofe; as firft we are to haue our recourfe vnto God
by earneft and feruent prayer, defiring and intreating that
he will annoint the blind eyes of our vnderftandings, with
the pretious eye falue of his holy fpirit, that we may fee our
owne wretchedneffe, miferie, pouertie, blindneffe and na-
kednefle, and that hee will foften our hard hearts, with the
oyle of his grace, and fo beate thefe ftonie rockes, that out
of the may flow plentifull ftreams of vnfained repentance.

Second-

Secondly, we are oftentimes to set the law as a glasse before vs that so we may see our deformities, and to examine our liues thereby as it were by a rule or square, that so wee may know both how often we haue erred & transgressed it in the time past, and how vnable we are to performe it for the time to come in that exact maner which God requireth. For as the deformities and spots in the face though they be great and many, cannot be descerned of those who haue them, vnlesse they looke themselues in a glasse, and though euery one els doth plainly see them, yet the party himselfe doth least of all perceiue them: so though our spirituall deformities and filthy spots of sinne, appeare most vgly and odious in the eies of God & men, so that euery one seemeth to point at them, yet wee our selues will neuer discerne them, vnlesse we set the looking glasse of the law before vs.

Thirdly, we are often and earnestly to meditate vpon the iustice and truth of God, in whose presence the heauens are not cleane, and *the Angels themselues are vnable to abide the rigour of his iustice, and how much more is man abominable and filthy, who drinketh iniquitie like water.* In whose sight our best righteousnesse is like a polluted cloth, and how much more filthy then are our sinnes and wickednesse, moreouer as he is most iust so as he cannot let sinne goe vnpunished, so also hee is most true, yea truth it selfe, neither can any of those threatnings fall to the ground vnexecuted, which he hath denounced against those who liue in their sinnes, and therefore there is no meanes to escape his fearefull iudgements, vnlesse we turne from our sinnes and meete the Lord by vnfained repentance.

Fourthly, let vs continually remember that we must once appeare before Gods tribunall seate of iudgement, there to render an accompt not onely of our words and workes but euen of our secret thoughts, when as the Lord himselfe who searcheth the hearts and reignes shalbe our iudge who will not acquit the guilty, nor respect the person of man, neither will he be satisfied with faire pretences and smooth excuses, nor corrupted with bribes and gifts. And therefore let vs

iudge

Iudge our selues that we may not be iudged of the Lord, and in bitternesse of soule and remorse of conscience let vs condemne our selues to be miserable sinners, thatthe Lord may acquite vs and make vs tast of his mercy.

5. Remembrance of those punishments due to the wicked. Lastly, let vs seriously meditate on those fearefull punishments, which are prepared for those who liue and die in their sinnes; for they shall for euer be seperated from the presence of God, the ioyes of heauen, and the sweete companie of the Saints and Angels, and be cast into eternall darknes, where they shall for euer and euer be tormented in flames vnquenchable, all which horrible punishments are due vnto

Gal. 3. 10. all, who *continue not in all which is written in the booke of the law to doe them,* and therefore how shall we escape who in stead of continuing in obedience to all Gods commandements, haue continualy broke them aland done the clean contrary, if we do not in the sense of the heauy burthen of our sinnes, humble our selues before God by vnfained repentance, and come vnto Christ by a true and liuely faith, that we may bee eased of this intollerable waight, and adorned with his righteousnesse and obedience.

§. Sect. 6. *The 2. thing required is that our sins be irkesome & greeuous vnto vs.* And so much concerning the first signe, whereby those may be discerned whom Christ calleth, namely the sight and sense of their sinnes. But it is not sufficient that we feele our sinnes like a heauie burthen, pressing vs down if we be content to bear it stil, but it must seeme irksom and grieuous vnto vs, and make vs exceeding weary of bearing it, we must with

1. Pet. 4. 3. the Apostle *Peter* thinke it *sufficiet that we haue spent the time past of our liues, after the lust of the Gentiles in abominable sinnes,* and for the time to come we are to liue after the will of God, dedicating our selues wholy to his worship and seruice. Otherwise, though we haue neuer so exquisite a sight and sense of our sins, yet if they seeme vnto vs a sweet burthen which we are content stil to beare without any great wearinesse, nay with pleasure and delight, if wee bee like the rich miser who though his backe should be almost broken with the waight of his owne gold, yet would not thinke it any trouble, nay would esteeme it for his chiefe felicity because his

burthen

burthen pleaseth him, so if we feeling that our sinnes are an huge and massy burthen, are neuerthelesse not troubled nor wearie of bearing them, but rather take our chiefe delight in being so loded; because the burthen is exceeding sweet and delightfull to vs, we may assure our selues that we are not in the number of those whom Christ calleth, for hee inuiteth them onely vnto him? who being heauy laden with the waight of their sinnes are wearie of their burthen, and sorrow and greeue, that they cannot shake it of, nor be freed from it. Crying out with the Apostle *Paule*, Rom.7.~4. *O wretched man that I am, who shall deliuer mee from the bodie of this death.*

The third signe, whereby wee may know those whome Christ calleth, is that being vexed with the heauy burthen of sinne, they earnestly desire to be eased and released of it; for as those who are ouerpressed with a heauy burthen, desire aboue all things to be freed from it, so those who feele the waight of sinne pressing them downe and are weary & tired in bearing of it, they most earnestly desire to bee eased of this intollerable burthen, and will neuer bee at rest till their desire bee accomplished.

§. Sect.7. *The 3. thinge is an earnest desire to be freed from our sinnes.*

This desire in the Scriptures is resembled to hunger and thirst; in which these two things concurre, first a sense of our want, and secondly an appetite or earnest desire to be satisfied, and to haue our want supplied; and so in these spirituall things, first we feele the want of Gods graces and Christes righteousnesse, and then wee earnestly desire that wee may be filled and satisfied with them. So that to hunger and thirst after the grace of God, and the righteousnesse of Christ, and to be wearie and heauie laden are much alike, & both are blessed of the Lorde; for as those who hunger, and thirst after righteousnesse, are blessed because they shall bee satisfied, as it is, Matth. 5. 6. So they are blessed who are wearie and heauie laden, with the burthen of their sinnes, for such Christ calleth vnto him, and hath promised to ease them, that is, to giue vnto them the remission of their sinnes, and to releafe them of this burthen, by taking it vpon his owne shoulders.

This desire resembled to hunger and thirst.

fhoulders. And as our Sauiour calleth and inuiteth vnto
him fuch as are wearie and heauie laden. Matth. 11. 28. So
in diuers other places, he inuiteth and calleth thofe, who hunger and thirft after his righteoufnes So Efa. 55. 1. *To euery one*
that thirfteth come yee to the waters, and yee that haue no filuer
come buie, and eate, come I fay buy wine, and milke, without mony.
and Iohn 7. 37. *Iefus cryed faying; If any man thirft, let him*

Apoc. 21.6.
and 22.17. *come vnto mee and drinke.* Apoc. 21. 6. *I will giue to him who*
is a thirft, of the well of the water of life freely. and 22. 17. *Let*
him that is a thirft come, and let whofoeuer will, take of the well
of the water of life freely. a notable example of this thirfting
wee haue in Dauid. Pfal. 63. 1. *O God thou art my God, early wil*
I feeke thee, my foule thirfteth for thee. and 42. 1. *as the hart bray-*
eth for the riuers of water, fo panteth my foule after thee O God.
2. *my foule thirfteth for God, euen for the liuing God.* and Pfal.
143. 6. *my foule th rfteth after thee, as the thirftie land.* Which
thirft whofoeuer feeleth, he may boldly affure himfelfe, that
hee is in the number of thofe whom Chrift calleth, and that
will fatiffie him.

Whofoeuer therefore hungreth and thirfteth after the
grace of God, and righteoufnes of Chrift, whofoeuer is wearie and heauie laden, that is, who fo hath a true fenfe, and
feeling of his finnes, and is vexed, and greeued, with the
burthen thereof, and withall, his heart defireth to to be eafed
of his loade, though he thinke himfelfe in a moft miferable
eftate, yet if he come vnto Chrift, and with blind *Bartemaus*
crie out O fonne of *Dauid* haue mercy on mee, I may fitly fay
vnto him, as it was fayde vnto this blind man : Bee of good
comfort, for Chrift caileth thee.

§. Sect. 8.
The laft thing
required is
that we come
vnto Chrift. The laft thing required in thofe whome Chrift calleth, is,
that they come vnto him. for to whom fhould wee come for
eafe, but vnto Chrift himfelfe, feeing their is neither faint nor
Angell, that can eafe vs, for the waight of one finne would
preffe them downe into hell; wheras our Sauiour Chrift is
able to beare the burthen of our finnes, nay he hath alreadie
borne them, that wee might bee deliuered from them. As it
is, 1. Pet. 2. 24. neither it is likely, that either faint or Angel,
would

would so willingly helpe vs as our Sauiour Chriſt Ieſus, who
ſo tenderly loued vs that hee came into the worlde, to lay
downe his own moſt precious life as a price for our redemption; and though they were willing, yet they haue not the
like abilitie vnto him, who hath all power in heauen, and
earth cōmitted vnto him, for working the worke of our re- Mat.11.27.
demption. And therfore, ſeeing he wanteth neither loue, nor
power, let vs goe vnto him, and him onely. Otherwiſe we
ſhal commit a double follie, that is, we ſhall leaue Chriſt, who
is the foūtaine of liuing water, & dig vnto our ſelues broken
ciſternes, which will hould no water. *For there is not ſaluation* Iere.2.13.
in any other, neither is their amonge men any other name giuen
vnder heauen, whereby we muſt be ſaued. as it is, Actes 4. 12.
Hee is the way which leadeth vnto euerlaſting happineſſe, he
is the truth, to inſtruct vs in all the counſailes of God, hee is
the life to reuiue vs, who were dead in our ſinnes, yea the life
of euerlaſting life, and the perfection of our heauenly happineſſe. Iohn 14. 6. *Hee hath taken vpon him our infirmities,*
and borne our paines, hee was wounded for our offences, and
ſmitten for our iniquities, the paine of our puniſhment was layd
vpon him, and with his ſtripes wee are healed. Eſa. 53. 4. 5. 6.
To whom therefore ſhould wee goe in our ſickeneſſe, but to
this our heauenly phyſition? whoſe helpe ſhould wee ſeeke
for the curing of our woundes, but the helpe of this our
bleſſed ſurgeon who will eaſily cure them all, with the precious balme of his bloud? whether ſhould wee returne after
our long wandring, but vnto the ſhepheard of our ſoules?
to whome ſhould wee ſeeke to bee preſerued from death,
and damnation, but to him, who is the Lorde of life, and
ſaluation? and therefore leauing all other meanes of our
owne diuiſing, let vs repaire vnto him, and him alone,
for hee calleth and inuiteth vs, promiſing that hee will
eaſe vs.

But how ſhould we come vnto Chriſt, and what is meant
hereby? ſurely wee are not to vnderſtand a corporall or lo-
cal comming vnto him, for hee is in heauen, and wee are
vpon the earth, but our comming is ſpirituall not of the

E e   **body**

body but of the foule.

And this is twofould, the comming of repentance, and the comming of faith, the comming of repentance, is perfectly to God the father, the comming of faith, is to Chrift Iefus, both which are mentioned, Act. 20. 21. *witneffing repentance towardes God, and faith towards Iefus Chrift.* For repentance is nothing, but a turning from our finnes, & a returning to God, & faith caufeth vs to goe out of our felues, vnto Chrift, feeking faluation in him aione.

So that our comming to Chrift, is to beleeue in him, for thus Chrift himfelfe expoundeth it, Iohn 6. 35. *Hee that commeth vnto mee fhall not hunger, and he that beleeueth n me, fhall neuer thirft.* So chap. 7. 37. 38. *If any man thirft, let h m come vnto me and drinke. He that beleeueth n mee as faith the fcriptures, out of his bellie fhall flow riuers of the water of life.* This then doth Chrift only require of all penitent finners, who are wearie, and heauie laden, with the burthen of their finnes, that they beleeue in him, that is, that by a liuely faith, they doe apply vnto themfelues Chrift Iefus, and all his benefites, and affure themfelues that whatfoeuer he hath done in the worke of mediation, and redemption, hee did it for their fakes; namely, that hee left the boofome of his father, and taking vpon him our flefh, became the fonne of man, that hee might make vs the fonnes of God, and heyres of his euerlafting kingdome, that hee was conceiued by the holy Ghoft, to fanctifie our conception, that hee here fuffered hunger, cold, wearineffe, and other miferies of this life, that hee might make vs partakers of all happineffe in the life to come, that hee performed perfect obedience to the law, that hee might decke and adorne vs with the rich robe of his righteoufneffe, that notwithftanding, hee was moft iuft and innocent, yet hee was condemned to death, before an earthly iudge, that we who were wicked, and vniuft, might bee acquitted, and abfolued, before the iudgement feate of God, that he died vpon the croffe, to preferue vs from euerlafting death of hell, that hee indured his fathers anger, that wee might bee reconciled vnto him, that

hee

hee bore the curfse of the law, that he might canfell the hand-writing of ordinances which made againft vs, that hee rofe againe and afcended into heauen, that hee might bee the firft fruites of them that flept, and by his entrance into heauen, might make way for vs alfo, that hee fitteth at the right hand of God, to make interceffion for vs, and to pro-tect and defend vs againft all our enemies, that hee fhall come to iudge both the quicke and the dead, to the end he may giue vnto vs, perfect redemption, and crowne vs with euerlafting glorie ; And if wee thus beleeue in Chrift, and applie him with all his benifites vnto vs, we may affure our felues that he will eafe vs of the heauie burthen of our fins, cloth vs, with the glorious aray of his righteoufneffe, and giue vnto vs the eternal poffeffion of thofe euerlafting ioies, which by his death and bloudfhed he hath dearely purcha-fed for vs.

CHAP. XXXII.

Of Sathan tentations which he vfeth againft thofe which are called, to bring them to defpaire.

§. Sect. I.
How Sathan
tēpteth thofe
which are
called to de-
fpaire.

ANd fomuch concerning thofe tentations of Sa-than, wherewith hee affaulteth them who are not yet effectually called, to the ende that hee may keepe them from turning vnto God by vnfained repentance, and comming vnto Chrift by a true and liuely faith : now wee are to fpeake of thofe tentations which he vfeth againft thofe who are called. And firft, when as he perceiueth that he can no longer blind them with ig-norance, nor keepe them ftill in carnall worldineffe & pre-fumptuous fecuritie, when as he feeth that they are refolued no longer to deferre their repentance and comming vnto Chrift by a true faith, neither can be perfwaded to content themfelues with fuch faith and repentance as are falfe and counterfait; then, and not before he appeareth in his owne likeneffe, and fheweth himfelfe a diuell indeed; for then he

accufeth

accuſeth them of their manifold and outragious ſins, where in they haue long continued, then he telleth them of their ſinnes paſt and preſent corruptions , whereby they are readie to fall into the like againe , then hee reuealeth vnto them their ſinnes of ignorance, and calleth to their remembrance thoſe ſinnes which they haue cōmitted againſt their knowledge and conſcience, then will hee aggrauate their ſinnes which in themſelues are but too too hainous, and ſet before them the iuſtice of God, the fearefull threatnings and terrible curſe of the law, the wrath of God and the intollerable and eternall torments of hell fire, which by their ſinnes they haue iuſtly deſerued; all which terrible ſights being in one view repreſented to their already timorous thoughts, he taketh occaſion of them al, to moue them to diſtruſt of Gods mercies and Chriſtes merites, and ſo to plunge them into vtter deſperation. Wouldeſt thou now vile wretch (will hee ſay) turne vnto God hoping to bee receaued to grace and mercy? why aſſure thy ſelfe it is too late, for are not thy ſins in number numberleſſe, and in their qualitie and nature moſt haynous and outragious; and haſt thou not continued in this thy rebellion againſt God a long time, refuſing to come vnto him though he hath often called, and careleſly neglecting all the meanes of thy ſaluation, when thy God hath gratiouſly offered them vnto thee? Now therefore the acceptable time and day of ſaluation is paſt neuer againe to be recalled, and though with *Eſau* thou ſeekeſt repentance with teares yet ſhalt thou neuer find it. Moreouer to the conſideration of thy horrible rebellion adde the remembrance of Gods iuſtice, which can in no wiſe ſuffer ſinne to goe vnpuniſhed, the terrible curſe of the law denounced by God who is trueth it ſelfe, againſt thoſe who continue not in all that is written in the booke of the law to doe it, the fearefull torments of hell prepared for ſinners amongſt which number thou art one of the chiefe; and therefore doe not flatter thy ſelfe with hope of mercy, but rather expect thoſe fearefull iudgements and endleſſe torments which are due vnto thee for thy rebellious wickedneſſe : and thus doth Sathan

labour

labour to bring the poore Chriftian to deepe defperation,
and to fill his confcience with horrour and feare, which if he
can accomplifh he refteth not there, but like a cruell coward
who can neuer be at quiet till he fee the death of his enemie,
fo our malitious enemie is neuer fatisfied till he fee our death
and vtter deftruction. And therfore when he hath grieuoufly vexed the Chriftians confciences with fearefull horrour,
and tormented him euen with the flafhings of hell fire,
in the next place he will perfwade him to feeke fome eafe of
his prefent torments by imbruing his hands in his owne
bloud, and putting himfelfe to fome violent death : which is
nothing els but (as the Prouerb is) to leape out of the frying
pan into the fire, and in feeking to eafe his terrours of confcience to plunge himfelfe into the torments of hell.

Againft which tentations whofoeuer would be ftrengthened and enabled to withftand their force and violence, they
muft not reft in themfelues, defiring in whole or in part to
be iuftified by their legall righteoufneffe, neither muft they
meafure out vnto themfelues Gods mercies according to
their owne merites and worthineffe, they muft not looke
onely vpon Gods iuftice, and vppon that exact obedience
which the law requireth of them, nor yet vpon thofe fearefull punifhments which by their finnes they haue iuftly
deferued, for then Sathan will eafily attaine vnto his purpofe, and fpeedily bring them to defperation and vtter deftruction. But they muft goe out of themfelues and reiecting their owne righteoufneffe, as altogether imperfect &
infufficient they are to reft and relie themfelues vppon the
alone righteoufneffe and obedience of Chrift Iefus, as being
in it felfe all fufficient both for our iuftification and faluation. And as they haue one eye on Gods iuftice to keepe them
from fecure prefumption, fo they muft haue the other firmly fixt on his infinite mercy to preferue them from falling
into defperation, as they haue one eye on the law to humble them, and to bring them out of themfelues to Chrift,
fo they muft haue the other eye on the fweet and comfortable promifes of the Gofpell to comfort and rayfe them

§. *Sect.2.*
*That if wee
will with-
ftand the for-
mer tentati-
on, wee muft
not reft on
our owne
righteouf-
neffe.*

vp. Finally as on the one side they behold the curse of the law, and the eternall torments prepared for the wicked : so on the other side they must stedfastly looke vpon the righteousnesse, death, and obedience of Christ, and also vpon those euerlasting ioyes which by his precious bloudshed hee hath purchased for them. And if thus being truely humbled and brought to vnfained repentance they goe out of themselues and reiect their owne righteousnesse, resting and relying vpon the alone righteousnesse of Christ for their iustification & saluation, they may most certainly assure themselues that they haue in Christ satisfied Gods iustice, & are by his death reconciled vnto him, that they are freed from the curse of the law, and from the wrath of God, that their scarlet sins are made as white as wooll, & all their imperfections perfected by Christs righteousnesse and obedience, that they are acquitted from the sentence of condemnation, and deliuered from the fearefull torments of hell.

§. Sect. 3.
Reasons to perswade the weake Christian of the forgiuenesse of his sinnes.

But forasmuch as those who labour vnder the burthen of their sinnes, and are continually vexed and mooued to desperation, by Sathans most subtil and violent tentations, are not so easily perswaded that their sins are forgiuen them, & they reconciled vnto God in Christ; therfore I will set down some arguments, whereby all those who truly repent, (that is sorrow for their sinnes past, and desire, and indeauour to forsake them in the time to come) and withall going out of themselues, doe earnestly hunger after Christ and his righteousnesse, and rest and relie vpon him for their saluation, may haue full assurance that their sinnes are forgiuen them, and that they are in Christ reconciled vnto God, and receiued into his loue and fauour.

The first argument drawne from Gods mercy.

The first argument, to assure all of the pardon and forgiuenesse of their sinnes, who will come vnto him, may be drawne from his mercy, which is one of his properties and attributes, so often attributed vnto him in the scriptures. Exod. 34. 6. 7. God thus describeth himselfe : *The Lord, the Lord, strong, mercifull and gracious, slow to anger, and abundant in goodnesse & truth. 2 reseruing mercy for thousands,*
forgiuing

forgiuing iniquitie, transgression and sinne. Out of which place
that famous & godly learned man *H. Zanchius* hath obserued matter fit for our purpose, & therefore it shall not be a-
misse to set downe his owne words: *For besides (saith he) that
the essence of God is only one, & that eternal most simple, most perfect, liuing, immortall, inuisible, incorruptible, infinite, omnipotent,
most wise; he is also wholy most good in whom nothing is wanting; a
louer of men, most meeke, most gentle, slow to anger, most ready
to forgiue iniuries, most patient, most true, most righteous, most iust,
most faithfull in performing his promises, finally hee is nothing els
then the soueraigne goodnesse, and the chiefe clemencie, as he hath
described, and liuely deciphered himselfe.* Exod. 34. *and else-
where.* And therefore we must note, although anger be attributed vnto God, yet notwithstanding it is in God nothing els but the
chiefe goodnesse and iustice, whereby he abhorreth euill and according to his iust iudgement doth at length punish it, if it be not
amended by his long suffering and patience. This herehence manifestly appeareth, because speaking of reuenge or taking punishment which is an effect of anger, he doth not say that he doth presently inflict punishment, or that hee is so ready to inflict it as to
shew mercy, but hee saith that hee is slow to anger. Signifying by
this maner of speach, that he is of his owne nature alwayes most
ready, to shew mercy, to graunt pardon to be beneficiall; but not so
ready to take punishment, but is forced herevnto as of himselfe,
vnwilling through our impenitencie. Hereunto also appertaineth
that ancient forme of prayer; O Lord whose propertie is alwaies
to haue mercy and forgiue. Herehence also we read in* Esai. ch.
28.21. *The Lord shall stand as in mount Perazim, hee shalbe
angry as in the valley Gibeon. That he may doe his worke, his
strange worke, that he may effect his act, his strange act. (that is,
he shall inflict the like punishments in his iust anger vpon his rebellious people, which hee exercised vpon his wicked enemies the
Philistines in mount Perazim, when as he ouerthrewe them, by
his seruant* Dauid, *and vpõ the* Amorites *in the valley of Gibeon
when as he smote them with stones from heauen.) Where the Prophet maketh a twofold kind of Gods workes, his proper and strange
works. The proper worke of God is to shew mercy, and to spare or*

*Zanch. de
Attrib. l. 2.
cap. 1. q. 2.*

Esa. 28. 21.
2. Sam. 5.
1. Chro. 14.
Ios. 10.

forgiue,

forgiue; his strange worke is to be angry and to punish. And therefore whereas hee calleth that the proper worke of God, and this his strangeworke; he plainely teacheth that mercy, goodnesse & long suffering are according to the nature of the deitie, but that to be angry is diuers from Gods nature, Yea which is more hee maketh it not his worke, that is to say, he is angrie that afterwards he may bring his worke to passe, that is, that he may haue mercie and preserue; for whilest (saith the Apostle) wee are iudged of the Lord, we are chastened that we should not be condemned with the world. 1. Cor. 11. 32. And what due these things teach vs, but that the nature of God is nothing els then goodnesse, mercy, loue especially of men, patience, benignitie, and most farre and remote from all vniust seueritie, cruelty, tyrannie, and pride. The which may minister vnto euery penitent sinner most sweet consolation; for when they see that God is angry by reason of their sins, & that he doth greeuously afflict them, & euen bring them as it were to the gates of hell, this must not make the to cast of al hope & to fal into vtter desperatio; but they must remember, that these are not the Lords proper works but strange vnto him, which he doth to this end, that he may bring to passe his owne proper works which are a-greeable to his nature, that is, that he may againe shew vnto vs the glorious beames of his louing coutenance in more full brightnesse, & bring vs fro death to life; fro affliction to ioy, from the gates of hell to the kingdome of heauen. According to that 1. Sam. 2. 6. the Lord killeth, & maketh aliue, he brin-geth downe vnto hell, and bringeth vp againe. As therefore when we see carpenters pulling downe a ruinous building our minds do not rest there, becaufe we know that this they doe is not their proper worke, but we goe further in our co-gitation thinking of a new house which they will build in the place of the old, for asmuch as wee know that it is not their proper worke to race downe but to build, or to race downe that they may build: fo when wee see the Lord an-gry and inflicting corrections let vs not rest here, but with the like foresight of mind, let vs consider that he doth these his strange and improper works, that afterwards he may do
those

1. Cor. 11. 32.

thofe which are proper and naturall, that is that he afflicteth that he may bring the more true cōfort, that he bringeth vs to the gates of hell, to the end hee may rayſe vs vp to bee partakers of the ioyes of heauen. But let vs conſider of ſome more teſtimonies of Gods infinite mercies. As the Prophet *Dauid* likewiſe ſaith Pſalm. 103. 8. *that the Lord is full of compaſſion and mercy, ſlow to anger, and of great kindneſſe.* and Pſal. 86. 5 *Thou Lord art good and mercifull, and of great kindneſſe vnto all them that call vpon thee.* So the prophet Ioel 2. 13. teſtifieth of the Lorde, that hee is *gratious and mercifull, ſlow to anger and of great kindneſſe.* And the apoſtle ſaith that he is *rich in mercie.*Eph.2.4. and 2.Cor. 1.3.He calleth him, *the father of mercies, and God of all cōfort.*

Seeing then, mercie is one of Gods attributes, therefore it is alſo of his eſſence, and being, for there is not in Godes moſt perfect nature, any qualities or accidentes, but whatſoeuer is in God, is God, ſo that God is mercie it ſelfe, and conſequently, to ſhew and excerciſe his mercie, is to ſhew and exerciſe his owne nature. Now wee know that naturall actions are not troubleſome, nor irkſome, neither is the ſunne troubled with giuing lighte, nor the fire with giuing heate, nor the tree with yeelding fruite, nor the beaſt with nouriſhing his young, nor man with receiuing nouriſhment, and ſleepe, becauſe it is their nature to be excerciſed in theſe actions, and therefore ſeeing mercie is of Gods eſſence, it is not painefull and troubleſome to excerciſe it towardes all repentant ſinners, bee their ſinnes neuer ſo many, and hanious, no more, then it is troubleſome to exerciſe his iuſtice, in puniſhing of thoſe who are obſtinate and rebellious, nay it is not onely not troubleſome and painefull, but alſo pleaſant and delightfull for God to ſhewe mercie vnto all thoſe who truely turne vnto him, and contrariwiſe it ſhould bee troubleſome and irkſome, (if I may ſo ſpeake,) for God not to ſhew and exerciſe his nature, and mercie, towardes repentant ſinners; for as the eye is delighed with ſeeing, and to bee reſtrayned there from is grieuous vnto it, as the eare is delighed with hearing, and is much moleſted if it be ſtoped,

§.Sect.4.
That God is delighted in exerciſing his mercie.

and

and as euerie part, and facultie of the bodie, and soule, are delighted in excercising their seuerall actions, and functions, and are much vexed, and cumbred, if by any meanes they should bee hindred; so is the Lord delighted, and well pleased, in shewing, and excercising his owne nature, and attributes, as his power, and prouidence, in gouerning the world, his iustice, in punishing wicked, obstinate, and rebellious sinners, and his mercy in pardoning, and remitting the sinnes of those, who are of an humble spirite and broken heart, and are wearie of this intollerable burthen, desiring nothing more, then to bee eased and freed from it. And not to thus excercise his nature, and attributes, woulde rather (that I may speake after the manner of men) bee vnto the Lord tedious and troublesome.

Of this pleasure and delight, which the Lorde taketh in pardoning repentant sinners, the Prophet Micha speaketh, chap. 7. 10. 18. who (saith he) *is a God like vnto thee, that taketh away iniquitie, and passeth by transgression of the remnant of his heritage : he retaineth not his wrath for euer, because mercie pleaseth him.* So the prophet Dauid Psal. 147. 11. saith that the *Lord is delighted in them that feare him and attend vpon his mercy; euen as though he reioyced much,* to haue an occasion offered, of excercising his mercy and goodnesse towardes those, who earnestly desiring it, wait vpon him, that they may bee made partakers of of it. For the obiect of Gods mercy, about which it is exercised, is mans miserie, and the action thereof, is to pittie, and helpe him, out of his wretched and miserable estate; and therefore, if there were no miserie, and wretchednesse, and no sinne to be forgiuen, there would be wanting that external obiect, about which Gods mercy should be exercised and manifested to all the world. And hence it is, that the Lorde willingly permitted the fall of our first parentes, to the ende that hee might make a way for the manifestation of his mercie , in pardoning repentant sinners, and his iustice in punishing the contemners of his grace. And as the apostle saith, Rom. 11. 32. *God hath shut vp all in vnbeleefe, that hee might haue mercie on all,* that

is

is to say, on all the elect, both Iewes, and Gentiles.

Seeing therfore God delighteth himselfe in excercising & manifesting his mercy, to the praise of the glorie of his grace, by pardōing & forgiuing repentant sinners, let not any who are grieuously laden, & grone for wearines vnder the heauie burthen of their sinnes, feare to come vnto the Lorde, and to implore his mercy for the forgiuenes of their sinnes, though neuer so grieuous and manifould, neither let them doubt, least God will reiect their suite, and refuse to receiue them, into his grace, and fauoure, becaufe of their great rebellions and vnworthinesse. For although there were not (as in truth there is not) any thing to bee respected in vs, sauing that wee are the creatures of God, and worke of his handes, yet the Lorde will haue compassion vpon vs, euen for his owne sake becaufe hee is exceedingly delighted in shewing mercy to all those who turne vnto him. And this the Lord himselfe professeth Esa. 43.25. *I euen I am he that putteth away thine iniquities for mine owne sake, and will not remember thy sinnes.* And therefore the prophet *Daniel* calling vpon the Lord for mercy, in the behalfe of himselfe and the people, disclaimeth their owne righteousnesse, and all respect of their owne merits and worthinesse; saying, wee do not present our supplications before thee for our own righteousnesse, but for thy great tender mercies : *O Lord heare, O Lord forgiue, O Lord confider and doe it; deferre not for thine owne sake.* Dan. 9. 18. 19.

But here fathan will be ready to obiect vnto the afflicted confcience, labouring vnder the burthen of sinne, that God indeede is mercifull, but yet he will neuer extend his mercy towards fuch haynous offenders, whofe finnes are in number numberlesse, and in qualitie and nature most grieuous and outragious. For answering of which tentation, we are to know that though our finnes bee neuer so innumerable and hainous, yet this should not discourage vs from comming to God by vnfained repentance, with assured hope of forgiuenesse, for though our finnes be great, his mercies are infinite, and consequently though it were imagined that

§. Sect. 5. That the grieuousnesse of sinne cannot debarre the repentant sinner of Gods mercy.

all

all the sinnes which were euer committed in the world were ioyned together, yet in comparison of Gods mercy they are without all comparison lesse then a mote in the Sunne to all the world. Neither is God like vnto man, whose bounty & mercy are limited in some straight bounds which they will not passe, and therefore they are soone weary both in giuing to those who want, and forgiuing those that offend, but his bounty is endlesse and his mercies infinite, and therefore he can and wil as easily forgiue vs the debt of ten thousand millions of pounds as one pennie, and as soone pardon the sinns of a wicked *Manasses* as of a righteous *Abraham*, if we come vnto him by vnfained repentance, and earnestly desire and implore his grace and mercy. And this our Sauiour Christ sheweth in the parable of the poore Publicāe, whose hainous

Luke 7.41. sinnes the Lord presently forgaue vpon his true conuersion. And in the parable of the two debters, where the lender our bountifull God as easily forgaue the 500. pence as the fiftie, that is innumerable great sinnes, as well as few and lesse. And the Apostle *Paule* teacheth vs, that *where sinne hath abounded, there grace hath much more abounded.* Rom.5.20.

That we must not so aggrauate our sins that we derogate from Gods mercy. Seeing therfore Gods mercy is infinite and without al limites, let not vs restraine it, neither let vs so aggrauate our sinnes as that in the meane time wee derogate from Gods mercy. If a Prince should send his generall pardon vnto a number of offendors, without any exception or limitation, and one amongst the rest should say this pardon doth not appertaine vnto me, because I am so great an offender, and therefore I will still stand in doubt of my Princes mercy, and suspect his word, who would not accuse sucn an one both of folly in refusing his pardon, and of vngratefulnes and diffidence in distrusting his gratious Prince, calling his great mercy and truth in his promisse into question ? Who would not thinke this offence greater then all the rest, but the Lord who is infinite in mercy, hath sent his generall pardon to all repentant and beleeuing sinners without all exception; why therefore should wee make question of his mercy, because of our hainous sinnes, why should we vnto our others sinnes

adde

adde this which is more hainous then all the reft, indoubting and diftrufting his word and promife, and in extenuating his infinite and endleffe mercies. For if wee thinke our debt fo great that God will neuer forgiue it, what doe we els but detract from Gods rich bounty and liberality, if we fuppofe our finnes may not bee forgiuen becaufe of their greatneffe, what do we els but imagine that they furpaffe Gods infinite mercy, which is a moft horrible blafphemy once to conceiue.

The mercy of the Lord extendeth it felfe to the beafts of the field, and hee gratioufly feedeth the Rauens and young Lions, which in their brutifh maner implore his helpe; & fhal he not extend his mercies to reafonable creatures that feeke after them? Yea the Lord *is good to all and his mercies are ouer all his workes*, as it is Pfal. 145.9. and will not the Lord be gratious to man, who is his moft excellent workemanfhip created according to his owne image, if hee fue vnto him for grace and defire to be partaker of his mercy? His goodneffe ftretcheth it felfe vnto his obftinate enemies, for *he caufeth his rayne to fall and his Sunne to fhine both vpon the euill and the good, on the iuft and vniuft*. Matth. 5.45. And fhall it be reftrained frō his repentant feruants? he multiplieth his mercies in temporall benefits vpon the wicked and reprobate, and fhall it be fcanted towards his elect, he is very gratious to malitious rebels, and will he denie grace to humble fuers for mercy and repentant finners. He fhewed his goodneffe and long fuffering vnto wicked *Achab* vpon his fained and hypocriticall humiliation, and will he not extend it towards thofe who being truely penitent vnfainedly turne vnto him? Yes affuredly, for though hee bee good to all euen fenfeleffe creatures, brute beafts, and rebellious finners, yet he is in efpeciall maner good to thofe who are of the houfhold of faith.

But if we cannot behold Gods mercies in their owne glorious brightneffe, let vs looke vpon them in fome fmall refemblance and little counterfaite, if we cannot comprehend them in their owne infinite nature, yet let vs view them in a fmall

§. Sect. 6.
That Gods mercy is ouer all his workes.

Pfal. 36.6.
&104.21.27
& 147.9.4
& 145.9.

§. Sect. 7.
That euen man is mercifull towards the penitent

and therefore much more God who is infinite in mercy. ſmall modell. Euen man himſelfe who hath but a ſparke of this mighty flame, and a ſmall drop of this bottomleſſe Ocean ſpareth his ſonne when he offendeth, pardoneth his ſeruant when he deſireth forgiueneſſe, yea is oftentimes reconciled to his enemie who hath many waies wronged him, when he ſueth for reconciliation, and confeſſeth his faults, ſhall therefore man who hath receaued a little ſparke from this euer burning flame of Gods goodneſſe, a ſmall drop of this endleſſe and bottomleſſe Ocean, and but a little modell of this infinite greatneſſe, whoſe greateſt mercy compared wirh Gods, is but ſauadge and barbarous cruelty; ſhall hee I ſay bee readie to ſpare his Sonne, forgiue his ſeruant, and bee reconciled vnto his enemy, and ſhall not God ſpare, forgiue, and bee reconciled vnto thoſe who turne from their ſinnes by vnfained repentance, and earneſtly ſue for grace; ſhall wee ſee, and acknowledge, the mercies of man, and ſhall wee doubt of the mercies of God which is the plentifull fountaine, from which like a pirling ſtreame they flow; ſhall wee confeſſe, that a droppe of water is moyſt, and affirme that the ocean is drie, ſhall wee be ſharpſighted in ſeeing the light of a ſmall ſparke, and bee ſtarke blinde, in behoulding the glorious beames of the ſunne. Nay let vs know, acknowledge, and aſſure our ſelues, that as much as the whole globe of the earth, exceedeth in quantitie the leaſt mote in the ſunne, as much as the whole ocean exceedeth the ſmalleſt drop of water, yea, aſmuch as the infinite creatour, exceedeth the finite creature, betweene which, there can bee imagined no degrees of compariſon, ſo much doth the mercie, and bountie of God, exceede the bountie and mercie of mortall man. And therefore if vpon repentance for our fault and earneſt deſire of reconciliation, wee hope of mercie and wounted kindnes, from our frinde or neighbour, let vs not make any queſtion, nor once doubt of the Lords loue and fauour towards vs, though our ſinnes bee neuer ſo grieuous, ſo wee truely repent and vnfainedly turne vnto him.

§. *Sect.*8.   But here the afflicted conſcience wilbe readie to ſay, that
though

though there bee no doubt of Gods mercie, but that it is in *That doubt-*
it selfe moft infinite, yet I doubt, leaft I fhall neuer be parta- *ing of Gods*
mercie: in re-
ker thereof becaufe of my manifold inperfections, and *fpect of our*
great vnworthineffe. To which I anfweare, that this dift- *vnworthineffe*
rufting of Gods mercies, in refpect of our vnworthineffe, *argueth pride*
proceedeth not from true humilitie, but from our naturall
pride, for if wee had denied our felues, and were nothing
in our owne eyes, if wee had wholy remooued our owne
righteoufneffe, and did wholy,and onely, reft on our fauiour
Iefus Chrift for our faluation, wee would neuer hope the
more in regard of our owne worthineffe, nor yet doubt in
refpect of our vnworthineffe.But it is our fecret and inbred
pride of heart,which makes vs to doubt of Gods mercy,vn-
leffe wee bring him a bribe and deferue it at his hands,and to
defire to make the Lorde beholding vnto vs rather then we
would be any whit beholding vnto him. Which is nothing
els but to difgrace Gods mercies, that we may grace our own
merits;& by labouring that we may be foething in our felus,
we wil not alow that God fhould be al in al & haue the whole
praife of our faluation. But we are to roote out of our hearts
this fpirituall pride, and to plant therein true humilitie, and
then we may affure our felues though our finnes bee great,
yet the mercies of God are farre greater, though wee bee
moft beggerly in merites, yet wee fhall bee made rich by
Chrift Iefus righteoufneffe; for the poorer wee are in defert,
the richer Gods mercie will appeare in accepting vs to his
grace and fauour; and where finne hath abounded, there
grace will abound much more.

Seeing therefore Gods mercies are infinite, and are not
any whit reftrayned by our vnworthineffe, let vs feeke vnto
the Lord by vnfained repentance, and affure our felues of
his loue and fauour in Iefus Chrift; *Let the wicked forfake*
his ways & the vnrighteous his own imaginations,and return vn-
to the Lord and he will haue mercie vpon him, and to our God,for
*he is very readie to forgiue,*as the Prophet exhoreth vs. Efay
55.7.

CHAP.

CHAP. XXXIII.

Of the second Argument grounded vpon Gods iustice.

§. *Sect. 1.*
That Gods
iustice will
not punish
those sinnes in
vs which are
already puni-
shed in Christ

He second argument to assure those of the forgiuenesse of their sinnes, who vnfainedly repent
and relye wholy vpon Iesus Christ for their saluation, by a liuely faith may bee drawne from
Gods iustice, for their sinnes are fully and sufficiently punished in Christ Iesus, and therefore it wil not stand with
the iustice of God, to punish them againe in any of those who
haue applyed vnto them the merites and sufferings of Christ
by a liuely faith; and as the Lord cannot in iustice let sinne
goe vnpunished, and therfore hath punished the sins of all
men either in Christ Iesus, or will throughly punish them in
the parties themselues, so the same iustice will not admit that
the same sinnes should be twise punished, once in our Sauiour, and againe in the faithfull. Now that our sauiour Christ
hath sufficiently suffered for all the sinnes of the faithfull,
it is euident by many places of the Scriptures. Esay 53.4.
Surely hee hath borne our infirmities and carried our sorrowes.
5. But hee was wounded for our transgressions, he was broken for
our iniquities, the chastisment of our peace was vpon him, and
with his stripes wee are healed. 2 Cor. 5. 21. *hee hath made him*
to bee sinne for vs which knewe no sinne, that wee should be made
the righteousnes of God in him. So the apostle He. 9. 26. saith that
our sauiour Christ *hath appeared once to put away sinne by the*
sacrifice of himselfe. And Pet. 1. epistle 2. 24. saith *that his own*
selfe bare our sinnes in his bodie on the tree, that wee being deli-
uered from sinne should liue in righteousnesse. Seeing then our
sinnes were laide vpon Christ and seuerely punished in him,
God in his iustice will not inflict any more punishmens vppon the faithfull but will pardon and forgiue them, which
pardon and forgiuenesse is a worke of his iustice as well as of
his mercie, and therefore it is said, Rom. 3. 25. that *God hath*
set forth our Sauiour Christ to be a reconciliation through faith
in his blood, to declare his righteousnesse by the forgiuenesse of
sinne

*sinnes that are passed through the patience of God. 26. to shewe
at this time his righteousnesse that hee might be iust, and a iusti-
fier of him who is of the faith of Iesus,* So it is said 1. Iohn 1.9.
that *If we acknowledge our sinnes, hee is faithfull and iust to forgiue vs our sinnes and to cleanse vs from all vnrighteousnesse.* So
that Gods righteousnes is declared in the forgiuenes of sins,
and hee sheweth his iustice in iustifying those who are of the
faith of Iesus, and in pardoning all their offences. And therefore if wee will beleeue in our Sauiour Christ and bring
forth the fruites of our faith in vnfained repentance, wee
need not seruilely to feare Gods iustice, nay wee may be af-
sured that because hee is iust, he will in Christ pardon and
forgiue our sinnes, and neuer inflict any punishment, which
by them in our selues wee haue iustly deserued.

But that the equitie hereof may bee more manifest, we are
to consider that our sinnes in the scriptures are called debtes;
for the Lord in our creation lent vnto vs the rich talents of
his graces, to be imployed for the setting forth of his glory,
all which wee wastfully mispent and brought our selues into such extreame beggerie, that we were altogether vnable
to pay to God the least part of that which we owed, nor to rē-
der accoumpt vnto our Lord & maister how in any good sort
we had bestowed his rich treasures; & therefore in his iustice
he sent his sergeant death to arest vs, and to cast vs in the prison of vtter darkenes, there to remaine in the custody of sathan our most malitious iaylor, till we had fully discharged
our debt and made full satisfaction to his iustice; which whē
we were altogeather vnable to perfourme, it pleased our sauiour Christ in his infinite loue towards vs, to become our
suerty, and to take vppon him the answering of our debt,
which he fully discharged in as exact a manner and measure
as the iustice of God required, for whereas wee are bound
to performe perfect obedience to the lawe, he performed it for vs; where as wee for our disobedience were
subiect to the sentence of condemnation, the curse
of the law, and death of body and soule, he was condemned for vs, and bore the curse of the lawe, and dyed in

§. Sect.2.
*That our sins
are debts and
therefore not
to be twice
paid.*

F f   our

our stead an ignominious death, whereas we deserued the anger of God, and to bee kept prisoners in the graue vnder the dominion of death, he endured his fathers wrathfull displeasure, and himselfe was for a time held captiue of death in the graue, that so he might reconcile vs to his father and set vs at libertie. In a word whatsoeuer we owed Christ discharged, whatsoeuer wee deserued hee suffered, if not in the selfe same punishments, (for hee could not suffer the eternall torments of hell) yet in proportion, the dignity of his person giuing value vnto his temporarie punishments, and making them of more valew and worth then if all the world should haue suffered the eternal torments of hell. Seing therefore our Sauiour Christ hath fully discharged our debt and made full satisfaction to his fathers iustice, God cannot in equitie exact of vs a second payment, no more then the creditours may iustly require that his debt should be twice payd, once of the suerty, and againe of the principal. Neither now hath Gods iustice any thing to shew against vs, for the lawe which was the hand writing of ordinances which made against vs, and as it were a bond whereby wee were obliged and bound to God the father either to performe obedience, or to vndergoe the penaltie; euen euerlasting death and condemnation, is now cancelled taken away; *and fastened to the crosse* of Christ, as the Apostle affirmeth, Col. 2. 14. So that now the Lord cannot in his iustice put vs in suite nor recouer any debt of vs, seeing our sauiour Christ our good and all sufficient suerty hath vndertaken the matter in our behalfe discharged our debt to the vtmost farthing, cancelled the handwriting or bond in which wee were obliged, and by the law acquitted vs of all paimentes which Gods iustice by vertue of the law might require of vs. and therefore if we turne vnto God by vnfained repentance, and lay hould vpon our sauiour Christ and his merites by a liuely faith, we haue our *quietus est* and generall acquittance, which God himselfe hath pronounced from heauen in the presence of many witnesses, saying, *This is my welbeloued son in whom I am well pleased,* that is in whome I am delighted, & rest fully satisfied, & wel cōtented. Mat. 3. 17.   CHAP.

CHAP. XXXIIII.

Of the third Argument grounded vpon Gods truth.

He third argument, whereby all thofe who re- §. *Sect.*1.
pent and beleeue may bee affured of the pardon *Of Gods truth*
& remiffion of their fins, is groūded vpon Gods *in his promi-*
truth; for the Lorde is moft true yea truth it *ſes.*
felfe, *and all his promifes in Chrift are yea, and amen. hee is a* 2.Cor.1.20.
faithfull and true witneffe. and whatſoeuer hee hath ſpoken Apoc.1.7.
ſhall be accomplifhed; ſo that though the heauens decay and
waxe olde like a garment, though the ſunne loofe his light,
and the moone be turned into bloud, though the earth tremble and quake, and the foundations of the mountaines bee
mooued and ſhake, yea though heauen and earth and all
things therein contained perifh and paffe away, *yet ſhall not* Matth.5.18.
one iote or title of his word fal to the ground vnaccomplifhed. And
therefore whatfoeuer the Lord hath promifed in his worde
that he wil moft vndoubtedly performe, for he is *Iehoua*, who
hauing his effence and being in and from himfelfe alone,
giueth being vnto all things elfe, efpecially to his worde and
promifes. But hee hath promifed to all beleeuers and repentant finners, that hee will in Chrift Iefus pardon al their fins,
and will receiue them into his grace and fauour, and therfore
if wee beleeue and reft vppon our Sauiour Chrift alone for
our faluation, truly repenting vs of all our finnes, wee may
affure our felues that though our fins be neuer fo many and
grieuous, yet the Lord will receiue vs to mercy, and pardon
and forgiue them.

But that the poore foule wounded with fin and groning for §. *Sect.*2.
wearines vnder this vnfupportable burthen, may haue fome *That Gods*
ground whereupon to reft, when it is ready to faint, & fome *regal ftile af-*
fpirituall weapons whereby it may defend it felfe, and beate *fureth vs of*
backe the violence of Sathans tentations, I will make choife *mercie and*
of fome amongft many of the comfortable promifes of the *forgiueneſſe.*
gofpell, made vnto all repentant finners. Firft therefore let

vs confider, that when the Lorde like a mightie monarch
would fet out his owne ftile as it were in faire text letters, to
be read of all his fubie&tes,he thus proclaymeth it,Exod. 34.
6. *The Lorde, the Lord,ftrong, mercifull and gracious, flowe to
anger, and aboundant in goodneffe and truth. 7. Referuing mercy
for thoufands,forgiuing iniquitie,and tranfgreffion ,and finners.*
wher we may obferue that the greateft part of his ftile cófift-
eth of his mercy,gratioufnes, long fuffering, goodnes & readines to forgiue the iniquities of repentant finners; as therfore wee cannot offer a greater difgrace to a mightie prince,
then to denie or call into queftion any part of his tytles or
regall ftile, fo we cannot more difhonour the prince of princes, and foueraigne king of heauen & earth, then by doubting of or denying any of thefe his titles which in his owne
ftile hee hath attributed vnto himfelfe, feeing then he profeffeth and proclaymeth himfelfe to bee a gratious, mercifull long fuffering God, who is alwaies readie to forgiue
repentant finners when they implore his mercie, let vs not
offer God that difgrace to rob him of any part of his glorious titles, nor depriue our foules of that true comfort which
the Lorde by them in his infinite goodneffe hath graunted
vnto vs.

§ .*Sect.3.*
That Gods
couenant af-
fureth vs of
the remiffion
of our finnes.

Moreouer this is one maine part of the couenant of grace,
which the Lord profeffeth that he will make with his church
and people, namely that he will *forgiue their iniquitie and remember their finnes no more.* Ier.31.34. the counterpaine of
which couenant we haue Heb. 10. 16. 17. and therefore if
we on our part performe the condition of this couenant betweene God and vs, that is, if we truely and vnfainedly repent vs of our finnes, and a reft and rely on Iefus Chrift for
our faluation by a liuely faith, wee may be affured that God
on his part will not goe one iote from his word, nor breake
the couenant which he hath made with vs. For he hath not
onely made this his couenant with vs by word of mouth,but
he hath alfo committed it to writing, and not contenting
himfelfe herewith that there might be no place left to doubting,hee hath confirmed and ratified his hand writing by
adding

adding thereunto his seales which are the Sacraments; as first the seale of Baptisme, whereby he assureth vs that being outwardly receiued into the body of the Church, and inwardly ingrafted into the body of Christ, wee haue all our sinnes and filthy corruptions washed away with his precious bloud, as the outward filth of the body is washed and purged by the washing of water. The vertue of which spirituall washing is not limited and restrained to the time past or present, as though it washed away onely our originall corruption, as some haue foolishly imagined, but extendeth it selfe to the whole course of our liues; So that if falling into many and greeuous sinnes we vnfainedly repent vs of them, and apply Christ Iesus and his merites vnto vs by a true and liuely faith, we may be assured of the pardon and forgiucnes of them all, for this was promised sealed, and confirmed vnto vs in our Baptisme. Secondly, the Lord hath further cō-firmed this his couenant by the Sacrament of his Supper, for he hath therefore instituted and ordained it, that thereby we should be put in mind of our sauiour Christes death and suffrings, to the end that we may gather more and more assurance, that our Sauiour gaue his blessed body to be crucified and shed his most pretious bloud, that hee might take away the curse of the law, and naile it vnto his crosse, free vs frō his fathers anger by bearing it himselfe, and by his death deliuer vs from euerlasting death, and by his bloudshed wash away all our sinnes and corruptions. And hence it is that the Apostle calleth the wine in the Lords supper, the new Testament in Christes bloud, because thereby the new Testament **1.Cor.11.** is sealed and confirmed vnto vs. And therefore whensoeuer **25.** wee receaue the Sacrament of the Lords supper, the Lord doth thereby certainly assure vs that our sinnes in Christ are pardoned and forgiuen, and that he hath receaued vs into his loue and fauour, yea the Lord hath not onely ratified & confirmed his couenant with vs, concerning the remission of our sinnes with his owne hand writing and seales annexed, but also by his oath; *For God willing more abundantly to shew vnto the heires of promise the stablenesse of his counsaile,*

     bound

bound himselfe by an oath: that by two immutable things wherein it is impossible that God should lye,we might haue strong consolation; as the Apostle speaketh, Heb.6.17.18. And therefore vnlesse wee would conceiue of God that hee is vntrue of his word,a couenant breaker,yea a periured person(which were most horrible blasphemie once to imagine)we may vndoubtedly assure our selues that he will pardon and forgiue vs all our sinnes, be they in number neuer so innumerable nor so hainous in their nature and qualitie, if wee will turne vnto him by vnfained repentance,and lay hould vpon Christ Iesus our sauiour,by a true and liuely faith.

§.Sect.4.
Of particular promises whereby wee may be assured of the remission of our sinnes.
But let vs more particularly consider of some of the speciall promises of God, contained in the couenant of grace, that so we may gather vnto our selues more full consolation and firme assurance of the pardon and forgiuenesse of our sinnes. The Prophet *Dauid* who had in himselfe often experience of Gods mercy telleth vs, Psal.32.10. that *whosoeuer trusteth in the Lords mercy shall compasse him.* The Prophet *Esay* exhorteth the wicked *to forsake his wayes,and the vnrighteous his owne imaginations,and to returne vnto the Lord, assuring them that he will haue mercy vpon them, for he is very ready to forgiue.* Esay.55.7. The Lord himselfe also doth make this gratious promise Ezech.18.21. *But* (saith he) *if the wicked will returne from all his sinnes which he hath committed,and keepe all my Statutes,and doe that which is lawfull and right,he shall surely liue and not dye.* 22. *All his transgressions that he hath committed shall not bee mentioned vnto him,but in his righteousnesse that he hath done he shall liue.* 23. *Haue I any desire that the wicked should dye saith the Lord God? or shall he not liue if he returne from his wayes?* vers.32. *For I desire not the death of him that dieth saith the Lord God; cause therefore one another to returne and liue yee,*and cap.33.ver.11.*As I liue saith the Lord I desire not the death of the wicked,but that the wicked turne from his way and liue.* So Mal.3.17. the Lord professeth that hee *will spare his people and children, as a man spareth his owne Sonne that serueth him.* Now we know that a louing father is ready to forgiue, & to receaue into his grace

and

and fauour his repentant Sonne, though he hath very often offended him : & fo furely the Lord who is infinitely rich in mercy, wil much more forgiue his children when they turne vnto him; nay he is not onely ready to receaue them into his grace and fauour, but it filleth him (as I may fay) with exceeding ioy and delight, when his repentant children forfake their finnes and euill wayes, and turne vnto him by vnfained repentance, as it appeareth moft euidently in the parable of the prodigall Sonne, of the ftrayed fheepe, and the loft groat. Moreouer our Sauiour Chrift had his name *Iefus* giuen him of God by the minifter of an Angell, becaufe hee faueth his people frō their finnes: as appeareth Math. 1.21.& he therfore came into the world, not to cal the righteous but finners to repentance. As it is Matt. 9 13. and he inuiteth and calleth vnto him all thofe who are wearie and heauie laden with the burthen of their finnes, promifing that hee will eafe them. Matt 11.28. yea fo certaine it is that they fhal haue remiffion of their finnes and euerlafting hapineffe who truly repent and beleeue, that our fauiour Chrift faith they haue it already as though they were in prefent poffeffion. Iohn 5.24. *Verily, verily I fay vnto you, he that heareth my word and beleeueth in him that fent me, hath euerlafting life, and fhall not come into condemnation but hath paffed from death to life.* So chap. 6. 47. and chap. 11.26. *whofoeuer liueth and beleeueth in mee fhall neuer die.* The apoftle *Peter* alfo plainly affirmeth that *God would haue no man to perifh, but would haue all men to come to repentance.* Seeing therefore the Lord hath made fo many gratious promifes in the Gofpel to all repentant and beleeuing finners, let vs vnfainedly turne vnto the Lord, and apply Chrift and his meritts vnto vs by a true & liuely faith, and then we may affure our felues that he will pardon and forgiue vs al our finnes, and receaue vs gratioufly into his loue and fauour.

But againft this which hath beene alleaged, Sathan wilbe ready to obiect to the afflicted confcience, that thefe promifes were made to the prophets, apoftles and holy men of God, but not to fuch haynous and rebellious finners who

§. *Sect.5.* *That al Gods promifes are made indefinitely to all that belieue.*

Ff 4　　　　　　　haue

haue moft iuftly deferued that God fhould poure out vppon them the violls of his wrath, and thofe fearefull punifhments threatned in the law, becaufe of the innumerable number of their finnes and the outragioufnefle of their wickednefle; and therefore fuch haue nothing to doe with the fweet promifles of the Gofpell, but are to apply vnto themfelues the terrible threatnings denounced in the law againft fuch grieuous finners

For the anfwering of which tentation, wee are to know that the Lords promifes made in the Gofpell, are general, indefinite and vniuerfall, excluding none, who turne from their finnes by vnfained repentance, and beleeue in Chrift Iefus, refting on him alone for their faluation. Neither is there any limitation or exception of this or that finne, for be they neuer fo greiuous and manifold, yet if wee performe the condition of faith and repentance, the Lord will make good his promifes vnto vs.

For the firft, namely that the promifes of the gofpell are indefinite, and generally made to al who repent and beleeue it, fhall manifeftly appeare if wee confider the particulars. Efa. 55. 1. the Lord calleth all vnto him indefinitly, faying, *to euery one who thirfteth come to the waters, and yee that haue no filuer come, buy and eate; Come I fay buy wine and milke without filuer and without money;* fo that though we haue no worthinefle and righteoufnefle of our owne, yet if we thirft after the mercy of God and righteoufnefle of Chrift, and come vnto God by vnfained repentance, and vnto our fauiour by a liuely faith, our thirft fhall be fatiffiyed and all our wantes fupplyed. So Ezech. 33. 11. the Lord folemnely fweareth that hee *will not the death of a finner, but that they turne from their wicked wayes and liue;* where hee fpeaketh not of this or that finner, but of all without exception who turne vnto him. Our fauiour Chrift likewife maketh this indefinite promife Marke 16.16. that *whofoeuer fhal beleeue and be baptifed fhalbe faued.* and Iohn 3. 14. he faith, *that as Mofes lift vp the ferpent in the wildernefle, fo muft the fonne of man be lift vp* 15. *that whofoeuer beleeueth in him fhould not perifh but haue*

eternall

eternall life. So that as al who were ſtunge of the fyrie ſerpent were healed if they looked vpon the braſen ſerpent, neither was their any exceptiõ or diſtinctiõ between thoſe who were deeply, or but a little pearſed with the ſting, for if they were ſtũg they died, if they vſed not the remedy ordained of God, though their wound were but ſmall and ſhallow, but if they looked vp to the braſen ſerpent according to God ordinãce, they were cured though their wound were neuer ſo deadly and deſperate, ſo thoſe who looke not vpon Chriſt Ieſus hanging on the croſſe with the eye of faith, are ſure to fall into euerlaſting death and damnation, bee their ſinnes neuer ſo few, and on the other ſide, they who lay hould vpon Chriſt and beleeue in him, are ſure to bee ſaued though their ſins bee neuer ſo many and grieuous. So in the 16. verſe it is ſaid, that God ſo loued the world, that hee hath giuen his onely begotten ſonne, that whoſoeuer beleeueth in him ſhould not periſh but haue euerlaſting life. and ve. 36. He that beleeueth in the ſonne hath euerlaſting life. &c. So that here is no exception of ſinnes, for the promiſes are made indefinitely to all that beleeue. In like maner our Sauiour hath promiſed Iohn 6. 37. *That whoſoeuer come vnto him hee will not caſt them away.* and ve. 40. he aſſureth vs that it is *the will of his father who ſent him, that euery man who beleeueth in him ſhould haue euerlaſting life.* And the Apoſtle Peter Actes 10. 43. ſaith that *vnto our Sauiour Chriſt giue all the prophets witneſſe, that through his name all that beleeue in him ſhall haue remiſſion of ſinnes.* And the Apoſtle Iohn likewiſe ſaith, 1. Ioh. 2. 1. *that if any man ſinne wee haue an aduocate with the father Ieſus Chriſt the righteous, and hee is the propitiation for our ſinnes, and not for ours onely but alſo for the ſinnes of the whole world,* that is for whoſoeuer repent and beleeue of euery kingdome, countrey, and nation. So that by all theſe places it is cleare and euident that none are excluded from being partakers of Gods mercifull promiſes, but thoſe who exclude themſelues through their infidelitie and vnrepentancie.

Neyther is there any ſins ſo innumerable in multitude & ſo hainous & grieuous, which will debarre vs from receiuing §. *Sect.* 6 the

That our sins cannot debarre vs of Gods mercy, so we repent and beleeue. the benefit of Gods mercie and Chrifts merites fo wee repent and beleeue, as may appeare alfo by plaine teftimonie, Efay. 1. 18. the Lord thus fpeaketh to the Iewes whom hee had defcribed to bee rebellious and moft outragioufly wicked. *Come now (faith the Lord) & let vs reafon together, though your finnes were as crimfon, they fhalbe made white as fnow: though they were red as fcarlet, they fhalbe as wooll.* The Apoftle *Paul* likewife witneffeth. Tit. 2. 14. that our fauiour Chrift *gaue himfelfe for vs, that he might redeeme vs from all iniquitie;* And the Apoftle *Iohn* faith, that *the bloud of Chrift cleanfeth vs from all finne, and if wee acknowledge our* 1.Ioh.17. 9. *finnes he is faithfull and iuft to forgiue vs our finnes, and to cleanfe vs from all vnrighteoufneffe.* So that here is no mention made of any finnes which are excepted, or which exclude vs from Gods mercy & Chrifts merits, fo that we repent & beleeue; neither are the promifes of the Gofpell limited or reftrained in refpect of the number or greeuoufneffe of our finnes, fo we performe the conditiō of faith and repentance, for whofoeuer is hartily forie for his finnes paft, and purpofeth for the time to come to leaue and forfake them, whofoeuer doth beleeue Gods promifes and refteth vpon Chrift Iefus alone, for his faluation by a true and liuely faith, he may be certainly affured, that the Lord hath pardoned and forgiuen all his finnes, and receaued him into his grace and fauour, though his finnes be neuer fo many and hainous; and on the other fide whofoeuer continueth in his vnrepentancie and infidelitie, fhalbe condemned though his other finnes be neuer fo few and fmall; neither will all our other finnes debarre vs of Gods mercy, vnleffe they bee ioyned with vnrepentancie and vnbeliefe, for obferue the condition of the promifes, faith and repentance, and all the promifes of the Gofpell belong vnto thee though thou were the greateft finner that euer liued. For whereas it may be obiected that the finne againft the holy Ghoft is vnpardonable, we are to know it is not fo much in regard of the hainoufneffe of the finne, as that becaufe it is alwaies feuered and difioyned from faith and repentance, God denying thefe his graces to thofe who

vpon

vpon desperate malice haue made a generall Apostasie, and haue persecuted the knowne truth. So that if it were possible for them to repent and beleeue, it were possible also that they should be saued.

Seing therefore the promises of the Gospell are generall excluding none,let not any man who is laden with the burthen of his sinnes, exclude himselfe through his want of repentance and infidelitie,for though their other sinnes are grieuous,yet this is more hainous and damnable then all the rest. For whereas the Lord saith,that he wil extend his mercy vnto all who come vnto him ; if wee reply,no he will not extēd it vnto me becaufe I am a grieuous sinner,what do we els but contradict the Lord, and giue truth it selfe the lie; not giuing credit to his word and promises. And therefore let vs take heed that wee do not so aggrauate our sinnes as that in the meane time wee extenuate and derogate from Gods infallible truth.

CHAP. XXXV.

Of other arguments drawne from the persons in the Trinty.

Nd these are the arguments which are drawne from the nature of God, whereby we may be assured of the remission of our sinnes; there may also other arguments bee drawne from euery person of the Trinitie. Firft God the father hath created vs of nothing,euen according to his own image, and when wee had defaced this his image in vs, and made our selues slaues to Sathan, he so tenderly loued vs his poore miserable creatures, that he spared not his dearely beloued & onely begotten Sonne, but sent him into the world to take our nature vpon him, that therein he might suffer all misery and affliction, and lastly the cursed and bitter death of the crosse,that so he might satisfie his iustice for our sinnes & perfect the worke of our redemption. And this the Euangelist witnesseth,Iohn 3.16, Al which loue the Lord shewed

§. Sect. 1.
Reasons drawne from the first person, God the father.

vnto

vnto vs euen for his owne names fake, when we neither deserued it nor yet defired it, for we were bondslaues vnto Sathan, and well contented to liue in his bondage, wee were children of wrath and dead in our sinnes, yea wee were enemies vnto God and all goodnesse. And therefore if our mercifull God so loued vs whilest we were in loue with our sinnes, at league with his enemie Sathan, & at enmitie with him, that hee sent his dearely beloued and onely begotten Sonne to dye for vs, that by his death and bloudshed hee might redeeme and saue vs out of this miserable estate, how much more will he now receiue vs to mercy and pardon, and forgiue our sinnes if we seeke and sue for grace? if hee loued vs so dearely when we hated him, and sought al means of reconciliation when wee were professed enemies against him, how much more will hee receaue vs into his fauour, when as we earnestly desire to be reconciled? If he so loued vs that he sent his Sonne to die for our sinnes, how much more will he remit those sinnes for which hee hath satisfied, when as with harty sorrow we doe bewaile them, and earnestly desire to be freed from them? if he hath giuen his Sonne to mankind to this end, that hee should saue and redeeme repentant sinners, why should any doubt of their redemption and saluation if they turne vnto him by vntained repentance, and lay hould on Christ by a liuely faith? and if he haue giuen vs his chiefe Iewell, his onely begotten and best beloued Sonne and that when wee were his enemies, what will he denie vs when in Christ we are reconciled vnto him and become his friends? And thus the Apostle reasoneth, Rom. 5.8. *God (saith he) setteth out his loue towards vs seeing that whilest we were yet sinners Christ died for vs. 9. much more then being now iustified by his bloud we shalbe saued from wrath through him. 10. For if we were enemies we were reconciled to God by the death of his Sonne, much more being reconciled we shalbe saued by his life.*

§. Sect.2.
Reasons drawne from the 2. person God the sonne

Secondly wee may drawe most firme argumentes to strengthen our assurance of the remission of our sinnes, from the second person in trinitie our Sauiour Iesus Christ; for first hee

hee is our Sauiour and redeemer, who therefore came into the world that hee might faue and redeeme vs out of the captiuitie of our fpirituall enemies, finne, death, and the diuell, and that hee might fatiffie his fathers iuftice, obtaine the remiffion of our finnes, and reconcile vs vnto him. Though then our finnes be many and grieuous, this fhould not hinder vs from comming to Chrift by a true faith, and firme affurance, that in him wee fhall haue the remiffion of our finnes, and be receaued into Gods loue and fauoure, nay rather this fhould bee a forceible argument to mooue vs, to feeke his helpe, when wee find our felues in a defperate cafe, deftitute of all meanes whereby wee may attaine vnto faluation, feeing our Sauiour Chrift came into the world to faue fuch as were loft in themfelues, and inthralled in the miferable bondage of finne and Sathan. And this is euident by the fcriptures, Matth. 9. 13. our Sauiour profeffeth that *he came not to call the righteous but finners to repentance.* and Luke 19. 10. *The fonne of man is come to feeke and to faue that which was loft.* 1. Tim. 1. 15. *This is a true faying and by all meanes worthie to bee receiued, that Iefus Chrift came into the worlde to faue finners.* the apoftle alfo affirmeth that our Sauiour Chrift hath *quickned vs who were dead in our fins & trefpaffes.* Eph. 2. 1. 5. And our fauiour Chrift Matth. 11. 28. doth not only call vnto him fmal finners, but thofe who are heauy ladē with an intollerable waight of fin, promifing that he will eafe them.

Seeing therefore hee came into the world to faue and redeeme grieuous and hainous finners, and to giue life vnto thofe who were euen ftarke dead in their finnes, feeing alfo hee calleth and inuiteth fuch vnto him as are heauily laden with an intollerable waight of wickednefle, and promifeth to eafe them; let vs not excufe our felues from comming becaufe our finnes are hainous and grieuous, but therefore let vs the rather goe vnto Chrift becaufe wee had need of his helpe. If a man being loded with a waightie burthen, fhould refufe the helpe of a friend, both able and willing to eafe him becaufe his burthen is very heauie, who would not laugh at fuch ridiculous follie, for therefore he fhould more

earneftly

earneſtly deſire, and more thankfully accept of his friendes offred courteſie, becauſe himſelfe is tyred, preſſed downe, and altogether vnable to beare this intollerable waight: but ſuch and greater follie doe they commit, who being pinched and oppreſſed with the heauie burthen of their ſinnes, doe through their infidelitie refuſe the healpe of Chriſt, offering himſelfe to releaſe and eaſe them vnder this pretēce, becauſe their burthen is ouer heauie; for becauſe to them it is intollerable, therefore they ſhould rather goe vnto Chriſt and erneſtly deſire to be eaſed and releaſed, ſeeing hee is not onely able, for his power is omnipotent, but alſo moſt willing, for he hath moſt gratiouſly promiſed and freely offred his helpe.

That the price which Chriſt hath paid for our redemption farre exceedeth all our ſinnes.

Moreouer we need not to doubt of the ſufficiencie of the price which our Sauiour hath paid for our redemption, for it is of infinite value and of more vertue and power to iuſtifie and ſaue, then all the ſinnes of the world to condemne and deſtroye; ſo that though wee were the greateſt ſinners that euer liued, yea though the waight of all ſinne which euer in the world hath beene cōmitted did lie vpō vs, yet the meritts of Chriſt and the price which hee paid for our redemption doe farre exceede them, and if we come vnto him by a liuely faith reſting vpon him alone for our ſaluation, hee will ſurely eaſe vs of this intollerable burthen. And therefore though the grieuouſneſſe of our ſinnes ſhoulde increaſe our repentance, yet they ſhould not diminiſh our faith and aſſurance of pardon and forgiueneſſe, for though our debt were neuer ſo great, our ſuerty Chriſt Ieſus hath paid it to the vttermoſt farthing, though our ſinnes are neuer ſo many and grieuous

1. Pet. 2. 24. our Sauiour *hath borne them all vpon the croſſe in his owne bodie* and fully ſatisfying Gods iuſtice for thē, hath freed and deliuered vs from this heauie burthen. Though wee were neuer ſo deeply inthraled in the bondage of our ſpiritual enemies, yet our almightie redeemer hath freed vs out of captiuitie & hath paid a ſufficient price for our raunſome; and though we had no right or intereſt in the kingdome of heauen, yet our ſauiour hath dearely purchaſed it for vs by his precious death and bloudſhed, and therefore ſeeing in Chriſt we haue fully ſatiſfied Gods iuſtice, and fully merited the pardon of

our

our sinnes, seeing in him wee haue not onely paied our debt, but also giuen a sufficient price for the purchasing of eternall happinesse, wee neede not to make any doubt of the pardō of our sins, and of possessing of our heauēly inheritance, for the Lord cannot in iustice hold that from vs which of right appertaineth vnto vs; nay we may assure our selues that though he could yet he would not; for who can imagine that the Lord who of his bountious liberallitie giueth vnto vs more then wee can deserue or desire, will keepe from vs that which of right appertayneth to vs? that he for his own names sake without any respect of our works or worthinesse freely multiplieth his benefites vpon vs, should with hould our rightfull inheritance in his heauenly kingdome from vs, which our sauiour Christ hath purchased for vs by his pretious death & bloudshed? and therefore seeing wee haue vndoubted right to the pardon of our sins becauſe Christ Iesus hath satisfied for them, & iust title to our heauenly inheritāce which our Sauiour hath purchased for vs with so deare and all-sufficient a price, let vs in the name of Christ goe bouldly vnto the throne of grace, desiring a generall acquittance of that debt which is alreadie paid, nay let vs not feare to approach the throne of Gods seuere iustice, and to claime our heauenly inheritance which Christ hath so dearly purchased.

§. *Sect.4.*

Furthermore we are to consider that our sauiour and redeemer is so gratious and bountifull, so rich in mercy, and so full of all power vertue and perfection, that our sinnes should not discourage vs from comming vnto him, for the more miserable wretched & sinful we are, the more fitt subiects we are, whereupon he may exercise and shew the infinite riches of bounty, mercy, vertue and all sufficiencie. If we were but a little soyled with sinne, it were not so great a matter to make vs cleane but when wee are most filthily defiled, and our polution is ingrayned in vs as it were with a scarlet die; when our vncleane corruptiō sticks as fast to our soules, as the *Ethiopian* blacknesse to their skins, then is the vertue of the excellent lauer of Christs bloud sufficiently manifested, when as he purgeth vs and maketh vs cleane, washing away all our filthy corruptions, and making our

That Chriſts power, mercy, and merites is more manifeſtied by forgiuing greeuous sinners.

scarlet

ſcarlet ſinnes as white as ſnow. Our ſauiour Chriſt is our
ſpirituall phyſitiō who can as eaſily cure deſperate diſeaſes e-
ue the remediles conſumptiō, the dead apoplexie & the filthy
leproſie of the ſoule, as ſome ſmall maladie, or little faintnes?
neither is he only able but alſo as willing to vndertake ſuch
deſperate cures as the leaſt infirmities, becauſe his ſkill will
be the more manifeſt and his praiſe the more extolled, for
the more deſperate the diſeaſe is, the more it argueth his
cūning who helpeth it, and the more cōmendations he ſhal
receaue who effecteth ſuch a cure. And therefore though
our diſeaſes are moſt daungerous & deſperate, yet let vs reſort to this our heauenly phyſitiō, for the more deſperate the
cure is, the more fitt occaſion ſhall he haue of ſhewing his
neuer failing ſkill, and of aduancing his immortall praiſe. He
is our heauenly ſurgeon, euen the good Samaritane which
powreth the ſoueraigne oyle of his grace, and the pretious
baulme of his bloud into our woūded ſoules, & therfore the
more greiſly our wounds are, the more praiſe and glory he
getteth in curing them, the more is the vertue of the ſoueraigne ſalue of his bloud manifeſted to all the world by healing of them.

Though therefore our ſoules are moſt filthy & polluted,
yet if we come to Chriſt he will ſurely waſh & purge vs, for
to this purpoſe he ſuffered his precious water and bloud to
iſſue out of his ſide, that thereby as with a liuing and cleare
ſtreame iſſuing from a moſt pure fountaine, he might cleanſe
vs from al our ſins, and waſh away all our filthy corruptions,
though we are moſt deſperatly ſicke, let vs come vnto our
ſpirituall phyſition, for he can cure the moſt remedileſſe diſ-
caſes as perfectly and as ſpeedily, as the moſt ſmall infirmitie
and faint weakneſſe : though our ſoules are wounded euen
to the death, with the deepe pearcing and deadly impoyſo-
ning ſting of ſinne, yet let vs ſeeke helpe of this our heauenly ſurgeon, who with the precious baulme of his bloud, can
as eaſily heale the moſt dangerous woūds, as ſmall ſcratches
or little cutts. Neither is he more able then willing, for hereby his vertue and power, his loue and bountie, is the more

mani-

manifested to his endlesse and immortall prayse.

But if we thinke our soules so filthy that he cannot purge them, what doe wee els but derogate from the vertue of his bloud, if we will not goe to this heauenly Phisition to craue his helpe, because our sicknesse is grieuous and dangerous, what doe we els but call his skill into question? If wee will not shew our wounds because they are griesly, what doe we els but notably detract from the cunning of this our spirituall surgeon, and doubt of the vertue and efficacie of the pretious baulme of his bloud: Whereas on the other side if we see our polluted filthinesse, and yet goe vnto Christ that we may be washed and cleansed, we acknowledge the vertue and excellencie of the spirituall lauer of his bloud? if wee plainely discerne that our sicknesse is desperate and yet goe to our soules Physition not doubting of recouery, we thereby extoll our Physitions skill, if our woundes be in themselues griesly and incurable, & yet we resort to our heauenly Surgeon to be healed of them, wee cannot more commend his all sufficient cunning. And therefore seing it is in these our extremities to our Sauiour Christ most honorable and acceptable, and to our selues most profitable and full of comfort, if we come vnto Christ not doubting of his helpe, let vs not pretend excuses eyther because we are vnfit, vnworthy, or in a desperate state, for by thus aggrauating our owne remedilesse misery we extenuate and call into question Gods mercy and Christs al-sufficiency, wee spoyle him of his honour, glorie, & our owne soules of all ioy & consolation.

That those who doubt of the remission of their sinnes derogate from the vertue of Christs merites.

Secondly, we may gather firme assurance of the pardon of our sinnes from the offices of Christ, for first he is our prophet who hath reuealed vnto vs all the will and counsayle of his father, he hath declared vnto vs the mysterie of our redemption and the meanes of our saluation, how we may attaine vnto the remission of our sinnes, and how wee may come out of that miserable and wretched estate, in which we are by nature, and attaine vnto eternall happinesse, he it is who by the bright beames of his word doth illuminate our vnderstandings, and by the operation of his holy spirit

§. Sect. 5. That the offices of Christ giue vs assurance of the remission of our sinnes. And first in that he is our Prophet.

doth

doth cause the sealesof ignorance to fall from our eyes, *Giuing knowledge of saluation to his people by rem ssion of sinnes.*
He is that glorious and bright shining day starre, *which from
an highe hath visited vs, to g ue light vnto them who sit in darkenesse and in the shadow of death, and to guide our feete into the
way of peace.* If therefore we will walke in the way which he
sheweth vs,and vse those meanes which hee reuealeth vnto
vs in his Gospell, namely turne vnto God by vnfained repentance,and beleeue in him by a liuely faith, wee shall not
need to feare our sinnes though neuer so grieuous and manifold, for this our heauenly Prophet hath truely reuealed
vnto vs a plaine way how wee may come out of our sinnes
and be reconciled vnto God, how we may be adorned with
the glorious robe of his righteousnesse and bee made partakers of all his merites; how we may become of the children
of wrath and firebrands of hell, the children of God, and
heires of heauen. And therefore let vs walke in this way and
assure our selues that wee shall come to the iourney end of
our desires,for truth it selfe is our guide so that we need not
to doubt of the way.

§. Sect. 6.
Reasõs drawn
from Christes
priesthood.

Secondly our sauiour Christ is our high priest, who hath
offered vp vnto his father an all-sufficient sacrifice and full
satisfaction for our sinnes, whereby Gods iustice is fully satisfied and his wrath appeased, who also sitting at the right
hand of his father,continually maketh intercession for vs.
The sacrifice which this our high priest offered was himselfe,
as the apostle testifieth Heb . 9. 26. euen his body to be crucified, and his bloud to be shed for the putting away of our
sinnes? the which oblation was offred on the altar of his die-
ty which sanctified the sacrifice, & gaue vnto it such sufficiē-
cy and valew,that it was a perfect price & ful satisfaction for
the sins of al the faithful,as the apostle witnesseth. 1 .Ioh.2.2.
*Hee is the propitiation for our sinnes, and not for ours only, but
for the sinnes of the whole world.* Seeing therefore this our high
priest hath giuen himselfe for vs, euen his body to be crucified, and his bloud to be shed to this end , that it might bee
a propitiatorie sacrifice and full satisfaction for our sinnes,
and

and ſeeing he was once offered to take away the ſinnes of ma
ny, as the Apoſtle ſpeaketh Heb. 9 28. wee need not doubt
of the remiſſion of our ſinnes if wee come vnto him by a
liuely faith, for to this end hee hath ſhed his bloud, that he
therby might offer vnto God a full ſatiſfaction for our ſinnes
and purge away all our wickedneſſe, and therefore if hee
ſhould not attaine vnto his end, that is if hee ſhould not ſatiſfie Gods iuſtice and appeaſe his wrath, by purging and take-
ing away all our ſinnes, his precious bloud ſhould be ſhed in
vaine.

Moreouer he is our mediatour and interceſſour, who continually ſitteth at the right hand of his father making interceſſion for vs, by ſhewing and pleading his owne meritts
righteouſneſſe and obedience whereby hee pacifieth his fathers diſpleaſure, and worketh vs into his loue and fauour.
And this the apoſtle witneſſeth. Rom. 8. 34. *It is Chriſt which
is dead yea or rather which is riſen againe, who is alſo at the right
hand of God, and maketh requeſt for vs.* So alſo Heb. 9. 24. it
is ſaid that our high prieſt Ieſus Chriſt *is entred into heauen, to
appeare in the ſight of God for vs.* and the Apoſtle Iohn ſayth.
1. Ioh. 2. 1. *If any man ſinne wee haue an aduocate with the father Ieſus Chriſt the iuſt, and hee is the propitiation for our ſinnes.*
neither need wee to doubt of his effectuall dealing for vs, for
if hee loued vs ſo dearely that hee ſpared not to giue his precious life for vs, there is no queſtion but he wilbe exceeding
earneſt in making requeſt for vs, neither will hee be ſparing
in wordes who hath not ſpared his deareſt bloud. And therfore ſeing our high prieſt doth continually make interceſſion
for vs, wee need not to doubt but that hee will obtaine his
ſuite, and procure the pardon of our ſinnes, and his fathers
loue and fauour. Eſpecially conſidering that hee intreateth
nothing which hee hath not deſerued and by his death purchaſed for vs, and conſequently when like an aduocate hee
pleadeth his full payment of our debt, and alleadgeth his all
ſufficient meritts and ſufferings, God cannot in his iuſtice
but graunt his moſt lawfull requeſt; conſidering alſo that he
maketh his ſuite not to a ſtranger or ſome common friend

*§. Sect. 7.
Reaſōs drawn
from Chriſtes
interceſſion.*

who

who will either preuent his suite with a strange and sterne
countenance, or denie it with some vaine excuse, but vnto
his most gratious & dearely louing father who willingly harkeneth vnto, and redily graunteth all his requests. And thus
our Sauiour himselfe testifieth Ioh. 11. 41 *father* (saith he)
I thanke thee because thou hast heard me. 42. *But I knowe thou
hearest mee alwaies &c.* And therefore considering Christs
merit in deseruing, and Gods mercie in graunting, Christs
importunitie in asking, and his fathers facilitie in yeelding;
seeing hee that intreateth for vs loued vs so intirely that hee
dyed for vs, and will vndoubtedly bee most earnest in soli-
citing our suite, and hee who is intreated so hartily affecteth
vs that he spared not to giue vnto vs his onely begotten and
dearely beloued sonne, that by his death he might purchase
for vs euerlasting life , let vs shake of all doubting *and goe
bouldly vnto the throne of grace, that wee may receiue mercie
and finde grace to helpe in time of need.* as the Apostle exhorteth

§.Sect.8.
Reasōs drawn
from Christes
kingly office.
Mat. 11. 25.

vs Heb. 4. 16. For our good high priest *is able perfectly to saue
them who come vnto God by him, seeing hee euer liueth to make
intercession for them.* as it is Heb. 7. 25.

Thirdly as our Sauiour Christ is our prophet and priest so
likewise he is our king, and this also may assure vs of the pardon and remission of our sins if we will come vnto him, for
hee who is our aduocate is also our soueraigne, hee that is
our mediatour is our iudge, hee that intreateth for vs, hath
power in his handes both to obtaine and graunt his owne
suite, hee that gaue his life a ransome for our sinnes hath all
power in heauen and earth committed vnto him, so as he is
able to remit all our sinnes and to blot out all our iniquities,
for (now) *the father iudgeth no man, but hath committed all
iudgment vnto the sonne.* as himselfe testifieth Ioh. 5. 22. and
euen when he was vpon the earth he excercised this authoritie, as appeareth Matth. 9. 2. whereas hee saith to the sick
of the palsie. *Sonne bee of good comfort thy sinnes are forgeuen
thee.* For which being chalenged hee defendeth his regall
priuiledges, affirming ver. 6. that the sonne of man hath
authoritie euen on earth to forgiue sinnes. Now what can

be

bee more comfortable vnto any soule wounded with sinne then the confideration of this vndoubted truth. For seeing our Sauiour who so tenderly loued vs, that hee spared not to giue his owne most precious bloud for the price of our redemption hath all-sufficient power in his owne handes to saue and deliuer vs out of the handes of all our enemies, who can imagine that hee will suffer vs to bee lost whom he hath so dearely bought? seeing he gaue his life to purchase for vs the remiffion of our sinnes, who can doubt that hauing thus dearely purchased it hee will not bestowe it and so suffer his bloud to be spilt in vaine, seeing he was content for our sakes to indure all miserie, mockings, reuilings, whipping, crucifying death it selfe, & the anger of his father more bitter then death, to this end that by all these his sufferings, he might procure the remiffion of our sinnes & euerlasting life, and that when we were rebellious traitours who did flee away from him; who can make any question, but that now hee will bestow these inestimable benefits which he hath of purpose bought for vs, they being in his owne power and custodie, if like humble seruants and penitent children we turne vnto him and implore his grace? if a malefactour had a deare friend who loued him so intirely, that he would not spare to giue his whole substance to procure his pardon, would this miserable offendour feare death or condemnation, if he were assured that now his pardon were in his friends hand, and that the matter were by his Prince referred to him, as vnto a supreame iudge absolutely to determine what hee will? But our Sauiour hath not giuen goods or gold, or any corruptible thing, but euen his owne most pretious body to be crucified, & his bloud to be shed, that by this inestimable price he might purchase our pardon of God our soueraigne king, now he hath the law in his own hands, and is appointed of God for our supreame Iudge to acquit vs at his owne pleasure, who therefore can make any doubt of grace and pardon, seeing his iudge is his Sauiour who hath loued him so dearely, that to this end he hath shed his precious bloud, that he might procure for him the remis-

fion

fion of his finnes and euerlasting happinesse, and therefore if he would not sticke to buy it at so high a rate, how much more hauing bought it onely for this purpose will he now bestow it if we seeke vnto him, and earnestly desire to bee partakers of his grace and mercy.

§. *Sect.9.*
Reasons drawne from Chrifts promises,confirmed by experience.

Moreouer as this our most gratious king and louing Sauiour hath sufficient power to pardon all our finnes, and in respect of his inestimable loue, is most certainely willing to blot out all our wickednesse, if wee repent and come vnto him, so also he hath bound himselfe hereunto by most free and faithfull promises. Matth.11.28. *Come vnto me all ye that labour and are heauy laden, and I will ease you.* Iohn 3.36. *Hee that beleeueth in the Sonne hath euerlasting life.* And Ioh. 6.37. He hath assuredly promised, that whosoeuer *commeth vnto him he will not cast away.* These and many such like gratious promises he hath made, of the performance wherof we need not to doubt, especially confidering that he gaue continuall experience in his practise here on earth, of his loue, goodnesse, mercy and trueth, for who euer came vnto him with any lawfull suite and receaued a repulse? who euer intreated his help, & was abadoned? who euer asked any thing of him which was profitable for him to receiue and did not obtaine his suite? whatsoeuer sicke came vnto him receaued their health, whatsoeuer lame desired his helpe receaued their lims, whatsoeuer blind resorted vnto him receaued their fight, whatsoeuer sinner implored the forgiuenesse of his finnes receaued full remission and pardon. Yea so gratious mercifull and louing was this our king and redeemer, that he preuented his poore miserable fubiectes with his grace, and fought all occasions of extending his loue and mercie towards them, giuing vnto them more then they desired; the sicke of the paulsie comming vnto him not onely was cured of his disease, but also receaued the remission of his finnes. Matth.9. *Zacheus* desired but to see his face, and he offereth vnto him his company and therewith eternall saluation. Luke 19. The woman of *Samaria* requested but elementall water, and hee offereth vnto her the water of life.
Ioh.

Ioh.4. The people followed him to be fed by miracle with corporall foode, and Chrift offereth vnto them the bread of life. Ioh.6. The poore blinde man defired that he might be by Chrift reftored to his bodily fight, and Chrift alfo illumi-nates the eyes of his foule, fo that as with his bodily eyes hee difcerned him to be a man, fo by the eie of faith he knew him to be his redeemer and Sauiour. By all which it clearly ap-peareth that there was neuer any more ready to aske then Chrift to giue, nay fuch was his goodneffe and loue, that he was alwaies more ready to graunt then they to intreat, and to graunt more then they euer defired. Now wee muft not thinke that our Sauiour is altered in nature, or that (as it is vfuall amongft men) honours haue changed manners, for he is God immutable in goodneffe, *and w thout change or fhadowe of change*, as it is Iam.1.17. and therefore wee may affure our felues if wee turne from our finnes by true repen-tance, and come vnto him by a liuely faith, we fhalbe recea-ued to grace and mercy, and receaue the pardon of our fins be they neuer fo hainous and innumerable.

Ioh 9.

Laftly, the vnion and communion which is betweene Chrift and all the faithful, may giue vnto them full affurance of the pardon and remiffion of all their finnes; for firft they are coupled vnto him in fpirituall matrimonie, and hee be-commeth the Bridegroome, they the fpoufe, he the husband, they the wife, now we know that in law there will no action of debt lie againft the wife whileft the husband liueth, be-caufe fhe is vnder couert barne, and therefore her husband who hath taken vpon him to maintaine and defend her, muft anfwere and follow all her fuites, and his goods are li-able for the paying of her debts. And thus it is alfo betweene Chrift the husband and the Church his fpoufe being marri-ed vnto her, he hath taken her vnder his charge and prote-ction, and hath vndertaken to anfwere all fuites and to fatif-fie all her debts, nay he hath difcharged them already, and therefore wee need not to feare any action which Sathan, the Law or Gods iuftice may lay againft vs, for our husband Iefus Chrift hath taken vpon him to follow all our fuites,

§.Sect.10.
Reafons drawne from our Commu-nion with Chrift.

and

and to satisfie all our debts, so that if eyther the Law, Gods iustice, or our enemy Sathan doe comence any suits against vs, we are not now to take vpon vs the answering of them in our owne persons, but wee are to send them to our husband Iesus Christ, who hath taken our causes in hand and will giue vnto them a sufficient answere.

The faithfull Christs members. Secondly the faithfull are vnited vnto Christ in a more neere vnion, for he is there head and they his members, as appeareth Ephe. 5. 23. 30. hee is the true vine and wee the branches, as himselfe speaketh Iohn 15 1. he is the fruitfull Oliue tree, we the sciences which are grafted into him. as it is Rom. 11. he is the foundation, wee the building, as the apostle affirmeth Ephe. 2. 20. 21. by reason of which neere vnion, it commeth to passe that those things which appertaine vnto Christ belong vnto vs, and ours vnto him, for as the head deriueth sence and motion vnto the members; and as the Oliue tree and vine doe communicate their vertue, fatnesse, and sap vnto their branches and sciences, by which they liue and bring forth fruite, and as the foundation doth sustaine and vphold all the building; so doth our Sauiour Christ our head, roote, and foundation communicate vnto vs his members and branches, the vertue of his merits and the iuce and sap of his precious bloud, whereby we are quickned and reuiued who were dead in trespasses, our sins washed away and purged and wee made fruitfull in all righteousnesse and holinesse, as in that his imputed righteousnesse whereby we are iustified before God, and that inhærent righteousnesse begunne in vs by his holy spirit, whereby we are iustified before men. And as he hath bestowed and communicated vnto vs his righteousnesse, death and obedience, so hath he taken vpon him from vs al our sins originall and actuall, of commission and omission, and in his owne person hath suffered all that punishment, which we by them had deserued, so as now he hauing taken vpon him our sinnes, and indued vs with his righteousnesse, merit, and obedience, wee need not to feare the exact rigour of Gods iustice, for by him and in him we are without sinne, pure and

vnde-

vndefiled, and perfe&ly righteous in Gods fight. Neither
fhall we need to feare the violence of all our fpirituall enemies,for our head Iefus Chrift is God almighty, and therefore none fhalbe able to plucke vs out of his hands againft
his will,and we are as deare vnto him as the members of his
body, and therfore looke how loath any careful head would
be to haue any of the members pulled from it by force and
violence,fo loath and vnwilling will our Sauiour and head
be, to haue any of his members plucked from him. And
therefore feing he wanteth neither will nor power to defend
vs, wee need not feare the raging malice and cunning violence of any of our fpirituall enemies, finne, the Diuell, the
world and the flefhe,for our head is all-fufficient, and alfo
moft willing to faue and defend vs, from all their force and
malice.

And fomuch concerning the reafons drawne from the fecond perfon,wherby euery repenting and beleeuing finner
may be affured of the pardon and remiffion of all his finnes.
Now we are to fpeake of thofe which may be drawne from
the third perfon the holy fpirit. Firft therefore wee are to
know that though our finnes be manifold, and our corruptions exceeding filthy, yet this holy fpirit will fanctifie and
purge vs from all our pollution ; fo that though in times
paft wee were moft hainous finners, idolaters, adulterers,
theeues,drunkards,raylers,extortioners,*yet now wee are wa-*
fhed, now wee are fanctified, now wee are iuftified in the name of
the Lord Iefus,and by the fpirit of our God. As the Apoftle fpeaketh,1.Cor.6.11.he is that heauenly fire which confumeth
and purgeth vs from all the droffe of our corruptions, hee is
that diuine water which wafheth away all our filthy pollution,it is hee who doth regenerate and beget vs a new who
were dead in our finnes, and whofoeuer are thus regenerated fhalbe heires of the kingdome cf heauen.

Secondly, we may hereby be affured of the remiffion of
our finnes, in that the fpirit of God ioyneth with vs in our
fuite and together with vs, maketh requeft vnto God in our
behalfe, and whereas wee are ignorant and *know not how to*
pray

§.Sect.11.
Reafons
drawne from
the 3. perfon
the holy fpi-
rit.

pray as we ought, the spirit it selfe helpeth our infirmities and maketh request for us w'th sighes which cannot be expressed. But
God who searcheth the hearts, knoweth what is the meaning of
the spirit: for he maketh request for the Saints according to the
will of God. As the Apostle speaketh. Rom. 8. 26, 27. who
therefore can doubt of obtaining his suite, euen the remission of his sinnes and reconciliation with God, seeing his
suite is framed and indited by Gods spirit, and consequently is most wise, iust, and as the Apostle saith according to the
will of God? yea it is sollicited and followed with great earnestnesse by the same spirit; and therefore our suite being
wise, iust, and framed by the spirit according to the will of
God, and by the same spirite in most earnest manner, sollicited and furthered, there is no question but wee shall obtaine it.

CHAP. XXXVI.

*Other reasons to perswade the weake Christian of the remission
of his sinnes.*

§. Sect. 1.
1. *That wee
are to beleeue
the remission
of our sinnes,
because it is
an article of
our Creede.*

Nd these are the reasons which may be drawn
from euery of the persons of the Trinitie, to
assure vs of the remission of our sinnes; to
which we may add diuers others. First, the beleeuing of the remission of our sinnes is an
article of our Creede, which we doe daily confesse and professe, which is not left vnto our choise to beleeue or not to
beleeue, but as we confesse it with the mouth, so we are boūd
to beleeue it with the heart, if we would be reckoned in the
number of Christians. Why then should we doubt of that
which we are bound to performe; and if wee doe not wee
grieuously sinne through infidelitie, which is more daungerous & damnable then all our other sins whatsoeuer? And
therefore though there were no other reason to mooue vs,
though our hainous and manifold sinnes should make it
seeme vnto vs neuer so incredible, yet let vs set aside all im-
                                                    pediments

pediments and breake through the violence of all obiections, and beleeue in obedience to Gods commaundements,
and becaufe it is our dutie, the performance whereof is very
acceptable vnto God, and the neglect whereof is a finne
moft daungerous and damnable. Which that we may perfourme, let vs carefully obferue the condition of the couenant of grace, that is, let vs reft and rely vpon Chrift Iefus
alone for our faluation by a liuely faith, and turne vnto God
by vnfained repentance, and then there is no place left to
doubting of that which in dutie we are bound to beleeue.

Secondly the afflicted foule labouring vnder finne may
receiue no fmall affurance by the teftimonie of Gods faithfull minifters; for the keyes of the kingdome of heauen are
committed vnto them, and they haue power giuen them of
God here on earth to bind and loofe; not as though they
could by their owne authoritie and in their owne name giue
pardon of finnes to whom they lift (as the papifts teach and
practife, for this is proper and peculiar vnto God alone, as
euen the Pharifes well knew whereof it was, that feeing our
Sauiour Chrift take vpon him to forgiue finnes whom they
imagined to bee a meere man, they affirmed that he blafphe-
med. For who (fay they can forgiue finne but God onely)
but they haue authoritie giuen them of God vpon due examination and tryall of their faith by the fruites thereof vnfained repentance, certainely to declare and pronounce vnto them that their finnes are forgiuen. Whofoeuer therefore
haue this teftimonie of Gods faithful minifters who are well
acquainted with their eftates giuen vnto thē, they may affure
themfelues that it is vndoubtedly true and moft certaine; for
who is it that dare oppofe himfelfe and contradict the teftimonie of Gods fpirite in the mouth of fo many his faithfull
ambaffadours? who dare bee fo prefumptuous as to take vppon him the difcerning of his ftate better then the minifters
of God, who being appointed of God to this function are
indued with a great meafure of his fpirit, whereby they are
inabled to difcerne and iudge of mens eftates better then
they themfelues? for he that is fpiritual difcerneth all things,

§. Sect.2.
2. The tefti-
monie of
Gods faith-
full mini-
fters.
Matth.16.

and.

and is made acquainted with the mind of Christ, as the A-
postle speaketh 1. Cor 2. 15. 16. And therefore if diuers of
Gods faithfull ministers with one consent pronounce vnto
any pænitent sinner the remission of their sinnes, and assure
them after the examination of their estate that they are in the
loue and fauour of God, it should be vnto them ten thousand
times more forcible an argument to perswade thē & to confirme their faith in the assurāce of Gods loue, then the cōtra-
rie testimonie of Sathan or their timorous vnbeleeuing flesh
to moue them to doubting thereof, if our bodies be sicke we
committ our selues to the skill and care of the phisition, and
good reason, because wee knowe he is better able to discerne
of our estate then we our selues, and beleeuing his iudgment
to bee good wee suffer him to applie such remedies as hee
thinketh most fitt; why then should wee not committ the
discerning of our estate to the phisition of the soule no lesse
careful, and in this respect much more skilful? for the others
rules in some patients may faile him, but the grounds whereupon the spirituall physition buildeth, are most infallible being the vndoubted truth of God. Why should we not rather
beleeue their often approoued iudgment then our owne timorous phantasies, or Sathans testimonie who is our malitious enemie?

§. Sect. 3.
The 3. Reason
drawne from
the contrarie
testimonie of
Sathan.   Thirdly the afflicted soule may gather assurance of the remission of sinnes from the contrarie testimonie of the diuel.
For when ther is any suggestion cast into our mindes which
is repugnant to the word of God and the testimonie of Gods
spirit in the heartes of the faithfull, we may assure our selues
that it is the speech of Sathan or of our corrupt fleshe the
messenger of Sathan both which come to one end; but those
motiues and suggestions, that God will not receiue vs to
mercie, that our sinnes are vnpardonable, that wee are reprobates and castawayes, that now it is too late to turne vnto God, proceed not from Gods spirit, for they are quite
contrarie to that which the scriptures teach vs, namely that
the mercies of God are infinite, and hee alwaies readie to receiue vs to grace when we turne vnto him; that if we wil earnestly

neftly repent and in the mediation of Chrift fue for mercie, hee will make our fcarlet finnes as white as fnow, that it is neuer to late to turne vnto God, for if wee repent hee hath promifed to remit our fins, and to receiue vs into his fauour. Neither are wee to imagine that the teftimonie of Gods fpirit in our confciences is contrarie to the teftimonie of the fame fpirit in the holy fcriptures, and therefore feeing thefe fuggeftions are flatly repugnant to the worde of God and teftimonie of the fpirit, wee are to affure our felues that they are the temptations of Sathan, eyther immediately fuggefted by himfelfe or mediately by his meffenger our corrupt flefhe.

Seeing then thefe fuggeftions come from Sathan who is our malicious enemie, and a lyar from the beginning yea the father of lies we are not to beleeue the, nay rather we may gather certaine affurance that the contrarie is true; for he fpeaketh onely lyes, or if at any time hee fpeake the trueth it is to this ende that hee may deceiue vs. For example hee telleth the fecure carnall man that hee is in the ftate of grace, and highly in Gods fauour, but vnto the humbled finner hee faith, that he is a reprobate & fhal moft certainly be damned; vnto the worldly fecure man hee faith that God is moft mercifull, then the which nothing can bee more true, but doth not fpeake this in his confcience, becaufe hee would haue him to taft thereof but to lull him a fleepe with this fweete fyren fong to his eternall perdition. On the other fide when hee hath to deale with the brufed heart and contrite fpirite, hee telleth him of nothing but of Gods exact iuftice, to the ende that hee may plunge him into vtter defperation : In a word whatfoeuer hee fpeaketh in the confcience of man, it is eyther falfe in it felfe or if true in them yet falfe in hypocrifie, if true in the generall, yet falfe in the particular application. As what can bee more true then that God is iuft? and what more falfe then that hee will excercife his iuftice in punifhing repentant and humbled finners ? what can be more true then that God is moft merciful? and what more falfe then that he wil fhew this his mercy in fauing thofe who

Ioh. 8. 44.
Sathan either lyeth or elfe fpeaketh the truth to deceiue.

liue

liue and die in their sins without repentance? & yet it is most
vsuall with Sathan to affirme both the one and the other, lying in both because hee doth misapply them. And therefore seeing Sathan doth neuer speake the truth or else doth
falsly apply it in respect of our estate, let vs acquaint our
selues with his false language; and so by hearing his lies wee
may bee the better assured of the truth; for example, when
hee telleth vs that our sinnes are vnpardonable, that it is now
too late to turne vnto the Lord, that wee are reprobates and
damned wretches, wee knowing that our malicious enemie
by his lies doth continually seeke our destruction, are contrariwise to assure our selues that Gods mercie and Christes
merites farre exceed our sinnes, that nowe is the acceptable time and day of saluation, if we will turne vnto God and
hearing his voice not harden our heartes, that wee are in the
state of saluation, the vessels of mercie. and beloued children
of God.

§ .Sect.4.
The last ar-
gument taken
from the ex-
perience of
Gods mercy
in pardoning
others. and
first of whole
cities and na-
tions.

Lastly those who are heauie laden with the burthen of
their sinnes, may gather vnto themselues assurance of the
forgiuenesse of them, by the consideration of Gods mercie
extended vnto other repentant sinners; for there was neuer
any from the beginning of the world to this day, were their
sinnes neuer so hainous or innumerable who haue not beene
receiued to mercie, and pardoned of our gratious God whensoeuer they did vnfainedly turne vnto him. And this may
appeare whether wee consider whole cities or nations, or else
particular men. Of the first wee haue a notable example in
the Israelites which liued in the time of the iudges, who
though they did many times negligently forget the greate
mercies and inestimable benefites of God shewed to their
forefathers, of which also themselues had beene partakers,
though they forsooke the Lorde not once or twise but very
often, euen then when he most bound them vnto him with
multiplying vpon them the benefitts of peace and plentie,
and though they let the raines loose vnto all wickednesse,
yea (which was most abhominable and odious in the sight
of God,) though they worshiped and serued *Baal* and *Aste-*
roth

roth and other idolls of the curfed nations, for which horrible idolatrie God had caft out the nations before them; yet whenfoeuer they turned vnto the Lorde hee pardoned their finnes, receiuing them into his former loue and fauour, and deliuered them out of the handes of all their enemies.

So likewife in the time of the prophet Efay, to what a notorious height of wickedneffe were the fame people growne as the Lord by his prophet doth decipher and defcribe them in the firft chapter of that prophecie. In the 2. ver. he calleth heauen and earth to witneffe their horrible rebellion, in the 3. verfe hee fheweth that their vnthankfulneffe for all his mercies, far exceeded the vngratitude of bruite beafts, in the 4. verfe hee exclaymeth out againft them calling them *a finfull nation, a people laden with iniquitie, a feed of the wicked corrupt children who had forfaken the Lord, and prouoked the holy one of Ifraell to anger.* In the 5. and 6. verfes he fheweth their hardneffe of heart and obftinacie in their rebellion which was fo great that though the Lord fent afflictions & caftizementes vpon them, yet they were no whit reformed but waxed worfe and worfe, and that this was not the cafe of fome few but of al the whole body of the people, for *the whole head was ficke and the whole heart was heauie. and that from the foule of the foote to the crowne of the head there was nothing found therein, but wounds, and fwellings, and fores full of corruption,* the cure whereof they vtterly neglected. In the 10. verfe hee matcheth the finnes of both prince and people, with thofe crying finnes and outragious wickedneffe of *Sodome* and *Gomorah* which brought down from heauen fire and brimftone to confume them. In the 11. 12. 13. and 14. verfes he complaineth of their filthie hypocrifie in Gods outward worfhip ioyned with the vtter neglect of true godlineffe and his fpirituall feruice, which caufed the Lord to deteft al their facrifices, fabbothes, and newe moones. So that their could not bee imagined greater wickedneffe in any people, refpecting thofe notable meanes which the Lorde continually graunted vnto them aboue all other nations for their owne conuerfion; and therefore who would not haue thought
their

The example of the Ifraelits in the time of the prophet Efay.
Efay 1. 5. to the 16.

their ſtate to be moſt deſperate, who would not haue looked dayly that the Lorde ſhould haue conſumed them with fire and brimſtone, or haue cauſed the earth to haue ſwallowed them vp aliue as it did *Corah* and his aſſotiats? but behould the infinite mercies of our gratious God, euen when they wallowed in this filthie ſinke of all impietie the Lord calleth them to repentance, and when as they had forſaken him and fled from him, deſiring nothing leſſe then to make or med-dle with him, the Lord calleth vnto them, and hee in whoſe power it was euery minute vtterly to deſtroy them, firſt of all deſireth a parley, he who might well abhorre to vouch-ſafe them his preſence, earneſtly deſireth conference with them, ſaying. ver. 18. Come now and let vs reaſon together ſaith the Lord; though your ſinnes were as crimſon, they ſhall bee made as white as ſnow; though they were red like ſcarlet, they ſhall be as wool.

§. Sect.6.
The example
of the Iſrae-
lites in the
time of our
ſauiourChriſt

In like manner in the time of our ſauiour Chriſt the ſame Iewes moſt wickedly rebelled againſt the Lorde; for when the Lord in his rich mercy ſent the promiſed *Meſſias*, to de-liuer them out of the handes of their enemies, they would not receiue him, nay they continually afflicted and perſecuted him, they mocked and reuiled him, they haled him before the iudgment ſeate, and cauſed him to bee condemned who came to iuſtifie and acquite them; they buffeted and whipped him, and preferred a wicked murtherer before him, who preferred their ſaluation before his owne life, laſtly in moſt ignominious ſort they crucified and killed him. After all which outragious wickedneſſe offered againſt the Lord of life, they continued in their hardneſſe of heart and impæni-tencie, neuer acknowledging their fault nor deſiring par-don, nay rather as they had perſecuted the head our Lord and Sauiour Ieſus Chriſt, ſo when they could offer no more wrong vnto him in his owne perſon, they were ready to ſa-tiſfie and glutt their malicious rage in perſecuting his poore members. Now what more helliſh impietie was euer com-mitted? what more outragious ſinne was euer heard of; who would euer haue imagined that there was any hope of

pardon

pardon for such rebellious bloudy wretches? but O the infinite and bottomelesse depth of Gods mercy, whilest their wickednesse was fresh in memorie, and their hands still imbrewed in the guiltlesse bloud of this innocent Lambe: when as they continued in their course, and ran headlong forward in their wickednes without any sence of sin or desire of pardon; the Lord sent his apostles vnto them to bring them to repentance, and to assure them that their sinnes were pardoned. Seeing therefore these obtained the remission of their sinnes, who needs to doubt of pardon who earnestly desires it? for did the Lord gratiously offer forgiuenesse to such rebellious wretches, and will hee not graunt it to lesse offenders if they desire it? did he offer them mercy before they sought it, and will he denie mercy vnto any who earnestly seeke and sue for it? Doth hee seeke to draw men to repentance and to turne vnto him; and will he not receiue them when they doe repent? was he so exceeding mercifull in times past, and shall we now thinke his arme shortned or his mercy abated? Nay assuredly he is immutable euer like himselfe one and the same most gratious, most merciful, & full of all goodnesse and compassion, towards all them that come vnto him. And therefore if we turne from our sinnes by vnfained repentance, wee may assure our selues though they be neuer so many and grieuous they shalbe pardoned, and we receaued into Gods loue and fauour.

Act.2.38.

To these examples of whole multitudes, we may ad the examples of particular sinners, who haue beene receyued to mercy and obteined pardon, though their sinnes haue beene. many and grieuous, as *Matthew, Zacheus, Leui*, who were sinfull Publicans that got their liuings by pilling & polling, oppression and extortion, men so notoriously wicked, that Publicans and sinners are ioyned together, as though they were sinners by profession, and therefore as Synonima or diuers words of one signification they interprete one another. And yet such was the riches of Gods mercy, that euen these professed sinners were conuerted, and receiued remission of all their outragious wickednesse. The like may bee

§. *Sect.7.*
Particular
examples of
Gods mercy.

Hh   said

said of *Mary Magdalene* who though shee had beene a woman of lewde behauiour and loose life, though she were possessed of many diuels, and commonly noted for an infamous
and notorious sinner, yet vpon her true repentance obtained
the remission of her sinnes : and whilest she washed the feet
of our sauiour Christ with her teares, hee purged and cleansed her body and soule from the filthy leprosie of sinne with
his owne most pretious bloud, whilest she wiped them with
the haires of her head, he beautified and adorned her with
the rich robe of his righteousnesse. Yea she was receiued into
an high degree of fauour with our sauiour Christ, so as shee
had in some things the preheminence before his chiefe Apo-
stels, for after Christes rising againe he first vouchsafed her
his presence, and vsed her as his messenger to certifie the rest
of his resurrection. So likewise the Apostle *Paul* before his
calling was not onely no louer but a bitter and fierce persecuter of the truth, and of all the professours thereof, impriso-
ning, stoning, and cruelly murthering the Saints of God;
but behold and admire the wonderfull mercy of God, euen
whilest his imbrued hands, were yet red with the bloud of
Gods faithfull children, and whilest his heart was so full of
burning rage, that hee breathed out still threatnings and
slaughter against the disciples of the Lord, it pleased God
wonderfully to conuert him, to assure him of the remission
of all these his horrible sinnes, and to make him of a bloudie
persecuter, a most excellent preacher of his Gospell, and of a
rauenous deuouring wolfe, a most vigilant and painefull
shepheard. To these wee might adde the example of the
theefe, who though he had spent his whole life wickedly &
prophanely, yet was conuerted at the howre of death and re-
ceauing the pardon of his sinnes, was presently assured of
euerlasting happinesse. But I shall not need to heape vp many particulars, onely I can not passe that notable example
of *Manasses* one of the most outragious sinners and pro-
phanest wretch that euer liued, as the holy Ghost hath de-
2. Kings 21. scribed him in the 21. chap. of the 2. booke of the *Kings*. For
there he affirmeth of him that he was a most horrible idolater,

ter, a most malitious enemy and cruell persecuter of Gods
truth, a defiler of Gods holy temple, a sacrificer of his owne
children vnto idols, that is diuels, a notable witch, and wicked sorcerer, a bloudy murtherer of exceeding many the
deare Saints and true Prophets of the Lord, one who did not
runne headlong alone into all hellish impietie, but also ledd
the people vnder his gouerment out of the way to doe more
wickedly then did the Heathen people whom the Lord di-
stroied before the children of Israel, and in a word wrought
more abominations and outragious wickednesse then the
cursed *Amorites* and *Cananites*, of whom notwithstanding
the land surfetted and spued them out for their crying sins.
And yet this *Manasses*, this wretch, more like a diuell incar-
nate then a Saint of God, repenting him of his sinnes from
the bottome of his heart, was receaued (I cannot speake it
without rauishing wonder of Gods bottomlesse & neuer sufficiently admired mercy) was receaued I say, to grace, and
obtained the pardon of all his horrible sinnes and most abominable wickednesse. Now all these examples are written
for our learning, and are recorded by the holy Ghost, to the
end that wee may continually laud and prayse the Lord for
his endlesse and infinite mercies, and gather vnto our selues
assurance, that though our sinnes were as grieuous and hainous as any of theirs before named , yet if with them wee
turne from our sinnes by vnfained repentance, and goe vnto Christ by a liuely faith, wee shall also with them receaue
the pardon of our sinnes, and be entertained into Gods loue
and fauour.

    And thus haue I set downe most infallible reasons, vpon *§. Sect.8.*
which as vpon immoueable firme grounds, the afflicted *That vnre-*
conscience may lay the foundation of sound comfort; now *pentant sin-*
if any abuse the Gospel of Iesus Christ, and gather out of this *ners haue*
heauenly doctrine this diuelish vse, that because Gods mer- *nothing to*
cies abound therefore they will abound in their sinnes with- *doe with the*
out repentance, and still more and more prouoke the wrath *former con-*
of the Lord against them, to these I answere with the Apo- *solation.*
stle that their damnation is iust, in that they abuse Gods *Rom.3,8.*

                        mercy

mercy, as an occasion to sinne, which should serue as a forcible argument to lead them to repentance, neither let such flatter themselues with vaine hope of Gods mercy, for despising the riches of his boūtifulnesse, patience, & long suffering, & cōtinuing in their hardnesse of hart & vnrepentancy, *they treasure vp vnto themselues wrath against the day of wrath, and of the declaration of the iust iudgemēt of God.* As the apostle plainely speaketh Rom.2.4.5. Neither let thē foolishly boulster vp themselues in their sinnes, by putting vnder their elbowes, the sweet soft pillowes of Gods mercifull promises, for as there is none so speciall which doe exclude the most hainous sinner that repenteth & beleeueth, so is there none so generall which do extend themselues to those who continue in their vnrepentancie and vnbeliefe; and therefore though there be no sinne so grieuous, which being repented of and forsaken will condemne vs if wee rest and relie vpon our Sauiour Christ for our saluation by a liuely faith; so there is no sinne so small and veniall which will not plunge vs into the bottome of hell, if we liue therein without repentance and doe not desire to leaue and forsake it. And therefore so long as wee liue in our sinnes, and doe not seriously turne vnto the Lord by vnfained repentance, let vs not in vaine arrogate and misapply vnto our selues the mercy of God, the merites of Christ, and the sweet promises of the Gospell, for vnto such appertaine the fearefull threatnings of the law as being still the children of wrath, dead in their sinnes, and subiect to Gods heauie wrath and displeasure.

CHAP. XXXVII.

How we may know whether we be effectually called or no.

§. Sect.1.
How Sathan
perswadeth
the weake
Christian,
that he is not
called.

Nd so much concerning those reasons whereby the humbled and repentant sinner may gather vnto himselfe certaine assurance of the pardon and remission of his sinnes: of all which consolations Sathan earnestly indeuoureth to spoile the afflicted
foule,

soule, by suggesting into his mind diuers subtill and dangerous tentations. As first, that all these gratious promises & sweet consolations of the gospell do onely belong vnto those who are called neither to all in this number, for many are called but few are chosen, but vnto those alone whose calling is effectuall, that is to say, who are seperated from the world giuen, vnto Christ and Christ vnto them, and who are ingrafted into him, and become liuely members of his body : but thou, will he say to the humbled sinner art not thus effectually called, and therefore do not flatter thy selfe with the hope of Gods promises, for though in themselues they are most certaine, yet they belong not vnto thee, but vnto those alone whose calling is effectuall.

Against which tentation if wee would strengthen our selues, we must examine our calling whether it be effectuall or no; and that both by considering the meanes whereby all are effectually called, and also the partes of effectuall calling, making application of both vnto our owne particular. For the first, wee may thus reason against our spirituall enemy, whosoeuer can find the meanes of effectuall calling, power fully working in himselfe, and conuerting him vnto God he is effectually called, but I haue and doe find these meanes thus working in me, and therefore I doe not flatter my selfe with vaine hope, but am certainely assured that I am effectually called and conuerted.

How we may withstand the former tentations.

The meanes whereby wee are effectually called, are first the sauing and fruitfull hearing of Gods word, by the ministery whereof the Lord calleth and inuiteth vs to come vnto him by vnfained repentance, and to our sauiour Christ by a liuely faith euen when wee are dead in our sinnes, without any desire to will or abilitie to performe any thing that is good, whilest wee are the bondslaues of Sathan and meere worldlings, not desiring nor once thinking vpon the means of our saluation. And this is done first by the preaching of the law, by which is reuealed vnto vs our innumerable hainous sinnes, and the fearefull punishments due vnto them : as that we by our continuall transgression are subiect to the

§. Sect.2. Of the means of our effectuall calling.

Ezech.16.6.

Eph.2.1.3. 12.13.

Rom.7.7.

curse

curſe of the law, vnable to perfourme obedience vnto any
of the commaundements or to make ſatisfaction to Gods
iuſtice for the leaſt of our ſins, and ſo conſequently that we
are obnoxious to Gods wrath, ſubiect to thoſe horrible torments prouided for the wicked, and therefore in reſpect of
our ſelues, our owne righteouſneſſe, ſatisfaction, or any
other meanes of our owne whatſoeuer in a moſt damnable and deſperate eſtate. Secondly, after the Lawe hath
thus ſhewed vnto vs our ſins & the puniſhments due vnto
them, the Lord by the miniſterie of the goſpel doth reueale
vnto vs a plaine way by which we may come out of this miſerable eſtate, and attaine vnto euerlaſting ſaluation, namely
by beleeuing and ayplying vnto our ſelues Chriſt Ieſus and
all his benefites. Thirdly with this outward miniſterie of the
word the Lord ioyneth the inwarrd cooperation of his holy
ſpirit, whereby hee openeth our deafe eares, and maketh vs

Pſal. 40.6.
Iohn 6. 44.
Act. 16. 14.
1.Ioh.2. 20.
27.
attentiuely to heare, and as with a precious eyeſalue illightens
the blind eyes of our vnderſtandings, enabling vs to conceiue and vnderſtand thoſe things which are deliuered vnto
vs, both out of the law, and out of the Goſpel.

§. *Sect.3.*
The 2. meanes
of our effect-
uall calling.
　　The ſecond meanes of our effectuall calling is the ſofte-
ning of our harde hartes, when as the Lorde taketh away
our ſtonie hartes, and giueth vs hartes of fleſh, as hee promiſeth Ezec.11.19. And breaketh vp theſe fallow grounds
fit in themſelues to bring forth no fruite but weedes and
thiſtles, that ſo they may bee prepared to receiue the ſeed of
his word, aud bee made fruitfull in all grace. And thus our
ſtubborne & rebellious hartes are ſoftened when as we particularly apply vnto our ſelues the doctrine of the law, wherby firſt wee come to the knowing and acknowledging of our
ſinnes, original and actual. Secondly our hartes are pricked,
and our conſciences wounded by apprehending and applying to our guiltie ſoules the curſe of the lawe, the anger of
God, and thoſe feareful puniſhments prepared for the wicked. Thirdly ſeeing this our miſerie, and finding no means
of our owne how wee may come out of this wretched eſtate,
wee are brought to deſpaire of our own ſtrength, righteouſneſſe

neſſe, and ſatisfaction,, finding them of no vertue for our iuſtification. By all which, being throughly humbled and caſt downe in our ſelues, the Lorde by the preaching of the goſpel doth reueale vnto vs a way how we may eſcape out of this miſerable eſtate, by applying vnto our ſelues Chriſt Ie-ſus, and all his meritts and obedience by a true and liuely faith; after which the humbled ſinner ſeeing his owne wants and niſerie by the lawe, and perceiuing that our ſa-uiour Chriſt is ſo rich in meritts, that hee can eaſily ſupply all his derects, and ſo gratious and powerfull that hee can and will free him out of his wretchedneſſe, he doth plainely diſcerne that hee ſtandeth exceedingly in need of Chriſt Ie-ſus and his righteouſneſſe. After which ſenſe of his owne wantes there is begott in him an earneſt and hungring deſire to bee made partaker of Ieſus Chriſt his righteouſneſſe, me-ritts, obedience, and of all thoſe ineſtimable benefitts which are purchaſed by them. And laſtly hee is mooued to appeale from the ſentence of the law, to the throne of grace, pleading not his owne righteouſneſſe or ſatiſfaction, but Chriſts me-ritts and obedience.

The third and laſt meanes of our effectuall calling is a true *The 3.meanes* and liuely faith, whereby we apprehend Chriſt Ieſus and all his benefitts giuen and applyed vnto vs by Gods ſpirite, reſt-ing vpon him alone for our iuſtification and ſaluation..

And theſe are the meanes of our effectuall calling, which *§.Sect.4.* whoſoeuer hath found powerfull working in themſelues for *That all who* their conuerſion after the manner before ſpoken of, *find the for-* they may moſt certainely aſſure themſelues that they are ef-*mer meanes* fectually called, and are alreadie partakers of Ieſus Chriſt *powerfull in them are ef-* and all his benefites. If therefore the Lorde whileſt wee did *fectually cal-* lye frozen in the dregs of our ſinnes, without all deſire of *led.* grace or meanes to eſcape out of our miſerie, hath vouchſa-fed vnto vs the miſterie of his holy word, if by the law hee hath reuealed our ſinnes vnto vs and the puniſhmentes due vnto them, and if by the goſpell hee hath ſhewed vs the way how we may come out of this miſerie; if by the inward cooperation of his holy ſpirit he hath opened our deafe eares, and with this precious eyesalue hath annointed the blinde eies of our vnderstandings so that we haue attentiuely heard, and in some measure vnderstoode those principles of our christian religion, which haue in the misterie of the worde beene deliuered vnto vs; if our hartes haue beene softened and pearced, and our consciences wounded with the sight and sense of our sinnes; if disparing in our owne strength, righteousnesse and all other meanes of our owne, wee haue gone out of our selues, and rested and relied vpon Christ Iesus alone for our iustification aud saluation, then are wee without all doubt effectually called and are in the number of Gods church and people to whom the promises of grace doe appertaine.

§. Sect. 5.
That we may know that we are effectually called by considering the seuerall parts thereof.
Secondly we may come to the knowledge of our effectuall calling, by considering the seuerall parts thereof. The first is our selection and separation out of the corrupt masse of mankind, whereby it commeth to passe that though wee be in the world, yet we are not of the world, and therefore wee neither loue it, nor the world vs; and this our Sauiour sheweth, Ioh. 15. 19. *If (saith he) yee were of the world the world would loue his owne, but because yee are not of the worlde, but I haue chosen you out of the world, therefore the world hateth you.*

1. Ioh. 2. 15. and the apostle Iohn affirmeth, that *if any man loue the worlde the loue of the father is not in him.* 1. Ioh. 2. 15. and the

Iam. 4. 4. apostle Iames telleth vs that *the amitie of the world is enmitie with God, and therefore whosoeuer will bee a friend of the worlde maketh himselfe the enemie of God.* If therefore our loue and affectiōs be weaned in some good measure from the world, and fixt on spirituall and heauenly things, if wee cease to be

Phil. 3. 29. citizens of the world, and begin to haue our *conuersation in in heauen from whence wee looke for a sauiour euen the Lorde Iesus Christ*; and if the world beginne to hate and scorne vs, then may we be assured that wee are seuered from the world, and intertained into Gods church and familie.

§. Sect. 6.
Sathans tentation answe
But here the tempter will obiect, that by this it plainely appeareth that wee are not yet effectually called nor seperated from the world, because we still loue the world af-
feeting

fecting and defiring the vaine pleasures, honoures, & riches
thereof, yea and also loue those who are meere worldlings,
and on the other side the world also loueth vs, giuing vs
good countenance and performing other duties vnto vs. For
the answering of which suggestion we must distinguish betweene our selues and our selues; for whilest we continue in
this life wee are partly flesh and partly spirit, and as there is
great enmitie betweene the spirit and the world, so is there
great amitie betweene the world and the flesh. So farre
forth therefore as wee are still carnall and corrupt flesh the
world loueth vs, but as much as is spirituall and regenerate
so much the world hateth and abhorreth. Moreouer we may
generally be considered as men, or more specially as we are
Christian men; in the first respect, the world that is wicked
worldlings may loue vs for some naturall partes or meere
morall vertues, or els in common humanitie as members of
the same ciuill or politicke body: but as wee are Christians
who haue giuen our names vnto God & diuoted our selues
to his worship and seruice, the world hateth vs and our profeffion, religion, and all the fruits and exercises of sanctification and holinesse, so that though in other naturall, worldly,
and more ciuill respects it loueth vs, yet in regard of our regeneration and the fruites thereof it cannot indure vs, and
our companie and conuersation is exceeding tedious, irksome and vnpleasant. So on the other side whereas Sathan
obiecteth that we loue the world that is carnal worldly men,
we may answere that euen as we are regenerate, it is lawfull
to loue them in the same respects which they loue vs, namely as they are men & the excellent creatures of God, as they
are indued with excellent naturall giftes or morall vertues,
as they are of the same ciuill body or kinred, or as they haue
beene vsed of God as his instruments for the bestowing of
any his benefits vpon vs: in which respects louing them, we
may notwithstanding with a true zeale hate & abhorre their
vices, their carnall worldlinesse, prophane irreligion, and
wicked conuersation. Neither will religion make vs to lay
aside all humanitie and transforme vs into some brutish, or

red whereby he perswa-deth the christian that he loueth the world and the world him.

rather

rather diuelish *Timon* who was a hater of men. For euen our
sauiour Chrift himfelf who was wholy exēpted from finne,
notwithftanding loued the worldly yong man for fome
good things he faw in him though he were not religious,yea
though he were fo carnall that hee preferred his vaine and
vncertaine riches before the faluation of his foule,as appeareth Mark.10.21.22. So alfo he vfed all humanitie and ciuill conuerfation euen amongft the Publicans and finners,
that he might haue the better opportunitie of conuerting all
thofe who belonged to Gods electiō. And therfore we need
not feare to follow Chrifts example fo it be with the fame ho
ly affection. For we alfo muft indeauour to gaine thofe vnto Chrift who are without,and by our holy cōuerfation giue
them occafion of glorifying God in the day of their vifitation as the apoftle exhorteth vs,1.Pet.2.12.which we can neuer doe by hatred, rough feueritie, and finicall inhumanitie,
but with louing curtefie,vpright behauiour, gentle admonitions and charitable reprehenfions. But if through our corruptiō we giue fathan occafion further to obiect, that vnder
thefe pretences we fet our harts too much vpon the world
louing worldings more then thofe who are of the houfhould
of faith and more delighting in their vaine conuerfation for
outward refpects then in the companie of the faithfull if not
alwaies yet oftentimes, we are to anfwere that though thefe
be finnes in vs, and notable fignes of our great corruption,
yet are they no ftronge arguments that we are not yet effectually called, or truely feuered frō the world,for as much as
we are not wholy feperated frō the world, but only fomuch
of vs as is fpirituall and regenerate; fo that it is no meruaile
if the the flefh and vnregenerate part ftill loue the world,be-
becaufe it is ftill worldly; but if in the inner man wee hate
this loue, and ftriue to bridle yea to mortifie it, if we are truly fory and difpleafed with our felues for this as for other fins
and labour to reforme it, wee may be affured that the fpirite of God is in vs,which hath feuered vs from the world, &
ioyned vs to the body of Iefus Chrift.

§.Sect.7.   The like alfo may be anfwered concerning the loue of
worldy

worldly things, honours, riches and pleasures; we may loue
them as they are the bleſſings of God, and deſire them ſo
farr foorth as they are temporall benefitts, and furtherances
or at leaſt no hinderances in the workes of holineſſe and righteouſneſſe, we may ſo loue them as that in the meane time
our loue be ſubordinate to the loue of God, our brethren &
ſpirituall things. But if our loue paſſe theſe limitts it is corrupt and carnall, yet no vndoubted argument to proue that
we are not effectually called, if we are diſpleaſed with it and
labour againſt it, though oftetimes we are ouercome therewith through the violence of our carnall affections and the
corruptions of the fleſh, yet if wee hate this ſinne in the inner man, if wee entertaine through violence, and not with
affection and delight, if it dwell in vs but doe not raigne
in vs, if but ſometimes it gett the vpper hand and doe
not continually ouerrule vs, it is no more wee that doe it
but ſinne that dwelleth in vs, that is the old man and corrupt fleſh, which whileſt wee liue in this life will beare ſome
ſway in vs.

How far forth we may loue worldly things.

Laſtly when as Sathan aſſaulteth the poere chriſtian with
his tentations, perſwading him that he is not yet called nor
ſeparated from the wicked world, becauſe it loueth him, he
may well ſuſpect his argument of falſhood, for Sathan doth
not hate thoſe whom the world loueth; but by his continuall aſſaulting of the weake chriſtian, and his dayly labouring to bring him through the violence of his tentations to
vtter deſtruction, it manifeſtly appeareth that Sathan like
a mortall enimie deadly hateth him; and therefore it is not
likely that he is beloued of the world though it may for a
time fawne vpon him, that by pretending loue and friend-
ſhipp it may worke him the greater miſchiefe.

That the world loueth them not wᵇᵒ Sathan hateth.

The ſecond part of our effectuall calling is the mutuall
donation of God the father, whereby he hath giuen Chriſt
Ieſus vnto vs to be our ſauiour and redeemer, and vs vnto
Chriſt to be ſaued and redeemed, by which alſo wee may
proue that we are effectually called. For this gift is mutuall and reciprocal, and therefore the one doth clearely proue
the

§.Sect. 8. *Of the ſecond part of our effectuall calling.*

the other, fo that if we can haue any aſſurance that Chriſt
is giuen vnto vs, then may we alſo be aſſured that we are
giuen vnto Chriſt, and contrariwiſe if we haue any aſſurance
that we are giuen vnto Chriſt, then may we be alſo aſſured
that Chriſt is giuen vnto vs, and conſequently that wee are
effectually called for this mutuall donation is one parte
thereof. Now wee may bee aſſured that Chriſt is giuen vnto vs if wee beleeue in him reſting vppon him alone for
our iuſtification and ſaluation, as appeareth Ioh. 3. 16. *So
God loued the world that hee hath giuen his onely begotten ſonne
that as many as beleeue in him ſhould not periſh but haue euerlaſting life,* and ſo alſo we may be aſſured that wee are giuen
vnto Chriſt, if wee heare his voice and follow him, as himſelfe ſpeaketh Ioh. 10.27. and ſubmitt our ſelues to bee led
and gouerned by his ſpirit, for *as many as are led by the ſpirite
of God they are the ſonnes of God, and whoſoeuer are ſonnes are
heires of God, and heires annexed with Chriſt.* as it is Rom. 8.
14.16.

How thoſe that are giuē to Chriſt, keep his word.

But here Sathan will obiect that thoſe who are giuen vnto
Chriſt haue kept his word, as himſelf alſo affirmeth Ioh.17.
6. How therefore will he ſay, canſt thou be aſſured that thou
art one of thoſe who are giuen vnto him, ſeeing thou keepeſt
it not but continually tranſgreſſeſt his commaundementes?
To which wee muſt anſwere that the worde of Chriſt is his
goſpell, wherein hee promiſeth euerlaſting life to all that beleeue in him, and bring forth the fruites of their faith in vnfained repentance. as it appeareth Ioh. 5. 38. where hee thus
ſpeaketh to the vnbeleeuing Iewes : *And his word* (ſaith he)
*haue yee not abiding in you: for whom he hath ſent, him yee be-
leeue not;* whereby it is manifeſt if Chriſts reaſoning bee of
ſound conſequence, that thoſe haue his word abiding in them
who beleeue in him, whom God hath ſent euen our Lorde
and Sauiour Ieſus Chriſt. So that we keepe the word of our
Sauiour when wee beleeue in him, reſting and relying vpon
him alone for our ſaluation, and truely repent vs of our ſins,
ſorrowing and grieuing that by them we haue offended and
diſpleaſed

diſpleaſed our louing God and mercifull father, hating our
ſinnes becauſe they are ſinnes, purpoſing and labouring to
forſake them, and indeuouring according to the meaſure of
ſtrength and grace receiued, to ſerue the Lord in holineſſe
and newneſſe of life. And therefore if wee can find in our
ſelues this faith and this repentance, wee may vndoubtedly
be aſſured notwithſtanding our manifould iails and greate
corruptions that we haue kept the word of Chriſt, and therefore are giuen vnto him of the father ; and conſequently
that we are effectually called and ſhalbe eternally glorified.
For it is the will of *the father that whoſoeuer beleeueth in his ſon
Ieſus Chriſt ſhoulde haue euerlaſting life*, as our Sauiour
teſtifieth Ioh. 6. 40. As for our corruptions they ſhall bee
waſhed away with the bloud of Chriſt, and our imperfections ſhall bee couered with the rich robe of his perfect righteouſneſſe, ſo that in him wee ſhall appeare perfect before
Gods iudgment ſeate, and there bee accepted as iuſt and
righteous.

The third part of our effectuall calling is our vnion and
communion with Chriſt, whereby he becommeth our head
and wee his members, of which whoſoeuer can bee aſſured,
they need not to make any queſton of their effectual calling;
but all thoſe who are indued with faith are vnited vnto
Chriſt, for it is a propertie thereof to apply vnto our ſelues
Chriſt and all his benefitts, it is the hand of the ſoule whereby wee lay hould vpon Chriſt, it is the mouth of the ſoule
wherby we ſpiritually feed vpō him, & he *that eateth his fleſh,
and drinketh his bloud dwelleth in Chriſt and Chriſt in him*, as
himſelfe ſpeaketh, Ioh. 6. 56. So alſo whoſoeuer are indued
with Gods ſpirit and haue ſubmitted themſelues to bee led
and gouerned thereby, they are ingrafted in the bodie of
Chriſt, for the ſpirit is the bloud of this vnion, and therefore
if wee can diſcerne the ſpirit of God in vs by any of the fruits
thereof, wee may bee aſſured that wee are the members
of Chriſt, and conſequently effectually called. Laſtly wee
may be aſſured that wee are ingrafted in the bodie of Chriſt
by our worke of ſaluation, either appertaining to Gods ſer-

§. *Sect. 9.*
*Of the third
part of our
effectuall
calling.*

Gal. 5. 22.

uice

uice or chriſtian righteouſneſſe towards our neighbour, for it is impoſſible that wee ſhoulde bring foorth any ripe grapes of godlineſſe if wee were not ingrafted in the true vine Ieſus Chriſt, as himſelfe affirmeth, Ioh. 15.4. *Abide in mee and I in you : as the branch cannot beare fruite of it ſelfe except it abide in the vine. no more can yee except yee abide in mee : 5. I am the vine, ye are the branches, hee that abideth in me and I in him the ſame bringeth forth much fruites for without mee yee can doe nothing.* And therefore if wee make conſcience of our wayes, and excerciſe our ſelues in ſome meaſure, in thoſe good workes which the Lorde hath commaunded in obedience to his will, and to this end that his name may be glorified, wee may aſſure our ſelues that wee are ingrafted into the true vine Chriſt Ieſus, for of our ſelues we are altogether vnfruitfull and could doe nothing.

§ *.Sect.10.*
That we may be vnited vnto Chriſt though we alwaies bring forth ſmall fruits and ſometime no fruites.

But here Sathan will obiect that this argument maketh againſt our ſelues, for we thereby make it manifeſt that we are not ingrafted into Chriſt, becauſe our fruites of holineſſe and righteouſneſſe are commonly exceeding ſmall, and ſometimes none at al, wheras the liuely branches of this vine are exceeding fruitfull, and abundant in good workes. To which we are to anſwere, that all the branches of the vine do not bring forth fruits in like aboundance, but ſome more and ſome leſſe, and yet notwithſtanding this doth not proue that theſe are not true branches as well as the other although they receiue leſſe ſappe and liuely iuyce from the roote and ſtocke, and ſo alſo it is in this myſticall vine; if the branches be not altogeather barren and fruitleſſe, though their fruites be not in ſo greate aboundance, yet if it bee right and of the ſame nature with the other, they may aſſure themſelues that they alſo are liuely branches of the true vine Ieſus Chriſt; neither is the quātity & nūber of our fruits ſo much in this regard to be reſpected; for if according to the quātitie of ſap & goodiuice which we receiue frō our root we bring forth fruit, that is, if according to that meaſure of grace & giftes of Gods holy ſpirit, which our ſauiour Chriſt hath beſtowed vpon vs, we ſpend our liues in Gods ſeruice which himſelfe hath commaunded

maunded to the end that we may glorifie his holy name, we may assure our selues that we are true branches of this vine, which our Sauiour *will purge and prune that wee may bringe forth more fruites,* as he hath promised. Ioh. 15. 2. moreouer whereas Sathan obiecteth, that wee are not branches of this vine, becaufe at fome times wee can fhew no fruits; wee are to anfwere that as the earthly vine hath not alwayes grapes, no not fo much as leaues vpon it, and yet notwithftanding it liueth, receiuing nourifhment from the roote, and bringeth forth fruit in due time and feafon, fo that the braunches of this mifticall vine are fome time without the fruites of good workes, yea, haue not fo much to bee feene vpon them as the faire greene leaues of an outward profeffion, as it is moft vfuall when as they are throughly nypped with the could winter of tentations, and haue all their beautie blafted and blowne away with the boyfterous blafts of fathans fierce incounters; and yet at the fame time they receiue the fapp, iuyce, and vertue of Gods fpirit from their roote Iefus Chrift, by which they feeming dead doe liue and receiue nourifhment; vntill at Gods good pleafure the comfortable beames of his loue and fauour do fhine vpon them, with which their frozen hartes being throughly warmed, doe againe bring forth not onely the leaues of profeffion, but alfo the ripe fruits of godlineffe and righteoufneffe, and therefore though prefently in fuch cafes wee haue no fruites to fhewe yet let not Sathan perfwade vs that we are not true branches of this vine? for if we can call to mind, that euer in former times we haue brought forth any right and kindly fruites of fanctification and true godlineffe, we are true branches of the vine Chrift which hee will lop and prune and againe make fruit-full; for out of him we could neuer haue brought forth fuch fruites, and thofe who are once ingrafted into him can ne-uer poffibly be plucked away by Sathan, the world, or al the powers of hell, though (as I faid) they may for a time bee nipped and fhrewdly weather beaten.

Ioh. 15. 4.
Ioh. 10. 28.

CHAP.

CHAP. XXXVIII.

Sathans tentations obiecting to the weake chriſtian unrepen-
tancie and hardneſſe of heart anſwered.

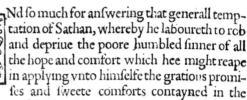

§. *Sect.*1.
How Sathan
perſwadeth
the weake
chriſtian that
he hath no
repentance.

Nd ſo much for anſwering that generall temptation of Sathan, whereby he laboureth to rob
and depriue the poore humbled ſinner of all
the hope and comfort which hee might reape
in applying vnto himſelfe the gratious promiſes and ſweete comforts contayned in the
goſpell, by perſwading him that hee is not effectually
called. Wherewith if hee cannot preuaile hee deſcendeth
from the generall to the particulars, and hauing as it were
a farre off diſcharged his ſhott of dangerous temptations
without inflicting deſired hurt and deſtruction, he approcheth neerer, and fighteth againſt the poore chriſtian with
handie blowes, that thereby hee may beate him downe into
deepe deſperation. Let it bee graunted will hee ſay that thou
art called, yet it followeth not hereof that thou art elected
and ſhalt bee ſaued; for Chriſt Ieſus himſelfe hath ſaide that
many are called but few are choſen and why maieſt not thou
bee in the greater number; neither is the calling thou ſpea-
keſt of ſufficient to make a chriſtian, vnleſſe it bee accompanied with vnfained repentance and a liuely faith. And the
promiſes of the goſpell wherein thou vainely hopeſt are not
made vnto all thoſe who are called, but vnto thoſe who are
indued with a true iuſtifying faith, which is alwaies ioyned
with the fruite thereof, vnfained repentance. But if thou examine thy ſelfe aright, thou ſhalt find that both theſe are
wanting in thee, for to beginne firſt with repentance which
is moſt ſenſible and to be diſcerned with greateſt eaſe if thou
ſearch thine hart without any affectionate partialitie or vaine
conceipt; thou ſhalt find that thou art altogeather deſtitute
thereof. For is not thy hart ſo obſtinately hard, and ſo ſtub-
bernely rebellious, that thou canſt not bewaile thy ſinnes
with

with any vnfained forrow, nor fcarce with much ftrayning force one teare, whereas for any worldly loffe, or temporarie affliction which indeed toucheth thee with true griefe, thou canft without any difficultie weepe more bitterly then the apoftle Peter, and fhed as many teares as *Marie Magdalene.* Befides wheras thofe who repent turne from their finnes with a true and vnreconcilable hatred of them, and fpend the reft of their life that remaineth in the feruice of God, whereas they haue their hard ftonic harts mollified and turned into harts of flefhe, which are flexible vnto holy obedience and full of alacritie and chearefulneffe in performing feruice to God, thou through thy hardneffe and heart that cannot repent liueft ftill in thy finnes, and fpendeft a great part of thy time in vanitie and worldly delightes, thy heart as hard as the adamat is ready fooner to breake then to bowe to Gods will, and when thou forceft thy felfe hereunto, thou canft not but difcerne the blindnes of thy vnderftanding in fpiritual thinges, which is fo fharpe and eaglefighted in matters concerning the world, thy fpirits fo dull & blockifh, & thine affectios fo glutted & tyred in performing feruice vnto God which are fo ful of life, & alacritie in following worldly vanities. And therefore it is impoffible that thou fhouldeft haue any true repentance, for how can repentance and hardnes of hart, a hart of flefh & an hart of ftone be at once in thee.

Againft which tentation of Sathan if we would arme our felues, it behoueth vs to bee verie carefull that wee doe not runne into two dangerous extreames; the one whereof is fecurely to flatter our felues with an opinion of our good eftate when as in turth it is moft dangerous and damnable, the other that we doe not too much fuffer our felues to bee deiected and caft downe, thoughe wee haue not as yet attained to fo greate perfection as our hearte defireth. And to this purpofe we are to know that hardneffe of heart is of two fortes, the firft is of them who being moft hard harted, notwithftanding doe not feele nor perceiue it; the other of thofe who feeling their hardneffe of heart are greeued therewith, and defire to haue it mollified, foftened, and

§. *Sect.2.*
For the answering that former tentation 2. extreames to be avoyded.

Two fortes of hardneffe of hart. 1. that which is infenfible.

euen

euen refolued into teares of vnfained repentance. The firft
fort is damnable or at leaft moft daungerous, for it lulleth vs
afleepe in carnall fecuritie, it taketh away all fenfe of finne,
and confequently all forrow whereby we fhould bewaile it;
it fcareth and brawneth the confcience, couering it as it were
on all fides with a thicke hard skinne, which will neuer or
moft hardly be pearced, either by Gods iuftice and threatnings to caufe vs to fear leaft we incurre his wrathful difpleafure, or by his mercies and gratious promifes to moue vs to
loue him, and to bring forth the fruits of our loue in acceptable obedience, it repelleth all the good motions of Gods fpirit & filleth the foule with fuch drowfie dulnes and blockifh
deadneffe, that it is altogether vnfit to perfourme any feruice
vnto God, and moft apt to entertaine any of Sathans tentations.   And this infenfible hardneffe of heart which is the
fpirituall lethurgie of the foule is of two kindes; the firft is
ioyned with wilfull obftinacie and affected rebellion, whereby men aduifedly and contemptuoufly withftand the outward minifterie of the word, and the inward motions of
Gods fpirit, with all other meanes which might mooue and
inuite them to ferious repentance; an example whereof wee
haue in *Pharaoh* who hardened his heart againft the Lord,
oppofing himfelfe againft his ambaffage deliuered vnto him
by *Moyfes*, and confirmed by fo many miracles, and alfo ob-
ftinately and with an high hand of rebellion checked, and
quenched the good motions of Gods fpirit, whereby he was
fometimes moued to confeffe his finne, and to acknowledge
the Lord righteous. As alfo in *Saul* who againft his confcience perfecuted *Dauid* becaufe the Lord loued & had made
choife of him to fucceed in his place, and howfoeuer fometimes by occafion of fome notable fruite of *Dauids* innocencie hee was moued to condemne himfelfe and to iuftifie
him, yet prefently hee hardned his heart againe and raged a-
gainft him with wonted malice. And thus likewife were
thofe Ifraelites hardened and frozen ftiffe in the dregs of
their finnes, of whom the Prophet *Efay* fpeaketh Efay.28.15
Yee haue faid (faith he) *wee haue made a couenant with death
and*

*The infenfi-
ble hardneffe
of hart is of
two fortes.
The firft ioy-
ned with ob-
ftinacie.*

Efay 28.15.

and with hell wee are at agreement : though a scourge runne ouer and passe through, it shall not come at vs : for we haue made falsehood our refuge and vnder vanitie are we hid. And those also of whom the Prophet *Zacharie* complaineth Zach. 7. 11. *who (obstinately) refused to harken, and pulled away the shoulder and stopped their eares that they should not heare, yea, and made their hearts as an Adamant stone, least they shou'd heare the law and the words which the Lord of hostes sent in his spirit by the ministerie of the Prophets.* Zach. 7. 11. And so also many of the Scribes and Pharisies hardened their hearts against our Sauiour Christ obstinately contemning the gratious and powerfull words, which proceeded out of his mouth, and quenched the good motions of Gods spirit, occasioned by his wonderfull miracles and admirable workes which none could performe, but he who was the very true and only begotten sonne of God. Now we are to know that this hardnesse of hart is most damnable, and whosoeuer are possessed therewith they can neuer escape Gods fearefull iudgements and euerlasting condemnation in the life to come.

The other kind of insensible hardnesse of heart proceedeth from carelesse retchlesnesse and carnall worldlinesse, when as men hauing their vnderstandings blinded doe not perceiue their filthie corruptions, prophane wickednesse, & extreame miserie, nor feele the burthen of their sinnes though they be growne to an intollerable waight, but flatter themselues with a vaine opinion of their good estate in themselues, without any other helpe, as though they needed not the meanes appointed of God for their conuersion which others vse. And therefore they neglect the ministerie of the word, as knowing and practizing inough already, or if they heare it they remoue farre from them the threatnings of the law denounced against impœnitent sinners as not appertaining to them, and checke all the good motions of Gods spirit which are commonly ioyned with the publike ministerie of the word, and the priuate admonitions of godly men, or with the example of Gods iudgement on others, or with the sense of their owne afflictions ; and so returne to their old prophanesse

§. *Sect.* 3.
Of that hardnesse of hart which proceedeth from carelesse retchlesnesse.

neſſe and lie wallowing in the dregs of their ſinnes without any remorſe or hatred of euill, or any true loue of that which is good. Vntill at length their harts are ſo hardned and their conſciences ſo ſcared with cuſtomable ſinning, and by often repelling and beating backe the meanes of their conuerſion the outward miniſtery of the word, and the inward motions of Gods ſpirit, that they proceed from careleſſe ſenſeleſneſſe, and negligent ſecuritie, to wilfull prophaneſſe and obſtinate rebellion. And this hardneſſe of heart is moſt commonly incident vnto worldlings and is nothing els but carnall ſecuritie, whereby they reſt contented with their miſerable and wretched eſtate, neither louing that which is good, nor hating that which is euill, nor vſing any means to better themſelues, becauſe they either thinke they are good inough or at leaſt neuer enter into conſideration of their eſtate, nor come to the ſenſe and feeling of their euill corruptions, in which they are wholy plunged & ouerwhelmed. Yea ſometimes and in ſome meaſure this befalleth the deare children of God through their careleſſe negligence, and want of the due examination of themſelues (as may appeare in the example of *Dauid,* who many moneths together liued in his ſinne of adulterie and murther, without any ſerious and ſound repentance, till it pleaſed the Lord to rouze him out of this ſpirituall lethurgie by the miniſterie of the Prophet *Nathan*) but yet the Lord doth not finally leaue them, but by the preaching of the word, godly admonitions and reprehenſions, and alſo with the inward motions and ſecrete operation of his holy ſpirit he pulleth them out of this wretched eſtate, giuing vnto them a ſight or feeling of their ſins, and mollifying their hard hearts, working in them an hatred and deteſtation of their ſinnes, and an earneſt deſire to be vnburthened of them. But howſoeuer this may befall the children of God, yet this can be no incouragement vnto any to continue ſtill in this wretched caſe, for howſoeuer they may be indeed the children of God, yet aſſuredly they can neuer haue any true aſſurance in their conſciences that they are his children and in his fauour, till their harts be mollified

lified and reſolued, into the teares of vnfained repentance at leaſt in ſome meaſure. And therefore let euery one beware of carnall ſecurity and of hardening their harts through careleſſe negligence, and by committing ſinnes againſt their knowledge and conſcience, let them beware of reſiſting the miniſterie of the word, and of quenching the good motions of Gods ſpirit, for though the conſcience at the firſt be moſt tender and the hart ſo ſoft, that euery ſinne will pricke and pearce it, and euery gentle admonition will make it relent, yet in continuance of time through cuſtomable ſinning, and reſiſting the meanes of our conuerſion and ſaluation, the conſcience is ſo ſeared that it becommeth ſenſeleſſe though it be oppreſſed and ſurcharged with a heauy maſſe of outragious wickedneſſe, and the heart groweth to ſuch Adamantiue hardneſſe, that the thundring Canon threatnings of the law, and of Gods fearefull and imminent iudgements cannot batter or bruiſe it, nor make any breach whereby true repentance may enter. In which reſpect the conſcience is not vnfitly compared to the eye, which of all other partes of mans body is moſt tender & impatient of the lighteſt touch, ſo that the ſmalleſt mote vexeth it, and the leaſt pricke cauſeth incredible torment : but if once it be affected with a diſeaſe called of *Oculiſts, ſcirrhoſis oculi* which ouercouereth it, but a hard fleſhy skinne, it becommeth of all other partes moſt inſenſible, ſo the conſcience of man is moſt tender of all other partes, and at the firſt ſmall ſinnes vexe & torment it, but if through cuſtome in ſinning it be ouerſpread with a *Callum* or thicke skinne, it becōmeth inſenſible and nothing will wound it.

CHAP. XXXIX.

Of that hardneſſe of heart which is ioyned with ſenſe and feeling thereof.

§. Sect. 1.
Of hardneſſe of hart, ioyned with ſenſe and feeling thereof.

He ſecond ſort of hardneſſe of hart, is that which is ioyned with ſenſe and feeling, when as we ſee and with ſorow feele our dulneſſe and blockiſhneſſe in Gods ſeruice, our obdurate inflexible-neſſe

Ii 3

neſſe to holy obedience, our hardneſſe of heart, which at the hearing either of the terrible threatnings of the law, or ſweet promiſes of the Goſpell, cannot relent nor reſolue it ſelfe into the teares of vnfained repentance; and this hardneſſe of heart is commonly incident vnto Gods deare children being at the ſame time in the ſtate of grace, and is a part of that inbred corruption and fleſhly old man which before our calling wholy poſſeſſeth and ouerruled vs, and after alſo beareth ſome ſway in vs euē when we are regenerate til with al our other corruptions we lay this aſide alſo by death. And this appeareth in the exāple of the Prophet *Dauid,* who deſireth the Lord *to create in him a cleane hart, & to renew a right*

Pſal.51. 10. *ſpirit within him.* Pſal. 51.10. in which words he implieth that his hardneſſe of heart was ſo great, and the corruption thereof ſo abominable that it was euen paſt mending, and there-

Ezech. 11. 19. fore he doth not pray the Lord to purge and reforme his old hart, but to create a new one, and to take quite away his ſtonie hart, & to beſtow vpon him a hart of fleſh, as though his hart were like a building exceeding ruinous which could no longer be repaired, vnleſſe it were razed downe euen to the foundation and all a new built vp againe. So whereas he praieth the Lord to renew his ſpirit in him, he giueth vs to vnderſtand that he hath loſt the feeling of the ſpirit of adoption crying in his hart Abba father, and that there was in him ſuch an intermiſſion & ſurceaſe of the actions & fruits therof that it ſeemed vtterly quenched and departed from him. So els where he praieth vnto the Lord to quickē him accor-

Pſal. 119. 88. ding to his louing kindneſſe, *that he might keepe the teſtimonies of his mouth.* Whereby hee intimateth his drowſineſſe and deadneſſe in Gods ſeruice. The Prophet Eſay likewiſe in the behalfe of himſelfe, and the people complaineth thus: Eſay

Eſay 63.17. 63.17. *O Lord why haſt thou made vs to erre from thy waies, and hardned our hart from thy feare.* By all which it appeareth that euen the deare children of God do oftentimes ſee and feele to their great griefe their hardneſſe of hart, which is ioyned with exceeding dulneſſe and drowſineſſe in Gods ſeruice. Yea in truth this kind of hardneſſe of hart is incident

dent

dent vnto them alone.For whileſt men are worldly and carnall though their harts are moſt hard and obdurate yet they
doe not diſcerne it, neither are they any whit diſpleaſed with
their eſtate, but fondly flatter themſelues imagining that
they are in exceeding good caſe and very deuout in Gods
ſeruice which indeed (as they perfourme it) is meerely formall,cuſtomable rather then conſcionable, in ſhew and ex-
ternall but not in ſpirit and truth; but when the Lord by the
miniſtery of his word made effectuall by the inward operation of his holy ſpirit, doth pull of the thicke skinne of carnall ſecuritie from of their hearts and cauſeth the ſeales of
ignorance to fall from their eyes, then and not before doe
they plainely diſcerne and ſenſibly feele that huge maſſe of
inbred corruption, their dulneſſe and drowſineſſe in Gods
ſeruice, their hardneſſe of hart and impænitencie,and now
they are much vexed and grieued with them, which in former times neuer troubled them. And therefore let not ſuch
be diſmaied nor debarre their ſoules of that côſolation which
of right belongeth to them, for fleſh and bloud hath not reuealed this their corruption, hardneſſe of hart, dulneſſe and
deadneſſe in Gods ſeruice but the good ſpirit of God, which
hath begunne already to worke in them,ſhewing them their
corruptions and moouing them to an vnfained diſlike of
them,and therefore they may aſſure themſelues,that he who
hath begunne this good worke in them, will alſo bring it in
his good time to perfection : Onely (as the Pſalmiſt exhorteth,) *Let them tarre the Lords leaſure, waite vpon and truſt* Phil.1.6.
in him and he ſhall comfort their hearts.

    Now this ſenſible or diſcerned hardneſſe of hart is alſo of
two ſortes : the firſt is of them who carefully vſe all good §. Sect.2.
meanes and indeauour with all diligence to better their 2. Sortes of
eſtate which they ſee to bee moſt miſerable and to mollifie neſſe of hart,
their hard hartes, and to attaine vnto harty and vnfained The firſt ioy-
repentance. Which who ſo doth hee may aſſure himſelfe ned with the
that hee is the child of God and in his loue and fauour; for vſe of the
earneſtly to deſire repentance, and carefully to vſe the by it may be
meanes whereby we may attaine thereunto, to be diſpleaſed ſoftned.

with our hardneſſe of heart and to labour that it may bee
mollified , to bee ſorry that wee can bee no more ſorry
and to bee diſpleaſed with our ſelues becauſe wee
can no more bee diſpleaſed with our ſinnes, is very acceptable in the ſight of God though wee ſee but a little progreſſe
in godlineſſe , and but a ſmall increaſe of repentance which
wee deſire in great meaſure, for the Lorde eſteemeth the
will for the deed, and the affection for the action, and wee
may aſſure our ſelues that if on our part wee be not wanting
in the vſe of the meanes, the Lord will not bee wanting on
his part to ſupply our wantes, and to ſatiſfie all our Godly
deſires.

Of this hardneſſe of heart which verie often befalleth the

Examples of this hardneſſe of heart. *Pſal.77.2.* deareſt of Gods children wee haue many examples. The
prophet *Dauid* thus complaineth Pſal. 77. 2. *In the day of my
trouble I ſought the Lorde, my ſore ranne and ceaſed not in the
night, my ſoule refuſed comfort. 3. I did thinke vppon God and
was troubled, I prayed and my ſpirit was full of anguiſh. 4. thou
keepeſt mine eyes waking; I was aſtonied and could not ſpeake.* So

Cant 3. 1. and 5.6. the church complaineth thus Cant.3.1. *In my bed I ſought
him by night whom my ſoule loued. I ſought him but I found him
not.* and chap. 5. ver. 6. *I opened to my welbeloued but my
welbeloued was gone and paſt : mine heart was gone when hee did
ſpeake I ſought him but I could not find him, I called him but hee
anſwered me not.* Whereby it is manifeſt that euen the deare
ſaints of God are often times deſtitute of all comfort and
voyde of all feeling of Gods fauour, and of the powerfull
working of the graces of Gods ſpirit which they haue receiued, though they vſe the meanes appointed of God for the
ſtirring vp and increaſing of grace in them, which commeth
to paſſe by reaſon of their hardneſſe of heart, and drowſie
dulneſſe of ſpirit in theſe ſpirituall excerciſes.

And hence it is that many of Gods children doe grieuouſly
afflict their ſoules becauſe they ſee theſe their corruptions
and imperfections, and hereby often times are mooued to
thinke that they are deſtitute of faith, and of all ſauing graces
of Gods ſanctifying ſpirite , becauſe though they vſe the
meanes

meanes ordayned of God for the begetting and increaſing of grace in them, yet they cannot perceiue any fruite that commeth thereby, nor feele in their ſoules any true comfort or ioy in theſe ſpirituall excercifes. For example ſome complaine that though they continually heare the word yet they feele no increaſe of any grace, no more knowledge, no more faith, no more zeale of Gods glory, no more mortification of their old corruptions, nor any reformation at all of their former ſinfull liues, and therefore they thinke that they heare the worde of God without any profit, nay that the more they heare it the more wicked and rebellious they are; and that for this cauſe it were much better not to heare the worde at all, for as much as it will but agrauate their ſinnes and increaſe their condemnation, *for hee that knoweth his maiſters will and doth it not, ſhalbe beaten* Luk.12. 47. *with many ſtripes.*

But let not ſuch poore mourning ſoules depriue themſelus of that true comfort which of right belongeth to them: and to this end let them know firſt that this is a vſuall complaint of thoſe children of God which profit moſt in hearing of the word though in truth they doe therein deceiue themſelues; for in complaining that they profit not, they ſhew they profit. For whereas men naturally blinded with ſelfe loue and carnall ſecuritie neuer diſcerne any ſuch want and corruption in themſelues, and therefore though they profit nothing by hearing the worde of God yet it neuer troubles them, nay they imagine that it is ſufficient to preſent their bodies into Gods aſſemblies and to heare Gods worde with their outward eares, though they vnderſtand it not nor retaine it in memorie, nor bring forth any fruits thereof; theſe humbled ſoules by the hearing of the worde are freed from this ſelfe loue and carnall ſecuritie, and haue the blind eies of their vnderſtandings opened ſo as they ſee their faultes and corruptions, and haue their harde harces ſoftened ſo as they are grieued and diſpleaſed with them, & their wills alſo are in ſome good meaſure ſanctified, ſo that they earneſtly deſire to be freed from their corruptions, and to heare the word

§. Sect. 2. Conſolations for ſuch as complaine of their imperfections in hearing the word.

word of God with more profit, whereby it appeareth that though they cannot profit so much as they desire yet they haue made a good progresse, and the Lord in his good time will perfect that good worke which hee hath begun in them; and the same spirit of God which hath wrought in them this desire of profitting by hearing the word, will also accomplish it, & so open their dull eares and soften their hard harts that they shall profit and reape manifould fruites of the seede of the word which is sowed in the furrowes of their hearts. In the meane while the Lorde may in his heauenly wisedome feed them for a time with a sparing hand to the end that hee may truly humble them vnder the sight and sense of their corruptions, and that he may hereby so sharpen their appetites that they may with more hungering desire, and earnest indeauour feed vpon the heauenly manna of his word; but as this should increase their diligence, so it should not decrease their hope and comfort, for most assuredly when the Lorde hath a while whetted their stomacke, and by pulling backe his hande mooued them more earnestly to desire, and more highly to esteeme this precious foode of their soules, he will fully satisfie their hungring desire, nourish them in all spirituall graces, and make them who are but babes strong men in Christ. In the mean time let them not faint, but wait vpon the Lorde, bee strong and trust in him and hee will surely comfort their heartes as the psalmist speaketh Psal. 27. 16.

§. Sect. 4.
Consolations for such as bewaile their want of feeling the fruits of their hearing.

Secondly wheras they complaine that they doe not after the hearing of the word, perceiue in themselues any increase of knowledge, faith or any sauing grace, they are to knowe that howsoeuer no man ought to rest contented in this estate but are to laboure more and more, not only to haue but also to discerne an increase of grace in them, and a progresse in al vertue and godlinesse, for otherwise though they may be the children of god who for a time liue in such a case yet they can not attaine vnto the assurance thereof nor feele the comfort of it in there owne consciences, neuertheles there is no reaso why they shoulde despaire or bee vtterly discouraged, for though they find no fruits of their hearing, yet if in obedience

ence to Gods commaundement, they will with care and diligence continue still hearers of the word, they shal vndoubtedly in the ende attaine vnto their desire and discerne in
themselues a greate increase of grace and godlinesse. Wee
knowe that the seede doth not presently bringe foorth
fruite when it is cast into the ground, but first it seemeth
to rott and perish and then it sprouteth vp in a
greene blade, and then it beareth an eare and a great
increase and much fruite; and so it fareth oftentimes
in hearing the worde of God, for at first it seemeth quite
lost and perished being sowne in some groundes, and
yet afterwardes it bringeth foorth not onely a faire greene
blade of an outward profession, but also a greate increase of
the ripe fruites of true godlinesse. So also the sicke patient
taking soueraigne physicke is not presently cured, nay in
stead of feeling any ease thereby hee is made much more
sicke in his owne sense and feeling, and yet after the physick
hath a while wrought with him and purged him of some
superfluous and hurtfull humours hee findeth some amendment, and so by little and little hee is restored to his former
health; and so it is also with the spirituall sicke patient, hee
doth not alwaies presently find ease and quiet peace of conscience, nay many times hee is tormented and vexed after
hee hath receiued the spiritual phisicke of the soule the word
of God, more then euer in former times, but yet notwithstanding in processe of time when this phisicke hath effectually wrought with him, it purgeth him from his filthie corruptions and strengtheneth him in all grace and godlinesse.
And therefore though we feele presently no profitable fruits
of hearing let not this discourage vs from hearing, nay rather let it serue as a sharpe spurre to pricke vs forwarde to
more diligence, and let vs ioyne therewith hartie prayer,
desiring the Lord to water the seed of his word sowne in our
hearts with the dew of his holy spirit, and then vndoubtedly the Lord in the end will heare vs, and to our exceeding
comfort shew vnto vs the plentifull fruits of all our labours.

Thirdly whereas they complaine that the more they heare §. *Sect.5.*

the

Confolations for fuch as complaine that the more they beare the more they abound in fin.
the greater are their finnes and rebellion againft God, in this they much deceiue themfelues; for the worde cf God doth not make them more finfull, but whereas heretofore they liued in carnall fecuritie and hardneffe of heart, hauing their vnderftandings darkned and their confciences feared fo as they could neither fee nor feele their fins though they were manifould and grieuous, now the worde of God made effectuall by the inward operation of his holy fpirit like a glorious light hauing difpelled the darke foggie mifts of ignorance, and illuminated the eyes of their vnderftandings with the knowledge of Gods law, they better difcerne their finnes and miferable eftate then in former times. And this the Apoftle Paul fheweth vnto vs in his own example Rom.7.9. *For* (faith he) *I was once aliue without the law, but when the commaundement came fin reuiued* 10. *but I died : and the fame commaundement which was ordeyned vnto life, was found to be vnto mee vnto death.* and ver.13. *.was that then which was good made death vnto mee ? God forbid: but finne that it might appeare, finne wrought death in mee by that which is good, that finne might bee out of meafure finfull by the commaundement.* So that the preaching of the law doth not make vs more finfull but reuealeth thofe finnes vnto vs which before we difcerned not. As therefore the funne fhining vpon fome filthie place doth not make it fo filthie, but onely doth make it manifeft which was not feene in the darke, and as the wholefome phyfieke is not the caufe of thofe corruptions which it purgeth out, but by expelling them out of the bodie fheweth them vnto vs, fo the heauenly light and foueraigne phyficke of Gods worde doth not worke in vs our filthie corruptions, and hurtfull humors of finne but it reuealeth them vnto vs whereas before times by reafon of our ignorance and blindneffe they were fecret and hidden,

§.Sect.6.
That we are not to neglect hearing the word becaufe of the former imperfections
When therefore out of the former premiffes this conclufion is inferred either by Sathan who continually like a malicious enemie feeketh our deftruction, or by our owne corrupt flefh (which is impatient of any rough handlinge, and therefore would rather haue vs ficke ftill then indure any paine in beeing cured) that it were better for vs to furceafe
the

the hearing of gods word as seruing to no other end but to
encrease our condemnation, let vs in any case resist such
motions as beeing most daungerous tentations which being entertained will bring vs to vtter ruine and endlesse
destruction; for if wee depriue our selues of this heauenly
light the diuell will easily lead vs hudwincke vnto all sin &
wickednesse, if we long abstaine from this comfortable food
of our soules they will be hungarstarued, and all the graces of
Gods spirit will waxe faint and die in vs, if wee disarme our
selues of this sword of the spirite, Sathan without any resistance will ouercome vs and take vs captiues, forcing
vs as his miserable slaues to commit all those workes of
darkenesse in which hee will imploy vs. And therefore as
wee tender the saluation of our owne soules, let vs not be
discouraged from hearing the word of God by any suggestions whatsoeuer, no not though we seeme vnto our selues e-
uery time wee come into the Church to goe a step towards
hell; for whilest we vse Gods ordinance which is appointed
as the meanes for our conuersion and saluation, there is some
good hope, but when we vtterly neglect it our state is most
desperate.

CHAP. XL.

*Consolations for such as bewayle their hardnesse of hart and
wants in prayer.*

Thers complaine that they are so ouerwhelmed
with their hardnesse of hart, and drowsie dulnesse of spirit that eyther they cannot pray at all,
or if they doe it is barrainely without all forme
or fashion; or if they haue the eloquence of the tongue &
good set formes of praier yet they perfourme it coldly and
drowsilie, without all earnestnesse and feruencie of spirit,
hauing their minds caried away with wandring thoughts,
so that their praiers are but meere liplabour, & therefore it
were better not to pray at all, because they cannot perfourme

*§. Sect. 1.
Consolations
for such as
cöplaienth a
they cannot
pray at all.*

this

this dutie in any good maner or meafure as God requireth.

And this is a tentation wherewith euen the deareſt children of God are much vexed and troubled, and therefore it
ſhall not be amiſſe to anſwere the ſeuerall branches of this
complaint. Firſt therfore, where as they complaine that they
cannot pray at all, this is to bee vnderſtood either generally
of all times, or ſpecially at ſometimes. If they ſay they can neuer pray, it is very likely that either they forget or much deceiue themſelues, for few or none who are altogether deſtitute of the ſpirit of ſupplication haue any vnderſ...:ding to
diſcerne their want, or any grace to bewaile it, but content
themſelues with their lip-labour as though they had perfourmed acceptable ſeruice vnto God. And it is a worke of
one and the ſame ſpirit to make vs ſee our infirmities with
hatred and diſlike of them, and to moue vs earneſtly to deſire of God that we may be freed from them, which earneſt
deſire is harty praier. But if they further affirme that they are
moſt ſure they doe neuer pray vnto God, I anſwere that
though this in it ſelfe be a moſt daungerous caſe, for it is a
ſigne of a worker of iniquitie, not to call vpon God as the
Pſalmiſt ſpeaketh, Pſal. 53. 4. yet they haue no cauſe to deſpaire, for the ſame ſpirit which hath reuealed vnto them this
their ſinne and infirmitie, and hath wrought in them a diſlike
thereof, will alſo remoue it and ſupply their want in Gods
good time, if they will labour for this good gift, and not
quench the good motions of the ſpirit when God offreth
them vnto them.

But if they cannot denie that ſometimes they haue had
the grace giuen them of God to call earneſtly vppon his
name, howſoeuer in this preſent time they are altogether
disfurniſhed thereof, then let them know that their caſe in
this reſpect is common withall the deare children of God,
for harty prayer is not in our owne power, neither doth it
attend vpon our owne will, but it is the gift of God which at
ſometimes in plentifull meaſure he beſtoweth vpon his children, and at other times he pulleth backe his liberall hand;
to the end that by the want thereof, we may learne to aſcribe
the

the glorie and praise of our harty prayers vnto God, who worketh in vs the will and the deed and is in truth the onely true authour of them which praise, otherwise in pride of hart we would arrogate vnto our selues, as being a naturall facultie and in our owne power; and also to the end we may more highly esteeme it, and with more ioy and diligence vse it when we haue it bestowed on vs, least through our negligence and slouthfulnesse we mooue the Lord to take it from vs.

Seeing therefore this hartie calling vpon Gods name is a gift of God, & a worke of his holy spirit in vs which at sometimes heretofore we haue discerned in our selues, let vs not altogether be discouraged though at sometimes we want it; for the *giftes of God are without repentance,* and though at sometimes they are withdrawne from our sense and feeling, yet shall they neuer be taken from vs; and if at any time we haue had assurance that the spirit of God hath dwelled in vs, by this worke thereof effectuall prayer, we may assure our selues that it hath not forsaken vs, but will againe *helpe our infirmities, and whereas we cannot tell how to pray as we ought, the spirit it selfe will make request for vs with sighes, which cannot be expressed.* $\quad$ Rom.8.16.

Secondly, whereas they complaine that they cannot pray in any good forme, but oftentimes fill Gods eares with impatient cries & vncomfortable roarings in stead of prayers, they are to know that this is often incident vnto the children of God, especially when his hand is heauy vpon them, either in some outward affliction of bodie, or some inward anguish of mind. For example the Prophet *Dauid* confesseth that when Gods hand was heauie vpon him day and night his prayers were but roarings. Psal. 32.3. So Ezechias saith, that whē he should haue praied *he chattered like a Crane or a Swallow, & mourned as a Doue,* Esa. 38.14. And the poore Publicāe oppressed with the heauy burthē of his sins in stead of a long & eloquent speach vttereth these fewe wordes; *O God be mercifull vnto me a sinner,* and yet our Sauiour Christ testifieth of him that he receaued the remission of his sinnes

Rom.11.29

§. Sect. 2.
Consolations
for such as
cōplaine that
they cannot
pray in any
good forme

Psal. 32.3.

Esa. 38.14.

and

Luke 18.13.
14.
and went home iustified. Luk. 18. 13. 14. Neither in trueth doth the Lord regard the eloquence of the tongue, but the earnestnesse of the hart, he respecteth not our well couched wordes and smooth vttered stile, but the feruencie of the spirit, and our humble and harty desires, which are acceptably heard of him though our tongues bee silent. *The sacrifices of God are not eloquent wordes but a contrite spirit, a*

Psal. 51. 17.
contrite and broken heart will not the Lord despise. as it is Psal. 51.17. The prayers indited by Gods spirite which also are according to the will of God, consist not in the wordes of the mouth, but in the sighes of the heart which cannot bee

Rom. 8. 26.
expressed, as the Apostle teacheth vs. Rom. 8. 26. And therefore if wee offer vnto God an humble and contrite spirit, if wee can sigh and grone earnestly, desiring those things wee want according to his holy will, though wee cannot expresse our mindes in any good order or in a continued forme of speech, yet if wee can from our hartes roare with *Dauid,* chatter with *Ezechias* and vtter this abrupt speech with the poore publicane, O God bee mercifull vnto mee a sinner, the Lorde will heare vs and that as speedily as though we could pray vnto him with the eloquence of men and angels. For to what end principally serue wordes, but that wee may by them expresse our mindes to men who otherwise could not vnderstand them; but the Lorde who searcheth the hartes vnderstandeth our sighes which cannot

Rom. 8. 26.
bee expressed, as it is Rom. 8. 26. 27. *and hee knowes our thoughts long before wee thinke them*, as the psalmist speaketh

Psal. 139. 2.
Psal. 139. 2. Hee is a spirit yea an allseeing spirit, and therefore our prayers vnto him are the desires of the heart, neither doth our wordes serue to perswade him, but to stirre vp our owne dul spirits, and to keepe vs from disorderly wandring

Exod. 14. 15
thoughts. So that if wee can with *Moses* lift vp our hearts vnto God with earnest desires, this will bee a strong crie in the eares of the Lorde, and hee will surely heare it. If we can

Psal. 38. 9.
vnfainedly say with the prophet *Dauid.* Psal. 38. 9. *Lorde I powre my whole desire before thee, and my sighing is not hid from thee*, we may be assured he will heare vs and graunt our request,

queſt, for *he heareth the deſire of the poore, he prepareth their hart and bendeth his eare vnto them.* as it is pſal.10.17. yea hee doth not only heare them and in ſome ſort incline to their requeſt, but hee *will fulfill the deſire of them that feare him, hee will heare their crie and ſaue them.* as the ſame prophet ſpeaketh. Pſal.145. 19. We know that a kind louing father if he ſee his ſonne exceeding ſicke wilbe verie carefull and tender ouer him, to prouide all things neceſſarie for him which may doe him good, and though with a faultering tongue and vnperfect ſpeech hee aſke any thing which is profitable for him to receiue, yet how readily will hee harken vnto him and graunt his deſire? yea if his ſickneſſe ſo increaſe that hee becommeth ſpeechleſſe vttering nothing but deepe grones, euen this language moues him to no leſſe care in vſing all meanes which may doe him good. Shall then wee daily obſerue ſuch fruites of loue in ſinfull man, and ſhall wee doubt of finding leſſe in the Lord, who is infinite in loue, mercie, and goodneſſe, farre bee it from vs. Nay let vs aſſure our ſelues, that though (our ſoules being ſicke in ſinne, and exceedingly dulled and beaten downe with ſome grieuous tentation) we cannot vtter any thing but vnperfect ſpeeches, yea though wee are through the grieuouſneſſe of our affliction and greatneſſe of our corruption ſtrucken dumbe and can vtter nothing but grones and ſighes, yet if wee deſire to be freed out of this wretched caſe and to haue the comfort of Gods ſpirit, the Lord who ſearcheth the hart and vnderſtandeth our ſecret thoughts wil harken vnto vs and graunt the deſires of our hart, at leaſt ſo farre forth as it will ſtand with his owne glorie and our euerlaſting good.

Thirdly whereas others complaine that their hartes are ſo harde and their ſpiritts ſo dull, that they cannot vtter vnto God a prayer with any earneſtneſſe or feruencie of ſpirit, but exceeding coldly and verie weakely, and therefore they feare that God will neuer heare them; they are to remember that the Lord heareth vs not nor graunteth our requeſts for the worthineſſe and excellencie of our prayers, but for his ſonne Ieſus Chriſts ſake who is our mediatour and interceſ-

Pſal. 10. 17

Pſal.145.19.

§. Sect.3.
Conſolations for ſuch as bewaile their coldneſſe and dulneſſe in prayer.

K k   ſour

four in whofe name we cal vpon God; and therefore though
our prayers bee full of infirmities and vttered with much
weakneffe, yet calling vpon the Lord in our fauiours name

Ioh.16.23. hee will furely heare vs as our fauiour hath promifed. Ioh.
1·6. 23. *Verily, verily I fay vnto you whatfoeuer ye fhall afke the*
father in my name he will giue it you. Moreouer we are to know
that we do not offer vp our prayers immediately vnto God
the father, but by the mediation of Iefus Chrift, who putting
our prayers into the goulden vialls which are full of the precious odours of his merites, thereby perfumeth them and

Apoc.5.8. maketh thē an offering of fweet fmelling fauour vnto God;
& by wafhing them in his owne moft precious blood he purgeth them from all their corruptions and perfecteth all their
wants and inperfections, fo as now though not in themfelues
yet in him they will bee acceptable vnto God and hee will
mercifully graunt our petitions.

§. Sect.4.
Confolations
for fuch as
bewaile their
diftractions
and wandring
thoughts in
prayer.
Fourthly whereas others complaine that their mindes are
carried away with worldly diftractions and wandring imaginations when they are making their prayers vnto God;
they are to knowe that this befalleth alfo euen the deareft
children of God, partly through their owne corruption, and
partly through the malice of Sathan who laboureth moft
to interrupt vs in thofe holy excercifes which hee knoweth
moft profitable and effectuall for our faluation. Whereof it
commeth to paffe that though diuers howers togeather we
can talke of worldly affaires and heare the fpeech of others
without any diftractiō of mind, or thinking of any thing but
of the fubiect of our prefent fpeach, yet when we heare God
fpeak vnto vs in the preaching of the word, or whē we fpeak
vnto God in prayer and fupplication, our mindes wander
hether and thether though wee ftriue neuer fo much to containe them, becaufe through our natural corruption wee are
foone wearie of thefe holy excercifes, and Sathan is ftill at
hand to fuggeft into our minds wandring thoughts in which
we take moft delight, but this fhould not difcourage vs from
taking in hand thefe holy actions, but rather the confideration hereof fhould ftrongly moue and prouoke vs to more
earneftneffe

earneſtnes care and diligence ſo as Sathan may not preuaile againſt vs; & if notwithſtāding ſometimes nay often wee receaue a foile, let it be an occaſiō to moue vs to take the more paines & to make a double requeſt vnto God, not onely that he will graunt vnto vs thoſe things which we deſire, but alſo that for Chriſts ſake he will pardon our ſins & infirmities in that wee haue begged them ſo coldly and negligently.

Laſtly, whereas our ſpirituall enemy taketh occaſion altogether to diſcourage vs from vndertaking theſe ſpirituall exerciſes, becauſe therein wee bewray notable corruptions and cannot though we ſtriue neuer ſo much performe them as we ought, let vs in no caſe yeeld vnto this tentation, but ſtrongly arme our ſelues againſt it; and to this end let vs conſider that if Sathan can perſwade vs to deſiſt from perfourming thoſe duties altogether which wee cannot performe as we ought, but with great weakeneſſe, corruption, and imperfection, we ſhall doe nothing at all which God requireth of vs, for example the Lord commaundeth vs to loue him with all our hearts, and with all our ſoule, and with all our ſtrength, which dutie of loue wee perfourme with great weakneſſe and exceeding coldly; but becauſe wee can not doe it as God requireth and as we ought, ſhall wee not therefore doe it at all? God forbid. So the Lord commaundeth vs to truſt and to put our whole affiance in him, but we are readie to reſt and relie vpon the arme of fleſh and inferiour meanes, either in whole or at leaſt in part, and when they faile vs, our truſt in God is very weake and mingled with much diffidence and doubting, but ſhall we therefore put no affiance in God, all becauſe we cannot doe it ſo perfectly as God requireth? be it farre from vs. So in the verie like maner the Lord expreſſly chargeth and commandeth vs to cal vpon his holy name, which dutie oftentimes we perfourme coldly and negligently, hauing our minds carried away with wandring thoughts and worldly imaginations, but ſhall ſathan working vpon our own corruption therefore perſwade vs altogeather to deſiſt from this holy exerciſe? no, in no caſe let vs not yeeld to this temptation. For it is not left vnto vs

§. Sect. 5.
That our wants and infirmities in prayer, ſhould not make vs neglect this holy exerciſe.

Kk 2   as

at our owne choiſe as a thing indifferent to pray or not to pray, but it is a notable parte of Gods worſhip and ſeruice, and a ſingular dutie which the Lord expreſly inioyneth vs to perfourme, whereunto he hath adioyned moſt comfortable promiſes which depend not vpon our worthineſſe, and the excellencie of our praiers, but on his owne free mercy and goodneſſe, and the merits and interceſſion of our Sauiour Chriſt. So Pſal. 50. 15. *Call vpon mee in the day of trouble, ſo will I deliuer thee and thou ſhalt glorifie mee.* And Matth. 7. 7. *Aske and it ſhalbe giuen you.* And Ioh. 16. 23. *Verily, verily I ſay vnto you, whatſoeuer you ſhal aske the father in my name hee will giue it you,* 24. *aske and ye ſhall receiue that your ioy may be full.* And the Apoſtle *Paul* chargeth vs. 1. Theſ. 5. 17. that *we pray continually.* Seeing therefore the Lord expreſly requireth this dutie at our hands; though our infirmities and corruptions be neuer ſo great, let vs labour continually to perforine it, aſſuring our ſelues that if in obedience to his commaundement we call vpō him, and labour and ſtriue againſt thoſe corruptions, which ſhew themſelues vnto vs in this holy action, he that hath inioyned vs this dutie will alſo giue vnto vs his holy ſpirit, if we will attend his leaſure which wil teach vs how to pray according to Gods wil with ſighes and grones, which cānot be expreſſed, whereas on the other ſide if our infirmities and corruptions wholy diſcourage vs, from performing this dutie we ſhall grieuouſly ſinne againſt God in tranſgreſſing his commaundement, and in robbing him of a chiefe part of his worſhip and ſeruice, and alſo wee ſhall plunge our ſelues into a moſt deſperate eſtate, adioyning our ſelues vnto the number of thoſe wicked Atheiſts of whom the Pſalmiſt ſpeaketh, who call not vpon God. Pſal. 53. 4.

And ſo much for anſwering thoſe tentations which Sathan and our corruption doe ſuggeſt to diſcourage vs from the ſeruice of God, which haue their occaſion and ground from our hardneſſe of hart, and drowſie dulneſſe, and deadneſſe in perfourming theſe holy exerciſes. The other kind of ſenſible hardneſſe of hart is ſeuered from the vſe of theſe holy meanes; for ſometimes it commeth to paſſe eſpecially

Marginal notes:
Pſal. 50. 15.
Matth. 7. 7.
Ioh. 16. 23. 24.
1. Theſ. 5. 17.
Pſal. 53. 4.
§. Sect. 6. Of the ſecond kind of ſenſible hardneſſe of hart.

in the ſpirituall combate of temptation, that euen Gods deare
children are ſo beſotted & aſtoniſhed, through the violence
of the temptations of Sathan, and huge waight of their owne
corruptions, that they cannot indeauour in no ſort to vſe
theſe meanes, whereby they might be comforted and releeued in this wretched eſtate, as the hearing of the word, calling vpon Gods name, meditating in the Scriptures, and holy cõferences; yea theſe holy exerciſes ſeeme for a time odious and loathſome vnto them, vntill it pleaſe the Lord by
his owne good ſpirit to awaken and raiſe them vp out of this
ſpirituall trance, and to giue vnto them againe the feeling of
his grace and fauour, and good motions & abilities to ſerue
him, and reape comfort vnto themſelues, by theſe holy duties. In the meane time ſuch are to ſupport themſelues from
falling into vtter deſperation by calling to their remẽbrance
their ſtate and condition in times paſt, for if euer they haue
had any delight in the holy exerciſes of religion, prayer, hearing the word & godly conferences, if euer they could diſcerne in themſelues any faith by the true fruits of ſanctification they may take comfort thereby, aſſuring themſelues
that they ſhall againe be reſtored vnto their former eſtate,
for the *gifts and calling of God are without repentance, and thoſe* Rom. 11. 29
whom he hath once loued, he loueth vnto the end. An example Ioh. 13. 1.
hereof we haue in *Dauid,* who being troubled and full of anguiſh in his ſpirit, his ſoule refuſing all comfort, and being ſo
aſtoniſhed that he could not ſpeake, yet hee conſidered the
daies of old, and the yeares of ancient time, hee called to re- Pſal. 77. 2.
mẽbrance his former ſonges in the night, occaſioned by the 3. 4.
great benefits which the Lord had beſtowed vpon him, & ſo
knowing that the Lord was vnchangeable in his mercy and
goodneſſe, he releeued his poore ſoule, which was ready to
faint vnder the heauy waight of preſent afflictions. And thus
alſo *Iob* being brought through the violence of thoſe heauie
croſſes which the Lord laied vpon him, euen to the brinke
of deſperation, ſo that hee ſpared not to vtter in the bitterneſſe of his ſoule, fearefull curſes and moſt impatient ſpeaches comming neere vnto blaſphemie, oftentimes comfor-

teth himselfe by calling to minde his former integritie
and righteousnesse , whose example if the poore humbled
soules will follow they may rayse themselues with true comfort, when they are sunke downe vnder their heauie burthen
of present corruptions.

CHAP. XLI.

How the weake Christian may bee assured that his repen-
tance is true and vnfained.

§ .Sect.1.
Of the signes
of true repen-
tance. & first
of the seuerall
degrees therof

Nd so much for answering Sathans tentations
drawn from hardnesse of hart, whereby he laboureth to perswade poore humbled sinners
that they are vtterly destitute of of repentance;
but if hee faile of his purpose then hee will indeauour to make them beleeue that though they haue some
shew of repentance yet it is not such as God requireth : for
either hee will affirme that it is hypocriticall and dissembled
rather for feare of punishment then for hatred of sinne or
true loue of God; or if it bee true yet it is not sufficient as
being in verie small measure and in no proportion answea-
rable to our hainous sinnes.

Against both which tentations it behooueth the humbled sinner to arme himselfe that he may repell them when
they are suggested; and to this purpose that hee may proue
his repentance true and vnfained, hee is to take a true search
of his owne heart and conscience, and to examine his repentance according to some vndoubted signes which may serue
as touchstones to discouer whether it be true and vnfained,
or dissembled & hypocriticall. The first vndoubted signe of
vnfained repentance is when wee can obserue in our selues
the seuerall degrees or partes thereof as they haue beene
wrought in vs by Gods spirit , for from the enumeration of
all the parts we may conclude that wee haue the whole. The
first degree is that by the law we come to the knowledg, and
acknowledgment that we are haynous and greeuous sinners
who

who haue broken & transgressed all Gods comaundements.
Secondly from this knowledge & acknowledgment of our
sinnes proceedeth a true sense and feeling of them and the
punishments due vnto them, and an apprehension and
applying to our selues the anger of God, the curse of the
law, and eternall condemnation due vnto vs for our sinnes.
Thirdly from this sense of our miserable estate there ariseth
in our consciences feare and horror of being ouertaken and
ouerwhelmed of those iudgments of God, and fearefull punishments which hang ouer our heads for our sins. Fourthly
from this feare and anguish of mind proceedeth sorrow and
bitter greefe, because wee haue thus hainously sinned, and
made our selues obnoxious to all these euills; and also in the
same respects a true hatred of sinne which still hangeth vpon
vs, and an earnest desire to be freed from it. Fiftly, this ha- Act.2.27.
tred of sinne and desire to be freed from it, maketh vs earnestly to seeke and inquire after some meanes whereby wee
may attaine vnto our desires, that beeing freed from all those
feareful euils which oppresse our consciences with the waight
of them, we may obtaine Gods loue and fauour and the assurance of our saluation. Sixtly, thus inquiring and searching
wee finde by the preaching of the Gospell, that our gratious God hath sent his sonne into the world, to the end that
he might saue and deliuer vs out of this miserable estate if we
beleeue in him, and also hath commaunded vs to beleeue.
Which being made effectuall by the inward operation of
Gods holy spirit, we haue true faith begott in vs, wherby we
are assured of Gods mercy in Iesus Christ, and of the full
remission of all our sinnes, the consideration whereof doth
comforte and rayse vs vp from falling into desperation
and vtter destruction. Seuenthly after this assurance of
Gods loue and of the forgiuenesse of our sinnes there followeth first a true hatred of sinne, because it is sinne, an vnfained
sorrow not so much in regarde of the punishment which by
our sinnes wee haue iustly deserued, as that because we haue
offended our so gratious a God and tender louing father.
Secondly this sorrow will not suffer vs to hide, excuse, or ex- 2.Cor.7.11

K k 4   tenuate

2.Cor.7.11. tenuate our sins, but moueth vs in all humilitie to prostrate our selues before Gods mercie seate, and in greefe of soule to confesse them, acknowledging that confusion and condemnation is due vnto vs, which by no meanes wee can escape but by Gods mercie, and the merites and righteousnesse of Iesus Christ.

Thirdly being assured of the pardon of our sinnes past, wee labour and striue for the time to come to leaue and forsake them, and to mortifie the flesh and corruptions thereof whereby we are led captiue vnto sinne, & also we indeauour with a feruent zeale of Gods glorie to serue the Lorde in holinesse and righteousnesse, that so by our godly liues wee may glorifie him and expresse our thankfulnesse for all his inestimable benefites. Fourthly if at any time besides or contrary to our purpose we be ouertaken by our corruption, and fall into sinne, there followeth in vs an holy anger and indignation with our selues, because wee did not more carefully looke to our waies; which godly anger preceedeth to the taking of a holy kind of reuenge, to the end that thereby our sinnes may be subdued and our corruptions mortified. For example hee that hath offended through gluttonie and drunkennesse being truly penitent and angry with himselfe for his sinne, will also tame the flesh by punishing the same through fasting and abstinence. He that hath offended by vsing excessiue pride in apparell, being angrie with him selfe vpon his true repentance doth withdraw from himselfe such costly attire as otherwise in respect of his calling hee might lawfully weare.

§.Sect.2.
The 2. signe
that it bee to-
tall and intire
and that both
in respect of
the subiect
and obiect. And thus may we come to the assurance that our repentance is true and vnfained if wee can finde these degrees thereof and these effects and fruits in our selues. The second signe of vnfained repentance is that it bee whole and intire and that both in respect of the subiect and also the obiect thereof. In respect of the subiect or of him in whome it is, it is required that it bee not of any part alone, or yet of all parts sauing one, but it must bee intire and totall of the whole man and of euerie of his seuerall partes, it must bee a reformation

in

in the forsaking of sin and imbracing of righteousnes, not in
the body or soule alone but of the both, & of al their seueral
faculties & powers, it must not only be of the outward actios,
but also of the inward affections and cogitations, it must not
only bee of the tongue and hande, but also of our wills and
hearts, according to that Iam. 4. 8. *Draw neere vnto God and* Iam. 4. 8.
*he will draw neere vnto you: clenfe your hands ye sinners, and
purge your heartes you wauering minded.* Otherwise if wee do
not turne vnto the Lorde with all our hearts, with all our
foules, with all our bodies and euery facultie and parte of
them, if we willingly entertaine finne, and purpolely fuffer
it to lurke in any fecret corner of vs, our repentance is hypocriticall and not acceptable in Gods fight. And hence it
is that *Dauid* faith, that if he fhould *regard wickednesse in his* Pfal.66.18.
hart the Lord would not heare him. Pfal. 66. 18.

Secondly, it muft bee whole and intire in refpect of the *We muft per-*
object: for it is not fufficient that we perfourme obedience *fourme obe-*
vnto fome of Gods commandements, if wee indeauour not *all Gods com-*
to fhew our obedience vnto all, it is not inough if we forfake *maundement*
fome of our finnes, if wee willingly and with delight entertaine and nourifh others, neuer ftriuing againft them nor labouring to mortifie them, but if we would approue our repentance to be fincere and vnfained both vnto God and our
owne confciences, we muft defire & indeauour to performe
obedience, as well to thofe commandements which feeme
hard and moft vnpleafant vnto vs, as vnto thofe which are
more eafie and delightfull, we muft not onely forfake thofe
finnes which are not fo pleafing vnto vs, but euen thofe
which otherwife are as deare vnto vs as our right had or eye;
for he that truely repenteth of one fin repenteth of al, he that
repenteth not of any one fin, repenteth of none as he ought;
he that wittingly and aduifedly neglecteth any one commandement will in time neglect all, whatfoeuer outward reformation may ferue to be in him; he that willingly enter-
taineth any one finne and nourifheth it as his deare dearling
in his boofome, will in the end make confcience of none; for
a little leauen leaueneth the whole lumpe, and euen fmall
finnes

sinnes if they be not mortified, will make roome for those which are greatest and most hainous.

The third signe of true repentance is, when our conuersion from sinne vnto God is not deferred in whole or in part from time to time but presently vndertaken : neither is it sufficient to vow repentance vnto God or to purpose it for the time to come, but wee must presently indeauour and labour in it; it is not inough that wee subdue some sinnes now and perfourme obedience vnto some of the commaundemēts, purposing to labour after more perfectiō whē we haue better opportunitie, but wee must presently labour and indeauour to perfourme obedience not to some, but to all Gods commaundements, and we must out of hand set vpon all our sinnes and labour to mortifie all our corruptions, for if the whole body of sinne be not beaten downe and subdued together, that which still liueth in vs, will giue life againe vnto that which is mortified, that which is still retained in the hart, will open a wide dore to let in that which is expelled. And so wee shall but take in hand an endlesse and fruitlesse worke, if wee doe not set aside all excuses, and instantly labour to destroy the whole body of sinne, breaking through all difficulties and impediments, for we shall neuer want hinderances in these holy actions, and excuses for want of fit occasion and conuenient opportunitie, will continually offer themselues vnto vs, and therefore he that will not turne wholly vnto God, till he haue a cleare passage & plaine way free from all thornie distractions which pull him backe, and worldly incumbrances, which like blocks lying before him hinder him in his iourney, may as well resolue to sit still and neuer returne vnto God by vnfained repentance.

The fourth signe of true repentance is if it be continuall from the first day of our conuersion vnto the end of our liues, for it is not sufficient to serue God by fitts, or that our religion should take vs like a tertian ague but euery other day; it is not that which God requireth, that wee should deuide our time betweene him and the world, or hauing be-

gun

gun in the spirit we should end in the flesh, but after wee are gone out of this *Sodome* of sinne, wee must goe forward in our iourney of holy obediēce, and neuer like *Lots* wife looke backe with a desire to inioy the pleasures thereof againe. We must so runne this spirituall race that we may obtaine, now we know that rūners of a race, as they do not stand stil after the watchword is giuen, but labour with all speed to set forth with the first, so they doe not sit downe in the midde way, much lesse run one while backward and another while forward, but they still hasten on till they come to the goale and obtaine the garland, and so it behooueth vs to runne speedily to the Lord by vnfained repentance, and not to desist in this our race till the end of our liues, if wee purpose to receaue that crowne of glory which the Lord hath promised vs. Our life therefore must be a continuall repentance, and so long as we liue so long must we greeue for our sinnes past and present, and striue after newnesse of life and a greater measure of sanctification.

The last signe of vnfained and true repentance is if it be mixed with faith; for true repentance is a fruit of faith, and they are neuer disioined the one from the other, neither can we euer sorrow for sinne as we ought, till we haue some assurance of Gods mercy and loue in Iesus Christ; for otherwise though our sorrow be neuer so great yet it is not so much for sinne as for the punishment thereof, not so much because wee haue thereby displeased God, as for those torments of conscience which we presently indure, and the torments of hell which for the time to come we feare. And therefore this desperate sorrow is it selfe to be sorrowed for, as being seuered from faith and therefore sinnefull, and not proceeding from any loue of God or hatred of sinne, but from the feare of punishment and condemnation. *§. Sect.5. The 5. signe when it proceedeth from faith.*

Rom. 14.23

But it may bee demaunded why amongst the signes of true repentance I haue not numbred teares and weeping for our sinnes; to which I answeare because howsoeuer it is a notable fruite of vnfained repentance, vnto which euerie christian with true compūction of hart is to accustome himselfe, *Why teares are not numbred amongst the signes of vnfained repentance.*

selfe,

selfe, yet notwithstanding it is not an inseparable propertie
thereof; for often times there is teares wheras their is no true
repentance, and there is true repentance whereas there is
few or no teares. For the first wee may plainely perceiue by
continuall experience that teares proceede from diuers other
causes then from true repentāce, sometimes frō excessiue ioy
whereby the pores and passages of the eyes are loosed and
opened, and sometimes from naturall and worldly sorrowe
whereby the said passages are constringed and straightned.
Somtimes from furious anger, & sometims from cōpassion
and pity; and in spirituall things sometimes these teares flow
from vnfained repentance, sometimes from desperat sorrow
conceiued vpon the apprehension of Gods horrible wrath or
of the fearefull torments and eternall condemnation prepared for them. Wherefore it commeth to passe that in the a-
bundance of their teares, they vtter from a heart full of raging malice, horrible blasphemies against God. An example
heareof wee haue in *Esau* who in the middest of his weeping
and howling comforted himselfe with the remembrance of
his fathers death and of that most wicked murther which he
intended vnto his innocent brother. Gen.27 41. So the rebellious Israelites being discouraged with the newes which
the spies brought who were sent to search the land, are said
to haue cried andwept, & yet in the middest of their lamen-
tation to haue murmured against God & his seruants *Moses*
and *Aaron*. So that simplie teares are not a signe of true repentance vnlesse they issue from a broken heart and contrite
spirit, from a true hatred of sinne, and from hartie sorrowe
conceiued because wee haue offended our gratious God. On
the other side if wee be in sinceritie of heart, ruely sorrie for
our sinnes in these respects because we hate our sinnes and
loue God, and are displeased with our selues because we haue
displeased our gratious father, indeauouring to forsake our
sinnes and to leade a newe life in holinesse and righteousnes,
then though wee can seldome or neuer shed teares which is
the ease of some of Gods dearest children yet our repentance
is true and vnfained, for in this action the broken and contrite

Gen. 27. 41.

Num. 14.1.2

trite hart is more to be respected then the blubred eyes howfoeuer most commonly they goe togeather.

And so much concerning the signes of true repentāce,
which if after due examination wee can finde in our selues,
we may be assured that we are truely pænitent; nay I will say
more for the comfort of all humbled sinners if after diligent
search they find not in their owne sense and feeling these
signes of true repentance in them at al or at least in very smal
measure, yet if they earnestly desire and sencerely indeuour
to attaine vnto true repentance vsing those good meanes ordained of God for this purpose, they may assure themselues
that they haue truely repented in the sight of God who accepteth of the will for the deed and of the affection for the action, as before I haue shewed.

And thus may we repell the tentation of Sathan and re- *§.Sect.6.*
ceiue comfort vnto our owne soules when hee laboureth to *That the af-*
perswade vs that our repentance is not true and vnfained, *surance of the*
but false and hypocriticall : but if the tempter cannot thus *remiffion of*
preuaile, in the next place hee will tel vs that our repentance *sinnes depen-*
though it be true yet it is not sufficient, neither is there any *the dignity of*
proportion betweene our small repentance and our great *ourrepentāce.*
sinnes as Gods iustice doth require, To which we must answeare that the remission of our sinnes and reconciliation
with God, dependeth not vpon the dignitie or quantitie of
our repentance, but vpon the righteousnesse and full satisfaction of our Sauiour Iesus Christ; neither doe wee repent
to the end that thereby wee may in whole or in part satisfie
for our sinnes; for though it could bee imagined that the
whole substance of our bodies should be resolued into teares,
yet woulde they not all of them satisfie and appease Gods
wrath for one breach of any of his commandements, neither
is it the water of our eyes no nor yet the bloud of our harts
wounded deepely with sorrow, which will purge vs from
our sinnes either in respect of the guilt, punishment, or corruptions themselues, but it is the water and bloud which
flowed from our crucified Lord which cleanseth our guiltie
soules from the filthie spotts of sinne, being applied vnto vs

by

by a true and liuely faith. And therefore let vs not with the popish rabble foolishly imagine that wee can by our repentance meritt any thing at Gods hand or satisfie his iustice for our sinnes, for so shall wee rob our Sauiour Christ of the glorie due vnto him for our saluation, and spoile our soules of all true comfort, but let vs repent and vnfainedly turne vnto God in obedience to his commaundement, and to the ende that thereby we may approue our faith before God, the world, & our owne consciences to be true by this liuely and vndoubted fruit thereof, For it cannot bee if we haue attayned to the assurance of Gods loue and the remission of our sins for the merits and satisfaction of Christ, but that we will loue God againe, and this loue cannot be idle but will shew it selfe in a feruent zeale of Gods glorie, and this zeale will make vs abhorre sinne whereby our gratious God is dishonoured, and loue righteousnesse whereby his holy name is glorified, and euen sorrow with bitter greefe when as we are ouertaken with our corruptions and fall into sinne, seeing our Sauiour Christ hath not spared his pretious bloud to purge vs, whē as nothing els could make vs cleane. Seeing therefore our repentance doth not satisfie Gods iustice nor purge away any sinne, let vs not be perswaded by Sathan that reconciliation with God, and the remission of our sinnes dependeth on the dignitie or quantitie of our repentance, but let vs assure our selues that it is onely the bloud of Christ applied vnto vs by a liuely faith, that purgeth vs from all our sinnes, and maketh full satisfaction vnto Gods iustice : And therefore though our repentance be but in small measure, yet so it be true and vnfained it is a certaine fruite of a liuely faith, and hee that beleeueth is made partaker of Christ and all his benefits.

§. *Sect.7.*
That wee are not to be discouraged in that some reprobates haue shewed more outward signes of sorrow then we.

Lastly Sathan will obiect that many who haue more bitterly sorrowed then we, & haue shewed more notable signes of exceeding repentāce, haue notwithstāding bene reiected and condemned. To which wee are to answere, that though such haue shewed more sorrow yet they haue had no true repentance, in that their sorrow hath bene destitute of faith
and

and not so much for any hatred of sinne or loue of God, or vnwillingnesse to displease him, as for horrour of conscience and desperate feare of eternall condemnation. And therefore though notwithstanding such sorrow, they haue bene condemned, yet we may be assured that vpon our true repentance, whereby on the one side wee looke vpon our sinnes and are grieued for them, and on the other side behould Gods mercifull and gratious countenance in Iesus Christ by a liuely faith, we shall haue the pardon of our sins and be made partakers of eternall saluation. For the promisses of the Gospell are not made to those who afflict themselues with a desperate sorrow, without any hope or desire of Gods mercy in Christ Iesus, but vnto those who turne vnto him by vnfained repentance which is ioyned with a true faith and assurance of the remission of our sinnes and euerlasting life.

CHAP. XLII.

How we may proue against Sathans tentations that wee haue true faith.

Nd so much for answering those tentations of Sathan, whereby he laboureth to proue that we haue no repentance or at least a false and insufficient repentance, and consequently that the sweete and gratious promisses of the gospell doe not belong vnto vs : now wee are to produce and answere such tentations as he alleageth and suggesteth into the minds of those who are effectually called against their faith ; and these are of two sortes : the first whereby hee laboureth to perswade them that they haue no faith ; the second that their faith (if they haue any) is so weake, so imperfect and so mixt with doubting that it is altogether insufficient for their saluation. For the first he will thus frame his tentation. Though thou boastest much of thy faith, and thereby presumest that thou shalt attaine vnto saluation , herein thou maiest much

§. Sect. 1.
How Sathan tempteth the weake Christian, to be-leeue that he hath no true faith.

deceiue

deceiue thy felfe & altogether faile of thy purpofe; for there may be in many fhewes and fhadowes of faith, and yet nothing in them but infidelitie, there are alfo many kinds of faith, and yet but one iuftifying and fauing faith, there is a generall or hiftoricall faith, there is a faith of working miracles which *Iudas* had as well as *Peter*, there is a temporarie or hypocriticall faith, there is a dead faith, there is alfo carnall prefumption, wherewith many who haue made goodly fhewes haue bene bewitched and deceiued to their perdition; feeing then there are many falfe faiths, for one true faith, it is likely that thine is one of the greateft number, and confequently no true faith. And therefore do not flatter and deceiue thy felfe in thy fond prefumption, by applying vnto thy felfe the fweete promiffes and gratious confolations of the gofpell, for they appertaine only vnto thofe who are indued with a true liuely and iuftifying faith, of which thou art altogether deftitute.

§. Sect.2.
Sathans te-ftimonie no good reafon, to proue that we haue no fayth.
Ioh.8.44.

　　And thus Sathan indeauoreth to perfwade the Chriftian exercifed in the combate of tentations that he hath no faith, to the end that he may deftroy it, and if it were poffible bring it indeed to nothing : to which tentation wee may firft anfwere thus generally, that Sathans teftimonie is no found argument to proue that we haue no faith, nor to be beleeued of vs, feeing he is not onely a malitious murtherer, who continually feeketh our deftruction. But alfo a falfe liar from the beginning, who hath not feared to bee lie men onely but euen God himfelfe accufing him of vntruth, enuie and want of power in that tentation wherewith hee affailed and ouercame our firft parents : and therefore if he be fo audatioufly impudent, as that he durft be lie God himfelfe, we may affure our felues he will make no fcruple of be lying vs. Seeing then Sathan is a malitious liar, who defireth nothing more then our deftruction, let vs not doubt of our faith becaufe of his teftimony, nay rather becaufe he faith wee want faith, we may affure our felues that we are indued therewith, for that he may worke our finall ouerthrow, it is his vfuall cuftome to tell the true beleeuing Chriftian that he is deftitute

tute of faith, and contrariwise the vnbeleeuing worldling that he hath a ftrong faith, whereas in truth there is nothing in him but fecure prefumption. And therefore let it fuffice vs that we know we haue a liuely faith by the teftimonie of Gods fpirit, and by trying and examining our faith by the touchftone of Gods words, for on thefe our faith dependeth and not on Sathans teftimonie.

But let vs after a more efpeciall manner arme our felues *§. Sect. 3.* against this tentation; and to this purpofe it behoouethys *How we may* firft that we prooue against Sathans falfe fuggeftions, that we *bee assured* haue faith : and fecondly that we arme our felues by al good *that we haue* meanes with the fhield of faith, feeking daily more ftrength *faith by fin-* and increafe thereof, vntil at laft wee attaine vnto that ful- *ding in our* neffe of faith which will fill our foules with true peace and *selues the de-* comfort, and alfo beat backe all the violence of Sathans fub- *grees thereof.* till and fearce tentations.

For the firft : wee may prooue that we haue a true iufti-fying faith by diuerfe argumentes , as firft by the degrees thereof, from which we may thus reafon? whofoeuer can truely find in himfelfe the feuerall degrees of a liuely faith, he may certainely be affured that he is indued therewith, but I (may euery chriftian man fay) doe truely howfoeuer in weake meafure finde thefe degrees of a liuely faith in mee, and therefore I am affured that I am indued therewith.

The firft degree vnto true faith, is the illumination of our *The 1. degree* darke and ignorant minds with the knowledge of the Gof- *of true faith,* pell, or with the maine principles thereof, wrought in our *the illumina-* minds by the outward meanes ordained of God, and the *tion of the* inward operation of his holy fpirit; whereby we giue our af- *minde.* fent to that truth of God in which the vnderftanding is in-fourmed. And of this the apoftle fpeaketh 1. Tim. 2. 4. where he faith that *it is the will of God, that all men fhould bee faued,* 1. Tim. 2. 4. *and come to the acknowledging of the truth,* that is to the know-ledge of the truth of God, and affenting therunto.

The fecond degree is an affurance that our finnes are par- *The 2. degree* donable, which is wrought in vs by the knowledge and due *a perfwafion* confideration of Gods infinite mercy, and Chrifts inualuable *that our fins are pardona-*

L l merits *ble.*

merites and indefinite promises of the Gospell, made with out exception to all repentant and beleeuing sinners;from whence also ariseth a generall hope that we shall receaue the pardon and remission of our sinnes, which hope is nourished and increased by this consideration, that the Lord hath placed vs in his church, and gratiously granted vnto vs the outward meanes wherby we may be brought vnto vnfained repentance, and haue a liuely faith wrought in vs, euen the ministerie of the word and administration of the sacraments, vpon which onely condition the couenant of grace and all the sweete promises of the Gospell, are made and assured vnto vs.

§. *Sect.*4.
The 3. *degree an hungring desire after grace.*

The third degree is a hungring desire after grace, that is not onely to be made partakers of Gods mercy, and Christs meritts and righteousnes by which we are iustified, reconciled vnto God, and receaue the pardon and remission of all our sinnes, but also after the meanes and instrumentall causes whereby the assurance of Gods mercy and Christs merits is deriued vnto vs, namely true faith and vnfained repentance, and the rest of the graces of Gods sanctifying spirit. The which desire of grace is the beginning of grace, neyther can wee desire it till in some measure it be wrought in vs;for regeneration and sanctification is begunne at the same time in all the parts and faculties of our bodies and soules, so that he who is truely regenerate in any facultie or part,is also regenerate in the whole man. And therefore whosoeuer hath his will renewed and sanctified to desire that which is good, is also sanctified and renewed in his vnderstanding, affections, and in all the powers and faculties of body and soule. Moreouer (as before I haue deliuered at large) our desire of grace,faith,and repentance,are the graces themselues which we desire,at least in Gods acceptation,who accepteth of the will for the deed, and of our affections for the actions. And therefore if we earnestly desire to repent & beleeue,we doe repent and beleeue in Gods sight : and the Lord hath made the like gratious promises to this earnest desire of grace, which hee hath made to those who find themselues plentifully

fully indued with the graces themselues. So Matth.5.6.*Bles*-
sed are they which hunger and thirst for righteousnesse, for they
shalbe filled. So the virgin *Marie* saith in her song, Luk.1.53. Luke 1.53.
That the Lord filleth the hungrie with good things, and sendeth a-
way the rich emptie. And our Sauiour Christ calleth vnto him
such as thus hunger and thirst, promising that he will satisfie
them. Iohn 7.37. Reuel.21.6. and 22,17. Lastly whosoeuer Ioh.7.37.
feeleth this desire in him ioyned with a carefull and continuall vse of the meanes whereby his desire may be satisfied,
he may assure himselfe that the Lord who hath wrought in
him, the will to desire, will also in his good time worke in
him abilitie to perfourme, and the graces which hee so earnestly desires; *for hee will fulfill the desire of them that feare*
*him; he will also heare their crie and will saue them.*As it is Psal. Psal.145.19
145.19.So Psal.10.17. *Lord thou hast heard the desire of the* & 10.17.
poore: thou preparest their heart and bendest thine eare vnto
them. And therefore if in the middest of our afflictions and
grieuous tentations, wee can crie out with the Prophet *Da-*
*uid,*Psalm.38.9. *Lord I powre my whole desire before thee, and* Psal.38.9.
my sighing is not hid from thee. We may be assured how miserable soeuer wee are in our owne sense and feeling, that
wee are in the state of grace, and shall haue our desires satisfied,for *he that hath begunne this good worke in vs, will also in* Phil.1.6.
his good time finish and perfect it. as the Apostle speaketh.Phil.
1.6.

    The fourth degree is an approaching vnto the throne of §. *Sect.5.*
mercy,that we may in all humilitie confesse our sinnes, and *The 4.degree*
acknowledge that wee are guiltie of death and condemna- *an approch-*
tion, and also that wee may in the name and mediation of *ing to the*
Christ obtaine the pardon and remission of them. And of *grace.*
this the Apostle speaketh. Heb. 4. 16. *Let vs therefore goe* Heb.4.16.
bouldly vnto the throne of grace, that wee may reeceiue mercy and
find grace to helpe in time of need. And the Prophet Hosea cap.
14.2. *O Israel returne vnto the Lord thy God: for thou hast fal-* Hos.14.2.
len by thine iniquity. 3. *Take vnto you words and turne vnto the*
Lord and say vnto him : take away all iniquitie, and receiue vs
graciously, so will we render the calues of our lips. An example

hereof

Psal.32.5. hereof we haue in the Prophet *Dauid*, Psal. 32. 5. *Then*(saith he) *I acknowledge my sinne vnto thee, neyther hid I mine iniquitie: for I thought I will confesse my wickednesse vnto the Lord, and thou forgauest the punishment of my sinne.* So likewise the prodigall Sonne hauing attained vnto the sight of his sinne and to a desire of forgiuenesse, resolueth to goe vnto his fa- Luk. 15 18. 19. ther, and to say; *Father I haue sinned against heauen and before thee; & am no more woorthie to be called thy sonne; make mee as one of thy hired seruants.*Luke 15.18.19.

§ .Sect.6.
The 5.degree
a special ap-
plication of
the promises.   The fift degree is a specially perswasion wrought in vs by Gods spirit whereby we particularly apply vnto vs the sweete promises of the gospell, and are assured of Gods loue and fauour, & of the remission of our sinnes for the merits, righteousnesse, and obedience of Iesus Christ, resting vpon him alone for our saluation. An example whereof wee haue Gala.2.20. in the Apostle Paul Gal. 2. 20. *Thus* (saith he) *I liue yet not I now but Christ liueth in me : and in that I now liue in the flesh, I liue by faith in the sonne of God, who hath loued mee and giuen himselfe for mee.* And this perswasion ought to goe before sense and experience , for first wee beleeue and are perswaded of the truth of Gods promises and resist diffidence and doubting, and afterwardes followes ioyfull sense and experience of Gods mercy, truth, and goodnes towards vs. And hence it is that the Apostle defineth faith to bee *the ground of things which are hoped for, and the demonstration or* Heb.11.1.
Ioh.20 29. *euidēce of things not seene.*Heb. 11.1.& to this purpose our sauiour Christ saith to Thomas. Ioh. 20. 29. *Thomas because thou hast seene me, thou beleeuest, blessed are they whiuh haue not seene and haue beleeued.* An example hereof wee haue in the Cananitish woman who though shee had no experience of Gods truth in his promises, yea though shee had many repulses yet beleeued, and afterwards to her comfort had ioy- Mat. 15.27. full experience of them, Mat. 15.27.

An these are the degrees of faith, which whosoeuer findeth in himselfe hee may be assured that hee hath a true liuely and iustifying faith notwithstanding all the tentations of Sathan. If therefore hauing heard the gospell wee haue at-

tained

tained vnto some measure of knowledge of the chiefe principles thereof, if we haue giuen our assent vnto this truth in
which our vnderstandings are informed ; if hereby we haue
attained vnto this assurance that our sinnes are pardonable
and haue conceiued some hope in consideration of Gods
infinite mercie and Christs merites that wee shall be forgiuen
and pardoned; if we haue an hungring desire after grace and
mercie and highly esteeme the merites and righteousnesse of
Iesus Christ , so that wee wish nothing more then to bee
made partakers of them; if by this desire wee haue beene
moued to flee vnto the throne of grace , and there humblie
acknowledging our sinnes haue earnestly desired pardon
and forgiuenesse. Lastly if at any time wee haue discerned in
in our selues a perswasion of Gods loue and of the pardon
and remission of our sinnes, and that we haue or doe rest vppon the alone merites and obedience of Christ Iesus for our
iustification and saluation, then may wee be assured that we
are indued with a true iustifying faith.

The second argument to proue that wee haue a true and
a liuely faith is the testimonie of Gods spirite; for as the A-
postle speaketh Rom. 8. 15. *Wee haue the spirite of adoption*
whereby we crie abba father. 16. *and the same spirit beareth*
witnesse with our spirit that we are the children of God. and ver.
26. *Likewise the spirite also helpeth our infirmities, for we know*
not what to pray as we ought, but the spirite it selfe maketh request
for vs with sighes which cannot be expressed &c. Whosoeuer
therefore haue this testimonie in their harts and consciences
that they are the children of God , whosoeuer at any time
feele or haue felt the spirit of God powerful in the, in powring out their soules in hartie prayer with sighes and grones
which cãnot be expressed, they may be assured that they haue
receiued the spirite of adoption and consequently are indued
with true faith , for the spirite and the fruites thereof (a-
mongst which faith is one of the chiefe) are neuer seuered.
Moreouer the Apostle saith 1. Cor. 2. 12. that *wee haue not*
receiued the spirit of the world, but the spirit which is of God that
wee might knowe the things that are giuen to vs of God. That is

§. *Sect.*7.
The second
argument to
proue that we
haue faith, is
the testimonie
of Gods spirie
Rom.8.15,
26.

Gal.5.22.

1.Cor.2.12.

not

not onely his spirituall graces in this life in which number
faith is one of the greatest, but those excellent ioyes in Gods
kingdome in the life to come, of which also wee haue some
knowledge and tast by the illumination of the same spirite.
Lastly the Apostle affirmeth 2. Cor. 1. 22. *that God hath sea-*

2.Cor.1.22.

led vs, and hath giuen the earnest of the spirit in our hartes, and
Ephe. 1. 13. Hee telleth the Ephesians that after they *had*

Ephe.1.13.

heard the gospel and beleeued, they were sealed with the holy spirit
of promise, which was the earnest of their inheritance, vntil the re-
demption of the possession purchased vnto the praise of the glorie of
God. Wheresoeuer therefore is this testimonie of the spirite
which as an earnest or seale assureth them that they are the
children of God there also is faith, for as the Apostle witnesseth after that wee beleeue we are thus sealed.

§.Sect.8.

The 3. *argu-*
ment is the
fight between
the flesh and
the spirit.

The third argument to proue that wee haue faith is the
conflict and fight which euerie christian feeleth in himselfe
betweene the spirit and the flesh, the world and the diuell,
and the combat which is betweene faith and doubting; for
so long as wee are destitute of the spirit and a liuely faith, we
are wholy ouerswayed with the fleshe, and Sathan like a
mightie tyrant houldeth vs captiue peaceably and without
any resistance; but when wee haue receiued the spirite of
God and haue faith wrought in our harts, then beginneth a
fierce battaile which neuer endeth till by death our spirituall
enemies get a final ouerthrowe. Though therefore this fight
be most sharpe and exceeding troublesome to the poore
christian, yet hee may thereby gather vnto himselfe sound
comfort and certaine assurance that hee is indued with the
spirit of God and a liuely faith; for when hee discerneth that
hee is assaulted with Sathan and his owne corrupt fleshe, he
may be assured that Sathan is diseased of his quiet possession
by a superior power which can be no other but the power of
Gods spirit, secondly by his assaulting it manifestly appeareth that hee findeth some resistance so as hee cannot peaceably reenter, thirdly that howsoeuer our faith seeme vnto
vs neuer so weak yet it is so strengthened cōtinually by vertue
of Gods spirit that sathā & al the power of hel cānot preuaile

against

againſt it, for otherwiſe how could ſuch weakeneſſe withſtãd ſuch might?

Laſtly being aſſured that it is the ſpirit of God which aſſiſteth and enableth vs to withſtand Sathan, we may alſo be aſſured that in the end we ſhall obtaine victorie, vnleſſe we would fondly imaginethat the diuell is ſtronger then God, and the violence of his tentations more forcible to deſtroy vs, then the ſpirit of God to protect and defend vs; for now they haue ioyned battle and either the one or the other muſt get the vpper hand, eyther the ſpirit of God muſt thruſt out ſathan, or Sathan the ſpirit of God; and therefore how can we doubt of conqueſt, ſeeing wee are aſſured that God cannot take the foyle, for his power is omnipotent and with a word of his mouth he is able to deſtroy Sathan and all his adhærents, and of his will wee neede not to make any queſtion, for it will not ſtand with his glory to receaue a repulſe by giuing Sathan place, after that he hath taken vpon him our protection.

Yea (will the tempter ſay) but how wilt thou know that this battle is fought in thee, how canſt thou be aſſured that it is the ſpirite of God which fighteth in thee againſt thy ſpirituall enemies, and not rather thine owne tumultuous paſſions and perturbations; and diuers tentations ſuggeſted by the ſame diuell. To which it is eaſie to make anſwere, for neither doth the fleſh fight againſt ſathan, nor ſathan againſt the fleſh, nor either of thẽ againſt thẽſelues, for ſo their kingdome being deuided could not poſſibly ſtand, as our ſauiour Chriſt himſelfe hath taught vs Mat.12.25.26. And therefore it muſt needs be ſoe other force which cauſeth this oppoſitiõ which can proceede from nothing elſe but the ſpirit of God.

But this will more manifeſtly appeare, if we conſider the contrarie affections and actions which plainely ſhew themſelues in this battle, for we find our faith aſſaulted with doubting and infidelitie, & theſe alſo againe beaten backe after they haue gotten ſome ground and ſubdued with the ſtrẽgth of faith; we diſcerne alſo our affiance in God ſhrewdly ſhaken with diffidence and diſtruſt, and afterwards this diſtruſt

§. Sect.9.
How we may know that this combate is fought betweene the fleſh and the ſpirite.

Mat.12.25.

vanquiſhed

vanquisheth againe by affiance, so as after we haue vttered
through the violence of tentation some diffident and impatient speeches, yet at the length we growe to *Iobs* resolution:
Though hee kill mee yet will I trust in him. Wee may also
discerne our zeale sometime so hot in Gods seruice that it
expelleth coldnesse and the fruit thereof dulnesse and drowsinesse of spirite, and sometimes by them it is cooled and in
outward appearance quenched; and the like may bee saide
of all the other fruits of the flesh and the spirit. Besides which
fight and stirring betweene them and their fruits the christian may obserue in himselfe a misliking of the corruptions of
the flesh, great greefe and vexation of mind, because hee is
still subiect vnto them and an earnest desire to be freed from
them, ioyned with an holy indeauoure in the vse of the
meanes which are ordayned of God for this purpose; and
howsoeuer through the violence of Sathans tentations and
his owne corruptions ye be sometimes led captiue into sinne
yet afterwardes hee is greeued for it, hee hateth and abhorreth it, and earnestly desireth and indeauoureth for the time
to come to leaue and forsake it, and to serue the Lorde in
newnesse of life. Now whence doth all this opposition and
contrarietie proceede? shall wee say from the flesh, why it
is against all reason; for as the Apostle *Iames* disputeth Iam.
3.11. *Doth a fountaine send out at one place sweete water and
bitter? can the figg tree bring forth oliues, or a vine figgs?* or rather as our sauiour Christ reasoneth Mat. 7. 16. *Doe men gather grapes of thorns or figgs of thistles?* so may I demaund can
the flesh in the which as the Apostle affirmeth dwelleth no
good thing, bring foorth the fruites of the spirite which are
quite contrarie to the nature thereof, namely sorrowe for
sinne, hatred of it selfe, and the corruptions thereof, and
earnest desire of sanctification and holines of life: it is impossible. And therfore we may conclude that they are the fruits
of Gods spirit in vs, and consequently that wee are the sons
of God who are indued with a true and liuely faith; for *as
many as are led by the spirite of God, they are the sonnes of God,*
which priuiledge belongeth onely to the faithfull as appeareth

Iob.13.15.

Iam.3.11.

Mat.7.16.

Rom.7.18.

Rom.8.

reth Ioh. 1. 12. *As many as receaued him to them hee gaue* Ioh. 1.12. *power to be the sons of God, euen to them that beleeue in his name.* So that whosoeuer haue the spirit haue faith also, for the spirit and faith which is a fruit thereof cannot be seuered.

The fourth argument whereby we may bee assured that §. *Sect. 10.* we haue faith, is our mortification and dying vnto sinne and *The 4. argu-* rising againe to newnesse of life; for the bloud of Iesus Christ *ment taken* which is applied vnto vs by faith as it doth washe away the *from our* guilt and punishment of our sinnes, so doth it also cleanse *sanctification* vs in some measure from the corruptions themselues; and as his death and obedièce hath meritted the pardon of our sins, so also Gods spirit by vertue whereof we are more and more freed from the bondage and seruitude of sinne and Sathan, and as by his resurrection hee hath made way for our second resurrection whereby wee rise to euerlasting happinesse, so also for our first resurrection whereby wee rise from sinne to newnesse of life. If therefore wee can find in our selues that our sins and corruptions are by little and little mortified, that wee striue and indeauour after holinesse and righteousnesse of life; if our vnderstandings bee somewhat inlightened in the knowledge of Gods truth and our stubberne wills incly-ned to holy obedience, if we discerne that our affections are in some measure changed and renewed, then may wee be as-sured that wee are indued with a true and liuely faith, which hath applied vnto vs Christ Iesus and his bloud shed, death, & merites, by vertue whereof this worke of regeneration is be-gunne in vs.

Lastly, we may be assured that we haue faith by the seue- §. *Sect. 11.* rall fruits of sanctification and regeneration which proceed *The last ar-* from it : for example when wee can sorrow and greeue for *gument ta-* our sinnes past, not for any worldly losse or feare of punish- *ken from the* ment, but because thereby we haue offended God, when as *seuerall fruits* we hate our present sinnes and corruptions, especially those *of sanctifica-* which stick fastest vnto vs, and are most pleasing to our cor- *tion.* rupt nature; when as we indeauour and striue to forsake and mortifie all sinne though our carnall affection be much in-deared to it, by reason of some great pleasure or profite which it bringeth with it, auoiding with no lesse care those sinnes which bring worldly benefitt, then those which are accompanied with shame and punishment, when as we loue God euen when he afflicteth vs and in obedience to his commaundement, perfourme such holy duties, and imbrace such vertues, not onely which are commendable in the world, but also those which are accompanied with shame and reproach, when as we loue our brethren, yea euen our enemies and shew this our loue by giuing vnto those who want, and forgiuing those who offend vs, and when more especially we extend this loue and the fruits thereof to those who are of the houshould of faith, and amongst these principally to Gods ministers who are instruments appointed of God, for our conuersion and saluation, when as wee can submit our selues vnto Gods will, and rest contented in all estates with his good pleasure, when as we loath this life and the vanities of the world, and desire our dissolution that we may be with Christ and be freed from our sinnes; when as we are patient in afflictions, and in the middest of them haue some hope of tasting Gods mercy and goodnesse, grounding our hope vpon Gods promisses and our owne former experience; when as we delight in the hearing and meditating in Gods word, and continue constant in the profession and practise of his truth, not onely when our obedience is good cheape, but also when it is deare and very costly, and as well when it is accompanied with losse, as when wee are in hope to gaine thereby. These and many other the braunches of sanctification are the vndoubted signes of a true and liuely faith, and therefore whosoeuer after due examination, find that they are indued with them, may also be assured notwithstanding all Sathans suggestions to the contrary that they haue faith, for this is the roote from which these fruits spring and they cannot be seuered.

CHAP. XLIII.

Sathans tentations grounded vpon our want of sense and feeling of faith, answered.

And

Nd these are the signes by which euery belee- §.*Sect.*1.
uer may be assured that he hath a true & liue- *Sathans ten-*
ly faith: which howsoeuer they bee to be ob- *tation where-*
serued in euery faithfull man, yet not at all *by he perswa-*
times, for oftentimes it commeth to passe that *deth vs tha*
the beleeuing Christian doth neither feele his faith nor the *we haue no*
fruites thereof, especially in the infancie of faith and in the *faith, because*
cumbate of tentations, which giueth occasion vnto Sathan *we feele it not*
of suggesting into his mind a daungerous tentation. Thou
braggest much (will he say) of thy faith, and thou confirmest,
this thy perswasion that thou art indued therewith with many signes and fruits which haue accompanied it; but if now
thou examine thy selfe a right thou shalt find in thee no such
matter; and not to stand vpon other arguments, I appeale
vnto the testimonie of thine owne conscience, whether at
this present thou hast any sense or liuely feeling of faith, or
canst discerne those fruits thereof which before thou hast
spoken of; if not, then doe not flatter thy selfe in vaine with
a fond perswasion, for though thou wilt not beleeue mee, yet
at least beleeue thine owne sense and feeling which plainely
telleth thee that either thou neuer haddest any true faith indeed, or if thou haddest yet that now it is quite lost and perished.

For the answering of which tentation wee must distin- *The answere*
guish betweene the habite of faith, and the act of faith; or be- *to the former*
tweene faith it selfe and the worke & function thereof, which *tentations.*
is to apprehend and apply Christs merits and Gods mercy
and louing fauour, with all the gratious promises of the gospell; as it is an habituall facultie of the mind, it alwaies continueth & abideth in Gods children, after it is once wrought
in them by the spirit of God, but in respect of the function
act or worke thereof it hath many intermissions, and oftentimes seemeth to be cast as it were into a dead sleepe. Now
we are to know that we cannot sensibly discerne faith, as it
is an habituall vertue or facultie of the mind although wee
haue it in great measure in vs, but onely so farre foorth as it
manifesteth it selfe in his actions, workes, & fruits; and there—
fore

fore it is an vnsound and false maner of reasoning, to inferre becau**se** we doe not sensibly feele and discerne that we haue faith, therfore we are destitute thereof; for the habite of faith or faith it selfe may be in vs, & yet for a time may be so hindred by outward accidents, that it cannot shew it selfe in his actions and fruits, by which alone it is sensibly discerned.

But I will make this more cleare and manifest by some familiar similitude and examples, we know that in the sicknesses and diseases of the body nature is so infeebled and o-uercome, that sometimes the partie affected falleth into a dead swoune wherein hee is depriued for a time, not onely of the vse of the vnderstanding, reason, and memorie, but also of his senses, motion, and vitall functions, so that in respect of sense and outward appearance, hee is quite depriued of all his vitall sensitiue and intellectuall faculties, but yet a while after by reason of some outward meanes vsed, or by the secrete power of nature working in him, hee is restored to the vse of all againe, and liueth, feeleth much and vnderstandeth as in former times, because hee had not lost these faculties but onely by some grieuous impediment was hindred of the vse of them in their actions and functions; so that here this manner of reasoning appeareth absurd and false, these faculties of the soule cannot be sensibly discerned, and therefore hee is quite destitute of them : And thus also it is in respect of our faith and other habituall vertues, oftentimes through the sicknes of the soule in sinne or the outward violence of Sathans tentations, it seemeth cast into a swoune & depriued of al the spirituall faculties and vertues thereof, faith, loue, zeale, hope, patience and the rest, but yet soone after by hearing the word, by godly admonitions, instructions, reprehensions, and consolations made effectuall by the inward operation of Gods spirit it is reuiued, and all the spirituall graces thereof shew themselues againe in their woonted strength; so that this inference is no lesse false then the other, there is no sensible appearance of these sanctifying gifts and graces, and therefore they are quite lost and perished, for the graces themselues remaine

though

thoughe for a time they appeare not in their actions and fruits.

So in the time of winter the fruitfull trees are so nipped with the cold frosts, and so weatherbeaten with tempestuous stormes that they appeare naked & bare, not only without fruite but also leaues, so as if wee shall iudge according to sence & outward appearance we should falsely conclude that they are dead; for by experience we know that they liue and sucke nourishment out of the earth, euen when they are most spoiled of their summer beautie, and though they are tossed with the winds yet hereby they are not hurt but rather take deeper roote and so are made capeable of more nourishment, and though they bee nipped with cold frosts yet hereby they are not made barren nay rather hereby their wormes and cankers are killed, and they prepared and made fitt to bring forth more fruite in the time of sommer, when the comfortable spring approacheth, and the sweet showers and warme sunne beames fall and descend vpon them. And thus it is with the spirituall graces in the poore christian, in the winter of affliction they are nipped with the cold frosts of feare and doubting, and weatherbeaten with the boysterous blasts of Sathans tentations, so as they seeme euen dead at the very roote if wee shall iudge according to outwarde sense & appearance, but yet by experience we find that it is farre otherwise, for hereby they are not ouerturned though they be shaken, and this shaking maketh them to take more deepe roote in godlinesse, and though they bee nipped and pinched with feares and doubtings yet they perish not, only the canker-worme of pride, fonde presumption, and selfe confidence is mortified and killed; and they hereby are prepared and fitted to bring forth more plentifull fruites of holinesse and righteousnesse, when the spring of true comfort commeth, wherein the sweete showers of Gods holy spirit distil vpon them, and the warme sunshine of Gods loue and fauour againe appeareth to them.

The fire is sometime so couered with ashes that it sendeth forth neither light nor heate, and therefore in outward sense and

and appearance it feemeth quite extinguifhed, but when the afhes are remooued and more wood added to it, it burfteth out into a great flame, and makes all the ftanders by to perceiue his heate and light; and fo the graces of Gods fpirite are fometimes fo couered with the afhes of our corruptions that there appeareth no fparke of them nor yet any heate of true comfort, but when our corruptions are remoued with vnfained repentance, and a new fupplie of grace miniftred vnto them by Gods fpirite, then doth their light appeare vnto vs and warme our harts with true côfort, and not to vs alone but euen thofe about vs fee our fhining light and glorifie our heauenly father.

A man hath not alwaies the vfe of his fenfes, reafon, and vnderftanding as in his fleepe, but becaufe we cannot fenfibly difcerne thefe faculties fhall wee therefore conclude that this man who is afleepe is fenfeleffe vnreafonable and without vnderftanding; it were moft abfurd; for if wee but expect a while till hee be throughly awakened our argument will appeare manifeftly falfe : and fo fometime the poore chriftian is ouertaken with the fleepe of drowfie fecuritie and is ouerwhelmed for a time with hardneffe of harte, and dulneffe of fpirite, fo as none of thofe fpirituall graces which are in him can fenfibly be difcerned by himfelfe or others, but fhall he or we conclude or beleeue Sathan fo concluding, that he neuer had them, or now is depriued of them? why it were as abfurd as the other. For when hee is awaked out of his drowfie fleepe by the voice of the Lorde founding in his eares, and by the good motions of his holy fpirite his faith, loue, zeale, and all other vertues and graces fhew themfelues in their fruits and actions, as manifeftly as in former times.

§. Sect. 3.
That we muft not conclude that we haue not faith becaufe we doe not fenfibly difcerne it.

Seeing then thofe arguments which are taken from fenfe and feeling fo often faile, let vs not be perfwaded by fathans tentations to beleeue that we are deftitute of faith and other fanctifying graces of Gods holy fpirit, becaufe at fometimes we cânot fenfibly difcerne them, for though now our foules feeme fo ficke in the fenfe of finne that there appeareth no

signe

figne of life, yet the Lord wil rayfe vs vp againe & reftore vs to perfect health, though now wee fee no fruites of faith whileft wee are nipped with the winter of tentations, yet the Lord will water vs with his holy fpirit, & warme our frozen hearts with the liuely beames of his loue and fauour fo as we fhal bring forth aboudant fruits in due time & feafo; though now there appeare not a fpark of grace in vs by reafo al is couered with the afhes of our corruptios, yet the Lord wil furely ad a frefh fupply & blow vpon vs by his holy fpirit fo that our light and heate fhall appeare to our felues & others, & though now our fpirits be oppreffed with drowfie dulneffe, yet the Lord in his good time will caufe vs to awake by hearing his voice, founding in our eares out of his holy word, and will againe quicken and reuiue vs with his holy fpirit, fo as after this fleepe wee fhalbe enabled to follow with chearefulneffe our labours and workes, both which concerne his feruice, and thofe duties alfo which concerne our brethren, onely let vs not tempt the Lord in prefcribing him a time, but waite his leafure & he will furely helpe vs.

CHAP. XLIIII.

How the weake Chriftian is to comfort himfelfe, when he is depriued of the fenfe of faith, and fenfibly feeleth the contrary corruptions.

Vt thou wilt fay how is it poffible that my foule fhould receyue any comfort, or that I fhould preferue my felfe from falling into vtter defperation, feeing I cannot feele in me any good thing, nor difcerne any fparke of grace? what hope remaineth when as I plainely difcerne in fteed of faith, doubting and infidelitie, in ftead of the loue of God, hatred and rebellion, in fteed of zeale, coldneffe and drowfie dulneffe, and in fteed of all fanctifying graces, nothing els but a heauy maffe of filthy corruptions? I anfwere that when thou haft no comfort in thy prefent fenfe, and feeling then

§. *Sect*.1. *That the Chriftian in the want of prefent fenfe, muft comfort himfelfe with his former feeling.*

thou

thou muſt call to thy remembrance the times paſt, in which
thou haſt by faith apprehended Gods loue, mercy, and goodneſſe towards thee, and brought foorth the fruits of thy faith
in the workes of holineſſe, appertaining to Gods ſeruice and
the workes of Chriſtian righteouſneſſe belonging to our
brethren, for we may aſſure our ſelues that if euer wee haue
truly diſcerned theſe graces of Gods ſpirit, by the fruits of
ſanctification in vs, they are not taken from vs, for the gifts
and calling of God are without repentance, as it is Rom. 11.
29 And where he hath begunne a good worke their he will
finiſh it and bring it to perfection, As the Apoſtle ſpeaketh
Phil. 1.6. Wee know that the woman being with childe feeleth no life nor motion of the child diuers moneths together, after the time of her conception, and after that ſhe hath
felt it ſtirre and moue oftentimes, there is an intermiſſion
wherein ſhe feeleth not the motion thereof a good ſpace together, and yet notwithſtanding becauſe in former times ſhe
hath felt it, ſhe is perſwaded that a liue child is in her, and cō-
fortably hopeth to haue happy trauaile. And thus it fareth
with Gods children oftentimes, after that by the ſeed of the
word faith is begotten and conceiued in them, they feele
no life, motion, nor vndoubted ſignes thereof a long while,
and after that they haue the remiſſion of their ſinnes and are
reconciled vnto God, they haue not the feeling and ſenſe of
pardon and reconciliation diuers moneths, yea ſometimes
many yeares together which the Lord in his wiſedome and
mercy doth that he may moue them hereby vnto more ſerious repentance, and earneſtly to hunger after a greater
meaſure of faith, carefully vſing the meanes ordained for
this purpoſe, and that they may more eſteeme and be more
thankefull for his inualuable benefits after that they haue
full aſſurance of them. And after they haue a feeling of faith
and other ſpirituall graces by their motions and fruits, oft-
times againe they are depriued of it, either becauſe they haue
wounded their conſciences by falling into ſome knowne
ſinne, or for that it pleaſeth the Lord to excerciſe their faith
and manifeſt his power in their weakeneſſe, moouing them

Rom.11.29.

Phil.1.6.

hereby

hereby to denie themselues and to rest wholy vpon him,
yeelding vnto him the whole glorie and praise of their saluation. What therefore is to bee done in such a case ? Surely
they are not vtterly to bee discouraged nor to suffer themselues to sinke into the gulfe of desperation; but as the sense
and feeling of their state ought to humble them vnder Gods
hand, and to mooue them to enter into a due examination
of themselues, and to a serious repentance for their sinnes,
so they must take comfort vnto themselues, and prop vp
their declining faith by calling to mind former times wherein the Lord hath shewed his mercifull and gratious countenance vnto them, and wherein they in token of thankefulnesse haue glorified God, by their holinesse and righteousnesse of life. An example whereof wee haue in the Prophet
Dauid, Psal. 77. who being grieuously afflicted, could not re-   Psal. 77.
ceaue in his soule any true comfort, for howsoeuer hee did
thinke vpon the Lord yet hee was still troubled, and though hee
prayed vnto him yet his spirit was full of anguish. What helpe
did he then find in this his present distresse? He telleth vs in
the first verse : *Then* (saith he) *I considered the dayes of old, and*
the yeares of ancient time ; I called to remembrance my song in
the night, namely his songs of thanksgiuing, whereby he had
praised God for his great benefits, and vers. 11. *I remembred*
the workes of the Lord, certainely I remembred thy wonders of
old. So the holy man *Iob* apprehending and conceyuing of   Iob. 31.
God as of his enemie, in respect of his present sense and feeling, and being mooued by his friends to doubt of his graces,
which he had receiued and to condemne himselfe for an hypocrite, comforteth himselfe and strengtheneth his faith in
the middest of al these grieuous tentations, by calling to his
remembrance his fruits of faith and workes of sanctification,
which he had discerned in himselfe in former times, as appeareth Chap. 31. Whose example if the children of God
in like distresse will follow, how miserable soeuer they are in
their present sense and feeling, yet they may receaue vnto
themselues comfort, because Gods gifts and calling are without repentance.

But

§.Sect.2.
*That true
faith resteth
faith in ourselfe
and feeling.*

But here Sathan will further obiect that we are not only without all sense and feeling of faith, but also that we doe sensibly feele the heauie burthen of Gods wrath, and plainely discerne his frowning and angrie countenance against vs, and therfore howsoeuer those children of God who are in his loue and fauoure may haue some faith in them although it doe not alwaies so sensibly appeare, yet it is impossibly that we should haue any sparke thereof seeing wee haue not any sense of Gods loue and fauour; nay doe sensibly perceaue the cleane contrary; to which wee are to answeare that faith doth not relie it selfe vpon our sence and feeling; for as the apostle saith *faith is the ground of things* (not presently inioyed but) *which are hoped for, and the euidence or demonstration of things* (not which are subiect to the senses and sensibly discerned but) *which are not seene,* Heb. 11.1 and we beleeue that such ioyes are prepared for vs *as neither eye hath seene, nor eare hath heard, nor the heart of man conceiued* as it is 1. Cor. 2.9. and it is a kind of infidelitie to beleeue onely those things which are subiect vnto our senses and vnderstandings; and therefore when *Thomas* would not beleeue that Christ was risen before it was made manifest to his senses hee is reproued for infidelitie, bee not (saith hee) faithlesse but faithfull. So that when our sense and feeling cease their faith beginneth his chiefe worke; & the most excellent faith sheweth it selfe most clearely when wee haue no sense and feeling, or when we discerne and feele the plaine contrarie; for it is an easie matter to be strong in faith when God sheweth himselfe gratious and mercifull; but when he appeareth vnto vs like an angrie iudge, when as his wrath flameth out against vs, then to behold his loue through the vizard of anger, to apprehend by faith his mercie and goodnesse towards vs, when our senses apprehend nothing but his wrath and displeasure, to growe to *Iobs* resolution in the middest of our bitter agonies and greiuous afflictions, *though hee kill me yet will I trust in him,* and when we haue receaued many repulses and bitter snubs yet with the Cananitish woman to continue our suite, argueth such a faith as is hardly found no

Heb.11.1.

1.Cor.2.9.

Iob.13.15.

Mat.15.

not

not in Ifraell. Our want of fenfe therefore of Gods loue and fauour doth not argue want of faith,for our faith is not grounded vppon our fenfe and feeling, but vppon Gods gratious promifes, immutable goodneffe , and infallible truth , and if euer we haue tafted of Gods loue and mercie, whatfoeuer wee apprehend in our prefent fenfe and feeling, faith concludeth that we are ftill in his loue and fauour, for *he is without change or fhadow of change* as the apoftle fpeaketh, Iam. 1. 17. *and* Iam. 1.1 7. *whom he loueth to the ende hee loueth them,* as our Sauiour hath taught vs. Ioh. 1 3. 1. Ioh. 13.1.

Though then our fenfe of Gods loue fayle yet may our faith continue ftrong, as appeareth plainely in the example of *Iob,* who though he conceiued of God in his fenfe and feeling that he had hiddē his face frō him & took him for his enemy, though he feemed to write bitter things againft him and made him to poffeffe the finnes of his youth, yet by a liuely faith he ftill refted and relied vpon him,protefting *that though he fhould flay him yet hee would truft in him.* as appeareth Iob. 13. 1 5.Yea Iob 13.15. our Sauiour Chrift himfelfe who could not finne through infidelitie, in refpect of his prefent fenfe and feeling complayneth that God had forfaken him.

If therefore Sathan goe about to perfwade vs that we are §. *Sect.*3. without faith becaufe we prefently apprehend not Gods loue *That we are* nor feele the fweete taft of his goodneffe wee are to anfweare *rather to be-* that wee are not to build our affurance vppon our owne fenfe *leeue Gods* and feeling, but vpon Gods vnchangable goodneffe and gra- *word then our* tious promiffes made vnto vs in Chrift Iefus;and if at any time *and feeling.* our fenfe and feeling tell vs one thing (namely that God hath withdrawne his loue from vs and will neuer againe looke gratioufly vpon vs) and the word of God affure vs of another thing (to witt that God will neuer forfake vs, but continue his loue towards vs vnto the end) wee are not to giue credit vnto our owne feeling but vnto Gods worde ; for otherwife what doe wee els but preferre our oft deceyuinge fenfe before Gods infallible truth,and imagine that wee can better difcerne and iudge of our eftate then God himfelfe ? but the worde of God telleth vs that if wee turne vnto the Lorde by vnfained

repentance

repentance forrowing for our finnes paft, hating our prefent corruptions, and defiring and indeauouring to mortifie the flefh and the lufts thereof and to ferue the Lord in holineffe and newneffe of life; and if we beleeue in Iefus Chrift refting vpon him for our faluation; or though prefently we feele not this faith and repentance yet if euer in former time wee haue difcerned it in vs, that then we are receiued into Gods loue and fauour and therefore fhall haue his loue continued vnto vs vnto the end, be made partakers of his gratious promifes & heires of euerlafting life; for the promifes of the gofpell are not reftrayned to thofe who feele their faith, but to thofe that haue faith, not to thofe who feele that they doe beleeue, but vnto thofe who doe beleeue.

§. Sect.4.
That conclu-
fions groun-
ded vpon our
fenfe are of-
ten falfe.

Neither is the not feeling of Gods loue and fauour a good argument to proue that wee are out of his loue and fauour, or the apprehenfion of his wrath and anger in our fenfe and feeling a found reafon to perfwade vs that wee are fubiect to his wrathfull difpleafure; feeing the being of a thing, and the fenfible difcerning of the thing to be, are diuers, and therefore howfoeuer at fometimes they concurre, yet oftentimes they are feuered and difioyned: fo that the conclufion which is inferred negatiuely from the fenfes, to proue the not being of their obiect is not onely commonly falfe, but alfo oftentimes abfurd and ridiculous; for example fometimes we fee not the beames of the funne, as in the night feafon, or whe̅ it is couered with fome thicke blacke cloud, but fhal we herehence co̅clude that the funne fhineth not, nor wil euer againe appeare vnto vs? So the bright beames of Gods loue and fauour are fometimes hidden from vs in the night of tentations, and fo fhadowed with the cloud of our grieuous finnes that we cannot fenfibly difcerne them, but fhall wee hence inferre that there is no grace and mercy to be found with God, or that he will neuer againe make them fhine vpon vs? The one is as abfurd as the other, and both groffly falfe. So fometimes the Sunne is eclipfed by the interpofition of the Moone, fo as we cannot difcerne his light or very dimly, but if any man fhould conclude from hence that it were quite ta-

ken

ken away, or that we were depriued vtterly of his life-preſeru-
uing influence, the experience of two or three howers would
ſhew the ſottiſh weakeneſſe of his ſenſible argumēt, and ſo in
like manner Gods fauour and loue are ſometimes ſo ecclipſed
with the interpoſition of ſome great afflictions, that wee cannot diſcerne them for a time or but very dimly, but if we ſhall
inferre hereof that they are quite taken from vs, and that they
caſt forth no comfortable influence on vs, our preſent preſeruation from being ſwallowed vp into vtter deſtruction, and
the ſpeedy returne of woonted ioy and conſolation, by the
apprehenſion of Gods loue and goodneſſe towards vs, will
euidently ſhew that this argument taken from the ſenſes is
void of reaſon.

Laſtly, it appeareth by the examples of Gods children from
time to time, that though they haue bene indued with a great
meaſure of faith, and in a high degree of fauour and loue with
almighty God, yet ſometimes in their owne ſenſe they haue
found in them, in ſtead of faith nothing but doubting, diffidence and infidelitie, and for Gods loue and fauour, they haue
apprehended nothing in their preſent feeling, but the wrathfull anger of God, and his greeuous diſpleaſure. Looke
vpon the holy man *Iob* who by Gods owne teſtimonie was
the iuſteſt man vpon earth, and highly in Gods loue and fauour, and you ſhal find that ſometimes he ſheweth in his grieuous afflictions no ſigne of faith, but groſſe doubting and in
outward apparance vtter deſpaire of Gods mercy and loue,
for he curſeth the day of his natiuitie, and wiſheth that he had
neuer beene borne, he complaineth that God was his enemy,
and had made him as a marke whereat hee ſhot venimed arrowes, that Gods terrors did fight againſt him, and that hee
did hide his louing countenance from him. So the Prophet
Dauid a man according to Gods owne hart ſheweth plainely
that ſometime he hath no ſenſe and feeling of the graces of
Gods ſpirit in him, as when he deſireth the Lord *to create in*
him a cleane hart and to renew a right ſpirit within him, to reſtore
him to the ioy of his ſaluatiō & to ſtabliſh him with his free ſpirit;
& ſometimes he apprehendeth in his preſent ſenſe & feeling,

§.Sect.5.
That Gods
deareſt chil-
dren haue not
at all times
ſenſibly diſ-
cerned Gods
loue, and the
graces of his
ſpirit in thē.

Pſal.51.10.
12.

M m 3

in stead of Gods loue and fauour, nothing but his wrath and displeasure, and therefore complaineth as one reiected and forsaken of God. So Psal. 22. 1. *My God, my God, why hast thou forsaken mee, and art so farre from my health, and from the words of my roaring.* 2. *O my God I crie by day but thou hearest not, and in the night and haue no audience.* And Psal. 77.7. he thus complaineth, *will the Lord absent himselfe for euer? and will he shew no more fauour?* 8. *Is his mercy cleane gone for euer? doth his promisse faile for euermore?* 9. *hath God forgotten to be merfull? hath he shut vp his tender mercies in displeasure?* 10. *And I said this is my death,&c.* So Psal. 88. 14. *Lord why doest thou reiect my soule and hidest thy face from me?* 15. *I am afflicted and at the point of death, from my youth I suffer thy terrors doubting of my life.* 16. *Thine indignations goe ouer me and thy feare hath cut me off.* The Prophet *Ieremy* likewise being grieuously afflicted in body and mind, was for a time depriued of the sense of Gods loue and fauour, apprehending nothing but present miserie, and in stead of faith, affiance in God, peace of conscience, and other sanctifying graces, he bewraieth his doubting, diffidence and impatiencie, cursing the day of his birth, and euen the man that brought first newes hereof to his father, and wishing that his mother had bene his graue, or her wōbe a perpetuall conception. As appeareth Ierem. 20. 14. 15. &c. The like may be said of the Apostle *Peter*, for where I pray you was the sense & feeling of his faith, affiance in God, zeale of his glorie, loue, feare, and other sanctifying graces, when as he shamefully denied his maister, yea forswore him with bitter cursing? and yet wee must eyther graunt that *Peter* at this time was indued with a liuely faith, or els that the prayer of our Lord and Sauiour Iesus Christ was not effectuall, for hee had praied for him that his faith might not faile, as appeareth Luk. 22. 32. But what should I insist in the examples of these the seruants of God, seeing the alone example of Christ himselfe is sufficient to cleare this point, for though hee were the onely begotten and best beloued Sonne of his heauenly father yet in his owne sense and feeling, hee apprehended nothing but Gods wrath and grieuous displeasure,

and

Psal. 22. 1.&
77.7. & 88.
14.

Ier. 20. 14.
15.

Luke 22. 32.

and lamentably complaineth as a man abandoned and caſt
out of all loue and fauour : My God, my God, why haſt thou
forſaken mee, which words ſhewe both Chriſts affiance in
God and his preſent apprehenſion in his ſenſe and feeling,
for in reſpeƈt of his affiance and truſt in God hee calleth him
ſtill his God, in reſpeƈt of his ſenſe and feeling hee complaineth that he is forſaken. Whereby it is manifeſt that a man
may be dearely beloued of God, and yet for a time apprehend
nothing but his wrath and diſpleaſure, that hee may haue
faith and affiance in God, yet at the ſame time be depriued
of all ſenſe and feeling of his loue and fauour. And therefore
when wee are excerciſed in the combate of tentations, let not
ſathan perſwade vs that we are vtterly depriued of the loue &
fauour of God, becauſe through the violence of his tentations and greeuouſneſſe of our affliƈtions we do not apprehend
it, nor that we are deſtitute of faith and all other ſpirituall graces becauſe we doe not ſenſibly diſcerne them in our feeling,
for this hath beene the ſtate of the deare children of God
from the beginning of the world and ſhall bee to the ende
thereof.

CHAP. XLV.

Of the meanes whereby our faith may be ſtrengthened and in-
creaſed.

Nd ſo much concerning thoſe reaſons whereby
we may proue that we haue faith, and alſo anſwere Sathans tentations whereby hee laboureth to perſwade vs that we are deſtitute thereof. The ſecond meanes whereby we may arme
our ſelues againſt Sathan and his ſuggeſtions, is that we moſt
earneſtly labour and indeauour after we haue found that wee
haue ſome faith to increaſe therein, and grow vp from faith
to faith vntill we come to that fulneſſe of perſwaſion which
will bring ſuch peace of conſcience as Sathan and all his tentations ſhall not be able to diſturbe. Otherwiſe we ſhall bee

§.Seƈt.1.
That all who
are indued
with true
faith, vſe the
means wher-
by it may bee
increaſed.

continually fubiect to feares and doubtings, and exceedingly
fhaken with Sathans tentations, and in truth not without
caufe if wee ftand ftill at a ftaie, for howfoeuer Sathan and all
the power of hell cannot preuaile againft the leaft meafure
of true faith to quench and vtterly to deftroy it, yet this will
bring no found comfort vnto thofe which reft contented with
this little quanticie and neuer labour after increafe, becaufe
this is a fhrewd prefumption that their faith is falfe and counterfaite, for affoone as the feede of true faith is fowne in vs,
and hath taken roote it fprooteth vp, and till it come to full
ripeneffe,in which refpect our Sauiour copareth it to a graine
of muftard feed, which though it be one of the leaft feeds of
the garden,yet it groweth to a great tree. Neither in truth is
it poffible that any who haue tafted of true faith, and of thofe
ineftimable benefits which it affureth vs of, fhould content
themfelues with a fmal pittance and neuer labour after more,
for who is it that hauing tafted and eaten a little bit of fome
delitious meate, doth not with a hungring appetite defire
more till he be filled and fatisfied, who is it that hath any
weake title and affurance of fome goodly inheritance, doth
not earneftly defire and vfe all good & lawfull means whereby his title may be ftrengthened and his affurance confirmed?
and can wee thinke that any haue truely tafted of faith and
the excellent benefits which accompany it, as namely affurance of Gods loue, and the remiffion of our finnes, peace of
confcience, ioy in the holy Ghoft, who content themfelues
with a little modicum and neuer hunger after more? or can
we imagine that wee haue any fmall title or true affurance of
thofe vnfpeakeable ioyes of Gods kingdome,and that vnualuable patrimonie of euerlafting glory, if we neuer vfe means
to confirme our title and ftrengthen our affurance? Surely it
is impoffible,and therefore if we would haue any found comfort and peace of confcience, if wee would euer attaine to a
certaine perfwafion that wee haue true faith indeed,let vs vfe
moft carefully and diligently all good meanes, whereby wee
may ftrengthen and confirme our faith, vntill it grow from a
fmall feed to a great tree, which will bring foorth plentifull
                                                         fruits

fruits of godlinesse and righteousnesse, and vntill it waxe of a small sparke vnto a great flame which will throughly warme our harts with true comfort, which are naturally frozen with feare and doubting, for howsoeuer Sathan cannot quench the least sparke of liuely faith, yet he will so couer it with the ashes of his tentations that we shall neither discerne the light nor feele the heate thereof.

Now the means which we are thus carefully to vse are of two sorts: the first tending to the encreasing and strengthening of our faith, the other seruing to preserue vs from doubting and desperation. The meanes to strengthen and increase our faith are diuers, the first is the frequent and attentiue hearing of Gods word, for as this is the ordinarie meanes whereby faith is begotten and begunne in vs, so is it a chiefe meanes to strengthen and confirme it; as it is that liuely seed from which faith doth spring, so is it that heauenly dewe whereby it is watered and increased from a litle plant to a great tree : and therefore as it is not sufficient for a fruitfull harueſt, that the blade or branch should sproute vp vnleſſe it bee watred continually with sweete dew and showers from heauen, and so preserued from dying and withering, so if euer we meane to reape the ripe fruits of faith to our euerlasting comfort, wee must bee carefull that not onely it take rooting, and bring foorth a blade of an outward profeſſion, but also that it may be watered with this heauenly dew of Gods word, otherwise when the sunne of affliction and perſecution ariseth it will die and wither.

§. Sect. 2.
The 1.meanes to increase faith, is the diligent hearing Gods word.

The second meanes to strengthen our faith is diligently to read and meditate in Gods word especially the Gospell, wherein is contained those sweete and gratious promisses which are made in definitely vnto all who repent of their sins, and beleeue in Iesus Christ, resting and relying vpõ him alone for their saluation. And to this purpose our Sauiour willeth the Iewes to *search the Scriptures, becauſe they are they which teſtifie of him.* Ioh. 5. 39. And hereby *Dauid* faith that hee was comforted in his troubles & euen quickned when he was dead. Pſal. 119. 50.

The 2. meanes meditation in Gods word.

Ioh.5.39.

Pſal.119. 50.

The

The 3. means holy conferēce

The third meanes is holy conference with our godly bre-thren; for hereby thofe which are falling are confirmed and the wearie handes and weake knees ftrengthened as *Eliphas*
Iob.4.3.4. fpeaketh Iob. 4.3.4. And thofe who are weake in faith are comforted and eftablifhed with the godly inftructions, profi-table exhortations, and fweete confolations of thofe who are more ftrange; and therefore the Apoftle *Paul* exhorts thofe who had attayned vnto a great meafure of faith that they ad-mitt fuch as were weake into their companie to be made par-takers of their Chriftian conferences to the ende that hereby they might be more and more ftrengthened and confirmed.
Rom.14.1 Rom. 14.1.

The 4. means the vfe of the facraments.

The fourth meanes is the holy vfe of the facraments; for the Lord hath added them as feales to the handwriting of his couenant of grace to confirme our faith in the full affurance of his promifes, and to take away all doubting. For whereas the weake confcience might make fome fcruple in refpect that the promifes of the gofpell in the preaching of the word are deliuered indefinitely and after a generall manner, in the vfe of the facraments they are affured vnto them particularly and as it were by name, and that not after fome obfcure and hidden maner, but moft familiarly by fuch common fignes as are fubiect to the fenfes and within the reach of the fhal-loweft capacitie.

The 5. means good workes.

A fitt meanes to confirme our faith is to be continually conuerfant in good workes, and to bring forth the fruites of holy obedience, for hereby our faith is excercifed and by ex-cercife ftrengthened and increafed; whereas contrariwife the neglect hereof doth wound the confcience and fo quench the liuely heate of faith that though it bee not quite extin-guifhed, yet it will not fenfibly be difcerned. As therefore the ftrength of the bodie is increafed by excercife and for want thereof waxeth faint and languifheth, and as the ftomacke is by outward excercife of the bodie made more fitt to per-forme his dutie of concoction ; fo our faith being excercifed in good workes is made more ftrong and fitt to performe his dutie in applying Chrift and the fweete promifes of the gofpel
vnto

vnto vs, and without this spirituall excercise it waxeth faint and the strength thereof abateth.

The last meanes to strengthen and increase our faith is continuall and feruent prayer, for faith is not in our owne power but *it is the free gift of God*, as the Apostle teacheth vs, Ephe. 2. 8. neither can any man come vnto our Sauiour Christ by a liuely faith except it be giuen him of the father, as himselfe speaketh. Ioh. 6. 65. And therefore when wee see the sm*all* measure of our faith, we are with the apostles to pray vnto the Lord that hee will increase it. Luk. 17. 5. And when wee perceiue that it is grieuously assaulted with doubting and infidelitie, we are in feruencie of spirit to crie out with the father of the possessed childe : *Lorde I beleeue helpe my vnbeleefe.* Mark. 9. 24. And then we may be assured that the Lord will heare vs and satisfie our godly desires, making vs to growe vp from faith to faith, till at length wee attaine vnto such a fulnesse of perswasion, that wee shall bee able truely to say with the Apostle; *I am perswaded that neither death nor life, nor angels, nor principalities, nor powers, nor things present, nor things to come, nor height, nor depth, nor any other creature shall bee able to seperate vs from the loue of God, which is in Christ Iesus our Lord.* as it is Rom. 8. 38. 39.

And these are the meanes which properly tende to the strengthening and increasing of our faith, which whosoeuer carefully and conscionably vse, they shall assuredly find them effectuall for this purpose : Now wee are to speake of those meanes whereby wee may bee preserued from doubting and desperation, of which I shal not neede to speake much, seeing the most of these points are handled before.

The first meanes to preserue vs from desperation is to call continually vnto our remembrance that the promisses of the gospell are generall and indefinite, excluding none how vnworthie and sinnefull soeuer they be, if they doe not exclude themselues through their owne infidelitie; So Mat. 11. 28. our Sauiour calleth all humbled and repentant sinners without exception, saying, *Come vnto me all yee that labour and are heauie laden and I will ease you.* and Ioh. 3. 16. *God so loued the world*

The 6. means feruent prayer

Ephe. 2. 8

Ioh. 6 65.

Luk. 17. 5.

Mark. 9. 24.

Ro. 8. 38. 39.

§. Sect. 3.
Of the means whereby we may be preserued from doubting and desperation.

The 1. means.

Mat. 11. 28.

Ioh. 3. 16.

world that he sent his only beloued son, that as many as beleue in him
Mat.9.13. *should not perish but haue euerlasting life.* So Matth. 9. 13. our
Sauiour saith *that hee came not to call the righteous but sinners to*
repentance; either then refuse the name of repentant sinner or
Ioh. 6. 40. acknowledge that he came to saue thee. and Ioh. 6. 40. our
sauiour saith *that it is his fathers will who sent him that euery man*
who beleeueth in him should haue euerlasting life. Seeing therefore God taketh no exception, nor excludeth any let vs not
exclude our selues through our want of faith and infidelitie.

The 2 means   Secondly we are to consider that the Lord hath not onely
propounded his gratious promises vnto vs, but also hath com-
Mark.1.15. maunded vs to beleeue them. So Mark. 1. 15. *Repent and*
1.Ioh 3.23. *beleeue the gospell.* and 1. Ioh. 3. 23. *This then is his commaun-*
dement, that wee beleeue in the name of his sonne Iesus Christ &c.
now to beleeue in Christ is not onely to beleeue that he is a sauiour, for this euē the diuels beleeue also, but to beleeue that he
is our sauiour & to rest wholy vpō him for our saluatiō, & to say
Gal.2. 20. with the Apostle *Paul*, Gal.2.20. *I liue by the faith in the sonne*
of God, who hath loued me and giuen himselfe for me. And to the
end that wee may be armed against doubting, and enabled to
perfourme this commaundement, it hath pleased the Lord to
Heb.6.18. adde vnto his word his oath, that *by two immutable things*
wherein it is impossible that God should lye wee should haue strong
consolation, as the apostle speaketh, Heb.6.18. Yea, he hath also vnto his word and handwriting annexed his Sacraments
as seales, that there might be no place left for doubting. Seeing therefore the Lord hath expresly commaunded vs to beleeue, and vsed al meanes to enable vs to perfourme his commaundement, let vs not now dispute the question whether
we are worthy to beleeue or no, or whether such grieuous sinners are bound to this dutie, but setting all excuses aside let vs
beleeue in obedience to Gods commaundement.

The 3. means.   Thirdly, we must not alwaies set before vs the innumerable multitude and huge waight of our sins, but withal cal to
our remembrance the infinite mercies of God and merits of
Christ, who hath offered vnto his father a propitiatorie sacri-
1.Iohn 2. 2. fice and full satisfaction for all our *sinnes, and not for ours onely*
but

but for the sinnes of all the world, as the Apostle speaketh, 1 Ioh. 2.2. Seeing therefore our debt how great soeuer it be is already discharged; and our sinnes how outragious soeuer they be, are fully punished long agoe in our Sauiour Christ, and seeing God himselfe who hath receiued this debt and taken this punishment, is of infinite iustice and mercy, why should we now despaire of pardon? Nay, why should wee not most certainely be assured that the roull and reckoning of our sins how long soeuer it be, is quite blotted out and cancelled, so as they shall neuer againe be laid to our charge.

Fourthly, wee are to consider that desperation it selfe is a most hainous and outragious sinne, for it causeth men to denie Gods truth in his promises & to account him a liar, as the Apostle plainely speaketh, 1.Ioh.5.10. *Hee that beleeueth not God hath made him a liar, because he beleeued not the record, that God witnessed of that his Sonne*, it maketh them to denie the infinitenes of his mercies as being ouermatched with the multitude of their sinnes, and the sufficiencie of Christs merites, as though they were not a full satisfaction for their horrible offences: yea it maketh them to denie Gods iustice in thinking that he will punish that sinne againe in them, which hath already beene punished in Christ, and exact that debt which he hath already discharged. Now to denie the truth, mercy, and iustice of God is to denie God himselfe, for his attributes are his essence, the truth of God is the true God, the mercy of God is the mercifull God, and the iustice of God is the iust God. So that he who despaireth falleth into the most horrible and capitall sinne of Atheisme euen the highest degree of wickednesse, and therefore more hainously offendeth God by this sinne alone, then by all his other sins whatsoeuer, though they appeare neuer so monstrous and abominable in his owne eies. For example the sinne of *Cain* in despairing of Gods mercy, was far more horrible then his monstrous sinne which he comitted in murthering his owne brother: the sinne of *Iudas* in despairing of Gods mercy, was without comparison greater then his sinne, in betraying his Lord and maister, in a word to commit Idolatrie, blasphemy, murther, adultery, &

such

§. Sect.4.
The 4. means to consider that desperation is a most haynous sin.
1.Ioh.5.10.

such like are hainous sinnes, but vtterly to despaire of Gods mercy is greater then they all. Though then wee haue committed other horrible wickednes against the Lord, yet in no case let vs despaire for this were to adde sinne vnto sinne, and to clogg our consciences more with the last then with all the former, til with their intollerable waight they presse vs down vnto hell; you would count him worse then madd who being oppressed with a heauy burthen should (in stead of vsing other meanes to ease himselfe) adde thereunto a double or treble waight, till hee were pressed downe groueling vnto the earth; but assuredly such and greater madnesse it is when wee feele our consciences clogged with a heauy burthen of sinne, in stead of seeking ease in comming to Christ by a liuely faith, to fall into vtter desperation and thereby to add a treble waight to the already intollerable burthen of sinne, which lieth vpon our consciences vntill they be pressed down into the torments of hell. Euery one would esteeme him a most desperate wretch, who hauing offended such a gratious Prince, as would most surely forgiue him vpon his vnfained sorrow for his fault, should in stead of humbling himselfe and asking pardon desperately refuse his Princes mercy, and with all denie his truth in his promises his mercy, iustice, and euen disauow him for being a lawfull Prince. But such and much more wickednesse doe they desperately commit who hauing offended God by their grieuous sinnes, who is so gratious & mercifull, that he would most certainely forgiue them vpon their true repentance, in stead of humbling themselues by vnfained sorrow, doe desperately refuse to bee partakers of his mercy, and not onely so but deny the infinitenes of his mercy; iustice, truth in his promisses, and consequently his godhead and being. And therefore when (the waight of sinne pressing vs) Sathan perswadeth vs to despaire of mercy and forgiuenes, let vs in any case resist this tentation, and boldly say vnto the tempter; it is inough and too much that I haue offended my gratious God with my other sinnes, though I doe not ad thereunto this sin which is greater then all the rest, the waight of my other wickednesse is already too too heauy vpō

my

my conscience,& therefore farre bee it frō me to load it with a farre more vnsupportable burthen; I haue already too much dishonoured my good God by my horrible sinnes, and therefore I will in no case more dishonour him, now then in committing all my other sinnes, by denying his mercie, iustice, truth, and euen the godhead it selfe; for what were this but being alreadie in a burning feauer to cast my selfe into the fire, or being gone ouer the shooes in the filthie puddle of sinne to plunge my selfe ouer head and eares, and euen to drowne my selfe in the bottomelesse gulfe of desperation? nay rather now I will breake of my sinnes by vnfained repentance and turne vnto the Lord whom I haue offended, assuring my selfe that his mercies are infinite, and therefore he is readie to forgiue, and the merites of Christ a full satisfaction for all my sinnes though many and hainous,and therefore in him I may bouldly chalenge forgiuenesse as a thing of right appertayning to me.

And thus are wee to resist Sathans tentations and though wee be often foyled yet to rise againe, in no case suffring him to plucke out of our hand the shield of faith, though he hath disarmed vs of the brest-plate of righteousnesse;for if once we be depriued of this part of this spirituall armour wee shall lie open to all his blowes and thrusts,vntil we be wounded to the very death.

But most lamentable it is to see the greeuous miserie of poore humbled sinners whereinto they are brought through the violence of Sathans tentations; for howsoeuer feeling the heauie waight of their other sinnes they earnestly desire to be freed frō the,howsoeuer being tormented with the greeuous smart of their other wickednesse they hate and abhorre it,yet they easily suffer themselues to bee plunged into desperation with euery friuoulous tentation;and quietly offer their hands to be manacled, and bound in these giues of hell without resistance. But let all such stirre vp themselues, and gather their oppressed spirites togeather,saying to their owne consciences I hate and detest from my heart my former wickednesse, and shall I now entertaine a sinne more horrible then all the rest;

§.*Sect.5.*
Though the afflicted conscience abhorreth other sinnes yet it easily inclyneth to desperation.

the

the burthen of my other sinnes oppresse me and make me earnestly to desire ease, and shall I adde a loade farre more intollerable to my afflicted conscience? I am filled with shame and confusion because by my former sinnes I haue dishonoured my gratious God? and shal I continue more to dishonour him by doubting of and denying his mercy, iustice, and truth in his promises? I haue heretofore with *Iudas* betrayed my Sauiour Christ vnto the death, yea and with my sinnes I haue whipped, mocked, and crucified him, and now hee hauing made full satisfaction for my sinnes, and called me vnto him that he may ease me of this intollerable burthen, should I with *Iudas* refuse to come desperately cast of al hope of mercie and become mine owne hangman? be it farre from mee, nay as I hate all other sinne so let me hate this aboue all the rest, as being more hainous then al the rest; as I desire to be eased and freed from the heauie burthen of other my wickednesse, so I will with all my power resist Sathan when he seeketh to loade me with this loade of desperation as being farre more intollerable; heretofore I haue dishonoured God by my sins, but now I will giue him glorie in beleeuing and acknowledging his infinite mercie, goodnesse, iustice, and truth in his promises; and seeing by my sinnes I haue crucified the Lorde of life, I will not ad hereunto this outragious wickednesse, to tráple his pretious bloud vnder my filthie feete as a thing vnholy and of no worth, neither will I through my vnbeleefe make it to be spilt in vaine; but now with all care and conscience I will gather it vp as a most precious balme, and with the hand of faith apply it to those greatly gashes, and deepe woundes which sinne hath made in my soule and conscience, and with this spirituall lauer I will washe my poluted soule till it bee throughly purged from all vncleanesse. And seeing I haue depriued my soule of that inherent righteousnesse wherewith it was indued by creation, now I will apply thereunto a farre more excellent righteousnesse by the hand of faith, euen the righteousnesse of Iesus Christ God and man, wherewith being adorned I may boldly offer my selfe into the presence of my heauenly father & receiue the blessing of euerlasting happines.

Lastly

Lastly we are to consider that as desperation is a sinne in §. *Sect.6.*
it owne nature most grieuous, so also it is vnto our selues most *That despe-*
pernitious, for whereas other sinnes make vs worthy of the *ration is a sin*
torments of hell and eternall condemnation, this as it aboue *most pernisti-*
al the rest intitleth vs vnto the right of this hellish inheritance, *ous.*
so also it entreth vs into the most certaine and present possession thereof euen whilest we liue vpon the earth. For what
are the torments of a despairing conscience but the flashings
of hell fire ? and what are their blasphemies which they vtter
against God, and their impatient cursinges of their accursed
selues, but the yelling cries of damned soules? And therefore
if we would not cast our selues into the iawes of hell, if wee
would not whilest we liue beginne to die an euerlasting death,
let vs in no case suffer our selues to bee plunged with the violence of Sathans tentations into this bottomelesse pitt of vtter
desperation.

Yea will the afflicted soule say but how should I auoyde §. *Sect.7.*
it, seeing I am forcibly pressed into it with the intollerable *That wee*
waight of my sinnes, and with the sense and apprehention *must hope a-*
of Gods fearefull wrath and displeasure, feeling no comfort *gainst hope*
nor assurance that euer I shall receiue pardon ? to which I an- *& beleeue a-*
swere that yet in no case they are to despaire, but to hope a- *gainst beliefe*
gainst hope, and to beleeue against beliefe, and as it were from
the bottome of hell to cast vp the eye of faith into heauen, laying hold of Gods mercies, and Christs merites; knowing that
faith is of things not seene neither with the bodely eye, nor
with the eye of reason, and that the Lord seemeth often to
hate those whome in truth hee dearely loueth. For so long
as wee beleeue Gods promises and haue some hope that
our sinnes are eyther pardoned or at least pardonable there
is certaine comfort; but when as all hope is cast of and that
we reiect all Gods promises through vnbeliefe and fall into
vtter desperation, there nothing remaineth but most certaine destruction; when sinne lieth vpon vs, it no question
exceedingly vexeth vs with the torments of conscience, but
if we despaire we presently in stead of obtaining ease cast our
selues into the torments of hell; the panges of conscience cau-

sed

fed by the fenfe of the heauy burthen of finne, are a good meanes to bring vs to Chrift, that we may be eafed of this burthen; but defpaire ftayeth vs in the midway, and vtterly debarreth vs from euer being partakers of Chrift or any of his benefits. And therefore though the burthen of finne be neuer fo irkefome and grieuous, yet let vs be contented to beare it till we come vnto Chrift for eafe, let vs beware in any cafe that we doe not faint through impatiencie and want of hope and fo fall into defperation, for fo fhall wee but increafe the waight of our finnes in exceeding meafure, which already we thinke an intollerable burthen, and confequently our horrour of confcience; fo fhall we bring our felues from a doubtfull or rather hopeful ftate, to moft certaine and prefent deftruction, fo fhall wee change our temporarie griefe for that which is euerlafting, and the terrours of confcience for the torments of hell; fo fhall that which wee moft feare and flee, prefently ouertake and ouerwhelme vs; for whileft in an horrible maner we feare the paines of hell, we caft our felues into them by falling into vtter defperation; as if a man for feare of death fhould cut his owne throate, or for feare of hanging fhould drinke fome deadly poyfon, whereby they are prefently tormented with that which they fearefully abhorred, and choofe rather to bee oppreffed with the euill they feared, then any longer to indure the feare it felfe. Which howfoeuer it may carry fome fhew of reafon in vndergoing a momentany and temporarie death, wherein oftentimes the feare is more intollerable then the paine feared; yet it is extreame madneffe to plunge a mans felfe body and foule into the eternall torments of hell, rather then for a time to indure the horrour thereof, feeing this horrour and feare is but a fmall fleabiting in refpect of thofe hellifh punifhments, and as it were but a fmoke of that eternall fire.

CHAP. XLVI.

Sathans tentations concerning fmalneffe, and weakneffe of faith anfwered.

And

Nd so much for answering those tentations, wher- §. *Sect.*1.
by Sathan laboureth to perswade the afflicted *There is no*
Christians that they haue no faith, wherewith if *such perfect*
he cannot preuaile, in the next place hee will tell *faith, which*
them that their faith is so small if it be any at all, so ouerwhel- *is not assaul-*
med with doubting, so vnfruitfull, and so mixt with imper- *ted with*
fections, that it will not bee effectuall and sufficient for their *doubting.*
saluation. Which tentation if we would withstand, we must
not dreame or imagine that to haue a true faith, is to haue a
perfect faith which is neuer assaulted with doubting nor shaken with any tentations, for there is no such faith to be found
in any of Gods childrē, seing the most perfect are partly flesh
and partly spirit, and as the fruite of the spirit is faith and affiance in God, so the fruit of the flesh is doubting and infidelitie, & these continually assault & fight one against another.

Againe wee are to know that there are diuers degrees of *That there*
true faith, and that all the children of God haue it not in the *are diuers*
like measure: for some haue attained to a strong and great *degrees of*
measure of faith, as those who are indued with much know- *faith in Gods*
ledge, and firmely assent vnto that which they know, and are *children.*
most certainely perswaded of their saluation in Christ, and
that all the gratious promises of the gospell doe belong vnto
them, so as nothing in the world shalbe able to seperate them
from the loue of God which is in Christ Iesus our Lord; o-
thers are weake and indued with a small measure of faith, as
those who haue little knowledge, weake assent and perswasion, being yet but babes in Christ, and growing vp from faith
to faith, as the Apostle speaketh Rom.1.17. till at length they *Rom.1.17.*
attaine to that fulnesse of perswasion, of which mention is
made, Heb.10.22. Now wee are to hould first that this small *Heb.10.22.*
and weake measure of faith is notwithstanding a true faith,
and therefore sufficient for the saluation of those who are indued therewith, neither are the promises of the gospell made
to those onely who haue a strong faith, but to those who haue
a true faith; Ioh.1.12. *As many as receiued him hee gaue to* *Ioh.1.12.*
them prerogatiue to be the sonnes of God, euen to them that beleeue
in his name. And Iohn 3.18. *He that beleeueth shalbe saued,* in *Ioh.3.18.*

which and such like places there is no measure of faith propounded, but the promises are made indefinitely to all that beleeue, how small and weake soeuer their faith be in respect of the qualitie and apprehension, so that in regard of the qualitie it be true and liuely.

§.Sect.2.
That a weake & smal faith may be a true and liuely faith.

That a weake and small measure of faith is true and liuely faith, it is manifest both by reason and also plaine testimonies of the Scripture; for the first: diuersitie of degrees in quantitie of a thing doth not take away and annihilate the existence & true being thereof; for example a smal drop of water is as well and truely water as the whole Ocean, a little sparke is true fire both in respect of substance & qualitie, as well as a mighty flame, a little man is as truly a man as a great Giant : and so a little faith is as well a true faith as a full perswasion; neither doth the small quantitie take away the being , nature, and truth thereof.   Secondly, this also manifestly appeareth by the Scriptures , whereas many are said to haue faith and to beleeue, who hearing the doctrine of Christ & seing his miracles beleeued, & acknowledged him to be the true Messias & their Sauiour, though at the same time they had attained to an exceeding small measure of knowledge, and were ignorant of many of the chiefe principles of Christian religion, because they nourished not this their ignorance, but resolued to vse all those good meanes of increasing in knowledge which God hath ordayned for this purpose. And thus many of the Samaritanes are sayd to haue beleeued for the saying of the woman and because of his owne word. Ioh. 4. 39. 41,

Ioh.4.39.41
ver. 52.

Thus a certaine ruler and all his houshould are saide to haue beleeued, when they sawe the miracle which our Sauiour wrought in curing the rulers sonne of his feauer only with his word, ver. 52. Yea the apostles themselues whose faith our Sauiour Christ compareth to a firme rocke against which the gates of hell should neuer preuaile, were notwithstanding indued with a weake and small measure of faith, before the ascension of our Sauiour, and sending of the holy ghost. For they were ignorant euen of the maine principles of christian religion, and of diuers articles of faith, and consequently could not beleeue,

leeue, assent, or be perswaded of those things which they did
not vnderstand. For example howsoever they knew and ac- Mat.16.18.
knowledged that our Sauiour Christ was the promised Messias, yet they were ignorant that he should redeeme mankind
by his death; for when he foretold that he should be deliuered into the hands of the Gentiles to bee crucified, it is saide
that they vnderstood none of these things. Mat. 20. 18. Luk. Mat.20. 18.
9.45.. So also they knew not that beeing dead he should rise Luk.9.45.
againe the third day as the Euangelist sheweth Mar. 9. 32. Mar.9.32.
And when they heard thereof by the women they thought
it a fained thinge as it is Luk. 24. 11. They were ignorant also Luk.24.11.
of his ascension as appeareth. Ioh. 13. 36. and 14. 5. and of Ioh.13.38.
his kingdome, for they dreamed of an earthly kingdome, and and 14.5.
of worldly preferments which they were to haue by him, as we Actes 1.6.
may see. Act. 1.6. Mar. 10. 37. By all which it plainely ap- Mar.10. 37.
peareth that though the Apostles were indued with a true
faith, yet their faith was exceeding weake and small, as also it
is most euident in that reprehention vsed by our sauiour when
they were in some appearance of danger. Matth. 8. 26. *where-* Mat.8.26.
fore are yee fearefull o yee of little faith.

  And therefore though wee find our faith to be weake §. *Sect.3.*
and small yet let not Sathan perswade vs that for this cause *That all pow-*
it is false and counterfaite, or that wee shall easily bee ouer- *er of hell can-*
come of euery tentation and neuer perseuer vnto the end that *not preuaile*
wee may bee saued; seeing a weake and small faith may bee a *against the*
true faith, against which how weake in it selfe soeuer it be, yet *smallest mea-*
the gates of hell shall neuer preuaile against it, for the wea- *sure of true*
ker our faith is, the stronger shall wee find Gods power in Phil. 3.12.
sustayning and preseruing vs, the more that Sathan laboureth
to winnow vs in the fiue of his tentations, the more effectually will our Sauiour Christ make intercession for vs that our
faith faile not; the feebler our faith is in apprehending Christ,
the more powerfull will his spirit bee in apprehending vs and
in ioyning vs inseparably in a holy communion with him. But
yet wee must not content our selues with a small and weake
measure of faith, but earnestly labour after more perfection,
and to grow from faith to faith, till we attaine vnto fulnesse of

perswasion.

That we must not content our selues with a small measure of faith   persuasion, Otherwise we shall make it manifest that we deceiue our selues with a shew and shadow of faith, and that as yet we haue no true faith indeede, which as it resembleth the graine of mustard seed in respect of the smalnes at the beginning thereof, so also in the growth & increase, & therefore if euer we would attaine vnto peace of conscience, and assurance that wee are indued with a true and liuely faith, we must earnestly labour in the vse of those meanes ordayned of God for the increase of faith, and feruently pray vnto God that he will not onely sowe the seede of faith in our harts, but also that he will so water it with the dew of his grace and holy spirite that it may grow from a small seede to a greate tree, and that he will neuer cease blowing this smoking flaxe with the breath of the same his holy spirit, till it increase from a little sparke to a mightie flame, whereby our hartes being warmed with true comfort, may with feruent zeale seeke to glorifie his holy name by our christian and holy conuersation.

§.Sect.4.
That the least faith is acceptable to God.
Mat.12.20.   Secondly we are to know that how weak & smal soeuer our faith be so it be true the Lord wil not reiect it, nor vs in regard of it, *for he wil not breake the bruised reed nor quench the smoking flax till he bring forth iudgment vnto victorie,* as himselfe hath spoken. Mat.12.20. He wil not contemne the least measure of his own grace which he hath bestowed vpon vs; for though it be in neuer so small a quantitie yet if it be true it is his owne gift, and his *gifts are without repentance,* neither doth he euer contemne that which himselfe hath giuen, nor take it away **Mat.25.29.** after it is once bestowed; nay rather *to him that hath shall bee giuen vntill hee haue abundance,* he that hath receiued 5. talents shall receaue 5. more, yea and hee that hath but one if hee doe not hide it, but vse it to his maisters glorie shall be accepted and haue his talent doubled. We reade in the scriptures that Christ reproued some for their small faith, but yet we neuer read nor heard that he reiected and cast of any, though their faith were neuer so weake if it were true, no not him who cried out in the sense of his owne weaknesse; *Lorde I beleeue,*
Mar.9.24 *helpe thou my vnbeliefe.* And therefore if with him wee find a true faith in vs, at least in some measure, and though it be exceedingly

ceedingly mingled with doubting and aſſaulted with infidelitie, yet if wee can with this man earneſtly pray the Lorde to
helpe our vnbeliefe, and with the Apoſtles hartily crie out :
O Lord increaſe my faith, the Lord will accept of our hartie
deſire, and graunt our requeſt which is made by his owne ſpirite in vs, and that according vnto his owne wil.

Thirdly we muſt vnderſtand that faith doth not iuſtifie *§. Sect.5.*
and ſaue vs by it ſelfe as it is a vertue or facultie of the mind *That faith*
and hart, or in reſpect of it owne excellencie, quantitie, and *doth not*
worthineſſe, (for what were this but to embrace againe the *iuſtifie vs as*
doctrine of the papiſts which we haue reiected, and to ſeeke *it is a worke*
for iuſtification in our ſelues, and for our owne merites and *or facultie in*
worthineſſe ?) but as an inſtrument whereby we lay hold of, *instrument*
and apply vnto our ſelues Chriſt Ieſus with his righteouſneſſe *which appli-*
and merites, by which onely wee appeare iuſt before God; *eth Chriſt*
now a weake faith as truly though not ſo powerfully doth ap- *vnto vs.*
prehend and apply Chriſt Ieſus and all his merites and obedience as a ſtronger faith, euen as a ſmall and weake hand if it
be able to reach vp the meate to the mouth, doth as well performe it dutie for the nouriſhment of the body as one of greater ſtrength; becauſe it is not the ſtrength of the hand but the
goodneſſe of the meate which nouriſheth the bodie : So a
weake faith laying hould of Chriſt and applying him and his
benefites, to the beleeuer, is ſufficient to nouriſh him to euerlaſting life as well as a ſtronger, becauſe it is not the worthines or excellencie of the inſtrument, but of Chriſt which it apprehendeth that is effectual for our iuſtification & eternal ſaluatiō. So in like maner as a ſmal & weak hãd is able to receiue
an almes as a ſtronger and greater, and as a little eye doth
ſee the whole body of ſunne, or ſome great mountaine as well
as a bigger : ſo our faith though weake and ſmall, doth apprehend Chriſt as truely and effectually for the ſaluation of the
beleeuer, as the greateſt and moſt ſtrong, our Sauiour Chriſt
compareth himſelfe to the braſen Serpent, and the beleeuing Ioh.3.14.
Chriſtian ſtong with the ſtinge of ſin to the Iſraelites which
did behold it to the end they might be cured : now we know
that all of them were not a like ſharpe ſighted, but ſome were

poreblind, ſome bleare eyed', ſome ſawe it but exceeding
weakely and dimly, but yet notwithſtanding as many as looked on it were cured and healed, though they were neuer ſo
weake ſighted; ſo whoſoeuer being ſtong with ſinne do looke
vpon Chriſt with the eye of faith, reſting vpon him alone for
their ſaluation, though they bee neuer ſo weake ſighted, yet
they ſhalbe reſtored to health and be eternally ſaued, becauſe
it is not in their ſight but in the obieƈt thereof Chriſt Ieſus to
iuſtifie before God, and to purchaſe for them eternall ſaluation.

CHAP. XLVII.

Other tentations concerning faith anſwered.

§.Seƈt.1.
Sathans ten-
tation con-
cerning the
certainty and
conſtancie of
faith anſwe-
red.

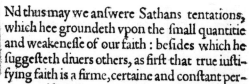

Nd thus may we anſwere Sathans tentations,
which hee groundeth vpon the ſmall quantitie
and weakeneſſe of our faith : beſides which he
ſuggeſteth diuers others, as firſt that true iuſtifying faith is a firme, certaine and conſtant perſwaſion, whereas ours if wee haue any at all is weake and feeble, inſtable, inconſtant and wauering, and that it is not onely
continually aſſaulted but alſo often foiled and ouercome with
doubting and infidelitie, and therefore that it is but a ſhadow
of faith, and not true faith indeed. The which tentation wee
may eaſily anſwere if wee but remember that which already
hath beene deliuered; namely that the beſt cannot attaine in
this life vnto ſuch perfeƈtion of faith as is quite freed from all
infirmities and corruption, that there is diuers degrees of true
iuſtifying faith, ſome weaker, ſome ſtronger, ſome in greater,
and ſome in ſmaller quantitie, ſome like ſmooking flaxe, and
a graine of muſtard ſeed, & ſome like a bright burning flame
which giueth light, and the liuely heat of true comfort to
thoſe who are indued therewith, and of as high growth as the
greateſt tree in the garden, and yet all true faith and ſufficient for ſaluation. That ſo long as wee continue in this life
our knowledge is but imperfeƈt and vayled with much darkneſſe

neffe and ignorance, *for we know but in parte,* as euen the apoftle fpeaketh in his owne perfon, 1.Cor.13.12. And therefore 1.Cor.13.12.
our affent and perfwafion muft needs be imperfect, and but
in part, and often affaulted with much doubting : that howfoeuer faith and doubting are oppofed in their owne nature,
yet notwithftanding they may be together in the fame fubiect in refpect of diuers partes. For wee are partly flefh and
partly fpirit, and thefe two with their feuerall fruits do continually fight and ftriue one againft the other, and fometimes
the flefh, fometimes the fpirit with their feuerall fruits get the
vpper hand, in the meane time both retaining their owne
nature and properties, howfoeuer they doe not fo euidently
appeare nor fo powerfully worke their feuerall actions, when
the aduerfe part preuaileth, and hath put them to the foile;
for example, faith which is a fruite of the fpirit, is continually
affaulted by doubting, which is a fruite of the flefh, and proceedeth from the roote of infidelitie, and fometime faith preuaileth and fometime it receiueth the foyle, but yet at the
fame time howfoeuer wee cannot fenfibly difcerne it, nor
the actions thereof, yet it retaines it owne nature and properties, neyther is it depriued of his firmeneffe, conftancie and
certainty howfoeuer they be for a time couered & hid out of
our fight, like the fire vnder the afhes, or the Sunne vnder a
cloud, as before I haue faid.

Though therefore we finde in vs much inconftancie and
doubting, yet let not Sathan perfwade vs that thefe are of
the nature and properties of our faith, and that therefore our
faith is not true but temporarie falfe and counterfaite, for this
inconftancie and doubting, proceedeth not from faith and
from the fpirituall and regenerate part, but from the flefh and
the part vnregenerate; and therefore howfoeuer it is affaulted, and fometimes foyled by them, yet in it owne nature it is
true certaine and conftant.

Secondly, he will fuggeft that the Saints mentioned in the §. Sect. 2.
Scriptures, had moft certaine & ftrong faith & in exceeding *Sathans ten-*
great meafure, that they brought forth cōtinually moft nota- *tation groū-*
ble fruits thereof, & were not fubiect to fuch infirmities and *ded on the*
                                                 doubtings, *ftrong faith*

of some of Gods children answered.

doubtings.as wee feele in our selues. To which we are to an-swere,that this tentation is full of vntruth,and hath no sound part in it : for first we are to assure our selues that they fell into manifold doubtings and were subiect vnto innumerable in-firmities and corruptions,which are not specified in the booke of God : neither was it fitte or expedient that it should be a register of all humane infirmities, and of their manifold falls, but onely that some should bee recorded for our warning, that wee might more warily watch ouer our selues, least wee should fall into the like sinnes, and for our comfort also when wee are fallen, in that our case is common with Gods dea-rest children; in which respect the Scriptures is not wan-ting Looke vpon *Abraham* the father of the faithfull whose faith was so strong that he aboue hope beleeued vnder hope, and you shall see that his faith notwithstanding was some-times shaken with diffidence and doubting, as when distru-sting Gods gratious promisses made vnto him, and not re-sting vpon his almighty power, he was content to take vnto him *Hagar* his maide and commit sinne with her, that so by his owne deuise he might make good Gods promisse and ob-taine the blessed seed, as though God could not perfourme that which he had spoken, vnlesse he helped him by such vn-lawfull meanes. So where was the strength and constancie of *Moyses* faith when hee dishonoured God before the peo-ple in not beleeuing his word, & by shewing his impatiencie.

Num.20.10 11.

Numb.20. 10. 11. where was the strength and constancie of *Dauids* faith, when he complaineth that he was forsaken, that God had fayled in his promisses, that he had forgotten to be mercifull and had shut vp his tender mercies in displeasure?

Psal.22.1. and 77.8.9.

Psal.22.1.and 77.8.9. Or of *Iobs* faith when he cursed the day of his birth and accounted God his enemy, who had set him vp as a marke against which he shot poisoned arrowes? or of *Ieremy* when he likewise wished that he had neuer bene borne and bewraieth great impatiency.Ier.20. Or of *Ionas* when he

Iere.10.

rebelled against Gods commaundement and fled from his presence, or when after his miraculous deliuerie, he murmu-red and vttered impatient speeches euen against God himself

for

for the lofle of a poore gourd which kept him from the heate of the funne; and when the Lord mercifully and mildly reproued him faying, doeft thou well to be angry for the gourd, he ftubbornely anfwered: I doe well to bee angry vnto the death. Ion.4.9. Or of the Apoftles themfelues when they fled away and forfooke their Lord and maifter Iefus Chrift for feare of worldly punifhment, and when after his death they would not beleeue the women reporting that hee was rifen againe, vntill their owne eyes had feene them? Laftly, though it be euident that diuers of the Saints mentioned in the Scriptures had a farre greater meafure of faith, and brought foorth much more plentiful fruits then we can difcerne in our felues, yet this is no good reafon to prooue that our weaker & fmaller faith is no faith, or vneffectuall for our faluation, for this is an abfurd confequence, the Moone giueth much leffe light then the Sunne, therefore it giueth no light at all, one hand is farre greater then another, therefore the leffer is not a true hand, this man excelleth another in the vfe of reafon, and therefore the other is vnreafonable, becaufe the diuers degrees in the quantitie of things doe not take away the truth of their being and exiftence fo long as they be of the fame nature and qualitie. Befides as the holy ghoft hath fet downe examples of moft ftrong faith in fome of Gods feruants, fo hath he made mention of fome who haue had but weake and little faith, to the end that we fhould fo labour to attaine vnto the higheft degree as that in the meane time we be not vtterly difcouraged with the loweft; for example as he hath remembred the faith of *Abraham* who beleeued aboue hope vnder hope, fo hee hath not forgotten his weake faith who cried I beleeue, Lord help thou mine vnbeliefe; as he hath mentioned the faith of *Iob* who grew to this refolution: Though hee kill me yet will I truft in him, fo he hath expreffed alfo the faith of *Nicodemus,* in knowledge weake and fimple, and in practife and profeffion cowardly and fearefull, as hee hath fet downe the ftrong faith of *Paul,* who grew to this fulneffe of perfwafion that nothing fhould be able to feparate him from the loue of God in Iefus Chrift, fo he hath not left out the little & weak

Ion.4.9.

faith

faith of *Thomas* who would not beleeue further then hee sawe and felt. Yea the Lord in his word hath reuealed vnto vs the

diuers degrees of faith in the same men in respect of diuers times; at one time like a graine of mustard seede, at another time like a great tree, at one time like a little smoke, and soone after bursting out into a great flame, now like a weake reed wauering and declyning with the smallest blast of any tryall, and within a while like an immoueable rocke which beateth backe huge billowes and euen a whole sea of violent tentations; in a word it setteth out to our vew as it were portrayed in a fresh and liue picture the diuers ages of a christian as he is in his conception and preparation to grace, and as he is in his new birth and first conuersion, as he is a babe, and as he groweth from his infancie to greater age and strength, till hee come to ripe yeares and to be a strong man in Christ. Besides it sheweth vnto vs his diuers relapses through sinne the sicknesse of the soule, and how oftentimes the spiritual growth is hindred, and the strength of Gods graces abated and much weakned by the cotidian ague of our corruptions and Sathans tentations, and also after these fitts bee driuen away by vertue of Gods spirit, how we receiue a greater increase of grace and measure of strength, whereby we grow more in christianitie and godlinesse in a yeere then we did in two before. All which is set downe to this end that we should not make our infancie our ἀκμὴν and full growth, but labour to increase in grace till we become of babes strong men in Christ; as also that finding our selues as weake as little infants wee bee not vtterly discouraged, for if we sucke the brests of our spirituall mother the true church, and receiue from her the milke and stronger meate of the word and sacraments, wee shall assuredly growe vp from grace to grace, and strength to strength, till of babes wee become strong men in Iesus Christ, and that though wee haue many great sicknesses of the soule, and relapses into sinne whereby our spirituall growth for a time is hindred, and our strength in Gods graces much abated, yet if we often feed vpon the comfortable foode of Gods worde and vse this spirituall physick prescribed by God himselfe we shall not only a-
gaine

againe recouer our former strength and health, but also find a great increase of Gods graces in vs.

Lastly, Sathan will suggest that though our faith be true, yet it is so exceeding small and weake, that with the violence of his tentations and huge masse of our own corruptions it will easily be ouerthrown and turned into infidelitie. To which we are to answere, that though hereby our faith may be shrewdly shaken yet it canneuer be ouerturned, though it may be couered with the ashes of our corruptions, yet it can neuer be vtterly quenched; though through our greiuous foyles and falls in the combate of tentations, it may be as it were brought into a traunce, so as we cannot sensibly discerne any action, motion or life of faith, yet the habite and grace it selfe, after it is once giuen of God is neuer taken away, neither is it possible that it should be quite destroied by all the power of hell. §. Sect.3. *That Sathan cannot preuaile against the weakest faith.*

And this may appeare by diuers reasons; first because faith is not *of our selues but the free gift of God*, as it is Ephe.2.8. And whatsoeuer sanctifyng and sauing grace the Lord giueth that he neuer taketh vtterly away; *for the gifts and calling of God are without repentance*, as the Apostle speaketh. Rom.11.29. Eph.2. 8.

Rom.11.29.

Secondly, whosoeuer truely beleeueth, he is truely knit and vnited vnto the body of Christ and is made partaker of his holy spirit which as it begetteth and beginneth all the sanctifying and sauing graces in vs, so also it nourisheth, strengtheneth and confirmeth them so as they can neuer vtterly faile, for whatsoeuer good worke he beginneth that will hee also perfect and accomplish. Phil.1.6. Phil.1. 16.

Thirdly, whosoeuer truely beleeueth he is truely iustified, and whosoeuer is iustified is elected called and shalbe glorified, for these inseparably goe together. Rom.8.30. and consequently he that hath true faith whereby he is iustified cannot fall away, seeing his iustification is as certaine as the eternall decree of Gods election. Rom.8.30.

§. Sect.4.

Lastly, God both can and will strengthen and confirme all those who are weake in faith, till they attaine vnto the end of their faith euen the saluation of their soules, and therefore it is impossible that they which once truely beleeue should fall away *That God both can and will vphould the weakest beleeuer.*

way

away and be cōdemned. Concerning Gods power no man can make any queſtion ſeeing it is omnipotent and almighty, and for his will he hath fully reuealed it both by his word and workes, namely that he will not take away that grace which he hath once giuen, but rather increaſe it till it bee perfected and accompliſhed. For the firſt the Lord ſaith that hee will comfort his Church and people, as the woman comforteth her child, Eſa. 66. 13. now wee know that the mother doth not a-bandon her child, nor depriue him of that comfort which ſhe can giue him becauſe he is ſicke and weake, but rather the ſic-ker and weaker he is, the more is her care and diligence in re-leiuing him in his diſtreſſe; when hee is not able to diſgeſt ſtrong meate ſhe prouideth for him cōfortable foode of light diſgeſtion, when he is ſo weake that he cannot goe ſhe carieth him in her armes or otherwiſe ſupporteth him, when he is ſo ſicke that he faleth downe to the ground in a ſwoune, ſhee rayſeth him vp & neuer reſteth till ſhee hath recouered life in him, is this loue in a naturall mother? then ſurely much more ſhall we finde in our heauenly father, for *though a mother may forget the fruit of her womb, yet wil the Lord neuer forget vs,* as he hath promiſed. Eſa. 49. 15. And therefore the greater our weakeneſſe is in grace, and the more greiuous our ſickneſſe is through ſinne, and the noiſome humors of our corruptions the more carefully will hee watch ouer vs, with the eye of his prouidence, and ſupport vs with his almighty power in our greateſt weakeneſſe, the more tenderly will he pitie vs, and in louing compaſſion will prouide for vs, ſuch comfortable food as wilbe fit to nouriſh vs and repaire our decaied ſtrength, when we cannot goe he will with his almighty hand vphould vs, and when we fall into a dead traunce he will not reſt till he hath againe reuiued and quickened vs with his holy ſpirite. Moreouer our Sauiour hath ſaide, *that hee will not breake the bruiſed reed nor quench the ſmoking flaxe.* Matth. 12.20. but he will ſupport our weakeneſſe with his almighty power, ſo that though with the reed we be borne downe to the ground, with the boyſterous blaſtes of Sathans tentations, yet we ſhal-be raiſed vp againe, according to that Pſal. 37.24. *Though hee*

fall

Eſa. 66. 13.
Gods loue compared to the loue of a tēder mother.

Eſa. 49. 15.

Math. 12.20

Pſal. 37. 24.

fall he shall not be cast off, for the Lord putteth vnder his hand, and he will blow vpon vs with the breath of his holy spirit, till he turne our small smoke to a great flame which shall neuer bee quenched by all the malice of our spirituall enemies. So Matth. 13. 12. our Sauiour Christ hath promissed, *that whosoeuer hath, to him it shal be giuen and he shall haue aboundance.* Neither doth he limit or define any quantitie lesse or more but indefinitely promisseth aboundant increase euen vnto the least, so farre is he from taking away that which he hath once bestowed. And whereas wee through our weakenesse and frailenesse are easily cast downe and fall away, and therefore haue good cause if we should onely looke vpon our infirmities to doubt and despaire of perseuerance, yet in respect of Gods omnipotent power, watchfull prouidence, and promissed assistance wee may confirme our selues in faith, hope, and certaine assurance of continuing vnto the end; for the Lord vpholdeth all that are falling, and lifteth vp those who are already downe, as the Psalmist speaketh, Psal. 145. 14. the power of God is manifested in our weakenesse, his riches in our beggerlinesse, his mercy and goodnesse in our frailenesse, and manifold corruptions, and with his holy spirit hee helpeth our infirmities, as it is Rom. 8. 26. *Wee haue not an high priest which cannot bee touched with the feeling of our infirmities, but was in all things tempted in like sort yet without sinne.* and therfore he *is able sufficiently to haue compassion on them that are ignorant and out of the way, because that hee also was compassed with our infirmities,* as the apostle reasoneth. Heb. 4. 15. and 5. 2

Secondly it appeareth manifestly by Gods workes, administration, and practise, that he wil not depriue any of that sanctifying grace which he hath once bestowed, though the measure thereof be neuer so small; neither can we obserue either by our reading the whole booke of God or by our owne experience that any man hauing receiued the least graine of true faith hath vtterly beene depriued of it, and reiected of God. Euen the disciples themselues when they were reprooued for their little faith, were by him strengthened and confirmed, so that all the power of hell could not preuaile against it,

and

Math. 13. 12

Psa. 145. 14

2. Cor. 12. 9.

Ro. 8. 26.

Heb. 4. 15.
& 5. 2.

§. Sect. 5.
The former point illustrated by examples.

and though Sathan indeauoured to fift them as wheate, yet Chrifts interceffion was more mightie to defend them, then the diuell to deftroye them, and his interceffion a ftronger propp to vphould them, then the waight of Sathans tentations to ouerthrow and bring them to ruine; fo he who cryed out I beleeue Lord helpe thou my vnbeliefe, though his faith was weak yet it perifhed not, but rather receiued a greater increafe. Yea he reiected not *Thomas* in his wilfull doubting and obfti-nate incredulitie, but offered all occafions of confirming his weake faith, and neuer ceafed till hee had fully affured him of his refurrection. In a word all the faintes of God at one time or other haue had experience of this mercy, power, and good-neffe of God in fupporting their weakneffe, vphoulding them in their great infirmities, and in rayfing them when they were fallen to the ground; and to this end our Sauiour was annoin-ted by Gods fpirite vnto the office of his mediation, that hee fhould *preach the gofpell vnto the poore, heale the broken harted, that he fhould preach deliuerance vnto captiues, and recouerie of fight to the blind, and fet at libertie them that are brufed.* Luk. 4.

Luk.4.18.

18. To this ende hee had familiar fociety with the fraile and weake, with thofe who had little faith, that he might increafe it, and no faith, that he might begett it, with publicanes and finners and men full of infirmities; to this purpofe he calleth fuch as thirft and hunger feeling their owne emptineffe of grace, and earneftly defiring to bee filled and fatisfied, and fuch alfo as labour and are heauie laden with the vnfupporta-ble waight of their corruptions promifing that hee will eafe them, laftly to this end he hath ordayned the minifterie of the worde and adminiftration of the facraments, not only to be-get faith where it is not, but to nourifh and increafe it where it is weake and feeble, and therefore though our faith be neuer fo weake and fmall let not Sathan perfwade vs that therefore it fhall bee ouerthrowne and turned into infidelitie, for the Lord hath affured vs both by his gratious promifes in his word and alfo by the performance thereof in his works from the be-ginning to this day, that where hee hath giuen the leaft meafure of faith or any other fanctifying grace, there he will

also

alſo increaſe, ſtrengthen, and confirme it, and where he hath begunne any good worke there hee will finiſh and perfect it, notwithſtanding our fraile weakneſſe, and the forcible violence of all our ſpirituall enemies.

CHAP. XLVIII.
Of our iustification.

Nd ſo much concerning thoſe tentations of Sathan which he ſuggeſteth to the end that hee may fruſtrate our effectuall calling. The next ſubordinate cauſe and means of our ſaluation is our iuſtification, for *whomſoeuer the Lord effectually calleth thoſe alſo he iuſti-fieth.* as it is Rom. 8. 30. In ſpeaking whereof I will firſt ſhew what it is, and afterwards anſwere ſuch tentations of Sathan as he ſuggeſteth into our mindes, to the end that hee may infringe the doctrine of iuſtification, and make it vaine and vnprofitable vnto vs.

§. *Sect. 1. Of the effi-cient cauſe of our iuſtifica-tion.* Rom. 8. 30.

For the firſt. Iuſtification is an action or worke of the whole trinitie the father, ſonne, and holy ghoſt, whereby God gratiouſly and freely imputing vnto euery faithfull man the righteouſneſſe and obedience of Chriſt the mediatour doth accept of him and pronounce him to be iuſt and righteous, for the glorie of his name and ſaluation of the beleeuer.

The efficiet cauſe of our iuſtificatiōis God alone as appeareth by manifeſt teſtimonies. Eſa. 43. 25. *I, euen I am he that putteth away thine iniquities for my owne ſake and will not remember thy ſinnes.* So Ezech. 16. 8. The Lord thus ſpeaketh to his church and people; *I ſpread my skirts ouer thee and couered thy filthineſſe. 9. Then I waſhed thee with water, yea I waſhed away thy bloud from thee and annointed thee with oyle. 10. I clothed thee with broydred worke &c.* whereby he ſignifieth that he purged it with the bloud of Chriſt from all ſinne, and adorned it with the rich robe of his righteouſneſſe. The Apoſtle likewiſe ſaith that it is God who iuſtifieth him who in himſelfe was vngodly. Rom. 4. 5. and 8. 33. *It is God who iuſtifieth, who ſhall condemne?* The reaſon hereof is manifeſt becauſe it is the Lord againſt whom we haue ſinned, as *Dauid* ſpeaketh Pſal. 51. 4. And he alone is our ſupreame iudge who hath authoritie to

Eſa. 43. 25. Ezec. 16. 8.

Rom. 4. 5. and 8. 33. Pſal. 51. 4.

O o   abſolue

abfolue or condemne vs, and therefore he onely can giue vnto vs the pardon and remiffion of our finnes and accept of vs as iuft and righteous.

And this worke is not peculiar vnto any one perfon, but is commune to the whole trinitie. For God the father being fully fatisfied by the full fatisfaction, righteoufneffe, and obedience of Chrift the fonne, applied vnto vs by the holy fpirit, doth pardon and forgiue vs all our finnes, and pronounceth and accepteth of vs as innocent, and indued with perfect righteoufneffe.

The motiue or impulfiue caufe, which moued the Lorde thus to iuftifie vs, was not any thinge in vs or out of himfelfe; but of his meere mercy, and free good will wherewith hee hath loued vs from the beginning, as it manifeftly appeareth Rom. 3. 24. Where the Apoftle fayth that _we are iuftified freely by his grace, through the redemption that is in Chrift Iefus._ and Tit. 3. 5. 7. _Not by the workes of righteoufneffe which we had done, but according to his mercie he faued vs, by the wafhing of the new birth and renewing of the holy ghoft._ 7. _That being iuftified by his grace, we fhould bee made heyres according to the hope of eternal life._

The inftrumentall caufes are of two forts : firft on Gods part the word and the facraments, whereby the Lord offreth, conuaigheth, fealeth, and affureth vnto vs his mercie & grace, Chrift Iefus with his merites, righteoufneffe, and obedience, the remiffion of our finnes, and euerlafting life.

Secondly on our part a true and liuely faith, whereby wee receiue and apply vnto our felues the mercy of God, Chrift Iefus & all his benefits, refting vpon him alone for our faluation.

The materiall caufe of our iuftification is the actiue and paffiue righteoufneffe and obedience of Iefus Chrift, his inhærent holineffe, his fulfilling of the law, his death, facrifice, and full fatisfaction. So that we are not iuftified by the effentiall righteoufneffe of the godhead, nor by our owne workes ioyned with Chrifts merites, nor by any inhærent righteoufnes infufed of God through the merites of Chrift; or by any other thing in our felues or any other meere creature, but by the alone righteoufneffe of our mediatour Iefus Chrift God

and

Rom. 3. 24.

Tit. 3. 5. 7.

§. Sect. 2.
The material
caufe.

and man, which is out of our ſelues and in Chriſt as the proper ſubiect thereof, and not belonging to vs till by the ſpirite of God and a liuely faith it be applyed vnto vs and ſo becommeth ours.

Of the formall cauſe.

The formall cauſe of our iuſtification is a reciprocall imputation or tranſmutation of the ſinnes of the beleeuer vnto Chriſt and of his righteouſneſſe vnto the beleeuer: whereby it commeth to paſſe that the faithfull man hath not his ſinnes imputed vnto him, nor the puniſhment due vnto them inflicted on him, becauſe Chriſt hath taken vpon him the guilt and puniſhment, and by making ful ſatisfaction vnto his fathers iuſtice, hath obtayned the pardon and remiſſion of al his ſinnes. And alſo is clothed with the glorious robe of Chriſt Ieſus righteouſneſſe, and ſo appearing before God both free from all ſinne and indued with perfect righteouſneſſe hee is iuſtified, reconciled, and eternally ſaued. And of this imputed righteouſnes the apoſtle ſpeaketh, Rom. 4. 5. *But to him that* Rom.4.5. *worketh not, but beleeueth in him that iuſtifieth the vngodly, his faith is counted for righteouſneſſe. 6. Euen as Dauid declareth the bleſſedneſſe of the man vnto whom God imputeth righteouſneſſe without workes,* ſaying. *7. Bleſſed are they whoſe iniquities are forgiuen, and whoſe ſinnes are couered. 8. bleſſed is the man vnto whom the Lord imputeth not ſinne.* and 2. Cor. 5. 19. *For God was* 2.Cor.5.19. *in Chriſt and reconciled the world vnto himſelfe, not imputing their ſinnes vnto them &c. 21. For hee hath made him to bee ſinne for vs which knewe no ſinne that wee ſhould be made the righteouſneſſe of God in him.* And the Apoſtle affirmeth 1. Cor. 1. 30. *That Ieſus Chriſt is made vnto vs of God, wiſdeme,* 1.Cor.1.30. *righteouſneſſe, ſanctification and redemption.* So that now Chriſts righteouſneſſe is our righteouſneſſe, his obedience our obedience, his merits our merites, as certainely, perfectly and effectually, euen as if we our ſelues had bene moſt innocent fulfilled the law, or made full ſatisfaction to Gods iuſtice. By which it appeareth that in reſpect of our ſelues wee are iuſtified freely of Gods meere mercy & grace, without any reſpect of our owne righteouſnes or worthineſſe; but yet through Chriſt and for his righteouſneſſe and obedience imputed

puted

Rom.3.23.
24.
puted to vs, both which are ſignified by the Apoſtle Rom.3.
23.24. where he ſaid that all in themſelues are wretched ſinners without difference, and thereby are depriued of the glory of Gods kingdome, 24. *and are iuſtified freely of his grace,*
through the redemption which is in Chriſt Ieſus.

§. Sect.3.
The finall
cauſe.
The finall cauſe of our iuſtification is two fold, the chiefe
and principall is the glory of God, for hereby the Lord hath
moſt notably manifeſted his infinite iuſtice and mercy, his
iuſtice in that he would rather puniſh our ſinnes in his onely
begotten Sonne, then he would ſuffer them to goe vnpuniſhed; his mercy in that for our ſakes hee ſpared not his beſt
beloued Sonne, but gaue him to ſuffer death, yea the death of
the croſſe, that by his one oblation he might make full ſatiſfaction for our ſinnes, and purchaſe for vs euerlaſting life; and
alſo in that he vouchſafeth vnto vs the outward means of his
word and Sacraments, and the inward aſſiſtance of his holy
ſpirit, whereby wee are vnited vnto Chriſt and haue a liuely
faith begotten in vs, which apprehending Chriſt his righteouſneſſe and merits wee are iuſtified, ſanctified, and eternally ſaued. And this end is ſignified by the Apoſtle Rom.3.24.25.

Rom.3.24.
& 5.21.
where hee ſaith that God hath *iuſtified vs freely by his grace,*
through the redemption which is in Chriſt Ieſus, to declare his
righteouſneſſe by the forgiueneſſe of ſinnes and might ſhew himſelfe
iuſt by iuſtifying him who is of the faith of Ieſus. And cap.5.21.he
ſaith, that as vnder the law *ſinne had raigned vnto death, ſo now*
grace raigneth by righteouſneſſe vnto eternall life through Ieſus
Chriſt our Lord. So Eph.2.5.6.7. hee affirmeth that God hath

Ephe.2.5.
6.7.
quickned vs in Chriſt who were dead in our ſins & hath rayſed vs vp in him; *that hee might ſhew in the ages to come the*
exceeding riches of his grace through his kindneſſe towards vs in
Chriſt Ieſus.

The inferiour and ſubordinate end is that our ſaluation
may hereby be firmely aſſured vnto vs, for now our ſaluation
is not in vs but in the hands of God, and it is grounded not
on our owne workes and worthineſſe, but vpon the righteouſneſſe and obedience of Ieſus Chriſt, which is a moſt certaine and firme foundation which will neuer faile vs. And this
the

the Apoſtle ſheweth Rom. 4. 16. whereas hee ſaith, that the Rom. 4. 16.
couenant of grace whereby wee are aſſured of euerlaſting ſaluation *is made by faith, that it might come by grace, and the pro-*
miſſe might be ſure to all the ſeed.

    The parts of our iuſtification are two, the remiſſion of our §. *Sect. 4.*
ſinnes, and the imputation of Chriſts righteouſneſſe, for as in *Of the parts*
euery naturall man there is the corruption, guilt, and puniſh- *of our iuſtifi-*
ment of ſinne, and the abſence or priuation of holineſſe and *cation.*
righteouſneſſe, ſo in Chriſt we haue a remedy for both : for the
firſt by his paſſion and ſuffering: for the other by his actuall o-
bediēce and perfect fulfilling of the law. And this is manifeſt
Rom. 4. 6. 7. where the Apoſtle diſtinctly maketh mention, of Rom. 4. 6. 7.
the righteouſneſſe of Ieſus Chriſt imputed without workes,
and of the forgiueneſſe, couering and not imputing of ſinne. *That Chriſts*
Neither was it ſufficient for the obtaining of euerlaſting life *actuall obe-*
and happineſſe, that our mediatour ſhould by his death make *dience, wher-*
full ſatisfaction for our ſinnes, both of commiſſion an d alſo *led the law is*
omiſſion, but alſo that he ſhould cloth vs with his actiue obe- *imputed vn-*
dience, whereby we might appeare perfectly righteous before *ted vnto vs.*
God.

    The truth hereof may further appeare, if we conſider firſt
that our Sauiour Chriſt was not bound to fulfill the law for
himſelfe, becauſe hee was from the firſt moment of his conception aſſumed into the hypoſtaticall and perſonall vnion
with the ſecond perſon in Trinitie, and conſequently was not
onely man but God alſo, and therefore not bound to any law,
neither needing any legall righteouſneſſe being already indued with a farre more excellent righteouſneſſe euen the
righteouſneſſe of God. So that either our Sauiour perfourmed obedience to the law to no purpoſe, or els to this end
that he might impute it vnto vs, and thereby indue vs with
ſuch a moſt perfect and euerlaſting righteouſneſſe as might
giue vnto vs the right of eternall life.

    Secondly, if onely our ſinnes were pardoned and wee not
not made partakers of Chriſts actiue righteouſneſſe, our imputed righteouſneſſe ſhould not excell the righteouſneſſe of
Adam before his fall, for he neither cōmitted ſinne of omiſ-

ſion

568   *Of our iustification.*

fion nor commiſſion till he tranſgreſſed Gods commaundement in eating of the forbidden fruit; but we are made partakers of a more excellent righteouſneſſe by faith, then we loſt
in *Adam*, euen *the righteouſneſſe of God by the faith of Ieſus*
Chriſt, as the Apoſtle ſpeaketh Rom. 3. 22. which conſiſteth
not onely in the abſence of euill and ſinne, but in the preſence
alſo of actuall holineſſe and righteouſneſſe.

    Thirdly and laſtly (becauſe it is my purpoſe onely to touch
this point by the way as not ſo properly belonging to this
treatiſe) wee are vnited vnto Chriſt Ieſus, and he is become
our head and we his members, by reaſon of which vnion as
he communicateth himſelfe vnto vs, ſo alſo that which belongeth vnto him as he is our mediatour, and conſequently not
onely his paſſiue obedience whereby he hath made full ſatiſfaction for our ſinnes , but alſo his actuall righteouſneſſe
whereby he perfectly fulfilled the law.

    And thus it appeareth that our iuſtification conſiſteth of
two parts, the firſt the remiſſion of our ſinnes for the full ſatisfaction of Chriſt by his death and ſufferings, the other the
imputation of his habituall and actiue righteouſneſſe.

    The remiſſion of ſinnes is the firſt part of iuſtification,
whereby God forgiueth for the death and full ſatisfaction of
Chriſt, all our ſinne both originall and actuall both in reſpect
of the guilt and puniſhment, ſo as they ſhall neuer be imputed
to our condemnation, neither in this life nor in the life to
come. And of this the pſalmiſt ſpeaketh, Pſal. 32.1. *Bleſſed*
is the man whoſe wickedneſſe is forgiuen, and whoſe ſinne is couered.
2. Bleſſed is the man vnto whom the Lorde imputeth not iniquitie.
So the Apoſtle ſaith that *God was in Chriſt , and reconciled the*
world to himſelfe not imputing their ſinnes vnto them. 2. Cor. 5.
19.

    The imputation of Chriſts righteouſneſſe is the other part
of our iuſtification, whereby God imputeth vnto euery beleeuer the righteouſneſſe of the mediatour Ieſus Chriſt as if it
were properly their owne and perfourmed by them, that being clothed therewith they may bee perfectly righteous in
Gods ſight, and ſo obtaine the right vnto euerlaſting life and
                           happineſſe.

Rom.3.22.

Pſal.32.1

2.Cor.5.19.

happines. And of this the apostle speaketh, Rom. 4. 6. *Euen* Rom.4.6.
as (saith hee) *Dauid declareth the blessednesse of the man vnto*
whom God imputeth righteousnesse without workes. and Rom. Rom.9.30.
9. 30. *The Gentiles which followed not righteousnesse haue at-*
tayned vnto righteousnesse, euen the righteousnesse which is of
faith. So Phil. 2. 8:9. The Apostle saith that hee accounted Phil.3.8.9.
all things losse and iudge them to bee dunge, that hee might
winne Christ, *and might be found in him not hauing his one righ-*
teousnesse which is of the law, but that which is of the faith of Christ,
euen the righteousnesse which is of God through faith. Ier. 23.6.

Now this righteousnesse of Christ is twofold, his habituall
and inharent holinesse and innocencie, whereby he was free
from all corruption and sinne both originall and actuall; and
indued with all holinesse and puritie of nature, from the first
moment of his conception. And of this the Apostle speaketh,
2, Cor. 5. 21. *He that knew no sinne, was made sinne for vs.* and 2.Cor.5.21.
1. Pet. 2.22. *Who did no sinne neither was there any guile found* 1.Pet.2.22.
in his mouth. So Heb. 4.15. He is said to be without sinne. And Heb.4.15.
1. Pet. 1. 19. Hee is called the lambe vndefiled and without 1.Pet.1.19.
spot. And himselfe challengeth the Iewes Ioh. 8. 46. *Which* Ioh.8.46.
of you can rebuke me of sinne. And this holinesse being imputed
vnto vs, is opposed to our originall sinne and naturall corruption. The other is his actuall righteousnesse, whereby he perfourmed perfect obedience vnto the law in all his thoughts,
words, and deeds, through the whole course of his life. And
this being imputed vnto vs, and becomming ours by reason
of that vnion which is betweene Christ and vs, is opposed vnto our actuall transgression, whereby wee haue broken the
whole law of God both in omitting the duties which are
commaunded, and in committing the vices and sinnes which
are forbidden.

The persons who are thus iustified are all the faithful, and
they onely who doe apply the righteousnesse of Iesus Christ
vnto themselues by a true and liuely faith. And thus the Apostle doth limmitt and restraine it. Rom. 3. 21. 22. Where hee Rom.3.21.
saith that *the righteousnesse of God is made manifest without the* 22. and 4. 5.
the law; to wit, the righteousnesse of God by the faith of Iesus Christ,

vnto

vnto all and vpon all that beleeue. and 4. 5. *To him that worketh not but beleeueth in him that iust fieth the vngodly, his faith is counted for righteousnesse.* And our Sauiour hath promised, that whosoeuer beleeueth in him *shall not come into iudgment, but hath passed from death to life.* Ioh. 5 24.

Ioh. 4. 24.

The time when we are thus iustified is first in this life as soone as true faith is begot in vs by the ministery of the word, whereby we particularly apply vnto our selues Christ Iesus and all his benefites, resting and relying vpon him alone for our iustification and saluation; the which shall bee fully perfected at the day of iudgment, when as our Sauiour Christ shall pronounce the sentence of absolution saying *Come yee blessed of my father, take the inheritance of the kingdome prepared for you from the foundation of the world.* Mat. 25. 34.

Mat. 25. 34.

CHAP. XLIX.

That we are not iustified by our workes and merites.

§. Sect. 1.
Sathans tentations concerning iustificatiō of two sorts.

A Nd so much breefely of the doctrine of Iustification. Now we are to speake of and to answere such tentations as are suggested by our spirituall enemie, to the end that hee may perswade vs that wee are not iustified, or that hee may moue vs to seeke for iustification where it is not to bee had, and so in the meane time neglect it where only it is to be found, and the alone meanes whereby it is to bee inioyed. In speaking whereof I shall not need to handle things so largly as those points which went before, partly because our iustification doth inseperably follow our effectuall calling, and therefore hee that is assured of the one needs not to doubt of the other, partly because the most of those tentations which Sathan suggesteth to impugne and make void our assurance that we are iustified are alreadie answered, namely those which concerne the remission of our sinnes;

and

and true faith in Ieſus Chriſt, and partly becauſe thoſe tentations which Sathan ſuggeſteth into the minds of afflicted chriſtians are the ſelfe ſame which the lims of Sathan the
antichriſt of Roome and all his apoſtaticall ſinagogue doe
hold and defend; and therefore I ſhall not need to intreat
hereof at large becauſe theſe points in controuerſie haue beene
alreadie and will be hereafter ſo copiouſly, learnedly, and reli-
giouſly handled by others of greater abilities, and farre more
excellent gifts.

But let vs come to the matter in hand. The tentations of
Sathan concerning this point are of two ſorts; the firſt tend
to perſwade vs to labour after and to reſt vpon an imperfect
and maymed righteouſneſſe for our iuſtification, whereby wee
can neuer be iuſtified in Gods ſight, & ſo in the meane time he
cauſeth vs to neglect the alſufficiēt & moſt perfect righteouſ-
neſof Ieſus Chriſt by which alone we are iuſtified before God
and eternally ſaued; the other tend to make vs doubt of our
true iuſtification, that ſo hee may either make this gratious
worke of God fruſtrate in vs, or els at leaſt depriue our ſoules
of that true conſolation and peace of cōſcience, which dependeth vpon the aſſurance of our iuſtification.

For the firſt, he will labour to perſwade vs that it is not the
righteouſneſſe of Ieſus Chriſt, imputed vnto vs by God and
apprehended and applied vnto vs by faith, whereby wee are
iuſtified in Gods ſight, for this imputatiue righteouſneſſe is
but meerely putatiue and imaginaty. but by that inharent
righteouſnes which is in our ſelues; for Chriſt (will he ſay) did
not fulfil the law & died, that this his righteouſnes & obediēce
ſhould become ours by imputation, but he died for vs to the
end he might merite for vs the ſpirit of God, which ſhould infuſe into vs an inharent righteouſnes. & he ſhed his blood to
the end that our good workes being dipped and died therein,
might become perfect and ſo iuſtifie vs in Gods ſight; and
therefore that wee are not iuſtified by faith alone, but by our
other graces and vertues alſo, and our good workes proceed-
ding from them; neither by faith at all as it is an inſtrument
which applieth Chriſt and his benefits vnto vs, but as it is a

§. *Sect.* 2.
*How Sathan
tempteth vs
to neglect
Chriſts righ-
teouſneſſe &
to reſt vpon
our owne.*

grace

grace or vertue infused into our selues. Against which tentation it behooueth vs m o st carefully to arme our selues as being most daungerous and pernicious, for it robbeth God and
our sauiour Christ of the whole glorie of our iustification and
saluation, and deriueth some, yea the greatest portion vnto
our selues, as being chiefly iustified by our owne meanes; and
also it depriueth our soules of all true comfort and full assurance that we are iustified & saued, by taking out of our hands
the strong staffe of our saluation, the perfect righteousnesse of
Iesus Christ and by putting into them the weake reed of our
owne workes, which will presently breake and faile vs, when
we most rest vpon it, and so we shall vnrecouerably fall into
the horrible pit of deepe desperation, when as we are abandoned of our chiefe hope, that is, when on the one side the huge
waight of our grieuous sinnes, and on the other side the great
imperfection of our most perfect righteousnesse, and the filthie pollution of our most glorious workes appeare vnto vs.

And to the end that we may be the better inabled to resist
this dangerous and damnable tentation, I will first shew that
we cannot be iustified before the tribunall of Gods iudgement
by our inhærent righteousnesse & good workes; and secondly that we are iustified by faith alone as it onely applieth vnto
vs Christ Iesus his righteousnesse and obedience.

§. *Sect.*3.
*That we are
not iustified
by our workes
proued by
the Scrip-
tures.*

Rom.3. 20.
21.22.
Phil.3.9.

That we are not iustified by our owne workes and righteousnesse, it manifestly appeareth both by plaine testimonies
of holy Scripture, and stronge arguments which are grounded vpon them. For the first, the Apostle plainely saith, that
*by the workes of the law shall no flesh be iustified in his sight, for by
the law commeth the knowledge of sinne : but now is the righteousnesse of God made manifest without the law, hauing witnesse of the
law and the Prophets; to wit the righteousnesse of God, by the faith
of Iesus Christ, vnto all and vpon all that beleeue.* Rom. 3. 20.
21.22. So Phil.3.9. He disclaimeth his owne righteousnesse,
& resteth vpon the alone righteousnesse of Christ Iesus, which
is made ours by faith for his iustification and saluation. *I haue
(saith he) counted all things losse and doe iudge them to be dunge
that I may winne Christ, and might bee found in him, not hauing
mine*

mine owne righteousnesse, which is of the law, but that which is through the faith of Christ, euen the righteousnesse which is of God through faith. Phil. 3.9. and Gal. 3. 10. 11. Hee affirmeth that *as many as rest in the workes of the law are vnder the curse;* and that *no man is iustified by the law in the sight of God, it is euident because the iust shall liue by faith.* So Rom. 4.5. *To him that worketh not but beleeueth in him that iustifieth the vngodly his faith is counted for righteousnesse.* And our Sauiour Christ teacheth vs to say and acknowledge when we haue done all to our vttermost power which is commaunded vs that we are still vnprofitable seruants Luk. 17. 10

Phil. 3.9.
Gal. 3. 10.
11
Rom. 4.5.
Lnk. 17. 10.

But vnto these and such like manifest places it is answered, that the Apostle speaketh not of the works of the morall law, but of the ceremonies onely, to which againe wee reply that no such friuolous distinction can be gathered out of the Apostles wordes, nay the plaine contrary euidently appeareth, by his maine scope and drift in his whole discourse of our iustification, and also by some particular places. His chiefe scope is to beate downe the pride of all, both Iewes and Gentiles to the end that the whole glory and praise of our iustification and saluation might be ascribed to the free mercy, grace, and goodnesse of God alone ; now it is most certaine that the morall duties are in themselues farre more excellent then the ceremoniall, and consequently more fit to puffe vs vp with a spirituall pride, and to make vs to rest in our selues for our iustification, ascribing at least some part of the praise vnto our owne workes and vertues ; so that if the Apostle had onely spoke of the works of the ceremoniall law, mans pride should not bee beaten downe, neither should God haue the whole praise of our saluation, and so his discourse should be vaine, as not tending to prooue & inforce that, for which end and purpose hee chiefly vndertakes it. Againe this should nothing concerne neither the Gentils in former times, nor any true Christians since the comming of Christ, forasmuch as they did not nor doe not, neither were nor are bound to obserue the ceremoniall law, & consequently could neuer once dreame of obtayning righteousnesse by fulfilling the ceremonies ; but

§. Sect. 4.
That the former places are to be vnderstood of the works of the morall law, and not of the ceremonies onely.

they

they would rather afcribe the glorie of their iuftification to their morall duties, to which they found themfelues bound by the law of nature written in their harts, or doe find themfelues bound by the morall law of God written in his worde ; and therfore it was necellarie for the beating downe of their pride, and that they might afcribe the whole glory vnto God of their iuftification and faluation, that the apoftles in this difcourfe fhould proue that they were not iuftified neither by obfer-uing the law of nature written in their hartes, nor yet the mo-rall law of God reuealed in his word. Whereby it manifeftly appeareth that howfoeuer the Apoftle excludeth the workes of the ceremoniall law from being caufes of iuftification, yet not them alone but the workes of the morall law alfo.

§. *Sect. 5.*
The former point prooued by particular teftimonies.

But this may more manifeftly appeare by particular pla-ces wherein the Apoftle plainly fheweth that he fpeaketh not onely of the ceremoniall law, but of the morall law alfo. In the fecond chapter of the Epiftle to the Romanes, he plainly difputeth as well of the law of nature, to the obedience where-

Rom. 3. 19. 20.

of the Gentiles were obliged as of the law giuen by *Mofes.* Chap. 3. 19. 20. Hee fayth that all the world are made culpa-ble before God, and therefore by the works of the law fhal no flefh be iuftified in his fight. Now if this confequence be good he fpeaketh not onely of the ceremoniall but of the moral du-ties, for the former belonged not to the gentiles, and there-fore the neglect of them did not make them culpable, nor de-

Rom. 10. 5. 6 barre them of being iuftified by their owne workes.

Gal. 3. 11. 12 21. 22. 24.

Secondly Rom. 10. 5. 6. and Gal. 3. 11. 12. 21. 22. 24. The Apoftle putteth a plaine difference betweene the righte-oufneffe which is by the law, and the righteoufneffe which is by faith, and maketh a flatt oppofition in the acte of iuftifica-tion not betweene morall & ceremonial duties, but betweene

Eph. 2. 8. 9. doing and beleeuing, faith and workes.

Thirdly hee faith, Eph. 2. 8. 9. that wee *are faued by grace through faith not of our felues,* nor of workes leaft any man fhould boaft himfelfe. If hee had fpoken only of workes they might (though foolifhly) haue wrefted it to ceremonies only feeing the Ephefians were not bound to the ceremoniall law,

as

as being strangers to the common wealth of Israel, as himselfe speaketh ver.12. but whē he saith also not of our selues, he excludeth al whatsoeuer is in vs from being the cause of our saluation, not onely ceremoniall but also morall duties. So writing to *Titus* he saith Tit.3.5. *Not by the workes of righteousnes which wee had done but according to his mercy, hee saued vs,* in which place we are necessarily to vnderstand the works of the morall law; for *Titus* being a Grecian was not bound to obserue the ceremoniall law, and therefore he was not so much as circumcised as the apostle plainely affirmeth, Gal.2.3. *verf.12.* *Titus 3.5.* *Gal.2.3.*

Fourthly *Paul* speaketh of that law by which wee come to the knowledge of sinne, as appeareth Rom.3.20. and 7.7. 8.9. But the knowledge of sinne came especially by the morall law, and therefore of this law the Apostle speaketh. *Rom. 3. 20. and 7.7.8.9.*

Lastly the Apostle speaking of the workes of the law alleadgeth these sentences. Gala. 3.10. *As many as are of the workes of the law are vnder the curse, for it is written cursed is euery man that continueth not in all thinges which are written in the booke of the law to doe them.* So that he speaketh not of the ceremoniall law alone but of the whole law of *Moses* and of all things contayned in it. and ver. 12. *And the law is not of faith, but the man that shall doe those things shall liue in them.* Which cannot be vnderstoode of the ceremoniall law alone, but of the workes of the morall law yea of them especially. *Gal.3.10.* *ver.12.*

Secondly it is answered that the apostle speaketh only of the workes of those who are not regenerate nor indued with faith, and not of the regenerate and faithfull. Which shifting cauill the apostle clearly taketh away, not only by applying his speeches vnto all men without any limitation; but especially in that example of *Abraham* which he bringeth for this purpose; who though hee were long before regenerate, indued with faith and exceeding plentifull in good workes, yet hee flatly excludeth all his workes from being any causes of his iustification. So Rom. 4.2. *If Abraham were iustified by works he had wherein to reioyce but not with God.* and ver. 3. *Abraham beleeued God and it was counted vnto him for righteousnesse.* 4.4. *Now to him that worketh, the wages is not counted by fauour but* *That the Apostle excludeth as well the workes of the regenerate, as of the vnregenerate.* *Rom.4.2.* *and ver.3.* *4.4.*

by

by debt. 5. But to him that worketh not, but beleeueth in him that iuſtifieth the vngodly his faith is counted for righteouſneſſe.

§.Seĉt.6.
*Reaſons to
proue that w
are not iuſti-
fie i by our
workes.*
Rom.8.1.33
34.
And ſo much cōcerning the teſtimonies of ſcripture which manifeſtly proue that we are not iuſtified by our works. The reaſons which may be brought to the ſame purpoſe are exceeding many, but I wil briefly touch ſome few only. Firſt iuſtification is manifeſtly oppoſed to cōdemnation:& they are both iudiciall words vſed in ciuill courts, & therefore to be vnderſtood both'iudicially & not after a diuers maner. But to condēne ſignifieth not to infuſe any fault or crime in to the perſon cōdēned; but to pronoūce him guiltie & faulty: And therfore to iuſtifie ſignifieth not to infuſe righteouſnes into the perſon iuſtified; but to declare, pronoūce, & repute him as iuſt & righteous.   Secondly, by the ſame meanes whereby we obtaine the remiſſion of our ſins, we are alſo iuſtified & made righteous; but wee obtaine the remiſſion of our ſinnes not for our workes or inhærent righteouſnes, or any vertue that is in our ſelues, but by and for the alone merites, obedience, and full ſatisfa&tion of Chriſt, apprehended and applyed vnto vs by a liuely faith, as appeareth Rom. 3. 25. And therefore by this meanes alone we are alſo iuſtified.

Rom. 3. 25.

Thirdly, whoſoeuer are iuſtified freely by grace they are not iuſtified by their owne merits, works, or inhærent righteouſneſſe: but the ſcriptures teſtifie that all the faithfull are iuſtified freely by Gods grace, as appeareth Rom. 3. 23. 24. *All haue ſinned and are depriued of the glorie of God. 24. And are iuſtified freely by his grace, through the redemption that is in Chriſt Ieſus.* So Eph. 1.7. *By whom we haue redemptiō through his bloud, euen the forgiueneſſe of ſinnes according to his rich grace. and 2. 8. By grace are you ſaued through faith, and that not of your ſelues, it is the gift of God.* and Tit. 3. *not by the works of righteouſneſſe which we had done, but according to his mercy he ſaued vs &c. 7. That we being iuſtified by his grace ſhould be made heires according to hope of eternall life.* And therefore none are iuſtified by their owne merits, workes, or inhærent righteouſneſſe.

Rō.3.23.24

Eph. 1.7.
& 2. 8.

Tit.3.5.7.

Laſtly, the apoſtle *Paul* himſelfe gathereth many abſurdities which would follow this doĉtrine of iuſtificatiō by works: firſt

firſt that our faith ſhould bee vaine, and the promiſſe of God voide, Rom.4.14. Secondly that Chriſt Ieſus ſhould die in vaine if we haue righteouſneſſe by the law. Gal.2.21. Thirdly that wee ſhould haue cauſe of boaſting and glorying in our ſelues.Eph.2.9.for if a man were iuſtified by his owne inhæ-rent righteouſneſſe, hee ſhould haue whereof to glory,and ſo God ſhould be robbed of the whole praiſe of our ſaluation. Rom.4.2.But the Lord of purpoſe hath iuſtified vs freely of his grace,and not for our workes and inharent righteouſnes, that all glorying in our ſelues might be excluded:as appeareth Rom.3.27.Eph 2.9. Fourthly it would follow hereupon that we ſhould ſtill be vnder the curſe of the law, which is denou̅-ced againſt all who continue not in all that is written in the booke of the law to do them, as the Apoſtle reaſoneth Gal.3. 10.Fiftly that the obedience and ſatisfaction of Chriſt ſhould be maymed and imperfect, vnleſſe it were patched vp with our owne righteouſneſſe : the contrary whereof the Apo-ſtle affirmeth Heb.7.25. namely that hee is able perfectly to ſaue all them who come vnto God by him. Laſtly, hereupon it would follow that wee ſhould continually wauer in doub-ting, in reſpect of our manifold corruptions and imperfect righteouſneſſe, and ſhould haue our ſoules depriued of that peace of conſcience which followeth iuſtification by faith, as it is Rom.5.1. Laſtly with the Iewes we ſhall bring our ſelues into moſt certaine da̅ger of being reiected and caſt of, from being the people and Church of God, if with them we goe a-bout to ſtabliſh our owne righteouſneſſe, in the meane time not ſubmitting our ſelues to the righteouſneſſe of God,which is of faith in Ieſus Chriſt,as it is Rom.10.4.6.

Rom.4.14.

Gal.2.21.

Eph.2.9.

Rom.4.2.

Rom.3.27. Eph.2.9.

Gal.3.10.

Heb.7.25.

Rom.5.1.

Rom.10.4. 6.

CHAP. L.

That faith alone iuſtifieth.

A Nd thus much concerning the firſt point, namely that wee are not iuſtified by workes : the ſecond is that we are iuſtified by faith alone: whereby we are not to vnderſtand that faith by it owne ver-tue,or as it is a facultie,habite,worke or action in vs, doth iu-

§. Sect.1.
How it is to be vnderſtood that faith alone iuſtifi-eth.

ſtifie

stifie vs, but as it is the alone instrument whereby we doe apprehend & apply vnto vs Christ Iesus, his righteousnesse & obedience, by which onely righteousnesse which is out of our selues in Christ as the proper subiect thereof, being offered in the word and Sacraments, and applied by faith we are iustified in Gods sight, as appeareth Phil. 2.9. Secondly whereas we say that faith alone iustifieth, we do not vnderstand such a faith, as is alone without workes, charitie, and other sanctifying graces, which were nothing els but imaginarie dead, and but as it were a carkase of faith which breatheth not; but that amongst all other graces, vertues & faculties of the soule faith alone, and not any of thē is the instrument whereby we apply Christ Iesus vnto vs, who being thus applied doth iustifie vs.

Phil. 2.9.

That though workes do not iustifie vs yet they are necessarily required as fruits of our iustification. Otherwise we affirme that other graces of Gods spirit and euen good workes which is a fruite of them all, doe necessarily accompany our iustification, not as instruments or causes thereof, but as inseparable effects and fruits thereof. So that howsoeuer we exclude workes from the act of iustifying, yet wee necessarily require them in the subiect or person iustified; we affirme that faith alone iustifieth, but wee denie that such a faith which is alone doth iustifie vs; we maintaine that we are iustified by faith alone without works, but withall we affirme that faith which is without workes doth not iustifie vs as being dead, false and imaginarie. This may bee made plaine by some similitudes: to the being of an honest man there is necessarily required honest actions, not as causes but as effects, neither are his honest actions the cause of his honesty, but his honesty the cause of his honest actions; to a liuing man there is necessarily required as well breathing which is an action or effect of life, as the soule which is the cause thereof, and so to a iustified man there is necessarily required, as well good works which are the effects of iustification, as faith which is the instrumentall cause thereof; for faith and workes are neuer seuered in the subiect or party iustified, although they are disioyned in the act of iustifying. So the eye onely seeth and not the forehead, but yet the eye seuered from the forehead seeth not, because it is but a dead eye, the hand writeth and not the
body

body, but the hand ſeuered from the body writeth not, becauſe it is a dead hand. The foote goeth and not the head or
heart, but the foote which is ſeuered from the head or heart
goeth not, and ſo faith onely iuſtifieth, and not hope, not
charitie, not workes, but the faith that is ſeuered from hope,
charitie, and workes, iuſtifieth not, becauſe it is but a dead
faith ; as therefore when we ſay the eye onely ſeeth, the hand
onely writeth, the foote onely walketh, our meaning is not
that theſe parts being alone, and ſeuered from the reſt, ſee,
write, and walke, but that amongſt all other parts, the action or function of ſeeing belongeth peculiarly vnto the eye,
writing to the hand, walking to the foote : ſo when we ſay
that onely faith iuſtifieth, our meaning is not that the faith
which is alone, and ſeuered from other graces and the fruites
of them good workes, iuſtifieth ; but that amongſt all other
graces this act of iuſtifying peculiarly and properly belongeth vnto faith, and not to any other grace, vertue, or workes.

Now that that faith alone, in this ſenſe vnderſtoode, iuſtifieth, appeareth plainely, both by teſtimonies of ſcripture
and apparant reaſons. For the firſt, it is manifeſt, Rom.3.28.
where after long diſputation concerning this poynt, the A-
poſtle expreſly concludeth thus. *Therefore we conclude that
a man is iuſtified by faith without the workes of the law.* And
chap.4.verſ.5. *To him that worketh not, but beleeueth in him,
that iuſtifieth the vngodly, his faith is counted for righteouſnes.*
So Gal.2.16. *Know that a man is not iuſtified by the workes of
the law but by the faith of Ieſus Chriſt: euen we I ſay haue beleeued in Ieſus Chriſt, that we might be iuſtified by the faith of
Chriſt, and not by the workes of the law, becauſe by the workes of
the law, no fleſh ſhall be iuſtified.* And cap.3.11. *And that no
man is iuſtified by the law in the ſight of God, it is euident : for
the iuſt ſhall liue by faith.* 12. *And the law is not of faith.* And
hence it is that the righteouſnes of Chriſt, whereby we are
iuſtified is called the *righteouſnes of faith.* Rom.9.30. becauſe
faith is the onely inſtrument, which apprehendeth and applieth this righteouſneſſe vnto vs, for our iuſtification.

The reaſons to proue that faith alone iuſtifieth are diuers.
Firſt, that which alone applieth vnto vs Chriſt Ieſus and his

§. Sect.2.
Teſtimonies to
proue that faith
alone iuſtifieth
vs.
Rom.3.28.

and 4.5.

Gal.2.16.

Gal.3.11.

Rom.9.30.

§. Sect.3.
Reaſons to
proue that faith
alone iuſtifieth.

P p   righteouſ-

righteouſneſſe,that onely iuſtifieth vs:but faith alone applyeth vnto vs Chriſt Ieſus and his righteouſneſſe,and not hope,
charitie, or any other grace : and therefore faith alone iuſtifieth.

Secondly, that which onely maketh the promiſes of the
Goſpell firme and ſure vnto vs,that alone iuſtifieth vs ; but
faith alone reſting vpon Gods mercie and Chriſts merits,
maketh the promiſes of the Goſpell firme and ſure vnto vs
(which would be moſt vncertaine if they ſhould depend on
the condition of our workes and worthineſſe ; ſeeing they
are moſt imperfect, and we moſt corrupt and vnworthie of
Gods leaſt mercie ; as the Apoſtle plainely ſheweth. Rom.

Rom.4.16.   4.16. *Therefore it is* (namely the couenant of grace) *by faith,
that it might come by grace, and the promiſe might be ſure to
all the ſeede:*and therefore faith alone iuſtifieth vs.

Ioh.3.14.15.   Laſtly, our Sauiour Chriſt Ioh.3.14.15. maketh this compariſon. *As Moſes lift vp the ſerpent in the wilderneſſe, ſo
muſt the ſonne of man be lift vp, that whoſoeuer beleeueth in
him ſhould not periſh but haue eternall life.* From which we may
thus reaſon ; As the Iſralites who were ſtung with fierie ſer-
pents, were cured not by any outward meanes of phyſicke
and ſurgerie, or any thing in themſelues, ſaue onely by looking vpon the braſen ſerpent, which for this purpoſe was
ſet vp by Gods commaundement ; ſo we being ſtung of the
old ſerpent, with the ſting of ſinne cannot be cured by any
meanes without or within our ſelues, but by beholding the
true ſubſtance Chriſt Ieſus,ſignified by this ſhadow,with the
eye of faith.

And thus haue I proued, firſt that we are not iuſtified by
our workes, and inherent righteouſneſſe ; and ſecondly that
we are iuſtified by faith alone: not as it is the chiefe and
principall cauſe, for in this reſpect God iuſtifieth; not as it
is the matter or meritorious cauſe of our iuſtification, for
in this reſpect the merits and righteouſneſſe of Ieſus Chriſt
iuſtifieth vs;but as it is the alone inſtrument and onely cauſe
in vs which applyeth that meritorious cauſe vnto vs, whereby alone we are iuſtified in Gods ſight.

§. Sect.4.   Secondly,the tempter will obiect,that this imputed righteouſneſſe

teouſneſſe wee ſpeake of, is but imaginarie, and a vaine phantaſie; as if a man who were defiled with durt ſhould be reputed cleane by the imputation of anothers cleaneſſe, or as if a begger ſhould be eſteemed rich, by imputation of anothers wealth. To which we are to anſwere, that the imputation of Chriſts righteouſneſſe vnto vs, is no imaginarie dreame, but a matter plainely expreſſed in Gods word, as alſo the not imputation of our ſinnes is therein ſpecified. In the fourth of the Romanes this word is vſed by the holy Ghoſt an eleuen times. So verſ.3. *Abraham beleeued God and it was imputed vnto him for righteouſneſſe.* And verſ.4. *To him that worketh not, but beleeueth in him that iuſtifieth the vngodly,his faith is imputed for righteouſneſſe.*And verſ.6.*Euen as Dauid declared the bleſſedneſſe of the man vnto whom God imputeth righteouſneſſe without workes.* And verſ.8. *Bleſſed is the man to whom the Lord imputeth not ſinne, &c.*

*That the impu-
tatiō of Chriſts
righteouſneſſe
is not putatiue
and imagina-
rie.*

Rom.4 3.4.

　　Yea will the tempter ſay, it is true that we are iuſtified by imputed righteouſneſſe; but not by the righteouſneſſe of Chriſt,which is out of our ſelues; but our faith, which is formed and perfected with charitie,and other graces,and good workes is imputed for righteouſneſſe : or more plainely, God accepteth of the workes of the faithfull, and their inherent righteouſneſſe, though imperfect and vnworthie in themſelues, for and through Chriſt, for ſuch righteouſneſſe which may iuſtifie vs in his ſight. For the anſwering of which obiection we are to know, that this word imputing, or imputation, is taken two waies in the Scriptures: firſt when as the thing imputed is in our ſelues, and ſo it is ſaid Pſal.106.31, that the fact of *Phinees* was imputed vnto him for righteouſneſſe ; ſo Rom.5.13, *But ſin is not imputed while there is no law.* Secondly, when as the thing imputed is out of our ſelues; and of this, mention is made Leuit.17.4. and Numb.18.27. And in this latter ſenſe the word is to be vnderſtoode in the doctrine of iuſtification, and not in the former. For our ſinnes were imputed vnto Chriſt, when he offered himſelfe to ſtand in our place, to pay our debt and to make full ſatiſfaction to his fathers iuſtice,by ſuffering thoſe puniſhments which we by our ſinnes had deſerued;in which

§. *Sect.5.*
*That not our
own but Chriſts
righteouſneſſe
is imputed vn-
to vs for our
iuſtification.*

Pſal.106.31.

Rom.5.13.

Leuit.17.4.

Numb.18.27.

Pp 2   reſpect

Mar.15.28.
2.Cor.5.21.

reſpect the Scriptures ſay that *he was reputed amongſt the wic-* *ked,*Mar.15.28. and that *he was made ſinne for vs,*2.Cor.5.21. not by infuſion of our ſinnes and corruptions into his moſt holy nature,but by imputation onely. And contrariwiſe, we are made iuſt or iuſtified not by infuſion of inherent righte-ouſneſſe into vs,but by imputation of Chriſts righteouſnes, when as beleeuing in him, notwithſtanding that our nature is ſtill defiled with ſinne and manifold corruptions,through the meere mercie and free grace of God for the merits and obedience of Chriſt wee are reputed iuſt, as though wee had neuer committed ſinne, and had perfourmed perfect obedi-ence vnto Gods commandements, and ſo adiudged heires of euerlaſting life.

So that this imputation conſiſteth not in Gods reputing of vs iuſt, in reſpect of our inherent righteouſneſſe infuſed into vs ; but in the free mercie and grace of God, which for Chriſt his ſake couereth our ſinnes, which are indeede inhe-rent in vs, ſo as they ſhall neuer be imputed vnto vs for our condemnation,& imputeth vnto vs the righteouſnes which is not in vs but in Chriſt, wherewith being fully poſſeſſed, he reputeth of vs as moſt innocent and perfectly righteous.

§.Sect.6.
The former
point prooued
by teſtimonies
of the Scrip-
tures.
Rom.4.4.5.

Now, that imputation is to be vnderſtood in this latter ſenſe,it is moſt manifeſt where ỹ Apoſtle *Paul* ſetteth down the word in both theſe ſenſes, denying that in this doctrine of iuſtification it is to be vnderſtood of the former,and affir-ming it of the latter. *To him(*ſaich he*)that worketh, the wages* *is not imputed by fauour,but by debt* (namely, becauſe he hath merited it by his owne righteouſnes) 5.*But to him that wor-**keth not, but beleeueth in him that iuſtifieth the vngodly, his* *faith is counted or imputed for righteouſnes ; euen as Dauid de-**clareth the bleſſednes of the man vnto whõ God imputeth righte-**ouſnes without works.*In which words he plainly ſheweth,that there is a kind of imputatiõ which hath his ground or foun-dation in works and inherent righteouſnes, and this he affir-meth is not of grace. And that there is another kind of im-putation, which hath not it ground and foundation in him to whom it is made,but in the free mercie of God iuſtifying the wicked without his workes,and therefore not onely de-

ſtitute

ftitute of inherent righteoufneffe whereby hee might be iuftified, but alfo guiltie of inherent corruption and actuall
tranfgreffion, whereby hee might bee condemned if God
fhould enter into iudgement with him. So alfo hee plainly
affirmeth Eph.2.8, that *we are faued by grace through faith,* Eph.2.8.
and that not of our felues; it is the gift of God. 9.Not of workes,
leaft any man fhould boaft himfelfe.

Secondly, this may be prooued by the example of *Abra-* §. Sect.7.
*ham,*vpon which the Apoftle in the former place infifteth; *The former*
for by that imputed righteoufneffe whereby he was iuftified, *point proued by*
wee are alfo iuftified: but the Apoftle plainly affirmeth that *the example of*
this imputation was not of *Abrahams* inherent righteouf- *Abraham.*
neffe,with the which notwithftanding he was plentifully indued; for (as he faith) *if Abraham were iuftified by workes,*
he had wherein to reioyce, but not in God; but that Abraham
beleeued in God, and this was counted to him for righteoufneffe, Rom.4.2.3.
as it is Rom.4.2.3: and therefore we are not iuftified by our
workes and inherent righteoufneffe, but by the righteoufneffe of Chrift imputed vnto vs.

Thirdly,that righteoufneffe which iuftifieth vs,muft con- §. Sect.8.
fift in perfect obedience and fulfilling of the law of God, in *That perfect*
that exact manner and meafure which Gods iuftice doth re- *righteoufneffe*
quire: but this cannot poffibly be done by any righteouf- *is required to*
neffe which is in vs, which is moft imperfect and mingled *our iuftifica-*
with many finnes and corruptions,*for in many things we finne* *tion.*
*all,*as it is Iam.3.2.and *he that faith he hath no finne is a liar,* as Iam.3.2.
Iohn fpeaketh 1.ep.1.8. and *our beft righteoufnes is like a pol-* 1.Ioh.1.8.
luted cloath, as it is Efa.64.6. but by the alone righteoufneffe Efa.64.6.
of Iefus Chrift, which being imputed vnto vs is fufficient to
anfwere and fatisfie Gods exact and moft perfect iuftice.
That our righteoufneffe whereby we are to be iuftified muft
be perfect, and fuch as the law and exact iuftice of God re- Rom.3.31.
quireth, it appeareth Rom.3.31. whereas the Apoftle plainly affirmeth,that when faith is imputed vnto righteoufneffe, Iam.2.10.
the law is not made voide, but rather confirmed and fulfilled. *Doe we then* (faith he) *make the law of none effect through*
faith? God forbid. Yea we eftablifh the law. But this cannot be
done by our righteoufneffe, which is imperfect and ming-

led

led with innumerable finnes, but by the alone moſt perfect
righteoufneſſe of Iefus Chriſt imputed vnto vs. Againe, the
Lord hath commaunded and ſtraitly charged , that in our
Deut.25.1. ciuill iudgements the righteous ſhall be iuſtified, and the
wicked condemned,Deut.25.1.And the wife man faith, that
Pro.17.15. he that *iuſtifieth the wicked , and he that condemneth the iuſt,
euen they both are abomination vnto the Lord*,Pro.17.15. And
Eſa.5.23. the Prophet *Eſay* denounceth a woe againſt them which
commit this finne, chap.5.verf.23. Now, ſhall the Lord require this of vs, and ſhall we thinke that he whofe will is the
rule of iuſtice,wil iuſtifie any whofe righteoufneſſe is imperfect,and not according to his law ? No, he hath told vs,that
Luk.16.17. it is more eaſie that heauen and earth ſhould paſſe away,
than that one title of the law ſhould fall vnaccompliſhed,
Luk.16.17. And therefore let vs not truſt vnto our owne imperfect righteoufneſſe, but wholy reſt vpon the alone righteoufneſſe of Iefus Chriſt by a liuely faith for our iuſtifica-
Iere.23.6. tion. For he *is the Lord our righteoufneſſe*,Iere.23.6.In him we
Eſa.45.24. *haue righteoufneſſe and ſtrength*,Eſa.45.24. *He is made vnto vs
of God wiſedome, righteoufneſſe, ſanctification and redemption,*
1.Cor.1.30. 1.Cor.1.30.*By his obedience many are made righteou*,Rom.5.
Rom.5.19. 19. *And that which was impoſſible to the law, in as much as it
was weake becauſe of the fleſh, God ſending his ſonne in the ſimi-*
Rom.8.3.4. *litude of ſinfull fleſh,and for ſinne, condemned ſinne in the fleſh,
that the righteoufneſſe of the law might be fulfilled in vs*; as it is
Rom.8.3.4. In a word, in him alone wee haue all our righteoufneſſe, in him we ſhine glorioufly in the ſight of God, and
he is that bright ſhining Sunne of righteoufnes,from whom
we borrow all our light,without whofe raies of holineſſe we
ſhould remaine in the darkneſſe of our finnes and corruptions.

Laſtly, the Apoſtle ſetteth downe the forme of our iuſtification, namely, the imputation of our finnes vnto Chriſt,
and the imputation of his righteoufnes vnto vs. 2.Cor.5.21.
2.Cor.5.21. *He which knew no ſinne was made ſinne for vs, that we might be
made the righteoufneſſe of God in him.* As therefore Chriſt was
made a finner for vs, ſo wee are made righteous before God
in him ; but Chriſt Iefus was not made a finner for vs by infufion

fufion of our finnes and corruptions into his nature (for hee
was alwaies moft holie,pure,vndefiled and without finne,as
the Apoftle witneffeth of him)but by imputation onely, as
being our furetie who had taken vpon him to difcharge
all our debt : and therefore in like manner wee are made
righteous,not by infufion of righteoufneffe, but by imputation onely.

1.Pet.1.18.19
and 2.21.

Now whereas they obiect, that to be iuftified by imputation is but an imaginarie mockerie,as if a poore man fhould
be reputed rich ; to this we are to anfwere,that it is but a friuolous cauill : for we doe not teach that God efteemeth and
reputeth vs righteous, being wholy defiled with finne and
quite deftitute of all righteoufnes; but that hee maketh vs
perfectly righteous, by wafhing away our fins with the precious bloud of Chrift, and by applying and appropriating
vnto vs his perfect righteoufnes and obedience by vertue of
his fpirit principally,& a liuely faith inftrumentally, wherby
we are vnited vnto Chrift and become members of his body,
and confequently haue right and full intereft vnto all that
which this our head hath done for vs ; and fo being made
partakers of his righteoufnes and merits,God reputeth vs as
we are in truth perfectly iuft and righteous. If a man being
poore and farre in debt fhould be accounted and reputed
exceeding rich and nothing indebted, it were indeede but a
meere imagination. But if another of great fufficiencie fhuld
take vpon him to be his furetie, and not onely difcharge all
his debts,but fhould beftow vpon him great fummes of money and much treafure, this man whatfoeuer hee was before
time in himfelfe,may now be efteemed rich and out of debt.
So if we (as wee are farre indebted to the iuftice of God and
exceeding beggerly,yea ftarke naked of all righteoufneffe)
fhould be reputed as we are thus in our felues righteous and
nothing indebted,it were but a meere mockerie ; but feeing
our Lord and Sauiour Iefus Chrift hath taken vpon him to
be our furetie who is himfelfe all-fufficient, and feeing hee
hath perfectly and fully anfwered all our debts wherein we
were ingaged to Gods iuftice;and not onely fo,but alfo hath
communicated and beftowed vpon vs the infinite rich trea-

§. Sect.3.
*That iuftifica-
tion by impu-
tation is not
imaginarie,
but reall and
in truth.*

fures

ſures of his righteouſnes and obedience, giuing vnto vs full intereſt and poſſeſſion hereof, outwardly by his hand-writing of the Goſpell, and his Sacraments as ſeales annexed thereunto, and inwardly by the vertue and cooperation of of his ſpirit applying them vnto vs : and laſtly, ſeeing we alſo haue recciued the full aſſurance of all this heauenly and ſpirituall rich treaſure by the hand of faith, wee are in truth quite out of debt, and exceeding rich with his righteouſnes which is now become ours, and therfore are ſo reputed and eſteemed in the ſight of God.

Chap. LI.

Sathans temptations mouing the weake Chriſtian to doubt of his iuſtification, anſwered.

§. Sect. 1.
*That our iuſtifi-
catiō is plain-
ly reuealed vn-
to vs in the
word of God.*

Nd ſo much for anſwering Sathans temptations, whereby he laboureth to perſwade vs to reſt vpon a falſe and imperfect righteouſneſſe for our iuſtification : now wee are briefly to ſpeake of thoſe which hee ſuggeſteth into the mindes of weake Chriſtians, to the end that hee may make them doubt of their iuſtification, that ſo hee might (if it were poſſible) make fruſtrate this worke of God, or at leaſt robbe their ſoules of all comfort and peace of conſcience, which alwaies accompanieth the aſſurance of our iuſtification ; for *being iuſtified by faith, wee haue peace towards God through our Lord Ieſus Chriſt*, as the Apoſtle ſpeaketh,

Rom. 5. 1. Firſt therefore he ſuggeſteth that our iuſtification is an action of God, and therefore vnknowne to vs ; ſo that we cannot poſſibly attaine vnto any certaine knowledge that we are iuſtified of God, vnleſſe he aſſure vs hereof by ſome ſpeciall and extraordinarie reuelation.

For the anſwering whereof, we are to vnderſtand that this act of God in iuſtifying a ſinner, is as cleerely reuealed ordinarily in the Scriptures, as any other thing concerning our ſaluation, and that euery true beleeuer may as certainly conclude by vndoubted arguments grounded on Gods infallible

lible truth,that he is iuſtified before God, as by naturall reaſon he can proue that he liueth and breatheth. For firſt our
effectuall vocation and iuſtification are inſeparably linked
together by the Apoſtle Rom.8.30. So that whoſoeuer can Rom.8.30.
proue that he is effectually called, he may alſo moſt certainly inferre that he is iuſtified. But euery true beleeuer
may come to the certaine knowledge that he is effectually
called (as before I haue ſhewed at large) and that not by
any ſpeciall reuelation, but by the will of God, reuealed in
his word by the inward teſtimonie of Gods ſpirit, and the
vndoubted ſignes of effectuall calling, which he obſerueth
in himſelfe ; and therefore without any particular reuelation we may attaine vnto the aſſurance alſo that we are iuſtified, that is, that our ſinnes are pardoned for the merits
and full ſatiſfaction of Ieſus Chriſt,and we cloathed with his
righteouſnes.

Secondly, whoſoeuer can come to the aſſurance that he
hath a true and liuely faith, he may alſo be aſſured that he is
iuſtified ; for it is the nature and an inſeparable propertie of
true faith, to apply vnto the beleeuer Chriſt Ieſus and his
righteouſneſſe, whereby hee is iuſtified before God; and
hence it is that the Scriptures plainely affirme that we are
iuſtified by faith and not by any thing elſe which is in vs, as
before I haue ſufficiently ſhewed. But we may come to the
certaine aſſurance that we haue a true faith,by the vndoubted ſignes and inſeparable fruites thereof, which wee may
diſcerne in our ſelues (as hath been alreadie plainely proued) though we neuer haue any ſpeciall reuelation : And
therefore without any ſuch particular reuelation we may
attaine vnto the certaine aſſurance that we are iuſtified in
Gods ſight.

Thirdly,that which the Goſpell aſſureth vs of, we neede
not to make any doubt thereof,or once call it into queſtion:
but the Goſpell aſſureth vs, that whoſoeuer beleeueth in
Chriſt Ieſus,and truely repent them of their ſinnes, ſhall be
made partakers of all the gracious promiſes of life and ſaluation therein contained ; So Ioh.3.16. *God ſo loued the* Ioh.3.16.
world that he hath giuen his onely begotten ſonne, that whoſoeuer
beleeueth

beleeueth in him ſhould not periſh,but haue euerlaſting life. And

Ioh.5.24.

chap.5.24. *Verely, verely, I ſay vnto you, he that heareth my word and beleeueth him that ſent me, hath euerlaſting life, and ſhall not come into condemnation, but hath paſſed from death to*

Matth.11.28.

life. And Matth.11.28. *Come vnto me all ye that labour and are laden, and I will eaſe you.* And therefore whoſoeuer beleeue in Ieſus Chriſt, approuing their faith to the world and their owne conſciences, to bee true and vnfained, by the fruite thereof, vnfained repentance, he may aſſure himſelfe of all the gratious promiſes of the Goſpell,and conſequently of the remiſſion of his ſinnes, and his iuſtification for the merits and righteouſneſſe of Ieſus Chriſt.

Laſtly, the Lord hath not onely after a generall manner propounded theſe promiſes vnto vs, and left vs to our owne libertie to beleeue or not to beleeue them, but hee hath bound vs to the performance of this dutie by his expreſſe

Mark.1.15.
1.Ioh.3.23.

commaundement, Mark.1.15. *Repent and beleeue the Goſpell.* And 1.Ioh.3.23. *This is his commaundement that we beleeue in his ſonne Ieſus Chriſt,* that is, that we doe not onely after a generall manner beleeue that he is the ſauiour of mankinde, but that we beleeue that he is our ſauiour,who hath redeemed,iuſtified,and wil moſt perfectly ſaue vs,and reſt wholy vpon him alone for our ſaluation. And he that thus beleeueth, needeth no other arguments to aſſure him that he is iuſtified and ſhall be ſaued; for he hath the witneſſe in himſelfe, euen the teſtimonie of Gods ſpirit, crying in his heart Abba father,and bearing witneſſe vnto his ſpirit that he is the childe of God : and not to beleeue this is to make God a lyer, becauſe wee *will not beleeue the record that hee hath*

1.Ioh.5.10.

witneſſed of that his ſonne, as the Apoſtle ſpeaketh. 1.Ioh.5. 10. Yea (as before I haue ſhewed at large) he hath added vnto the hand writing of his word, which containeth alſo his oath for our better confirmation,his ſacraments; whereby he particularly conuayeth and giueth vnto euery beleeuer, as it were proper poſſeſſion of Chriſt Ieſus and all his benefits, to the end that there ſhould bee no place left to doubting, nor any neede of any particular reuelation, for our further aſſurance.

Secondly,

Secondly, Sathan will ſuggeſt that thoſe who are iuſtified
are made iuſt, and thoſe who are made iuſt doe continually the workes of righteouſneſſe; but thou,will he ſay to the
humbled ſinner, continueſt ſtill in thy corrupcions, and thy
wickedneſſe cleaueth faſt to thee, and compaſſeth thee a-
bout; and in ſtead of doing the workes of righteouſneſſe,
thou continually heapeſt vp the full meaſure of thy ſinnes;
yea thy beſt actions are ſo ſtained with imperfections and
ſo full of infirmities, that they iuſtly prouoke Gods wrath
againſt thee.

§. Sect.2.
*That we are
made iuſt not
by infuſion but
by imputation
of righteouſnes.*

To which we muſt anſwere, that indeede whoſoeuer is
iuſtified is made iuſt, but not by infuſion of inherent righteouſneſſe into our ſelues, but by imputation of Chriſts moſt
perfect righteouſneſſe, as before I haue ſhewed; for hereby
our ſinnes are pardoned, he hauing taken them vpon himſelfe, and ſatiſfied Gods iuſtice by ſuffering thoſe puniſhments which wee had deſerued; and alſo he hath perfectly
fulfilled the law, that hee might make vs partakers of his
actiue obedience; and ſo imputing both vnto vs,hath made
vs perfectly iuſt and righteous in Gods ſight.

So that now the Lord doth not require obedience to his
law at our hands, to the end that wee ſhould be iuſtified in
whole or in part, by our owne righteouſneſſe;neither are we
to this end to obſerue Gods commandements,that we may
offer vnto God our workes and inherent righteouſneſſe,
deſiring thereby to be iuſtified;for,as I haue ſhewed,our beſt
righteouſneſſe is imperfect, and mingled with manifold
corruptions, ſo as it would rather condemne vs, then iuſtifie
vs,if the Lord ſhould examine it according to the exact rule
of his moſt perfect iuſtice: but we offer vnto God for our
iuſtification, the moſt perfect righteouſneſſe and full ſatiſfaction of Ieſus Chriſt, which by his merits and ſufferings he
hath once made for vs, deſiring thereby wholy and onely to
be iuſtified and ſaued.

As for our workes and inherent righteouſneſſe, they are
not cauſes but effects and fruites of our iuſtification; neither
is it poſſible that we ſhould doe any good worke acceptable
in Gods ſight, till we are iuſtified, and reconciled vnto God

§. Sect.3.
*That our workt
are not cauſes
but effects of
our iuſtifica-
tion.*

in

in Iesus Christ, for our workes cannot pleafe him, till our perfons pleafe him, and whatfoeuer we doe, before faith hath purified the heart, it is finne and odious in the fight of God: but as foone as we haue faith begotten in vs, prefently it apprehendeth, Christ and his rightcoufnes, whereby we are iuftified, and then being iuftified, faith worketh by loue and bringeth forth in vs the fruites of fanctification ; which though they bee mingled with much corruption, and manifold imperfections, yet God in Christ accepteth of them as perfect, and will crowne them with glorie, and immortalitie.

That now the Lord doth not require of vs perfect righteoufneffe.

Neither doth the Lord now require of vs, that wee perfectly at once fhake off all our corruptions, but that we labour as much as in vs lieth, to mortifie and fubdue them according to the meafure of his grace, and holy fpirit, which he hath beftowed on vs; he doth not ftraightly commaund that we fhould inftantly banifh and expell finne from dwelling in vs, but that we doe not fuffer it to raigne in vs, nor willingly obey the flefh in the lufts thereof, fubmitting our felues vnto finne, as feruants and vaffals to their Lord and maifter ; he doth not inioyne vs that we fhould wholy vanquifh our corruptions, and obtaine a full victorie ouer them, but that we proclaime open warres againft them, and manfully fight and ftriue vnder the conduct of his fpirit, againft the flefh, and the finfull lufts thereof; and when we are taken captiue of finne, that we labour to attaine vnto our former freedome, in the meane time forrowing and groning vnder the heauie waight of our corruptions, and crying out

Rom.7.

with the Apoftle, *wretched man that I am, who fhall deliuer me from the body of this death* ; and that we confeffe our miferable eftate vnto our captaine and leader Iefus Chrift, defiring him to affift vs with the power of his holy fpirit, that thereby we may be freed out of the hands of thefe our fpirituall enemies, whofe bondage and captiuitie is fo irkfome and grieuous vnto vs. Neither doth the Lord now require that we performe abfolute and perfect obedience to his commaundements, but that *to will* be prefent in vs, that we confent and approue his law to be good and delighting in it
concerning

concerning the inner man, that we deſire and indeauour to
performe that good we cannot, and forgetting that which
is behinde, indeauour our ſelues to that which is before, and
follow hard towards the marke, though we cannot attaine
vnto the end of our race, till wee come to the end of our
iues. Finally, the Lord doth not require of vs a whole harueſt of goodnes and righteouſnes, but the firſt fruites thereof; he doth not ſtand ſo much vpon our actions, as vpon our
affections, vpon the perfection of our workes, as vpon the
alacritie of our willes, and integritie of our hearts; the righteouſnes which he requireth is an humble confeſſion of our
vnrighteouſneſſe, a ſincere hatred of our ſinnes, a holy indeauour in the vſe of the meanes to mortifie our corruptions,
and to riſe from the death of ſinne, to holineſſe and newnes of life; which whoſoeuer can offer vnto God, they may
assure themſelues that they ſhall be accepted through
Chriſt, as righteous in Gods ſight, notwithſtanding their manifold imperfections
and corruptions.

Phil.3.13.14.

The end of the ſecond Booke.

THE THIRD BOOKE
INTREATING OF SANCTIFI-
CATION AND PERSEVERANCE,
as alſo of Sathans temptations which he ſuggeſteth
againſt them both, and of ſuch anſweres wherewith the Chriſtian may refute and
repell them.

Chap. I.
Of Sanctification, and the cauſes thereof.

§. Sect.1.
*That God is
the principall
efficient of our
ſanctification.*

Nd ſo much for the anſwering of ſuch
temptations of Sathan as concerne our
iuſtification. Now wee are to ſpeake of
our ſanctification, which is the next effect of Gods election, and inſeparably
ioyned with our iuſtification : wherein I
will obſerue my former order, firſt ſet-
ting downe the doctrine of ſanctification, and then anſwering thoſe temptations of Sathan which doe moſt impugne it.

*Sanctification,
what it is.*

For the firſt, *Sanctification is an action of the whole Trinitie,
whereby the beleeuer already iuſtified, is by little and little renued according to Gods image in holineſſe and righteouſneſſe, by
the mortification of the fleſh, with the corruptions thereof, and
the quickening of the ſpirit.*

And this is our ſanctification, which is expreſſed in the
Scriptures by diuers names and phraſes ; for it is called regeneration, the new birth, renouation, the putting off or mortifying

fying of the old man, and the putting on or quickening of
the new man and such like.

The efficient cause of our sanctification is God himselfe,
who as he alone iustifieth vs and freeth vs from the guilt and
punishment of sinne, so he onely sanctifieth vs and deliuereth vs from the tyrannie of sinne, so that it shall no longer
raigne in our mortall bodies, freeing vs in such measure as
pleaseth him from our naturall corruptions, which hereto- Leuit.20.8.
fore wholy ouerswayed vs. And this appeareth by plaine testimonies of holy Scriptures. Iohn 1.13. It is said that the Iohn 1.13.
faithfull are borne, *not of blood, nor of the will of the flesh, nor of*
the will of man, but of God. So Ephes.2.10. we are said to be Ephes 2.10.
Gods workemanship, created in Christ Iesus vnto good workes:
which phrase the Apostle vseth to note vnto vs, that as God
onely did create vs, so he onely doth renue and regenerate
vs. The Lord likewise doth appropriate this worke vnto
himselfe as belonging to another. Ezech.36.26. *A new heart* Ezech.36.26.
will I giue you, and a new spirit will I put into you, and I will take and 34.28.
away the stony heart out of your body, and I will giue you an heart
of flesh. And hence it is that the Apostle desiring the sanctification of the Thessalonians beggeth it at Gods hand,
1.Thes.5.23. *The very God of peace sanctifie you throughout.* 1.Thes.5.23.
And *Dauid* finding the want hereof in himselfe, hath his re- Psalm.51.13.
course vnto God. Psalm.51.10. *Create in me a cleane heart*
O God, and renue a right spirit within me. So that as God doth
begin in vs this worke of sanctification, so likewise he doth
accomplish and finish it. And therefore as we are wholy to
ascribe vnto God our election, vocation and iustification, so
also our sanctification, that he may be all in all in the worke
of our saluation. For as he onely formed vs, so he onely can
reforme vs, as he is the author of our naturall generation, for Gen.1.28.
by his blessing we haue our being, so also of our spirituall regeneration, for by his spirit onely wee are renued. Neither
must we imagine that it is in mans power to renew himselfe,
no more than to beget himselfe: for as well may the Black-
moore change his skinne, or the Leopard his spots, as wee
doe good who are accustomed to doe euill, Ierem.13.23. Ierem.13.23.
yea, as easily may the dead man raise himselfe, as wee may

raise

Eph.2.1.

raise our selues from the death of sinne to newnesse of life,
Eph.2.1. It is onely the water of Gods spirit that can wash
away our Ethiopian blacknesse, and turne our spotted vncleannesse into snowie whitenesse; it is onely the God of
life that can make vs rise from the death of sinne to newnesse of life.

But here it may be demaunded, that if sanctification bee
wholie the worke of God, and not in our owne power, why
doe the Scriptures exhort vs to sanctifie our selues, to mortifie our sinnes, and to walke in newnesse of life? I answere,
that though sanctification bee wholy from God, yet these
exhortations are necessarie; for hee worketh this worke in
vs, not as in stocks and stones, but as in reasonable creatures,
of whom he requireth consent of will, desire and endeuour
in the vse of the meanes ordained of God, for the beginning
and perfecting of this worke of sanctification in vs. And although this will, desire, and endeuour, be his work likewise,
yet these exhortations to godlinesse are to good purpose;
for with the exhortation God ioyneth the operation of his
spirit, and whilest he commandeth vs, he giueth power also
to performe that which he commandeth; whilest he exhorteth vs to sanctification, hee himselfe sanctifieth vs with his
spirit.

§. Sect.2.
*That the work
of sanctifica-
tion is com-
mon to the
three persons in
Trinitie.*
Tit 3.5.
Eph.2.4.5.
Heb.9.14.

Now further wee are to know, that as all other workes of
God which he exerciseth towards his creatures, so this work
of sanctification likewise is common vnto the three persons
in the Trinitie: for first God the Father sanctifieth vs by giuing vs his sonne and sending his spirit, and therefore this
work is ascribed vnto him, Tit.3.5.Eph.2.4.5.God the sonne
sanctifieth vs, by mortifying our sins by vertue of his bloud,
purging our consciences from dead workes, that wee may
serue the liuing God, and by vertue of his resurrection raising vs also from the death of sinne to newnesse of life: and
lastly, by his death hath merited for vs Gods spirit, and rising againe hath sent him vnto vs, whereby wee are regenerate: and therefore hee also is said to haue sanctified vs, and
God is said to haue sanctified vs in him, Eph.5.26. 1.Cor.2.

Eph.5.26..
1.Cor.2.11.

11. God the holy Ghost also sanctifieth vs, by applying the
vertue

vertue of Chrifts death and refurrection vnto vs, and fo immediatly beginneth, continueth, and perfecteth this worke
in vs, and therefore moft vfually in the Scriptures this worke
is afcribed vnto him, Ioh.3.5,6. Act.11.16. Tit.3.5.

Ioh.3.5.6.
Act.11.16.
Tit.3.5.

And thus it appeareth that God himfelfe is the principall
and onely efficient caufe of our fanctification; vpon which
point I haue the longer infifted, to the end that wee fhould
not in this worke reft vpon our owne ftrength, for then wee
fhall be fubiect to many difcouragements, and lie open to
innumerable temptations, grounded vpon our fmall meafure and flow progreffe in our fanctification, as alfo vpon the
great difficulties and manifolde difcouragemenrs, which
both ftay vs in the birth, and hinder our full growth in true
godlineffe; all which in refpect of our owne power prooue
this worke not onely hard, but euen impoffible for vs to be
perfected and accomplifhed. But rather that wee relie our
felues vpon the Lords infinite power and gracious promifes, whereby wee are affured, notwithftanding our owne exceeding weakneffe, that he will not onely begin, but alfo finifh and perfect this good worke in vs.

And thus much concerning the principall efficient caufe
of our fanctification: the motiue caufe which mooued the
Lord to fanctifie vs, was his owne mercie and Chrifts merits. The firft is expreffed by the Apoftle 1.Pet.1.3. whereas
it is faid, that God *according to his abundant mercie hath be-*
gotten vs again, &c. The other is implied by *Paul* Eph.2.5.
where hee faith, that God hath quickened vs in Chrift; who
by his death merited not onely the remiffion of finne for vs,
but alfo Gods fpirit, whereby wee are fanctified. So that it
was not any good inclination vnto holineffe in vs, or any
thing els wherein we excelled others, which moued God to
fanctifie vs, for wee were all alike the *children of wrath and*
dead in our finnes, but onely his owne boundleffe mercie and
the alfufficient merits of Chrift our Sauiour, were the onely
caufes which moued the Lord to giue vs his fpirit, whereby
we are regenerate and raifed from the death of finne to holineffe and newneffe of life. And therefore let vs not arrogate the praife of our fanctification in whole or in part vnto

§. Sect.3.
The motiue
caufe Gods
fole mercie.
1.Pet.1.3.

Ephef.2.5.

Eph.2 1.3.

our

our selues, but ascribe all the glorie to God who is the sole author and finisher of it.

§. *Sect.4.*
*Of the instru-
mentall causes
of our sanctifi-
cation.*
Ioh 15.3.
and 17.17.
Iam.1.18.
1.Pet.1.23.

The instrumentall causes of our sanctification, are either externall or internall; the external are first the word of God, of which our Sauiour speaketh Ioh.15.3. *Now are you cleane through the word which I haue spoken vnto you.* And cap.17.17. *Sanctifie thē with thy truth: thy word is truth.* So the Apostle *Iames* chap.1.18. *Of his owne will begat he vs with the word of truth, &c.* And the Apostle *Peter* affirmeth, that we are *borne anew not of mortall seede, but of immortall by the word of God, &c.* The word of God therefore is an instrumentall cause of our sanctification. In which respect also the Ministers, by whose ministerie wee are conuerted and regenerate, are said

1.Cor.4.15.
Philem.v.10.

to be our spirituall fathers who haue begotten vs vnto God: as appeareth 1.Cor.4.15. and Philem.vers.10.in both which places *Paul* chalengeth this title vnto himselfe. Another ex-ternall cause of our sanctification are the Sacraments, espe-cially the Sacrament of Baptisme; whereof it is that *Ananias*

Act.22.16.
Eph.5.26.

saith vnto *Paul* Act.22.16. *Arise and be baptized & wash away thy sins.* So Eph.5.26. it is said that Christ gaue himself *for his Church, that he might sanctifie it and cleanse it by the washing of water through the word.* The which places as they are to be vnderstood principally of the washing of iustification, wher-by we are purged from the guilt and punishment of sinne; so also of the washing of sanctification, whereby we are clean-sed from the sinnes and corruptions themselues.

The internall instrument of our sanctification is a liuely faith, without which the other outward instruments are vn-effectuall, in those who are of yeeres; neither must we think that the bare action of hearing, or the outward washing, take away our sins and corruptions, vnlesse the word and things signified in the Sacraments bee applied vnto vs by a true faith. For the word which we heare profiteth not, vnlesse it

Heb.4.2.
Act.8.37.

be mixed with faith in those that heare it, Heb.4.2. And vn-lesse those that are capable of faith beleeue with all their heart, it is to no purpose to be baptized, Act.8.37: and there-fore vnto the other we must ioyne this instrument of a liuely faith, if wee would attaine vnto true sanctification. For faith
purifieth

purifieth the heart, and is fruitfull in the workes of loue, as Act. 15.9. Gal. 5.6. the Scripture speaketh.

And thus haue I set downe the efficient causes of our san- §. Sect. 5. ctification; in the next place let vs consider of the manner *Of the manner* how this worke is wrought in vs. For the vnderstanding *how our sancti-* whereof we are to know, that wee being vnited vnto Christ, *fication is* principally by Gods spirit, and instrumentally by a liuely *wrought.* faith, and so made members of his mysticall bodie, doe participate the vertue of his death, buriall, and resurrection, whereby not onely our iustification but also our sanctification is deriued vnto vs. For first, by vertue of his death our sinnes are mortified, and our corruptions crucified together with him : as appeareth Rom. 6. 6. *Knowing this, that our old* Rom. 6. 6. *man is crucified with him, that the bodie of sinne might be destroyed, that hencefoorth we should not serue sinne.* Secondly, by vertue of his buriall, this death of sinne is as it were further continued, and thereby our sinnes and corruptions are more and more subdued and kept vnder, that they cannot rise and rebel against the spirit. And of this the Apostle speaketh Rom. 6. 3. where he saith, that we *are buried with Christ* Rom. 6. 3. *into his death.* Thirdly, by vertue of his resurrection there is a quickening power deriued into vs, whereby wee are reuiued and raised vp from the death of sinne to holinesse and newnesse of life. And of this mention is made Coloss. 2. 12. 13. Col. 2. 12. 13. where it is said, that *as we are buried with Christ, so likewise wee* Rom. 6. 4. *are raised vp and quickened together with him :* and Rom. 6. 4. the Apostle saith, that we are *buried with him by baptisme into his death, that like as Christ was raised vp from the dead by the glorie of the father, so wee also should walke in newnesse of life.*

And this is the manner according to which God wor- §. Sect. 6. keth sanctification in vs ; now wee are briefly to speake of *Of the ends of* the other causes, as they lie in order. The materiall and for- *our sanctifica-* mall causes of our sanctification may best be considered in *tion.* the parts thereof. The finall cause is two-fold: Gods glorie, 1 which is the chiefe and principall cause of our sanctification; and the eternal saluation of those who are sanctified, 2 which is subordinate to the other. For the first, that Gods

glorie

glorie is the end of all our good actions and holy conuersation,it appeareth Mat.5.16. *Let your light so shine before men*
that they may see your good works,and glorifie your father which
is in heauen. So 1.Pet.2.12. *Haue your conuersation honest a-*
mong the Gentiles, that they which speake euill of you as of euill
doers,may by your good workes which they shall see glorifie God
in the day of visitation. And the Apostle *Paul* willeth vs, that
*we doe all things whatsoeuer to the glorie of God,*1.Cor.10.31.

    For the other,we are therefore sanctified that wee may be
saued,and also be assured of our saluation : and this we may
gather out of the Apostles words Tit.3.5.7. where hee saith,
that *God hath saued vs by the washing of the new birth, and re-*
nuing of the holy Ghost, that we should be made heires of eternall
*life.*Neither can we euer inioy euerlasting happinesse,vnlesse
we be regenerate,according to that Ioh.3.3.*Except a man be*
*borne againe,he cannot see the kingdome of God.*So the Apostle
saith, that *flesh and bloud cannot inherit the kingdome of God,*
*neither doth corruption inherit vncorruption,*1.Cor.15.50.And
Apoc.21.27. it is said, that *no vncleane thing shall enter into*
Gods kingdome : and therefore the Apostle Heb.12.14. vseth
this as an effectuall argument to mooue vs to embrace sanctification, because *without this holinesse no man shall see the*
Lord. On the other side,if wee bee regenerate and shew the
fruites thereof in a holy conuersation, by dying to sinne and
rising againe to newnesse of life,then may wee bee certainly
assured of our saluation : and therefore the Apostle willeth
vs by these workes of holinesse to *make our calling and elec-*
tion sure, affirming that *if wee doe these things wee shall neuer*
*fall.*2.Pet.1.10.

(marginal references:)
Matth.5.16.
1.Pet.2.12.
1.Cor.10.31.
Tit.3 5.7.
Ioh.3.3.
1.Cor.15.50.
Apoc 21.27.
Heb.12.14.
2.Pet.1.10.

CHAP. II.
Of the effects,subiect obiect,and time of our
sanctification.

§. *Sect.*1.
Of the effects
of our sancti-
fication.

THe principall effects of our sanctification, are a de-
testation of our former sinnes in which wee haue
taken our pleasure and delight,and an hartie loue
of righteousnesse and holinesse,which before our regeneration

tion were loathfome and vnpleafant vnto vs; when notwithftanding our infirmities and often falles wee can fay
with the Apoftle *Paul*, that wee would faine doe that good
we cannot, and hate that euill which we doe, and howfoeuer
wee cannot performe perfect obedience to all Gods com-
mandements, yet we *delight in the law of God in the inner man,*   Rom.7.15.19.
Rom.7.15.19.22. Secondly, from thefe affections of louing   22.
good and hating euill, there arifeth an earneft defire to embrace the one and flee the other , and from this defire proceedeth a fetled purpofe of heart, and a carefull endeuour to
mortifie our flefh with the corruptions thereof, and for the
time to come to frame our liues according to the rule of
Gods word, the which purpofe and endeuour is ioyned with
the diligent vfe of all good meanes, wherby we may attaine
vnto our defire. Thirdly, when as this defire and endeuour
to leade a godly life is hindred by our fpiritual enemies, the
flefh, the world and the diuell, there followeth in the man regenerate a fpirituall combat, wherein hee ftrugleth and ftriueth to withftand their temptations, and to goe forward in
his courfe of holy obedience. And if hee preuaile and foyle
his fpirituall enemies, then there followeth peace of confcience and ioy in the holy Ghoft; but if hee bee ouercome
and led captiue vnto finne, through the violence of their
temptations, then doth hee not lie ftill and fuffer finne to
raigne in him, but hee feeketh to rife againe by vnfained repentance, which is accompanied with thefe feuen fruites :
Firft, a care to leaue that fin into which he is fallen. Secondly,   2.Cor.7.11.
an vtter condemning of himfelfe for it. Thirdly, an holy an-
ger againft himfelfe for his fall. Fourthly, a feare leaft againe
he fhould fall into the fame finne. Fiftly, a defire euer after
to pleafe God. Sixtly, a zeale of the fame. Seuenthly, reuenge
vpon himfelfe for his former offence. And thefe are the effects of true fanctification, which whofoeuer can finde in
himfelfe, he may be affured that he is fanctified and fhall be
faued.

The fubiect in which this worke of fanctification is   §. *Sect.*2.
wrought, is all and euery one of Gods elect, and them only :   *Of the fubiect*
neither is there any fanctified but thofe onely that are e-   *of our fanctifi-*
lected   *cation.*

lected and shall be saued, as appeareth Ephef.1.4. Neither is this worke begun in any one part of them alone, but in all the parts, powers, and faculties of soule and bodie, as appeareth 1.Thef.5.23. The *God of peace sanctifie you throughout:* The minde is inlightned with the true knowledge of Gods will reuealed in his word, which before was blinded with ignorance. The memorie is inabled to retaine those holy things which the vnderstanding conceiueth. The will fleeth that which is euill, and imbraceth that which is good. The affections are purged from their corruptions, and made seruiceable to holy reason. The body also is sanctified, and made a fit temple for the holy Ghost: so that whereas heretofore the members thereof were the *readie seruants of vnrighteousnesse vnto sinne, they are now become the seruants of righteousnesse vnto holinesse.* Lastly, the actions and outward conuersation which heretofore were sinfull and scandalous, are now holy and righteous, seruing both for the aduancement of Gods glorie, and the edification of our christian brethren. In a word, whosoeuer are truely sanctified, they are also wholy sanctified, that is, as the Apostle speaketh, sanctified throughout, in euery part and facultie of bodie and soule. And therefore whosoeuer would bee assured that he hath attained true sanctification, he is to labour to compose and frame the whole man, his minde and imagination, his will and affections, his outward actions, life and conuersation, according to the exact rule of Gods law: in all of them mortifying the old man, and his inbred corruption, and imbracing the contrarie duties of holinesse and righteousnesse. Otherwise if our sanctification be not of the whole man, and euery part in their seuerall measure, it will in the end be vaine and fruitlesse; for as it is to no purpose for citizens being besieged, to fortifie one place of the wall, and leaue another part vnfortified, or to keepe strait watch at some of the gates and leaue others open; so it will not auaile vs to fortifie some parts against the power of sinne, and to leaue others weake and naked, nor to garde some of the outward passages of the senses, and neglecting some other, suffer them to lie as an open entrance to let in

our

Marginal references:
Pfal.119.18.
Col.1.9.
Pfal.119.11.
Rom.7.18.

1.Cor.3.16.

Rom.6.19.

our fpirituall enemies, for fo they will eafily furprife vs, and leade vs captiue vnto finne; but if we would be in any fafetie in this ftrait fiege, we muft fet a ftrong garde, and a carefull watch, ouer euery part and facultie of our bodies and foules.

The obiect of our fanctification about which it is exercifed, is finne and corruption, and holineffe and righteoufneffe, that we may flie the one and imbrace the other, mortifie the flefh and the lufts thereof, and be quickned in the fpirit that we may be conformable in all holy obedience vnto the law of God, auoyding that which he hath forbidden, and labouring to performe that which hee hath commaunded.

§. *Sect.*3. *Of the obiect and time of our fanctification.*

The time when fanctification is wrought in vs, is prefently after we are effectually called and iuftified; for as foone as the vertue and power of Chrifts obedience, death, and refurrection, is applied vnto vs by a liuely faith, it doth not onely free vs from the guilt and punifhment of finne, but alfo mortifie the flefh with the corruptions thereof, and quickneth vs in the inner man, enabling vs to forfake our former finnes, and to ferue the Lord in holineffe and newneffe of life. But howfoeuer our fanctification bee begun prefently after our conuerfion, yet it is not fo foone finifhed; but as the feede being caft into the ground, doth firft take roote, and then is fcarcely difcorned, afterwards fhooteth forth into a blade, and fo fpringeth vp by little and little, till it bringeth forth an eare, and laftly it ripeneth and yeeldeth to the fower plentifull increafe: fo when firft the feedes of fanctification are fowne in vs, by vertue of Gods fpirit, they haue a time to take rooting, when as they make little or no fhew to our felues or others, but afterwards they fend forth as it were a blade of a holy profeffion, and the ripe fruites of godlineffe. Notwithftanding thefe fruites in this life are not purely cleane, and without mixture; but as in the faireft field there is amongft the cleaneft wheate fome tares and cockell: fo in thofe that are moft fanctified, there are many corruptions of the flefh, mixed with the good fruites of the fpirit, the which the chriftian is ftill in weeding Apoc. 22, 11.

Qq 4   and

and plucking vp by the rootes so long as he liueth, but yet can neuer ouercome this great worke, till the winter of death wholy nippeth and killeth thefe weedes of finne. We muft not therefore prefently after our conuerfion, dreame of a perfection in fanctification; no nor yet at the firft, eftimate the truenefe thereof by the greatnefe of the meafure: for as it is in the naturall generation and growth of the body, fo alfo in fpirituall regeneration; all is not finifhed at the firft, but perfected by degrees. As foone as we are conuerted, we are but babes in Chrift, and, in refpect of our infancie in knowledge faith and other graces, fuch as haue neede rather of *milke than of ftrong meate:* in the reft of our life we grow vp from ftrength to ftrength, till we come to mans eftate, vnto which age we cannot properly be faid to haue attained, till by death we wholy lay afide the old man, and the corruptions thereof: and laftly we attaine to our confummation and full perfection, when at the latter day wee fhall rife againe, and both in body and foule bee indued with perfect holinefe, whereby we fhall be enabled to performe obedience to Gods will, in that degree which his iuftice requireth.

Heb. 5. 14.

Rom. 8. 29.

Chap. III.

Of the parts of Sanctification.

§. *Sect.* 1.
That fanctification containeth two parts, mortification, and viuification.

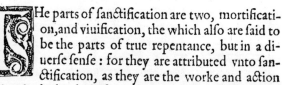He parts of fanctification are two, mortification, and viuification, the which alfo are faid to be the parts of true repentance, but in a diuerfe fenfe : for they are attributed vnto fanctification, as they are the worke and action of God, who by his holy fpirit doth mortifie and quicken vs, and is the fole author and caufe of our fanctification; and vnto repentance as they haue reference vnto vs, who being regenerate and indued with Gods fpirit, doe labour in the mortification of our corruptions, and indeauour to ferue the Lord in newneffe of life ; for, *Spiritu fancto acti agimus,* we being firft moued and fet a worke by Gods fpirit,

doe

doe worke together with him. This diuision hath it ground and warrant in many places of holy Scriptures, in which it is expreſſed in diuers phraſes and formes of ſpeech. Pſal.34. 14, *Eſcew euill and doe good.* Eſa.1.16.17, *Ceaſe to doe euill, learne to doe well.* Rom.6.11, likewiſe, *thinke ye alſo that ye are dead to ſinne, but are aliue to God in Ieſus Chriſt our Lord.* And v.18. *Being free from ſin ye are made the ſeruants of righteouſneſſe.* Epheſ.4.22,*That ye caſt of concerning the conuerſation in time paſt the old man which is corrupt through the deceiuable luſts.* 23. *And be renewed in the ſpirit of your minde.* 24. *And put on the new man which after God is created in righteouſneſſe and true holineſſe.* So Rom.7.4. 8.13. 1.Cor.5.7. Col.2.12. 3.9. Gal.5.16. 1.Pet.2.24. 3.11.By al which places and many others it is cleere and manifeſt, that our ſanctification conſiſteth of theſe two parts, the mortifying of the fleſh, and the quickning of the ſpirit.

Mortification is the firſt part of ſanctification, wherein the ſpirit of God applying vnto vs the vertue and power of Chriſts death and buriall, doth by little and little weaken, ſubdue, and kill in vs our naturall corruption, the fleſh and the luſts thereof, ſo that they are not ſo powrfull as in times paſt to ſtirre vp in our mindes euill motions which are contrarie to the will and word of God.

In this deſcription is ſet downe firſt the cauſe of our mortification,which is the vertue and efficacie of Chriſts death and buriall, communicated and applied vnto vs by the ſpirit of God, whereby wee are ingrafted into the body of Chriſt, and ſo made partakers of the power and vertue of Chriſts death, which being deriued vnto vs, doth not onely take away the guilt and puniſhment of ſinne, but alſo doth mortifie and kill our naturall corruptions, which heretofore wholy ruled and ouerſwaied vs. Secondly, the forme manner and progreſſe of this worke is here expreſſed, namely, the weakning, ſubduing, and killing of our corruption by little and little ; ſo that this worke is not perfected at once, and in an inſtant, but by degrees: firſt it is weakned and the power thereof ſomewhat abated, ſo as though it beare ſway in vs, yet it doth not wholy ouerrule vs without reſiſtance,

as

Pſal.34 14. and 37.27. Eſa.1.16.17. Rom.5.11.18 Eph.4.22.23.

§. Sect.2. *Of Mortification what it is and how it is wrought.*

Rom.6.4.5,

as it was vfed to doe in the time of our ignorance : then being further enabled by vertue of Gods fpirit, working in vs, we preuaile againft it,fo that though it often rebell, yet doe we fubdue it and obtaine victorie. Laftly obtaining a greater meafure of the fpirit, we mortifie and kill it; that is, though we doe not vtterly depriue it of life and motion, yet we giue it fuch a deadly wound that it neuer recouereth his former ftrength , but ftill pineth and languifheth , till with the death of the bodie it alfo dieth and is wholy abolifhed. Now whileft it is in this confumption and neere vnto death, hauing a long time before been weake, oftentimes it feemeth to recouer ftrength, and to offer fome violence vnto the regenerat part:but this muft not difcourage vs,as though now it were on the mending hand, and like to be reftored to it former health and ftrength : for as it fareth with thofe that lie vpon their deathbead; fo it is with our ficke flefh, and the corruptions thereof, after that nature feemeth fpent, and the power thereof wholy decayed, oftentimes falling into fome grieuous fit, wherein there is a fight betweene life and death, their ftrength feemeth redoubled and farre greater than euer it was: but bee of good comfort, it is no figne of health,but a pange of death which neare approacheth.

And thus you fee the death of finne and our naturall corruption. Now as in the death of the body there is a certaine progreffe therein, namely,when the dead carcafe is alfo buried;fo alfo there is not only a death of finne, but alfo a buriall, the which is wrought by the vertue of Chrifts buriall applied vnto vs by Gods fpirit,whereby it commeth to paffe that finne which is already flaine and dead, doth fo remaine and continue;fo that this buriall of finne is nothing elfe but the further progreffe and continuance of our mortification. Of this the Apoftle fpeaketh, Rom.6.4. *We are buried then with him by baptifme into his death,&c.* So Col.2.12.

And thus haue I fhewed what our mortification is, which as it is a worke moft hard,fo alfo moft neceffary:the difficulty appeareth by the name which is borrowed from the practife of Chirurgeons, who before they cut off any member, doe firft mortifie it, that after they may take it away with

leffe

Rom.6.4.
Col.2.12.
and 3.3.5.

Rom.6.4.

§. Sect.3.
That the worke of mortification is hard and neceffarie.

Of Mortification.

leſſe ſenſe of paine. And this is implyed by our Sauiour Chriſt, whereas hee inioyneth vs, if our right hand or eye offend vs,to cut it off and plucke it out: and plainely expreſ-ſed by the Apoſtle *Paul* Col.3.5. *Mortifie therefore your members which are in the earth, fornication, vncleaneneſſe, the inordinate affection, euill concupiſcence and couetouſneſſe,&c.* where calling theſe ſinnes by the name of members,he inti-mateth thus much,that they are as deare vnto vs as the mem-bers of our body, and alſo that it is as vnpleaſant and paine-full vnto vs to forſake our naturall corruptions, as to be de-priued of the hand, eye, or foote. But though this worke be moſt hard, yet it is moſt neceſſary ; for the beſt things that are in the fleſh and vnregenerate part , euen the *wiſedome thereof is death and enmitie againſt God, becauſe it is not ſub-iect to the lawe of God,neither in deede can be,*Rom.8.6,7. nei-ther can we doe any thing pleaſing vnto God ſo long as we are in the fleſh,as it is verſe 8. Laſtly,if we liue after the fleſh, we ſhall dye,euen the euerlaſting death of body and ſoule; but if wee mortifie the deeds of the body by the ſpirit wee ſhall liue,euen the life of holineſſe and righteouſneſſe vpon earth, and the life of glory and eternall happineſſe in Gods kingdome. And therefore if it be neceſſary to be in amitie with God,whoſe *louing kindneſſe is better than life*; or to per-forme obedience vnto the lawe of God,or to doe any thing pleaſing in his ſight,or to eſcape death and damnation,or to inioy life and eternall ſaluation, then is it alſo neceſſarie to mortifie the fleſh and the luſts thereof, how hard and vn-pleaſant ſoeuer this worke ſeemeth vnto vs. So that the dif-ficulty muſt not diſcourage vs, but rather double our dili-gence; and becauſe it is a paine intollerable to part with our ſinnes, ſo long as they remaine like liuely members of the body of our fleſh, therefore as Chirurgians (to make the paine tollerable to the patient) doe firſt vſe meanes to mor-tifie the member which they purpoſe to cut off; ſo let vs vſe all good meanes to weaken the ſtrength of ſinne, and to mortifie our carnall affections,and then we ſhall ſuffer them to be quite cut off and taken from vs without any extraordi-narie paſſion or ſenſe of paine.

And

Col.3.5.

Rom.8.6,7,8.

Pſalm.63.4.

§. Sect.4.
Of Viuificati-
on, what it is,
and the causes
thereof.

And so much concerning our mortification, viuification is the second part of our sanctification, wherein the spirit of God communicating and applying vnto vs the vertue and efficacie of Chrifts refurrection, doth raife vs vp from the death of finne to holinefle and newnefle of life.

The caufe of our viuification is the vertue and efficacie of Chrifts refurrection applied vnto vs by Gods fpirit; the which vertue flowing from his deitie, was firft powerfull in his owne flefh, raifing it out of graue, and giuing it victorie ouer finne and death, and being deriued from our head, and communicated vnto vs who are members of his body, it doth alfo reuiue vs who were dead in our finnes, and inableth vs to leade a new life in holinefle and righteoufnefle, according to the rule of Gods word. This appeareth, Rom. 6.4. where he faith that we are buried with him by baptifme into his death, that like as Chrift was raifed vp from the dead by the glory of the father, fo we alfo fhould walke in new-

Phili 3.10.11. nefle of life. So Philip.3.10,11. where *Paul* defireth not onely to bee clothed with the righteoufnefle of Chrift applied by faith for his iuftification, but alfo to know *and feele the vertue of Chrifts refurrection, that by this meanes he might attaine vnto the refurrection of the dead.* And as *Paul* earneftly defired this, fo alfo he attained vnto it, as himfelfe profef-

Gal.2.20. feth. Galath.2.20. *Thus* (faith hee) *I liue, yet not I now but Chrift liueth in me, and in that I now liue in the flefh, I liue by faith in the fonne of God, who hath loued me and giuen himfelfe for me.* Now this efficacie and vertue of Chrifts refurrection is applied vnto vs by Gods fpirit, which vniteth vs vnto Chrift our head, and therefore vfually in the Scriptures this

Rom. 8.11. worke is afcribed vnto him. So Rom.8.11. *But if the fpirit of him that raifed vp Iefus from the dead dwell in you, he that raifed vp Chrift from the dead fhall alfo quicken your mortall bodies, becaufe his fpirit dwelleth in you.*

§. Sect.5.
Of the manner
how our viui-
fication is
wrought.

And thus haue I fhewed the author of our viuification: the manner how it is wrought followeth to bee fpoken of. Firft, the fpirit of God difpelleth the cloudes of ignorance, and illuminateth the eyes of our vnderftanding with the beames of true fauing knowledge, wherewith being inlightened,

tened,we rightly iudge that folly and madnesse,in which we thought formerly our chiefe wisdome consisted, and approue that as onely wise, which before wee condemned as extreame foolishnesse. Of this the Apostle speaketh, Ephes. 1.17. where he prayeth that God would bestow vpon them *the spirit of wisdome and reuelation through the knowledge of him, that the eyes of their vnderstanding might bee inlighte-* Ephes. 1.17. *ned,&c.* After the vnderstanding is thus inlightened, then also the will is changed; and whereas before regeneration it was corrupt,peruerse,and rebellious, now being sanctified, it beginneth to hate and auoide that euill which in former times it loued and imbraced, and to like and delight in that good which formerly it loathed and abhorred: so that the regenerate man saith with the Apostle,that to will is present with him, though hee finde no meanes to performe that which is good;and that he is *delighted in the lawe of God con-* Rom.7.18.22. *cerning the inner man,*though *the law of his members rebelling against the law of his mind,leade him captiue to the law of sinne.* Finally, the vnderstanding being inlightened, and the will reformed,there followeth the renewing of all the affections, the thoughts, imaginations, powers and faculties of the soule : and lastly, the internal parts being quickened, there insueth the renuing of the body, the outward actions, life and conuersation.

And thus haue I set downe the manner and forme of our §. Sect.6. spirituall renewing : now as the worke of mortification, so *That the worke* this of viuification,is not perfected and finished in an in- *of sanctificati-* stant,but in continuance of time and by degrees; neither *on is not fini-* doe we so long as we continue in this life, receiue any great *shed in an in-* measure thereof, but onely *the first fruites,* which is but as it *stant.* were a little handfull in respect of that large haruest of godlinesse which we shall attaine vnto in Gods kingdome, as the Apostle speaketh, Rom. 8. 23. Whereas therefore the Rom.8.23. Church is saide to bee perfectly purged from all spottes of sinne,Ephes.5.26,27. it is to be vnderstood of our iustifica- Ephe.5.26,27 tion, whereby the faithfull are deliuered from the guilt and punishment of sinne, and adorned with Christs perfect righteousnesse;and not of our sanctification, which is onely

begun

begun in this life, but not perfected till the life to come, as it
2.Cor.5.1,2. &c.
is notably set downe 2.Cor.5.1,2,3,4.

CHAP. IIII.

Sathans temptations, Whereby he laboureth to intice vs to commit sinne, answered.

§.Sect.1.
Of the kinds of Sathans temptations whereby he indeauoreth to hinder our sanctification.

Nd so much for the doctrine of sanctification, the right vnderstanding wherof serueth much for the answering of all contrarie cauils and obiections, which are suggested into our mindes by our spirituall enemies. Now, ha-uing shewed the trueth of this doctrine, let vs in the next place propound Sathans temptations, which he commonly vseth to hinder this worke of sanctification : to the end that the weake christian may bee the better inabled to answere them in the day of triall.

The temptations which Sathan suggesteth to hinder our progresse in godlinesse are of two sorts : either allurements to intice vs to goe aside out of the narrow path of holi-nesse, into the broade way of sinne and wickednesse; or dis-couragements to disharten and wearie vs, in trauailing this spirituall iourney. By the first, he sweeteneth the bitter pill of sinne that it may seeme pleasant to our carnall appetites, to the end that we may greedely swallow it to our euerla-sting bane; by the other hee laboureth to make holsome godlinesse loathsome and altogether vnpleasant to our sen-suall taste. Those hee commonly vseth before we haue sin-ned, to cause vs presumptuously to fall into it : and these af-ter wee haue sinned and wounded our consciences, to the end hee may moue vs desperately to surcease our labour in the workes of sanctification, as being not only difficult, but altogether impossible.

§. Sect.2.
Of Sathans temptation, whereby he al-lureth vs to fall into sinne.

The first sort of his temptations whereby he laboureth to draw vs into sinne, he inforceth by extenuating the sinne vn-to which he allureth vs, by putting vs in minde of the mer-cies of God, and merits of Christ, and by hiding from vs
the

the curſe of the law, and the puniſhments threatned againſt ſinne both in this life and the life to come. Why (will hee ſay) makeſt thou ſuch ſcruple of committing this ſinne which is ſo pleaſant or profitable vnto thee; ſeeing it is in it owne nature but very ſmall, and almoſt no offence at all, being compared with the great tranſgreſſions which others haue committed, who notwithſtanding are ſaid euen in the Scriptures to haue been moſt godly and righteous, yea, and highly in Gods loue and fauour; why therefore ſhouldeſt thou who art farre inferiour vnto them, ſtumble at this ſmall ſtrawe, ſeeing theſe great blockes could not hinder euen the moſt religious from inioying the pleaſures of ſinne? Conſider alſo the common frailtie of mankinde, and the naturall corruptions of the beſt, whereby they are ready to fall when the leaſt occaſions are offered, into ſinnes farre greater then this which ſo much pleaſeth thee. Remember that thou canſt not be a ſaint in this life, nor freed from that corruption which ſo faſt cleaueth vnto thee; and therefore ſeeing thou muſt needs ſinne; now ſinne, when thereby thou maiſt haue pleaſure or profit, for doe what thou canſt, yet thou ſhalt often fall. And why wilt thou not rather be lead with delight, then be drawne with neceſſitie? Conſider likewiſe that thy God is moſt mercifull, and therefore ſtill ready to pardon thy ſinnes; and the rather, becauſe he knoweth thy fraile weakeneſſe in reſiſting ſinne, and inability to performe obedience to his lawe: and alſo that Chriſt died, not for the iuſt but the vniuſt, not for the righteous, but for the ſinner: and therefore be thy ſinnes neuer ſo many, yet applying the merits of Chriſt by faith, neither their guilt nor puniſhment ſhall be imputed vnto thee. Call to minde alſo the gracious promiſes of pardon and forgiueneſſe, which are made vnto thee in the Goſpell; for the obtaining whereof, nothing is required of thee but faith and repentance: now this faith thou haſt already, and this repentance thou maiſt haue hereafter when thou haſt inioyed the pleaſure or profit of this ſinne. Neither doth repentance goe before, but followeth the committing of ſinne; ſo that vnleſſe thou firſt ſinne, thou haſt no cauſe of repentance nor neede to repent.

And

§. Sect.3.
That the world and the flesh further the former temptation.

And thefe and fuch like are Sathans baites, wherewith he allureth vs to intangle our felues in the fnares of finne : into which wee are more readie to fall through the corruption of the flefh, which naturally louing finne, doth, with the euill motions and defires thereof, further Sathans temptations; and the inftigation of the world which pricketh vs forward and draweth vs on into the fteepe defcending way of wickedneffe, into which we are readie to runne headlong of our owne accord; partly alluring vs with pleafures , riches and worldly glorie, the defired obiects of our carnall defires; and partly drawing vs with euill examples, firft to a liking, and then to the practizing of thofe finnes, which we fee committed by others.

Againft all which temptations that we may be the better armed, let vs in the next place propound fome arguments whereby wee may bee withheld from falling into Sathans fnares of finne, into which his fuggeftions, the worlds allurements, and our owne corruptions leade and draw vs: and then being hereby moued to a true deteftation of our finnes, and an earneft defire of hauing a diuorce fued betwixt vs and them, I will afterwards fet downe fome meanes, by the carefull vfe whereof we may be inabled to ftand in the day of temptation, and preferued from falling into thofe finnes which we alreadie condemne in our iudgements and diflike in our affections.

§. Sect.4.
The preferuatiues to keepe vs from finne, of two forts.

The reafons whereby wee may bee perfwaded to refift finne are of two forts: the firft, tying vs to holy obedience in the bands of loue : the other, binding vs from falling into finne with the cords of feare. Of the former ranke are thefe and fuch like holy confiderations.

The first reafon taken from Gods loue towards vs.

Firft, wee are to fet before vs the infinite loue of God towards vs bafe and vile creatures , altogether vnworthie of his leaft fauour by reafon of our finnes; the which his loue as it plainly appeareth in all other his mercies and manifolde benefits beftowed on vs, fo efpecially in fending his onely begotten and dearely beloued fonne , not onely to fuffer fome fmall miferie, but euen death it felfe, yea that curfed ignominious and cruell death of the croffe for vs, who were

not

not his louing friends or faithfull seruants, but opposed enemies and rebellious traytors, who had renounced his seruice
and yeelded our selues as slaues to Sathan readie to doe his
will. Seeing therefore our good God hath so dearely loued
vs, who were altogether vnworthie his loue, and most worthie of his anger and heauie iudgements, O why should not
this flame of his loue towards vs, kindle some sparkles of
loue towards him againe, who is in himselfe the chief goodnesse, and to vs most kinde and gratious? If for our sakes who
were his abiect enemies, hee hath not spared his owne sonne
but gaue him to die for vs; should wee not for his sake, who
is our chiefest friend, bee as willing to part with our sinnes,
and to kill and crucifie all our carnall corruptions? Neither
can wee by any other meanes so cleerely shew our loue to
God as by hating sinne, which aboue al things in the world
is most hatefull and odious vnto him, and the onely cause
which maketh him abhorre euen his excellent creatures, so
that though hee loued them as being his owne workes, yet
he detested them being defiled with the filthie spots of sin;
yea so odious is sinne vnto our righteous God, that he could
not chuse but punish it in his dearely beloued sonne, who
bare our transgressions and sustained our persons, and when
there was no other way to subdue the power of sinne, hee
gaue it a mortall wound euen through the bodie of our
blessed Sauiour, and deliuered him to be crucified, that by
this meanes he might also kill and crucifie our corruptions.
Seeing therefore sinne is most odious and detestable in the
eyes of God, wee cannot better shew our loue towards him,
which his loue towards vs hath so well deserued, than by
hating and flying that which he so much abhorreth.

Secondly, let vs call to our remembrance his innumerable
benefits, which are the vndoubted signes of his loue towards vs. First hee hath elected vs vnto eternall life that wee
should be holy. Seeing therfore he hath made special choise
of vs amongst many who are reiected, therfore let vs exceed
others in a holy care of seruing him, and auoiding those
things which are displeasing in his sight; hee also hath created vs to the end we should worship and serue him our Lord

§. Sect. 5.
The second
reason, taken
from Gods be-
nefits.
Ephes. 1. 4.

R r   and

Act.17.28.
and Creator: and therefore seeing we haue our being from him,let vs in al our actions seeke his glorie and auoid sinne, whereby he is dishonoured. Yea hee hath not made vs the vilest of his creatures, but reasonable men according to his owne image and likenes, and therefore let vs not deface this glorious workmanship with the filthie spots of sinne.He hath redeemed vs out of the cruell bondage of our spirituall enemies,by giuing his sonne to be the price of our redemption,and therefore seeing we are bought with a price so inestimable,let vs not wilfully again make our selues the bond-

1.Cor.6.20.
Luk.1.74.75.
2.Cor.5.15.
Rom.6.6.8.18
slaues of sinne and Sathan, but *glorifie our redeemer in our bodies and in our soules, seruing him in holinesse and righteousnesse all the daies of our liues.* He hath effectually called vs and selected vs out of the corrupt masse of mankinde, and there-

1.Thess 4.17.
fore *let vs walke worthie our vocation, for God hath not called vs vnto vncleannesse but vnto holinesse.* He hath freely iustified vs, imputing vnto vs Chrifts righteousnesse, and pardoning all our sinnes,both in respect of the guilt and punishment; and therefore being made free from sinne,let vs no longer liue therein,but now become the seruants of righteousnesse;

Luk.7 47.
and seeing he hath forgiuen much,let vs alfo loue much, labouring to manifest our loue by the fruites of holy obedience. He hath reconciled vs vnto himselfe in his sonne, and therefore let vs not by our sinnes make him our enemie, nor againe build vp this wall of separation which Chrift our Sa-

Col.1.21.22.
Eph.2.14.
uiour hath broken downe. He hath adopted vs in Chrift to be his sonnes and heires of euerlafting life,and therfore seeing we are the sonnes of God,let vs yeeld obedience to our heauenly father, and not liue in our finnes like the flaues of Sathan,leaft prouoking his iuft displeafure againft vs by our rebellious wickednesse, wee should bee difinherited of our heauenly patrimonie. He hath granted vnto vs the peace of confcience and ioyes in the holy Ghoft, and therefore let vs not by our sinnes difturbe our peace and wound our confciences,turning our fweete ioy and comfort into griefe and bitter heauineffe. Finally,he hath added vnto thefe fpirituall gifts,innumerable temporarie benefits,health,wealth,libertie,foode,apparell,and therefore let vs not abufe his gifts by
prophaning

prophaning them with our sinnes, but rather vse them as incouragements whereby we may be moued with all cheerefulnes to serue so bountifull a master. In a word, as the gifts of God are infinite which concerne this life and the life to come; so are the reasons drawne from them infinite, which may serue to restraine vs from sinne, and containe vs in the course of holie obedience: the which if wee continually retaine in memorie (euen those benefits which are common to all true Christians, and those which euery one receiueth in his particular place and calling) wee will not (vnlesse our vngratefulnes bee intollerable) easily hearken to Sathans temptations, nor for the vaine pleasures, vncertaine riches and momentanie honours of this wicked world be hired to commit sinne, which we know to be displeasing and odious in the sight of God, who in his endlesse loue hath bestowed vpon vs such innumerable benefits.

Thirdly, when wee are tempted vnto sinne, let vs call to minde the death and suffring of our Sauiour Christ, and say vnto our owne soules, Hath Christ my redeemer paid for my redemption euen his dearest bloud, and shall I sell my soule to sinne againe for this vaine pleasure or base commoditie? Hath he not spared to powre out the full streames of his most precious bloud, that in this pure lauer I might be purged and cleansed from the filthie spots of sinne; and shall the world cause me with her Syrens songs to leape againe into this filthie puddle? Should he suffer himselfe to be crucified that by his death he might kil sin, and shall I now put life into it againe, reuiuing that which hee hath mortified? Did he in his infinite loue giue himselfe for me, and shall I trample this precious gift vnder foote, preferring before it the trifling vanities of this wicked world? Should honour allure me to commit sinne, seeing the glorious sonne of God hath abased himselfe and vndergone ignominious shame to free me from it? Should pleasures intice me to breake Gods comandements, seeing my Sauiour Christ left the bosome of his father, at whose right hand there is fulnes of pleasures & ioyes for euermore, and endured the griefe and miseries of a wretched life and cursed death, that thereby hee might satis-

§. *Sect.6.*
The third reason, taken from the death and suffrings of our Sauiour Christ.

fie

fie Gods iuftice for my tranfgreffions? Should I be perfwaded to commit finne, with the bafe hire of vncertaine riches,

1.Pet.1.18.19 feeing *Chrift hath redeemed me, not with filuer or gold, or any
other corruptible thing, but with the ineftimable price of his moft
precious bloud?* Should my fenfuall tafte and curious pallate,
moue me to finne in drunkenneffe and gluttonie, feeing
Chrift to redeem me hath hungred and thirfted, and in fteed
of drink had offred vnto him gall & vineger? Shall I be moued to finne by anger, and to feeke vniuft reuenge, feeing

Efa.53.7. Chrift being iniured *opened not his mouth, but like an innocent
lambe fuffred himfelfe to be led to the flaughter?* Farre be from
me fuch a defire; nay rather becaufe my Sauiour Chrift hath
fuffred all this for me, to redeeme me out of my fpirituall
bondage, I will refolue rather to be depriued of all worldly
benefits, and endure patiently the greateft miferies and afflictions, than by wilfull falling into finne make my felfe again
the flaue of Sathan. And thus haue I fhewed how the remembrance of Chrifts death and paffion is a notable corra-
fiue to kill our corruptions : and as men are accuftomed to
fhew vnto Elephants the iuyce of the Grape or Mulberie, to
make them more fierce and encourage them to a more couragious fight; fo haue I by offring to our view the precious
bloud of this immaculate Lambe, endeuoured to redouble
our valour in fighting this battell of temptations againft
our fpirituall enemies.

§. Sect.7.
*The fourth
reafon, taken
from the vnion
which is be-
twixt Chrift
and vs.*
Fourthly, let vs remember the vnion that is between Chrift
and vs, whereby he is become our husband, we his fpoufe, he
our head, and wee his members. The confideration whereof
may ferue as a forcible argument to reftraine vs from falling
willingly into any finne; for if wee bee the fpoufe of Chrift,
farre be it from vs to behaue our felues like Sathans ftrum-
pets, proftituting our foules to finne that we may receiue the
gaine of fome worldly vanities, and to incurre the grieuous
difpleafure of our moft louing husband, for the pleafing of
our carnall lufts & fenfuall appetites; if we be the members
of Chrifts bodie, farre be it from vs to make his members

2.Cor.6.15. the inftruments of finne and feruants of vnrighteoufneffe;
for what were this but as much as in vs doth lie, to draw our
holy

holy head into the communion of our sinnes and wickednesse, and to make our Sauiour who in himselfe hath wholy
vanquished and glorioussy tryumphed ouer sinne and Sathan, in his members to recciue a foyle? Nay rather seeing
we are the spouse of Christ,let vs labour to adorne our selues
with the glorious goulden garment of holinesse and righteousnesse; and though we haue some spots of our naturall
infirmities in our outward parts,yet let vs in a glorious manner decke our selues within with integritie and vpright-
nesse of heart; and so the King our heauenly husband shall
take pleasure in our beautie, and place vs at his right hand
in his kingdome of eternall glorie. Seeing also we are the
members of Christs body,therefore let vs endeauour to conforme our selues to the holinesse of our head, and by our
righteous liues and conuersations make it manifest, that we
are quickned and led by the same spirit.

Psal.45.

Lastly,let vs cal to minde that our bodies are the temples
of the holy Ghost, which once were polluted and vncleane,
but now sanctified and purged by this our holy guest, that
they may be fit habitations for himselfe to dwell in. And
then let vs consider that it is a most horrible indignitie a-
gainst the maiestie of God, to prophane with our filthie
sinnes the holy temples of his most holy spirit, and to make
them more fit to be sties for filthie swine and vncleane spirits,than mansion houses for God to dwell in ; that by our
sinnes we vexe and grieue the good spirit of God, and make
his lodging lothsome vnto him, and so as much as in vs lyeth, we driue him away, and as it were thrust him out of
dores,if not by violence,yet at least by our hard and vnciuill
entertainement : yea that by our sinnes we doe not onely
defile,but euen destroy the temple of God, and thereby also
cast our selues headlong into eternall destruction. *For if any*
man destroy the temple of God, him shall God destroy, as it is
1.Cor.3.16. If therefore wee would not prophane Gods
temple, abuse his glorious presence, vexe our holy guest,
destroy his mansion and our selues also, let vs most carefully auoyde sinne, and nourish all the good motions of Gods
spirit,wholy submitting our selues with cheerefull alacritie

§. Sect.8.
The fift reason
taken from the
spirit of God
dwelling in vs.
1.Cor.3.16.
Eph.2.21.22.

Eph.4.30.

1.Cor.6.17.

Rr 3

to

1.Pet.2.5.

to be guided and gouerned by his directions, and ſo we ſhal perfume theſe holy temples with the odours and incenſe of holy obedience, which ſmelling ſweetely in Gods noſtrils will moue him to dwell in vs with pleaſure and delight, all the daies of this our pilgrimage, and afterwards to tranſport vs into thoſe eternall manſions of his kingdome of glorie, where we ſhall continue in all ioy and happineſſe for euermore.

Chap. V.

Of the ſecond ſort of preſeruatiues to keepe vs from ſinne.

§. Sect.1.
The firſt reaſon taken from Gods all-ſeeing wiſedome and all-filling preſence.

Nd ſo much concerning the firſt ſort of arguments grounded vpon loue; the ſecond ſorte whereby we may be withdrawne from committing ſinne, may be taken from that feare and reuerence of God, which ought to be in euery one of vs: vnto which we may be moued by diuers effectuall reaſons. As firſt by the conſideration of Gods all-ſeeing wiſedome, and all-filling preſence, whereby he ſeeth euen our moſt ſecret thoughts, and is a preſent witneſſe of all our hidden actions. For this being remembred, who dare in ſuch a glorious preſence commit that wickedneſſe, which he knoweth hatefull vnto him, before whom he committeth it? He is counted an vngracious childe, who will wittingly breake his fathers commaundement euen before his face; and he is eſteemed a deſperat malefactor who dare preſumptuouſly offend againſt the law in preſence of his iudge; how then can our vngracious impudencie and deſperate preſumption be excuſed, who dare offend and ſinne in the ſight and preſence of a father ſo gracious, and of a iudge ſo iuſt?

§. Sect.2.
The ſecond reaſon taken from Gods exact iuſtice.

Secondly, let vs call to minde Gods iuſtice, which is ſo exact, that rather then he would let ſinne goe vnpuniſhed, he puniſhed it in his deerely beloued ſonne. If therefore thou ſin, thou canſt not corrupt him with bribes, nor pacifie him with

with faire words, nor ouercome him by intreatie, nor ftop
the courfe of iuftice,with the interceffió of friends. For, hath
he not fpared his fonne,and will he fpaire his feruants? hath
he punifhed fin in his owne childe, and will he winke at it
in a common fubiect? could neither the intreatie, nor
teares, nor grones, nor ftrong cryes, nor bloodie fweate
of his beft beloued fonne, appeafe his wrath and fatiffie
his iuftice, but that ftanding in our place hee muft needes
beare our punifhment, and being furetie for finners he muft
die for finne? and fhall they who are the principalls efcape,
who in ftead of pleading his paiment, doe contemptuoufly
refufe it, and as it were tread it vnder foote? It is true indeede that Chrift fuffered for vs that we might efcape, and
paid our debt that it might not be required at our hand; but
feeing all finners haue not their part of Chrift and his merits, but onely thofe that are in Chrift; and thofe onely are
in Chrift,who walke not after the flefh, but after the fpirit;
feeing alfo thofe onely are partakers of all the gracious promifes made in him, who approue their faith by the liuely
fruite thereof vnfained repentance; and thofe onely doe
truely repent,who forrow for their fins paft, hate their prefent corruptions, and defire and indeauour to ferue God in
newneffe of life; how can we haue any affurance that Gods
iuftice is fatiffied for vs, and that we haue efcaped condemnation,if we quench the good motions of Gods fpirit, and
obey the flefh in the lufts thereof, and if ftill being in loue
with our finnes, we refolue to goe forward in our courfe of
wickedneffe?

Thirdly,let vs cal to our remembrance Gods fearce wrath §. Sect.3.
conceiued againft finne,and his fearefull iudgements which *The third rea-*
he hath executed vpon finners, and that not onely particular *fon taken from*
men, but alfo whole ftates and common-wealthes. Let vs *Gods fierce an-*
call to minde the generall deluge in which all mankinde *ger againft fin,*
fauing eight perfons were drowned; the deftruction of So- *fhewed in his*
dome and Gomorrah by fier and brimftone;the rooting out *fearefull iudg-*
of the whole nation of the Cananites; the reiection of the *ments executed*
Iewes; the ouerthrow and vtter defacing of thofe famous *vpon finners.*
Churches of the Corinthians,Galathians,Ephefians, Philip-
pians,

Rr 4

pians, Collossians, Thessalonians, and the rest mentioned in
the Reuelation. And to the examples of former times adde
those which euery man obserueth in his owne experience;
and then consider withall that the cause which moued the
Lord to execute in his iust displeasure these heauie iudgements vpon mankinde, was nothing else but sinne, and it
will be a forcible reason to withdraw vs from it. For the
Lord is immutable and vnchangeable in his course of iustice,
and he hateth sinne now as deadly as in former ages; neither
will he spare vs more than others, if we liue in our sinnes
without repentance: nay certainly as our sinnes being ag-
grauated by many circumstances are more odious vnto
him, so will the Lord proportionably inflict more heauie
iudgements vpon vs then he hath vpon others, whose sinnes
haue not been so great and presumptuous. For if the Lord
giue vs now extraordinarie knowledge, or at least the
meanes thereof, and we sinne against this knowledge and
against our owne consciences; if he hath in most abundant
measure, multiplied his mercies vpon vs, and we hereby be
made more vnkind and vngratefull; if he hath giuen vs
warning by innumerable examples of his heauie iudgements executed vpon others in former times, and in our
own daies, yea euen in our owne sight, layeth heauie punishments vpon such as haue committed no other sinnes then
wee our selues are guiltie of, and yet wee continue in our
sinnes without repentance, how is it possible but that wee
should prouoke Gods fierce wrath against vs, and draw
downe violently vpon our selues with these cartropes of
iniquitie, Gods fearefull plagues and heauie iudgements.
It is true indeede that God is long suffering and slow to
anger, but if hereby wee take occasion to continue in our
sinnes, and doe delay our repentance, what doe we else but
treasure vp against our selues wrath against the day of wrath,

Rom. 2. 5.

and the declaration of the iust iudgement of God? It is most
certaine that God is not easily prouoked to wrath and anger, but let not this incourage vs to continue in our sinnes;
for if it be once inflamed, it is so fierce and terrible, that with
the heate thereof it drieth vp the seas; and so powerfull
that

that he maketh therewith the earth to tremble and the mountaines to melt like waxe in his presence, and the voyce of his furie doth breake and rent in sunder the ceaders, yea the mightie strong ceaders of Libanus, as the scripture speaketh. As therefore fire doth burne more hotly in such solid matter as is long in kindling, then in flaxe or straw which is soone inflamed, and soone extinguished; so the anger of God is not easily inflamed, but if it be once kindled, it burneth so furiously that nothing will quench it, but the blood of Christ applied by faith, and the streaming teares of vnfained repentance. Seeing then Gods iudgements are so fearefull, and his anger so terrible, let vs carefully take heede of prouoking his wrath against vs by our sinnes, *for it is a fearfull thing to fall into the hands of the liuing* He 1. 10. 3 1. *God.*

Fourthly, let vs meditate vpon the day of iudgement, when as we must giue an account not onely of our words and workes, but also of our secret thoughts, before a most iust iudge, who with the all-seeing eye of his diuine knowledge searcheth and beholdeth the very heart and reynes, in the presence also of men and Angels. And this will restraine vs from falling into sinne, though it may be so secretly acted that we neede not to feare in this life, either shame or punishment. For let it be supposed that we can hide our sinnes from the sight of all men, yet what wil this benefit vs if God against whom we sinne, and before whom as our supreme iudge, we must giue an account doe looke vpon vs? what will it profit vs though time weare our offences out of mans remembrance, if God keepe a faithfull regifter of them, and ingraue our reckoning with a penne of yron? what will it helpe vs if by our cunning conueyances, we can hide our sinnes and auoyde shame, or with an impudent forehead can face them out without blushing, if our nakednesse be discouered, and our shame proclamed in the presence of God and all his Saints and Angels? What will it auaile vs to be exempted from punishment in this life, through our great power and vncontrouleable authoritie, or to escape the penaltie of humaine lawes by the intercession of friends, or by

§. *SeEt.* 4.
The fourth reason taken from them day of iudgement.

by corrupting the iudge, or by procuring the princes pardon; if againe we muſt be arraigned before ſuch an vpright iudge, as reſpeƈteth no perſons, receiueth no rewards, and being found guiltie, be condemned vnto the eternall torments of hell fire? When therefore we heare the voyce of Sathans temptations alluring vs to commit ſinne, let vs alſo haue the voyce of the Archangell ſounding in our eares, *Ariſe ye dead and come vnto iudgement* : when the world tempteth vs vnto ſinne on the one ſide by intiſing promiſes of honors, pleaſures, and riches, and on the otherſide, by terrifying threatnings of loſſe, daunger, or puniſhment, let vs call to minde the day of iudgement, when either we muſt

Matth.25.

heare the ſentence of ſaluation, *Come ye bleſſed of my father and inherit the kingdome prepared for you &c,* or the ſentence of condemnation, *Depart ye curſed into hell fire which is prepared for the diuell and his angels:* and then ſhall not the momentanie vanities of the world ſo forcibly draw vs into the

2.Pet.3.11.
Iude.14.15.

ſnares of ſinne, as the remembrance of the heauenly ioyes prepared for vs in Gods kingdome will retaine vs in holy obedience; then will not the worlds threats of temporarie miſeries ſo ſtrongly vrged vs to wound our conſciences with the ſting of ſinne, as the feare to heare the definitiue ſentence of eternall condemnation will reſtraine vs from it.

§. Sect.5.
*The fifth rea-
ſon taken from
the manifold
euils of ſinne.*

Laſtly, let vs call to minde the manifold euils, wich ſinne cauſeth both to body and ſoule, in this life and the life to come; and ſo though the vglineſſe of it ſelfe will not make vs to flee from it, yet the miſerable effeƈts which it produceth may moue vs to abhorre it. Conſider therefore that there is no euill vnder the ſunne, in this life or afterwards, which is not a fruit of this curſed roote: it ſubieƈteth the bodie to ſickneſſe and diſeaſes, hunger and thirſt, cold and wearineſſe; the minde to ignorance and blindneſſe, the will to peruerſneſſe, the affeƈtions to all prepoſterous diſorder; it ruinateth the eſtate, and bringeth a man to pouertie and extreame miſerie; it maketh the whole man obnoxious to the curſe of the law, the anger of God, and all thoſe innumerable euils, which euer accompanie them. In this world
it

it bringeth the body to death and corruption, and in the
world to come both body and foule to condemnation, and
endieffe deftruction; it depriueth vs of our heauenly inheritance, and the euerlafting ioyes of Gods kingdome, and
plungeth vs into the lake which burneth with fire and brimftone. In a word there is no euill which can be imagined
which doth not proceede from this euill of finne, and therefore though it feeme neuer fo fweete to our carnall appetites, yet being mixed with this gall and wormewood of innumerable euils, let vs loath and abhorre it; when the vaine
and vncertaine benefits which it promifeth moue vs to imbrace it, let the miferable euils which accompanie it, and
the moft affured and furpaffing ioyes which it depriueth vs
of, make vs to auoyde it as a deadly ftinging ferpent.

Chap. VI.

*Of fome fpeciall meanes whereby we may be preferued from
falling into finne.*

Nd thefe are the reafons whereby euery one may
be armed againft Sathans fuggeftions, tempting
him vnto finne; and be moued vnto a chriftian
refolution, of poffeffing body and foule in holineffe and puritie: now we are to fpeake of fome fpeciall
meanes, whereby the chriftian thus refolued may be preferued from falling into fuch grieuous finnes, as wound the
confcience, and hinder him in the courfe of fanctification.
Firft, he that would auoyde finne, muft carefully alfo auoyde
the occafions thereof, which are ftrong inducements to
draw him vnto finne; for as it is great folly for a man who
dreadeth burning to be alwaies medling with fire and gun-
powder; fo is it no leffe madneffe to thinke that we can preferue our felues from finne, and yet intertaine all occafions
thereof, continually fuffering the fparkes of Sathans temptations to fall as it were into the tindar of our corrupt affections. It is not poffible that he who is inclined to gluttonie and drunkenneffe fhould containe himfelfe from thefe
finnes,

§. Sect. 1.
*The firft
meanes is to
auoyde the oc-
cafion of finne.*

1. Thef. 5. 22.

sinnes,if he giue himselfe to companie keeping,and take his chiefe delight in pleasing his tast with the daintiest meates and drinkes: or that he who is cholericke, should refraine from anger, and yet thrust himselfe into needlesse controuersies and hot contentions: or for him that is lasciuious to abstaine from vncleanesse, and yet frequent vnchast companie,reade wanton bookes,view obscure spectacles,vse filthie communication, and pamper himselfe in gluttonie, and drunkennesse. In a word we cannot auoyde any sinne, vnlesse wee also flee and shunne the occasions and meanes thereof; and therefore let vs be as carefull and watchfull in the one as the other, or els we shall most certainely loose our labours.

§. *Sect.2.*
The second meanes, to make conscience of the least sinnes.

Secondly, if wee would not fall into greater sinnes, we must also make conscience of those which are lesse; and thinke with our selues that no sinne is small, seeing the least deserueth the anger of God and euerlasting death: otherwise if we willingly intertaine euen small corruptions, we shall at length make no conscience of heynous transgressions;and these little theeues being let in,wil in time set wide open the doore of our hearts, that the greatest and grossest may easily enter,and so robbe and spoyle vs of all grace and goodnesse.

§. *Sect.3.*
The third meanes is continually to stand vpon our guard.

Thirdly,let vs continually stand vpon our guard, carefully watching ouer our owne hearts, that we be not surprised at vnawares; for thousands are the baites which are laid to intrap vs, and tenne thousand snares doth Sathan lay to intangle vs; and therefore it behooueth vs to looke narrowly to our waies, and to be alwaies as readie to giue Sathan the repulse, as he to make the encounter. And considering that if we doe not assault sinne, it will most surely set vpon vs, and at one time or other will giue vs the foyle if we onely lie at warde and neuer offer blow against this our enemie; therefore it behooueth euery christian souldier,not onely to giue sinne a repulse, but also to wound it in the head, and beate it downe, that it may not againe assault him, or at least not with wonted power and violence : and for as much as he hath many enemies which cannot at once be ouercome,

come, therefore he is to labour to get euery day the maste-
rie of some sinne, and to bring it in subiection, that so in
continuance of time he may vanquish all, and obtaine a full
and finall victorie our all his corruptions.

Fourthly, if we would not fall into grieuous sinnes, wee
must not stand in our owne power, nor trust in our owne
strength, but wholy rest and relie vpon Gods promised assistance. For if once we robbe God of his glorie, and arrogate the praise of our victorie ouer sinne and Sathan vnto
our selues, the Lord will withdraw his helping hand, and
leaue vs vnto our selues, till by our grieuous falles we haue
learned to acknowledge our owne weakenesse, and to rest
wholy in the power of his might. For as all other sinnes are
odious vnto God, so especially the sinne of pride, because
it maketh vile man corriuall with God in his praise and glorie, of which he is most iealous; and therefore the Lord suffereth, euen his owne children, to fall into grieuous sinnes,
that hereby they may be humbled; and so vseth other sinnes
as a counterpoyson to cure pride.

§. Sect. 4. The fourth meanes, to rest on Gods assi- stance and not on our owne power.

Lastly, seeing we stand not by our owne strength but by
the power of Gods might, let vs as often as we see our owne
weakenesse and aptnesse to fall, haue our recourse vnto God,
by feruent and effectuall prayer; crauing his ayde and assistance that thereby we may be enabled to stand in the day
of temptation. And when by vertue thereof we haue giuen
sinne the foyle, and repelled Sathans suggestions; let vs
remember to returne praise and thankesgiuing to the Lord
by whose helpe wee haue beaten backe our spirituall enemies: and then wee may bee assured that the Lord will vphold vs by the power of his spirit from falling into sinne; or
if we doe fall, he will speedily raise vs vp by vnfained repentance.

§. Sect. 5. Ths fift meanes is feruent pray- er.

CHAP. VII.

*That in the moſt ſanctified, remaine ſome reliques of
ſinne, and the cauſes thereof.*

§.Sect.I.
Sathans temp-
tation, whereby
he diſcoura-
geth the Chri-
ſtian in the
worke of ſan-
ctification.

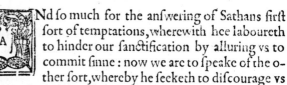

ANd ſo much for the anſwering of Sathans firſt ſort of temptations, wherewith hee laboureth to hinder our ſanctification by alluring vs to commit ſinne: now we are to ſpeake of the other ſort, whereby he ſeeketh to diſcourage vs in this worke, as being not only hard and difficult, but euen impoſſible. And theſe alſo are of two kindes; the firſt taken from the great maſſe of our naturall corruptions and ſmall meaſure of our ſanctification; the other from ſome actuall ſinnes which we haue committed. Concerning the firſt, hee thus frameth his temptations: Thou laboureſt much (will hee ſay) and tireſt thy ſelfe in attaining vnto ſanctification, but all in vaine; for doeſt thou not ſee on the one ſide the vnreſiſtable violence of thy natural corruptions, which continually choake in thee all the good motions of Gods ſpirit, and forcibly draw thee into all ſinne and wickedneſſe; and on the other ſide, thy ſmall meaſure of grace and ſanctification, which is exceedingly ſtained with thy manifold imperfections? How therefore can ſuch weakneſſe withſtand ſuch power? And how is it poſſible that thy feeble ſpirit ſhould ouercome thy ſtrong fleſh, eſpecially ſeeing it is aſſiſted with the ſtrong aides of the puiſſant world, and the mightie power of innumerable diuels? Neither art thou vainly to imagine that God will enable thee to ouercome all theſe difficulties, for he hath giuen thee ouer to thine own weakneſſe, otherwiſe if it were his will to make thee one of his holy ones, he could with the powerfull operation of his ſpirit, long ago haue perfectly purged thee from al thy corruptions, and giuen vnto thee a great meaſure of ſanctification. Seeing then it is impoſſible, in reſpect of thy weakneſſe and thine enemies power, to accompliſh this worke which thou haſt taken in hand, and ſeeing thou haſt no aſſurance

that

that God wil ſtrengthen thee with his ſpirit,which thou haſt a long time reſiſted and vexed, by quenching the good motions thereof; thou haſt now no ſhew of hope to effect that which thou deſireſt; and therefore it were much better for thee to ceaſe ſtriuing againſt the ſtreame of thy corruptions, and to follow the naturall current of thy deſires : for when thou takeſt all the paines thou canſt,thou art in one day caried further backward toward thine old conuerſation, than thou canſt in many moneths get forward in the courſe of ſanctification.

And thus doth Sathan diſcourage the weake Chriſtian with his falſe ſuggeſtions , to the end hee may hinder him from trauailing this way of holineſſe which leadeth to Gods kingdome ; for the anſwering whereof we are to know, that the ſanctification of the moſt holie is imperfect, both in reſpect of the reliques of ſinne, and corruptions which continually cleaue to them, and in reſpect of the manifold wants and defects of their beſt actions. Neither are wee ſo waſhed in the lauer of regeneration,but that there remain in vs ſome ſtaines of that ſcarlet-ingrained dye of our corruptions ; we haue not ſo clerely eſcaped out of our old captiuitie of ſinne, but that we retaine ſtill ſome gaules and bruſes,which make vs to goe haltingly in the waies of righteouſneſſe ; we haue not ſo vanquiſhed this ſpirituall enemie, but that ſtill it will aſſault vs,yea and often foyle vs,though it cannot ſubdue vs; we haue indeede ouercome theſe curſed Canaanites, ſo that they cannot rule and raigne in vs as in former times, but wee haue not vtterly expelled them from dwelling amongſt vs ; ſo that doe we what wee can, yet ſtill they will be as thornes in our ſides to vexe and grieue vs. Heretofore the luſts of our fleſh like tyrannicall Lords did againſt all law and iuſtice ouerrule vs;but now by vertue of Gods ſpirit aſſiſting vs,we haue weakened their force and brought them vnder,yet not ſo but that ſtill they will rebell againſt the ſpirit,and continually exerciſe vs in the ſpirituall warfare. So that the regenerate man is not wholy ſpirit, as the carnall man is wholy fleſh,but is diuided into two factions or parts,and alwaies is at ciuill warres within himſelfe : for ſo farre foorth as hee is

§. Sect.2.
That our ſanctification is imperfect and mingled with our corruptions.

regenerate

regenerate he is holie,pure,and vndefiled,but fo farre foorth as he is carnall, he is finfull,corrupt and full of al pollution : as hee is regenerate hee wholy loueth and embraceth true holineffe and righteoufneffe,and abhorreth and fleeth finne and wickedneffe, but as hee is vnregenerate he loueth finne and the vaine pleafures thereof, and loatheth righteoufneffe as irkfome and vnpleafant. In the fpirituall part he contemneth the world,and hauing his conuerfation aboue he mindeth heauenly things; but in the carnall part hee loueth the world, and is preffed downe with the cares and pleafures thereof, fo that his minde cannot as it would mount aloft in diuine meditations ; in the fpirit he ferueth the law of God, in the flefh the law of finne.

§. Sect.3.
That we muft not dreame of perfection in our fanctification.

We muft not therefore imagine,that to be fanctified is to be wholy purged from al corruption,to be endued with perfect righteoufneffe,and to haue the fpirit in full meafure;but to haue the corruptions of finne leffened and their power abated, fo that they cannot wholy ouerfway vs as in former times ; to haue fome holy defires and good endeuours of feruing God in holineffe and righteoufneffe,which alfo wee expreffe in our actions,although in great weakneffe and imperfection;to haue the firft fruites of the fpirit in this life,expecting the whole harueft in the life to come : neither let vs yeeld to Sathan,fuggefting vnto vs,that we are not at al fanctified, becaufe wee haue fome reliques of our old corruptions and manifold imperfections in our beft actions; or that therefore our holineffe which we haue, is fo fmal that it is to no purpofe,and that which we want fo great and hardly come by,that it is not poffible we fhould euer attaine vnto it ; feeing thefe fuggeftions are fufficiently confuted both by the Scriptures and examples of all Gods children.For the Scriptures teach vs,that *in many things we finne all*; that *if wee fay we haue no finne, we deceiue our felues, and there is no truth in vs:* and therefore becaufe wee continually offend, our Sauiour requireth that as wee aske our daily bread,fo alfo wee fhould pray daily for the forgiueneffe of our finnes. The Apoftle alfo telleth vs,that there is a continuall fight in euerie Chriftian,the *flefh lufting againft the fpirit,& the fpirit againft the*

Iam.3.2.
1.Ioh. 1.8.

Gal.5.17.

the flefh, the one tempting vs vnto finne, the other ftirring vs vp to holy obedience. Moreouer, the examples of Gods faints are pregnant for this purpofe, neither was there euer any fo perfectly fanctified, but there remained in them fome reliques of their naturall corruptions, which alfo fhewed themfelues in actuall finnes and grieuous tranfgreffions; as appeareth plainly in the examples of the Patriarches, *Dauid, Peter,* and all others. But moft cleerely doth the Apoftle *Paul* fhew this in his owne perfon, propounding himfelfe as Rom.7. a true patterne of a man regenerate; for though he had attained vnto a great meafure of fanctification, yet he complaineth of the great force and violence of his inbred corruptions, Rom.7: for fo great ftrength thereof remained in him, that it forced him to abufe the law of God, taking occafion thereby to work in him all manner of concupifcence, and fo in fteed of killing finne did reuiue it in him, verf.8,9; that it made him to omit the good he would, and to do the euill that he hated, verf.15.19; that it rebelled againft the law of his minde, and led him captiue to the law of finne, ver.23; that he faw no poffible meanes in himfelfe to fubdue vtterly thefe corruptions, and therefore feeketh for helpe elfwhere, crying out, *Wretched man that I am, who fhall deliuer me from the body of this death?* v.24.

Seeing therefore this is the ftate of all Gods children, let §. Sect.4. not Sathan perfwade vs that wee are not yet fanctified, or *That our wants* that it is loft labour to goe forward in this worke, becaufe of *and corrupti-* the great power of our corruptions and fmall meafure of *ons fhould not* fanctification, which is ftained alfo with manifold imperfe- *but redouble* ctions; but rather let the ftrength of our corruptions re- *our care and* double our care and diligence that wee may fubdue them: *diligence.* and confidering that there are diuers degrees of holineffe, let vs as foone as wee haue afcended one ftep, neuer reft ftriuing till we haue afcended a higher, vntill at length we come to the top of perfection and the higheft ftep of true holineffe; according to the exhortation of the Apoftle Apoc.22. 11. *He that is righteous let him be righteous ftill, he that is holy* Apoc.22.11. *let him be holy ftill,* that is, let him continue and daily increafe in righteoufneffe and holineffe.

Sf　　　　　　And

§ *Sect. 5.*
That our re-
liques of finne
fhall not be im-
puted vnto vs.

And to the end that wee may not be difcouraged in thefe
our holy endeuours, with Sathans temptations drawne from
the reliques of our finnes, the ftrength of our corruptions,
and the imperfections and fmall meafure of our fanctification; let vs further confider, firft, that thefe reliques of finne
fhall not bee imputed vnto vs, nor come in iudgement before God to our condemnation, becaufe by faith we are vnited vnto Chrift, and fo made partakers of the vertue and merits of his death and paffion, whereby he hath fatisfied Gods
iuftice for our finnes, fo that they cannot now condemne vs,
nor draw vpon vs any punifhment; and likewife wee are
made partakers of his perfect righteoufneffe and obedience
to the law, which as a rich robe doth couer and hide our
patched ragges of imperfection. So then though we fee the
reliques of finne and our manifold imperfections, let vs not
be difcouraged hereby from labouring in the worke of fanctification, but rather ftriue and endeuour to mortifie our
finnes, and afpire to more and more perfection. And if befides our purpofe wee be led captiue of fin, let vs remember
that we haue *an aduocate with the father Iefus Chrift the iuft,*
and that he is the reconciliation for our finnes; fo that though
they make vs condemne our felues in our own confciences,
yet they fhall neuer condemne vs before God. And this the
Apoftle *Paul* fheweth vnto vs : for hauing in the feuenth
chapter of his epiftle to the Romanes declared, that the
faithfull haue remaining in them the flefh and reliques of
their old corruptions, which powerfully hinder them from
doing the good they would, and moue them to commit the
euill which they would not, leaft any hereby fhould be difcouraged in the fight and fenfe of his corruptions, hee prefently addeth in the beginning of the eighth chapter, that
notwithftanding the flefh and the corruptions therof, which
before he had fpoken of, remained in vs, yet *there was no con-*
demnation to thofe who were in Chrift Iefus: and hee yeeldeth
this reafon, *becaufe the law of the fpirit of life which is in Chrift*
Iefus, had freed them from the law of finne and of death, that is,
becaufe the power and vertue of the fpirit of God (which is
the author of life, by vniting vs as members vnto the bodie

of

of Chrift in whom we liue, and by fprinkling our confciences with his precious bloud) had deliuered them from the force and power of finne and death, fo that now it could not condemne them, nor oblige and binde them to guilt and punifhment as in former times. Seeing therefore the fting of finne is taken away that it cannot condemne vs, let vs not fo feare it as that it fhould moue vs defperately to caft away our weapons not daring to encounter it; for though this our enemie may affault vs, yet it cannot ouercome vs; though it may wound vs, yet it cannot kill vs; though it may giue vs a foyle, yet in the end wee are fure of victorie, if we manfully refift and labour to fubdue it.

Secondly, let vs confider that the Lord doth not require of vs vnder the Gofpel fuch exact and perfect righteoufnes, as was required vnder the Law, which is altogether impoffible to our corrupt nature, and was neuer to be found in any man (our Sauiour Chrift excepted) but onely that wee ftriue and labour to attaine vnto it; he doth not require of vs that we fhould at once free our felues from the flefh and the corruptions thereof, but that we endeuour to mortifie it, according to the meafure of grace and ftrength which wee haue receiued from him; he doth not require of vs that wee be without finne, but that finne doe not rule in our mortall bodies, that wee fhould like flaues obey it willingly in the lufts thereof, and that alfo wee hating and abhorring it doe continually make warre againft it, and fubdue it by little and little, feeing we cannot at once wholy vanquifh it. He doth not now require of vs ẏ we fhould performe perfect obedience to the law, which Chrift hath performed for vs, but that we doe our beft endeuour, and though we cannot attaine to our defire, yet at leaft that wee be delighted *in the law of God* *concerning the inner man* and *confent vnto it that it is good, holy and iuft.* In a word, this is the Chriftian mans righteoufnes which God requireth, that he hate finne, and loue godlines, that hee defire and endeuour to mortifie the flefh and corruptions thereof, and labour to leade a new life in holy obedience; and if contrarie to his defire and purpofe he doe the euill which hee hateth, or leaue vndone the good which hee

§ *Sect. 6.*
That the Lord in the Gofpell requireth not perfect obedience to the law.

Rom. 7. 11. 22.

loueth;

loueth; that he sorrow and grieue for his sinnes and imperfections, and making confession hereof before the throne of grace, doe implore mercie and forgiuenesse in Christ Iesus. And if wee offer vnto God this righteousnesse, it will be acceptable vnto him, notwithstanding our manifold imperfections; for hee measureth our deede by our will, and esteemeth more of our affections than of our actions; *Nec intuetur Deus quantum quilibet valeat, sed quantum velit, & quicquid vis & non potes Deus factum computat:* He respecteth not what we can doe, but what we would do, and that which we would performe and cannot, he esteemeth it as though it were performed. So that hee reputeth him righteous who earnestly desireth and laboureth to be righteous, and him perfect who acknowledging and bewailing his imperfections striueth to attaine to more perfection. Wherein he fitly may be compared vnto a tender louing father, who esteemeth of the least endeuours of his beloued sonne, more than of the best actions of a seruant, because hee regardeth not so much the excellencie of the action, as the person and cheerefull will of the agent.

August.

§. Sect. 7. VVhy the Lord accepteth of our imperfect righteousnesse.

Now the reasons why the Lord being perfectly iust, will notwithstanding accept of our imperfect righteousnesse, is first because (we being made members of Christs bodie) our persons are acceptable vnto him, and therefore our workes also (not in their own worthines, or for their own merit, but in and for Christ) are accepted; the corruptions and staines of them being washed away in his bloud, and the imperfections of them being couered with Christs perfect righteousnesse. And thus being adorned in the garment of our elder brother Christ Iesus, we obtaine the blessing of our heauenly father. Secondly, our righteousnesse and holinesse doth proceede from the spirit of God dwelling in vs; and from hence our workes being imperfect in themselues, doe receiue their dignitie, excellencie, and estimation in Gods sight, as being the fruites of his own spirit, howsoeuer mingled with our corruptions.

§. Sect. 8.

Thirdly, let vs remember that our sinnes and corruptions which we hate and labour to mortifie, will neuer mooue the

Lord

Lord to reiect and caft vs out of his loue and fauour; for we are the Lords children, and he our gratious father : now we know that a louing father will not reiect his childe, becaufe he is ficke,lame,or in miferable eftate, but rather he is more tender ouer him,till hee be recouered of his infirmities : but what are our finnes but the ficknefle, wounds and miferie of the foule, with which wee are vexed and turmoyled whileft we continue in this life ? and wil our heauenly father, whofe loue infinitely furpaffeth the loue of the moft tender mo-ther, caft vs out of his fauour, becaufe our foules are ficke in finne, and molefted with many miferies which doe accom-panie it ? It is impoffible ; efpecially confidering that we de-fire nothing more than to bee cured of thefe difeafes, and to be reftored to perfect health. The Lord is our heauenly huf-bandman, and wee his husbandrie ; now wee know that the good husbandman doth not forfake his land , becaufe it bringeth foorth thornes and thiftles, but rather is fo much the more diligent and painful in weeding and tilling it, that it may be fitted for good feed and bring vnto him plentiful increafe;and fo the Lord wil not caft vs off,becaufe we natu-rally bring foorth the weedes and thiftles of finne and cor-ruption,but in his infinite loue he will with the operation of his holy fpirit,plow vp the fallow grounds of our hearts,and weed out our corruptions,that fo we may like good ground well husbanded, bring foorth the ripe fruites of holinefle and righteoufnefle.

Fourthly , let vs confider that the Lord our God, who could eafily if it had pleafed him, haue throughly purged vs from all finne and corruption, and indued vs with perfect righteoufnefle and holineffe , hath notwithftanding left re-maining in vs fome reliques of fin, and many imperfections in our fanctification,both for the manifeftation of his owne glorie,and for the furthering of our owne eternall faluation. For firft hereby it commeth to paffe, that the Lord hath the whole praife of our faluation, feeing hee faueth vs of his meere mercie , and not for our workes and worthineffe. Whereas if our righteoufnefle and fanctification were per-fect,we would be readie to fhare with God,afcribing part in

the

the worke of our saluation vnto our selues, and not wholy attribute it to Gods mercie and Chrifts onely and all-fufficient merits: and therefore the Lord hath left in vs the reliques of finne and manifold imperfections, that hereby it may appeare that we are not faued for our owne woithinesse and deferts, but of his free grace and vndeferued loue.

§. Sect.10.
That there might be a fit obiect of his mercie and patience.

Secondly, he hath left in vs thefe reliques of fin and manifold imperfections, to the end that there might be continuall matter and a fit obiect, wherein he might exercife, and by exercifing manifeft, to the praife of his grace, his patience, long fuffring, loue, goodneffe, and infinite mercie, in the pardoning and forgiuing of them, which would not fo plainly appeare if at once hee had indued vs with perfect righteoufneffe.

§. Sect.11.
That he might shew his power in our weaknes.

Thirdly, that hereby he might make way for the manifeftation of his power in our weakneffe and imperfections. If wee were perfectly righteous and indued with all grace, it were no wonder if wee fhould withftand Sathans temptations and get the vpper hand in the fpirituall combat; but feeing we are of our felues finfull, exceeding weake and full of all imperfections, hereby is the infinite power of God manifefted, in that we are notwithftanding enabled, to withftand Sathan and all the power of hell which oppofe themfelues againft vs, feeing nothing els could vpholde fuch feeble weakneffe againft fuch puiffant might. Of this the A-

2.Cor.12.8.9.

poftle fpeaketh 2.Cor.12.8, 9: for hauing oftentimes befought the Lord to bee freed from the corruptions of his flefh, he receiueth this anfwere, that *Gods grace was fufficient for him, and that his power was made perfect through weakneffe.*

§. Sect.12.
That he might stirre vs vp to continuall thankfulnes.

Fourthly, hereby the Lord continually putteth vs in mind of his mercie and manifold benefits, to the end that we daily tafting of them, may alfo daily returne vnto him thanks and praife. If he fhould at once free vs from finne, and indue vs with a full meafure of grace and perfect righteoufneffe, wee would foone be forgetfull of his abundant mercies, and this forgetfulneffe would worke in vs vnthankfulneffe, and this vnthankfulneffe would make vs neglect his worfhip and feruice. And therefore he doth not at once inrich vs, but lets vs continue

continue in our pouerty, that so we may continually depend vpon him: and like a wise housholder hee doth not suddenly aduance vs to our highest preferments, for then wee would leaue his seruice and betake vs to our ease and pleasure; but he bestoweth his benefits by little and little, and so keeping vs still in expectation of receiuing more, he retaineth vs still in his seruice, and euery day increasing his bountie, hee putteth also into our mouthes new songs of thankesgiuing, and giueth vs daily new occasion of praising his magnificence.

Secondly, as the Lord hereby aduanceth his owne glorie, so also he worketh our good, and furthereth our eternall saluation. For first by leauing in vs these reliques of sinne and manifolde imperfections, hee worketh in vs true humilitie, which of all other graces is most acceptable vnto him, and mortifieth our pride, which of all other vices is most odious and abominable in his sight. For when we see our manifold infirmities and corruptions of sinne, all cause of pride and selfe-conceit is taken away, and we in all humilitie are moued to confesse, that *it is Gods mercie that wee are not consumed*; how much more that notwithstanding our vilenesse and vnworthinesse, he hath made vs his sonnes and heires of euerlasting glorie. And thus, of the flesh of this Viper sinne, doth the Lord make a soueraigne antidote against the deadly poyson of pride. And as good Chirurgeons doe not suddenly heale vp the wound, but keepe it open till they haue drawne out the core and healed it to the bottome, for otherwise it would putrifie and become more dangerous; so the Lord will not at once heale the wounds of our sinnes, but leaueth them as it were open and vncured till hee haue drawne out the core of pride, which being left in vs (though we were healed of all our other sinnes) would more indanger vs than all the rest. Wherein the Lord confirmeth and furthereth vs in the way of saluation; for nothing more weakneth and disableth vs than pride, nothing more strengtheneth and vpholdeth vs than humilitie, because the strength whereby we stand and repell our spirituall enemies is not our owne abilitie, but the power of Gods might, and the Lord withdraweth his assisting hand from the proud, to

§. Sect. 13.
That he may hereby worke in vs true humilitie.

Lam. 3. 22.

the end that hee may learne to be more humble by his grieuous falles; yea he resisteth him, and therefore how is it possible that he should stand? but contrariwise he giueth grace
to the humble, and filleth him who acknowledgeth his own
emptinesse with good things, but the proud who is full in
his owne conceit he sendeth emptie away.

§. *Sect.*14.
*That we may
be moued to
rest on Christ
alone.*

§. *Sect.*15.
*That we may
be exercised in
the Christian
warfare.*

Secondly, he leaueth in vs corruptions and imperfections,
to the end that wee should not rest in our owne righteousnes for our iustification and saluation (which though it were
as great as *Adams* in the state of innocencie, yet it were no
sure ground to rest vpon) but in the alone righteousnesse of
Christ Iesus, which is all-sufficient and a foundation so vn-
remoueable, that all the power of hell cannot ouerturne it,
nor any that are built vpon it. Vpon which sure pillar wee
would hardly relie, so long as we haue in our hand the reede
of our owne righteousnesse, wee being naturallie inclined rather to seeke for saluation in our selues than else-
where.

Thirdly, he leaueth in vs these spirituall enemies, that wee
may exercise our selues in fighting against them, and so bee
kept from idlenesse the mother and nurse of all euill ; and as
he would not at once cast out the Canaanites before the Ifraelites, but by little and little; least the land should grow vnto a wildernesse, and the wilde beasts should multiplie a-
gainst them: so he would not suddenly cast out our spirituall enemies, but suffreth vs to preuaile against them by little
and little, least giuing our selues vnto idlenesse when there is
no opposition made against vs, there grow in vs as in a wildernes the noysome weeds and thornes of sin, and the wild
beasts of all outragious wickednesse, which would deuoure
and vtterly destroy vs. Whereas contrariwise when wee are
assaulted outwardly with the forces of sathan and the world,
and inwardly with the flesh and our natural corruptions, we
haue enemies against whom wee may exercise our faith, affiance, hope, patience, courage, and all other graces which we
haue recciued, and by exercise increase them : wee fight the
Lords battailes like his valiant souldiers, and being assisted
by his holie spirit wee obtaine victorie, and with our conquest

1.*Pet.*5.5.
*Luk.*1.53.

quest a more excellent crowne of eternall glorie : as appea- Reuel.2.26. 27.and.3.21.
reth Reuel.2.26,27.and 3.21.

Lastly, he suffereth vs to be molested and vexed with the §. Sect.16. *That we may be moued to loath the world and to long for eternall life.*
reliques of our sinnes, that hereby he may make vs to loath
this world and vale of miserie, wherein we can doe nothing
but breake the commaundements of our deare louing father; and may be moued to desire that heauenly life in Gods
kingdome, when hauing laid aside all corruption, we shall
be indued with all perfection, and be fully enabled to performe such obedience vnto God as he requireth. For seeing
sinne is not fully vanquished till it be subdued by our death,
nor we euer at rest and free from the assaults thereof, till we
rest in the graue; therefore the children of God are content
to forsake the world, becaufe they can no otherwife forfake
their sinnes; and defire rather to indure death, than they
would haue sinne to liue with them, as appeareth in the example of the Apostle *Paul* Phil.1.22.23. Phil.1.22,23.

And thus haue I shewed the wifedome and power of God, §. Sect.17. *The conclufion of the former point.*
who turneth euen the sinnes of his children to their good,
which are in their owne nature euill ; and therefore though
we are continually to bewaile them,& to defire by al meanes
to be freed from them, yet we are not defperatly to sinke
vnder them, not daring to encounter them, feeing now they
cannot condemne vs,nay not fo much as hurt vs, but rather
are fo ordered by Gods all-wife prouidence, that they ferue
for the manifeftation of his glorie, and furthering of our
faluation,fo that we doe not with willing delight nor flauifh
feare yeeld vnto them, but to the vttermoft of our power
make refiftance, and defire and indeauour to ouercome
them.

Now in the fift and laft place let vs confider,that though §. Sect.18. *The laft confo-lation taken from our affu-red victorie a-gainft finne.*
our flesh be neuer fo ftrong, and the innumerable corrupti-
ons thereof feeme vnrefiftable,and though on the other fide
our fpirituall man feeme neuer fo weake and feeble, yet we
are not hereby to be difcouraged, feeing the regenerate
part fhall moft certainely obtaine the victorie in the end,
though in the conflict it receiueth many foyles. And though
this little *Dauid* feeme in the eyes of a carnall *Saul*, to be
farre

farre to weake, and altogether vnable to encounter that great *Goliah*, the flesh with the powerfull lusts thereof, yet in the end it will most certainly preuaile and get the conquest; becaufe the fpirit is the Lords champion which goeth out in the name of the Lord to fight againft his enemies; the flesh the diuels fouldier who is Gods enemie : That,is ftrengthened and fupported with the power of God which being infinit is vnrefiftable; this by the power of Sathan,and the world,whofe power is finite, and fo reftrained and ouerruled by Gods might, that they cannot ftirre without his leaue and permiffion. Vnleffe therefore we would blafphemoufly imagine,that the flesh and his affiftants are of greater power than God himfelfe, or that God will fuffer this difgrace that his champion fhould be ouerthrowne by his profeffed enemies; we may moft certainely affure our felues that we shall get the day and obtaine a famous victorie.And therefore let not Sathan difcourage vs,by fetting before our eyes our owne weakneffe , and the mightie oppofitions which are made againft vs; but arming our felues with the chriftian armour, and trufting wholy in the power of Gods might,let vs valiantly incounter our fpirituall enemies, and neuer giue ouer fighting till by death we haue giuen vnto them a finall ouerthrow,and fo shall we be crowned with an vnualuable crowne of immortall glorie.

Chap. VIII.

Sathans temptations drawne from our flow progreffe in fanctification,anfwered.

§. Sect.1.
Sathans temptation grounded vpon our little profiting in chriftianitie.

Nd fo much for anfwering Sathans temptations, drawne from the reliques of finne which remaine in vs, and the fmall meafure of our fanctification : the fecond temptation whereby he laboreth to difcourage the weake chriftian,from going forward in his courfe of true godlineffe, he takech from his flow progreffe and flacke proceedings in fanctification, vpon which occafion he thus affaulteth him.

Thou

Thou laborest much (will he say) and toylest thy selfe with intollerable paines that thou maiest become a sanctified man, but all in vaine; for though thou hearest the word often, and readest much, and prayest continually, and beatest thy braines with daily care, to the end that thou mayest attaine vnto some perfection in christianitie; yet, dost thou not see how little thou profitest by all thy labours, seeing thy knowledge is still small, thy faith weake, thy charitie cold, thy heart dull and hard, thy good workes few and imperfect, and all thy zealous resolutions easily hindred and quite ouerthrowne with euery small temptation? Why then dost thou striue against the streame, and vndertake a taske which is to thee not onely hard but euen impossible? for doe what thou canst, yet all will bee to little purpose, seeing this worke is full of great difficulties, thy selfe disabled with manifold corruptions, and thy enemies which oppose against thee exceeding strong and mightie, as thy selfe findest by lamentatble experience, and thy much laboring and little profiting doe clearely proue. Cease therefore thy bootlesse trauaile, and rather imbrace thy pleasing delights, than turmoyle thy selfe with vaine labour.

For the answering of which temptation we are to know, that if we dislike our own dulnesse and backwardnes in profiting and growing forward in sanctification, if we be truely sorrowfull and bewaile our great wants and imperfections, and labour earnestly in the vse of the meanes whereby we may attaine vnto knowledge, faith, and all other sanctifying graces, and also be enabled to bring forth the fruites of holy obedience; then are we accepted of God and shall in the end most certainely obtaine our desire, though yet we can see but small profit of all our labours; neither shall all the power of our spirituall enemies so farre preuaile against vs, as vtterly to hinder vs in this worke, but that we shall vndoubtedly goe forward although not so speedely as we desire. For this holy desire of profiting in godlinesse, this indeauour and carefull vse of those meanes which are ordained by God for this purpose, are not naturall, but the worke of Gods spirit begun in vs; and we are with the Apostle to *be perswaded*

§. *Sect.*2.

That the dislike of our dulnesse and backwardnesse is accepted of God.

Phil.1.6.

perfwaded *of this fame thing*; *that he that hath begun this good worke in vs will performe it vntill the day of Iefus Chrift*, Phil. 1.6. We are to aſſure our felues with the Prophet *Dauid*, Pfal.145.19.

that *the Lord* will *fulfill thefe holy defires of thofe that feare him*, Pfal.145.19. We are vndoubtedly to beleeue that the

1.Cor.10.13.

Lord will not fuffer vs to be tempted aboue our power, but will giue a good iffue with the temptation, 1.Cor.10.13. We are not to imagine that he will *breake this brufed reede, nor quench*

Matth.12.20.

this fmoking flaxe feeing he hath promifed the contrarie, Matth 12.20.And though this little graine of muſtard feede for a time lie hidden in the earth, and when it fprouteth vp fpringeth fo flowly that wee cannot fenfibly difcerne the growing thereof;yet in Gods good time being watred with the dew of his holy fpirit, it will become one of the greateft trees in the Lords garden. For feeing the Lord hath giuen vs this grace, not to be wanting in the vfe of all good meanes, we may moſt certainely aſſure our felues that the Lord for his part will not be wanting,in giuing his bleſſing

Luk.11.13.

and graunting the aſſiſtance of his holy fpirit,which he hath promifed to thofe that defire it.

§.*Sect*.3.

That Gods fpirit dwelling in vs,will in the end perfect this worke.

Secondly, let vs confider that thefe fmall beginnings of grace and firſt fruites of the fpirit,are moſt vndoubted fignes that he dwelleth in vs: now wherefoeuer he dwelleth,he fanctifieth his own lodging,and is not idle till he haue effected this worke which he hath vndertaken and begun. Though therefore this worke in regarde of thy flowe proceedings feeme hard, yea, euen impoſſible, yet confider that that which is impoſſible to man, is poſſible to God; though thou feeft many difficulties and mighty oppofitions by thy powrefull enemies, yet let not this difcourage thee, feeing the Lord who is with thee is almightie,and therefore able to repell the violence of all oppofers, and to make the moſt heauie and pinching yoke light and eafie. Though in thy

Matth.11.30.
Eph.6.10.
Phil.4.13.

felfe thou art moſt weake and feeble, yet thou *art ſtrong in the power of Gods might, and enabled to doe all things through the helpe of Chrift which ſtrengtheneth thee.*

§.*Sect*.4.

Thirdly,let vs confider,that as the Lord hath decreed our faluation,and promifed vnto vs eternall life : fo he hath alfo

as certainly decreed and promifed the meanes tending *That the Lord*
thereunto, which are the effects of his election and the fore- *hath as cer-*
runners of our faluation;but one efpeciall effect of his electi- *tainly decreed*
on is our fanctification, and the way to faluation is the path *and promifed*
our fanctifica-
of righteoufneffe and holineffe; and therefore this is no leffe *tion as our fal-*
certainely affured vnto vs, that we fhall be fanctified, and *uation.*
enabled to walke in this way of righteoufneffe and holineffe, then that we are elected and fhall be faued. Though
then we are weake and vnftable, yet *the foundation of God* 2.Tim.2.19.
remaineth euer fure ; though in regarde of our owne feebleneffe, and manyfould imperfections, the worke of fanctification feeme altogether impoffible, yet this fhould not
moue vs to doubting nor difcourage vs in our courfe,feeing
it hath not any ground vpon our owne ftrength, but vpon
Gods immutable decree,and neuer failing promifes. When Eph.1.4.
then our fmall progreffe in true godlineffe, caufed through Ioh.14.16.17.
the violence of our corruptions and oppofitions of our fpi- Ezech.11.19.
and 36.26.
rituall enemies,difcourageth vs,making this worke of fanc- Ier.31.33.34.
tification feeme impoffible,let vs cal to minde that the Lord Ioel.2.28.29.
hath as certainely decreed, that we fhould be his faints here
vpon earth as his faints in heauen, that he hath moft faithfully promifed, that he will direct vs with his holy fpirit,
take away from vs our ftonie hearts and giue vs flefhy
hearts, illuminate our blinde vnderftandings with true fauing knowledge, indue vs with a liuely faith, and with all
other fanctifying graces, enable vs to performe in fome
meafure holy obedience to his heauenly will,mortifying our
corruptions and enabling vs to ferue him in newnes of life ;
all which gracious promifes we are as vndoubtedly to beleeue, as thofe which concerne either the remiffion of our
finnes, or euerlafting happines. And therefore though our
owne dulneffe,backwardneffe, and little profiting in fanctification, fhould worke in vs true forrow, yet this fhould not
difcourage vs doubting of the iffue of all our labours, but
knowing that God is alike true in all his promifes, let vs,
fetting afide all difficulties,beleeue againft beliefe, and vndoubtedly perfwade our felues that the Lord will finifh that
good worke which hee hath begun in vs, though as yet it
hath

hath but small proceedings,if we hungar after more perfection, and carefully vse the meanes whereby we may attaine
to true holines.

Chap. IX.

*Sathans temptations whereby he aggranateth our
sinnes in generall,answered.*

§ Sect. 1.
*How Sathan
terrifieth the
Christians con-
science by ag-
grauating his
sinne.*

Nd so much concerning those temptations of
Sathan,which he groundeth vpon our naturall
corruptions and our small measure of sanctification. Now wee are to speake of such as hee
suggesteth after we haue committed some ac-
tuall sinnes: and these are either in respect of our sinnes in
generall, or els some speciall sinne into which wee haue fallen. Concerning the first, when the weake Christian (who
hath a tender conscience, and therefore cannot bee perswaded to lie securely in his sinne) hath through the strength of
his own corruptions,and violence of his temptations, committed any sinne against his knowledge and conscience,
then doth the tempter (who before his fall exceedingly ex-
tenuated & minced his sin,now after that he is fallen into it)
out of measure aggrauate the grieuousnesse and hainousnes
of his offence,partly in respect of the nature and qualitie of
the sinne it selfe, and partly in respect of the circumstances,
as being committed after his calling,against his knowledge,
in such a time or place,& by such a person, as God is therby
most dishonoured,and his brethren offended by his bad example. And thus hauing as it were stretched out his sinne
vpon the tentars of his temptations, and with the blasts of
his false suggestions made of euery small drop a great
bubble, then doth hee also set before him the curse of the
law, Gods fearefull iudgements, the plagues and punishments of this life,and euerlasting death and condemnation
in the life to come, continually accusing and terrifying him
as being guiltie of all these fearefull euils, by reason of his
sinnes,to the end that hereby being vtterly discouraged,hee

may

may defperately caft off all care of continuing in his former
courfe of godlineffe, as if now it were altogether in vaine
and to no purpofe.

The which temptation if wee would withftand in the day §*Sect.2.*
of triall, it behooueth vs not to reft in the remembrance of *The meanes to*
our former faith and repentance, but as wee haue renewed *withftand the*
our finne,fo alfo muft we renew our forrow for it,bewailing *former tempta-*
our corruptions, which haue fo preuailed againft vs as to *nued faith and*
moue vs to tranfgreffe Gods commandements, hating and *repentance.*
detefting our finne into which wee haue fallen,and purpofing for the time to come to leaue and forfake it,and to ferue
the Lord in holineffe and newneffe of life. And this our repentance wee muft approue to be vnfained by thofe fruites
thereof which the Apoftle mentioneth,2.Cor.7.9,10,11.that *2.Cor.7.9,10,*
is, wee muft ftudie and endeuour to amend, confeffe our fin *11.*
vnto God in all humilitie, and moft earneftly craue remiffion both of the fault and punifhment , haue a godly indignation againft our felues becaufe wee haue finned,and
a fonnelike feare not fo much in refpect of the punifhment,
as of offending and difpleafing God our moft gratious louing father; and an earneft defire that we may be fo renued,
that we be not againe fo ouertaken ; a more feruent zeale in
louing God and keeping his commandements than before
our fall ; and laftly, wee muft take a holy reuenge of our
felues, that thereby wee may fo tame our flefh,that it may
not hereafter be fo powerfull in vs,as to ouercome and leade
vs captiue vnto finne.

And thus hauing renewed our repentance, wee muft alfo
renew our faith,by applying vnto our felues all the gratious
promifes of the Gofpel, concerning life and faluation in
Chrift Iefus,made vnto all repentant finners;and by calling
to our remembrance that Chrift the iuft hath borne the punifhment due vnto vs who were vniuft; that with his death
and merits he hath fully fatisfied Gods iuftice, appeafed his
wrath,and wafhed away our finnes with his bloud; that hee
hath fulfilled the law for vs, and taken vpon him our curfe,
that we in him might be bleffed; that by fuffring for vs, hee
hath freed vs from all punifhments of this life and the life

to

to come, that hee euer liueth to make intercession for vs; so that though we sinne, yet there is no feare of condemnation, seeing *wee haue an aduocate with the father, Iesus Christ the iust, who is the reconciliation for our sinnes,* 1.Ioh.2.1,2.

1.Ioh.2.1.2.

§. *Sect.3.*
Sathans temptation perswading vs that we are still in the flesh.
Rom. 8. 1.

But here the tempter will obiect vnto the weake Christian, that these promises of the Gospell can yeeld vnto him no sound comfort, seeing they are restrained to those onely who are members of Christ Iesus, in which number are none but those who are regenerate, renewed, and gouerned by Gods spirit, according to that Rom.8.1. *There is no condemnation to those which are in Christ Iesus, which walke not after the flesh but after the spirit.* But thou (will hee say) art not in Christ, for being ingrafted in this vine thou wouldest bring foorth the grapes of godlinesse, whereas there springeth nothing from thee but the briars and brambles of iniquitie; neither walkest thou after the spirit, for then in thy life thou wouldest shew the fruites thereof, but after the flesh, which wholy ouerruleth thee and casteth thee headlong into all sin and wickednesse.

§. *Sect.4.*
VVhat it is to walke after the flesh and after the spirit.

Rom.7.

For the answering of which temptation we are to know, that it is not the committing of a sinne or of many sinnes, which prooueth that wee walke not after the spirit but after the flesh, (for so should all the children of God bee carnall and not spirituall, yea euen the Apostle *Paul* himselfe who complained that he did the euill which he hated, and found no meanes to doe that which was good, but when he would doe good, euill was present with him: and that there was a law in his members rebelling against the law of his minde, which led him captiue vnto the law of sinne) but to walke after the flesh is willingly to obey it in the lusts thereof; to commit sinne with pleasure and delight; to embrace that which is euill with full consent of will cheerefully and with all readinesse; to runne headlong into wickednesse stubbornly, presumptuously and securely; to haue sinne not onely dwelling but also raigning in our mortall bodies; to liue therein without repentance, neuer grieuing for it, nor endeuouring to forsake it, nay rather greatly louing and making such high account of it, that wee had rather part with our

liues

liues than bee diuorced from our finnes. Whofoeuer therefore through his weakneffe and infirmitie is led captiue vnto finne, and being enthralled by this tyrant earneftly defireth libertie, and doth not willingly run, but is violently drawne by Sathans temptations and his owne corruptions, and hauing finned is not therewith delighted, but exceedingly grieued that by his finne hee hath difpleafed God; and feeing his owne weakneffe and infirmities doth bewaile them, and fleeth vnto God by feruent prayer, defiring the affiftance of his holy fpirit, whereby hee may be enabled to mortifie his flefh and the corruptions thereof which hee deadly hateth, and to ferue God in holineffe and newneffe of life; fuch a one may affure himfelfe that hee walketh not after the flefh but after the fpirit, and that hee is in Chrift Iefus, and hath efcaped condemnation, though through his infirmitie and ftrength of his inbred corruptions hee falleth often into finne.

Though therefore the fanctified man finneth, yet this doth not prooue that he is ftill in the flefh and vnregenerate; feeing there is great difference betweene his finnes into which he now falleth, and thofe which hee committed before hee was fanctified, or thofe which they commit which ftill liue in the flefh. For firft the vnregenerate man doth continuallie finne, heaping vp one wickedneffe vpon another, the man regenerate but fometimes, when hee is ouercome by his corruptions; the wicked man committeth finne with greedineffe, the godly man with fome kinde of irkfomneffe and after a fort vnwillingly; the one drawes finne vnto him as it were *with cartropes*, the other is violently drawne to finne with the ftrength of his corruptions; the one hunteth after finne and the occafions thereof, the other is hunted by finne and Sathans temptations, till being out of breath and fainting for wearineffe hee is ouertaken and led prifoner. The carnall man finneth with full confent of will, and with pleafure and delight, the fpirituall man doth not yeeld without fome refiftance of the regenerate part, and as it were grudgingly and with the mifliking of the fpirit; he that is vnregenerate fuffreth finne to raigne in him, and yeeldeth vnto

§ *Sect. 5.*
The differences betweene the finnes of the regenerate man and the vnregenerate.

Efa.5.18.

Tt   it

it fuch willing and heartie obedience as the loyall fubiect
doth to his lawfull King, but the fanctified man obeyeth it
as though it were an vfurping tyrant, repiningly and by cō-
ftraint, rather drawne with force than moued by any loue or
liking. The wicked man committeth finne vpon deliberation, aduifedly and of fet purpofe; but the regenerate man
for the moft part fuddenly, befides his purpofe and contrary
to his refolution. The vngodly mans heart and confcience
feldome or neuer controules him for his finne, or if it doe,
yet it fuddenly vanifheth like a flafh of lightning; but there
is a fight in the hart of the godly man, the carnall part drawing one way and the fpirituall part another. When the carnall worldling offendeth hee is in his common way, for hee
maketh an occupation of committing finne; but when the
regenerate man finneth hee is out of his courfe, and is neuer
at reft till he commeth into his way of righteoufneffe again:
when the wicked man hath committed one finne, that is an
argument to moue him to commit another, *becaufe iudgement is deferred,* and hee hath efcaped punifhment; but the
true Chriftian (like one who runneth a race for fome great
wager) if he ftumble and fall, when he rifeth againe he doth
more carefully looke to his feete, and ftriueth to runne the
more fwiftly in the way of righteoufneffe, that fo he may redeeme with more than vfuall fpeed the loft time wherein he
was hindred by his fall. Finally, the vnregenerate man being
fallen into the puddle of finne, doth wallow therein with
pleafure and delight, and neuer ftriues to rife againe by a-
mendment of life, but the man regenerate though hee fall,
yet he rifeth vp againe by true repentance, and neuer refteth
till hee haue throughly wafhed his polluted foule with the
bloud of Chrift applied vnto him by a liuely faith. The one
remembreth his finnes which he hath committed, with gladneffe and reioycing, yea bragging and boafting of his outragious wickedneffe; the other neuer thinketh vpon them
but with griefe and forrow, neither is there any thing in the
world whereof he is more afhamed than of his finnes. Seeing therefore there is fuch great and manifold differences,
betweene the finnes of the fanctified and thofe who are vn-
fanctified,

Eccl.8.11.

fanctified,let not Sathan perfwade vs that wee are ftill in the
flefh and vnregenerate, becaufe will we nill we,we often fall
into finne, if in our manner of finning wee can finde thefe
differences which we neuer difcerned in former times.

Chap. X.

Sathans temptations taken from particular finnes
into which we haue fallen,anfwered.

Nd fo much concerning thofe temptations which
Sathan fuggefteth in refpect of our finnes in generall : now we are to fpeake of fuch as concerne
particular finnes, and thefe are of two forts ; for
either Sathan feeketh to ouerthrow our faith,and to difcourage vs from going forward in our courfe of godlineffe, by
fetting before vs and exceedingly aggrauating thofe finnes
which indeede wee haue committed, or by perfwading vs
falfely that we haue committed fuch finnes, as being vnpardonable are not incident to the childe of God. The former
fort of temptations are taken either from fome hainous fin
once committed,or from the often falling into the fame fin.
Concerning the firft, he aggrauateth the finnes of the faithfull two efpeciall waies, either becaufe they haue been committed after repentance , or voluntarily againft knowledge
and confcience.In the former refpect he is ready to fuggeft,
that the children of God doe not commit any finne after
they haue truly repented of it;and if any doe,either he neuer
truly repented, or if he did,yet after his fall there is no place
to a fecond repentance, nor hope of Gods mercie. For anfwering whereof wee are to know, that howfoeuer the ftate
of thofe who thus finne is fomewhat dangerous, and they
more hardly recouered than others (euen as thofe difeafes
are perilous and hardly cured,into which wee fall by a re-
lapfe after the recouerie of health) yet this is incident to the
children of God who haue truly repented,and notwithftanding this grieuous kinde of falling they are not debarred of
Gods mercie in Chrift Iefus. And this appeareth partly by

§. *Sect.*1.
That fins com-
mitted after
repentance, ex-
clude vs not
from pardon.

reafons,

reasons, and partly by examples. For first, the gracious promises of the Gospell concerning the remission of sinnes, are indefinite and without limitation, of time, or sinnes, whether committed before or after repentance. So Matth. 11. 28.

Matth. 11.28.
1.Ioh.2.1,2.

Come vnto me all ye that labour and are heauie laden, and I will ease you: and 1.Iohn 2.1,2. *If any man sinne, we haue an aduocate with the father, &c.* In which and in many other places, the Lord assureth vs that he will receiue to mercy all repentant sinners, of what nature and qualitie soeuer their sinnes are. Secondly, in the lawe were sacrifices appoynted for the sinnes of the people, not onely those who were newly receiued into the Lords couenant for their sinnes past, but also for those sinnes which were daily committed, after that they had long been therein. Thirdly, the Lord inoyneth vs that we forgiue our brother seuentie times seuen times, if so often hee offend vs and repent of his fault; and therefore himselfe much more, whose mercy is infinite, and more exceedeth ours than the whole sea a little droppe, will pardon vs if as we often sinne, so also wee often turne vnto him by vnfained repentance. This also manifestly appeareth by examples, for did not the Prophet *Dauid* after his true conuersion fall grieuously by committing murther and adulterie, the Apostle *Peter* by denying his Lord and Sauiour, *Noah* by drunkennesse, *Lot* by incest, and yet afterwards they truly repented againe and were receiued to mercy? So that this poynt is cleere and manifest, that the deare childe of God, after his true conuersion and vnfained repentance may fall into grieuous sinnes, and yet truly repenting of them, may haue them remitted, and bee receiued againe into Gods wonted loue and fauour.

§ Sect.2.
An obiection answered.
Heb.6.4,5,6.

But here the tempter will obiect that the Apostle affirmeth Heb.6.4,5,6. *That it is impossible that those who haue been once inlightened, &c. if they fall away should be renewed by repentance: seeing by so sinning, they crucifie againe to themselues the Sonne of God, and make a mocke of him.* And therefore whosoeuer sinneth after his true conuersion, can neither repent nor receiue mercy. To which we must answere, that the Apostle in this place doth not speake of euery falling into to finne, for fo he fhould be contrary to the other Scriptures before alledged, but of a generall falling away by apoftafie, and of a malitious perfecuting of the knowne truth, which is the finne againft the holy Ghoft, the which is ioyned with continuall impenitency, and therefore cannot be pardoned. And this appeareth manifeftly by the words of the text; for he doth not fimply fay if he fall into finne, but if he fall away, namely by a generall and malitious apoftafie : and againe, he fheweth of what manner of falling he meaneth in the words following, whereas he faith, that fuch as thus fall away, crucifie vnto themfelues the fonne of God, and make a mocke of him. Now they are faid to crucifie Chrift againe, who with an vnplacable hatred doe fcorne and deride Chrift crucified, renouncing all part and hope in his death and fufferings, as did fome of the malitious Iewes, and as fome apoftates doe in thefe dayes. And therefore this place maketh nothing againft the repentance and receiuing to mercie of fuch as fall through infirmitie into fome particular finnes, though neuer fo hainous.

And fo much for anfwering Sathans temptations drawne from our finnes committed after repentance. The fecond fort are taken from finnes committed voluntarily againft our knowledge and confcience ; which if we haue fallen into, he prefently fuggefteth that we haue finned prefumptuoufly againft God, and therefore cannot be reckoned in the number of Gods children, nor conceiue any hope of pardon and forgiueneffe. For the anfwering vnto which temptation, we are to knowe thefe two things ; firft, that all finnes committed againft knowledge and confcience are not prefumptuous : fecondly, that though we fhould fall into prefumptuous finnes, yet we may be the children of God, who are neither debarred of true repentance nor of Gods mercy. For the firft, we are to know that not the hainoufneffe of the finne committed maketh it to bee prefumptuous, but the manner of the fact, and the minde of the offender ; for howfoeuer *Peter* fell grieuoufly, yet we cannot fay that hee fell prefumptuoufly, becaufe he finned through infirmitie and feare of danger, whereas to finne prefumptuoufly, is to finne

§. Sect. 3.
That all finnes of knowledge are not prefumptuous.

VVhat it is to finne prefumptuoufly.

of

of a stubborne wilfulnesse, either through the neglect of Gods iustice and iudgements, or through the abuse of his mercy and benefits. In the first respect they offend, who hauing diuers times themselues sinned, and yet escaped punishment, or hauing seene others in the like case, doe take occasion hereby to sinne againe, hoping to escape as in former times : and of such the wise man speaketh, Ecclef.8.11,

Because sentence against an euill worke is not executed speedily, therefore the heart of the children of men is fully set in them to doe euill. In the other respect, such offend as take occasion vpon Gods mercy and long suffering to fall into sinne, presuming before they commit it, that God vpon their repentance will in his infinite mercy forgiue them : and thus they abuse Gods mercy and goodnesse which should leade them to repentance, as an argument to make them more desperately to runne into all wickednesse. So that to sinne presumptuously, is not to sinne vpon knowledge, and against a mans conscience onely, vnlesse there be ioyned therewith a presumptuous hope to escape punishment, or that notwithstanding the sinne committed, he shall receiue pardon in respect of Gods infinite mercy. Now many of Gods children may fall against their knowledge and conscience, and yet not presume either to escape Gods iudgements or to be partakers of his mercy, as namely those who are caried headlong into a sinne without any time of deliberation through the violence of their corruptions, or ouercome by feare of some present danger, or some other vnruly passion.

But here the tempter will obiect, that though these sinnes against knowledge and conscience bee not presumptuous, yet they are vnpardonable, seeing the committers of them haue no part in Christs sacrifice, and consequently can hope for no mercy at Gods hands : and this he will indeauour to proue by that saying of the Apostle, Hebr.10.26. *For if we sinne willingly after that we haue receiued the knowledge of the truth, there remaineth no more sacrifice for sinnes, but a fearefull looking for of iudgement &c.* For the answering whereof, we are to know, that the Apostle in his doctrine is not contrary to our Sauiour Christ : but hee hath taught vs, that not onely sinnes

Margin notes:
- Ecclef.8.11.
- Rom.2.4.
- §.Sect.4. *That sinnes of knowledge are pardonable.*
- Heb.10.26.

sinnes against knowledge are pardonable vpon true repentance, but euen horrible blasphemies against the maiestie of God, yea, all sinnes whatsoeuer sauing the sinne against the holy Ghost. Matth.12.31,32. Secondly, we knowe by expe- Mat.12.31,32
rience, that both *Dauid* and *Peter* fell grieuously against their knowledge and conscience, wittingly, and in a sort willingly, and yet they both repented and were receiued to mercie : and therefore the Apostle speaketh not of all kinde of voluntary falling, but first of sinne committed with full consent of will, pleasure, and delight : the which kinde of sinnes are neuer committed by Gods children after their true conuersion; for as they are in part carnall and vnregenerate, so are they in part spirituall and regenerate, which is to be vnderstoode, not onely of the vnderstanding part, but also of the will and affections. So farre forth therefore as their will is regenerate, they doe not will nor yeeld vnto sinne ; and though they consent vnto sinne, yet this consent is not absolute and intire, but with some dislike, grudging, and resistance of the spirituall part; the which dislike and resistance, though sometimes it cannot easily be discerned in the very act of sinne, whereas the weake motions of the spirit are violently ouerborne, through the violent strength of their naturall corruptions, and so ouershadowed by the cloudie mists which their vnruly passions cast before their vnderstãding, that they cannot at all perceiue any dislike or resistance against the temptation : yet after the sinne is committed, and the good motions of the spirit are againe reuiued out of their deadly swound, then doe they hate and detest that sinne which before seemed pleasant vnto them, and earnestly desire with the Apostle to be freed from it. Lastly, the Apostle in that place doth not speake of euery particular sinne committed with full consent of will, for so also the elect offend before their conuersion, but of a generall and malitious apostasie from the knowne truth, and a scornefull reiecting of the sacrifice of Christ once offered for sinne : so that the sense is thus much, that if wee wilfully and malitiously sinne, by renouncing the sacrifice of Christ offered for sinne, we cannot hope to be saued by any other sacrifice, but

Tt 4   are

are to expect iudgement and condemnation, seeing such treade vnder foote the sonne of God, and count the blood of the testament an vnholy thing, and euen despite the spirit of grace, as he explaneth himselfe in the verses following.

§. Sect.5.
That the chri-
stian may fall
into presumptu-
ous sinnes, and
that so falling,
he may be re-
ceiued to mer-
cie.

And so much concerning the first question; the second is whether the christian man may fall into presumptuous sins, and if hee doe, whether they be pardonable or no. For the first, though it must needes bee confessed that it is a fearefull case, to neglect Gods iustice and iudgements because of his long suffering, or to take occasion vpon the abundance of Gods mercies and readinesse to forgiue, to prouoke him continually by our sinnes; yet it cannot be denied, but that a true christian, through the strength of his inbred corruptions, may fall into these presumptuous sinnes; neither is there any priuiledge in the holy Scriptures to exempt them from any sinne whatsoeuer, but that either before or after their conuersion they may fall into it, sauing onely that vnpardonable sinne which is committed against the holy Ghost. Moreouer, *Dauid* prayeth the Lord to keepe him from *pre-*

Psalm.19.13.
sumptuous sinnes, and that he would not suffer them *to raigne ouer him*, Psalm.19.13. where first he sheweth that of himselfe he was apt to fall into such sinnes, if the Lord did not preserue him from them; and secondly he implieth, that the Lord might for good causes knowne vnto himselfe, suffer him to commit these sinnes of presumption, and therefore he further prayeth that if hee should fall into such sinnes, it would please the Lord to raise him by true repentance, and not suffer them to rule and raigne in him. So that it appeareth that a true christian may fall into these sinnes: now, that hauing fallen he may rise againe by true repentance, and receiue pardon and forgiuenesse, it is likewise manifest. For if once the Lord receiue vs into the couenant of grace, and acknowledge vs for his children, then nothing in the world, no not the most grieuous sinnes which we can fall into, can separate vs from the loue of God which is in Christ Iesus our

Rom.8.38,39.
Lord, as the Apostle speaketh, Rom.8.38,39. Secondly, our Sauiour telleth vs, that *euery sinne and blasphemy shall be forgi-*

Mat.12.31.32.
uen vnto men vpon true repentance, sauing onely the blasphemie

phemie againſt the ſpirit which is alwaies ioyned with finall
impenitencie. Matth. 12.31,32. Thirdly, the promiſes of the
the Goſpell are generall and indefinit, excluding no ſortes
of ſinnes whatſoeuer, ſo they performe the condition of
faith and repentance. And therefore alſo preſumptuous
ſinners, repenting and beleeuing, are aſſured of mercie and
forgiueneſſe. Laſtly, if *Dauid* might fall into theſe ſinnes,
then *Dauid* alſo might repent and receiue pardon, ſeeing he
was truely iuſtified, ſanctified, and a choſen veſſell of the
Lord elected to euerlaſting life.

And ſo much concerning the temptations which are taken from thoſe ſinnes which are once committed; now we
are to ſpeake of them which he ſuggeſteth vnto the weake
conſcience, after the committing of one and the ſame ſinne
diuers times; vpon which occaſion he is readie to perſwade
the weake chriſtian, that he neuer truely repented, otherwiſe
he would neuer againe fall into the ſame ſinne; and that
howſoeuer the child of God may fall into diuers ſinnes,
through want of care and experience, yet it is not incident
to any of this number to fall againe and againe into the
ſame wickedneſſe, after they haue had warning and ſufficient
knowledge of the euils thereof. For the anſwering whereof
we are to know, that in truth it is a grieuous and fearefull
caſe to be thus ouertaken, and to be ſo beſotted with the
pleaſures of ſinne, that neither inſtruction nor our owne experience can make vs to ſee the euils of ſinne, and worke in
vs a care to auoyde and ſhunne it. The burnt childe (as the
prouerbe is) dreadeth the fire; he that hath been deceiued
and thereby much indamaged, is afterwards more warie;
he that hath caſt himſelfe into any grieuous diſeaſe through
ſome vnholeſome meates, is euer after more carefull of
his diet; he that hath once been aſſaulted by his enemie at
vnawares, and hath receiued griefly woundes, will after he
is cured goe better armed and furniſhed, that he may not
againe be ouertaken of the like daunger. And therefore ſeeing experience of all other euils doth teach vs to auoyde
them, what a lamentable thing is this, that no warning will
make vs take heede of ſinne, which is the greateſt euill and

§ Sect.6.
That it is a
fearefull thing
to fall often in-
to the ſame ſin
willingly.

cauſe

caufe of all the reft? that hauing drunke this deadly poyfon
and been grieuoufly ficke thereof in our confciences, wee
fhould being recouered be inticed with the pleafant tafte
thereof to fwallow it downe againe? and that hauing receiued grieuous wounds, we fhould after take no better heede,
and goe no better armed and prepared to make refiftance,
but for want of care and watchfulneffe expofe our felues
againe to the like daunger of our fpirituall enemies? But

That the child
of God may fall
often into the
fame finne and
yet be receiued
to mercie.

yet we are to know that this fometimes, through our great
frailtie and corruption, may be the eftate of a true chriftian
and faithfull feruant of God, to fall againe and againe into
the fame finne, neither doth any thing priuiledge them
from committing that finne againe which they haue once
committed. For firft the fame inbred corruption ftill dwelleth in them and is readie againe to giue them the foyle and
to leade them captiue into the fame finne, if the Lord vphold them not, fo that inrefpect of their owne ftrength they
may fall againe as in former times. Secondly, the fame caufes ftill remaine which may moue the Lord to leaue them
to themfelues, and fuffer them to fall, namely that hereby
they may be more humbled, and more ferioufly bewaile
their corruptions, that they may more earneftly implore his
mercie, and he more manifeft it in pardoning their finnes to
the praife of his glorie. Thirdly, howfoeuer this is not vfuall
with the children of God, to fall diuers times into a finne
which is great and grieuous, yet euery one findeth in his
owne experience that he often committeth fuch finnes as
are not fo heynous, through infirmitie and weakneffe; as to
heare the word negligently and careleffely, to be diftracted
with wandering thoughts in prayer, to fall into vniuft anger,
to lie and vfe idle communication and fuch like, of which
notwithftanding repenting he is receiued vnto mercie. So
that it is not the often falling into the fame finne, that excludeth vs out of the number of Gods children, or debarreth vs of pardon, fo that we often repent and lay holde vpon Chrift with a liuely faith. Neither do the fcriptures limit
and reftraine Gods mercie, and the vertue of Chrifts merits,
to the pardoning and taking away of diuers finnes, once
committed,

committed, but extend them also to the same sinne committed diuers times, yea to all sinnes whatsoeuer of which we truely repent.

CHAP. XI.

Sathans temptations perswading the christian that he hath sinned against the holy Ghost, answered.

Nd thus haue I answered Sathans temptations §. *Sect.*1. drawne from these sinnes which the weake *Of the sinne* christian hath fallen into ; but if he cannot so *against the holy* preuaile, then he will falsely accuse them of *Ghost.* those sinnes which they neuer committed, and especially of that vnpardonable sinne against the holy Ghost, taking aduantage of their ignorance, that so he may plunge them into desperation, and vtterly discourage them from going forward in the course of godlinesse. The which his temptation is so vsuall and common, that there is scarce any who are exercised in this spirituall warfare, if they be conuerted vnto God out of their ignorance, whom he doth not encounter with this weapon. For as much therefore as ignorance is the chiefe ground of this temptation, therefore the best meanes to strengthen our selues against it, is to know what this sinne is, which if we once vnderstand, there is no daunger of being foyled in this assault.

The sinne against the holy Ghost, is a generall deniall and *What the sinne* oppugning of the truth and all religion, of which the vnder- *against the holy* standing and conscience by the illumination of the spirit *Ghost is.* are perswaded and conuicted, proceeding from an obstinate will and purposed malice against God and his truth. The which sinne is committed of two sortes of men; first, of those who haue made profession of the truth, and afterwards become Apostataes, not from some part onely but from all religion, condemning, blaspheming, and persecuting as hereticall and impious, that truth which before they professed, and of which they were perswaded. And thus did *Hymenæus* and *Alexander* sinne, of whom *Paul* speaketh 1.*Tim.*1,20. 1.*Tim.*

1.Tim.1.20. Secondly, of those who were neuer profeſſors thereof, whoſe conſciences notwithſtanding are conuicted of that truth which they doe oppugne : an example whereof we haue in the Scribes and Phariſes, Matth.12.24.31. and in many of the learned Papiſts in theſe dayes, who maliciouſly deny and perſecute that truth which they know and are con-uicted of.

Matth.12.24. 31.
Steuen Gard-ner. See his ſto-rie in the booke of Martyrs.

§. *Sect.*2.
How to diſtin-guiſh the ſinne againſt the holy Ghoſt from other ſinnes.

    Hereby therefore it appeareth that not euery grieuous ſinne againſt knowledge and conſcience is the ſinne againſt the holy Ghoſt, for thus *Dauid* offended who was a man ac-cording to Gods owne heart ; nor euery denying of the knowne truth, if it proceede from feare and infirmitie, and not from malice and obſtinat rebellion,for thus *Peter* ſinned in denying his maiſter ; nor all kinde of oppoſing and per-ſecuting of the truth, if it bee not againſt knowledge and conſcience, but vpon blindneſſe and ignorance, for thus *Paul* offended before his conuerſion, as appeareth 1.Tim.1. 13. and many of the Iewes who crucified Chriſt, as the Apo-ſtle *Peter* teſtifieth, Act.3.17. nor all malicious oppoſing againſt euery knowne truth, but of the truth in generall and all true religion, for this ſinne is an vniuerſall apoſtaſie from God and his truth, and not onely a defection from ſome particular point thereof. So that though a man ſinne againſt knowledge and conſcience, through infirmitie and not of malice; though he deny the truth through feare and weake-neſſe, though he perſecute it through blindneſſe and igno-rance ; though he wittingly oppoſe againſt and willingly perſecute ſome particular point thereof, and yet hold and profeſſe the generall, howſoeuer he hath moſt hainouſly of-fended, yet he hath not committed this vnpardonable ſinne againſt the holy ſpirit, and therefore is not excluded from repentance, nor vpon his repentance from pardon and for-giueneſſe.Whereby it manifeſtly appeareth that theſe poore chriſtians which labour vnder the burthen of ſinne , are meerely deluded by Sathans falſe ſuggeſtions, and groſely abuſed through their owne ignorance, when as he maketh them beleeue that they haue ſinned againſt the holy Ghoſt. But let ſuch know to their comfort that ſo long as they would

1.Tim.1.13.

Act.3.17.

would not commit this sinne, or feare leaft they haue alreadie fallen into it, they are as yet moft free from it, feeing it
is not done of infirmitie or at vnawares, but vpon a malitious will,cleare knowledge and fetled refolution.

But here the poore chriftian is readie to complaine, that
he is continually troubled with impious thoughts, and horrible blafphemies againft God and his holy fpirit, which he
feareth to be the finne againft the holy Ghoft. I anfwere as
before, that feeing thefe thoughts are a trouble vnto him,
and feeing he feareth to commit this finne, thereby it is manifeft that he is not fallen into it, as appeareth by that which
hath been faid. Secondly,he is to know that his ftate is common with Gods faithfull children, who are thus vexed e-
fpecially in the conflict of temptations, and before they
haue receiued a great meafure of faith, and fulneffe of perfwafion of Gods loue and fauour, whereby they are moued
intirely to loue him againe. Neither needes this to feeme
ftrange vnto any who confidereth of that maffe of naturall
corruption which remaineth in vs, euen after regeneration,
which continually boyleth and fometh vp the filthie
fcumme of wicked thoughts and blafphemous imaginations ; and of the malice of our fpirituall enemie Sathan, who
is ftill readie to tempt vs by his fuggeftions to the moft horrible and outragious finnes, if not in hope to ouercome vs,
yet at leaft to vexe and trouble vs. As we may fee in the example of the holy man *Iob,* whom he fpared not to tempt
vnto fearefull blafphemie.

But though we cannot keepe the diuell from affaulting
vs, let not this difcourage vs, nay rather let vs be moued
hereby with more care and watchfulneffe to withftand him,
for if we *refift him he will flee from vs.* Iam.4.7. But in this our
refiftance two things efpecially muft be obferued : the firft
is the meanes whereby we muft giue him the repulfe; which
is partly by the fword of the fpirit,the word of God,where-
by we beate backe the temptation by prouing the wickedneffe thereof by fome teftimonie of fcripture, according to
our Sauiours example; and partly by lifting vp our mindes
vnto God in prayer,defiring ftrength to withftand the temptation.

§.*Sect.*3.
Of impious and blasphemous suggestions.

Iam.4.7.

tation. Secondly, we muſt take heede that we doe not re-uolue the temptation in our mindes, but preſently repell it, leaſt theſe helliſh ſparkes taking hold of the tindar of our corruptions, doe at length inflame vs with horrible wicked-neſſe, which at their firſt falling might eaſily haue been ex-tinguiſhed. And if we thus ſpeedely repell theſe horrible blaſphemies ſuggeſted by Sathan, they ſhall neuer be im-puted vnto vs, but vnto him from whom they proceede, and that both in reſpect of the fault and puniſhment.

Chap. XII.

Arguments to proue the certaintie of our perſeuerance groun-ded vpon Gods will and immutabilitie.

§ Sect.1.
Sathans temp-
tation mouing
the chriſtian to
doubt of his
perſeuerance.

And thus haue I anſwered Sathans temptations which concerne our ſanctification. Now in the laſt place wee are to intreate of our perſeue-rance which he impugneth with no leſſe ſub-tiltie and violence. For though the chriſtian man haue attained to ſome aſſurance, that he is elected, cal-led, iuſtified, and ſanctified, yet Sathan will not giue him ouer, but laboreth to perſwade him, that notwithſtanding all this he may finally fall away and become a reprobate. Let it be graunted (will he ſay) that thy ſtate now is ſuch as thou ſuppoſeſt, yet thou art in no ſafetie, neither canſt thou promiſe vnto thy ſelfe any aſſurance of attaining vnto euer-

Matth. 24.3. laſting life and happineſſe, ſeeing thoſe onely *which continue vnto the end ſhall be ſaued:* whereas thou haſt no aſſurance of thy perſeuerance, nay contrariwiſe thou art in reſpect of thy frailtie and mutabilitie, certaine of nothing more then thine vncertaintie. Call to thy remembrance the example of thy firſt parents, who were perfectly righteous and holy, more accompliſhed in all graces than any of their poſteritie, more ſtrong and able to indure and reſiſt all temptations, as be-ing indued with free-will, and therefore able both to chuſe the good and refuſe the euill, who notwithſtanding all this were ouercome, and of the children of God made the ſlaues

of

of sinne and Sathan. Did they therefore fall who were perfectly righteous, and canst thou who are most imperfect
hope to stand? were not they who were full of all graces
able to indure the incounter in the day of triall, and canst
thou hope to make resistance who art full of sinne and corruption? were they vanquished who were strong champions, and dost thou who art weake and feeble hope for victorie? were they allured by Sathans temptations, to commit sinne, and fall from God, who could freely will the good
and nill the euill; and canst thou hope to perseuer and
continue constant, whose will is captiued and ouerruled by
thy corruption? Consider further thy mutabilitie and vn-
constancie, thy exeeding weaknesse and frailtie, thy corruptions and imperfections; and on the other side set before
thee, the mightie power, the subtill pollicie, the vigilant
watchfulnesse, and vnwearied diligence, of thy spirituall e-
nemies who continually assault thee: and then thinke with
thy selfe if there be any possibilitie, that thy weaknes should
withstand their power, thy ignorant simplicitie their prudent wisedome, and thy carelesse negligence their carefull
diligence. Lastly, call to minde the manifold examples
which thou hast both read and seene, of such as haue been
of greater gifts and graces, and made a much fairer shew
then thou, of holinesse towards God and righteousnesse
towards men, who notwithstanding haue finally fallen away
and become reprobates, and therefore why maiest not thou
be one of this number? Seeing then the case thus standeth
doe not foolishly flatter thy selfe with a vaine hope, that because thou art elected, called, iustified, and sanctified, therefore thou shalt be saued; for though now thou art elected,
yet hereafter thou maiest become a reprobate; though to
day thou art a childe of God, and in his fauour, yet to morrow thou mayest through thy sinnes, be a childe of the diuell, and in Gods displeasure be reiected; though now thou
art a member of Christ, thou maiest become a limme of Sathan; and though now thou art indued with the spirit of
God, and with all the graces and gifts thereof, yet by thy
sinne thou mayst easily loose both it and them; and bee
wholy

wholy and finally giuen ouer to run on in thy former wickednes vnto eternall death and condemnation.

And thus doth Sathan perswade the christian man to doubt of his perseuerance; the which temptations, if we would withstand, it behoueth vs not to ground the certaintie of our perseuerance vpon our owne resolution, strength and graces which we haue receiued, for these are altogether insufficient to vphold vs against the assaults of our spirituall enemies, who are farre more stronger then we; but wholy distrusting in our owne abilitie, let vs rest and rely wholy vpon the Lord, for as it is he alone who hath bestowed vpon vs all the gifts and graces which we haue receiued, so also haue wee our growth and perseuerance in them from him onely. And so we may be assured of our perseuerance, notwithstanding our owne weakenesse and inconstancie, for

2.Cor.1.21.

it is God which stablisheth vs in Christ, as it is 2.Cor.1.21. Though in respect of any thing that is in vs we might euery hour fall away, yet we are sure to continue in those graces which we haue receiued, mauger the malice and power of all our enemies, for wee stand not in our owne strength but

1.Pet.1.4.

are kept by the power of God through faith vnto saluation, as the Apostle speaketh 1.Pet.1.4. Though we should euery day loose euerlasting life and happinesse through negligence, or sell it away for the vanities of the world and pleasures of sinne if it were in our owne hands, yet all this is not sufficient to disinherit vs of our heauenly patrimonie, for it is not

Col.3.3.

at our own disposition *but our life is hid with Christ in God*, as it is Col.3.3. And therefore though in our selues we are as weake as reedes, and as vnconstant and changeable as the wind and weather, yet are we tenne thousand times more sure to perseuer in that grace which we haue receiued vnto euerlasting life, than *Adam* in the state of innocencie; for he stoode by his owne strength, which though it were great, yet it was finite, but we by the almightie power of God; he by the vertue of his owne free will, which was mutable and subiect to alteration, but we by the will of God which being immutable admitteth of no change.

But let vs come more specially to speake of this maine
controuersie

controuerfie betweene the true Chriftian and the enemies of his faluation, the ftate whereof ftandeth thus ; whether hee that is elected in Gods eternall counfaile, and is effectually called, that is, feuered from the world, giuen to Chrift, and ingrafted into Chrift by the fpirit of God and a liuely faith, iuftified, fanctified, and indued with the fanctifying gifts and graces of Gods fpirit, may after all this fall away, lofe the fpirit of God and the graces thereof, and become as prophane and wicked as euer he was before his conuerfion, lofe alfo his iuftification, be cut off from the bodie of Chrift, and finally become a reprobate. This the enemies of our faluation affirme, but we denie as being a thing impoffible, not in regard of our owne ftrength, conftancie, or great meafure of grace which wee haue receiued, but in refpect of Gods will and power who vpholdeth vs, Chrifts interceffion who prayeth for vs, and Gods holy fpirit alwaies dwelling in vs, wherby we are fo ftrengthened and confirmed, that al the power of hell cannot preuaile againft vs.

The ftate of the Controuerfie.

This our affertion we will firft confirme by vnfallible reafons, and afterwards anfwere the contrary obiections which are made againft this truth by the enemies of our faluation.

§. *Sect.*4.
The firft argument grounded vpon Gods wil, confidered in his decree of election.

The reafons which may be alledged for this purpofe are many; the firft fort are taken from Gods owne nature, as it is defcribed in his word and exercifed in his workes towards vs. As firft we may be affured of our perfeuerance, becaufe it is grounded vpon Gods will, which may be confidered either in his fecret counfaile and decree of election, or in his will reuealed in his word. From the firft wee may thus reafon; Whomfoeuer the Lord in his eternall counfaile hath elected to euerlafting life, they fhall moft certainly be faued, and perfeuere in the meanes tending thereunto, which are no leffe contained in Gods decree than our faluation it felf. But the Lord in his eternall counfaile hath elected all the faithfull vnto eternall life. And therefore nothing can hinder their faluation, nor yet their perfeuerance, without which it is impoffible they fhould be faued. The firft part of this reafon is cleere and manifeft : for not to effect that which one hath decreed and purpofed, argueth either impotencie and

want

want of power, or vnconſtancie, neither of which without
blaſphemie can bee aſcribed vnto God; *for there is nothing* Iere.32 17.
hard vnto him. Iere.32.17, but *he deth whatſoeuer he will*,Pſal. Pſalm.115.3.
115.3, yea euen *thoſe things which vnto men are impoſſible are* Matth. 19.26.
poſſible vnto him,Mat.19.26, *for he can doe all things*,Iob,42.2. Iob.42 2.
Neither is the will of God mutable, for this argueth a want
of wiſedome, whereas *his wiſedoms is infinite and knoweth* Pſal.145.5.
no end, Pſal.145.5; and hee perfectly ſeeth and knoweth all
things in one view, paſt, preſent,and to come,Heb.4.13:and Heb.4.13.
therfore we may conclude with the Apoſtle, that *the purpoſe*
of God in his election remaineth ſure, Rom.9.11. and *the foun-* Rom.9.11.
dation of God (that is, his vnchangeable decree)*continueth*
firme,and hath this ſeale,The Lord knoweth who are his,2.Tim. 1.Tim.2.19.
2.19. Whoſoeuer then are elected they ſhall moſt certainly
be ſaued,neither is it poſſible that they ſhould fall away: as
our Sauiour implieth Matth.24.24. whereas he ſaith,that the
falſe Prophets ſhould ſhew ſuch great ſignes, that if it were
poſſible they ſhould deceiue the very elect. Noting hereby
that this is altogether a thing impoſſible,that they ſhould be
deceiued and ſeduced with falſe Chriſts and falſe Prophets.

   The ſecond part of this reaſon, namely, that all the faithfull are elected, is alſo of moſt vndoubted trueth; for whoſoeuer haue a true faith they are iuſtified, whoſoeuer are iuſtified are alſo effectually called, elected, and ſhall be glorified; What ſaid I? ſhall be? nay are alreadie glorified, as the
Apoſtle affirmeth,to note the vndoubted certaintie of their Rom.8.30.
ſaluation,Rom.8.30. Moreouer,the Apoſtle maketh faith an
inſeparable fruite of our election, and proper and peculiar
vnto the elect, calling it the *faith of Gods elect*, Tit.1.1. And Tit.1.1.
Act.13.48.it is ſaid, that *as many as were ordained vnto eternall* Act.13.48.
life beleeued, where hee maketh Gods election the cauſe of
faith. And contrariwiſe our Sauiour telleth vs, that they beleeue not, who are not his ſheepe, Ioh.10.26. So that it is Ioh.10.26.
manifeſt that thoſe who beleeue are elected, and thoſe who
are elected ſhall be ſaued.

§. Sect.5.   The ſecond reaſon may be taken from his wil reueiled in
his word ; for whatſoeuer God thus willeth,that ſhall moſt
certainly

certainly come to paffe : but God willeth that all fhould haue euerlafting life whom he hath giuen to Chrift,in which number are all thofe who are effectually called, as our Sauiour teftificth Ioh.6.39, *And this is the fathers will which hath fent me,that of all which he hath giuen me I fhould lofe nothing,but fhould raife it vp again at the laft day.*And he willeth likewife,*that he that beleeueth in the fonne fhould be faued,* as it is verf.40. And therefore thofe who are effectually called and beleeue in Chrift, cannot poffibly perifh,but fhall moft certainly haue eternall life.

The fecond reafon, grounded on his will reuealed. Ioh 6.39.40.

The third reafon may bee taken from the conftancie and immutabilitie of God, both in his loue towards vs, and alfo in his gifts. In the former refpect wee may thus reafon : Whomfoeuer the Lord loueth with a conftant and immutable loue,thofe fhall moft certainly be faued,feeing it is the nature of loue to defire the good of the partie beloued, and to feeke his welfare as much as it can ; but the Lord loueth his faithfull ones with a conftant and perpetual loue,as himfelfe teftifieth Iere.31.3. *I haue loued thee with an euerlafting loue,therefore with mercie haue I drawne thee.* So Ioh.13.1. *Forafmuch as he loued his owne which were in the world,vnto the end he loued them.* And therefore all the faithfull may affure themfelues that they fhall be faued, and being once affured of Gods loue, they may with the Apoftle bee vndoubtedly perfwaded,that nothing in the world fhall be able to feparate them from the loue of God which is in Chrift Iefus our Lord.

§. Sect.6. *The third reafon, taken from Gods immutabilitie in his loue.*

Iere.31.3.

Ioh.13.1.

But againft this it may be obiected, that the finnes of the faithfull doe prouoke the Lord vnto anger,and mooue him to caft them off in his iuft difpleafure,and to withdraw from them his wonted loue and fauour : and therefore feeing fin feparateth them from Gods loue, it may alfo plunge them into condemnation. To which I anfwere, that indeede the finnes of the faithfull doe in themfelues deferue the euerlafting wrath of God and eternall death, if they were not taken away by Chrift, who hath by his precious bloudfhed fatisfied his fathers iuftice; and that euen now they fo offend by their finnes their gracious father, that they had neede to

§. Sect.7. *An obiection againft the former reafon anfwered.*

renew

renew their faith and repentance, before they can haue any
sensible assurance that they are reconciled vnto him, and receiued into his loue and fauour. It is most true that God is
displeased with the sinnes of his children, according to that

Esa.64.5.
How God is
said to be an-
grie with his
children.

Esa.64.5. *Behold thou art angrie, for we haue sinned.* But this
anger doth not exclude them out of his loue, seeing it is not
the anger of an enemie but of a gracious father, who is not
angrie with their persons to destroy them, but with their sins
to conuert and saue them. As therefore children with their
faults prouoke their parents to anger, and mooue them to
turne their fatherly smiles into bitter frownes, and the fruits
of their loue into the effects of hatred in outward shew, as
namely seuere countenances, sharpe reproofes, and rigorous
chastizements; and in respect of these outward signes and effects of their anger they are vsually said to be out of fauour
and in their fathers displeasure, howsoeuer in truth at the
same time they intirely loue them, and vse all this holesome
seueritie not because they hate, but because they would reforme them: So Gods children when by their sinnes they do
offend him and prouoke his anger against them, are said to
be out of his fauour, not that God doth euer change his fatherly affection or purposeth vtterly to reiect them, but because hee changeth the effects of his loue into the effects of
hatred in outward shew, as when inwardly hee suffreth them
to be vexed with the terrors of conscience, and with the apprehension of his anger and displeasure, and outwardly
whippeth and scourgeth them with temporarie afflictions;
all which he doth not for any hatred to their persons, for he
neuer hateth those whom hee hath once loued in Christ, but
for the hatred of their sinnes, and loue of the sinner, whom
by this meanes hee bringeth by the rough and vnpleasant
way of repentance, vnto the eternall pleasures of his kingdome.

§. Sect.8.
Our perseue-
rance proued
by Gods immu-
tabilitie in his
gifts.

And thus it appeareth that Gods loue and anger may
stand together, and that notwithstanding his momentanie
displeasure his loue may be eternall. Now secondly wee are
to know, that as God is immutable in his loue so also in his
gifts, as faith, repentance, hope, affiance, charitie, &c. according

ling to that Rom.11.29, *The gifts and calling of God are with-* Rom.11.29.
out repentance. But yet this is to bee vnderstood with diuers
cautions; for first it is not to be vnderstood of all the gifts of
God, not of temporarie gifts, nor of the gifts of the spirit
which are common to the wicked with the godly, for these
being not essentiall to a Christian nor necessarie to saluation, the Lord giueth or taketh away, as in his infinite wisedome he thinketh best; neither yet are we to vnderstand it
of all gifts of the spirit which are proper to the elect, for
some also of these being not of the essence of faith, but only
effects and fruites thereof, he taketh away from his children
for a time; as namely, the puritie of their conscience, and the
peace which doth accompanie it, the sense and feeling of
Gods loue and fauour, cheerefulnes of spirit, ioy in the holie   Psal. 51.9,10,
Ghost, patience, the gift of prayer and such like; because his   11,12,15.
loue and the saluation of the faithfull may stand with the
want of these gifts for a time. Neither are wee to vnderstand
this of the actions and sensible fruites of Gods graces, for
these also haue their intermissions, the graces themselues
notwithstanding remaining: for as the Sunne doth alwaies
shine, and yet sometimes the beames thereof are not discerned, being hindred from spreading themselues by the inter-
position of the clowds or of the earth, and the fire doth continue light and hot in it selfe, and yet being couered with
ashes doth giue neither light nor heate to the standers by; so
these graces of Gods spirit, faith, hope, affiance, loue and
such like, may in respect of their substance habitually remaine in vs, and yet for a time not send foorth the light and
heate of ioy, comfort, peace and the rest; and though they retaine their nature still, yet they may be hindred from exercising their actions and functions; as namely, when as the
conscience is wounded with some wilfull sinne committed
against the knowledge, or in the spirituall conflict of temptations, as before I haue shewed at large. Lastly, this is not to
be vnderstood of their measure and degree, for these graces
haue their full and waine, their ebbe and tide, their perfect
strength and their faint languishing; but of their substance
and true being, in which respect they neuer vtterly faile but

V v 3   continue

continue without intermiſſion vnto the end, for as the gift of faith, ſo all other the like graces are the worke of God, as our Sauiour teacheth vs, Iohn 6.29: and we may aſſure our ſelues of this, *That he that hath begunne this good worke in vs, will alſo finiſh and perfect it vntill the day of Ieſus Chriſt,* as the Apoſtle ſpeaketh, Philip.1.6.

— — —

CHAP. XIII.

Of the fourth and fifth reaſon to proue the certaintie of our perſeuerance, grounded vpon Gods power and truth.

§. Sect.1. The fourth reaſon grounded vpon Gods omnipotencie.

THe fourth reaſon may be taken from Gods omnipotencie and almighty power : for if God in reſpect of his infinite loue, bee willing that we ſhall bee ſaued, and perſeuere in the meanes of our ſaluation; and bee immutable alſo and vnchangeable in his loue and will; and likewiſe in reſpect of his power infinit and almighty, able to effect whatſoeuer hee willeth: then ſurely being aſſured that we are in the ſtate of grace, and in Gods loue and fauour, there is no doubt but we ſhall bee ſaued, and perſeuere in the meanes which are inſeparably ioyned with our ſaluation. But as the Lord in reſpect of his loue is moſt willing, ſo in reſpect of his power hee is able, continually to vpholde vs in the ſtate of grace, and to fruſtrate and defeate all the malice and might of all our enemies, who labour to hinder our ſaluation; for he *is omnipotent and mighty to ſaue,* as it is Eſa.63.1. And though through our frailety and weakeneſſe we might continually bee vanquiſhed and drawne from God, yet now there is no doubt hereof, ſeeing we doe not ſtand in our owne ſtrength, *but are kept by the power of God through faith vnto ſaluation,* as it is 1.Pet. 1.5. though in our ſelues wee are impotent and feeble, yet we are *ſtrong in the Lord, and in the power of his might,* and being armed with the armour of God, we are inabled *to ſtand againſt the aſſaults of the diuell,* as the Apoſtle ſpeaketh, Epheſ.6.10,11. Though wee are of little force in regard of our owne ſtrength and able to doe nothing, yet are *we able*

Iohn 6.29.

Phil.1.6.

Eſa.63.1.

1.Pet.1.5.

Eph.6.10,11.

to

to doe all things through the helpe of Christ which strengthneth Phil.4.13.
vs, as it is, Philip.4.13: though we be weake in faith, and vnable to stand, yet being the seruants of God *we shall be esta-* Rom.14.4.
blished; for God is able to make vs stand, Rom.14.4. In a word,
though our spirituall enemies are stronger than we, yet shall
they not bee able to plucke vs from Christ; *For the father* Ioh.10.28,29.
*which gaue vs to him is greater than all, and none is able to take
vs out of the fathers hand*, as our Sauiour reasoneth, Iohn 10.
28,29. And therefore when we are discouraged and ready to
faint, in the fight and sense of our owne weakenesse, and our
enemies mighty power, let vs comfort our selues in the
Lord, saying with the Apostle, *I knowe whom I haue beleeued*, 2.Tim.1.12.
and I am perswaded he is able to keepe that which I haue committed to him against that day, as it is 2.Tim.1.12.

The fifth reason is grounded vpon Gods truth and fideli- §. *Sect.2.*
tie, which is so infallible, that whatsoeuer hee hath spoken, *The fifth rea-*
promised, or couenanted, that he will most certainely per- *son grounded
on Gods truth*
forme: for *God is a faithfull and true witnesse*, Apoc.1.5. and *in his coue-*
all his promises in Christ are Yea and Amen, 2.Corinth.1.20. *nant.*
So that *it is more easie that heauen and earth should passe a-* Apoc.1.5.
way, than that one title of Gods word should fall vnaccompli- 2.Cor.1.20.
shed, Luke 16.17. But the Lord in his word hath assured Luke 16.17.
all that beleeue, that hee will vpholde them and preserue
them vnto euerlasting life, against all the furie of their e-
nemies; as may appeare both by his couenant which he hath
made with his Church in generall, and also by particular
promises made to all the faithfull. Concerning the first,
the Lord maketh this couenant with his Church, Esa.59.21.
I will (saith hee) *make this my couenant with them ; my spirit* Esa.59.21.
*that is vpon thee and my words which I haue put in thy mouth,
shall not depart out of thy mouth, nor out of the mouth of thy
seede, nor out of the mouth of the seede of thy seed, saith the Lord,
from henceforth euen for euer.* If therefore Gods spirit neuer
departeth from them, and they for euer confesse and professe his word and truth, then certainely they can neuer fall
away nor loose their heauenly inheritance. For, *if the spirit of* Rom.8.11.
*him that raised vp Iesus from the dead dwell in vs, hee shall also
quicken our mortall bodies, because his spirit dwelleth in vs*, as it

Rom.8.11.14. is Rom.8.11. And as many as *are led by the spirit of God, they*
17. *are the sonnes of God,* verf.14. *And if we be children,we are*
Ier.32.38,39, *also heyres,&c.* verf.17. So Ierem.32.38. *I will bee their God,*
40. *and they shall be my people.* Verf.39. *And I will giue them one*
heart and one way,that they mav feare me for euer,for the wealth
of them and of their children after them. 40. And *I will make*
an euerlasting couenant with them,that I will neuer turne away
from them to doe them good, but I will put my feare in their
hearts,that they shall not depart from me,&c. If therefore the
Church and people of God shall feare him for euer, if his
couenant be euerlasting, if he will neuer depart from them,
nor they from him, then certainely there is no doubt of their
Ier.31.31.32.' perfeuerance.And chapter 31.31.32, The Lord faith that he
will make a new couenant with his Church, not according to the
couenant which he made with their fathers. 33. *But this shall*
be the couenant that I will make with the houfe of ifrael after
those dayes (faith the Lord) *I will put my lawe in their inward*
parts,and write it in their hearts,and will be their God, and they
shall be my people,&c. And I will forgiue their iniquitie, and I
will remember their sinnes no more. In which words the Lord
couenanteth,that his law should euer remaine so deeply in-
grauen in their hearts,that nothing should blot it out & that
Rom.2.15. they should continually meditate and delight themfelues
2.Cor.3.2. therein; for thus this phrafe of writing in the heart is vfually
taken in the Scriptures. So likewife he affureth them of the
perpetuall pardon of their finnes,fo that their finnes should
neuer make fruftrate that couenant which he had made with
Hof.2.19.20. them. So Hof.2.19. *And I will marrie thee vnto me for euer,*
yea, I will marry thee vnto me in righteoufneffe and in iudge-
ment,and in mercy and compaffion. 20. *I will marrie thee vnto*
me in faithfulneffe, and thou shall knowe the Lord. If therefore
the Church of God shall bee married vnto him for euer in
righteoufneffe and faithfulneffe, and in mercy and compaffion, then can neither their faith and righteoufneffe towards
God,nor his mercy and compaffion towards them fayle,but
both shall continue vnto the end. Seeing then the couenant
which is betweene God and vs doth affure vs of the continuance of his loue and mercy,and of our perfeuerance in his
feare

feare and holy obedience we neede not to doubt either of
the ceasing of his loue, or our falling away. For though the
mountaines remoue and the hils fall downe, yet shall not
his mercie depart from his children, neither shall the couenant of his peace fall away. As the Lord himselfe protesteth
Esa.54.10.

Esa 54.10.

And thus haue I proued the certaintie of our perseuerance,
by the couenant of grace which God hath made with his
Church; for whatsoeuer ÿ Lord promiseth to the whole body of the Church, that he also promiseth to euery particular
member thereof, seeing the whole containeth all his parts:
so that whatsoeuer belongeth to the whole body, that also
belongeth to all the members. But it may be obiected that
howsoeuer this couenant on Gods part is firme and eternall, yet by our fault and transgression it may be made voyde
and frustrate. I answere that so likewise the couenant made
with the Israelites was firme on Gods part, but made frustrate by their sinnes, but the Lord hath made a new couenant with vs, not of workes but of grace, vpon the condition of faith and repentance, which being obserued on our
part our sinnes and vnworthinesse cannot make it frustrate and of none effect; as before I haue shewed more at
large.

§. Sect.3.
An obiection
taken from our
faitinesse an-
swered.

Secondly, we are assured of our perseuerance, by Gods
particular promises made to his faithfull ones. Psal.1.3. it is
said of the righteous man, that he shall be like a *tree planted
by the riuers of waters that will bring forth her fruites in due
season, whose leafe shall not faid,&c.* As therefore the tree planted by the riuer side doth not wither, because continually
it sucketh moysture, whereby it is quickned and refreshed:
so the righteous man perseuereth in his righteousnesse, because he is continually reuiued and quickned with that spirituall moysture, which he sucketh from Christ who is the
liuely roote, whereof he is a branch. Psal.15 5, *He that doth
these things shall neuer be moued.* Psal.37.24. *Though (the
righteous man)fall,he shall not be cast off; for the Lord putteth
vnder his hand.* Psal.112.6, *Surely he shall neuer be moued, but
the righteous shall be had in euerlasting remembrance.* And

§ Sect.4.
Of the particu-
lar promises of
our perseue-
rance.
Psal.1.3.
Ezech.47 22.

Psal.15.5.
Psal.37.24.

Psal.112.6,

verս.ɡ.

Verf.9.
Pfal.125.1.

Ioh 4.14.

Ioh.7.38,39.

Ioh.6.35.37.
∾.54.

Ioh.5.24.
and 10.28.

verf.9. *His righteousnesse remaineth for euer.* Pfal.125.1.*They that trust in the Lord shall be as mount Syon, which cannot be remoued,but remaineth for euer.* Ioh.4.14.*Whosoeuer drinketh of the water that I shall giue him, shall neuer be more a thirst, but the water which I shall giue him shall be in him a well of water, springing vp to euerlasting life.* Where by this water we are to vnderstand the holy Ghost, as appeareth Ioh.7.38. *He that beleeueth in me as saith the scripture, out of his belly shall flow riuers of the water of life.* 39. *This* (saith the Euangelist)*spake he of the spirit which they that beleeued in him should receiue.* So that to drinke of this water is through faith in Christ to be made partakers of the holy Ghost, whom whosoeuer receiueth shall retaine him vnto the end. As therefore he that hath a liuing fountaine continually springing in him cannot be a thirst; so they who haue this fountaine of life perpetually springing in them, they shall neuer thirst any more, but it shall continually refresh and quicken them, till they haue attained vnto euerlasting life. Ioh.6.35. *I am the bread of life, he that commeth to me shall not hunger, and he that beleeueth in me shall neuer thirst.* And verf.37. *All that the father giueth me shall come vnto me ; and him that commeth to me I cast not away.* And verf.51. *I am the liuing bread which came downe from heauen, if any man eate of this bread he shall liue for euer.* And verf.54. *Whosoeuer eateth my flesh and drinketh my blood, hath eternall life, and I will raise him vp at the last day,&c.* Now whosoeuer beleeue in Christ,they eate his flesh and drinke his blood; for faith is the mouth of the soule whereby we feede on this heauenly foode; and therefore all the faithfull shall haue euerlasting life;nay as he saith they haue it alreadie and *shall not come into condemnation, but haue passed from death to life*, as it is Ioh.5.24. and Ioh.10.28. *I will giue vnto them eternall life, and they shall neuer perish, neither shall any plucke them out of my hand.* 29. *My father which gaue them me is greater than all, and none is able to take them out of my fathers hand.* In which words he both sheweth his will in his promise, and his power to performe it, and therefore whosoeuer are the sheepe of Christ, they cannot be taken from him, neither for a time nor eternally, for

so

so it should follow if Chrifts reafon be of any force, that they who tooke them from him fhould be ftronger than Chrift and his father, which were a horrible blafphemie for any to imagine.

But here it is obieated that thefe promifes are made to all the faithfull fo long as they continue faithfull, and to the fheepe of Chrift fo long as they are his fheepe, who abide in his word and follow him. But when they ceafe to beleeue and to be his fheepe, they doe not appertaine vnto him, for they onely remaine the Difciples of Chrift who abide in his word, and haue his word abiding in them, Ioh.8 31. and 15.7. To which I anfwere that this is an idle trifling in a circular difputation, and a vaine begging of the queftion in controuerfie. For the queftion is, whether the faithfull may be affured of their perfeuerance in faith, whether a member of Chrift may be affured to continue a member of Chrift, whether a fheepe of Chrift may affure himfelfe that he is to remaine for euer a fheepe of Chrift; we hold the affirmatiue part and proue it by diuers teftimonies; they deny that thefe promifes are abfolute, but on this condition, that we are affured none can plucke vs from Chrift, fo long as we continue and retaine the nature of the members and fheepe of Chrift. But I would faine know what it is to be plucked from Chrift, but to ceafe to bee a member or fheepe of Chrift, and to loofe their nature : and what it is to be a fheepe of Chrift but to heare his word and to follow him. When as then our Sauiour Chrift promifeth that none fhall plucke his fheepe from him, he promifeth that none fhall be able to make them ceafe to be his fheepe, nor de-priue them of their nature which is the effentiall forme which maketh them to be fheepe, rather than other who neither heare his word nor follow him. Whereas therefore they affirme, that thefe promifes doe affure vs to perfeuere, fo long as we continue and retaine the nature of the fheepe and members of Chrift, what is it but idly to repeate the fame thing? namely that Gods promifes doe affure vs to per-feuere, fo long as wee doe perfeuere; that we fhall not bo plucked from Chrift fo long as we remaine with Chrift; that

§. *Sect.5.*
An obieftion tending to fruftrate the for-mer promifes, anfwered.
Ioh.8.31.
and 15.7.

we

we fhall continue the members and fheepe of Chrift, fo long as we continue to be his fheepe and members; that we fhall not loofe our faith fo long as we continue faithfull. And what is it to fay that the fheepe of Chrift fhall fo long continue to be his fheepe as they retaine their nature, but to graunt alfo that they may loofe their nature, & confequently ceafe to be Chrifts fheepe, and fo be plucked from him which is quite contrarie to his promife?

Chap. XIIII.

Of eight other reasons which proue the certaintie of our perfeuerance.

§ *Sect.* 1.
The fixt reafon taken from Chrifts interceffion.

Ioh 11.42.

Luk.22.32.
Ioh.17.9.11.
15.21.

He fixt reafon to affure vs of our perfeuerance may be taken from the interceffió of Chrift for vs to God the father. For whatfoeuer Chrift himfelf maketh requeft for in the behalfe of his faithfull, that without doubt the father graunteth vnto him, for *God heareth him alwaies,* Ioh.11.42. But he continually maketh requeft for them that their faith faile not, as appeareth Luk.22.32. He prayeth for them, Ioh.17.9. that the father would keepe *them in his name whom he had giuen vnto him, That they may be one, as he and the father are one,* verf.11; *That he would preferue them from euill,* verf.15; and what greater euill than to fall from grace and God alfo? *That they all may be one, as the father is in Chrift and Chrift in him,* verf.21. *That they be with Chrift where he is, and may behold his glorie,* verf.24. He maketh alfo interceffion for all thofe whom he hath redeemed, that they may be faued, notwithftanding their finnes into which they fall through the ftrength of their corruptions, as appeareth 1.Ioh.2.1.2. And therefore all thefe things are graunted vnto him by the father, for the faithfull. So that now they may fay with the Apoftle Rom.8.33. *It is God that iuftifieth.* 34. *Who shall condemne? It is Chrift Which is dead, yea or rather which is rifen againe, Who is alfo at the right hand of God and maketh requeft for vs.* 35. *Who shall feparate vs from the loue of God &c?* And though

Verf. 24.

1.Ioh.2.1.2.

Rom.8.33,34,
35.

though our corruptions be many and our weakeneſſe great yet we neede not doubt of our perſeucrance to euerlaſting life. *For we haue an high prieſt who is able perfectly to ſaue them that come vnto God by him, ſeeing he euer liueth to make interceſſion for them,* as it is Heb.7.25.

Heb.7.25.

The ſeuenth reaſon may be taken from that vnion which is betweene Chriſt and the faithfull,whereby he becommeth their head, and they his members. For there is no head that will willingly permit any of it members to bee rent and torne from it, becauſe then it ſhould haue a maimed and vnperfect body. But Chriſt Ieſus is the head of all the faithfull, and they the members of his body. Epheſians.5.30. And therefore hee will not ſuffer any of them to bee pulled from him, and ſo periſhing make a maime in his body, ſeeing hee is alſo omnipotent and able to ſaue all thoſe who depend vpon him. Moreouer ſeeing our Sauiour Chriſt who is our head, hath paſt all daungers, and now liueth and raineth with God his father, wee are alſo aſſured that we ſhall liue and raigne with him. For he hath obtained this eternall glorie, not for himſelfe alone, but alſo for all the members of his body, as appeareth Ioh.17. 21.24. and therefore now there is no doubt of periſhing, *ſeeing our life is hid with Chriſt in God,* as it is Col.3.3 ; and conſequently no leſſe ſafe than his who now raigneth and triumpheth ouer his enemies. Whereof it is that they are ſaid in reſpect of the certaintie of their aſſurance, to haue alreadie euerlaſting life, and to haue paſſed from death to life, Ioh.5.24. 1.Ioh.3.14.

§. Sect.2.
The ſeuenth reaſon taken from our vnion with Chriſt.

Eph.5.30.

Ioh.17.21.24.

Col.3.3.

Ioh.5.24.
1.Ioh.3.14.

The eight reaſon may be taken from the ſpirit of God dwelling in vs ; for ſo long as it hath his abiding with vs,we muſt needs perſeuer in grace; neither is it poſſible we ſhould fall away, ſeeing it is the fountaine and roote from which all graces flow and ſpring,and ſeeing it continually fighteth againſt and ſubdueth the fleſh and the luſts thereof. But after we haue receiued the ſpirit of God it continually dwelleth and abideth with vs ; for this is that ſpirituall water of which whoſoeuer *drinketh ſhall neuer be more a thirſt, but it ſhall be a well of water ſpringing vp into euerlaſting life,* as it

§. Sect.3.
The eight reaſon taken from the ſpirit of God dwelling in vs.

Ioh 4.14.
and 7.39.

may

may appeare by comparing Ioh.4.14. with chapt.7.39. So

Ioh.14.16.
1.Ioh.2.27.

1.Ioh.3.9.

Ioh.14.16. *I will pray the father and he shall giue you another Comforter, that hee may abide with you for euer.* 17. *Euen the spirit of truth, whom the world cannot receiue, because it seeth him not, neither knoweth him ; but ye know him, for he dwelleth with you and shall be in you.* And 1.Ioh.3.9. *Whosoeuer is borne of God sinneth not,* (that is, with full consent of will) *for his seede remaineth in him; neither can he sinne, because he is borne of God:* where the spirit is called the seede of God, because by vertue thereof wee are begotten vnto God. If therefore by vertue of this spirit wee are so preserued that wee cannot sinne with full consent of will, nor haue it raigning in vs as it did before our regeneration, then certainly wee shall bee preserued thereby from falling away, and notwith-standing our sinnes wee shall perseuere in grace to euerla-sting life.

§. *Sect.4.*
The ninth rea-
son taken from
the effects of
the spirit.
1.Ioh.2.20.27
Rom.8.14.17.

1.Ioh.5.18.

Rom.16.17.

Eph.1.14.
2.Cor.1.22.
Eph.4.30.

The ninth argument may be taken from the effects of the spirit dwelling in vs ; for first it teacheth and guideth vs in the way of Gods truth, as appeareth 1.Ioh.2.20.27. And *as many as are led by the spirit of God, they are the sonnes of God,* Rom.8.14 : and those that are sonnes *are also heires, euen the heires of God, and coheires with Christ,* vers.17. Neither is it possible that those who are guided with the spirit should sinne with full consent of will, much lesse fall away. For who-soeuer is borne of God sinneth not, namely after this man-ner, neither can euer their spirituall enemies finally preuaile against them ; for he that is *begotten of God keepeth himselfe, and the wicked one toucheth him not,* as it is 1.Ioh.5.18. Se-condly, the spirit of God witnesseth to our spirits that wee are the sonnes of God, and consequently heires of his king-dome, as it is Rom.16.17. and his testimonie is true and in-fallible. It also is *the earnest of our inheritance,* and a pledge to assure vs that God will make good his promises vnto vs, Eph.1.14. 2.Cor.1.22. and thereby also wee are *sealed vnto the day of redemption,* Ephes.4.30. And therefore seeing the Lord hath confirmed our assurance by the testimonie of his spirit, by this earnest, pledge, and seale, we neede not to feare our falling away or to doubt of our perseuerance. But of this

I

I haue alreadie written at large in treating of the certaintie of our election.

The tenth reaſon may be taken from Gods continuall aid in all trials and temptations ; for if hee be alwaies readie to ſtrengthen and ſupport vs, wee can neuer finally bee ouerthrowne,but though wee fall, yet we ſhall not fall away,but ſhall be raiſed vp againe in deſpite of all our enemies. For *God is faithfull, and will not ſuffer vs to be tempted aboue our power, but will giue a good iſſue with the temptation, that we may be able to beare it,* as it is 1.Cor.10.13. And *he knoweth to deliuer the godly out of temptation,* as the Apoſtle ſpeaketh 2.Pet. 2.9. And therefore be our weakneſſe neuer ſo great, yet let vs not feare our finall falling away, but knowing whom we haue beleeued, let vs perſwade our ſelues of our perſeuerance, knowing that hee *is able to keepe that which we haue committed vnto him,* as it is 2.Tim.1.12.

§. Sect.5.
The tenth reaſon, taken from Gods continual aide.

1.Cor.10.13.

2.Pet.2.9.

2.Tim.1.12.

And theſe are the reaſons drawne frō Gods nature in himſelf and his actions towards vs,wherby we may vndoubtedly be aſſured of our perſeuerance. The ſecond ſort of arguments may bee taken from our ſelues,and firſt from the nature of true faith wherewith wee are endued, which is not temporarie but conſtant and permanent. For he that hath a true and liuely faith,is like the houſe builded vpon the rock, which neither the raine nor floods nor windes could ouerthrow, Matth.7.24,25:neither *ſhall the gates of hell ouercome him,* chap.16.verſ.18 : he is like the good ground in which the ſeede falling is not ſtollen away, nor choked vp,nor withereth for want of root, but *he receiueth the ſeed and keepeth it, and bringeth foorth fruite with patience,* as it is Luk.8.15. And contrariwiſe it is a moſt vndoubted marke of an hypocrite who neuer was indued with a true faith, when as his faith is temporarie, and hee falleth away, according to that 1.Ioh.2 19.*They went out from vs,but they were not of vs; for if they had been of vs they would haue continued with vs. But this commeth to paſſe that it might appeare that they are not all of vs.*

§ Sect.6.
The eleuenth reaſon taken from the nature of faith.

Matth.7.24.
25.and 16.18.

Luk.8.15.

1.Ioh.2.19.

The ſecond reaſon may bee taken from the example of thoſe who haue grieuouſly fallen,and yet haue continued in the

§.Sect.7.

The twelfth reason, taken from examples.
Pfal. 51.10.11

the ftate of grace, and haue been raifed and reftored againe by vnfained repentance: and thus did *Dauid* fall and that moft grieuoufly, and yet was not depriued of Gods fpirit, as appeareth Pfal. 51.10.11. Thus did *Peter* fail by denying his mafter, *Noah* by drunkenneffe, *Lot* by inceft, and yet they were not depriued of thofe graces which they had receiued; howfoeuer for the time they were much eclipfed and weakened, neither were they reiected by God, but vpon their true repentance were receiued into his former loue and fauour.

§. *Sect. 8.*
The laft reafon, taken from the inabilitie of the caufes which fhould hinder our perfeuerance.
Rom. 1. 35.

2. Cor. 4. 17.

The laft reafon may be taken from the weakneffe and inabilitie of the caufes which fhould hinder our perfeuerance and make vs fall away. For there is nothing in the world fo powerfull, but it is altogether too weake to worke this defection. For firft, afflictions cannot depriue vs of grace, nor hinder our perfeuerance, as it is Rom. 8. 35 : for though they are the firie trial, yet they do not burne vs, but refine vs from our droffe, neither doe they hinder our faluation, but rather *caufe vnto vs a farre moft excellent and eternall waight of glorie*, as it is 2. Cor. 4. 17 : nor yet our flefh, for though it be neuer fo ftrong, yet the fpirit of God dwelling in vs, will in the end mortifie and fubdue it. Not the world, for our Captaine Chrift hath ouercome it, not onely for himfelfe but alfo for

Iohn 16. 33.
1. Ioh. 5. 4.

his members, Ioh. 16. 33: yea and hee enableth vs alfo by his holy fpirit to ouercome it. *For all that is borne of God ouercommeth the world, and this is the victorie that ouercommeth the world, euen our faith*, as it is 1. Ioh. 5. 4. Not the diuell, for

Iam. 4. 7.
1. Ioh. 5. 18.

if Wee refift him, he will flee from vs, Iam. 4. 7. And *he that is borne of God keepeth himfelfe, and the wicked one toucheth him not*, 1. Ioh. 5. 18. Not our finnes, for they are punifhed and fully fatisfied for in Chrift; and *if we fin, we haue an aduocate*

1. Ioh. 2. 1, 2.

with the father, &c. 1. Ioh. 2. 1, 2. And for the corruption of fin,

Rom. 6. 12.
1. Ioh. 3. 9.

though it dwell in vs, yet it fhall not raigne in vs, Rom. 6. 12. Though we fall into it, yet not with full confent of will, 1. Ioh. 3. 9. for the regenerate man finneth not, but his cor-

Rom. 7.

rupt flefh dwelling in him, as it is Rom. 7. Not any temptation, for the *Lord is faithfull, and will not fuffer vs to be temp-*

1. Cor. 10. 13.

ted aboue our power, but will giue a good iffue vnto it, 1. Cor. 10.

Rom. 8. 38. 39.

13. Not any thing in the world, Rom. 8. 38. 39, for all things whatfoeuer

whatsoeuer shall be so disposed by the wise prouidence of God, that though they bee neuer so hurtfull in their owne nature, and apt to draw vs from God, *yet they shall worke together for the best vnto them which loue God,* as it is Rom.8.28.

And thus haue I prooued the certaintie of our perseuerance, both by plaine testimonies of Scripture, and also infallible reasons : I had purposed (as in the other points going before) to haue answered such obiections as are commonly suggested by Sathan, and stifly vrged by his instruments the Popish rabble against this truth, and accordingly had almost finished that which I intended ; but diuers reasons moued me to desist from my purpose, as first and especially his earnest desire who is at the chiefe charge of printing these my labours, who fearing that the greatnesse and dearenesse of the booke might be a hindrance to the sale thereof, intreated me to forbeare the publishing of this controuersie, which being somewhat long, would haue increased the volume and consequently the price. To whose request I more willingly condescended, partly because the controuersie before handled, of the certaintie of faith and assurance of our saluation, is of the like nature, so that the proouing of the one is the confirming of the other, and the answering of those obiections which are made against the certaintie of our assurance, is a sufficient refutation of those which are obiected against our perseuerance, many of the testimonies of Scriptures and other reasons which are alledged against both, being the very same : And partly because I vnderstand, that my godly learned and most deare brother, purposeth presently to publish his Lectures vpon the 15 Psalme, wherin this controuersie is largely and much more excellently handled and determined, than I was any waies able to haue written of it. Notwithstanding, if my book seeme maimed in respect of this defect, & if I see it be desired that it should be intire and full in it self, I will hereafter most willingly supplie that which yet is wanting, if I perceiue that my labours are approoued as profitable for the Church of God. In the meane time I commend them to

X x   Gods

Gods blessing, who onely is able by the assistance of his holy spirit to make them effectuall for those ends for which I intended them, he being the sole fountaine of all true comfort and consolation : desiring the Christian reader who shal finde fruite and profit by these my labours, that as I haue not been wanting vnto him in my paines and best endeuours; so he will not be wanting to remember me in his prayers vnto Almightie God, for the continuance, increase, and holie vse of all his gifts and graces which hee hath bestowed on me.

To this God most wise, most gracious, and most infinite in all perfections, the Father, Sonne and Holie Ghost, be ascribed all glorie, praise, power and dominion both now and euermore, *Amen.*

FINIS.

Christian Reader, becauſe there was ſome haſte required in printing of this booke, part thereof from pag.371 to pag.578 was committed to another Printer, who wanting a Corrector ſuffred theſe faults to eſcape which are materiall. As for others which are apparant at the firſt view, I haue left vnobſerued.

THE ERRATA.

Pag.25.line 14. reade muſt needes be. pag.48 l.13,r.anothers, p.371.l.4.r.fleſhy, p.375.l.6.r.repeateth. p.378.l.13 r.thinke ye. p.391.l.30.r.ſelues.p.396.l.5.r. all accompany. p.399.l.29. r.goodly ſhewes.l.34. r.health p.405.l.6. r. alſo haue them. p.408.l.23 r mocke repentance. p.409. l 3.r.doe not.l.12. r. κοπιῶντϛ.l. 14.r.προοσπιζμένοι. p.412.r. he freeth thoſe. p.418.l.4. r. Ho euery. l.18. r. and that he will. l.24.r.and with all his heart deſireth to be. p.420.l 4,5.r is properly to God.p.425. l 24.r.(as of himſelf vnwilling)l 27 r.hainous,no more then.p.417.l 5.r.mercies. The.l.27.r.hainous,no more then. p 438.l.29.r.and reſt p.440.l.18.r.Lord,mercie. p.442 l 22.r,Ho euery.p.446.l 31.r if when we were p.449.l.10.r that he who for. l.30.r.of his bountie.p 451 l.27.r.honour and glorie.p.455.l 6.r.and now he.p.463. l.30.r.true in theſi,yet falſe in hypotheſi. p.473.l.26.r powerfully.l.33.r.miniſterie. p.474.l.4.r.miniſterie p.475.l 22 r.and meere ciuill.p.477.l.10.r.and though. l.13.r.entertaine it. p.479.l 32.r.the bond of this lin.laſt r.works of ſanctification. p.481.l.10.r.ſo the branches.p 484 l 5 r.it ſeareth.p.486.l.4.r. ſeared l.29.r.ſight and feeling. p.487 l 24 r with an hard,p.501.l.29.r. in God at al.p 507.l.14.r.may ſeeme to be p.510 l.30.r.truly ſorie. l.36.r.the caſe. p.514.l.25.r.deſtruction,but. p.522.l.11.r.vanquiſhed.l.10.r.ſtriuing p.526.l.8.r.ſimilitudes. l.19 r moueth and p 53.l 20.r the 5 verſe p.538.l.10 r.vp vntill it.l.19 r hauing any.p.540.l.7.r,more ſtrong.p.553.l 29.r almes atwell as l 33.r.ſtrong.Our.p.557.l.9.r ſeene him?p 566. l.13.r one oblation.lin.21.r.where he p.569.l.7.r and iudged lin.8 r. his owne. p.571.l.26.r.imaginarie. p.574 l.7.r.Apoſtle. p.578.l.19.r. neceſſarily.